# See what students love al LearningCurve.

Macmillan Education

**LearningCurve** learningcurveworks.com

**Students using LaunchPad receive access** to LearningCurve for *A History of World Societies*.

Each chapter-based LearningCurve activity gives students **multiple chances to understand key concepts**, return to the narrative textbook if they need to reread, and answer questions correctly.

Over 90% of students report satisfaction with LearningCurve's **fun and accessible game-like interface**.

## "With LearningCurve, students engage with the content and retain it better."

— Melissa Walker,
*Converse College*

Assigning LearningCurve in place of reading quizzes is easy for instructors, and the **reporting features help instructors track overall class trends** and spot topics that are giving students trouble so that they can adjust lectures and class activities.

To learn more about LearningCurve, visit **learningcurveworks.com**.

*LearningCurve: Everyone's got a learning curve — what's yours?*

THE CONTEMPORARY WORLD

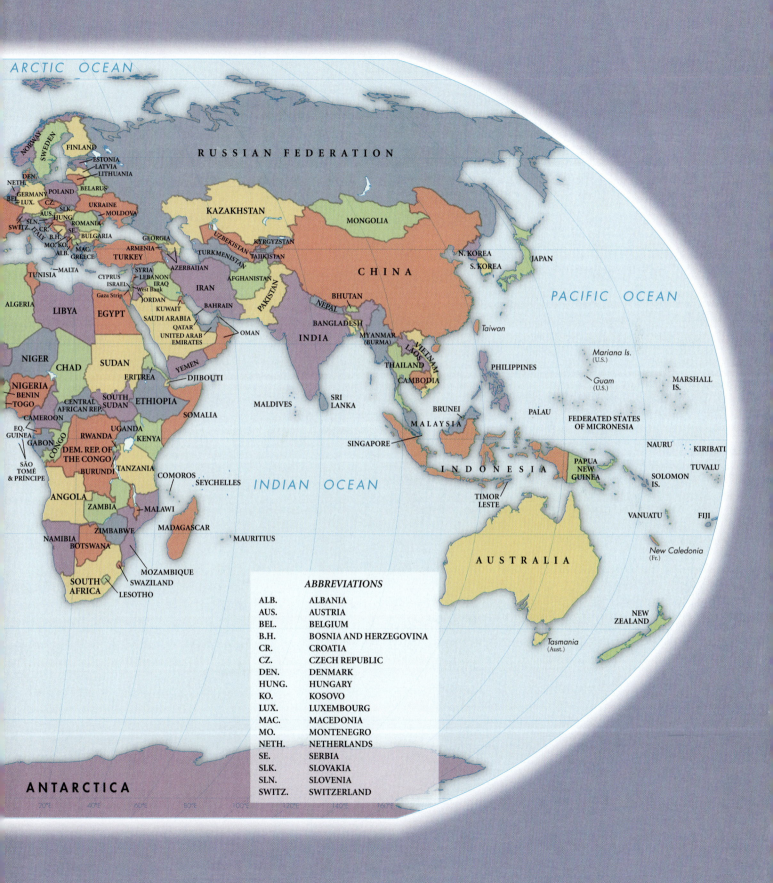

# A HISTORY OF
# World Societies

Tenth
EDITION

Volume B
From 800 to 1815

# A HISTORY OF
# World Societies

**John P. McKay** • *University of Illinois at Urbana-Champaign*

**Bennett D. Hill** • *Late of Georgetown University*

**John Buckler** • *Late of University of Illinois at Urbana-Champaign*

**Patricia Buckley Ebrey** • *University of Washington*

**Roger B. Beck** • *Eastern Illinois University*

**Clare Haru Crowston** • *University of Illinois at Urbana-Champaign*

**Merry E. Wiesner-Hanks** • *University of Wisconsin–Milwaukee*

**Jerry Dávila** • *University of Illinois at Urbana-Champaign*

Bedford/St. Martin's | BOSTON • NEW YORK

## FOR BEDFORD/ST. MARTIN'S

*Director of Development for History:* Jane Knetzger
*Senior Developmental Editor:* Sara Wise
*Senior Production Editor:* Christina M. Horn
*Production Supervisor:* Samuel Jones
*Executive Marketing Manager:* Sandra McGuire
*Associate Editor:* Robin Soule
*Editorial Assistant:* Arrin Kaplan
*Production Assistant:* Erica Zhang
*Copy Editor:* Jennifer Brett Greenstein
*Indexer:* Leoni Z. McVey

*Cartography:* Mapping Specialists, Ltd.
*Page Layout:* Boynton Hue Studio
*Photo Researcher:* Bruce Carson
*Senior Art Director:* Anna Palchik
*Text Design:* Marsha Cohen
*Cover Design:* Donna Lee Dennison
*Cover Art:* Portrait of Arjumand Banu (1592–1631). The Granger Collection, New York City.
*Composition:* Jouve
*Printing and Binding:* RR Donnelley and Sons

Copyright © 2015, 2012, 2009, 2007 by Bedford/St. Martin's

All rights reserved. No part of this book may be reproduced, stored in a retrieval system, or transmitted in any form or by any means, electronic, mechanical, photocopying, recording, or otherwise, except as may be expressly permitted by the applicable copyright statutes or in writing by the Publisher.

Manufactured in the United States of America.

9  8  7  6  5  4
f  e  d  c  b  a

*For information, write:* Bedford/St. Martin's, 75 Arlington Street, Boston, MA 02116    (617-399-4000)

ISBN 978-1-4576-5993-5 (Combined Edition)
ISBN 978-1-4576-8544-6 (Loose-leaf Edition)
ISBN 978-1-4576-5994-2 (Volume 1)
ISBN 978-1-4576-8547-7 (Loose-leaf Edition, Volume 1)
ISBN 978-1-4576-5995-9 (Volume 2)

ISBN 978-1-4576-8549-1 (Loose-leaf Edition, Volume 2)
ISBN 978-1-4576-8518-7 (Volume A)
ISBN 978-1-4576-8519-4 (Volume B)
ISBN 978-1-4576-8522-4 (Volume C)

## ACKNOWLEDGMENTS

*Acknowledgments and copyrights appear on the same page as the text and art selections they cover; these acknowledgments and copyrights constitute an extension of the copyright page. It is a violation of the law to reproduce these selections by any means whatsoever without the written permission of the copyright holder.*

The tenth edition of *A History of World Societies* continues to provide the social and cultural focus, comprehensive regional organization, and global perspective that have long been hallmarks of the book. All three of these qualities have been greatly enhanced by the addition of a new member to the author team, Jerry Dávila from the University of Illinois, who brings expertise in Latin America and the twentieth century. A renowned scholar of Brazil whose work focuses on race and social policy, Jerry offers a fresh perspective to our coverage of Latin America and to the final chapters in the book, which he has completely reconceptualized.

Not only do we thus continue to benefit from a collaborative team of regional experts with deep experience in the world history classroom, but we are also pleased to introduce a suite of digital tools designed to save you time and to help students gain confidence and learn historical thinking skills.

## New Tools for the Digital Age

Because we know that your classroom needs are changing rapidly, we are excited to announce that *A History of World Societies* is available with **LaunchPad**. Free when packaged with the book, LaunchPad's course space and interactive e-book are ready to use as is (or can be edited and customized with your own material) and can be assigned right away. Developed with extensive feedback from history instructors and students, LaunchPad includes the complete narrative e-book, as well as abundant primary documents, maps, images, assignments, and activities. The aims of key learning outcomes are addressed via formative and summative assessments, short-answer and essay questions, multiple-choice quizzing, and **LearningCurve**, an adaptive learning tool designed to get students to read before they come to class. Available with training and support, LaunchPad can help you take your teaching into a new era. To learn more about the benefits of LearningCurve and LaunchPad, see "Versions and Supplements" on page xv. In addition, the following sections will show you how specific skills-based features of *A History of World Societies* can be enhanced by the ability to assign and track student work in LaunchPad.

## The Story of *A History of World Societies*

In this age of global connections, with their influence on the global economy, global migration patterns, popular culture, and global warming, among other aspects of life, the study of world history is more vital and urgent than ever before. An understanding of the broad sweep of the human past helps us comprehend today's dramatic changes and enduring continuities. People now migrate enormous distances and establish new lives far from their places of birth, yet migration has been a constant in history since the first humans walked out of Africa. Satellites and cell phones now link nearly every inch of the planet, yet the expansion of communication networks is a process that is thousands of years old. Children who speak different languages at home now sit side by side in schools and learn from one another, yet intercultural encounters have long been a source of innovation, transformation, and at times, unfortunately, conflict.

This book is designed for twenty-first-century students who will spend their lives on this small interconnected planet and for whom an understanding of only local or national history will no longer be sufficient. We believe that the study of world history in a broad and comparative context is an exciting, important, and highly practical pursuit. It is our conviction, based on considerable experience in introducing large numbers of students to world history, that a book reflecting current trends in scholarship can excite readers and inspire an enduring interest in the long human experience.

Our strategy has been twofold. First, we have made social and cultural history the core elements of our narrative. We seek to re-create the lives of ordinary people in appealing human terms and also to highlight the interplay between men's and women's lived experiences and the ways they reflect on these to create meaning. Thus, in addition to foundational works of philosophy and literature, we include popular songs and stories. We present objects along with texts as important sources for studying history, and this has allowed us to incorporate the growing emphasis on material culture in the work of many historians. At the same time, we have been mindful of the need to give great economic, political, and intellectual developments the attention they deserve. We want to give individual students and instructors an integrated perspective so that they can pursue — on their own or in the classroom — the themes and questions that they find particularly exciting and significant.

Second, we have made every effort to strike an effective global and regional balance. The whole world interacts today, and to understand the interactions and what they mean for today's citizens, we must study the whole world's history. Thus we have adopted a comprehensive regional organization with a global perspective that is clear and manageable for students. For example, Chapter 7 introduces students in depth to East Asia, and at the same time the chapter highlights the cultural connections that occurred via the Silk Road and the spread of Buddhism. We study all geographical areas, conscious of the separate histories of many parts of the world, particularly in the earliest millennia of human development. We also stress the links among cultures, political units, and economic systems, for these connections have made the world what it is today. We make comparisons and connections across time as well as space, for understanding the unfolding of the human story in time is the central task of history.

## Primary Sources for Teaching Critical Thinking and Analysis

*A History of World Societies* offers an extensive program of primary source assignments to help students master a number of key learning outcomes, among them **critical thinking**, **historical thinking**, **analytical thinking**, and **argumentation**, as well as learning about the **diversity of world cultures**. When assigned in LaunchPad, all primary source features are accompanied by multiple-choice quizzes that help you ensure students come to class prepared.

For the tenth edition, we have augmented our Viewpoints primary source feature to highlight the diversity of the world's people in response to reviewers' enthusiastic endorsement of this feature. The new edition offers in each chapter two sets of paired primary documents on a topic that illuminates the human experience, allowing us to provide more concrete examples of differences in the ways people thought. Anyone teaching world history has to emphasize larger trends and developments, but students sometimes get the wrong impression that everyone in a society thought alike. We hope that teachers can use these passages to get students thinking about diversity within and across societies. The **66 Viewpoints assignments**—two in each chapter—introduce students to working with sources, encourage critical analysis, and extend the narrative while giving voice to the people of the past. Each includes a brief introduction and questions for analysis, and in LaunchPad they are also accompanied by multiple-choice questions. Carefully chosen for accessibility, each pair of documents presents views on a diverse range of topics. **NEW** Viewpoints topics include "Addressing the Gods in Mesopotamia and Egypt"; "The Inglorious Side of War in the *Book of Songs* and the *Patirruppattu*"; "Hellenistic and Chinese Spells"; "Freeing Slaves in Justinian's *Code* and the Qur'an"; early Chinese and Portuguese accounts of Africa; Protestant and Neo-Confucian ideas on behavior; "Jahangir and Louis XIV on Priorities for Monarchs"; "Jean-Jacques Rousseau and Mary Wollstonecraft on Women's Nature and Education"; perspectives on Indian cotton manufacturing in India and Britain; "African Views of the Scramble for Africa"; the abolition of slavery in the Americas; and women activists in Mexico.

Each chapter also continues to include a longer primary source feature titled **Listening to the Past**, chosen to extend and illuminate a major historical issue considered in each chapter. The feature presents a single original source or several voices on the subject to help instructors teach the important skills of **critical thinking** and **analysis**. Each opens with an introduction and closes with questions for analysis that invite students to evaluate the evidence as historians would, and again, in LaunchPad, multiple-choice questions are provided. Selected for their interest and significance and carefully placed within their historical context, these sources, we hope, allow students to "hear the past" and to observe how history has been shaped by individuals. **NEW** topics include "The Teachings of Confucius"; "Gregory of Tours on the Veneration of Relics"; "Courtly Love Poetry"; "Stefan Zweig on Middle-Class Youth and Sexuality" (in early-twentieth-century Europe); "Reyita Castillo Bueno on Slavery and Freedom in Cuba"; "C. L. R. James on Pan-African Liberation"; and lyrics from a Brazilian band on globalization.

In addition to using documents as part of our special feature program, we have quoted extensively from a wide variety of **primary sources within the narrative**, demonstrating in our use of these quotations that they are the "stuff" of history. Thus primary sources appear as an integral part of the narrative as well as in extended form in the Listening to the Past and expanded Viewpoints chapter features.

New assignable **Online Document Projects** in LaunchPad offer students more practice in interpreting primary sources. Each project, based on the Individuals in Society feature described in the next section, prompts students to explore a key question through analysis of multiple sources. Chapter 22's project, for example, asks students to analyze documents on the complexities of the Haitian Revolution and the conditions that made Toussaint L'Ouverture's story possible. Auto-graded multiple-choice questions based on the documents help students analyze the sources.

Finally, we have revised our **primary source documents collection**, *Sources for World Societies*, to add more visual sources and to closely align the readings with the chapter topics and themes of the tenth edition. The documents are now available in a fully assignable and assessable electronic format within each LaunchPad unit, and the accompanying multiple-choice questions measure comprehension and hold students accountable for their reading.

## Student Engagement with Biography

In our years of teaching world history, we have often noted that students come alive when they encounter stories about real people in the past. To give students a chance to see the past through ordinary people's lives, each chapter includes one of the popular **Individuals in Society** biographical essays, each of which offers a brief study of an individual or group, informing students about the societies in which the individuals lived. This feature grew out of our long-standing focus on people's lives and the varieties of historical experience, and we believe that readers will empathize with these human beings who themselves were seeking to define their own identities. The spotlighting of individuals, both famous and obscure, perpetuates the book's continued attention to cultural and intellectual developments, highlights human agency, and reflects changing interests within the historical profession as well as the development of "micro-history." As described previously, in LaunchPad, this feature includes an associated Online Document Project. **NEW** features include essays on Sudatta, a lay follower of the Buddha; Cosimo and Lorenzo de' Medici; Malintzin; and Sieng, a Mnong refugee living in the United States.

## Connecting History to Real-World Applications

Back again are the popular **Global Trade** features, essays that focus on a particular commodity, exploring the world trade, social and economic impact, and cultural influence of that commodity. Each essay is accompanied by a detailed map showing the trade routes of the commodity. We believe that careful attention to all these essays will enable students to appreciate the complex ways in which trade has connected and influenced various parts of the world. All the Global Trade features are fully assignable and assessable in LaunchPad.

## Geographic and Visual Literacy

We recognize students' difficulties with geography and visual analysis, and the new edition retains our **Mapping the Past map activities** and **Picturing the Past visual activities**. Included in each chapter, these activities ask students to analyze a map or visual and make connections to the larger processes discussed in the narrative, giving them valuable practice in reading and interpreting maps and images. In LaunchPad, these activities are assignable and students can submit their work. Throughout the textbook and online in LaunchPad, more than **100 full-size maps** illustrate major developments in the chapters. In addition, **82 spot maps** are embedded in the narrative to show specific areas under discussion.

## Chronological Reasoning

To help students make comparisons, understand changes over time, and see relationships among contemporaneous events, each chapter ends with a **chapter chronology** that reviews major developments discussed in the chapter. A **unified timeline** at the end of the text, and available from every page in LaunchPad, allows students to compare developments over the centuries.

## Active Reading

With the goal of making this the most student-centered edition yet, we paid renewed attention to the book's reading and study aids:

- **Focus questions** at the start of each main heading help guide students in their reading. These questions are repeated in the chapter review section.

- In LaunchPad, instructors can assign the **NEW Guided Reading Exercise** for each chapter, which prompts students to read actively to collect information that answers a broad analytic question central to the chapter as a whole.

- The chapter-closing **Connections** feature synthesizes main developments and makes connections and comparisons between countries and regions to explain how events relate to larger global processes, such as the influence of the Silk Road, the effects of the transatlantic slave trade, and the ramifications of colonialism.

- A **NEW Chapter Summary** reinforces key chapter events and ideas for students.

- **Review and Explore** at the end of each chapter includes a list of key terms, chapter focus questions, and **NEW Make Connections questions** that prompt students to assess larger developments across chapters.

- **Key terms** are bolded in the text, defined in the margin, and listed in the chapter review to promote clarity and comprehension, and **phonetic spellings** are located directly after terms that readers are likely to find hard to pronounce.

All our changes to the book, large and small, are intended to give students and instructors an integrated perspective so that they can pursue—on their own or in the classroom—the historical questions that they find particularly exciting and significant.

## Organizational and Textual Changes

To meet the demands of the evolving course, we have made several major changes in the organization of chapters to reflect the way the course is taught today. The most dramatic changes are the reordering of Chapter 17: The Islamic World Powers, 1300–1800 (formerly Chapter 20) and a complete overhaul of the final section of the book covering the postwar era. This new placement for our coverage of Islam reflects a growing interest among instructors and students in the Islamic world and highlights early Islamic cultural contributions.

To address the concerns of instructors who teach from the second volume of the text, we have added a new section on the Reformation to Chapter 18 so that students whose courses begin with Chapters 15 or 16 will now receive that coverage in Volume 2. The new section includes the Protestant and Catholic Reformations as well as religious violence and witch-hunts.

In its examination of the age of revolution in the Atlantic world, Chapter 22 now incorporates revolutions in Latin America. In order to provide a more global perspective on European politics, culture, and economics in the early modern period, Chapter 23 on the Industrial Revolution considers industrialization more broadly as a global phenomenon with a new section titled "The Global Picture." Together, the enhanced global perspectives of these chapters help connect the different regions of the globe and, in particular, help explain the crucial period when Europe began to dominate the rest of the globe.

The final section of the text, covering the post-1945 period, has also been completely reworked. In addition to updating all the postwar chapters through 2014, Jerry Dávila substantially rewrote the last four chapters and streamlined them into three, creating a more tightly focused and accessible section that now divides the period chronologically as follows: Chapter 31: Decolonization, Revolution, and the Cold War, 1945–1968; Chapter 32: Liberalization, 1968–2000s; Chapter 33: The Contemporary World in Historical Perspective. The last three chapters are now organized around two dominant themes of the postwar world: liberation movements that challenged power structures such as colonialism and racial supremacism; and the spread of liberalization that characterized the end of the Cold War in particular, marking the rise of free markets and liberal political systems. The final chapter examines the significance of social movements in shaping a contemporary world that continues to struggle with historic conflicts and inequalities.

In terms of specific textual changes, we have worked hard to keep the book up-to-date and to strengthen our comprehensive, comparative, and connective approach. Moreover, we revised every chapter with the goal of readability and accessibility. Highlights of the new edition include:

- Chapter 1 includes new information on the recent archaeological find at Göbekli Tepe in present-day Turkey that suggests that cultural factors may have played a role in the development of agriculture.
- Chapter 2 has new coverage on Egyptian society and a discussion of gender distinctions in Sumerian society.
- In Chapter 6, the section on the founding of Rome has been completely rewritten.
- Chapter 8 contains a new section on Christian missionaries and conversion, and it explains the process of the Christianization of barbarian Europe.
- Chapter 11 now centers on the ways in which systems of religious belief shaped ancient societies of the Americas and provided tools people used to understand and adapt to their world. It also looks at the role of sources produced after the European encounter in shaping our understanding of the histories of indigenous American empires.
- An expanded discussion of witchcraft in Chapter 15 now includes practices of indigenous peoples in the New World.
- Chapter 18 has enhanced coverage of Russian imperial expansion as well as a new section called "People Beyond Borders" that includes piracy and gives students a feeling for the ways in which imperial borders were often more real on the map than in real life.
- In Chapter 19, a new section called "The Early Enlightenment" clarifies the mixture of religious, political, and scientific thought that characterized the early period of the Enlightenment.

- Chapter 22 emphasizes the indigenous origins of the Haitian revolution by highlighting the African backgrounds of slaves and the considerable military experience many of them had, which helps explain how they could defeat the French and British.
- Chapter 23 has been heavily revised to reflect new scholarship on industrialization and to provide a broader, more comparative perspective.
- A new section in Chapter 24 on social and economic conflict connects the industrialization of continental Europe with the political coverage of the revolutions of 1848.
- Chapter 27 now focuses on the Americas within the framework of liberalism and examines connections between the experiences of settlement, state formation, and economic integration in the United States and Latin America.
- Chapter 29 contains more detail on the reforms of Amanullah Khan in the section on the modernization of Afghanistan.
- As noted previously, the final three chapters of the book have been entirely rewritten by new author Jerry Dávila.

In sum, we have tried to bring new research and interpretation into our global history because our goal is to keep our book stimulating, accurate, and current for students and instructors.

## Acknowledgments

It is a pleasure to thank the many instructors who critiqued the book in preparation for this revision:

Stewart Anderson, *Brigham Young University*
Brian Arendt, *Lindenwood University*
Stephen Auerbach, *Georgia College*
Michael Bardot, *Lincoln University*
Natalie Bayer, *Drake University*
Michael Bazemore, *William Peace University*
Brian Becker, *Delta State University*
Rosemary Bell, *Skyline College*
Chris Benedetto, *Granite State College*
Wesley L. Bishop, *Pitt Community College*
Robert Blackey, *California State University–San Bernardino*
Edward Bond, *Alabama A&M University*
Nathan Brooks, *New Mexico State University*
Jurgen Buchenau, *The University of North Carolina at Charlotte*
Paul Buckingham, *Morrisville State College*
Steven B. Bunker, *University of Alabama*
Kate Burlingham, *California State University, Fullerton*
David Bush, *The College of the Siskiyous*
Laura M. Calkins, *Texas Tech University*
Robert Caputi, *Erie Community College–North Campus*
Lucia Carter, *Mars Hill College*

Lesley Chapel, *Saginaw Valley State University*
Nevin Crouse, *Chesapeake College*
Everett Dague, *Benedictine College*
Jeffrey Demsky, *San Bernardino Valley College*
Peter de Rosa, *Bridgewater State University*
Nicholas Di Liberto, *Newberry College*
Randall Dills, *University of Louisville*
Shawn Dry, *Oakland Community College*
Roxanne Easley, *Central Washington University*
John Fielding, *Mount Wachusett Community College*
Barbara Fuller, *Indian River State College*
Dolores Grapsas, *New River Community College*
Emily Fisher Gray, *Norwich University*
Gayle Greene-Aguirre, *Mississippi Gulf Coast Community College*
Neil Greenwood, *Cleveland State Community College*
Christian Griggs, *Dalton State College*
W. Scott Haine, *Cañada College*
Irwin Halfond, *McKendree University*
Alicia Harding, *Southern Maine Community College*
Jillian Hartley, *Arkansas Northeastern College*
Robert Haug, *University of Cincinnati*
John Hunt, *Utah Valley University*
Fatima Imam, *Lake Forest College*
Rashi Jackman, *De Anza College*
Jackie Jay, *Eastern Kentucky University*
Timothy Jenks, *East Carolina University*
Andrew Kellett, *Harford Community College*
Christine Kern, *Edinboro University*
Christopher Killmer, *St. Johns River State College*
Mark Klobas, *Scottsdale Community College*
Chris Laney, *Berkshire Community College*
Erick D. Langer, *Georgetown University*
Mary Jean Lavery, *Delaware County Community College*
Mark Lentz, *University of Louisiana, Lafayette*
Darin Lenz, *Fresno Pacific University*
Yi Li, *Tacoma Community College*
Jonas Liliequist, *Umeå University*
Ron Lowe, *University of Tennessee at Chattanooga*
Mary Lyons-Carmona, *University of Nebraska at Omaha*
Elizabeth S. Manley, *Xavier University of Louisiana*
Brandon D. Marsh, *Bridgewater College*
Sean F. McEnroe, *Southern Oregon University*
John McLeod, *University of Louisville*
Brendan McManus, *Bemidji State University*
Christina Mehrtens, *University of Massachusetts–Dartmouth*
Charlotte Miller, *Middle Georgia State College*
Robert Montgomery, *Baldwin Wallace University*
Curtis Morgan, *Lord Fairfax Community College*
Richard Moss, *Harrisburg Area Community College*
Larry Myers, *Butler Community College*
Erik Lars Myrup, *University of Kentucky*
April Najjaj, *Mount Olive College*
Katie Nelson, *Weber State University*
Lily Rhodes Novicki, *Virginia Western Community College*

Monica Orozco, *Westmont College*
Neal Palmer, *Christian Brothers University*
Jenifer Parks, *Rocky Mountain College*
Melinda Pash, *Fayetteville Technical Community College*
Tao Peng, *Minnesota State University–Mankato*
Patricia Perry, *St. Edward's University*
William Plants, *University of Rio Grande/Rio Grande Community College*
Joshua Pollock, *Modesto Junior College*
Fabrizio Prado, *College of William & Mary*
Daniel Prosterman, *Salem College*
Tracie Provost, *Middle Georgia College*
Melissa Redd, *Pulaski Technical College*
Charles Reed, *Elizabeth City State University*
Leah Renold, *Texas State University*
Kim Richardson, *Front Range Community College*
David Ruffley, *Colorado Mountain College*
Martina Saltamacchia, *University of Nebraska at Omaha*
Karl Schmidt, *South Dakota State University*
Kimberly Schutte, *SUNY–The College at Brockport*
Eva Seraphin, *Irvine Valley College*
Courtney Shah, *Lower Columbia College*
Jeffrey Shumway, *Brigham Young University*
David Simonelli, *Youngstown State University*
James Smith, *Southwest Baptist University*
Kara D. Smith, *Georgia Perimeter College*
Ilicia Sprey, *Saint Joseph's College*
Rachel Standish, *San Joaquin Delta College*
Kate Staples, *West Virginia University*
Brian Strayer, *Andrews University*
Sonia Chandarana Tandon, *Forsyth Technical Community College*
James Todesca, *Armstrong Atlantic State University*
Elisaveta Todorova, *University of Cincinnati*
Dianne Walker, *Baton Rouge Community College*
Kenneth Wilburn, *East Carolina University*
Carol Woodfin, *Hardin-Simmons University*
Laura Zeeman, *Red Rocks Community College*

It is also a pleasure to thank the many editors who have assisted us over the years, first at Houghton Mifflin and now at Bedford/St. Martin's. At Bedford/St. Martin's, these include senior development editors Sara Wise and Laura Arcari; associate editor Robin Soule; editorial assistant Arrin Kaplan; former executive editor Traci Mueller Crowell; director of development Jane Knetzger; publisher for history Mary Dougherty; photo researcher Bruce Carson; text permissions editor Eve Lehmann; and senior production editor Christina Horn, with the assistance of Erica Zhang and the guidance of Sue Brown, director of editing and design, and managing editor Michael Granger. Other key contributors were page makeup artist Cia Boynton, copy editor Jennifer Brett Greenstein, proofreaders Linda McLatchie and Angela Morrison, indexer Leoni McVey, and cover designer Donna Dennison. We would also like to thank former vice president for editorial humanities Denise Wydra and former president Joan E. Feinberg.

Many of our colleagues at the University of Illinois, the University of Washington, the University of Wisconsin–Milwaukee, and Eastern Illinois University continue to provide information and stimulation, often without even knowing it. We thank them for it. The authors recognize John P. McKay, Bennett D. Hill, and John Buckler, the founding authors of this textbook, whose vision set a new standard for world history textbooks. The authors also thank the many students over the years with whom we have used earlier editions of this book. Their reactions and opinions helped shape our revisions to this edition, and we hope it remains worthy of the ultimate praise they bestowed, that it is "not boring like most textbooks." Merry Wiesner-Hanks would, as always, like to thank her husband, Neil, without whom work on this project would not be possible. Clare Haru Crowston thanks her husband, Ali, and her children, Lili, Reza, and Kian, who are a joyous reminder of the vitality of life that we try to showcase in this book. Roger Beck thanks Ann for supporting him while she was completing her Ph.D. He is also grateful to the World History Association for all past, present, and future contributions to his understanding of world history. Jerry Dávila thanks Liv, Ellen, and Alex, who are reminders of why history matters.

Each of us has benefited from the criticism of his or her coauthors, although each of us assumes responsibility for what he or she has written. Merry Wiesner-Hanks has written and revised Chapters 1, 2, 5, 6, 8, 14, and 15; Patricia Buckley Ebrey has written and revised Chapters 3, 4, 7, 9, 12, 13, 17, 21, and 26; Roger B. Beck has written and revised Chapters 10, 20, 25, and 28–30; Clare Haru Crowston has written and revised Chapters 16, 18, 19, and 22–24; and Jerry Dávila has completely rewritten Chapters 11, 27, and 31–33.

Adopters of *A History of World Societies* and their students have access to abundant print and digital resources and tools, including documents, assessment and presentation materials, the acclaimed Bedford Series in History and Culture volumes, and much more. And for the first time, the full-featured LaunchPad course space provides access to the narrative with all assignment and assessment opportunities at the ready. See below for more information, visit the book's catalog site at bedfordstmartins.com/mckayworld/catalog, or contact your local Bedford/St. Martin's sales representative.

### Get the Right Version for Your Class

To accommodate different course lengths and course budgets, *A History of World Societies* is available in several different formats, including three-hole-punched loose-leaf Budget Books versions and low-priced PDF e-books, such as the *Bedford e-Book to Go for A History of World Societies* from our Web site and other PDF e-books from other commercial sources. And for the best value of all, package a new print book with LaunchPad at no additional charge to get the best each format offers—a print version for easy portability and reading with a LaunchPad interactive e-book and course space with loads of additional assignment and assessment options.

- **Combined Volume** (Chapters 1–33): available in paperback, loose-leaf, and e-book formats and in LaunchPad
- **Volume 1, To 1600** (Chapters 1–16): available in paperback, loose-leaf, and e-book formats and in LaunchPad
- **Volume 2, Since 1450** (Chapters 16–33): available in paperback, loose-leaf, and e-book formats and in LaunchPad
- **Volume A: To 1500** (Chapters 1–14): available in paperback
- **Volume B: From 800 to 1815** (Chapters 11–22): available in paperback
- **Volume C: From 1775 to the Present** (Chapters 22–33): available in paperback

As noted below, any of these volumes can be packaged with additional titles for a discount. To get ISBNs for discount packages, see the online catalog at bedfordstmartins.com/mckayworld/catalog or contact your Bedford/St. Martin's representative.

### NEW • Assign LaunchPad — a Content-Rich and Assessment-Ready Interactive e-Book and Course Space

Available for discount purchase on its own or for packaging with new books at no additional charge, LaunchPad is a breakthrough solution for today's courses. Intuitive and easy to use for students and instructors alike, LaunchPad is ready to use as is, and can be edited, customized with your own material, and assigned in seconds. *LaunchPad for A History of World Societies* includes Bedford/St. Martin's high-quality content all in one place, including the full interactive e-book and the *Sources of World Societies* documents collection, plus LearningCurve formative quizzing, guided reading activities designed to help students read actively for key concepts, additional primary sources, images, videos, chapter summative quizzes, and more.

Through a wealth of formative and summative assessments, including short-answer and essay questions, multiple-choice quizzing, and the adaptive learning program of LearningCurve (see the full description ahead), students gain confidence and get into their reading *before* class. Map and visual activities engage students with visual analysis and critical thinking as they work through each unit, while special boxed features become more meaningful through automatically graded multiple-choice exercises and short-answer questions that prompt students to analyze their reading.

LaunchPad easily integrates with course management systems, and with fast ways to build assignments, rearrange chapters, and add new pages, sections, or links, it lets teachers build the courses they want to teach and hold students accountable. For more information, visit launchpadworks.com or contact us at history@bedfordstmartins.com to arrange a demo.

### NEW • Assign LearningCurve So Your Students Come to Class Prepared

Students using LaunchPad receive access to LearningCurve for *A History of World Societies*. Assigning LearningCurve in place of reading quizzes is easy, and the reporting features help you track overall class trends and spot topics that are giving students trouble so you can adjust your lectures and class activities. This online learning tool is popular with students because it was designed to help them rehearse content at their own pace in a nonthreatening, gamelike environment. The feedback for wrong answers provides instructional coaching and sends students back to the book for review. Students answer as many questions as necessary to reach a target score, with repeated chances to revisit material they haven't mastered. When LearningCurve is assigned, students come to class better prepared.

## Take Advantage of Instructor Resources

Bedford/St. Martin's has developed a rich array of teaching resources for this book and for this course. They range from lecture and presentation materials and assessment tools to course management options. Most can be found in Launch-Pad or can be downloaded or ordered at **bedfordstmartins .com/mckayworld/catalog**.

**Instructor's Resource Manual.** The instructor's manual offers both experienced and first-time instructors tools for preparing lectures and running discussions. It includes chapter content learning objectives, teaching strategies, and a guide to chapter-specific supplements available for the text, plus suggestions on how to get the most out of Learning-Curve and a survival guide for first-time teaching assistants.

**Guide to Changing Editions.** Designed to facilitate an instructor's transition from the previous edition of *A History of World Societies* to the tenth edition, this guide presents an overview of major changes as well as changes in each chapter.

**Computerized Test Bank.** The test bank includes a mix of fresh, carefully crafted multiple-choice, short-answer, and essay questions for each chapter. All questions appear in Microsoft Word format and in easy-to-use test bank software that allows instructors to add, edit, re-sequence, and print questions and answers. Instructors can also export questions into a variety of formats, including Blackboard, Desire2Learn, and Moodle.

**The Bedford Lecture Kit: PowerPoint Maps and Images.** Look good and save time with *The Bedford Lecture Kit*. These presentation materials are downloadable individually from the Instructor Resources tab at **bedfordstmartins .com/mckayworld/catalog**. They include all maps, figures, and images from the textbook in JPEG and PowerPoint formats.

## Package and Save Your Students Money

For information on free packages and discounts up to 50 percent, visit **bedfordstmartins.com/mckayworld/catalog**, or contact your local Bedford/St. Martin's sales representative. The products that follow all qualify for discount packaging.

**The Bedford Series in History and Culture.** More than 100 titles in this highly praised series combine first-rate scholarship, historical narrative, and important primary documents for undergraduate courses. Each book is brief, inexpensive, and focused on a specific topic or period. For a complete list of titles, visit **bedfordstmartins.com/history/series**.

**Rand McNally Atlas of World History.** This collection of almost 70 full-color maps illustrates the eras and civilizations in world history from the emergence of human societies to the present.

**The Bedford Glossary for World History.** This handy supplement for the survey course gives students historically contextualized definitions for hundreds of terms—from *abolitionism* to *Zoroastrianism*—that they will encounter in lectures, reading, and exams.

**World History Matters: A Student Guide to World History Online.** Based on the popular "World History Matters" Web site produced by the Center for History and New Media, this unique resource, edited by Kristin Lehner (The Johns Hopkins University), Kelly Schrum (George Mason University), and T. Mills Kelly (George Mason University), combines reviews of 150 of the most useful and reliable world history Web sites with an introduction that guides students in locating, evaluating, and correctly citing online sources.

**Trade Books.** Titles published by sister companies Hill and Wang; Farrar, Straus and Giroux; Henry Holt and Company; St. Martin's Press; Picador; and Palgrave Macmillan are available at a 50 percent discount when packaged with Bedford/St. Martin's textbooks. For more information, visit **bedfordstmartins.com/tradeup**.

**A Pocket Guide to Writing in History.** This portable and affordable reference tool by Mary Lynn Rampolla provides reading, writing, and research advice useful to students in all history courses. Concise yet comprehensive advice on approaching typical history assignments, developing critical reading skills, writing effective history papers, conducting research, using and documenting sources, and avoiding plagiarism—enhanced with practical tips and examples throughout—have made this slim reference a bestseller.

**A Student's Guide to History.** This complete guide to success in any history course provides the practical help students need to be successful. In addition to introducing students to the nature of the discipline, author Jules Benjamin teaches a wide range of skills from preparing for exams to approaching common writing assignments, and explains the research and documentation process with plentiful examples.

# Contents

 Access the interactive content online. See inside the front cover for more information.

## 12 Cultural Exchange in Central and Southern Asia

### 300–1400   329

## 13 States and Cultures in East Asia

### 800–1400   363

## 14 Europe in the Middle Ages
### 800–1450  391

## 15 Europe in the Renaissance and Reformation
### 1350–1600  425

## 18 European Power and Expansion
### 1500–1750 519

## 19 New Worldviews and Ways of Life
### 1540–1790 555

# Maps, Figures, and Tables

## FIGURES AND TABLES

# Special Features

## INDIVIDUALS IN SOCIETY

## GLOBAL TRADE

# A HISTORY OF
# World Societies

**Moche Portrait Vessel**

A Moche artist captured the commanding expression of a ruler in this ceramic vessel. The Moche were one of many cultures in Peru that developed technologies that were simultaneously useful and beautiful, including brightly colored cloth, hanging bridges made of fiber, and intricately fit stone walls. (Private Collection/Photo © Boltin Picture Library/The Bridgeman Art Library)

**LearningCurve**

After reading the chapter, go online and use LearningCurve to retain what you've read.

# Chapter Preview

When peoples of the Americas first came into sustained contact with peoples from Europe, Africa, and Asia at the turn of the sixteenth century, their encounters were uneven. Thousands of years of isolation from other world societies made peoples of the Americas vulnerable to diseases found elsewhere in the world. When indigenous peoples were first exposed to these diseases through contact with Europeans, the devastating effects of epidemics facilitated European domination and colonization. But this exchange also brought into global circulation the results of thousands of years of work by peoples of the Americas in plant domestication that changed diets worldwide, making corn, potatoes, and peppers into the daily staples of many societies.

The ancient domestication of these crops intensified agriculture across the Americas that sustained increasingly complex societies. At times these societies grew into vast empires built on trade, conquest, and tribute. Social stratification and specialization produced lands not just of kings but of priests, merchants, artisans, scientists, and engineers who achieved extraordinary feats.

In **Mesoamerica**—the region stretching from present-day Nicaragua to California—the dense urban centers of Maya, Teotihuacan, Toltec, and Mexica city-states and empires featured great monuments, temples, and complex urban planning. Roadways and canals extended trade networks that reached from South America to the Great Lakes region of North America. Sophisticated calendars guided systems of religious, scientific, medical, and agricultural knowledge.

These achievements were rivaled only in the Andes, the mountain range that extends from southernmost present-day Chile north to Colombia and Venezuela. Andean peoples adapted to the mountain range's stark vertical stratification of climate and ecosystems to produce agricultural abundance similar to that of Mesoamerica. The technological, agricultural, and engineering innovations of ancient Andean civilizations allowed people to make their difficult mountain terrain a home rather than a boundary.

# Societies of the Americas in a Global Context

☐ How did ancient peoples of the Americas adapt to, and adapt, their environment?

Ancient societies of the Americas shared many characteristics that were common to other premodern societies around the world that stretched from the Pacific Rim to the Mediterranean. But many elements were also unique to the ancient peoples of the Americas, and we must consider these on their own terms. Since societies of the Americas developed in isolation, their history offers a counterpoint to premodern histories of other parts of the world. Like people everywhere, civilizations of the Americas interpreted the meaning of the world and their place in the cosmos. They organized societies stratified not just by gender, class, and ethnicity but also by professional roles and wealth, and they adapted to and reshaped their physical and natural world. But they did all this on their own, without outside influences and within a distinct environment.

If the differences between civilizations in the Americas and other world regions are remarkable, the similarities are even more so. By studying the peoples of the Americas before their encounters with other world societies, we gain a clearer view of universal aspects of the human experience.

## Trade and Technology

The domestication of crops and animals created an abundance of food and livestock, which allowed people to take on new social roles and to develop specialized occupations. As cities emerged, they became hubs of a universal human activity: trade. These cities were home to priests who interpreted the nature of our world, as well as a nobility from which kings emerged, some of whom forged vast empires based on their ability to coordinate conquest, trade, tribute from conquered subjects, and systems of religious beliefs.

The differences in the development and application of three different kinds of technologies—the wheel, writing and communications systems, and calendars—capture this essential nature of human adaptability.

Before their encounters with other world peoples that began in 1492, societies in Mesoamerica and the Andes did not use wheeled transportation. Had they failed to invent one of the basic technologies used elsewhere in the world? No, they had not. As it happens, wheels were used in children's toys, just not for transportation. Tools emerged (or did not emerge) from specific needs. In Mesoamerica there were no large animals like horses or oxen to domesticate as beasts of burden,

so there was no way to power wagons or chariots. In the Andes, domesticated llamas and alpacas served as pack animals and were a source of wool and meat. But in the most densely settled, cultivated, and developed areas, the terrain was too difficult for wheeled transportation. Instead Andean peoples developed extensive networks of roads that navigated steep changes in altitude, supported by elaborate suspension bridges made from woven vegetable fibers.

Peoples of the Americas also did not develop an alphabet or character-based writing systems, but this did not mean they did not communicate or record information. If we separate our understanding of the alphabetical reading you are doing right now from its functions—communicating and storing of information—we can appreciate the ways in which Andean and Mesoamerican civilizations accomplished both. Peoples of the Americas spoke thousands of languages (hundreds are still spoken today). Mesoamericans, beginning with the Olmecs (1500–400 B.C.E.), used pictographic glyphs similar to those of ancient Egyptian writing to record and communicate information. Later civilizations continued to adapt these systems. The Aztecs produced hieroglyphic books written on paper and deerskin.

The Andean innovation for recording information was particularly remarkable. The **khipu** (KEY-pooh) was an assemblage of colored and knotted strings. The differences in color, arrangement, and type of knot, as well as the knots' order and placement, served as a binary system akin to a contemporary computer database. As archaeologists and linguists struggle to decode khipus, they have discerned their role in recording demographic, economic, and political information that allowed imperial rulers and local leaders to understand and manage complex data.

Mesoamerican peoples used a sophisticated combination of calendars. These were based on a Calendar Round that combined a 365-day solar calendar with a 260-day calendar based on the numbers thirteen and twenty, which were sacred to peoples of Mesoamerica. Annual cycles were completed when twenty 13-day bundles converged with thirteen 20-day bundles. Together with the solar calendar, these formed a fifty-two-year cycle whose precision was unsurpassed in the premodern world. It also provided an incredibly intricate mechanism not only for following the solar and lunar years but also for connecting these to aspects of daily life and religion, helping users of the calendar to interpret their world.

- **Mesoamerica** The term used to designate the area of present-day Mexico and Central America.

- **khipu** An intricate system of knotted and colored strings used by early Andean cultures to store information such as census and tax records.

**Inca Khipu** Khipus like these (above) were used by communities and by Inca imperial officials to store and communicate data. The dyes, weaves, and knots made by their users recorded data much like contemporary binary computer storage, allowing users (right) to read information about populations, production, and tribute. (khipu: The Granger Collection, NYC — All rights reserved; illustration: from *Historia y Genealogia Real de los Reyes Incas del Peru, de sus hechos, constumbres, trajes y manera de Gobierno*, known as the *Codice Murua* [vellum], 16th century/ Private Collection/The Bridgeman Art Library)

## Settlement and Environment

Ancient settlers in the Americas adapted to and adapted diverse environments ranging from the high plateau of the Andes and central plateau of Mesoamerica to the tropical rain forest and river systems of the Amazon and Caribbean, as well as the prairies of North and South America. But, given the isolation of these societies, where did the first peoples to settle the continent come from?

The first settlers migrated from Asia, though their timing and their route are debated. One possibility is that the first settlers migrated across the Bering Strait from what is now Russia to Alaska and gradually migrated southward sometime between 15,000 and 13,000 B.C.E. But archaeological excavations have identified much earlier settlements along the Andes in South America, perhaps dating to over 40,000 years ago, than they have for Mesoamerica or North America. These findings suggest that the original settlers in the Americas arrived instead (or also) as fishermen circulating the Pacific Ocean.

Like early settlers elsewhere in the world, populations of the Americas could be divided into three categories: nomadic peoples, semi-sedentary farming communities, and dense agricultural communities capable of sustaining cities. Urban settlement and empire formation centered around two major regions. The first area, Lake Titicaca, located at the present-day border between Peru and Bolivia, is the highest lake in the world (12,500 feet high) and the largest lake in South America (3,200 square miles). The second area was in the Valley of Mexico on the central plateau of Mesoamerica, where empires emerged from the cities around Lake Texcoco. Access to these large freshwater lakes allowed settlers to expand agriculture through irrigation, which in turn supported growing urban populations.

The earliest farming settlements emerged around 5000 B.C.E. These farming communities began the long process of domesticating and modifying plants, including maize (corn) and potatoes. Farmers also domesticated other crops native to the Americas such as peppers, beans, squash, and avocados.

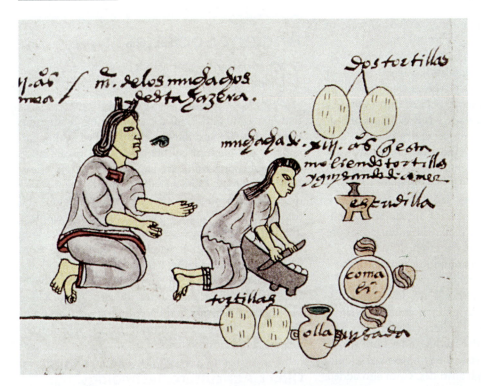

**Making Tortillas** A mother teaches her daughter to roll tortillas on a metate. The dough at the right of the metate was masa made with maize and lime. The preparation process, known as nixtamalization, enriched the maize paste by adding calcium, potassium, and iron. (Page from the *Codex Mendoza*, Mexico, c. 1541–42 [pen and ink on paper], Bodleian Library, Oxford, UK/The Bridgeman Art Library)

The origins of maize in Mesoamerica are unclear, though it became a centerpiece of the Mesoamerican diet and spread across North and South America. Unlike other grains such as wheat and rice, the kernels of maize—which are the seeds as well as the part that is eaten for food—are wrapped in a husk, so the plant cannot propagate itself easily, meaning that farmers had to intervene to cultivate the crop. In addition, no direct ancestor of maize has been found. Biologists believe that Mesoamerican farmers identified a mutant form of a related grass called teosinte and gradually adapted it through selection and hybridization. Eaten together with beans, maize provided Mesoamerican peoples with a diet sufficient in protein despite the scarcity of meat. Mesoamericans processed kernels through **nixtamalization**, boiling the maize in a solution of water and mineral lime. The process broke down compounds in the kernels, increasing their nutritional value, while enriching the resulting *masa*, or paste, with dietary minerals including calcium, potassium, and iron.

The masa could then be cooked with beans, meat, or other ingredients to make tamales. It could also be rolled flat on a stone called a *metate* and baked into tortillas. Tortillas played roles similar to bread in wheat-producing cultures: they could be stored, they were light and easy to transport, and they were used as the basic building block of meals. Aztec armies of the fifteenth century could travel long distances because they carried tortillas for sustenance. Along their route, communities were obligated to provide tribute in tortillas. The rapid military expansion of the Aztec Empire was sustained in part by the versatility of the tortilla, which gave soldiers the ability to fight far from home.

Andean peoples cultivated another staple of the Americas, the potato. Potatoes first grew wild, but selective breeding produced many different varieties. For Andean peoples, potatoes became an integral part of a complex system of cultivation at varying altitudes. Communities created a system of "vertical archipelagos" through which they took advantage of the changes of climate along the steep escarpments of the Andes. Different crops could be cultivated at different altitudes, allowing communities to engage in intense and varied farming in what would otherwise have been inhospitable territory.

The settlement of communities, including what would become the largest cities, often took place at an altitude of nearly two miles (about 10,000 feet), in a temperate region at the boundary between ecological zones for growing maize and potatoes. The notable exception was the Lake Titicaca basin, at an elevation of 12,500 feet, where the abundance of fresh water tempered the climate and made irrigation possible. Communities raised multiple crops and engaged in year-round farming by working at different altitudes located within a day's journey from home. Some of these zones of cultivation were so distant—sometimes over a week's journey—that they were tended by

• **nixtamalization** Boiling maize in a solution of water and mineral lime to break down compounds in the kernels, increasing their nutritional value.

temporary or permanent colonies, called *mitmaq*, of the main settlement.

At higher elevations, members of these communities cultivated potatoes. Arid conditions across much of the altiplano, or high-plains plateau, meant that crops of potatoes could sometimes be planted only every few years. But the climate—dry with daily extremes of heat and cold—could be used to freeze-dry potatoes that could be stored indefinitely. Above the potato-growing zone, shepherds tended animals such as llamas and alpacas, which provided wool and dried meat, or *ch'arki* (the origin of the word *jerky*). They also served as pack animals that helped farmers bring in the crops from their high- and low-altitude plots. The animals' manure served as fertilizer for farming at lower altitudes.

At middle altitudes, communities used terraces edged by stone walls to extend cultivation along steep mountainsides to grow corn. In the lowlands, they cultivated the high-protein grain quinoa, as well as beans, peppers, and coca. Farmers chewed coca (the dried leaves of a plant native to the Andes from which cocaine is derived) to alleviate the symptoms of strenuous labor at extremely high altitudes. Coca also added nutrients such as calcium to the Andean diet and played an important role in religious rituals. In the lowlands communities also grew cotton, and in coastal areas they harvested fish and mussels. Fishermen built inflatable rafts made of sealskin.

**MAP 11.1 The Olmecs, ca. 1500–300 B.C.E.** Olmec civilization flourished in the coastal lowlands of southern Mexico along the Caribbean coast. Olmec patterns of settlement, culture, religion, organization, and trade are known almost solely through excavation of archaeological sites.

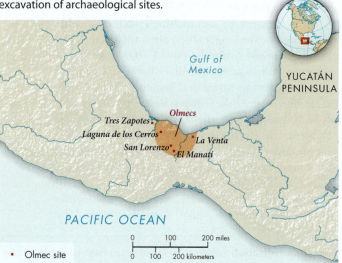

# Ancient Societies

☐ What patterns established by early societies shaped civilization in Mesoamerica and the Andes?

Between 1500 and 1200 B.C.E. emerging civilizations in Mesoamerica and the Andes established lasting patterns of production, culture, and social organization that would long influence societies of the Americas. In Mesoamerica, Olmec civilization brought together practices of farming and trade, as well as religious and technological innovations that served future empires. The imprint of Olmec civilization spread across long networks of trade that would one day extend from Central America to the Mississippi Valley and the Great Lakes of North America. In the Andes, Chavín and Moche civilizations formed the early part of a long cycle of centralization and decentralization. This political and economic centralization helped spread technology, culture, and religion.

## Olmec Agriculture, Technology, and Religion

The **Olmecs** were an early civilization that shaped the religion, trade practices, and technology of later civilizations in Mesoamerica. They flourished in the coastal lowlands of Mexico along a region stretching from Veracruz to the Yucatán from 1500 to 300 B.C.E. The Olmecs formed the first cities of Mesoamerica, and these cities served as centers of agriculture, trade, and religion (Map 11.1). Through long-distance trade, the Olmecs spread their culture and technology across Mesoamerica, establishing beliefs and practices that became common to the civilizations that followed.

The Olmecs settled and farmed along rivers in coastal lowlands, where they cultivated maize, squash, beans, and other plants and supplemented their diet with wild game and fish. But they lacked many other resources. In particular, they carried stone for many miles for the construction of temples and for carving massive monuments, many in the shape of heads. Across far-flung networks the Olmecs traded rubber, cacao (from which chocolate is made), pottery, clay figures, and jaguar pelts, as well as the services of artisans such as painters and sculptors, in exchange for obsidian, a volcanic glass that could be carved to a razor-sharp edge and used for making knives, tools, spear tips, and other weapons.

These ties between the Olmecs and other communities spread religious practices, creating a shared framework of beliefs among later civilizations. These practices included the construction of large pyramid temples, as well as acts that ranged from blood sacri-

**MAP 11.2 Major North American Agricultural Societies, ca. 600–1500 C.E.**
Many North American groups used agriculture to increase the available food supply and allow greater population density and the development of urban centers. This map shows three of these cultures: the Mississippian, Anasazi, and Hohokam.

fice, in which nobles ritually cut and bled themselves but did not die, to human sacrifice, in which the subject died. In addition to the manner of worship, archaeologists can trace the nature of the deities common in Mesoamerica. Olmec deities, like those of their successors, were combinations of gods and humans, included merged animal and human forms, and had both male and female identities. People practicing later religions based their gods on the fusion of human and spirit traits along the lines of the Olmec were-jaguar: a half-man, half-jaguar figure.

The Olmecs also used a Long Count solar calendar—a calendar based on a 365-day year. This calendar begins with the year 3114 B.C.E., though its origins and the significance of this date are unclear. Archaeologists presume that the existence of the Long Count calendar meant that the Calendar Round combining the 260-day and 365-day years already existed as well. All the later Mesoamerican civilizations used at least one of these calendars, and most used both of them.

## Hohokam, Hopewell, and Mississippian Societies

Mesoamerican trading networks extended into southwestern North America, where by 300 B.C.E. the Hohokam people and other groups were using irrigation canals, dams, and terraces to enhance their farming of arid lands (Map 11.2). Like the Olmecs and other Mesoamerican peoples, the Hohokam built ceremonial platforms and played games with rubber balls that were traded over a long distance in return for turquoise and other precious stones. Along with trade goods came religious ideas, including the belief in local divinities who created, preserved, and destroyed. The Mesoamerican feathered serpent god became important to desert peoples. They planted desert crops such as agave, as well as cotton and maize that came from

• **Olmecs** The oldest of the early advanced Mesoamerican civilizations.

Mexico. Other groups, including the Anasazi (ah-nah-SAH-zee), the Yuma, and later the Pueblo and Hopi, also built settlements in this area using large sandstone blocks and masonry to construct thick-walled houses that offered protection from the heat. Mesa Verde, the largest Anasazi town, had a population of about twenty-five hundred living in houses built into and on cliff walls. Roads connected Mesa Verde to other Anasazi towns, allowing timber and other construction materials to be brought in more easily. Eventually drought, deforestation, and soil erosion led to decline in both the Hohokam and Anasazi cultures.

To the east, the Mississippian culture also engaged in monumental mound building beginning around 2000 B.C.E. One of the most important mound-building cultures was the Hopewell (200 B.C.E.–600 C.E.), named for a town in Ohio near the site of the most extensive mounds. Some mounds were burial chambers holding either a powerful individual or thousands of more average people. Other mounds formed animal or geometric figures. Hopewell earthworks also included canals that enabled trading networks to expand, bringing products from the Caribbean far into the interior. Those trading networks also carried maize, allowing more intensive agriculture to spread throughout the eastern woodlands of North America.

At Cahokia (kuh-HOE-kee-uh), near the confluence of the Mississippi and Missouri Rivers in Illinois, archaeologists have uncovered the largest mound of all, part of a ceremonial center and city that housed perhaps thirty-eight thousand people. Work on this complex of mounds, plazas, and houses—which covered 5½ square miles—began about 1050 C.E. and was completed about 1250 C.E. A fence of wooden posts surrounded the center of the complex. Several hundred rectangular mounds inside and outside the fence served as tombs and as the bases for temples and palaces. Within the fence, the largest mound rose in four stages to a height of one hundred feet and was nearly one thousand feet long. On its top stood a large building, used perhaps as a temple.

Cahokia engaged in long-distance trade reaching far across North America and became a highly stratified society. Mississippian mound builders relied on agriculture to support their complex cultures, and by the time Cahokia was built, maize agriculture had spread to the Atlantic coast. Particularly along riverbanks and the coastline, fields of maize, beans, and squash surrounded large, permanent villages containing many houses, all encompassed by walls made of earth and timber. Hunting and fishing provided animal protein, but the bulk of people's food came from farming.

At its peak in about 1150 Cahokia was the largest city north of Mesoamerica. However, construction of the interior wooden fence stripped much of the surrounding countryside of trees, which made spring floods worse and eventually destroyed much of the city. An earthquake at the beginning of the thirteenth century furthered the destruction, and the city never recovered. The worsening climate of the fourteenth century, which brought famine to Europe, probably also contributed to Cahokia's decline, and its population dispersed. Throughout Mississippian areas, the fifteenth century brought increased warfare and migration. Iroquois-speaking peoples in particular migrated into the region, sometimes displacing, through war, groups that had been living in these areas.

## Kinship and Ancestors in the Andes

As in Mesoamerica, in the Andes social organization and religion shaped ideas of spiritual kinship as well as patterns of production and trade. The *ayllu* (EYE-you), or clan, served as the fundamental social unit of Andean society. Kinship was based on a shared ancestor, or *huaca*, who could be a once-living person whose remains were mummified and preserved, but could also be an animal spirit or a combination of the two. Members of an ayllu considered their huaca as more than a spirit: it owned lands the ayllu farmers tended, and the huaca served as the center of community obligations such as shared labor.

Ancestor worship provided the foundations of Andean religion and spirituality, served as the basis of authority, and guided food production. All members of the ayllu owed allegiance to *kuracas*, or clan leaders, who typically traced the most direct lineage to the ancestor, or huaca. This lineage made them both temporal and spiritual leaders of their ayllu: the kuraca was the living member of the community who had the most direct communion with the spirit world inhabited by the huaca. An Andean family's identity came from membership in an ayllu's ancestral kinship, and its subsistence came from participation in the broader community's shared farming across vertical climate zones. People often labored collectively and reciprocally. Within the ayllu, a reciprocal labor pool first tended to the fields of the huaca and the kuraca, then to the fields of widows and the infirm, and then to the other fields of the ayllu members.

Andean history unfolded in a cycle of centralization and decentralization. There were three great periods of

• **Moche** A Native American culture that thrived along Peru's northern coast between 100 and 800 C.E. The culture existed as a series of city-states and was distinguished by an extraordinarily rich and diverse pottery industry.

• **Inca** The name of the dynasty of rulers who built a large empire across the Andes that was at its peak around 1500.

centralization, which archaeologists call the Early, Middle, and Late Horizon. The Late Horizon, which included the Inca Empire, was the briefest, cut short by the Spanish conquest (see page 324). The first period, the Early Horizon (ca. 1200–200 B.C.E.), centered on the people of Chavín, upland from present-day Lima. The Chavín spread their religion along with technologies for the weaving and dyeing of wool and cotton. Weaving became the most widespread means of recording and representing information in the Andes.

After the end of the Early Horizon, regional states emerged, including **Moche** (MOH-cheh) civilization, which flourished along a 250-mile stretch of Peru's northern coast between 100 and 800 C.E. Rivers that flowed out of the Andes into the valleys allowed the Moche people to develop complex irrigation systems, with which they raised food crops and cotton. Each Moche valley contained a large ceremonial center with palaces and pyramids surrounded by settlements of up to ten thousand people. Their dazzling gold and silver artifacts, as well as elaborate headdresses, display a remarkable skill in metalwork. The Moche were also skilled potterymakers and weavers of cotton and other fibers. Their refined vessels, like the one shown at the beginning of this chapter, offer a rich look into their aesthetics and their world.

Politically, the Moche were organized into a series of small city-states rather than one unified state, and warfare was common among them. Beginning about 500 the Moche suffered several severe El Niños, changes in ocean current patterns in the Pacific that bring searing drought and flooding. They were not able to respond effectively to the devastation, and their urban population declined.

Pan-Andean cultures re-emerged during the Middle Horizon (500–1000 C.E.), centered to the south in Tiwanaku, near Lake Titicaca, and to the north at Wari, near present-day southern Peru. The city-state of Wari's dominion stretched from the altiplano north of Lake Titicaca to the Pacific coast, drawing on Moche cultural influences. Its reach between mountain and coastal regions led to extensive exchanges of goods and beliefs between ecologically different farming zones. The city-state of Tiwanaku extended its influence in the other direction, south of the lake. Both Wari and Tiwanaku practiced ancestor worship, and Tiwanaku religion centered on the figure of Viracocha, the god creator and father of humanity, who was identified with the sun and storms.

Storms and climate shifts were central to Andean people's worldview because changes in climate, particularly abrupt changes brought by El Niño, could devastate whole civilizations. El Niño disrupted Moche culture and contributed to the decline of Wari and Tiwanaku. The remains of elaborate projects designed to extend irrigation and reclaim land for farming along Lake Titicaca reveal the social and political impact of drought in already-arid Andean environments. As the Middle Horizon ended, the cities of Tiwanaku and Wari endured on a smaller scale, but between 1000 and 1200 C.E. they lost their regional influence. The eras between the Early, Middle, and Late Horizon, known as Intermediate Periods, were times of decentralization in which local cultures and practices re-emerged. It was out of these local developments that new centralizing empires would over time emerge.

# The Incas

❑ What were the sources of strength and prosperity, and of problems, for the Incas?

**Inca** was the name of a ruling family that settled in the basin of Cuzco and formed the largest and last Andean empire. The empire, whose people we will call the Incas, was called Tawantinsuyu (TAH-want-een-soo-you), meaning "from the four parts, one," expressing the idea of a unified people stretching in all directions.

## The Inca Model of Empire

In the Late Intermediate Period (1200–1470), the Pan-Andean influences of Wari and Tiwanaku waned. City-states around Lake Titicaca competed and fought with each other. The strongest ones to emerge again followed the division between the region north of the lake and toward the coast, and south of the lake and across the altiplano. To the north, the Chimu claimed the legacy of the Moche and Wari. To the south, the city of Cuzco became the hub of a growing kingdom under the hereditary control of the Inca (Map 11.3). *Inca* refers to the empire's ruler, while the empire was called Tawantinsuyu. According to their religious beliefs, the Inca rulers invented civilization. In reality, they inherited it from the civilizations of the Titicaca basin and the Chimu on the northern coast.

From the 1420s until 1438 Viracocha Inca emerged as the first Inca leader to attempt permanent conquest. Unlike the *sinchis* (SEEN-cheese), or kings, of earlier and rival city-states, Viracocha Inca fashioned himself an emperor and, in adopting the name Viracocha, connected himself to the god of creation. In 1438 rivals invaded Viracocha Inca's territories and he fled. His son, Pachacuti, remained in Cuzco and fended off the invaders. He crowned himself emperor and embarked on a campaign of conquest. Pachacuti Inca (r. 1438–1471) conquered the Chimu near the end of his reign, and he incorporated beliefs and practices from this northern civilization.

After conquering the Chimu, Pachacuti instituted practices that quickly expanded the empire across the Andes. He combined Andean ancestor worship with the Chimu system of a split inheritance, a combination that drove swift territorial expansion and transformed Tawantinsuyu into one of the largest empires in the world within less than fifty years. Under the system of ancestor worship, the Incas believed the dead emperor's spirit was still present, and they venerated him through his mummy. Split inheritance meant that the dead emperor retained all the lands he had conquered, commanded the loyalty of all his subjects, and continued to receive tribute. A *panaqa* (pan-AH-kah), a trust formed by his closest relatives, managed both the cult of his mummy and his temporal affairs. Chimu split inheritance became the political structure that determined the Inca emperor's authority.

When the ruler died, his corpse was preserved as a mummy in elaborate clothing and housed in a sacred and magnificent chamber. A sixteenth-century account of the death of Pachacuti Inca in 1471 described the practices for burying and honoring him:

> He was buried by putting his body in the earth in a large new clay urn, with him very well dressed. Pachacuti Inca [had] ordered that a golden image made to resemble him be placed on top of his tomb. And it was to be worshiped in place of him by the people who went there. . . . [He had] ordered those of his own lineage to bring this statue out for the feasts that were held in Cuzco. When they brought it out like this, they sang about the things that the

Inca did in his life, both in the wars and in his city. Thus they served and revered him, changing its garments as he used to do, and serving it as he was served when he was alive.[1]

The panaqa of descendants of each dead ruler managed his lands and used his income to care for his mummy, maintain his cult, and support themselves, all at great expense. When a ruler died, one of his sons was named the new Inca emperor. He received the title, but not the lands and tribute—nor, for that matter, the

## ☐ Mapping the Past

**MAP 11.3    The Inca Empire, 1532** Andean peoples turned their stark mountain landscape to their advantage by settling and farming in vertical archipelagos. Settlements were located at temperate altitudes, while farming and herding took place at higher and lower altitudes.

**ANALYZING THE MAP** In what ways did Andean peoples turn their mountain landscape from an obstacle into a resource?

**CONNECTIONS** What types of geographic features did other peoples of the Americas, or peoples in other regions of the world, adapt to their advantage? How did adaptation to their geography shape those societies?

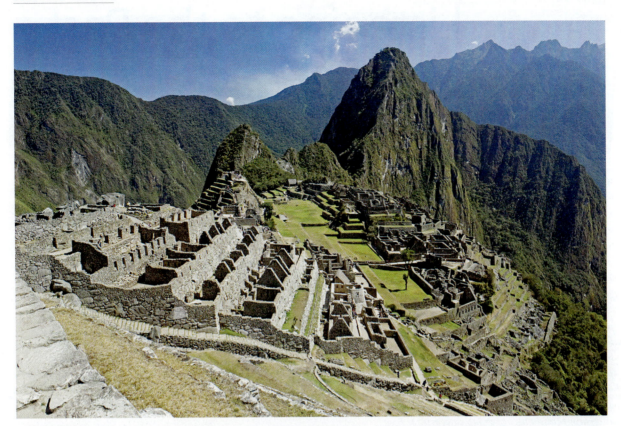

**Machu Picchu** The Inca ruins of Machu Picchu rise spectacularly above the steep valley of the Urubamba River. The site was built around 1450 as a royal estate and abandoned after the Spanish conquest. (Tony Camacho/Photo Researchers, Inc.)

direct allegiance of the nobility, bound as it was to the deceased ruler. The new emperor built his own power and wealth by conquering new lands.

## Inca Imperial Expansion

The combination of ancestor worship and split inheritance provided the logic and impulse for expanding Inca power. The desire for conquest provided incentives for courageous (or ambitious) nobles: those who succeeded in battle and gained new territories for the state could expect to receive lands, additional wives, servants, herds of llamas, gold, silver, fine clothes, and other symbols of high status. Even common soldiers who distinguished themselves in battle could be rewarded with booty and raised to noble status. Under Pachacuti Inca and his successors, Inca domination was extended by warfare to the frontier of present-day Ecuador and Colombia in the north and to the Maule River in present-day Chile in the south, an area of about 350,000 square miles. Eighty provinces, scores of ethnic groups, and 16 million people came under Inca control.

The Incas pursued the integration of regions they conquered by imposing their language and their gods. Magnificent temples scattered throughout the expanding empire housed images of these gods. Priests led prayers and elaborate rituals, and during occasions such as terrible natural disasters or great military victories they sacrificed humans. The Incas forced conquered peoples to adopt **Quechua** (KEH-chuh-wuh), the official language of the empire, which extinguished many regional languages, although another major Andean language, Aymara, endured. Though Quechua did not exist in written form until the Spanish in Peru adopted it as a second official language, it is still spoken by millions in Peru and Bolivia, as well as in regions of Ecuador, Argentina, and Chile.

The pressure for growth strained the Inca Empire. Open lands became scarce, so the Incas tried to penetrate the tropical Amazon forest east of the Andes — an effort that led to repeated military disasters. Traditionally, the Incas waged war with highly trained armies drawn up in massed formation and fought pitched battles on level ground, often engaging in hand-to-hand combat. But in dense jungles the troops could not maneuver or maintain order against enemies, who used

- **Quechua** First deemed the official language of the Incas under Pachacuti, it is still spoken by most Peruvians today.

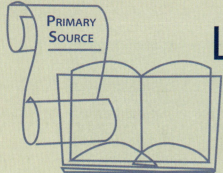

PRIMARY SOURCE

# Listening to the Past

## Felipe Guaman Poma de Ayala, *The First New Chronicle and Good Government*

*Felipe Guaman Poma de Ayala (1550?–1616) came from a noble indigenous family in Peru. He spoke Quechua, Aymara, and Spanish and was baptized as a Christian. As an assistant to a Spanish friar and a Spanish judge, he saw firsthand the abuses of the Spanish authorities in what had been the Inca Empire. In the early seventeenth century he began writing and illustrating what became his masterpiece, a handwritten book of almost eight hundred pages of text and nearly four hundred line drawings addressed to the king of Spain that related the history of the Inca Empire and the realities of Spanish rule. He hoped to send the book to Spain, where it would convince the king to make reforms that would bring about the "good government" of the book's title. (The book apparently never reached the king, though it did make its way to Europe. It was discovered in the Danish Royal Library in Copenhagen in 1908.) In the following section, Guaman Poma sets out certain traditional age-group categories of Inca society, which he terms "paths," ten for men and ten for women.*

“ The first path was that of the brave men, the soldiers of war. They were thirty-three years of age (they entered this path as young as twenty-five, and left it at fifty). These brave men were held very much apart and distinguished in every manner possible. The Inca [the Inca ruler] selected some of these Indians to serve in his battles and wars. He selected some from among these brave Indians to settle as *mitmaqs* (foreigners) in other provinces, giving them more than enough land, both pasture and cropland, to multiply, and giving each of them a woman from the same land. He did this to keep his kingdom secure; they served as overseers. . . .

The Fifth Path was that of the *sayapayac* [those who stand upright]. These were the Indians of the watch, aged from eighteen to twenty years. They served as messenger boys between one pueblo and another, and to other nearby places in the valley. They also herded flocks, and accompanied the Indians of war and the great lords and captains. They also carried food. . . .

The Eighth Path was that of boys aged from five to nine years. These were the "boys who play" (*puellacoc wamracuna*). They served their mothers and fathers in whatever ways they could, and bore many whippings and thumpings; they also served by playing with the toddlers and by rocking and watching over the babies in cradles. . . .

The Tenth Path was that of those called *wawa quirawpi cac* (newborn babies at the breast, in cradles), from the age of one month. It is right for others to serve them; their mothers must necessarily serve them for no other person can give milk to these children. . . .

The First Path was that of the married women and widows called *auca camayocpa warmin* [the warriors' women], whose occupation is weaving fine cloth for the Inca, the other lords, the captains, and the soldiers. They were thirty-three years of age when they married; up until then, they remained virgins and maidens. . . . These wives of brave men were not free [from tribute obligations]. These women had the occupation of weaving fine *awasca* cloth and spinning yarn; they assisted the commons in their pueblos and provinces, and they assisted with everything their titled noble lords decreed. . . .

The Sixth Path was that of those called *coro tasqui-cunas*, *rotusca tasqui*, which means "young girls with short-cropped hair." They were from twelve to eighteen years of age and served their fathers, mothers, and grandmothers. They also began to

guerrilla tactics against them. Another source of stress came from revolts among subject peoples in conquered territories. Even the system of roads and message-carrying runners couldn't keep up with the administrative needs of the empire. The average runner could cover about 175 miles per day—a remarkable feat of physical endurance, especially at a high altitude—but the larger the empire became, the greater the distances to be covered grew. The round trip from the capital at Cuzco to Quito in Ecuador, for example, took from ten to twelve days, so an emperor might have to base urgent decisions on incomplete or out-of-date information. The empire was overextended.

## Imperial Needs and Obligations

At its height, the Inca Empire extended over 2,600 miles. The challenges of sustaining an empire with that reach, not to mention one built so fast, required extraordinary resourcefulness. The Inca Empire met these demands by adapting aspects of local culture to meet imperial needs. For instance, the empire demanded that the ayllus, the local communities with shared ancestors, include imperial tribute in the rotation of labor and the distribution of harvested foods. (See "Listening to the Past: Felipe Guaman Poma de Ayala, *The First New Chronicle and Good Government*," above.)

serve the great ladies so that they could learn to spin yarn and weave delicate materials. They served as animal herders and workers in the fields, and in making *chica* [corn beer] for their fathers and mothers, and they assisted in other occupations insofar as they could, helping out . . . they were filled with obedience and respect, and were taught to cook, spin, and weave. Their hair was kept cropped until they reached the age of thirty, when they were married and given the dowry of their destitution and poverty.

The Seventh Path was that of the girls called flower pickers. . . . They picked flowers to dye wool for *cumpis*, cloth, and other things, and they picked the edible herbs mentioned above, which they dried out and stored in the warehouse to be eaten the following year. These girls were from nine to twelve years of age. . . .

The Ninth Path was that of the girls aged one and two, who were called *llucac warmi wawa* ("young girls who crawl"). They do nothing; instead, others serve them. Better said, they ought to be served by their mothers, who should be exempt [from tribute] because of the work of raising their children. Their mothers have to walk around carrying them, and never let go of their hands. 🙶

Source: Felipe Guaman Poma de Ayala, *The First New Chronicle and Good Government* (abridged), translated by David Frye (Cambridge, Mass.: Hackett Publishing Company, 2006). Copyright © 2006 by Hackett Publishing Company, Inc. Reprinted by permission of Hackett Publishing Company, Inc. All rights reserved.

### QUESTIONS FOR ANALYSIS

1. The "First Path" among both men and women is the one with the highest status. Judging by the way Guaman Poma describes these, what do the Incas especially value? How do his descriptions of other paths support your conclusions about this?

2. In what ways are the paths set out for boys and men different from those for girls and women? In what ways are they similar? What does this suggest about Inca society?

3. Guaman Poma wrote this about eighty years after the Spanish conquest of Peru. How do the date and the colonial setting affect your evaluation of this work as a source?

Guaman Poma's line drawing shows a woman weaving fine cloth on a back-strap loom. (De Agostini Picture Library/ The Bridgeman Art Library)

As each new Inca emperor conquered new lands and built his domain, he mobilized people and resources by drawing on local systems of labor and organization. Much as ayllus had developed satellite communities called mitmaq, populated by settlers from the ayllu in order to take advantage of remote farming areas, the emperor relocated families or even whole villages over long distances to consolidate territorial control or quell unrest. What had been a community practice became a tool of imperial expansion. The emperor sent mitmaq settlers, known as *mitmaquisuna*, far and wide, creating diverse ethnic enclaves. The emperor also consolidated the empire by regulating marriage, using maternal lines to build kinship among conquered peoples. Inca rulers and nobles married the daughters of elite families among the peoples they conquered. Very high-ranking Inca men sometimes had many wives, but marriage among commoners was generally monogamous.

The reciprocal labor carried out within ayllus expanded into a labor tax called the *mit'a* (MEE-tuh), which rotated among households in an ayllu throughout the year. Tribute paid in labor provided the means for building the infrastructure of empire. Rotations of laborers carried out impressive engineering feats, allowing the vast empire to extend over the most difficult and inhospitable terrain. An excellent system of roads—averaging three feet in width, some paved and others not—facilitated the transportation of armies and the rapid communication of royal orders by runners. Like Persian and Roman roads, these great feats of Inca engineering linked an empire. The government also made an ayllu responsible for maintaining state-owned granaries, which distributed grain in times of shortage and famine and supplied assistance in natural disasters.

On these roads Inca officials, tax collectors, and accountants traveled throughout the empire, using elaborate khipus to record financial and labor obligations, the output of fields, population levels, land transfers, and other numerical records. Khipus may also have been used to record narrative history, but this is speculation, as knowledge of how to read them died out after the Spanish conquest. Only around 650 khipus are known to survive today, because colonial Spaniards destroyed them, believing khipus might contain religious messages that would encourage people to resist Spanish authority.

# The Maya and Teotihuacan

☐ How did the Maya and Teotihuacan develop prosperous and stable societies in the classical era?

In Mesoamerica the classical period (300 C.E. to 900 C.E.) saw major advances in religion, art, architecture, and farming, akin to those of the classical civilizations of the Mediterranean (see Chapters 5 and 6). It saw the rise of many city-states, and although the **Maya** city-states, which peaked between 600 C.E. and 900 C.E., were the longest lasting, others were significant as well. The city of **Teotihuacan** in the Valley of Mexico emerged as a major center of trade (300–650 C.E.). It was followed by the postclassical Toltec Empire (900–1200 C.E.), which adapted the cultural, ritual, and aesthetic practices that influenced later empires like the Aztecs.

## Maya Agriculture and Trade

The Maya inhabited the highlands of Guatemala and the Yucatán peninsula in present-day Mexico and Belize. Their physical setting shaped two features of Maya society. First, the abundance of high-quality limestone allowed them to build monumental architecture. Second, limestone formations created deep natural wells called *cenotes* (say-NOH-tehs), which became critical sources of water in an often-arid environment. Cenotes were essential to farming and also became important religious and spiritual sites. The staple crop of the Maya was maize, often raised in small remote plots called *milpas* in combination with other foodstuffs, including beans, squash, chili peppers, some root crops, and fruit trees. They farmed on raised narrow rectangular plots that they built above the seasonally flooded low-lying land bordering rivers.

The entire Maya region may have had as many as 14 million inhabitants. Sites like Uxmal, Uaxactún, Copán, Piedras Negras, Tikal, Palenque, and Chichén Itzá (Map 11.4) emerged as independent city-states, each ruled by a hereditary king. These cities produced

### Palace Doorway Lintel at Yaxchilan, Mexico

Lady Xoc, principal wife of King Shield-Jaguar, who holds a torch over her, pulls a thorn-lined rope through her tongue to sanctify with her blood the birth of a younger wife's child—reflecting the importance of blood sacrifice in Maya culture. The elaborate headdresses and clothes of the couple show their royal status. (© The Trustees of the British Museum/Art Resource, NY)

**MAP 11.4  The Maya World, 300–900 C.E.** The Maya built dozens of cities linked together in trading networks of roads and rivers. Only the largest of them are shown here.

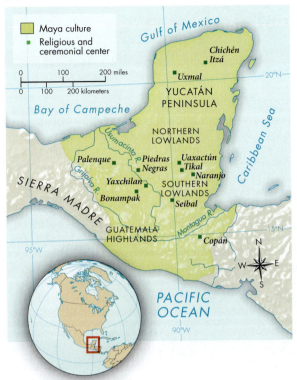

They recorded important events and observations in books made of bark paper and deerskin, on pottery, on stone pillars called steles, and on temples and other buildings. Archaeologists and anthropologists have demonstrated that the inscriptions are historical documents that record major events in the lives of Maya kings and nobles. As was common for elites everywhere, Maya leaders stressed the ancient ancestry of their families. "In the year 3114 B.C.E. my forefathers were present, during the Creation of the World," reads one stele in the city of Tikal, recording the lineage of the Maya lord Kan Boar.[2]

Learning about Maya religion through written records is difficult. In the sixteenth century Spanish religious authorities viewed Maya books as demonic and ordered them destroyed. Only a handful survived, offering a window into religious rituals and practices, as well as Maya astronomy. (See "Viewpoints 11.1: Creation in the *Popol Vuh* and in Okanogan Tradition," page 312.) From observation of the earth's movements around the sun, the Maya used a calendar of eighteen 20-day months and one 5-day month, for a total of 365 days, along with the 260-day calendar based on 20 weeks of 13 days. When these calendars coincided every fifty-two years, the Maya celebrated with feasting, ball-game competitions, and religious observance. These and other observances included blood sacrifice by kings to honor the gods.

Using a system of bars, where a single bar equals five (— = 5) and a single dot equals one (• = 1), the Maya devised a form of mathematics based on the vigesimal (20) rather than the decimal (10) system. More unusual was their use of the number zero, which allows for more complex calculations than are possible in number systems without it. The zero may have actually been discovered by the Olmecs, who used it in figuring their calendar, but the Maya used it mathematically as well. The Maya's proficiency with numbers made them masters of abstract knowledge—notably in astronomy and mathematics.

Between the eighth and tenth centuries the Maya abandoned their cultural and ceremonial centers. Archaeologists attribute their decline to a combination of agricultural failures due to drought, land exhaustion, overpopulation, disease, and constant wars fought for economic and political gain. These wars brought widespread destruction, which aggravated agricultural problems. Royalty also suffered from the decline in Maya

polychrome pottery and featured altars, engraved pillars, masonry temples, palaces for nobles, pyramids where nobles were buried, and courts for ball games. The largest site, Tikal, may have had forty thousand people and served as a religious and ceremonial center. A hereditary nobility owned land, waged war, traded, exercised political power, and directed religious rituals. Artisans and scribes made up the social level below. Other residents were farmers, laborers, and slaves, the latter including prisoners of war.

At Maya markets, jade, obsidian, beads of red spiny oyster shell, lengths of cloth, and cacao beans—all in high demand in the Mesoamerican world—served as media of exchange. The extensive trade among Maya communities, plus a common language, promoted unity among the peoples of the region. Merchants traded beyond Maya regions, particularly with the Zapotecs of Monte Albán, in the Valley of Oaxaca, and with the Teotihuacanos of the central valley of Mexico. Since this long-distance trade played an important part in international relations, the merchants conducting it were high nobles or even members of the royal family.

## Maya Science and Religion

The Maya developed the most complex writing system in the Americas, a script with nearly a thousand glyphs.

- **Maya** A highly developed Mesoamerican culture centered in the Yucatán peninsula of Mexico. The Maya created the most intricate writing system in the Western Hemisphere.

- **Teotihuacan** The monumental city-state that dominated trade in classical era Mesoamerica.

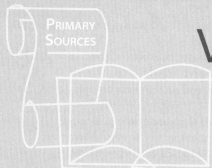

# Viewpoints 11.1

## Creation in the *Popul Vuh* and in Okanogan Tradition

• *Every people of the world appears to have had a creation account that describes the way the world and the people within it came to be. These are excerpts from the accounts of the Maya people, as recorded in the sixteenth century in the* Popul Vuh, *and of the Okanogan people of the Pacific Northwest, as recorded in the twentieth century from oral traditions.*

### *Popul Vuh*

“ Heart of Sky arrived here with Sovereign and Quetzal Serpent [three creator gods] in the darkness, in the night. . . . They thought and they pondered. They reached an accord, bringing together their words and their thoughts. . . . Then the earth was created by them. Merely their word brought about the creation of it. In order to create the earth, they said, "Earth," and immediately it was created. . . . Then were conceived the animals of the mountains, the guardians of the forest, and all that populate the mountains — the deer and the birds, the puma and the jaguar, the serpent and the rattlesnake. . . . This, then, is the beginning of the conception of humanity, when that which would become the flesh of mankind was sought. Then spoke they who are called She Who Has Borne Children and He Who Has Begotten Sons, the Framer and the Shaper [four other gods associated with creation], Sovereign and Quetzal Serpent: "The dawn approaches, and our work is not completed. A provider and a sustainer have yet to appear — a child of light, a son of light. Humanity has yet to appear to populate the face of the earth," they said. Thus they gathered together and joined their thoughts in the darkness, in the night. They searched and they sifted. Here they thought and they pondered. Their thoughts came forth bright and clear. They discovered and established that which would become the flesh of humanity. . . . Thus their frame and shape were given expression by our first Mother and our first Father. Their flesh was merely yellow ears of maize and white ears of maize. . . . And so there were four who were made, and mere food was their flesh. . . . Then their companions, their wives, also came to be. It was the gods who conceived them as well. ”

### Okanogan Tradition

“ The earth was once a human being: Old One made her out of a woman. "You will be the mother of all people," he said.

Earth is alive yet, but she has been changed. The soil is her flesh, the rocks are her bones, the wind is her breath, trees and grass are her hair. She lives spread out, and we live on her. When she moves, we have an earthquake.

After taking the woman and changing her to earth, Old One gathered some of her flesh and rolled it into balls, as people do with mud or clay. He made the first group of these balls into the ancients, the beings of the early world. . . .

Besides the ancients, real people and real animals lived on the earth at that time. Old One made the people out of the last balls of mud he took from the earth. He rolled them over and over, shaped them like Indians, and blew on them to bring them alive. They were so ignorant that they were the most helpless of all the creatures Old One had made.

Old One made people and animals into males and females so that they might breed and multiply. Thus all living things came from the earth. When we look around, we see part of our mother everywhere. ”

Sources: Allen Christensen, trans., *Popul Vuh: The Sacred Book of the Maya.* Reproduced with permission of UNIVERSITY OF OKLAHOMA PRESS in the format Republish in a book via Copyright Clearance Center; "Creation of the Animal People" from Ella C. Clark, *Indian Legends of the Pacific Northwest.* Reproduced with permission of UNIVERSITY OF CALIFORNIA PRESS in the format Book via Copyright Clearance Center. Reproduced in electronic form by permission of the Association of American Indian Affairs.

### QUESTIONS FOR ANALYSIS

1. Who carries out the creation of the world and human beings in each of these accounts? How does the process of creation combine the spiritual and the material world?

2. How are humans created? What does this process suggest about the relations between humans and the rest of creation?

## □ Picturing the Past

**Maya Calendar** This Maya calendar (at right) from Yaxchilan, Mexico, bears a date equivalent to February 11, 526 C.E. The animals represent blocks of time, while the dots and profiles of gods mark numbers. The monkey (right column, second from top) signals a day date. The day is defined by the god's head in its hand, which means six, and the skull beneath the hand, which means ten: sixteen days. (Otis Imboden/National Geographic Creative)

**ANALYZING THE IMAGE**
Calendars show not only dates but also the sense of time of the people who used them. What do the figures in this calendar show you about the Maya and their world?

**CONNECTIONS** How does the Maya system of numbers (near right) resemble other numerical systems with which you are familiar?

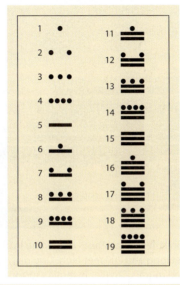

civilization: just as in good times kings attributed moral authority and prosperity to themselves, so in bad times, when military, economic, and social conditions deteriorated, their subjects saw the kings as the cause and turned against them.

Decline did not mean disappearance. The Maya ceased building monumental architecture around 900 C.E., which likely marked the end of the era of rule by powerful kings who could mobilize the labor required to build it. The Maya persisted in farming communities, a pattern of settlement that helped preserve their culture and language in the face of external pressures. They resisted invasions from warring Aztec armies by dispersing from their towns and villages and residing in their milpas during invasions. When Aztec armies entered the Yucatán, communities vanished, leaving Aztec armies with nothing to conquer. This tactic continued to serve the Maya under Spanish colonial rule. Though Spaniards claimed the Yucatán, the Maya continued to use the strategy that had served them so well in resisting the Aztecs. Many communities avoided Spanish domination for generations. The last independent Maya kingdom succumbed only in 1697, and resistance continued well into the nineteenth century.

## Teotihuacan and the Toltecs

The most powerful city in classical Mesoamerica emerged at Teotihuacan, northwest of the lands of the Maya. By 100 C.E. it had a population of 60,000. At its height, between 300 and 600 C.E., its population reached as high as 250,000, making it one of the largest cities in the world at that time. The heart of Teotihuacan was a massive ceremonial center anchored by a colossal Pyramid of the Sun, 700 feet wide and 200 feet tall, and a Pyramid of the Moon. Connecting them was the Avenue of the Dead, 150 feet wide and 2 miles long, along which stood the homes of scores of priests and lords. The monuments of Teotihuacan were so massive that centuries later the Aztecs thought they had been built by giants. A cave under the Pyramid of the Sun suggests the ceremonial center's origins. Caves symbolized the womb from which the sun and moon were born. It is possible that, like other pilgrimage sites around the world that became important marketplaces, the cave served as both a ceremonial and trade center.[3]

The monuments of the ceremonial district of Teotihuacan were matched in grandeur by the city's markets, which extended its influence across Mesoamerica.

**The Pyramid of the Sun at Teotihuacan** Built in several stages beginning in about 100 C.E., the Pyramid of the Sun has sides measuring 700 feet long and 200 feet high. Originally it was covered with lime plaster decorated with brightly colored murals. Smaller pyramids surround it in what was the heart of the bustling city of Teotihuacan. (© age fotostock/SuperStock)

The city's trade empire lay in its control of a resource vital to Mesoamerican society and religion: obsidian, a glasslike volcanic rock that could be worked into objects with both material and spiritual uses. Obsidian knives were used for daily tasks and for important rituals such as the blood sacrifice practiced by the Maya. Teotihuacan merchants traded directly with Maya and Zapotec kings, whose local control of obsidian enhanced their power. Teotihuacan's power was unrivaled in its time, so it was able to extend its influence through trade networks, which included a colony in Kaminaljuyu, near present-day Guatemala City. This outpost in another obsidian-rich area allowed Teotihuacan to dominate the obsidian market.[4]

Religion followed trade. Teotihuacan was a religious and cultural center whose influence extended over large distances. One factor in the city's success was its ethnic diversity. Teotihuacan grew through the migration of outsiders along trade networks, and these groups built separate ethnic neighborhoods. Two gods that were particularly important to classical period civilizations were Tlaloc (Chac in Maya), the god of rain, and Quetzalcoatl, the plumed serpent. The worship of these deities became an enduring aspect of Mesoamerican religion that the Toltecs and the Aztecs embraced.

In fact, after their defeat by the Spanish, Aztecs would invoke prophesies of Quetzalcoatl as foretelling the arrival of the Spaniard Hernán Cortés.[5]

Teotihuacan thrived because it controlled trade of the most valuable goods. This helped it grow, and in turn the trade networks it sustained helped other regions in Mesoamerica develop through intensified contact with other groups and the spread of technologies. Over time, improvements in other regions decreased Teotihuacan's comparative advantage, as its trading partners produced increasingly valuable goods, spurring competition. By 600 its influence had begun to decline, and in 650 the residents of the city seem to have burned its ceremonial center in what may have been a revolt against the city's leadership. The city had ceased to be a major trade center by 900 C.E.[6]

The Toltecs (900–1200 C.E.) filled the void created by Teotihuacan's decline. The Toltecs inaugurated a new era, the postclassical, which ended with the Spanish conquest of the Aztec Empire. The postclassical period saw fewer technological or artistic advances. Instead it was a time of intensified warfare in Mesoamerica and a time of rapid and bold imperial expansion through conquest. After the decline of Teotihuacan, whose rulers had considered the Toltecs barbarians and kept

**The Toltecs,
ca. 900–1200 C.E.**

■ Toltec site
■ Zapotec site

# The Aztecs

❑ How did the Aztecs build on the achievements of earlier Mesoamerican cultures and develop new traditions to create their large empire?

According to their oral tradition, between 1300 and 1345 a group of **Nahuatl**-speaking people, the **Mexica**, migrated southward from what is now northern Mexico, settling on the shores and islands of Lake Texcoco in the central valley of Mexico (Map 11.5). They formed a vast and rapidly expanding empire centered around the twin cities of Tenochtitlan (tay-nawch-TEET-lahn) and Tlatelolco, which by 1500 were probably larger than any city in Europe except Istanbul. This was the Aztec Empire, a network of alliances and tributary states with the Mexica at its core. Examining the means by which they formed and expanded their empire, as well as the vulnerabilities of that empire, can help us build a rich understanding of Mesoamerican society.

## The Mexica: From Vassals to Masters

In the early fourteenth century, the Mexica, a migrant, seminomadic group, arrived in the crowded and highly cultured Valley of Mexico. They found an environment that, since the collapse of the Toltec Empire in the twelfth century, had divided into small, fragile alliances that battled to claim the legacy of the Toltecs. At the moment of their arrival, control over much of the valley lay in the hands of the Tepanec Alliance. The Mexica negotiated the right to settle on a swampy island on Lake Texcoco in exchange for military service to the Tepanecs.

Residents of the city-states that ringed the lake looked down upon the Mexica. But the Mexica adopted the customs of their new region, organizing clan-based communities called *calpolli*, incorporating the deities of their new neighbors, and serving the Tepanecs. They gradually reclaimed land around their island to form two urban centers, Tenochtitlan and Tlatelolco. They adopted a farming technique used in parts of Lake Texcoco called *chinampa* (chee-NAHM-pah) agriculture. Though later chroniclers would frequently refer to chinampas as floating gardens, they were a means of land reclamation by which farmers built up reeds and mud along the margins of Lake Texcoco to gradually extend farming well into the lake.

them out of the Valley of Mexico, the Toltecs entered and settled in Tula. The Toltecs' legend of their origins held that in 968 C.E. their people were led into the valley by a charismatic leader who fused himself to the plumed serpent god and called himself Topiltzin-Quetzalcoatl. In 987, amid infighting, Topiltzin-Quetzalcoatl and his followers were expelled from Tula. They marched south, where they conquered and settled in a Maya region.

The Toltec origin myth later merged with the mythology of the Aztecs, who fashioned themselves modern Toltecs, and in turn these myths were adapted in the sixteenth century in order to explain conquest by the Spanish. Through this long and distorted course, the legend went like this: Topiltzin-Quetzalcoatl and his followers marked their journey into exile by shooting arrows into saplings, forming crosslike images. Settled in the east, he sent word that he would return to take back his rightful throne in the Mesoamerican calendar year Ce Acatl. And by tradition, the god Quetzalcoatl's human manifestation was bearded and light skinned. Ce Acatl corresponded to the European year 1519, when Hernán Cortés marched into the Aztec capital Tenochtitlan (light skinned, bearded, and coming from the east bearing crosses). Perhaps the demise of the Aztec Empire at the hands of a vengeful god had been foretold by half a millennium.

The Toltecs built a military empire and gradually absorbed the culture, practices, and religion of their neighbors in the Valley of Mexico. Their empire waned amid war, drought, and famine over the eleventh and twelfth centuries. After the demise of the Toltec Empire, city-states in the Valley of Mexico competed with each other militarily and to cast themselves as the legitimate descendants and heirs of the Toltecs.

• **Nahuatl** The language of both the Toltecs and the Aztecs.

• **Mexica** The dominant ethnic group of what is now Mexico, who created an empire based on war and religion that reached its height in the mid-1400s; in the nineteenth century the people became known as Aztecs.

**MAP 11.5  The Aztec (Mexica) Empire in 1519**  The Mexica migrated into the central valley of what is now Mexico from the north, conquering other groups and establishing an empire, later called the Aztec Empire. The capital of the Aztec Empire was Tenochtitlan, built on islands in Lake Texcoco.

At its peak, the chinampa farming system formed vast areas of tidy rectangular plots divided by canals that allowed for canoe transportation of people and crops. When the Spanish entered **Tenochtitlan** (which they called Mexico City) in November 1519, they could not believe their eyes. The Aztec city, built in 1325, impressed them greatly. Bernal Díaz del Castillo, one of Cortés's companions, reported:

> When we saw all those cities and villages built in the water, and other great towns on dry land, and that straight and level causeway leading to Mexico, we were astounded. These great towns and cues (temples) and buildings rising from the water, all made of stone, seemed like an enchanted vision. . . . Indeed, some of our soldiers asked whether it was not all a dream.[7]

Over time, the Mexica improved their standing in the Valley of Mexico by asking a powerful neighboring city-state to name a prince considered to be of noble

Toltec descent to rule them, forming a dynasty that would become the most powerful in Mesoamerica. The new ruler, or *tlatoani* (tlah-toh-annie), Acamapichtli (ah-camp-itch-lee), brought the Mexica higher social rank and the ability to form alliances. While the naming of a new ruler of noble origins initially made the Mexica into closer allies of their neighbors, it gave them their own noble dynasty of rulers who gradually made the Mexica more militarily powerful and more competitive with neighboring states, which they would eventually dominate.

By the end of Acamapichtli's reign (1372–1391), the Mexica had fully adapted to their new environment and had adopted the highly stratified social organization that would encourage the ambitions of their own warrior class. Under the rule of Acamapichtli's successors Huitzilihuitl (r. 1391–1417) and Chimalpopoca (r. 1417–1427), the Mexica remained subordinate to the Tepanec Alliance. But in 1427 a dispute over the succession of the Tepanec king created an opportunity for the Mexica.

Anthropologist Ross Hassig described the manner in which Mexica ruler Itzcoatl (r. 1427–1440) turned the dispute to his advantage: "Itzcoatl sent his nephew,

● **Tenochtitlan**  A large and prosperous Aztec city that was built starting in 1325. The Spanish admired it when they entered in 1519.

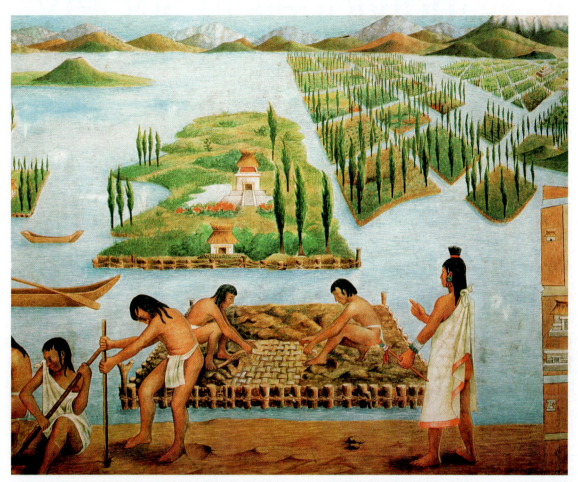

**Chinampa Farming** This illustration shows farmers in the Aztec Empire building chinampa farming plots by reclaiming land from Lake Texcoco. Farmers created the plots by packing them with vegetation and mud from the lake, supporting their boundaries by planting willow trees. Chinampas allowed for intensive farming in a region that had limited rainfall, and the canals between them permitted easy transportation. (© Gianni Dagli Orti/Corbis)

Tlacaelel, to Azcapotzalco [the Tepanec capital], where he asked first if peace was possible. On learning it was not, he smeared pitch on the king and feathered his head, as was done with the dead, and gave him a shield, sword, and gilded arrows—the insignia of the sovereign—and thus declared war." In 1428, the Mexica formed a coalition with other cities in the Valley of Mexico, besieged the Tepanec capital for nearly three months, and then defeated it. A powerful new coalition had emerged: the Triple Alliance, with the Mexica as its most powerful partner. The Aztec Empire was born.[8]

To consolidate the new political order, Tlatoani Itzcoatl, guided by his nephew Tlacaelel, burned his predecessors' books and drafted a new history. Tlacaelel advised his tlatoani: "It is not necessary for all the common people to know of the writings: government will be defamed, and this will only spread sorcery in the lands; for they contained many falsehoods."[9]

The new history placed the warrior cult and its religious pantheon at the center of Mexica history, making the god of war, Huitzilopochtli, the patron deity of the empire. Huitzilopochtli, "Hummingbird of the South," was a god unique to the Mexica who, according to the new official origin stories of the Mexica people, had ordered them to march south until they found an island where he gave them the sign of an eagle eating a serpent, which appeared to them in Tenochtitlan. (See "Individuals in Society: Tlacaelel," page 318.)

Under the new imperial order, government offices combined military, religious, and political functions. Eventually, tlatoanis formalized these functions into distinct noble and common classes. This gave soldiers opportunities for social advancement. After securing five sacrificial victims in battle, a commoner soldier entered the lower nobility, which freed him from paying tribute. He could show his new status by publicly wearing feathers and flowers. The Valley of Mexico had sustained itself through chinampa agriculture, but as the empire grew, crops provided as tribute from distant

# Individuals in Society

## Tlacaelel

**THE HUMMINGBIRD GOD HUITZILOPOCHTLI WAS** originally a somewhat ordinary god of war and of young men, but in the fifteenth century he was elevated in status among the Mexica. He became increasingly associated with the sun and gradually became the most important Mexica deity. This change appears to have been primarily the work of Tlacaelel, the very long-lived chief adviser to the emperors Itzcoatl (r. 1427–1440), Moctezuma I (r. 1440–1469), and Axayacatl (r. 1469–1481).

Tlacaelel first gained influence during wars in the 1420s in which the Mexica defeated the rival Tepanecs, after which he established new systems of dividing military spoils and enemy lands. At the same time, he advised the emperor that new histories were needed in which the destiny of the Mexica people was made clearer. Tlacaelel ordered the destruction of older historical texts, and under his direction the new chronicles connected Mexica fate directly to Huitzilopochtli. Mexica writing was primarily pictographic, drawn and then read by specially trained scribes who used written records as an aid to oral presentation, especially for legal issues, historical chronicles, religious and devotional poetry, and astronomical calculations.

**Tlacaelel emphasized human sacrifice as one of the Aztecs' religious duties.** (From the *Codex Magliabechiano* [vellum]/Biblioteca Nazionale Centrale, Florence, Italy/The Bridgeman Art Library)

According to these new texts, the Mexica had been guided to Lake Texcoco by Huitzilopochtli; there they saw an eagle perched on a cactus, which a prophecy foretold would mark the site of their new city. Huitzilopochtli kept the world alive by bringing the sun's warmth, but to do this he required the Mexica, who increasingly saw themselves as the "people of the sun," to provide a steady offering of human blood.

The worship of Huitzilopochtli became linked to cosmic forces as well as daily survival. In Nahua tradition, the universe was understood to exist in a series of five suns, or five cosmic ages. Four ages had already passed, and their suns had been destroyed; the fifth sun, the age in which the Mexica were now living, would also be destroyed unless the Mexica fortified the sun with the energy found in blood. Warfare thus brought new territory under Mexica control and provided sacrificial victims to nourish the sun-god. With these ideas, Tlacaelel created what Miguel León-Portilla, a leading contemporary scholar of Nahua religion and philosophy, has termed a "mystico-militaristic" conception of Aztec destiny.

Human sacrifice was practiced in many cultures of Mesoamerica, including the Olmec and the Maya as well as the Mexica, before the changes introduced by Tlacaelel, but historians believe the number of victims increased dramatically during the last period of Mexica rule. A huge pyramid-shaped temple in the center of Tenochtitlan, dedicated to Huitzilopochtli and the god of rain Tlaloc, was renovated and expanded many times, the last in 1487. To dedicate each expansion, priests sacrificed war captives. Similar ceremonies were held regularly throughout the year on days dedicated to Huitzilopochtli and were attended by many observers, including representatives from neighboring states as well as masses of Mexica. According to many accounts, victims were placed on a stone slab, and their hearts were cut out with an obsidian knife; the officiating priest then held the heart up as an offering to the sun. Sacrifices were also made to other gods at temples elsewhere in Tenochtitlan, and perhaps in other cities controlled by the Mexica.

Estimates of the number of people sacrificed to Huitzilopochtli and other Mexica gods vary enormously and are impossible to verify. Both Mexica and later Spanish accounts clearly exaggerated the numbers, but most historians today assume that between several hundred and several thousand people were killed each year.

Sources: Miguel León-Portilla, *Pre-Columbian Literatures of Mexico* (Norman: University of Oklahoma Press, 1969); Inga Clendinnen, *Aztecs: An Interpretation* (Cambridge: Cambridge University Press, 1991).

### QUESTIONS FOR ANALYSIS

1. How did the worship of Huitzilopochtli contribute to Aztec expansion? To hostility toward the Aztecs?
2. Why might Tlacaelel have believed it was important to destroy older texts as he created this new Aztec mythology?

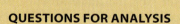
## LaunchPad
### Online Document Project

**Why did Tlacaelel believe the Aztec Empire needed a new history?** Read documents that examine Aztec history and culture, and then complete a quiz and writing assignment based on the evidence and details from this chapter.

*See inside the front cover to learn more.*

conquered peoples increasingly fed the valley's rapidly growing population. The Mexica sustained themselves through military conquest, imposing their rule over a vast part of modern Mexico.

## Life in the Aztec Empire

The Aztecs wrote many pictographic books recounting their history, geography, and religious practices. They also preserved records of their legal disputes, which amounted to vast files. The Spanish conquerors subsequently destroyed much of this material, but surviving documents offer a rich picture of the Mexica people at the time of the Spanish invasion.

Few sharp social distinctions existed among the Aztecs during their early migrations, but by the early sixteenth century Aztec society had changed. A stratified social structure had emerged, and the warrior aristocracy exercised great authority. Men who had distinguished themselves in war occupied the highest military and social positions in the state. Generals, judges, and governors of provinces were appointed by the emperor from among his servants who had earned reputations as war heroes. These great lords, or *tecuhtli* (teh-COOT-lee), dressed luxuriously and lived in palaces. Acting as provincial governors, they exercised full political, judicial, and military authority on the emperor's behalf. In their territories they maintained order, settled disputes, and judged legal cases; oversaw the cultivation of land; and made sure that tribute was paid.

Beneath the great nobility of military leaders and imperial officials was the class of warriors. Theoretically, every free man could be a warrior, and parents dedicated their male children to war, burying a male child's umbilical cord with arrows and a shield on the day of his birth. In actuality, the sons of nobles were more likely to become warriors because of their fathers' positions and influence in the state. At the age of six, boys entered a school that trained them for war. They were taught to fight with a *ma-cana*, a paddle-shaped wooden club edged with bits of obsidian, and learned to live on little food and sleep and to accept pain without complaint. At about age eighteen, a warrior fought his first campaign. If he captured a prisoner for ritual sacrifice, he acquired the title *iyac*, or warrior. If in later campaigns he succeeded in killing or capturing four of the enemy, he became a *tequiua*—one who shared in the booty and was thus a member of the nobility. If a young man failed in several campaigns to capture the required four prisoners, he became a *macehualli* (plural *macehualtin*), a commoner.

The macehualtin were the ordinary citizens—the backbone of Aztec society and the vast majority of the population. The word *macehualli* means "worker" and implies boorish speech and vulgar behavior. Members of this class performed agricultural, military, and domestic services and carried heavy public burdens not required of noble warriors. Government officials assigned them to work on the temples, roads, and bridges. Unlike nobles, priests, orphans, and slaves, macehualtin paid taxes. Macehualtin in the capital, however, possessed certain rights: they held their plots of land for life, and they received a small share of the tribute paid by the provinces to the emperor.

Beneath the macehualtin were the *tlalmaitl*, the landless workers or serfs who provided agricultural labor, paid rents in kind, and were bound to the soil— they could not move off the land. In many ways the tlalmaitl resembled the serfs of western Europe, but unlike serfs they performed military service when called on to do so. Slaves were the lowest social class. Most were prisoners captured in war or kidnapped from enemy tribes. People convicted of crimes could be sentenced to slavery, and people in serious debt sometimes voluntarily sold themselves. Female slaves often became their masters' concubines. Mexica slaves differed fundamentally from European ones, for they could possess goods; save money; buy land, houses, and even slaves for their own service; and purchase their freedom. If a male slave married a free woman, their offspring were free. Most slaves eventually gained their freedom.

Women of all social classes operated within the domestic sphere. As the little hands of the newborn male were closed around a tiny bow and arrow indicating his warrior destiny, so the infant female's hands were wrapped around miniature weaving instruments and a small broom: weaving was a sacred and exclusively female art, and the broom signaled a female's responsibility for the household shrines and for keeping the home swept and free of contamination. Save for the few women vowed to the service of the temple, marriage and the household were a woman's fate, and marriage represented social maturity for both sexes. Pregnancy became the occasion for family and neighborhood feasts, and a successful birth launched celebrations lasting from ten to twenty days.

## The Limits of the Aztec Empire

Mesoamerican empires like that of the Aztecs were not like modern nation-states that consolidate control of the territory within their borders. Instead the Aztec Empire was a syndicate in which the Mexica, their allies, and their subordinates thrived on trade and tribute backed by the threat of force.

When a city succumbed, its captive warriors were marched to Tenochtitlan to be sacrificed. The defeated city was obligated to provide tribute to be distributed within the empire, including corn and other foods, flowers, feathers, gold, and hides. But conquest stopped

**Huitzilopochtli** This painting of the hummingbird god of war carrying a shield in one hand and a serpent-headed knife in the other was made by Aztec priests in a book written on bark paper about the time of the Spanish conquest. He is shown descending from a step-pyramid, perhaps a reference to the great pyramid in the center of Tenochtitlan, where he was worshipped. (© Foundation for the Advancement of Mesoamerican Studies, Inc., www.famsi.org)

short of assimilation. Rulers and nobles remained in place. Subjects were not required to adopt Mexica gods. Some children of nobles would be sent to Tenochtitlan for their education and were encouraged to intermarry with the nobles of other states within the empire, but otherwise local communities and their leaders remained intact.

The death of a ruler is always a time of uncertainty, and this was especially true in Mesoamerica under the Aztec Empire. For peoples of the Valley of Mexico and beyond, this meant war was sure to arrive. The council of high nobles who served the deceased ruler chose the new tlatoani, who was often the commander of the army. Once the new tlatoani was named, he would embark on a military campaign in order to answer the questions his succession raised: Would he bring sacrificial victims to the gods and thus ensure prosperity and fertility during his reign? Could he preserve and strengthen the alliances that composed the empire? Could he keep rivals at bay?

A success in the tlatoani's inaugural military campaign provided new tribute-paying subjects, produced a long train of sacrificial victims captured in battle, maintained the stability of the empire's alliances, warned off potential foes, and kept conquered areas in subordination. After the successful campaign, the new tlatoani invited the rulers of allied, subject, and enemy city-states alike to his coronation ceremony—a pageant of gifts, feasts, and bloody sacrifice that proclaimed Tenochtitlan's might.

But success was not always possible, as the troubled rule of Tizoc (r. 1481–1486) demonstrated. His wars sometimes resulted in a greater number of casualties among his own forces than of sacrificial victims for his altars. Five years after he was crowned, he was poisoned by his own subjects. His successor, Ahuitzotl (r. 1486–1502), faced the challenge of reinvigorating the empire through renewed displays of strength. He had little margin for failure. To symbolize the restoration of Tenochtitlan's power, he waged wars of conquest that defied precedence in their scale, culminating in two coronation ceremonies, the second of which incorporated sacrificing over eighty thousand captive warriors.

Blood sacrifice was not new to the Aztecs. For centuries Mesoamerican peoples had honored their gods this way. For instance, the cult honoring Xipe Totec, the god of spring renewal, involved two emblematic sacrifices. Priests wore the skin of a sacrificial victim to symbolize the shedding of leaves and new growth, and they greeted the arrival of spring by binding a human sacrifice to a post and shooting his body full of arrows with slits carved along their shafts. Blood channeled off the arrows and dripped to the ground, symbolizing the spring rains.

The Aztecs elevated the warrior cult as the central observance. They were the chosen people, who faced a bleak struggle to stave off the apocalypse. The Mexica believed the earth had been destroyed and re-created four times. The end of creation loomed after their age, the fifth sun. Since this apocalypse might be forestalled through divine intervention, their sacrifice could show that humans were worthy of divine intervention. If ancient deities had given their lives to save the sun, how could mortals refuse to do the same? Their service to the gods culminated on the altar of the temple to Huitzilopochtli, where priests cut into the chests of warriors with their obsidian knives to pull out their beating hearts and raise them in sacrifice to the sun.

Such sacrifice evoked the power of Aztec rulers, but the ceremony observing the end of each fifty-two-year bundle better reflected the Mexica worldview. Had humans sacrificed enough for the gods to intercede and ensure the sun would rise again? In preparation for the end, families broke their earthenware vessels, cleansed their homes, and extinguished all fires. As the new day came, priests made a fire on the chest of a living, powerful captive warrior. Noble warriors lit torches from this new fire and relayed the flame of creation into each hearth in the empire. For the next fifty-two years, all would know the fire in their hearth, like the rising of the sun itself, was the fruit of a sacred warrior sacrifice.

The need for sacrifice, as well as the glorification of the warriors who provided it through battle, was a powerful rationale for the expansion of the Aztec Empire. The role of the Aztecs' sacrifice-based religious system is the subject of scholarly debate: Did the religious system guide imperial expansion? Or did imperial expansion guide the religious system? These views are by no means incompatible: for the Aztecs, the peoples who came under their rule, and the peoples who resisted them, the twin goals of empire building and service to the gods were inseparable.

# American Empires and the Encounter

☐ What did the European encounter mean for peoples of the major American empires?

By 1500 the Incas and Aztecs strained under the burdens of managing the largest empires the Americas had seen. Both faced the challenges of consolidating their gains, bearing the costs of empire and of the swelling nobility, and waging war in increasingly distant and difficult conditions.

## The Fall of the Aztecs

In 1502 Moctezuma II, the last Mexica to rule before the arrival of the Spaniards, was named tlatoani. His reign presents a paradox. On one hand, we know the most about it because it was narrated in detail both by Spanish chroniclers and by indigenous informants (the defeated Mexica continued to create books narrating their history for decades after the conquest). On the other hand, we interpret this information knowing that between 1519 and 1521 the Aztec Empire fell to the Spanish conquistador Hernán Cortés, and our tendency is to analyze Moctezuma II's reign with the knowledge that six hundred foreigners could topple the most powerful empire ever seen in Mesoamerica. Was the Aztecs' loss the result of an empire in crisis? Was it a technological failure? A political failure? A mismatch between a more advanced and a less advanced civilization?

Moctezuma inherited a strained empire. His predecessors had expanded the empire's reach from the Caribbean coast to the Pacific. At the margins of the empire the Aztecs encountered peoples who were semi-nomadic or who, like the Maya, abandoned their cities to resist conquest. An empire that had expanded rapidly through conquest found itself with little room to grow.

Aztec leaders had sought targets for conquest that were easy to overpower or were strategic for trade, or that possessed resources or produced goods that made for valuable tribute. This created an empire riddled with independent enclaves that had resisted conquest. The most powerful of these was Tlaxcala, at the edge of the Valley of Mexico. In addition, even those areas nominally under Aztec rule retained local leadership and saw themselves as subjected peoples, not as Aztecs. An Aztec army en route to conquer new lands frequently had to reconquer cities along its path.

Finally, the costs of expanding and sustaining the empire had become onerous. Generations of social mobility through distinction in combat had produced a bloated nobility both exempt from and sustained by tribute. Tenochtitlan became dependent on tributary maize in order to feed itself. Materially, the lack of new peoples to conquer meant the empire had little promise of increased prosperity. Spiritually, the dwindling flow of sacrificial victims meant the Mexica might be losing the great cosmic struggle to keep creation from ending.

Faced with these challenges, Moctezuma II reformed the empire. His predecessors had formalized social stratification and defined both the classes of nobility and the means by which to ascend into them. Moctezuma reduced the privileges (and thus the costs to the empire) of the lesser nobility and narrowed the pathways of social mobility. The austerity he imposed in the imperial capital caused unrest. He also pressed the consolidation of territory by seeking to conquer the autonomous enclaves left by his predecessors. As Moctezuma targeted these enclaves, their ability to resist sapped their resources and strained their morale without

# Viewpoints 11.2

## Inca and Spanish Views on Religion, Authority, and Tribute

• *In 1532 Inca emperor Atahualpa traveled to Cajamarca to meet with the band of Spaniards led by Francisco Pizarro. At the meeting, Pizarro's men captured Atahualpa. Before the capture, a remarkable exchange took place. The priest accompanying Pizarro, Friar Vicente de Valverde, read to Atahualpa, through a translator, a document prepared in Spain in 1513 called the* Requerimiento. *The document presented core Christian teachings about Jesus Christ and explained the establishment of the Roman Church, led by the pope, who granted Spanish emperor Charles V the right to conquer and Christianize the Americas. Conquistadors were legally obligated to read the* Requerimiento *in front of witnesses before waging a war of conquest. A portion of the friar's reading and Atahualpa's response are related here by Garcilaso de la Vega, the son of an Andean woman and a Spanish soldier, who published a history of the Inca Empire and the Spanish conquest in 1609.*

### Friar Vicente de Valverde Presents the *Requerimiento*

❝ It is proper that you should know, most famous and most powerful king, that it is necessary that Your Highness and all your subjects should not only learn the true Catholic faith but that you should hear and believe the following. . . .

Therefore the holy pope of Rome . . . has conceded the conquest of these parts to Charles V, . . . the most powerful king of Spain and monarch of all the earth. . . . The great emperor Charles V has chosen as his lieutenant and ambassador Don Francisco Pizarro, who is now here, . . . so that Your Highness and all your realms will become tributaries; that is to say, you will pay tribute to the emperor, and will become his vassal and deliver your kingdom wholly into his hands, renouncing the administration of it, as other kings and lords have done. . . . If you seek obstinately to resist, you may rest assured that God will suffer that you and all your Indians shall be destroyed by our arms, even as Pharaoh of old and all his host perished in the Red Sea. ❞

### The Inca Atahualpa Responds

❝ I will be no man's tributary. I am greater than any prince upon the earth. Your emperor may be a great prince; I do not doubt it, when I see that he has sent his subjects so far across the waters; and I am willing to hold him as a brother. As for the pope of whom you speak, he must be crazy to talk of giving away countries that do not belong to him. For my faith, I will not change it. Your own God, as you say, was put to death by the very men he created. But mine . . . [pointing to the sun] still lives in the heavens, and looks down upon his children. . . .

You threaten us with war and death . . . and say that I must renounce my kingdom and become the tributary of another, either willingly or by force. Whence I deduce one of two things: either your prince and you are tyrants who are destroying the world, depriving others of their realms, slaying and robbing those who have done you no harm and owe you nothing, or you are ministers of God, whom we call Pachacámac, who has chosen you to punish and destroy us. . . . [If so,] you should therefore act like divine messengers and ministers and put a stop to the slayings and lootings and acts of cruelty. . . .

You have mentioned five great men I should know. The first is God three and one, or four, whom you call the creator of the universe: he is perchance the same as our Pachacámac and Viracocha. The second is he whom you say is the father of all other men on whom they have all heaped their sins. The third you call Jesus Christ, the only one who did not lay his sins on the first man, but he was killed. The fourth you call pope. The fifth is Charles, whom you call the most powerful and monarch of the universe and supreme above the rest, without regard for the other four. If this Charles is prince and lord of the whole world, why should he need the pope to give him a new grant and concession to make war on me and usurp these kingdoms? If he has to ask the pope's permission, is not the pope a greater lord than he, and more powerful, and prince of all the world? Also, I am surprised that you say that I must pay tribute to Charles and not to the others, for you give no reason for paying the tribute, and I have certainly no obligation whatever to pay it. If there were any right or reason for paying tribute, it seems to me that it should go to the God you say created everyone and the man you say was the father of all men and to Jesus Christ . . . and finally it should go to the pope who can grant my kingdoms and my person to others. But if you say I owe these nothing, I owe even less to Charles, who was never lord of these regions and has never set eyes on them. . . .

I wish also to know about the good man called Jesus Christ who never cast his sins on the other and who you say died — if he died of a sickness or at the hands of his enemies; and if he was included among the gods before his death or after it. I also desire to know [if] you regard these five you have mentioned to me as gods, since you honor them so. For in this case, you have more gods than we, who adore only Pachacámac as the Supreme God and the Sun as the lower god, and the Moon as the Sun's wife and sister. **"**

Sources: Excerpts "It is proper that you should know" and "You threaten us with war" from Garcilaso de la Vega, *Royal Commentaries of the Incas, and General History of Peru*, translated by H. V. Livermore (Austin: University of Texas Press, 1989). Used by permission of the University of Texas Press; excerpt "I will be no man's tributary" from William Prescott, *History of the Conquest of Peru*, vol. 1. 1892 [1847], p. 370.

## QUESTIONS FOR ANALYSIS

1. According to Atahualpa, what is the source of his authority? What is the source of the Spaniards' authority?

2. Why does Atahualpa believe that the Spaniards have more gods than the Incas?

3. How does Atahualpa perceive the Spaniards and their intentions?

producing a corresponding reward for the empire in sacrifice or tribute.

Would Moctezuma have been able to consolidate these reforms and help the empire make the transition from expansion to stable maturity? Or was he a modern version of Tizoc, whose failures led to his assassination and a successor who responded to his predecessor's weakness with a surge of human sacrifice? The Aztec Empire had no real military or political rivals. As a result, the empire was well poised to continue despite its limitations, but it was also vulnerable to disruption upon the arrival of Europeans.

By the time he reached the gates of Tenochtitlan in 1519, Hernán Cortés had forged alliances with foes of the Aztec Empire, particularly Tlaxcala, which had so ably resisted conquest. The Tlaxcalans saw in the foreigners an opportunity that could aid their struggle against the Mexica and formed an alliance with the Spanish. Cortés's band of six hundred Spaniards arrived in Tenochtitlan accompanied by tens of thousands of Tlaxcalan soldiers. In Tlaxcala the defeat of Tenochtitlan would be seen as the Tlaxcalans' victory, not that of the handful of Spaniards.

Mexica accounts from after the Spanish conquest are filled with prophecies that foretold the conquest of Tenochtitlan and the fall of the Aztec Empire. One of the most evocative was the myth of the return of Quetzalcoatl. Surely Moctezuma could not resist a man he believed to be a powerful god descended from the Toltecs. Whatever he made of the strangers, he received them as guests, probably because he sought to understand the nature of this encounter and its significance for his empire. Perhaps Moctezuma hesitated, losing the opportunity to act against them. Perhaps he concluded that he had no chance of defeating them, since at that moment most of the men he could count on in battle were tending to their crops and the capital had been so riddled with division and resentment of his reforms that he was powerless to act.

Either way, Cortés and his men managed the encounter skillfully and succeeded in taking Moctezuma prisoner. When the residents of Tenochtitlan rose up to expel the Spaniards, Moctezuma was killed, either at the hands of the Spaniards or by his own subjects, depending on the account. Though the Spaniards were cast out of the city, they left an unwelcome guest, smallpox. The first epidemic of the disease swept through the city in 1520, killing Moctezuma's successor, Cuitlahuac, within a matter of months. Cuauhtemoc, the last tlatoani of the Mexica, was named that same year.

The Aztec Empire and the Mexica people were not defeated by technology, cultural superiority, or a belief that the Europeans were gods. Instead the Mexica suffered a political defeat: they fell because of ruptures in

**Past and Present Meet in Mexico City**   Construction for the Pino Suárez metro station unearthed the Aztec ceremonial altar of Ehecatl, the Aztec god of wind. (David Hiser/National Geographic/SuperStock)

their leadership due to the death of Moctezuma and his successor, as well as the willingness of allies and enemies alike to join with the Spaniards against them when they perceived an opportunity.

Through the lens of history, the destruction of the Aztec Empire seems sudden and swift, but Tenochtitlan resisted for two years, surrendering only in 1521. During this time the Spaniards and Tlaxcalans brokered alliances across the Valley of Mexico and beyond, leaving the Mexica virtually alone in their fight. In this sense, the end of the Aztec Empire looked a lot like its beginning: people who had obeyed the Mexica now took advantage of the opportunity to defeat them, just as the Mexica had done with the Tepanec Alliance. Even so, abandoned by their allies, the besieged Mexica fought on through famine and disease, defending their city street by street until they were finally vanquished.

## The Fall of the Incas

In 1525 Huayna Capac Inca, the grandson of Pachacuti Inca, became ill while carrying out a military campaign in present-day Ecuador, at the northern frontier of the empire. Campaigns of conquest always take place at

frontiers (even if these frontiers are between enclaves within an empire, as was the case for the Aztecs). But in this case, because of split inheritance, Huayna Capac's entire dominion would have to be created by expanding outward beyond the frontiers of his father's empire. His illness was plague, introduced by Europeans waging wars of conquest in Mesoamerica, and it would kill him. But as he waged war, he also received news of the foreigners in the north and anticipated that they would come southward. From his deathbed, he urged his successor to make peace with them.

But peace did not follow Huayna Capac's death. Instead civil war erupted between two of his sons over succession to the throne. Huascar claimed it as the firstborn. His half-brother Atahualpa, Huayna Capac's favorite and an experienced military commander who had accompanied him in his Ecuadorean campaign, claimed it as well. Atahualpa asserted that Huayna Capac's dying wish was that Atahualpa succeed him. The brothers fought for seven years, turning the empire's armies against each other. In 1532 Atahualpa vanquished and imprisoned his brother and consolidated his rule in Cuzco. That same year a group of Spaniards led by Francisco Pizarro landed on the Peruvian coast, pursuing rumors of a city of gold in the mountains.

Atahualpa agreed through emissaries to meet the Spaniards at the city of Cajamarca in northern Peru. In a demonstration of his imperial authority, he entered Cajamarca carried on a golden litter, accompanied by four military squadrons of eight thousand men each. Other members of the nobility followed, carried on their own litters. Their procession was preceded by a multitude of servants who cleared the ground, removing all stones, pebbles, and even bits of straw. Atahualpa met the Spanish intending not to fight a battle, but to understand them and hear them out. The meeting between Atahualpa and Pizarro reflected two deeply different worldviews. (See "Viewpoints 11.2: Inca and Spanish Views on Religion, Authority, and Tribute," page 322.)

In the scuffle that ensued at the meeting, the Spaniards took Atahualpa prisoner, and they eventually executed him. The Spaniards named a new indigenous leader, Manco Capac, whom they hoped to control. But Manco Capac turned against the Spaniards. He, and later his son Tupac Amaru, led resistance against the Spaniards until 1567. Each time the Inca forces besieged a Spanish-controlled city or town, however, their proximity to the Spaniards exposed them to European diseases. They were more successful in smaller-scale attacks, which delayed and limited Spanish colonization, but did not undo it.

## Chapter Summary

The Inca and Aztec Empires that encountered Spanish conquerors were short-lived products of the cycle of centralization and decentralization that had characterized the Andes and Mesoamerica for thousands of years. In this sense, there was nothing new in the toppling of these empires. The empires preceding those of the Incas and Aztecs had been undone when their own people turned against them, when climate changes disrupted them, or when they faced outside competition. What was new in the sixteenth century was that this outside competition came from Europeans.

The civilizations of the Andes and Mesoamerica from which the Incas and Aztecs emerged had remarkable similarities with and differences from other ancient and premodern civilizations in other regions of the world. Without being influenced by developments in Africa, Asia, or Europe, indigenous societies of the Americas developed extensive networks of trade. In Mesoamerica and the Andes, the domestication of crops led to the kind of bountiful production that allowed for diversification of labor among farmers, priests, nobles, merchants, and artisans. In these environments, cycles of centralization occurred in which powerful city-states emerged and embarked on campaigns of conquest, bringing vast regions under their political, religious, and cultural influence.

But civilizations of the Americas developed in unique ways as well. This was particularly true in the Andes, where peoples developed specialized patterns of farming in vertical archipelagos in their inhospitable mountain environment. Similarly, though Andean peoples did not develop writing, they instead developed the khipu into a sophisticated system of recording and communicating information.

Ultimately, the history of the peoples of the Americas was defined by their diverse experiences as they coped with varied climates, ecology, and geography. Chinampa agriculture in the Valley of Mexico and raised-bed farming practiced by the Maya are examples. And peoples' experiences of adapting to their environments, and of transforming those environments to meet their needs, shaped the ways they understood their world. These experiences led them to produce

### CHRONOLOGY

| | |
|---|---|
| ca. 40,000–13,000 B.C.E. | Initial human migration to the Americas |
| ca. 5000 B.C.E. | Intensification of agriculture |
| ca. 2000 B.C.E. | Earliest mound building in North America |
| ca. 1500–300 B.C.E. | Olmec culture |
| ca. 1200 B.C.E. | Emergence of Chavín culture in the Andes |
| ca. 100–800 C.E. | Moche culture |
| ca. 300–650 C.E. | Peak of Teotihuacan's influence |
| ca. 600–900 C.E. | Peak of Maya culture |
| ca. 1050–1250 C.E. | Construction of mounds at Cahokia |
| ca. 1325 C.E. | Construction of Aztec city of Tenochtitlan begins |
| ca. 1428–1521 C.E. | Aztec Empire dominates Mesoamerica |
| ca. 1438–1532 C.E. | Inca Empire dominates the Andes |

precise calendars, highly detailed readings of the stars, and an elaborate architecture of religious beliefs through which they interpreted their relationships to their world and their place in the cosmos.

## NOTES

1. *Narrative of the Incas by Juan de Betanzos*, trans. and ed. Roland Hamilton and Dana Buchanan from the Palma de Mallorca manuscript, p. 138.
2. "Maya Writing," Authentic Maya, http://www.authenticmaya.com/maya_writing.htm.
3. Michael Coe, *Mexico from the Olmecs to the Aztecs*, 5th ed. (New York: Thames and Hudson, 2002), p. 107.
4. Ross Hassig, *War and Society in Ancient Mesoamerica* (Berkeley: University of California Press, 1992), p. 56.
5. Ibid., p. 49.
6. Ibid., pp. 81, 85.
7. Bernal Díaz, *The Conquest of New Spain*, trans. J. M. Cohen (New York: Penguin Books, 1978), p. 214.
8. Ross Hassig, *Aztec Warfare* (Norman: University of Oklahoma Press, 1988), p. 143.
9. Miguel León-Portilla, "Mexico to 1519," in *Cambridge History of Latin America*, ed. Leslie Bethell, vol. 1 (Cambridge: Cambridge University Press, 1984), p. 14.

## CONNECTIONS

Though we often think of history unfolding along differences between peoples (Spaniards versus Aztecs, for instance), a more common division is often evident: rural versus urban experiences. The disruption of American societies and cultures after the encounter with Europeans occurred in both rural and urban areas, but there were deep differences in the effects of colonization upon urban and rural peoples of the Americas.

The early sixteenth century marked the end of independent empires of the Americas and the gradual integration of American peoples into global empires seated in Europe. Spaniards were the most motivated and had their greatest success when they encountered dense, organized urban areas. Here they displaced existing overlords as the recipients of tribute in goods and labor. The Spanish were less interested in sparsely settled areas that did not have well-established systems of trade and tribute and were harder to subdue. As a result, European conquest was a surprisingly drawn-out process. Peoples of the Americas resisted conquest until well into the nineteenth century.

The incidental companion of conquest—disease—was also uneven in its effects. Over the course of the sixteenth century, epidemic diseases decimated the population of the Americas, which fell from 50 million to just 5 million. But epidemics of diseases that are spread through human contact, such as measles and smallpox, are primarily urban phenomena: these diseases emerged as ancient cities grew large enough that the diseases could spread quickly among dense populations. As a result, the impact of the diseases brought by Europeans was the most severe and the most destructive in the cities of the Americas.

Since cities faced the brunt of both disease and wars of conquest, the disruptions caused by the encounter were disproportionally felt there. Whole systems of knowledge, sets of artisanal skills, political cultures, and religious thought resided in cities. As epidemics erupted, as besieging armies tore down buildings stone by stone, and as survivors dispersed, many of the most remarkable aspects of American civilizations were lost. Rural peoples and cultures were much more resilient. It was in rural areas that languages, foodways, farming practices, and approaches to healing—indeed whole worldviews—endured and evolved. This process occurred either in isolation from or in dialogue with European cultures, but local practices in rural regions were not obliterated, as they were in major cities. In the end, the European encounter destroyed the urban cultures and systems of knowledge in the Americas.

# Review and Explore

## Make It Stick

### LearningCurve
Go online and use LearningCurve to retain what you've read.

## Identify Key Terms

Identify and explain the significance of each item below.

**Mesoamerica** (p. 298)       **Moche** (p. 305)        **Teotihuacan** (p. 310)

**khipu** (p. 299)             **Inca** (p. 305)         **Nahuatl** (p. 315)

**nixtamalization** (p. 301)   **Quechua** (p. 307)      **Mexica** (p. 315)

**Olmecs** (p. 302)            **Maya** (p. 310)         **Tenochtitlan** (p. 316)

## Review the Main Ideas

Answer the focus questions from each section of the chapter.

1. How did ancient peoples of the Americas adapt to, and adapt, their environment? (p. 299)
2. What patterns established by early societies shaped civilization in Mesoamerica and the Andes? (p. 302)
3. What were the sources of strength and prosperity, and of problems, for the Incas? (p. 305)
4. How did the Maya and Teotihuacan develop prosperous and stable societies in the classical era? (p. 310)
5. How did the Aztecs build on the achievements of earlier Mesoamerican cultures and develop new traditions to create their large empire? (p. 315)
6. What did the European encounter mean for peoples of the major American empires? (p. 321)

## Make Connections

Analyze the larger developments and continuities within and across chapters.

1. Why didn't societies of the Americas adopt the wheel for transportation, as peoples of other world regions did?
2. How does the connection between religion and imperial expansion among the Aztecs and Incas resemble the role of religion in other societies?
3. Much of what we know of ancient societies of the Americas is based on archaeological data rather than written sources. How does the reliance on archaeological data shape our understanding of history? What does it help us understand? What is hard for us to interpret from it?

**⊔LaunchPad**

**Online Document Project**

## The Making and Remaking of Aztec History

**Why did Tlacaelel believe the Aztec Empire needed a new history?**
Read documents that examine Aztec history and culture, and then complete a quiz and writing assignment based on the evidence and details from this chapter.

*See inside the front cover to learn more.*

## Suggested Reading

Carassco, David, and Scott Sessions. *Daily Life of the Aztecs: People of the Sun and Earth*. 2008. An overview of Aztec culture designed for general readers.

Clendinnen, Inga. *Aztecs: An Interpretation*. 1992. Pays particular attention to the role that rituals and human sacrifice played in Aztec culture.

Coe, Michael D. *The Maya*. 2011. A new edition of a classic survey that incorporates the most recent scholarship.

Coe, Michael D. *Mexico: From the Olmecs to the Aztecs*. 2013. A rich examination of Mesoamerican peoples with the exception of the Maya.

Conrad, G. W., and A. A. Demarest. *Religion and Empire: The Dynamics of Aztec and Inca Expansionism*. 1993. Compares the two largest American empires.

Freidel, David. *A Forest of Kings: The Untold Story of the Ancient Maya*. 1990. A splendidly illustrated work providing expert treatment of the Maya world.

Hassig, Ross. *Mexico and the Spanish Conquest*. 2006. A study of indigenous participation in the conquest by a leading historical anthropologist.

Kehoe, Alice Beck. *America Before the European Invasion*. 2002. An excellent survey of North America before the coming of the Europeans, by an eminent anthropologist.

León-Portilla, Miguel. *The Aztec Image of Self and Society: An Introduction to Nahua Culture*. 1992. A rich appreciation of Aztec religious ritual and symbolism.

Mann, Charles C. *1491: New Revelations of the Americas Before Columbus*. 2006. A thoroughly researched overview of all the newest scholarship, written for a general audience.

Mumford, Jeremy Ravi. *Vertical Empire: The General Resettlement of Indians in the Colonial Andes*. 2012. A study of Andean mountain life between Inca and Spanish rule.

Ramirez, Susan. *To Feed and Be Fed: The Cosmological Bases of Authority and Identity in the Andes*. 2008. Examines the relationships between ancestors, the spiritual world, and the physical world that shaped Andean societies.

Restall, Matthew, and Amara Solari. *2012 and the End of the World: The Western Roots of the Maya Apocalypse*. 2011. Reflects on popular interpretations of the Maya calendar and cosmology.

### Mongol Woman

Women played influential roles among the Mongols. The Mongol woman portrayed in this painting is Chabi, wife of Khubilai Khan. Like other Mongols, she maintained Mongol dress even though she spent much of her time in China. (The Granger Collection, NYC — All rights reserved.)

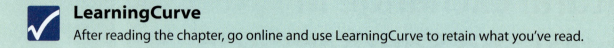

**LearningCurve**

After reading the chapter, go online and use LearningCurve to retain what you've read.

# Chapter Preview

**Central Asian Nomads**

**Chinggis Khan and the Mongol Empire**

**East-West Communication During the Mongol Era**

**India, Islam, and the Development of Regional Cultures, 300–1400**

**Southeast Asia, the Pacific Islands, and the Growth of Maritime Trade**

The large expanse of Asia treated in this chapter underwent profound changes during the centuries examined here. The north saw the rise of nomadic pastoral societies, first the Turks, then more spectacularly the Mongols. The nomads' mastery of the horse and mounted warfare gave them a military advantage that agricultural societies could rarely match. From the fifth century on, groups of Turks appeared along the fringes of the settled societies of Eurasia, from China and Korea to India and Persia. Often Turks were recruited as auxiliary soldiers; sometimes they gained the upper hand. By the tenth century many were converting to Islam (see Chapter 9).

Much more dramatic was the rise of the Mongols under the charismatic leadership of Chinggis Khan in the late twelfth and early thirteenth centuries. A military genius with a relatively small army, Chinggis subdued one society after another from Byzantium to the Pacific. For a century Mongol hegemony fostered unprecedented East-West trade and contact. More Europeans made their way east than ever before, and Chinese inventions such as printing and the compass made their way west.

Over the course of several centuries, Arab and Turkish armies brought Islam to India, but the Mongols never gained power there. In the Indian subcontinent during these centuries, regional cultures flourished. Although Buddhism declined, Hinduism continued to flourish. India continued to be the center of a very active seaborne trade, and this trade helped carry Indian ideas and practices to Southeast Asia. Buddhism was adopted in much of Southeast Asia, along with other ideas and techniques from India. The maritime trade in spices and other goods brought increased contact with the outside world to all but the most isolated of islands in the Pacific.

# Central Asian Nomads

☐ What aspects of nomadic life gave the nomads of Central Asia military advantages over nearby settled civilizations?

One experience Rome, Persia, India, and China all shared was conflict with **nomads** who came from the very broad region referred to as Central Asia. This region was dominated by the **steppe**, arid grasslands that stretched from modern Hungary, through southern Russia and across Central Asia (today's Tajikistan, Turkmenistan, Kazakhstan, Kyrgyzstan, and Uzbekistan) and adjacent parts of China, to Mongolia and parts of present northeast China. Initially small in number, the nomadic peoples of this region used their military superiority to conquer first other nomads, then the nearby settled societies. In the process they created settled empires of their own that drew on the cultures they absorbed.

## Nomadic Society

Easily crossed by horses but too dry for crop agriculture, the grasslands could support only a thin population of nomadic herders who lived off their sheep, goats, camels, horses, or other animals. Following the seasons, they would break camp at least twice a year and move their animals to new pastures, going north in the spring and south in the fall.

In their search for water and good pastures, nomadic groups often came into conflict with other nomadic groups pursuing the same resources, which the two would then fight over, as there was normally no higher political authority able to settle disputes. Groups on the losing end, especially if they were small, faced the threat of extermination or slavery, which prompted them to make alliances with other groups or move far away. Groups on the winning end of intertribal conflicts could exact tribute from those they defeated, sometimes so much that they could devote themselves entirely to war, leaving the work of tending herds to their slaves and vassals.

To get the products of nearby agricultural societies, especially grain, woven textiles, iron, tea, and wood, nomadic herders would trade their own products, such as horses and furs. When trade was difficult, they would turn to raiding to seize what they needed. Much of the time nomadic herders raided other nomads, but nearby agricultural settlements were common targets as well. The nomads' skill as horsemen and archers made it difficult for farmers and townsmen to defend against them. It was largely to defend against the raids of the Xiongnu nomads, for example, that the Chinese built the Great Wall.

**Manichaean Priests**  Many religions spread through Central Asia before it became predominantly Muslim after 1300. This fragment of a tenth- to twelfth-century illustrated document, found at the Silk Road city of Turfan, is written in the Uighur language and depicts Manichaean priests. (Archives Charmet/The Bridgeman Art Library)

Political organization among nomadic herders was generally very simple. Clans—members of an extended family—had chiefs, as did tribes (coalitions of clans). Leadership within a group was based on military prowess and was often settled by fighting. Occasionally a charismatic leader would emerge who was able to extend alliances to form confederations of tribes. From the point of view of the settled societies, which have left most of the records about these nomadic groups, large confederations were much more of a threat, since they could plan coordinated attacks on cities and

- **nomads**  Groups of people who move from place to place in search of food, water, and pasture for their animals, usually following the seasons.

- **steppe**  Grasslands that are too dry for crops but support pasturing animals; they are common across much of the center of Eurasia.

towns. Large confederations rarely lasted more than a century or so, however, and when they broke up, tribes again spent much of their time fighting with each other, relieving some of the pressure on their settled neighbors.

The three most wide-ranging and successful confederations were those of the Xiongnu—Huns, as they were known in the West—who emerged in the third century B.C.E. in the area near China; the Turks, who had their origins in the same area in the fourth and fifth centuries C.E.; and the Mongols, who did not become important until the late twelfth century. In all three cases, the entire steppe region was eventually swept up in the movement of peoples and armies.

## The Turks

The Turks were the first of the Inner Asian peoples to have left a written record in their own language; the earliest Turkish documents date from the eighth century. Turkic languages may have already been spoken in dispersed areas of the Eurasian steppe when the Turks first appeared; today these languages are spoken by the Uighurs in western China; the Uzbeks, Kazakhs, Kyrghiz (KIHR-guhz), and Turkmens of Central Asia; and the Turks of modern Turkey. The original religion of the Turks was shamanistic and involved worship of Heaven, making it similar to the religions of many other groups in the steppe region.

In 552 a group called Turks who specialized in metalworking rebelled against their overlords, the Rouruan, whose empire dominated the region from the eastern Silk Road cities of Central Asia through Mongolia. The Turks quickly supplanted the Rouruan as overlords of the Silk Road in the east. When the first Turkish khagan (ruler) died a few years later, the Turkish empire was divided between his younger brother, who took the western part (modern Central Asia), and his son, who took the eastern part (modern Mongolia). Sogdians—who were influential merchants along the Silk Road—convinced the Turks to send a delegation to both the Persian (see Chapter 9) and the Byzantine courts (see Chapter 8). Repeated diplomatic overtures in both directions did not prevent hostilities, however, and in 576 the Western Turks captured the Byzantine city of Bosporus in the Crimea.

The Eastern Turks frequently raided China and just as often fought among themselves. The Chinese history of the Sui Dynasty, written in the seventh century, records that "the Turks prefer to destroy each other rather than to live side-by-side. They have a thousand, nay ten thousand clans who are hostile to and kill one another. They mourn their dead with much grief and swear vengeance."[1] In the early seventh century the empire of the Eastern Turks ran up against the growing military might of the Tang Dynasty in China and soon broke apart.

In the eighth century a Turkic people called the Uighurs (Wee-gurs) formed a new empire based in Mongolia that survived about a century. It had close ties to Tang China, providing military aid but also extracting large payments in silk. During this period many Uighurs adopted religions then current along the Silk Road, notably Buddhism, Nestorian Christianity, and Manichaeism. In the ninth century this Uighur empire was destroyed by another Turkic people from north of Mongolia called the Kyrghiz. Some Uighurs fled to what is now western China. Setting up their capital city in Kucha, the Uighurs created a remarkably stable and prosperous kingdom that lasted four centuries (ca. 850–1250). Because of the dry climate of the region, many buildings, wall paintings, and manuscripts written in a variety of languages have been preserved from this era. They reveal a complex urban civilization in which Buddhism, Manichaeism, and Christianity existed side by side, practiced by Turks as well as by Tokharians, Sogdians, and other Iranian peoples.

Farther west in Central Asia other groups of Turks, such as the Karakhanids, Ghaznavids, and Seljuks, rose to prominence. Often local Muslim forces would try to capture them, employ them as slave soldiers, and convert them. By the mid- to late tenth century many were serving in the armies of the Abbasid caliphate. Also in the tenth century Central Asian Turks began converting to Islam (which protected them from being abducted as slaves). Then they took to raiding unconverted Turks.

In the mid-eleventh century Turks had gained the upper hand in the caliphate, and the caliphs became little more than figureheads. From there Turkish power was extended into Syria, Palestine, and Asia Minor. (Asia Minor is now called Turkey because Turks migrated there by the thousands over several centuries.) In 1071 Seljuk Turks inflicted a devastating defeat on the Byzantine army in eastern Anatolia (see page 246). Other Turkish confederations established themselves in Afghanistan and extended their control into north India (see page 349).

In India, Persia, and Anatolia the formidable military skills of nomadic Turkish warriors made it possible for them to become overlords of settled societies. Just as the Uighurs developed a hybrid urban culture along the eastern end of the Silk Road, adopting many elements from the mercantile Sogdians, the Turks of Central and West Asia created an Islamic culture that drew from both Turkish and Iranian sources. Often Persian was used as the administrative language of the states they formed. Nevertheless, despite the presence of Turkish overlords all along the southern fringe of the steppe, no one group of Turks was able to unite them all into a single political unit. That feat had to wait for the next major power on the steppe, the Mongols.

## The Mongols

In the twelfth century ambitious Mongols did not aspire to match the Turks or other groups that had migrated west, but rather wanted to be successors to the Khitans and Jurchens, nomadic groups that had stayed in the east and mastered ways to extract resources from China, the largest and richest country in the region. The Khitans and Jurchens had formed hybrid nomadic-urban states, with northern sections where tribesmen continued to live in the traditional way and southern sections politically controlled by the non-Chinese rulers but settled largely by taxpaying Chinese. The Khitans and Jurchens had scripts created to record their languages and adopted many Chinese governing practices. They built cities in pastoral areas that served as trading centers and places to enjoy their newly acquired wealth. In both the Khitan and Jurchen cases, their elite became culturally dual, adept in Chinese ways as well as in their own traditions.

The Mongols lived north of these hybrid nomadic-settled societies and maintained their traditional ways. Chinese, Persian, and European observers have all left descriptions of the daily life of the Mongols, which they found strikingly different from their own. They lived in tents called **yurts** rather than in houses. The yurts, about twelve to fifteen feet in diameter, were constructed of light wooden frames covered by layers of wool felt, greased to make them waterproof. Yurts were round, since this shape held up better against the strong winds that blew across the treeless grasslands. The floor of a yurt was covered first with dried grass or straw, then with felt, skins, or rugs. In the center, directly under the smoke hole, was the hearth. The master's bed was on the north. Goat horns attached to the frame of the yurt were used as hooks to hang joints of meat, cooking utensils, bows, quivers of arrows, and the like. A group of families traveling together would set up their yurts in a circle open to the south and draw up their wagons in a circle around the yurts for protection.

The Mongol diet consisted mostly of animal products. The most common meat was mutton, supplemented with wild game. When grain or vegetables

**Gold Belt Plaques** Like earlier nomads, the Mongols favored art with animal designs, such as these two gold belt plaques, which depict deer under trees or flowers. Belts and horses were often exchanged to seal or commemorate an alliance. (Nasser D. Khalili Collection of Islamic Art, © Nour Foundation. Courtesy of the Khalili Family Trust)

could be obtained through trade, they were added to the diet. Wood was scarce, so dried animal dung or grasses fueled the cook fires.

The Mongols milked sheep, goats, cows, and horses and made cheese and fermented alcoholic drinks from the milk. A European visitor to Mongolia in the 1250s described how they milked mares, a practice unfamiliar to Europeans:

> They fasten a long line to two posts standing firmly in the ground, and to the line they tie the young colts of the mares which they mean to milk. Then come the mothers who stand by their foals, and allow themselves to be milked. And if any of them be too unruly, then one takes her colt and puts it under her, letting it suck a while, and presently taking it away again, and the milker takes its place.[2]

He also described how they made the alcoholic drink koumiss from the milk, a drink that "goes down very pleasantly, intoxicating weak brains."[3]

Because of the intense cold of the winter, the Mongols made much use of furs and skins for clothing. Both men and women usually wore silk trousers and tunics (the silk obtained from China). Over these they wore robes of fur, for the very coldest times in two layers—an inner layer with the hair on the inside and an outer layer with the hair on the outside. Hats were of felt or fur, boots of felt or leather. Men wore leather belts to which their bows and quivers could be attached.

• **yurts** Tents in which the pastoral nomads lived; they could be quickly dismantled and loaded onto animals or carts.

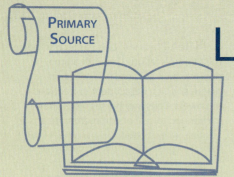

# Listening to the Past

## The Abduction of Women in *The Secret History of the Mongols*

*Within a few decades of Chinggis Khan's death, oral traditions concerning his rise were written down in the Mongolian language in* The Secret History of the Mongols. *The account begins with the cycles of revenge among the tribes in Mongolia, many of which began when women were abducted for wives. The following passages relate how Temujin's (Chinggis Khan's) father, Yesugei, seized Hogelun, Temujin's future mother, from a passing Merkid tribesman; how twenty years later three Merkids in return seized women from Temujin; and how Temujin got revenge.*

❝ That year Yesugei the Brave was out hunting with his falcon on the Onan. Yeke Chiledu, a nobleman of the Merkid tribe, had gone to the Olkhunugud people to find himself a wife, and he was returning to the Merkid with the girl he'd found when he passed Yesugei hunting by the river. When he saw them riding along Yesugei leaned forward on his horse. He saw it was a beautiful girl. Quickly he rode back to his tent and just as quick returned with his two brothers, Nekun Taisi and Daritai Odchigin. When Chiledu saw the three Mongols coming he whipped his dun-colored horse and rode off around a nearby hill with the three men behind him. He cut back around the far side of the hill and rode to Lady Hogelun, the girl he'd just married, who stood waiting for him at the front of their cart. "Did you see the look on the faces of those three men?" she asked him. "From their faces it looks like they mean to kill you. As long as you've got your life there'll always be girls for you to choose from. There'll always be women to ride in your cart. As long as you've got your life you'll be able to find some girl to marry. When you find her, just name her Hogelun for me, but go now and save your own life!" Then she pulled off her shirt and held it out to him, saying: "And take this to remember me, to remember my scent." Chiledu reached out from his saddle and took the shirt in his hands. With the three Mongols close behind him he struck his dun-colored horse with his whip and took off down the Onan River at full speed.

The three Mongols chased him across seven hills before turning around and returning to Hogelun's cart. Then Yesugei the Brave grasped the reins of the cart, his elder brother Nekun Taisi

rode in front to guide them, and the younger brother Daritai Odchigin rode along by the wheels. As they rode her back toward their camp, Hogelun began to cry, . . . and she cried till she stirred up the waters of the Onan River, till she shook the trees in the forest and the grass in the valleys. But as the party approached their camp Daritai, riding beside her, warned her to stop: "This fellow who held you in his arms, he's already ridden over the mountains. This man who's lost you, he's crossed many rivers by now. You can call out his name, but he can't see you now even if he looks back. If you tried to find him now you won't even find his tracks. So be still now," he told her. Then Yesugei took Lady Hogelun to his tent as his wife. . . .

[Some twenty years later] one morning just before dawn Old Woman Khogaghchin, Mother Hogelun's servant, woke with a start, crying: "Mother! Mother! Get up! The ground is shaking, I hear it rumble. The Tayichigud must be riding back to attack us. Get up!"

Mother Hogelun jumped from her bed, saying: "Quick, wake my sons!" They woke Temujin and the others and all ran for the horses. Temujin, Mother Hogelun, and Khasar each took a horse. Khachigun, Temuge Odchigin, and Belgutei each took a horse. Bogorchu took one horse and Jelme another. Mother Hogelun lifted the baby Temulun onto her saddle. They saddled the last horse as a lead and there was no horse left for [Temujin's wife] Lady Borte. . . .

Old Woman Khogaghchin, who'd been left in the camp, said: "I'll hide Lady Borte." She made her get into a black covered cart. Then she harnessed the cart to a speckled ox. Whipping the ox, she drove the cart away from the camp down the Tungelig. As the first light of day hit them, soldiers rode up and told them to stop. "Who are you?" they asked her, and Old Woman Khogaghchin answered: "I'm a servant of Temujin's. I've just come from shearing his sheep. I'm on my way back to my own tent to make felt from the wool." Then they asked her: "Is Temujin at his tent? How far is it from here?" Old Woman Khogaghchin said: "As for the tent, it's not far. As for Temujin, I couldn't see whether he was there or not. I was just shearing his sheep out back." The soldiers rode off toward the camp, and Old Woman Khogaghchin whipped the ox. But as the cart moved faster its axletree

Women of high rank wore elaborate headdresses decorated with feathers.

Mongol women had to work very hard and had to be able to care for the animals when the men were away hunting or fighting. They normally drove the carts and set up and dismantled the yurts. They also milked the sheep, goats, and cows and made the butter and cheese.

In addition, they made the felt, prepared the skins, and sewed the clothes. Because water was scarce, clothes were not washed with water, nor were dishes. Women, like men, had to be expert riders, and many also learned to shoot. They participated actively in family decisions, especially as wives and mothers. In *The Secret History of the Mongols*, a work written in Mongolian in

snapped. "Now we'll have to run for the woods on foot," she thought, but before she could start the soldiers returned. They'd made [Temujin's half brother] Belgutei's mother their captive, and had her slung over one of their horses with her feet swinging down. They rode up to the old woman shouting: "What have you got in that cart!" "I'm just carrying wool," Khogaghchin replied, but an old soldier turned to the younger ones and said, "Get off your horses and see what's in there." When they opened the door of the cart they found Borte inside. Pulling her out, they forced Borte and Khogaghchin to ride on their horses, then they all set out after Temujin. . . .

The men who pursued Temujin were the chiefs of the three Merkid clans, Toghtoga, Dayin Usun, and Khagatai Darmala. These three had come to get their revenge, saying: "Long ago Mother Hogelun was stolen from our brother, Chiledu." When they couldn't catch Temujin they said to each other: "We've got our revenge. We've taken their wives from them," and they rode down from Mount Burkhan Khaldun back to their homes. . . .

Having finished his prayer Temujin rose and rode off with Khasar and Belgutei. They rode to [his father's sworn brother] Toghoril Ong Khan of the Kereyid camped in the Black Forest on the Tula River. Temujin spoke to Ong Khan, saying: "I was attacked by surprise by the three Merkid chiefs. They've stolen my wife from me. We've come to you now to say, 'Let my father the Khan save my wife and return her.'" . . .

[Temujin and his allies] moved their forces from Botoghan Bogorjin to the Kilgho River where they built rafts to cross over to the Bugura Steppe, into [the Merkid] Chief Toghtoga's land. They came down on him as if through the smoke-hole of his tent, beating down the frame of his tent and leaving it flat, capturing and killing his wives and his sons. They struck at his door-frame where his guardian spirit lived and broke it to pieces. They completely destroyed all his people until in their place there was nothing but emptiness. . . .

As the Merkid people tried to flee from our army running down the Selenge with what they could gather in the darkness, as our soldiers rode out of the night capturing and killing the Merkid, Temujin rode through the retreating camp shouting out: "Borte! Borte!"

Lady Borte was among the Merkid who ran in the darkness and when she heard his voice, when she recognized Temujin's voice, Borte leaped from her cart. Lady Borte and Old Woman Khogaghchin saw Temujin charge through the crowd and they ran to him, finally seizing the reins of his horse. All about them was moonlight. As Temujin looked down to see who had stopped him he recognized Lady Borte. In a moment he was down from his horse and they were in each other's arms, embracing. 🙶

Source: Paul Kahn, trans., *The Secret History of the Mongols: The Origin of Chinghis Khan*. Copyright © 1984. Reprinted with permission of Paul Kahn.

Chinggis and his wife Borte are seated together at a feast in this fourteenth-century Persian illustration. (Bibliothèque Nationale, Paris, France/The Bridgeman Art Library)

## QUESTIONS FOR ANALYSIS

1. What do you learn from these stories about the Mongol way of life?

2. "Marriage by capture" has been practiced in many parts of the world. Can you infer from these stories why such a system would persist? What was the impact of such practices on kinship relations?

3. Can you recognize traces of the oral origins of these stories?

about 1240, the mother and wife of the Mongol leader Chinggis Khan frequently make impassioned speeches on the importance of family loyalty. (See "Listening to the Past: The Abduction of Women in *The Secret History of the Mongols*," above.)

Mongol men kept as busy as the women. They made the carts and wagons and the frames for the yurts. They also made harnesses for the horses and oxen, leather saddles, and the equipment needed for hunting and war, such as bows and arrows. Men also had charge of the horses, and they milked the mares. Young horses were allowed to run wild until it was time to break them in. Catching them took great skill in the use of a long springy pole with a noose at the end. One specialist among the nomads was the blacksmith, who made stirrups, knives, and other metal tools.

Kinship underlay most social relationships among the Mongols. Normally each family occupied a yurt, and groups of families camping together were usually related along the male line (brothers, uncles, nephews, and so on). More distant patrilineal relatives were recognized as members of the same clan and could call on each other for aid. People from the same clan could not marry each other, so men had to get wives from other clans. When a woman's husband died, she would be inherited by another male in the family, such as her husband's brother or his son by another woman. Tribes were groups of clans, often distantly related. Both clans and tribes had chiefs who would make decisions on where to graze and when to retaliate against another tribe that had stolen animals or people. Women were sometimes abducted for brides. When tribes stole men from each other, they normally made them into slaves, and slaves were forced to do much of the heavy work. They would not necessarily remain slaves their entire lives, however, as their original tribes might be able to recapture them or make exchanges for them, or their masters might free them.

Even though population was sparse in the regions where the Mongols lived, conflict over resources was endemic, and each camp had to be on the alert for attacks. Defending against attacks and retaliating against raids was as much a part of the Mongols' daily life as caring for their herds and trading with nearby settlements.

Mongol children learned to ride at a young age, first on goats. The horses they later rode were short and stocky, almost like ponies, but nimble and able to endure long journeys and bitter cold. Even in the winter the horses survived by grazing, foraging beneath the snow. The prime weapon boys had to learn to use was the compound bow, which had a pull of about 160 pounds and a range of more than 200 yards; it was well suited for using on horseback, giving Mongol soldiers an advantage in battle. Other commonly used weapons were small battle-axes and lances fitted with hooks to pull enemies off their saddles.

Hunting was a common form of military training among the Mongols. Each year tribes would organize one big hunt; mounted hunters would form a vast ring perhaps ten or more miles in circumference, then gradually shrink it down, trapping all the animals before killing them. On military campaigns a Mongol soldier had to be able to ride for days without stopping to cook food; he ate from a supply of dried milk curd and cured meat, which could be supplemented by blood let from the neck of his horse. When time permitted, the soldiers would pause to hunt, adding dogs, wolves, foxes, mice, and rats to their food.

As with the Turks and other steppe nomads, religious practices centered around the shaman, a religious expert believed to be able to communicate with the gods. The high god of the Mongols was Heaven/Sky, but they recognized many other gods as well. Some groups of Mongols, especially those closer to settled communities, converted to Buddhism, Nestorian Christianity, or Manichaeism.

# Chinggis Khan and the Mongol Empire

☐ How did Chinggis Khan and his successors conquer much of Eurasia, and how did the Mongol conquests change the regions affected?

In the mid-twelfth century the Mongols were just one of many peoples in the eastern grasslands, neither particularly numerous nor especially advanced. Why then did the Mongols suddenly emerge as an overpowering force on the historical stage? One explanation is ecological. A drop in the mean annual temperature created a subsistence crisis. As pastures shrank, the Mongols and other nomads had to look beyond the steppe to get more of their food from the agricultural world. A second reason for their sudden rise was the appearance of a single individual, the brilliant but utterly ruthless Temujin (ca. 1162–1227), later and more commonly called Chinggis Khan (sometimes spelled Genghis or Ghengis).

## Chinggis Khan

What we know of Temujin's early career was recorded in *The Secret History of the Mongols*, written within a few decades of his death. In Temujin's youth, his father had built a modest tribal following. When Temujin's father was poisoned by a rival, his followers, not ready to follow a boy of twelve, drifted away, leaving Temujin and his mother and brothers in a vulnerable position. Temujin slowly collected followers. In 1182 Temujin was captured and carried in a cage to a rival's camp. After a daring midnight escape, he led his followers to join a stronger chieftain whom his father had once aided. With the chieftain's help, Temujin began avenging the insults he had received.

Temujin proved to be a natural leader, and as he subdued the Tartars, Kereyids, Naimans, Merkids, and other Mongol and Turkish tribes, he built up an army of loyal followers. He mastered the art of winning allies through displays of personal courage in battle and gen-

• **Chinggis Khan** The title given to the Mongol ruler Temujin in 1206; it means Great Ruler.

**The Tent of Chinggis Khan** In this fourteenth-century Persian illustration from Rashid al-Din's *History of the World*, two guards stand outside while Chinggis is in his tent. (From a book by Rashid al-Din [1247–1318] [vellum], Persian School [14th century]/Bibliothèque Nationale, Paris, France/The Bridgeman Art Library)

erosity to his followers. To those who opposed him, he could be merciless. He once asserted that nothing gave more pleasure than massacring one's enemies, seizing their horses and cattle, and ravishing their women. Sometimes Temujin would kill all the men in a defeated tribe to prevent later vendettas. At other times he would take them on as soldiers in his own armies. Courage impressed him. One of his leading generals, Jebe, first attracted his attention when he held his ground against overwhelming opposition and shot Temujin's horse out from under him. Another prominent general, Mukhali, became Temujin's personal slave at age twenty-seven after his tribe was defeated by Temujin in 1197. Within a few years he was leading a corps of a thousand men from his own former tribe.

In 1206, at a great gathering of tribal leaders, Temujin was proclaimed **Chinggis Khan**, or Great Ruler. Chinggis decreed that Mongol, until then an unwritten language, be written down in the script used by the Uighur Turks. With this script a record was made of the Mongol laws and customs, ranging from the rules for the annual hunt to punishments of death for robbery and adultery. Another measure adopted at this assembly was a postal relay system to send messages rapidly by mounted courier, suggesting that Chinggis already had ambitions to rule a vast empire.

With the tribes of Mongolia united, the energies previously devoted to infighting and vendettas were redirected to exacting tribute from the settled populations nearby, starting with the Jurchen (Jin) state that extended into north China (see Map 13.2, page 370). Because of his early experiences with intertribal feuding, Chinggis mistrusted traditional tribal loyalties, and as he fashioned a new army, he gave it a new, nontribal decimal structure (based on units of ten). He conscripted soldiers from all the tribes and assigned them to units that were composed of members from different tribes. He selected commanders for each unit whom he could remove at will, although he allowed commanders to pass their posts on to their sons.

After Chinggis subjugated a city, he would send envoys to cities farther out to demand submission and threaten destruction. Those who opened their city gates and submitted without fighting could join the Mongols, but those who resisted faced the prospect of mass slaughter. He despised city dwellers and would sometimes use them as living shields in the next battle. After the Mongol armies swept across north China in 1212–1213, ninety-odd cities lay in rubble. Beijing, captured in 1215, burned for more than a month. Not surprisingly many governors of cities and rulers of small states hastened to offer submission.

Mongol campaign before 1240
Mongol campaign after 1240
Route of Marco Polo, 1271–1295

## ▢ Mapping the Past

**MAP 12.1 The Mongol Empire** The creation of the vast Mongol Empire facilitated communication across Eurasia and led to both the spread of deadly plagues and the transfer of technical and scientific knowledge. After the death of Chinggis Khan in 1227, the empire was divided into four khanates ruled by different lines of his successors. In the 1270s the Mongols conquered southern China, but most of their subsequent campaigns did not lead to further territorial gains.

**ANALYZING THE MAP** Trace the campaigns of the Mongols. Which ones led to acquisition of territory, and which ones did not?

**CONNECTIONS** Would the division of the Mongol Empire into separate khanates have made these areas easier for the Mongols to rule? What drawbacks might it have had from the Mongols' point of view?

Chinggis preferred conquest to administration and did not stay in north China to set up an administrative structure. He left that to subordinates and turned his attention westward, to Central Asia and Persia, then dominated by different groups of Turks. In 1218 Chinggis proposed to the Khwarizm shah of Persia that he accept Mongol overlordship and establish trade relations. The shah, to show his determination to resist, ordered the envoy and the merchants who had accompanied him killed. The next year Chinggis led an army of one hundred thousand soldiers west to retaliate. Mongol forces destroyed the shah's army and sacked one Persian city after another, demolishing buildings and massacring hundreds of thousands of people.

After returning from Central Asia, Chinggis died in 1227 during the siege of a city in northwest China. Before he died, he instructed his sons not to fall out among themselves but instead to divide the spoils.

## Chinggis's Successors

Although Mongol leaders traditionally had had to win their positions, after Chinggis died the empire was divided into four states called **khanates**, with one of the lines of his descendants taking charge of each (Map 12.1). Chinggis's third son, Ögödei, assumed the title of khan, and he directed the next round of invasions.

In 1237 representatives of all four lines led 150,000 Mongol, Turkish, and Persian troops into Europe. During the next five years, they gained control of Moscow and Kievan Russia and looted cities in Poland and Hungary. They were poised to attack deeper into Europe when they learned of the death of Ögödei in 1241. To participate in the election of a new khan, the army returned to the Mongols' new capital city, Karakorum.

Once Ögödei's son was certified as his successor, the Mongols turned their attention to Persia and the Middle East. In 1256 a Mongol army took northwest Iran, then pushed on to the Abbasid capital of Baghdad. When it fell in 1258, the last Abbasid caliph was murdered, and the population was put to the sword. The Mongol onslaught was successfully resisted, however, by both the Delhi sultanate (see page 349) and the Mamluk rulers in Egypt (see page 246).

Under Chinggis's grandson Khubilai Khan (r. 1260–1294), the Mongols completed their conquest of China. South China had never been captured by non-Chinese, in large part because horses were of no strategic advantage in a land of rivers and canals. Proceeding deliberately, the Mongols first surrounded the Song empire in central and south China (discussed in Chapter 13) by taking its westernmost province in 1252, as well as Korea to its east in 1258; destroying the Nanzhao kingdom in modern Yunnan in 1254; and then continuing south and taking Annam (northern Viet-

nam) in 1257. A surrendered Song commander advised the Mongols to build a navy to attack the great Song cities located on rivers. During the five-year siege of a central Chinese river port, both sides used thousands of boats and tens of thousands of troops. The Mongols employed experts in naval and siege warfare from all over their empire—Chinese, Korean, Jurchen, Uighur, and Persian. Catapults designed by Muslim engineers launched a barrage of rocks weighing up to a hundred pounds each. During their advance toward the Chinese capital of Hangzhou, the Mongols ordered the total slaughter of the people of the major city of Changzhou, and in 1276 the Chinese empress dowager surrendered in hopes of sparing the people of the capital a similar fate.

Having overrun China and Korea, Khubilai turned his eyes toward Japan. In 1274 a force of 30,000 soldiers and support personnel sailed from Korea to Japan. In 1281 a combined Mongol and Chinese fleet of about 150,000 made a second attempt to conquer Japan. On both occasions the Mongols managed to land but were beaten back by Japanese samurai armies. Each time fierce storms destroyed the Mongol fleets. The Japanese claimed that they had been saved by the *kamikaze*, the "divine wind" (which later lent its name to the thousands of Japanese aviators who crashed their airplanes into American warships during World War II). Twelve years later, in 1293, Khubilai tried sending a fleet to the islands of Southeast Asia, including Java, but it met with no more success than the fleets sent to Japan.

Why were the Mongols so successful against so many different types of enemies? Even though their population was tiny compared to the populations of the large agricultural societies they conquered, their tactics, their weapons, and their organization all gave them advantages. Like other nomads before them, they were superb horsemen and excellent archers. Their horses were extremely nimble, able to change direction quickly, thus allowing the Mongols to maneuver easily and ride through infantry forces armed with swords, lances, and javelins. Usually only other nomadic armies, like the Turks, could stand up well against the Mongols. (See "Viewpoints 12.1: Chinese and European Accounts About the Mongol Army," page 340.)

The Mongols were also open to trying new military technologies. To attack walled cities, they learned how to use catapults and other engines of war. At first they employed Chinese catapults, but when they learned that those used by the Turks in Afghanistan were more powerful, they adopted the better model. The Mongols also used exploding arrows and gunpowder projectiles developed by the Chinese.

---

**khanates** The states ruled by a khan; the four units into which Chinggis divided the Mongol Empire.

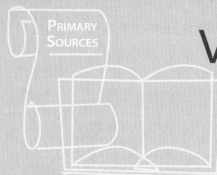

# Viewpoints 12.1

## Chinese and European Accounts About the Mongol Army

• *The Mongols received little attention from historians until they were united under Chinggis and began their military conquests. The following documents offer different perspectives on the Mongol army. The first, one of the earliest surviving accounts, was written about 1220 by a Chinese historian, Li Xinchuan, living in south China under the Song Dynasty. He would have learned of the Mongols secondhand, as the Song had diplomatic relations with Jin, which was then under attack by the Mongols. He reported how the Tartars—referring to the Mongols—gained control of north China in 1213–1214. The second excerpt refers to the time that the state of Song in south China sustained its first major attack by the Mongols in 1236, when Mongol armies entered the western province of Sichuan and destroyed major cities like Chengdu. A man who survived the slaughter, Zhu Sisun, later reported what he went through. Marco Polo, encountering the Mongols a half century later, after most of their conquests through Eurasia were complete, had a different view of the warriors.*

### Li Xinchuan

❝ In the spring of 1213 [the Tartars] attacked Yanjing [modern Beijing] and that fall Yunji [the Jin emperor] was killed. Chinggis left Samohe in charge of Yanjing and incorporated the 46 divisions of the surrendered [Jin] armies of Yang Boyu and Liu Bolin into the great Tartar armies, which were divided into three divisions to conquer the prefectural cities of [the circuits of] River North, River East, and Mountains East. . . . At this time the troops of the various circuits of north China pulled back to defend the region west of the mountains, but there were not enough troops, so commoners were drafted as soldiers and put on the tops of the city walls to defend them. The Tartars drove their family members to attack them, and fathers and sons or brothers often got close enough to recognize and call out to each other. Because of this, [the drafted soldiers] were not firmly resolved, and all of the cities surrendered as soon as the fighting began. From the twelfth month of 1213 to the first month of 1214, more than ninety prefectures fell. Every place the armies passed through was devastated. For several thousand *li*, throughout River East, River North, and Mountains East, the people were slaughtered. Gold and silk, boys and girls, oxen and sheep, horses and other animals were all "rolled up" and taken away. Houses were burnt down and defensive walls smashed. ❞

### Zhu Sisun

❝ Here is how the people of Sichuan went to their deaths: groups of fifty people were clustered together, and the Mongols impaled them all with swords and piled up the corpses. At sunset, those who did not appear dead were again stabbed. Sisun lay at the bottom of a pile of corpses, and by chance the evening stabbing did not reach him. The blood of the corpses above him dripped steadily into his mouth. Halfway through the night Sisun began to revive, and crawling into the woods he made his escape. ❞

### Marco Polo

❝ They are brave in battle, almost to desperation, setting little value upon their lives, and exposing themselves without hesitation to all manner of danger. Their disposition is cruel. They are capable of supporting every kind of privation, and when there is a necessity for it, can live for a month on the milk of their mares, and upon such wild animals as they may chance to catch. The men are habituated to remain on horseback during two days and two nights, without dismounting, sleeping in that situation whilst their horses graze. No people on earth can surpass them in fortitude under difficulties, nor show greater patience under wants of every kind. ❞

Sources: Li Xinchuan, *Jianyan yilai chaoye zaji* (Beijing: Zhonghua shuju, 2000), pp. 847–851, trans. Patricia Ebrey; Paul J. Smith, "Family, *Landsmann*, and Status-Group Affinity in Refugee Mobility Strategies: The Mongol Invasions and the Diaspora of Sichuanese Elites, 1230–1330," *Harvard Journal of Asiatic Studies* 52.2 (1992): 671–672, slightly modified; *The Travels of Marco Polo, the Venetian*, ed. Manuel Komroff (New York: Boni and Liveright, 1926), p. 93.

### QUESTIONS FOR ANALYSIS

1. How would you explain the differences in what these writers chose to mention?

2. If you were writing a history of the Mongols, would you consider these sources as equally valid evidence, or do you find some more reliable than others? Does anything in the accounts seem exaggerated? How can you judge?

The Mongols made good use of intelligence and tried to exploit internal divisions in the countries they attacked. Thus in north China they appealed to the Khitans, who had been defeated by the Jurchens a century earlier, to join them in attacking the Jurchens. In Syria they exploited the resentment of Christians against their Muslim rulers.

## The Mongols as Rulers

The success of the Mongols in ruling vast territories was due in large part to their willingness to incorporate other ethnic groups into their armies and governments. Whatever their original country or religion, those who served the Mongols loyally were rewarded. Uighurs, Tibetans, Persians, Chinese, and Russians came to hold powerful positions in the Mongol governments. Chinese helped breach the walls of Baghdad in the 1250s, and Muslims operated the catapults that helped reduce Chinese cities in the 1270s.

Since, in Mongol eyes, the purpose of fighting was to gain riches, the Mongols would regularly loot the settlements they conquered, taking whatever they wanted, including the residents. Land would be granted to military commanders, nobles, and army units to be governed and exploited as the recipients wished. Those working the land would be given to them as serfs. The Mongols built a capital city called Karakorum in modern Mongolia, and to bring it up to the level of the cities they conquered, they transported skilled workers from those cities. For instance, after Bukhara and Samarkand were captured in 1219–1220, some thirty thousand artisans were enslaved and transported to Mongolia. Sometimes these slaves gradually improved their status. A French goldsmith from Budapest named Guillaume Boucher was captured by the Mongols in 1242 and taken to Karakorum, where he gradually won favor and was put in charge of fifty workers to make gold and silver vessels for the Mongol court.

The traditional nomad disdain for farmers led some commanders to suggest turning north China into a gigantic pasture after it was conquered. In time, though, the Mongols came to realize that simply appropriating the wealth and human resources of the settled lands was not as good as extracting regular revenue from them. A Chinese-educated Khitan who had been working for the Jurchens in China explained to the Mongols that collecting taxes from farmers would be highly profitable: they could extract a revenue of 500,000 ounces of silver, 80,000 bolts of silk, and more than 20,000 tons of grain from the region by taxing it. The Mongols gave this a try, but soon political rivals convinced the khan that he would gain even more by letting Central Asian Muslim merchants bid against each other for licenses to collect taxes any way they could, a system called **tax-farming**. Ordinary Chinese found this

## MONGOL CONQUESTS

| | |
|---|---|
| **1206** | Temujin made Chinggis Khan |
| **1215** | Fall of Beijing (Jurchens) |
| **1219–1220** | Fall of Bukhara and Samarkand in Central Asia |
| **1227** | Death of Chinggis |
| **1237–1241** | Raids into eastern Europe |
| **1257** | Conquest of Annam (northern Vietnam) |
| **1258** | Conquest of Abbasid capital of Baghdad; conquest of Korea |
| **1260** | Khubilai succeeds to khanship |
| **1274** | First attempt at invading Japan |
| **1276** | Surrender of Song Dynasty (China) |
| **1281** | Second attempt at invading Japan |
| **1293** | Mongol fleet unsuccessful in invasion of Java |
| **mid-14th century** | Decline of Mongol power |

method of tax collecting much more oppressive than traditional Chinese methods, since there was little to keep the tax collectors from seizing everything they could.

By the second half of the thirteenth century there was no longer a genuine pan-Asian Mongol Empire. Much of Asia was in the hands of Mongol successor states, but these were generally hostile to each other. Khubilai was often at war with the khanate of Central Asia, then held by his cousin Khaidu, and he had little contact with the khanate of the Golden Horde in south Russia. The Mongols adapted their methods of government to the existing traditions of each place they ruled, and the regions went their separate ways.

In China the Mongols resisted assimilation and purposely avoided many Chinese practices. The rulers conducted their business in the Mongol language and spent their summers in Mongolia. Khubilai discouraged Mongols from marrying Chinese and took only Mongol women into the palace. Some Mongol princes preferred to live in yurts erected on the palace grounds rather than in the grand palaces constructed at Beijing. Chinese were treated as legally inferior not only to the Mongols but also to all other non-Chinese. In cases of assault the discrepancy was huge, as a Mongol who murdered a Chinese could get off with a fine, but a Chinese who hit a Mongol to defend himself would face severe penalties.

**tax-farming** Assigning the collection of taxes to whoever bids the most for the privilege.

In Central Asia, Persia, and Russia the Mongols tended to merge with the Turkish groups already there and, like them, converted to Islam. Russia in the thirteenth century was not a strongly centralized state, and the Mongols allowed Russian princes and lords to continue to rule their territories as long as they turned over adequate tribute (thus adding to the burden on peasants). The city of Moscow became the center of Mongol tribute collection and grew in importance. In the Middle East the Mongol Il-khans (as they were known in Persia) were more active as rulers, again continuing the traditions of the caliphate. In Mongolia itself, however, Mongol traditions were maintained.

Mongol control in each of the khanates lasted about a century. In the mid-fourteenth century the Mongol dynasty in China deteriorated into civil war, and in the 1360s the Mongols withdrew back to Mongolia. There was a similar loss of Mongol power in Persia and Central Asia. Only on the south Russian steppe did the Golden Horde maintain its hold for another century.

As Mongol rule in Central Asia declined, a new conqueror emerged, Timur, also known as Tamerlane (Timur the Lame). Not a nomad but a highly civilized Turkish noble, Timur in the 1360s struck out from his base in Samarkand into Persia, north India (see page 349), southern Russia, and beyond. His armies used the terror tactics that the Mongols had perfected, massacring the citizens of cities that resisted. In the decades after his death in 1405, however, Timur's empire went into decline.

## East-West Communication During the Mongol Era

☐ How did the Mongol conquests facilitate the spread of ideas, religions, inventions, and diseases?

The Mongol governments did more than any earlier political entities to encourage the movement of people and goods across Eurasia. With these vast movements came cultural accommodation as the Mongols, their conquered subjects, and their trading partners learned from one another. This cultural exchange involved both physical goods and the sharing of ideas, including the introduction of new religious beliefs and the adoption of new ways to organize and rule the Mongol Empire. It also facilitated the spread of the plague and the unwilling movement of enslaved captives.

### The Movement of Peoples

The Mongols had never looked down on merchants the way the elites of many traditional states did, and they welcomed the arrival of merchants from distant lands.

Even when different groups of Mongols were fighting among themselves, they usually allowed caravans to pass without harassing them.

The Mongol practice of transporting skilled people from the lands they conquered also brought people into contact with each other in new ways. Besides those forced to move, the Mongols recruited administrators from all over. Especially prominent were the Uighur Turks of Chinese Central Asia, whose familiarity with Chinese civilization and fluency in Turkish were extremely valuable in facilitating communication. Literate Uighurs staffed much of the Mongol administration.

One of those who served the Mongols was Rashid al-Din (ca. 1247–1318). A Jew from Persia and the son of an apothecary, Rashid al-Din converted to Islam at the age of thirty and entered the service of the Mongol Il-khan of Persia as a physician. He rose in government service, traveled widely, and eventually became prime minister. Rashid al-Din became friends with the ambassador from China, and together they arranged for translations of Chinese works on medicine, agronomy, and statecraft. Aware of the great differences between cultures, he believed that the Mongols should try to rule in accord with the moral principles of the majority in each land. On that basis he convinced the Mongol khan of Persia to convert to Islam. Rashid al-Din undertook to explain the great variety of cultures by writing a world history more comprehensive than any previously written. (See "Viewpoints 12.2: Circulating Paper Money," at right.)

The Mongols were remarkably open to religious experts from all the lands they encountered. More Europeans made their way as far as Mongolia and China in the Mongol period than ever before. Popes and kings sent envoys to the Mongol court in the hope of enlisting the Mongols on their side in their longstanding conflict with Muslim forces over the Holy Land. European visitors were also interested in finding Christians who had been cut off from the West by the spread of Islam, and in fact there were considerable numbers of Nestorian Christians in Central Asia. In 1245 Pope Innocent IV wrote two letters to the "King and people of the Tartars" asking him to become a Christian and cease attacks against Europe. They were delivered to a Mongol general in Armenia. The next year another envoy, Giovanni di Pian de Carpine, reached the Volga River and the camp of Batu, the khan of the Golden Horde. Batu sent him on to the new Great Khan in Karakorum with two Mongol guides, riding so fast that they had to change horses five to seven times a day. Their full journey of more than three thousand miles took a remarkably short five and a half months. Carpine spent four months at the Great Khan's court but never succeeded in convincing the khan to embrace Christianity or drop his demand

# Viewpoints 12.2

## Circulating Paper Money

• *In China the Mongols maintained the established practice of circulating paper money (see page 378), which amazed visitors from other parts of Eurasia. The three texts below give different perspectives on the use of paper money. The first is a legal ruling issued in 1291 by the Mongols in China, the second is Marco Polo's description of the practice as he witnessed it in the 1290s, and the third is Rashid al-Din's account of the failed attempt to introduce the practice in Mongol-ruled Persia in 1294.*

### The Yuan Code of 1291

❝ At any Treasury for Note Circulation, when a person comes to exchange worn-out notes for new notes, the responsible official shall oversee the counting of the notes in the presence of the owner. If none of the notes are patched or counterfeited, the official shall apply the stamp "Exchanged" to them and place them in the treasury and hand over new notes to the owner. The supervising authorities shall send inspectors to make frequent inspections. Any violator of these provisions shall be investigated and punished. ❞

### Marco Polo

❝ The coinage of this paper money is authenticated with as much form and ceremony as if it were actually pure gold or silver; for to each note a number of officers, specially appointed, not only subscribe their names, but affix their seals also. . . . When thus coined in large quantities, this paper currency is circulated in every part of the Great Khan's dominions; nor dares any person, at the peril of his life, refuse to accept it in payment. All his subjects receive it without hesitation, because, wherever their business may call them, they can dispose of it again in the purchase of merchandise they may require; such as pearls, jewels, gold, or silver. With it, in short, every article may be procured. . . .

When any person happens to be possessed of paper money which from long use has become damaged, they carry it to the mint, where, upon the payment of only three per cent, they receive fresh notes in exchange. Should any be desirous of procuring gold or silver for the purpose of manufacture, such as of drinking-cups, girdles, or other articles wrought of these metals, they in like manner apply to the mint, and for their paper obtain the bullion they require. ❞

### Rashid al-Din

❝ On Friday [July 27, 1294], Akbuka, Togachar, Sadr al-Din, and Tamachi-Inak went to Tabriz to launch the paper money [*chao*]. They arrived there on [August 13], promulgated the decree, and prepared a great quantity of paper money. On Saturday [September 12, 1294], in the city of Tabriz, they put the paper money into circulation. The decree laid down that any person who refused to accept it would be summarily executed. For one week, in fear of the sword, they accepted it, but they gave very little in return. Most of the people of Tabriz perforce chose to leave, taking the textiles and foodstuffs from the bazaars with them, so that nothing was available, and people who wanted to eat fruit went secretly to the orchards. The city, which had been so populous, was completely emptied of people. Vagabonds and ruffians looted whatever they found in the streets. Caravans ceased to go there. . . .

Sadr al-Din, affected by the words [of a dervish], and with the assent of the retainers after this ruination, obtained a decree authorizing the sale of foodstuffs for gold. Because of this people became bold and transacted business openly in gold, and the absent returned to the city, and within a short time it was flourishing again. In the end, the attempt to introduce paper money did not succeed. ❞

Sources: *Dayuan tongzhi tiaoge* (Taipei: Huasheng shuju, 1980), 14.1b–2a, trans. Patricia Ebrey; Manuel Komroff, ed., *The Travels of Marco Polo* (New York: Boni and Liveright, 1926), pp. 159–161; Bernard Lewis, ed. and trans., *Islam from the Prophet Muhammad to the Capture of Constantinople*. Vol. 2: *Religion and Society* (New York: Oxford University Press, 1987), 292w from p. 192, slightly modified. © 1974 by Bernard Lewis. Used by permission of Oxford University Press, USA.

### QUESTIONS FOR ANALYSIS

1. What do you learn about the processes of cultural borrowing from these sources?

2. What features of paper money most impressed Marco Polo?

3. What made it difficult to introduce paper money in Tabriz?

that the pope appear in person to tender his submission to the khan. When Carpine returned home, he wrote a report that urged preparation for a renewed Mongol attack on Europe. The Mongols had to be resisted "because of the harsh, indeed intolerable, and hitherto unheard-of slavery seen with our own eyes, to which they reduce all peoples who have submitted to them."[4]

A few years later, in 1253, Flemish friar William of Rubruck set out with the permission of King Louis IX of France as a missionary to convert the Mongols. He too made his way to Karakorum, where he found many Europeans. At Easter, Hungarians, Russians, Georgians, Armenians, and Alans all took communion in a Nestorian church.

The most famous European visitor to the Mongol lands was the Venetian Marco Polo (ca. 1254–1324). In his famous *Travels*, Marco Polo described all the places he visited or learned about during his seventeen years away from home. He reported being warmly received by Khubilai, who impressed him enormously. He was also awed by the wealth and splendor of Chinese cities and spread the notion of Asia as a land of riches. In Marco Polo's lifetime some skeptics did not believe his tale, and even today some scholars speculate that he may have learned about China from Persian merchants he met in the Middle East without actually going to China. But Mongol scholars staunchly defend Marco Polo, even though they admit that he stretched the truth to make himself look good in several places.

## The Spread of Disease, Goods, and Ideas

The rapid transfer of people and goods across Central Asia spread more than ideas and inventions. It also spread diseases, the most deadly of which was the plague known in Europe as the Black Death, which scholars identify today as the bubonic plague. In the early fourteenth century, transmitted by rats and fleas, the plague began to spread from Central Asia into West Asia, the Mediterranean, and western Europe. When the Mongols were assaulting the city of Kaffa in the Crimea in 1346, they were infected by the plague and had to withdraw. In retaliation, they purposely spread the disease to their enemy by catapulting the bodies of victims into the city of Kaffa. Soon the disease was carried from port to port throughout the Mediterranean by ship. The confusion of the mid-fourteenth century that led to the loss of Mongol power in China, Iran, and Central Asia undoubtedly owes something to the effect of the spread of the plague and other diseases. (For more on the Black Death, see Chapter 14.)

Traditionally, the historians of each of the countries conquered by the Mongols portrayed them as a scourge. Russian historians, for instance, saw this as a period of bondage that set Russia back and cut it off from western Europe. Among contemporary Western historians, it is now more common to celebrate the genius of the Mongol military machine and treat the spread of ideas and inventions as an obvious good, probably because we see global communication as a good in our own world. There is no reason to assume, however, that people benefited equally from the improved communications and the new political institutions of the Mongol era. Merchants involved in long-distance trade prospered, but those enslaved and transported hundreds or thousands of miles from home would have seen themselves not as the beneficiaries of opportunities to encounter cultures different from their own but rather as the most pitiable of victims.

The places that were ruled by Mongol governments for a century or more—China, Central Asia, Persia, and Russia—do not seem to have advanced at a more

**Planting Trees**  The illustrations in early copies of Marco Polo's book show the elements that Europeans found most interesting. This page illustrates Khubilai's order that trees be planted along the main roads. (Illumination from *Le Livre des Merveilles du Monde* [Travels of Marco Polo], by the Paris studio of the Boucicaut Master, c. 1412/Bibliothèque Nationale, Paris/akg-images)

**Horse and Groom** Zhao Mengfu (1254–1322), the artist of this painting and a member of the Song imperial family, took up service under the Mongol emperor Khubilai. The Mongol rulers, great horsemen themselves, would likely have appreciated this depiction of a horse buffeted by the wind. (*Horse and Groom in Winter* [ink on paper], Chao Meng-Fu, or Zhao Mengfu [1254–1322], National Palace Museum, Taipei, Taiwan/The Bridgeman Art Library)

rapid rate during that century than they did in earlier centuries, either economically or culturally. By Chinese standards, Mongol imposition of hereditary status distinctions was a step backward from a much more mobile and open society, and placing Persians, Arabs, or Tibetans over Chinese did not arouse interest in foreign cultures. Many more styles of foreign music, clothing, art, and furnishings were integrated into Chinese civilization in Tang times than in Mongol times.

In terms of the spread of technological and scientific ideas, Europe seems to have been by far the main beneficiary of increased communication, largely because in 1200 it lagged farther behind than the other areas. Chinese inventions such as printing, gunpowder, and the compass spread westward. Persian and Indian expertise in astronomy and mathematics also spread. In terms of the spread of religions, Islam probably gained the most. It came to dominate in Chinese Central Asia, which had previously been Buddhist.

# India, Islam, and the Development of Regional Cultures, 300–1400

☐ **What was the result of India's encounters with Turks, Mongols, and Islam?**

South Asia, although far from the heartland of the steppe, still felt the impact of the arrival of the Turks in Central Asia. Over the course of many centuries, horsemen from both the east and the west (Scythians, Huns, Turks, and Mongols) all sent armies south to raid or invade north India. After the Mauryan Empire broke apart in 185 B.C.E. (see page 84), India was politically divided into small kingdoms for several centuries. Only the Guptas in the fourth century would emerge to unite much of north India, though their

rule was cut short by the invasion of the Huns in about 450. A few centuries later, India was profoundly shaped by Turkish nomads from Central Asia who brought their culture and, most important, Islam to India. Despite these events, the lives of most Indians remained unchanged, with the majority of the people living in villages in a society defined by caste.

## The Gupta Empire, ca. 320–480

In the early fourth century a state emerged in the Ganges plain that was able to bring large parts of north India under its control. The rulers of this Indian empire, the Guptas, consciously modeled their rule after that of the Mauryan Empire, and the founder took the name of the founder of that dynasty, Chandragupta. Although the Guptas never controlled as much territory as the Mauryans had, they united north India and received tribute from states in Nepal and the Indus Valley, thus giving large parts of India a period of peace and political unity.

The Guptas' administrative system was not as centralized as that of the Mauryans. In the central regions they drew their revenue from a tax on agriculture of one-quarter of the harvest and maintained monopolies on key products such as metals and salt (reminiscent of Chinese practice). They also exacted labor service for the construction and upkeep of roads, wells, and irrigation systems. More distant areas were assigned to governors who were allowed considerable leeway, and governorships often

**The Gupta Empire, ca. 320–480**

became hereditary. Areas still farther away were encouraged to become vassal states, able to participate in the splendor of the capital and royal court in subordinate roles and to engage in profitable trade, but did not have to provide much revenue.

The Gupta kings were patrons of the arts. Poets composed epics for the courts of the Gupta kings, and other writers experimented with prose romances and popular tales. India's greatest poet, Kalidasa (ca. 380–450), like Shakespeare, wrote poems as well as plays in verse. His most highly esteemed play, *Shakuntala*, concerns a daughter of a hermit who enthralls a king who is out hunting. The king sets up house with her, then returns to his court and, owing to a curse, forgets her. Only much later does he acknowledge their child as his true heir. Equally loved is Kalidasa's one-hundred-verse poem "The Cloud Messenger" about a demigod who asks a passing cloud to carry a message to his wife, from whom he has long been separated. At one point he instructs the cloud to tell her: "I see your body in the sinuous creeper, your gaze in the startled eyes of deer, your cheek in the moon, your hair in the plumage of peacocks, and in the tiny ripples of the river I see your sidelong glances, but alas, my dearest, nowhere do I see your whole likeness."[5]

In mathematics, too, the Gupta period could boast of impressive intellectual achievements. The so-called Arabic numerals are actually of Indian origin. Indian mathematicians developed the place-value notation system, with separate columns for ones, tens, and hundreds, as well as a zero sign to indicate the absence of units in a given column. This system greatly facilitated calculation and had spread as far as Europe by the seventh century.

The Gupta rulers were Hindus, but they tolerated all faiths. Buddhist pilgrims from other areas of Asia reported that Buddhist monasteries with hundreds or even thousands of monks and nuns flourished in the cities. The success of Buddhism did not hinder Hinduism with its many gods, which remained popular among ordinary people.

The great crisis of the Gupta Empire was the invasion of the Huns in about 450. Mustering his full might, the Gupta ruler Skandagupta (r. ca. 455–467) threw back the invaders, but they had dealt the dynasty a fatal blow.

**Wall Painting at Ajanta** Many of the best surviving examples of Gupta period painting are found at the twenty-nine Buddhist cave temples at Ajanta in central India. The walls of these caves were decorated in the fifth and sixth centuries with scenes from the former lives of the Buddha. This scene shows members of different castes. (SEF/Art Resource, NY)

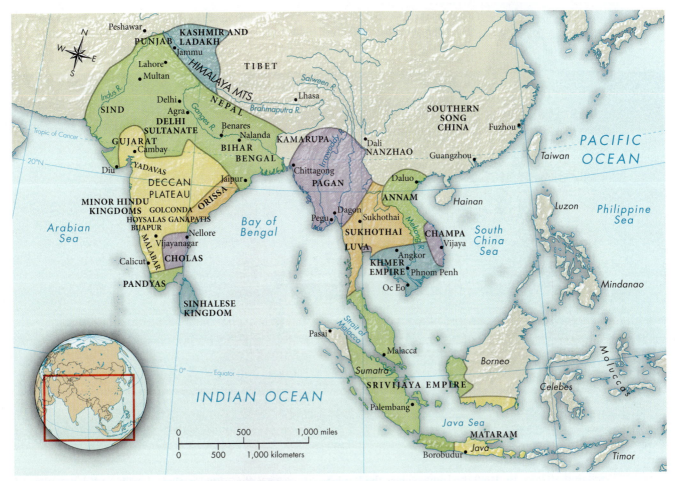

**MAP 12.2  South and Southeast Asia in the Thirteenth Century** The extensive coastlines of South and Southeast Asia and the predictable monsoon winds aided seafaring in this region. Note the Strait of Malacca, through which most east-west sea trade passed.

## India's Medieval Age and the First Encounter with Islam

After the decline of the Gupta Empire, India once again broke into separate kingdoms that were frequently at war with each other. Most of the dynasties of India's medieval age (ca. 500–1400) were short-lived, but a balance of power was maintained between the major regions of India, with none gaining enough of an advantage to conquer the others. Particularly notable are the Cholas, who dominated the southern tip of the peninsula, Sri Lanka, and much of the eastern Indian Ocean to the twelfth century (Map 12.2).

Political division fostered the development of regional cultures. Literature came to be written in India's regional languages, among them Marathi, Bengali, and Assamese. Commerce continued as before, and the coasts of India remained important in the sea trade of the Indian Ocean.

The first encounters with Islam occurred in this period. In 711, after pirates had plundered a richly laden Arab ship near the mouth of the Indus, the Umayyad governor of Iraq sent a force with six thousand horses and six thousand camels to seize the Sind area in western India (modern Pakistan). The western part of India remained part of the caliphate for centuries, but Islam did not spread much beyond this foothold. During the ninth and tenth centuries Turks from Central Asia moved into the region of today's northeastern Iran and western Afghanistan, then known as Khurasan. Converts to Islam, they first served as military forces for the caliphate in Baghdad, but as its authority weakened (see pages 339, 341), they made themselves rulers of an effectively independent Khurasan and frequently sent raiding parties into north India. Beginning in 997 Mahmud of Ghazni (r. 997–1030) led seventeen annual forays into India from his base in modern Afghanistan. His goal was plunder to finance his wars against other Turkish rulers in Central Asia. Toward this end, he systematically looted Indian palaces and temples, viewing religious statues as infidels' idols. Eventually the Arab conquerors of the Sind

**Kandariyâ Mahâdeva Hindu Temple** Built around 1050 by a local king in central India, this is one of the best-preserved Hindu temples from the medieval period. The main spire rises 100 feet, and the sides are decorated with more than six hundred stone statues. (Yvan Travert/akg-images)

fell to the Turks. By 1030 the Indus Valley, the Punjab, and the rest of northwest India were in the grip of the Turks.

The new rulers encouraged the spread of Islam, but the Indian caste system (see page 69) made it difficult to convert higher-caste Indians. Al-Biruni (d. 1048), a Persian scholar who spent much of his later life at the court of Mahmud and learned Sanskrit, wrote of the obstacles to Hindu-Muslim communication. The most basic barrier was language, but the religious gulf was also fundamental:

> They totally differ from us in religion, as we believe in nothing in which they believe, and vice versa. On the whole, there is very little disputing about theological topics among them; at the utmost they fight with words, but they will never stake their soul or body or property on religious controversy. . . . They call foreigners impure and forbid having any connection with them, be it by intermarriage or any kind of relationship, or by sitting, eating, and drinking with them, because thereby, they think, they would be polluted.[6]

> **protected people** The Muslim classification used for Hindus, Christians, and Jews; they were allowed to follow their religions but had to pay a special tax.

After the initial period of raids and destruction of temples, the Muslim Turks came to an accommodation with the Hindus, who were classed as a **protected people**, like the Christians and Jews, and allowed to follow their religion. They had to pay a special tax but did not have to perform military service. Local chiefs and rajas were often allowed to remain in control of their domains as long as they paid tribute. Most Indians looked on the Muslim conquerors as a new ruling caste, capable of governing and taxing them but otherwise peripheral to their lives. The myriad castes largely governed themselves, isolating the newcomers.

Nevertheless, over the course of several centuries Islam gained a strong hold on north India, especially in the Indus Valley (modern Pakistan) and in Bengal at the mouth of the Ganges River (modern Bangladesh). Moreover, the sultanate seems to have had a positive effect on the economy. Much of the wealth confiscated from temples was put to more productive use, and India's first truly large cities emerged. The Turks also were eager to employ skilled workers, giving new opportunities to low-caste manual and artisan labor.

The Muslim rulers were much more hostile to Buddhism than to Hinduism, seeing Buddhism as a competitive proselytizing religion. In 1193 a Turkish raiding party destroyed the great Buddhist university at Nalanda in Bihar. Buddhist monks were killed or forced to flee to Buddhist centers in Southeast Asia, Nepal, and Tibet. Buddhism, which had thrived for so long in peaceful and friendly competition with Hinduism, subsequently went into decline in its native land.

Hinduism, however, remained as strong as ever. South India was largely unaffected by these invasions, and traditional Hindu culture flourished there under native kings ruling small kingdoms. (See "Individuals in Society: Bhaskara the Teacher," page 350.) Devotional cults and mystical movements flourished. This was a great age of religious art and architecture in India. Extraordinary temples covered with elaborate bas-relief were built in many areas. Sexual passion and the union of men and women were frequently depicted, symbolically representing passion for and union with the temple god.

## The Delhi Sultanate

In the twelfth century a new line of Turkish rulers arose in Afghanistan, led by Muhammad of Ghur (d. 1206). Muhammad captured Delhi and extended his control nearly throughout north India. When he fell to an assassin in 1206, one of his generals, the former slave Qutb-ud-din, seized the reins of power and established a government at Delhi, separate from the government in Afghanistan. This sultanate of Delhi lasted for three centuries, even though dynasties changed several times.

The North African Muslim world traveler Ibn Battuta (see "Individuals in Society: Ibn Battuta," page 256) served for several years as a judge at the court of one of the Delhi sultans. He praised the sultan for his insistence on the observance of ritual prayers and many acts of generosity to those in need, but he also considered the sultan overly violent. Here is just one of many examples he offered of how quick the sultan was to execute:

> During the years of the famine, the Sultan had given orders to dig wells outside the capital, and have grain crops sown in those parts. He provided the cultivators with the seed, as well as with all that was necessary for cultivation in the way of money and supplies, and required them to cultivate these crops for the [royal] grain-store. When the jurist 'Afif al-Din heard of this, he said, "This crop will not produce what is hoped for." Some informer told the Sultan what he had said, so the Sultan jailed him, and said to him, "What reason have you to meddle with the government's business?" Some time later he released him, and as 'Afif al-Din went to his house he was met on the way by two friends of his, also jurists, who said to him, "Praise be to God for your release," to which our jurist replied, "Praise be to God who has delivered us from the evildoers." They then separated, but they had not reached their houses before

this was reported to the Sultan, and he commanded all three to be fetched and brought before him. "Take out this fellow," he said, referring to 'Afif al-Din, "and cut off his head baldrickwise," that is, the head is cut off along with an arm and part of the chest, "and behead the other two." They said to him, "He deserves punishment, to be sure, for what he said, but in our case for what crime are you killing us?" He replied, "You heard what he said and did not disavow it, so you as good as agreed with it." So they were all put to death, God Most High have mercy on them.[7]

A major accomplishment of the Delhi sultanate was holding off the Mongols. Chinggis Khan and his troops entered the Indus Valley in 1221 in pursuit of the shah of Khurasan. The sultan wisely kept out of the way, and when Chinggis Khan left some troops in the area, the sultan made no attempt to challenge them. Two generations later, in 1299, a Mongol khan launched a campaign into India with two hundred thousand men, but the sultan of the time was able to defeat them. Two years later the Mongols returned and camped at Delhi for two months, but they eventually left without taking the sultan's fort. Another Mongol raid in 1306–1307 also was successfully repulsed.

Although the Turks by this time were highly cosmopolitan and no longer nomadic, they had retained their martial skills and understanding of steppe warfare. They were expert horsemen, and horses thrived in northwest India. The south and east of India, however, like the south of China, were less hospitable to raising horses. In India's case, though, the climate of the south and east was well suited to elephants, which had been used as weapons of war in India since early times. Rulers in the northwest imported elephants from more tropical regions. The Delhi sultanate is said to have had as many as one thousand war elephants at its height.

During the fourteenth century, however, the Delhi sultanate was in decline and proved unable to ward off the armies of Timur (see page 342), who took Delhi in 1398. Timur's chronicler reported that when the troops drew up for battle outside Delhi, the sultanate had 10,000 horsemen, 20,000 foot soldiers, and 120 war elephants. Though alarmed at the sight of the elephants, Timur's men dug trenches to trap them and shot at their drivers. The sultan fled, leaving the city to surrender. Timur took as booty all the elephants, loading them with treasures seized from the city. Ruy Gonzalez de Clavijo, an ambassador from the king of Castile (now part of Spain), who arrived in Samarkand in 1403, was greatly impressed by these well-trained elephants. "When all the elephants together charged abreast, it seemed as though the solid earth itself shook at their onrush," he observed, noting that he thought each elephant was worth a thousand foot soldiers in battle.[8]

# Individuals in Society

## Bhaskara the Teacher

IN INDIA, AS IN MANY OTHER SOCIETIES, ASTRONOMY AND mathematics were closely linked, and many of the most important mathematicians served their rulers as astronomers. Bhaskara (1114–ca. 1185) was such an astronomer-mathematician. For generations his Brahmin family had been astronomers at the Ujjain astronomical observatory in north-central India, and his father had written a popular book on astrology.

Bhaskara was a highly erudite man. A disciple wrote that he had thoroughly mastered eight books on grammar, six on medicine, six on philosophy, five on mathematics, and the four Vedas. Bhaskara eventually wrote six books on mathematics and mathematical astronomy. They deal with solutions to simple and quadratic equations and show his knowledge of trigonometry, including the sine table and relationships between different trigonometric functions, and even some of the basic elements of calculus. Earlier Indian mathematicians had explored the use of zero and negative numbers. Bhaskara developed these ideas further, in particular improving on the understanding of division by zero.

A court poet who centuries later translated Bhaskara's book titled *The Beautiful* explained its title by saying Bhaskara wrote it for his daughter named Beautiful (Lilavati) as consolation when his divination of the best time for her to marry went awry. Whether Bhaskara did or did not write this book for his daughter, many of the problems he provides in it have a certain charm:

> On an expedition to seize his enemy's elephants, a king marched two yojanas the first day. Say, intelligent calculator, with what increasing rate of daily march did he proceed, since he reached his foe's city, a distance of eighty yojanas, in a week?*
>
> Out of a heap of pure lotus flower, a third part, a fifth, and a sixth were offered respectively to the gods Siva, Vishnu, and the Sun; and a quarter was presented to Bhavani. The remaining six lotuses were given to the venerable preceptor. Tell quickly the whole number of lotus.†
>
> If eight best variegated silk scarfs, measuring three cubits in breadth and eight in length, cost a hundred nishkas, say quickly, merchant, if thou understand trade, what a like scarf, three and a half cubits long and half a cubit wide will cost.‡

In the conclusion to *The Beautiful*, Bhaskara wrote:

> Joy and happiness is indeed ever increasing in this world for those who have *The Beautiful* clasped to their throats, decorated as the members are with neat reduction of fractions, multiplication, and involution, pure and perfect as are the solutions, and tasteful as is the speech which is exemplified.

Bhaskara had a long career. His first book on mathematical astronomy, written in 1150 when he was thirty-six, used mathematics to calculate solar and lunar eclipses or planetary conjunctions. Thirty-three years later he was still writing on the subject, this time providing simpler ways to solve problems encountered before. Bhaskara wrote his books in Sanskrit,

**The observatory where Bhaskara worked in Ujjain today stands in ruins.** (Dinodia Photo Library)

already a literary language rather than a vernacular language, but even in his own day some of them were translated into other Indian languages.

Within a couple of decades of his death, a local ruler endowed an educational institution to study Bhaskara's works, beginning with his work on mathematical astronomy. In the text he had inscribed at the site, the ruler gave the names of Bhaskara's ancestors for six generations, as well as of his son and grandson, who had continued in his profession.

### QUESTIONS FOR ANALYSIS

1. What might have been the advantages of making occupations like astronomer hereditary in India?
2. How does Bhaskara link joy and happiness to mathematical concepts?

*Quotations from Haran Chandra Banerji, *Colebrooke's Translation of the Lilavati*, 2d ed. (Calcutta: The Book Co., 1927), pp. 80–81, 30, 51, 200. The answer is that each day he must travel 22/7 yojanas farther than the day before.

†The answer is 120.

‡The answer, from the formula $x = (1 \times 7 \times 1 \times 100) / (8 \times 3 \times 8 \times 2 \times 2)$, is given in currencies smaller than the nishka: 14 drammas, 9 panas, 1 kakini, and $6\frac{2}{3}$ cowry shells. (20 cowry shells = 1 kakini, 4 kakini = 1 pana, 16 panas = 1 dramma, and 16 drammas = 1 nishka.)

## LaunchPad
## Online Document Project

**What ideas and beliefs were central to Indian culture?** Read a Persian account of medieval India, and then complete a quiz and writing assignment based on the evidence and details from this chapter.

*See inside the front cover to learn more.*

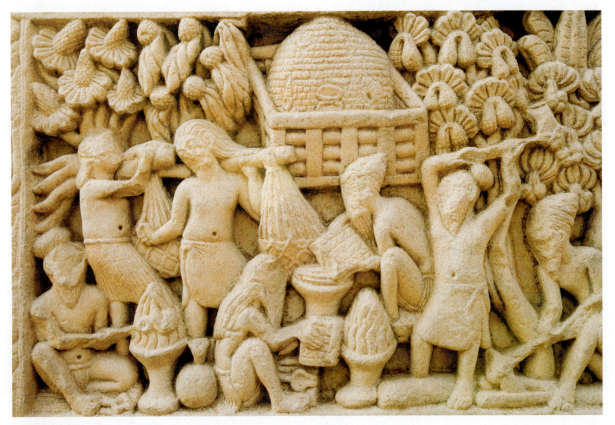

**Men at Work** This stone frieze from the Buddhist stupa in Sanchi depicts Indian men doing a variety of everyday jobs. Although the stone was carved to convey religious ideas, we can use it as a source for such details of daily life as the sort of clothing men wore while working and how they carried loads. (Dinodia Photo Library)

Timur's invasion left a weakened sultanate. The Delhi sultanate endured under different rulers until 1526, when it was conquered by the Mughals, a Muslim dynasty that would rule over most of northern India from the sixteenth into the nineteenth century.

## Life in Medieval India

Local institutions played a much larger role in the lives of people in medieval India than did the state. Craft guilds oversaw conditions of work and trade, local councils handled law and order at the town or village level, and local castes gave members a sense of belonging and identity.

Like peasant societies elsewhere, including in China, Japan, and Southeast Asia, agricultural life in India ordinarily meant village life. The average farmer worked a small plot of land outside the village. All the family members pooled their resources — human, animal, and material — under the direction of the head of the family. These joint efforts strengthened family solidarity.

The agricultural year began with spring plowing. The traditional plow, drawn by two oxen wearing yokes and collars, had an iron-tipped share and a handle with which the farmer guided it. Rice, the most important grain, was sown at the beginning of the long rainy season. Beans, lentils, and peas were the farmer's friends, for they grew during the cold season and were harvested in the spring, when fresh food was scarce. Cereal crops such as wheat, barley, and millet provided carbohydrates and other nutrients. Some families cultivated vegetables, spices, fruit trees, and flowers in their gardens. Sugarcane was another important crop.

Farmers also raised livestock. Most highly valued were cattle, which were raised for plowing and milk, hides, and horns, but Hindus did not slaughter them for meat. Like the Islamic and Jewish prohibition on the consumption of pork, the eating of beef was forbidden among Hindus.

Local craftsmen and tradesmen were frequently organized into guilds, with guild heads and guild rules. The textile industries were particularly well developed. Silk (which had entered India from China), linen, wool, and cotton fabrics were produced in large quantities and traded throughout India and beyond. The cutting and polishing of precious stones was another industry associated closely with foreign trade.

# Global Trade

## Spices

**Spices** were a major reason from ancient times on for both Europeans and Chinese to trade with South and Southeast Asia. Pepper, nutmeg, cloves, cinnamon, and other spices were in high demand not only because they could be used to flavor food but also because they were thought to have positive pharmacological properties. Unlike other highly desired products of India and farther east — such as sugar, cotton, rice, and silk — no way was found to produce the spices close to where they were in demand. Because of the location where these spices were produced, this trade was from earliest times largely a maritime trade conducted through a series of middlemen. The spices were transported from where they were grown to nearby ports, and from there to major entrepôts, where merchants would take them in many different directions.

Two types of pepper grew in India and Southeast Asia. Black pepper is identical to our familiar peppercorns. "Long pepper," from a related plant, was hotter. The Mediterranean world imported its pepper from India; China imported it from Southeast Asia. After the discovery of the New World, the importation of long pepper declined, as the chili pepper found in Mexico was at least as spicy and grew well in Europe and China.

By Greek and Roman times trade in pepper was substantial. According to the Greek geographer Strabo (64 B.C.E.–24 C.E.), 120 ships a year made the trip to India to acquire pepper, the round trip taking a year because sailors had to wait for the monsoon winds to shift direction. Pliny in about 77 C.E. complained that the Roman Empire wasted 50 million sesterces per year on long pepper and white and black pepper combined.

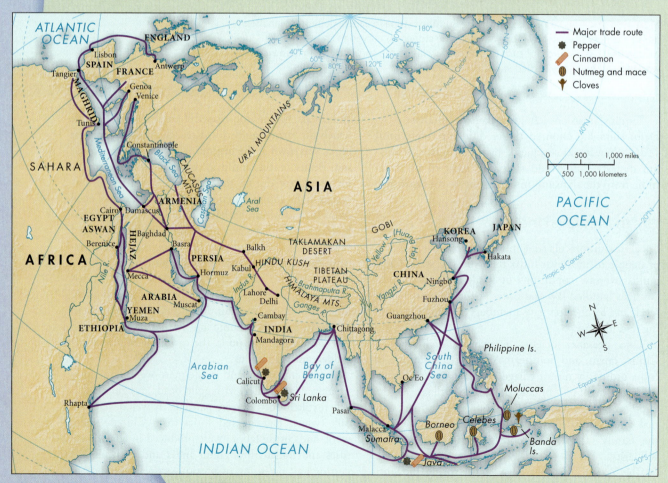

**MAP 12.3** The Spice Trade, ca. 100 B.C.E.–1500 C.E.

Cloves and nutmeg entered the repertoire of spices somewhat later than pepper. They are interesting because they could be grown in only a handful of small islands in the eastern part of the Indonesian archipelago. Merchants in China, India, Arab lands, and Europe got them through intermediaries and did not know where they were grown. An Arab source from about 1000 C.E. reported that cloves came from an island near India that had a Valley of Cloves, and that they were acquired by a silent barter. The sailors would lay the items they were willing to trade out on the beach, and the next morning they would find cloves in their place.

The demand for these spices in time encouraged Chinese, Indian, and Arab seamen to make the trip to the Strait of Malacca or east Java. Malay seamen in small craft such as outrigger canoes would bring the spices the thousand or more miles to the major ports where foreign merchants would purchase them. This trade was important to the prosperity of the Srivijayan kingdom. The trade was so profitable, however, that it also attracted pirates.

In the Mongol era, travelers like Marco Polo, Ibn Battuta, and Odoric of Pordenone (in modern Italy) reported on the cultivation and marketing of spices in the various places they visited. Ibn Battuta described pepper plants as vines planted to grow up coconut palms. He also reported seeing the trunks of cinnamon trees floated down rivers in India. Odoric reported that pepper was picked like grapes from groves so huge it would take eighteen days to walk around them. Marco Polo referred to the 7,459 islands in the China Sea that local mariners could navigate and that produced a great variety of spices as well as aromatic wood. He also reported that spices, including pepper, nutmeg, and cloves, could be acquired at the great island of Java, perhaps not understanding that they had often been shipped from the innumerable small islands to Java.

Gaining direct access to the spices of the East was one of the motivations behind Christopher Columbus's voyages. Not long after, Portuguese sailors did reach India by sailing around Africa, and soon the Dutch were competing with them for control of the spice trade and setting up rival trading posts. Pepper was soon successfully planted in other tropical places, including Brazil. India, however, has remained the largest exporter of spices to this day.

In the cities shops were open to the street; families lived on the floors above. The busiest tradesmen dealt in milk and cheese, oil, spices, and perfumes. Equally prominent but disreputable were tavern keepers. Indian taverns were haunts of criminals and con artists, and in the worst of them fighting was as common as drinking. In addition to these tradesmen and merchants, a host of peddlers shuffled through towns and villages selling everything from needles to freshly cut flowers.

The Chinese Buddhist pilgrim Faxian (FAH-shehn), during his six years in Gupta India, described it as a peaceful land where people could move about freely without needing passports and where the upper castes were vegetarians. He was the first to make explicit reference to "untouchables," remarking that they hovered around the margins of Indian society, carrying gongs to warn upper-caste people of their polluting presence.

During the first millennium C.E., the caste system reached its mature form. Within the broad division into the four varnas (strata) of Brahmin, Kshatriya, Vaishya, and Shudra (see page 69), the population was subdivided into numerous castes, or **jati**. Each caste had a proper occupation. In addition, its members married only within the caste and ate only with other members. Members of high-status castes feared pollution from contact with lower-caste individuals and had to undertake rituals of purification to remove the taint.

Eventually Indian society comprised perhaps as many as three thousand castes. Each caste had its own governing body, which enforced the rules of the caste. Those incapable of living up to the rules were expelled, becoming outcastes. These unfortunates lived hard lives, performing tasks that others considered unclean or lowly.

Villages were often walled, as in north China and the Middle East. The streets were unpaved, and the rainy season turned them into a muddy soup. Cattle and sheep roamed as freely as people. Some families kept pets, such as cats or parrots. Half-wild mongooses served as effective protection against snakes. The pond outside the village was its main source of water and also a spawning ground for fish, birds, and mosquitoes. Women drawing water frequently encountered water buffalo wallowing in the shallows. After the farmers returned from the fields in the evening, the village gates were closed until morning.

The life of the well-to-do is described in the *Kama-sutra* (Book on the Art of Love). Comfortable surroundings provided a place for men to enjoy poetry, painting, and music in the company of like-minded friends. Courtesans well trained in entertaining men added to the pleasures of wealthy men. A man who had more than one wife was advised not to let one wife

---

• **jati**  The thousands of Indian castes.

speak ill of the other and to try to keep all of them happy by taking them to gardens, giving them presents, telling them secrets, and loving them well.

For all members of Indian society regardless of caste, marriage and family were the focus of life. As in China, the family was under the authority of the eldest male, who might take several wives, and ideally sons stayed home with their parents after they married. The family affirmed its solidarity by the religious ritual of honoring its dead ancestors—a ritual that linked the living and the dead, much like ancestor worship in China (see pages 92–94). People commonly lived in extended families: grandparents, uncles and aunts, cousins, and nieces and nephews all lived together in the same house or compound.

Children were viewed as a great source of happiness. The poet Kalidasa described children as the greatest joy of their father's life:

> With their teeth half-shown in causeless laughter,
> and their efforts at talking so sweetly uncertain,
> when children ask to sit on his lap
> a man is blessed, even by the dirt on their bodies.[9]

Children in poor households worked as soon as they were able. Children in wealthier households faced the age-old irritations of learning reading, writing, and arithmetic. Less attention was paid to daughters than to sons, though in more prosperous families they were often literate. Because girls who had lost their virginity could seldom hope to find good husbands and thus would become financial burdens and social disgraces to their families, daughters were customarily married as children, with consummation delayed until they reached puberty.

A wife was expected to have no life apart from her husband. A widow was expected to lead the hard life of the ascetic: sleeping on the ground; eating only one simple meal a day, without meat, wine, salt, or honey; wearing plain, undyed clothes without jewelry; and shaving her head. She was viewed as inauspicious to everyone but her children, and she did not attend family festivals. Among high-caste Hindus, a widow would be praised for throwing herself on her husband's funeral pyre. Buddhist sects objected to this practice, called **sati**, but some Hindu religious authorities declared that by self-immolation a widow could expunge both her own and her husband's sins, so that both would enjoy eternal bliss in Heaven.

Within the home the position of a wife depended on her own intelligence and strength of character. Wives were supposed to be humble, cheerful, and diligent, even toward worthless husbands. As in other patriarchal societies, however, occasionally a woman ruled the household. For women who did not want to accept the strictures of married life, the main way out was to join a Buddhist or Jain religious community (see pages 190–191).

# Southeast Asia, the Pacific Islands, and the Growth of Maritime Trade

☐ How did states develop along the maritime trade routes of Southeast Asia and beyond?

Much as Roman culture spread to northern Europe and Chinese culture spread to Korea, Japan, and Vietnam, in the first millennium C.E. Indian learning, technology, and material culture spread to the mainland and islands of Southeast Asia. The spread of Indian culture was facilitated by the growth of maritime trade, but this interchange did not occur uniformly, and by 1400 there were still isolated societies in this region, most notably in the Pacific Islands east of Indonesia.

Southeast Asia is a tropical region that is more like India than China, with temperatures hovering around 80°F and rain falling dependably throughout the year. The topography of mainland Southeast Asia is marked by north-south mountain ranges separated by river valleys. It was easy for people to migrate south along these rivers but harder for them to cross the heavily forested mountains that divided the region into areas that had limited contact with each other. The indigenous population was originally mostly Malay, but migrations over the centuries brought many other peoples, including speakers of Austro-Asiatic (such as Vietnamese and Cambodian), Austronesian (such as Malay and Polynesian), and Sino-Tibetan-Burmese (such as Burmese and possibly Thai) languages, some of whom moved to the islands offshore and farther into the Pacific Ocean.

## State Formation and Indian Influences

Southeast Asia was long a crossroads. Traders from China, India, Africa, and Europe either passed through the region when traveling from the Indian to the Pacific Ocean, or came for its resources, notably spices. (See "Global Trade: Spices," page 352.)

The northern part of modern Vietnam was under Chinese political control off and on from the second century B.C.E. to the tenth century C.E. (see pages 196–197), but Indian influence was of much greater significance for the rest of Southeast Asia. The first state to appear in historical records, called Funan by Chi-

---

• **sati** A practice whereby a high-caste Hindu woman would throw herself on her husband's funeral pyre.

## □ Picturing the Past

**Bayan Relief, Angkor** Among the many relief sculptures at the temples of Angkor are depictions of royal processions, armies at war, trade, cooking, cockfighting, and other scenes of everyday life. In the relief shown here, the boats and fish convey something of the significance of the sea to life in Southeast Asia. (Hervé Champollion/akg-images)

**ANALYZING THE IMAGE** Find the boat. What do the people on it seem to be doing? What fish and animals do you see in the picture? Can you find the alligator eating a fish?

**CONNECTIONS** Why would a ruler devote so many resources to decorating the walls of a temple? Why include scenes like this one?

nese visitors, had its capital in southern Vietnam. In the first to sixth centuries C.E. Funan extended its control over much of Indochina and the Malay Peninsula. Merchants from northwest India would offload their goods and carry them across the narrowest part of the Malay Peninsula. The ports of Funan offered food and lodging to the merchants as they waited for the winds to shift to continue their voyages. Brahmin priests and Buddhist monks from India settled along with the traders, serving the Indian population and attracting local converts. Rulers often invited Indian priests and monks to serve under them, using them as foreign experts knowledgeable about law, government, architecture, and other fields.

Sixth-century Chinese sources report that the Funan king lived in a multistory palace and the common people lived in houses built on piles with roofs of bamboo leaves. The king rode around on an elephant, but narrow boats measuring up to ninety feet long were a more important means of transportation. The people enjoyed both cockfighting and pig fighting. Instead of drawing water from wells, as the Chinese did, they made pools, from which dozens of nearby families would draw water.

After the decline of Funan, maritime trade continued to grow, and petty kingdoms appeared in many places. Indian traders frequently established small settlements, generally located on the coast. Contact with

**Angkor Wat Temple**  The Khmers built several stone temple complexes at Angkor. This aerial view catches something of the scale of the largest of these complexes, Angkor Wat. *(© Roy Garner/Alamy)*

the local populations led to intermarriage and the creation of hybrid cultures. Local rulers often adopted Indian customs and values, embraced Hinduism and Buddhism, and learned **Sanskrit**, India's classical literary language. Sanskrit gave different peoples a common mode of written expression, much as Chinese did in East Asia and Latin did in Europe.

When Indian traders, migrants, and adventurers entered mainland Southeast Asia, they encountered both long-settled peoples and migrants moving southward from the frontiers of China. As in other extensive migrations, the newcomers fought one another as often as they fought the native populations. In 939 the north Vietnamese became independent of China and extended their power southward along the coast of present-day Vietnam. The Thais had long lived in what is today southwest China and north Myanmar. In the eighth century the Thai tribes united in a confederacy

and expanded northward against Tang China. Like China, however, the Thai confederacy fell to the Mongols in 1253. Still farther west another tribal people, the Burmese, migrated to the area of modern Myanmar in the eighth century. They also established a state, which they ruled from their capital, Pagan, and came into contact with India and Sri Lanka.

The most important mainland state was the Khmer (kuh-MAIR) Empire of Cambodia (802–1432), which controlled the heart of the region. The Khmers were indigenous to the area. Their empire eventually extended south to the sea and the northeast Malay Peninsula. Indian influence was pervasive; the impressive temple complex at Angkor Wat built in the early twelfth century was dedicated to the Hindu god Vishnu. Social organization, however, was modeled not on the Indian caste system but on indigenous traditions of social hierarchy. A large part of the population was of slave status, many descended from non-Khmer mountain tribes defeated by the Khmers. Generally successful in a long series of wars with the Vietnamese, the Khmers reached the peak of their power in 1219 and then gradually declined.

• **Sanskrit**  India's classical literary language.

• **Srivijaya**  A maritime empire that held the Strait of Malacca and the waters around Sumatra, Borneo, and Java.

# The Srivijayan Maritime Trade Empire

Far different from these land-based states was the maritime empire of **Srivijaya**, based on the island of Sumatra in modern Indonesia. From the sixth century on, it held the important Strait of Malacca, through which most of the sea traffic between China and India passed. This state, held together as much by alliances as by direct rule, was in many ways like the Gupta state of the same period in India, securing its prominence and binding its vassals and allies through its splendor and the promise of riches through trade.

Much as the Korean and Japanese rulers adapted Chinese models (see pages 197–198), the Srivijayan rulers drew on Indian traditions to justify their rule and organize their state. The Sanskrit writing system was used for government documents, and Indians were often employed as priests, scribes, and administrators. Using Sanskrit overcame the barriers raised by the many different native languages of the region. Indian mythology took hold, as did Indian architecture and sculpture. Kings and their courts, the first to embrace Indian culture, consciously spread it to their subjects. The Chinese Buddhist monk Yixing (d. 727) stopped at Srivijaya for six months in 671 on his way to India and for four years on his return journey. He found a thousand monks there, some of whom helped him translate Sanskrit texts.

After several centuries of prosperity, Srivijaya suffered a stunning blow in 1025. The Chola state in south India launched a large naval raid and captured the Srivijayan king and capital. Unable to hold their gains, the Indians retreated, but the Srivijayan Empire never regained its vigor.

During the era of the Srivijayan kingdom, other kingdoms flourished as well in island Southeast Asia. Borobudur, the magnificent Buddhist temple complex, was begun under patronage of Javan rulers around 780. This stone monument depicts the ten tiers of Buddhist cosmology. When pilgrims made the three-mile-long winding ascent, they passed numerous sculpted reliefs depicting the journey from ignorance to enlightenment.

Buddhism became progressively more dominant in Southeast Asia after 800. Mahayana Buddhism became important in Srivijaya and Vietnam, but Theravada Buddhism, closer to the original Buddhism of early India, became the dominant form in the rest of mainland Southeast Asia. Buddhist missionaries from India and Sri Lanka played a prominent role in these developments. Local converts continued the process by making pilgrimages to India and Sri Lanka to worship and to observe Indian life for themselves.

# The Spread of Indian Culture in Comparative Perspective

The social, cultural, and political systems developed in India, China, and Rome all had enormous impact on neighboring peoples whose cultures were originally not as technologically advanced. Some of the mechanisms for cultural spread were similar in all three cases, but differences were important as well.

In the case of Rome and both Han and Tang China, strong states directly ruled outlying regions, bringing their civilizations with them. India's states, even its largest empires, such as the Mauryan and Gupta, did not have comparable bureaucratic reach. Outlying areas tended to be in the hands of local lords who had consented to recognize the overlordship of the stronger state. Moreover, most of the time India was politically divided.

The expansion of Indian culture into Southeast Asia thus came not from conquest and the extension of direct political control but from the extension of trading networks, with missionaries following along. This made it closer to the way Japan adopted features of Chinese culture, often through the intermediary of Korea. In both cases, the cultural exchange was largely voluntary, as the Japanese or Southeast Asians sought to adopt more up-to-date technologies (such as writing) or were persuaded of the truth of religious ideas they learned from foreigners.

# The Settlement of the Pacific Islands

Through most of Eurasia, societies became progressively less isolated over time. But in 1400 there still remained many isolated societies, especially in the Islands east of modern Indonesia. As discussed in Chapter 1, *Homo sapiens* began settling the western Pacific Islands very early, reaching Australia by 50,000 years ago and New Guinea by 35,000 years ago. The process did not stop there, however. The ancient Austronesians (speakers of Austronesian languages) were skilled mariners who used double-canoes and brought pottery, the root vegetable taro, pigs, and chickens to numerous islands of the Pacific in subsequent centuries, generally following the coasts. Their descendants, the Polynesians, learned how to sail into the open ocean with only the stars, currents, wind patterns, paths of birds, and perhaps paths of whales and dolphins to help them navigate. They reached Tahiti and the Marquesas Islands in the central Pacific by about 200 C.E. Undoubtedly, seafarers were sometimes blown off their intended course, but communities would not have developed unless the original groups had included women as well as men, so probably in many cases they were looking for new places to live.

After reaching the central Pacific, Polynesians continued to fan out, in some cases traveling a thousand or more miles away. They reached the Hawaiian Islands in about 300 C.E., Easter Island in perhaps 1000, and New Zealand not until about 1000–1300. There even were groups who sailed west, eventually settling in Madagascar between 200 and 500.

In the more remote islands, such as Hawai'i, Easter Island, and New Zealand, the societies that developed were limited by the small range of domesticated plants and animals that the settlers brought with them and those that were indigenous to the place. Easter Island is perhaps the most extreme case. Only 15 miles wide at its widest point (only 63 square miles in total area), it is 1,300 miles from the nearest inhabited island (Pitcairn) and 2,240 miles from the coast of South Amer-

ica. At some point there was communication with South America, as sweet potatoes originally from there made their way to Easter Island. The community that developed on the island raised chickens and cultivated sweet potatoes, taro, and sugarcane. The inhabitants also engaged in deep-sea fishing, catching dolphins and tuna. Their tools were made of stone, wood, or bone. The population is thought to have reached about fifteen thousand at Easter Island's most prosperous period, which began about 1200 C.E. It was then that its people devoted remarkable efforts to fashioning and erecting the large stone statues that still dot the island.

What led the residents of such a small island to erect more than eight hundred statues, most weighing around ten tons and standing twenty to seventy feet tall? When the first Europeans arrived in 1722, no stat-

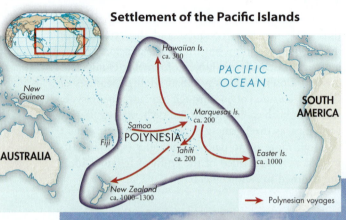

**Settlement of the Pacific Islands**

**Easter Island Statues** Archaeologists have excavated and restored many of Easter Island's huge statues, which display remarkable stylistic consistency, with the heads disproportionately large and the legs not visible. (Jean-Pierre De Mann/Robert Harding World Imagery)

ues had been erected for several generations, and the local residents explained them as representing ancestors. One common theory is that they were central to the islanders' religion and that rival clans competed with each other to erect the most impressive statues. The effort they had to expend to carve them with stone tools, move them to the chosen site, and erect them would have been formidable.

After its heyday, Easter Island suffered severe environmental stress with the decline of its forests. Whether the rats that came with the original settlers ate too many of the trees' seeds or the islanders cut down too many of the trees to transport the stone statues, the impact of deforestation was severe. The islanders could not make boats to fish in the ocean, and bird colonies shrank as nesting areas decreased, also reducing the food supply. Scholars still disagree on how much weight to give the many different elements that contributed to the decline in the prosperity of Easter Island from the age when the statues were erected.

Certainly, early settlers of an island could have a drastic impact on its ecology. When Polynesians first reached New Zealand, they found large birds up to ten feet tall. They hunted them so eagerly that within a century the birds had all but disappeared. Hunting seals and sea lions also led to their rapid depletion. But the islands of New Zealand were much larger than Easter Island, and in time the Maori (the indigenous people of New Zealand) found more sustainable ways to feed themselves, depending more and more on agriculture.

## Chapter Summary

The pastoral societies that stretched across Eurasia had the great military advantage of being able to raise horses in large numbers and support themselves from their flocks of sheep, goats, and other animals. Nomadic pastoralists generally were organized on the basis of clans and tribes that selected chiefs for their military talent. Much of the time these tribes fought with each other, but several times in history leaders formed larger confederations capable of coordinated attacks on cities and towns.

### CHRONOLOGY

| | |
|---|---|
| ca. 320–480 | Gupta Empire in India |
| ca. 380–450 | Life of India's greatest poet, Kalidasa |
| ca. 450 | Huns invade northern India |
| ca. 500 | Srivijaya gains control of Strait of Malacca |
| ca. 500–1400 | India's medieval age; caste system reaches its mature form |
| 552 | Turks rebel against Rouruan and rise to power in Central Asia |
| ca. 780 | Borobudur temple complex begun in Srivijaya |
| 802–1432 | Khmer Empire of Cambodia |
| ca. 850–1250 | Kingdom of the Uighurs |
| 1030 | Turks control north India |
| ca. 1100–1200 | Buddhism declines in India |
| ca. 1200–1300 | Easter Island society's most prosperous period |
| 1206 | Temujin proclaimed Chinggis Khan; Mongol language recorded; Delhi sultanate established |
| ca. 1240 | *The Secret History of the Mongols* |
| 1276 | Mongol conquest of Song China |
| ca. 1300 | Plague begins to spread throughout Mongol Empire |
| 1398 | Timur takes control of the Delhi sultanate |

From the fifth to the twelfth centuries the most successful nomadic groups on the Eurasian steppes were Turks who gained ascendancy in many of the societies from the Middle East to northern India. In the early thirteenth century, through his charismatic leadership and military genius, the Mongol leader Chinggis Khan conquered much of Eurasia. Those who submitted without fighting could become vassals, but those who resisted faced the prospect of mass slaughter or enslavement.

After Chinggis's death, the empire was divided into four khanates ruled by four of Chinggis's descendants. For a century the Mongol Empire fostered unprecedented East-West contact. The Mongols encouraged trade and often moved craftsmen and other specialists from one place to another. They were tolerant of other religions. As more Europeans made their way east, Chinese inventions such as printing and the compass made their way west. Europe especially benefited from the spread of technical and scientific ideas. Diseases also spread, including the Black Death, carried by fleas and rats that found their way into the goods of merchants and other travelers.

India was invaded by the Mongols but not conquered. After the fall of the Gupta Empire in about 480, India was for the next millennium ruled by small kingdoms, which allowed regional cultures to flourish. For several centuries Muslim Turks ruled north India from Delhi. Over time Islam gained adherents throughout South Asia. Hinduism continued to flourish, but Buddhism declined.

Throughout the medieval period India continued to be the center of active seaborne trade, and this trade helped carry Indian ideas and practices to Southeast Asia. Local rulers used experts from India to establish strong states, such as the Khmer kingdom and the Srivijayan kingdom. Buddhism became the dominant religion throughout the region, though Hinduism also played an important role. The Pacific islands east of Indonesia remained isolated culturally for centuries.

## NOTES

1. Trans. in Denis Sinor, "The Establishment and Dissolution of the Türk Empire," in *The Cambridge History of Early Inner Asia*, ed. Denis Sinor (Cambridge: Cambridge University Press, 1990), p. 307.
2. Manuel Komroff, ed., *Contemporaries of Marco Polo* (New York: Dorset Press, 1989), p. 65.
3. Ibid.
4. Cited in John Larner, *Marco Polo and the Discovery of the World* (New Haven, Conn.: Yale University Press, 1999), p. 22.
5. Quoted in A. L. Basham, *The Wonder That Was India*, 2d ed. (New York: Grove Press, 1959), p. 420. Copyright © Picador, A. L. Basham. Reprinted by permission of Pan Macmillan, London.
6. Edward C. Sachau, *Alberuni's India*, vol. 1 (London: Kegan Paul, 1910), pp. 19–20, slightly modified.
7. H. A. R. Gibb, *The Travels of Ibn Battuta* (Cambridge: Cambridge University Press for the Hakluyt Society, 1971), pp. 700–701. Reprinted by permission of David Higham Associates on behalf of the Hakluyt Society.
8. Guy le Strang, trans., *Clavijo, Embassy to Tamerlane, 1403–1406* (London: Routledge, 1928), pp. 265–266.
9. Quoted in Basham, *The Wonder That Was India*, p. 161. Copyright © Picador, A. L. Basham. Reprinted by permission of Pan Macmillan, London.

## CONNECTIONS

The societies of Eurasia became progressively more connected to each other during the centuries discussed in this chapter. One element promoting connection was the military superiority of the nomadic warriors of the steppe: first the Turks, then the Mongols, who conquered many of the settled civilizations near them. Invading Turks brought Islam to India. Connection between societies also came from maritime trade across the Indian Ocean and East Asia. Maritime trade was a key element in the spread of Indian culture to both the mainland and insular Southeast Asia. Other elements connecting these societies included Sanskrit as a language of administration and missionaries who brought both Hinduism and Buddhism far beyond their homelands. Some societies did remain isolated, probably none more than the remote islands of the Pacific, such as Hawai'i, Easter Island, and New Zealand.

East Asia was a key element in both the empires created by nomadic horsemen and the South Asian maritime trading networks. As discussed in Chapter 13, before East Asia had to cope with the rise of the Mongols, it experienced one of its most prosperous periods, during which China, Korea, and Japan became more distinct culturally. China's economy boomed during the Song Dynasty, and the scholar-official class, defined through the civil service examination, came more and more to dominate culture. In Korea and Japan, by contrast, aristocrats and military men gained ascendancy. Although China, Korea, and Japan all drew on both Confucian and Buddhist teachings, they ended up with elites as distinct as the Chinese scholar-official, the Korean aristocrat, and the Japanese samurai.

# Review and Explore

## Make It Stick

 **LearningCurve**
Go online and use LearningCurve to retain what you've read.

## Identify Key Terms

Identify and explain the significance of each item below.

**nomads** (p. 331)          **khanates** (p. 339)          **sati** (p. 354)

**steppe** (p. 331)          **tax-farming** (p. 341)          **Sanskrit** (p. 356)

**yurts** (p. 333)          **protected people** (p. 348)          **Srivijaya** (p. 357)

**Chinggis Khan** (p. 337)          **jati** (p. 353)

## Review the Main Ideas

Answer the focus questions from each section of the chapter.

1. What aspects of nomadic life gave the nomads of Central Asia military advantages over nearby settled civilizations? (p. 331)
2. How did Chinggis Khan and his successors conquer much of Eurasia, and how did the Mongol conquests change the regions affected? (p. 336)
3. How did the Mongol conquests facilitate the spread of ideas, religions, inventions, and diseases? (p. 342)
4. What was the result of India's encounters with Turks, Mongols, and Islam? (p. 345)
5. How did states develop along the maritime trade routes of Southeast Asia and beyond? (p. 354)

## Make Connections

Analyze the larger developments and continuities within and across chapters.

1. How do the states established by Arabs in the seventh and eighth centuries compare to those established by Turks in the tenth and eleventh centuries?
2. What similarities and differences are there in the military feats of Alexander the Great and Chinggis Khan?
3. How does the slow spread of Buddhism and Indian culture to Southeast Asia compare to the slow spread of Christianity and Roman culture in Europe?

## LaunchPad
### Online Document Project

**Intellectual and Religious Life in India**

**What ideas and beliefs were central to Indian culture?**
Read a Persian account of medieval India, and then complete a quiz and writing assignment based on the evidence and details from this chapter.

*See inside the front cover to learn more.*

## Suggested Reading

Abu-Lughod, Janet L. *Before European Hegemony: The World System* A.D. *1250–1350*. 1989. Examines the period of Mongol domination from a global perspective.

Ali, Daud. *Courtly Culture and Political Life in Early Medieval India*. 2004. Explores the growth of royal households and the development of a courtly worldview in India from 350 to 1200.

Chaudhuri, K. N. *Asia Before Europe*. 1990. Discusses the economy and civilization of cultures within the basin of the Indian Ocean.

Findley, Carter Vaughn. *The Turks in World History*. 2005. Covers both the early Turks and the connections between the Turks and the Mongols.

Fischer, Steven Roger. *A History of the Pacific Islands*. 2002. A broad-ranging history, from early settlement to modern times.

Foltz, Richard. *Religions of the Silk Road: Premodern Patterns of Globalization*. 2010. Considers the spread of religions from the perspective of a region that was home to many universal religions in succession.

Franke, Herbert, and Denis Twitchett, eds. *The Cambridge History of China*. Vol. 6: *Alien Regimes and Border States*. 1994. Clear and thoughtful accounts of the Mongols and their predecessors in East Asia.

Golden, Peter B. *Central Asia in World History*. 2011. Concise and up-to-date account.

Jackson, Peter. *The Delhi Sultanate*. 2003. Provides a close examination of north India in the thirteenth and fourteenth centuries.

Jackson, Peter. *The Mongols and the West, 1221–1410*. 2005. A close examination of many different types of connections between the Mongols and both Europe and the Islamic lands.

Lane, George. *Daily Life in the Mongol Empire*. 2006. Treats many topics, including food, health, dwellings, women, and folktales.

Lieberman, Victor. *Strange Parallels: Southeast Asia in Global Context, c. 800–1830*, 2 vols. 2003, 2009. Ambitious and challenging effort to see Southeast Asia as a part of Eurasia.

Ratchnevsky, Paul. *Genghis Khan: His Life and Legacy*. 1992. A reliable account by a leading Mongolist.

Rossabi, Morris. *Khubilai Khan: His Life and Times*. 1988. Provides a lively account of the life of one of the most important Mongol rulers.

Shaffer, Lynda. *Maritime Southeast Asia to 1500*. 1996. A short account of early Southeast Asia from a world history perspective.

**Song Chancellor**
Known for his stern demeanor, Sima Guang (1019–1086) was an eminent historian and a leading official. (The Granger Collection, NYC — All rights reserved.)

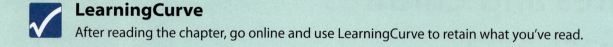

**LearningCurve**

After reading the chapter, go online and use LearningCurve to retain what you've read.

# Chapter Preview

**The Medieval Chinese Economic Revolution, 800–1100**

**China During the Song and Yuan Dynasties, 960–1368**

**Korea Under the Koryŏ Dynasty, 935–1392**

**Japan's Heian Period, 794–1185**

**The Samurai and the Kamakura Shogunate, 1185–1333**

During the six centuries between 800 and 1400, East Asia was the most advanced region of the world. For several centuries the Chinese economy had grown spectacularly, and China's methods of production were highly advanced in fields as diverse as rice cultivation, the production of iron and steel, and the printing of books. Philosophy and the arts all flourished. China's system of government was also advanced for its time. In the Song period, the principle that the government should be in the hands of highly educated scholar-officials, selected through competitive written civil service examinations, became well established. Song China's great wealth and sophisticated government did not give it military advantage, however, and in this period China had to pay tribute to militarily more powerful northern neighbors, the Khitans, the Jurchens, and finally the Mongols, who conquered all of China in 1279.

During the previous millennium, basic elements of Chinese culture had spread beyond China's borders, creating the East Asian cultural sphere based on the use of Chinese as the language of civilization. Beginning around 800, however, the pendulum shifted toward cultural differentiation as Japan, Korea, and China developed in distinctive ways. In both Korea and Japan, for several centuries court aristocrats were dominant both politically and culturally, and then aristocrats lost out to military men with power in the countryside. By 1200 Japan was dominated by warriors—known as samurai—whose ethos was quite unlike that of China's educated elite. In both Korea and Japan, Buddhism retained a very strong hold, one of the ties that continued to link the countries of East Asia. In addition, China and Korea both had to deal with the same menacing neighbors to the north. Even Japan had to mobilize its resources to fend off two seaborne Mongol attacks.

# The Medieval Chinese Economic Revolution, 800–1100

☐ What made possible the expansion of the Chinese economy, and what were the outcomes of this economic growth?

Chinese historians traditionally viewed dynasties as following a standard cyclical pattern. Founders were vigorous men able to recruit capable followers to serve as officials and generals. Externally they would extend China's borders; internally they would bring peace. They would collect low but fairly assessed taxes. Over time, however, emperors born in the palace would get used to luxury and lack the founders' strength and wisdom. Families with wealth or political power would find ways to avoid taxes, forcing the government to impose heavier taxes on the poor. As a result, impoverished peasants would flee, the morale of those in the government and armies would decline, and the dynasty would find itself able neither to maintain internal peace nor to defend its borders.

Viewed in terms of this theory of the **dynastic cycle**, by 800 the Tang Dynasty (see pages 194–196) was in decline. It had ruled China for nearly two centuries, and its high point was in the past. A massive rebellion had wracked it in the mid-eighth century, and the Uighur Turks and Tibetans were menacing its borders. Many of the centralizing features of the government had been abandoned, with power falling more and more to regional military governors.

Historically, Chinese political theorists always assumed that a strong, centralized government was better than a weak one or than political division, but, if anything, the Tang toward the end of its dynastic cycle seems to have been both intellectually and economically more vibrant than the early Tang had been. Less control from the central government seems to have stimulated trade and economic growth.

A government census conducted in 742 shows that China's population was still approximately 50 million, very close to what it had been in 2 C.E. Over the next three centuries, with the expansion of wet-field rice cultivation in central and south China, the country's food supply steadily increased, and so did its population, which reached 100 million by 1100. China was certainly the largest country in the world at the time; its population probably already exceeded that of all the Islamic countries of the time or that of all the countries of Europe put together.

Agricultural prosperity and denser settlement patterns aided commercialization of the economy. Farmers in Song China no longer merely aimed at self-

**Chinese Paper Money** Chinese paper currency indicated the unit of currency and the date and place of issue. The Mongols continued the use of paper money, as this note from the Mongol period attests. (National Museum of Chinese History, Beijing, China/Ancient Art and Architecture Collection Ltd./The Bridgeman Art Library)

sufficiency. They had found that producing for the market made possible a better life. Farmers sold their surpluses and used their profits to buy charcoal, tea, oil, and wine. In many places farmers specialized in commercial crops, such as sugar, oranges, cotton, silk, and tea. (See "Global Trade: Tea," page 366.) The need to transport the products of interregional trade stimulated the inland and coastal shipping industries, providing employment for shipbuilders and sailors and business opportunities for enterprising families with enough capital to purchase a boat. Marco Polo, the Venetian merchant who wrote of his visit to China from about 1275 to 1292, was astounded at the boat traffic on the Yangzi River. He claimed to have seen no fewer than fifteen thousand vessels at one city on the river, but he commented, "And yet there are other towns where the number is still greater."[1]

• **dynastic cycle** The theory that Chinese dynasties go through a predictable cycle from early vigor and growth to subsequent decline as administrators become lax and the well-off find ways to avoid paying taxes, cutting state revenues.

# Global Trade

**Tea** is made from the young leaves and leaf buds of *Camellia sinensis*, a plant native to the hills of southwest China. As an item of trade, tea has a very long history. By Han times (206 B.C.E.–220 C.E.) tea was already being grown and drunk in southwest China, and for several centuries thereafter it was looked on as a local product of the region with useful pharmacological properties, such as countering the effects of wine. By Tang times (608–907) it was being widely cultivated in the Yangzi River Valley and was a major item of interregional trade. Tea was common enough in Tang life that poets often mentioned it in their poems. In the eighth century the Chinese poet Lu Yu wrote an entire treatise on the wonders of tea.

The most intensive time for tea production was the harvest season, since young leaves were of much more value than mature ones. Mobilized for about a month each year, women would come out to help pick the tea. Not only were Chinese tea merchants among the wealthiest merchants, but from the late eighth century on, taxes on tea became a major source of government revenue.

Tea circulated in several forms, loose and compressed (brick), powder and leaf. The cost of tea varied both by form and by region of origin. In Song times (960–1279) the cheapest tea could cost as little as 18 coins per unit of weight, the most expensive 275. In Kaifeng in the 1070s the most popular type was powdered tea. The tea exported from Sichuan to Tibet, however, was formed into solid bricks for ease of transport.

The Song Dynasty established a government monopoly on tea. Only those who purchased government licenses could legally trade in tea. The dynasty also used its control of tea to ensure a supply of horses, needed for military purposes. The government could do this because its neighbors that produced horses — Tibet, Central Asia, Mongolia — were not suitable for growing tea. Thus the Song government insisted on horses for tea.

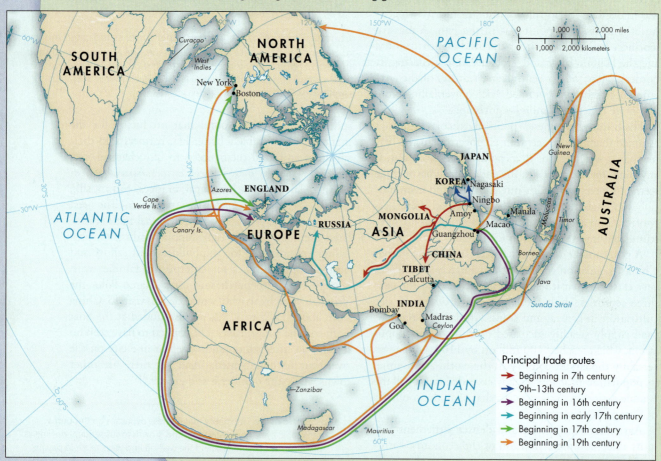

**MAP 13.1** The Tea Trade

Tea reached Korea and Japan as a part of Buddhist culture. Buddhist monks drank it to help them stay awake during long hours of recitation or meditation. The priest Saichō, patriarch of Tendai Buddhism, visited China in 804 and reportedly brought back tea seeds. Tea drinking did not become widespread in Japan, however, until the twelfth century, when Zen monasteries popularized its use. By the fourteenth century tea imported from China was still prized, but the Japanese had already begun to appreciate the distinctive flavors of teas from different regions of Japan. With the development of the tea ceremony, tea drinking became an art in Japan, with much attention to the selection and handling of tea utensils. In both Japan and Korea, offerings of tea became a regular part of offerings to ancestors, as they were in China.

Tea did not become important in Europe until the seventeenth century. Tea first reached Russia in 1618, when a Chinese embassy presented some to the tsar. Under agreements between the Chinese and Russian governments, camel trains would arrive in China laden with furs and would return carrying tea, taking about a year for the round trip. By 1700 Russia was receiving more than 600 camel loads of tea annually. By 1800 it was receiving more than 6,000 loads, amounting to more than 3.5 million pounds. Tea reached western Europe in the sixteenth century, both via Arabs and via Jesuit priests traveling on Portuguese ships.

In Britain, where tea drinking would become a national institution, tea was first drunk in coffeehouses. In his famous diary Samuel Pepys recorded having his first cup of tea in 1660. By the end of the seventeenth century tea made up more than 90 percent of China's exports to England. In the eighteenth century tea drinking spread to homes and tea gardens. Queen Anne (r. 1702–1714) was credited with starting the custom of drinking tea instead of ale for breakfast. Afternoon tea became a central feature of British social life in the 1800s.

By the end of the eighteenth century Britain already imported so much tea from China that it worried about the outflow of silver to pay for it. Efforts to balance trade with China involved promoting the sale of Indian opium to China and efforts to grow tea in British colonies. Using tea seeds collected in China and a tea plant indigenous to India's Assam province, both India and Sri Lanka eventually grew tea successfully. By the end of the nineteenth century huge tea plantations had been established in India, and India surpassed China as an exporter of tea.

The spread of the popularity of drinking tea also stimulated the desire for fine cups to drink it from. Importation of Chinese ceramics, therefore, often accompanied adoption of China's tea customs.

As marketing increased, demand for money grew enormously, leading eventually to the creation of the world's first paper money. The decision by the late Tang government to abandon the use of bolts of silk as supplementary currency had increased the demand for copper coins. By 1085 the output of coins had increased tenfold to more than 6 billion coins a year. To avoid the weight and bulk of coins for large transactions, local merchants in late Tang times started trading receipts from deposit shops where they had left money or goods. The early Song authorities awarded a small set of these shops a monopoly on the issuing of these certificates of deposit, and in the 1120s the government took over the system, producing the world's first government-issued paper money. (See "Viewpoints 12.2: Circulating Paper Money," page 343.)

With the intensification of trade, merchants became progressively more specialized and organized. They set up partnerships and joint stock companies, with a separation of owners (shareholders) and managers. In the large cities merchants were organized into guilds according to the type of product sold, and they arranged sales from wholesalers to shop owners and periodically set prices. When government officials wanted to requisition supplies or assess taxes, they dealt with the guild heads.

Foreign trade also flourished in the Song period. In 1225 the superintendent of customs at the coastal city of Quanzhou wrote an account of the foreign places Chinese merchants visited, with sketches of major trading cities from Srivijaya and Malabar in Southeast Asia to Cairo and Baghdad in the Middle East. Pearls were said to come from the Persian Gulf, ivory from the Red Sea port of Aden, pepper from the Indonesian islands of Java and Sumatra, and cotton from the various kingdoms of India. Chinese ships began to displace Indian and Arab merchants in the South Seas, and ship design was improved in several ways. Watertight bulkheads improved buoyancy and protected cargo. Stern-mounted rudders improved steering. Some of the ships were powered by both oars and sails and were large enough to hold several hundred men.

Also important to oceangoing travel was the perfection of the **compass**. The ability of a magnetic needle to point north had been known for some time, but in Song times the needle was reduced in size and attached to a fixed stem (rather than floated in water). In some instances it was put in a small protective case with a glass top, making it suitable for sea travel. The first reports of a compass used in this way date to 1119.

The Song also witnessed many advances in industrial techniques. Heavy industry, especially iron, grew

---

• **compass** A tool for identifying north using a magnetic needle; it was made useful for sea navigation in Song times when placed in a protective case.

astoundingly. With advances in metallurgy, iron production reached around 125,000 tons per year in 1078, a sixfold increase over the output in 800. At first charcoal was used in the production process, leading to deforestation of parts of north China. By the end of the eleventh century, however, bituminous coke had largely taken the place of charcoal. Much of the iron was put to military purposes. Mass-production methods were used to make iron armor in small, medium, and large sizes. High-quality steel for swords was made through high-temperature metallurgy. Huge bellows, often driven by water wheels, were used to superheat the molten ore. The needs of the army also brought Chinese engineers to experiment with the use of gunpowder. In the twelfth-century wars against the Jurchens (see page 333), those defending a besieged city used gunpowder to propel projectiles at the enemy.

Economic expansion fueled the growth of cities. Dozens of cities had 50,000 or more residents, and quite a few had more than 100,000, very large populations compared to other places in the world at the time. China's two successive capitals, Kaifeng (kigh-fuhng) and Hangzhou (hahng-joh), each had an estimated 1 million residents. Marco Polo described Hangzhou as the finest and most splendid city in the world. He reported that it had ten marketplaces, each half a mile long, where 40,000 to 50,000 people would shop on any given day. There were also bathhouses; permanent shops selling items such as spices, drugs, and pearls; and innumerable courtesans, whom Marco Polo described as "adorned in much finery, highly per-fumed, occupying well-furnished houses, and attended by many female domestics."[2]

The medieval economic revolution shifted the economic center of China south to the Yangzi River drainage area. This area had many advantages over the north China plain. Rice, which grew in the south, provides more calories per unit of land and therefore allows denser settlement. The milder temperatures often allowed two crops to be grown on the same plot of land, first a summer crop of rice and then a winter crop of wheat or vegetables. The abundance of rivers and streams facilitated shipping, which reduced the cost of transportation and thus made regional specialization economically more feasible. In the first half of the Song Dynasty, the capital was still at Kaifeng in the north, close to the Grand Canal (see page 191), which linked the capital to the rich south.

The economic revolution of Song times cannot be attributed to intellectual change, as Confucian scholars did not reinterpret the classics to defend the morality of commerce. But neither did scholar-officials take a unified stand against economic development. As officials they had to work to produce revenue to cover government expenses such as defense, and this was much easier to do when commerce was thriving.

Ordinary people benefited from the Song economic revolution in many ways. There were more opportunities for the sons of farmers to leave agriculture and find work in cities. Those who stayed in agriculture had a better chance of improving their situations by taking up sideline production of wine, charcoal, paper,

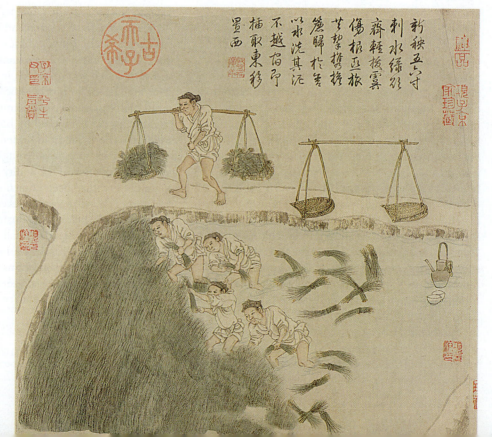

**Transplanting Rice** To get the maximum yield per plot and to make it possible to grow two crops in the same field, Chinese farmers grew rice seedlings in a seedbed and then, when a field was free, transplanted the seedlings into the flooded field. Because the Song government wanted to promote up-to-date agricultural technology, in the twelfth century it commissioned a set of twelve illustrations of the steps to be followed. This painting comes from a later version of those illustrations. (*Tilling Rice*, Yuan Dynasty [ink and colour on paper], Qi, Cheng [13th century] [attr. to]/ Freer Gallery of Art, Smithsonian Institution, Washington, D.C., U.S.A./The Bridgeman Art Library)

or textiles. Energetic farmers who grew cash crops such as sugar, tea, mulberry leaves (for silk), and cotton (recently introduced from India) could grow rich. Greater interregional trade led to the availability of more goods at the rural markets held every five or ten days.

Of course, not everyone grew rich. Poor farmers who fell into debt had to sell their land, and if they still owed money they could be forced to sell their daughters as maids, concubines, or prostitutes. The prosperity of the cities created a huge demand for women to serve the rich in these ways, and Song sources mention that criminals would kidnap girls and women to sell in distant cities at huge profits.

# China During the Song and Yuan Dynasties, 960–1368

☐ How did the civil service examinations and the scholar-official class shape Chinese society and culture, and what impact did the Mongol conquest have on them?

In the tenth century Tang China broke up into separate contending states, some of which had non-Chinese rulers. The two states that proved to be long lasting were the Song, which came to control almost all of China proper south of the Great Wall, and the Liao, whose ruling house was Khitan and which held the territory of modern Beijing and areas north (Map 13.2). Although the Song Dynasty had a much larger population, the Liao was militarily the stronger of the two. In the early twelfth century the Liao state was defeated by the Jurchens, another non-Chinese people, who founded the Jin Dynasty and went on to conquer most of north China, leaving Song to control only the south. After a century the Jurchens' Jin Dynasty was defeated by the Mongols, who extended their Yuan Dynasty to control all of China by 1276.

## The Song Dynasty

The founder of the Song Dynasty, Taizu (r. 960–976), was a general whose troops elevated him to emperor (somewhat reminiscent of Roman practice). Taizu worked to make sure that such an act could not happen in the future by placing the armies under central government control. To curb the power of his generals, he retired or rotated them and assigned civil officials to supervise them. In time these civil bureaucrats came to dominate every aspect of Song government and society. The civil service examination system established during the Sui Dynasty (see page 191) was greatly expanded to provide the dynasty with a constant flow of men trained in the Confucian classics.

Curbing the generals' power ended warlordism but did not solve the military problem of defending against the nomadic Khitans' Liao Dynasty to the north. After several attempts to push the Liao back beyond the Great Wall, the Song concluded a peace treaty with them. The Song agreed to make huge annual payments of gold and silk to the Khitans, in a sense paying them not to invade. Even so, the Song rulers had to maintain a standing army of more than a million men. By the middle of the eleventh century military expenses consumed half the government's revenues. Song had the industrial base to produce swords, armor, and arrowheads in huge quantities, but had difficulty maintaining enough horses and well-trained horsemen. Even though China was the economic powerhouse of the region, with by far the largest population, the horse was a major weapon of war in this period, and it was not easy to convert wealth to military advantage.

In the early twelfth century the military situation rapidly worsened when the Khitan state was destroyed by another tribal confederation led by the Jurchens. Although the Song allied with the Jurchens, the Jurchens quickly realized how easy it would be to defeat the Song. When they marched into the Song capital in 1126, they captured the emperor and former emperor and took them and the entire court into captivity. Song forces rallied around one of the emperor's sons who had escaped capture, and this prince re-established a Song court in the south at Hangzhou (see Map 13.2). This Southern Song Dynasty controlled only about two-thirds of the former Song territories, but the social, cultural, and intellectual life there remained vibrant until the Song fell to the Mongols in 1279.

## The Scholar-Officials and Neo-Confucianism

The Song period saw the full flowering of one of the most distinctive features of Chinese civilization, the **scholar-official class** certified through highly competitive civil service examinations. This elite was both broader and better educated than the elites of earlier periods in Chinese history. Once the **examination system** was fully developed, aristocratic habits and prejudices largely disappeared. Ancestry did not matter as

- **scholar-official class** Chinese educated elite that included both scholars and officials. The officials had usually gained office by passing the highly competitive civil service examination. Scholars without office had often studied for the examinations but failed repeatedly.

- **examination system** A system of selecting officials based on competitive written examinations.

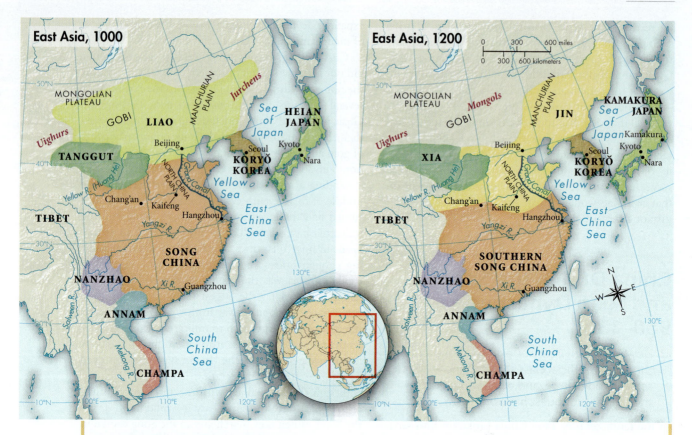

## ☐ Mapping the Past

**MAP 13.2  East Asia in 1000 and 1200** The Song empire did not extend as far as its predecessor, the Tang, and faced powerful rivals to the north — the Liao Dynasty of the Khitans and the Xia Dynasty of the Tanguts. Koryŏ Korea maintained regular contact with Song China, but Japan, by the late Heian period, was no longer deeply involved with the mainland. By 1200 military families dominated both Korea and Japan, but the borders were little changed. On the mainland the Liao Dynasty had been overthrown by the Jurchens' Jin Dynasty, which also seized the northern third of the Song empire. Because the Song relocated its capital to Hangzhou in the south, this period is called the Southern Song period.

**ANALYZING THE MAP**  What were the countries of East Asia in 1000? What were the major differences in 1200?

**CONNECTIONS**  What connections do you see between the length of their northern borders and the histories of China, Korea, and Japan?

much when office depended more on study habits than on connections.

The examination system came to carry such prestige that the number of scholars entering each competition escalated rapidly, from fewer than 30,000 early in the eleventh century, to nearly 80,000 by the end of that century, to about 400,000 by the dynasty's end. To prepare for the examinations, men had to memorize the classics in order to be able to recognize even the most obscure passages. They also had to master specific forms of composition, including poetry, and be ready to discuss policy issues, citing appropriate historical examples. Those who became officials this way had usually tried the exams several times and were on

average a little over thirty years of age when they succeeded. Because the competition was so fierce, the great majority of those who devoted years to preparing for the exams never became officials.

The invention of printing should be given some credit for the trend toward a better-educated elite. Tang craftsmen developed the art of carving words and pictures into wooden blocks, inking the blocks, and pressing paper onto them. Each block held an entire page of text. Such whole-page blocks were used for printing as early as the middle of the ninth century, and in the eleventh century **movable type** (one piece of type for each character) was invented, but it was rarely used because whole-block printing was cheaper. In China,

觸袖野花多自舞
避人幽鳥不成啼

## □ Picturing the Past

**On a Mountain Path in Spring** With spare, sketchy strokes, the court painter Ma Yuan (ca. 1190–1225) depicts a scholar on an outing accompanied by his boy servant carrying a lute. The scholar gazes into the mist, his eyes attracted by a bird in flight. The poetic couplet was inscribed by Emperor Ningzong (r. 1194–1124), at whose court Ma Yuan served. It reads: "Brushed by his sleeves, wild flowers dance in the wind. / Fleeing from him, hidden birds cut short their songs." (National Palace Museum, Taipei, Taiwan/photo © AISA/The Everett Collection)

**ANALYZING THE IMAGE** Find the key elements in this picture: the scholar, the servant boy, the bird, the willow tree. Are these elements skillfully conveyed? Are there other elements in the painting that you find hard to read?

**CONNECTIONS** What do you think is the reason for writing a poetic couplet on this painting? Does it enhance the experience of viewing the painting or detract from it?

as in Europe a couple of centuries later, the introduction of printing dramatically lowered the price of books, thus aiding the spread of literacy.

Among the upper class the availability of cheaper books enabled scholars to amass their own libraries. Song publishers printed the classics of Chinese literature in huge editions to satisfy scholarly appetites. Works on philosophy, science, and medicine were also avidly consumed, as were Buddhist texts. Han and Tang poetry and historical works became the models for Song writers. One popular literary innovation was the encyclopedia, which first appeared in the Song period, at least five centuries before the publication of the first European encyclopedia.

The life of the educated man involved more than study for the civil service examinations and service in office. Many took to refined pursuits such as collecting antiques or old books and practicing the arts—especially poetry writing, calligraphy, and painting. (See "Viewpoints 13.1: Painters of Uncanny Skill in China and Rome," page 372.) For many individuals these cultural interests overshadowed any philosophical, political, or economic concerns; others found in them occasional outlets for creative activity and aesthetic pleasure. In the Song period, the engagement of

**movable type** A system of printing in which one piece of type is used for each unique character.

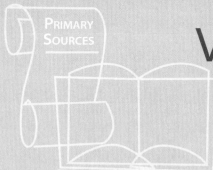

# Viewpoints 13.1

## Painters of Uncanny Skill in China and Rome

> • *Chinese art critics often expressed astonishment at the ability of exceptional painters to evoke an emotional reaction in viewers. A good example is the account of the eighth-century painter Wu Daozi, written by a ninth-century critic, Zhu Jingxuan, in his* Famous Painters of the Tang Dynasty. *It can be compared to remarks on painters by the Roman man of letters Pliny the Elder (23–79 C.E.).*

### Zhu Jingxuan on the Painter Wu Daozi

❝ A poor orphan, Wu Daozi was so talented by nature that even before he was twenty he had mastered all the subtleties of painting. When he was in Luoyang, the emperor heard of his fame and summoned him to court. . . .

The General Pei Min sent a gift of gold and silk to Wu Daozi and asked him to paint the walls of the Paradise Buddhist monastery. Wu Daozi returned the gold and silk with a note saying, "I have long heard of General Pei. If he would do a sword dance for me, that would be reward enough, and the sight of such vigor will inspire my brush." So the general, even though in mourning, did the sword dance for Wu Daozi, and when the dance was finished Wu made his brush fly with such strength that the painting was done in no time, as though some god was helping him. Wu Daozi also did the laying on of the colors himself. One can still see the painting in the western corridor of the temple. . . .

During the Tianbao period (742–755), the emperor Xuanzong suddenly longed for the Jialing River on the road to Sichuan. So he allowed Wu Daozi the use of post horses and ordered him to go there and make sketches of the scenery. On his return, in response to the emperor's query, Wu said, "I have not brought back a single sketch, but everything is recorded in my mind." He was commanded to depict it on the walls of Great Accord Hall. He painted a landscape of more than 300 *li*, finishing it all in a single day. . . . He also painted five dragons in the Inner Hall whose scales seemed to move. Whenever it was about to rain, mist would emanate from them. . . .

Early in the Yuanhe period (806–820), while I was taking the civil service examinations and living in Dragon Rising Buddhist Temple, an elderly official, more than eighty years old, told me that when Master Wu was about to paint the halo of a god on the central gate of Xingshan Buddhist monastery, residents of the city, old and young, gathered around to watch, standing as deep as a hedge. He raised his brush then swirled it around with the force of a whirlwind, apparently with divine help. I also heard from an old monk of Scenic Clouds Monastery that when Master Wu painted a Hell scene at the temple, butchers and fishmongers who saw it became so frightened by it that they decided to change their profession and turn to doing good works. ❞

### Pliny on the Painters Arellius and Lepidus

❝ Not long before the time of the god Augustus, Arellius had earned distinction at Rome, save for the sacrilege by which he notoriously degraded his art. Always desirous of flattering some woman or other with whom he chanced to be in love, he painted goddesses in the person of his mistresses, of whom his paintings are a mere catalogue. The painter Famulus also lived not long ago; he was grave and severe in his person, while his painting was rich and vivid. He painted an Athena whose eyes are turned to the spectator from whatever side he may be looking. . . .

While on the subject of painting I must not omit the well-known story of Lepidus. Once during his triumvirate he had been escorted by the magistrates of a certain town to a lodging in the middle of a wood, and on the next morning complained with threats that the singing of the birds prevented him from sleeping. They painted a snake on an immense strip of parchment and stretched it all round the grove. We are told that by this means they terrified the birds into silence and that this has ever since been a recognized device for quieting them. ❞

Sources: Zhu Jingxuan, *Tangchao minghua lu*, in *Tang Wudai hualun* (Changsha: Hunan Meishu Chubanshe, 1997), pp. 83–85, trans. Patricia Ebrey; *The Elder Pliny's Chapters on the History of Art*, trans. K. Jex-Blake (London: Macmillan, 1896), pp. 149–150.

### QUESTIONS FOR ANALYSIS

1. What assumptions, if any, did the Chinese and Roman authors share about artistic creativity?

2. In what ways did painters gain fame in these two societies?

the elite with the arts led to extraordinary achievement in calligraphy and painting, especially landscape painting. A large share of the social life of upper-class men was centered on these refined pastimes, as they gathered to compose or criticize poetry, to view each other's art treasures, and to patronize young talents.

The new scholar-official elite produced some extraordinary men able to hold high court offices while pursuing diverse intellectual interests. (See "Individuals in Society: Shen Gua," page 375.) Ouyang Xiu spared time in his busy official career to write love songs, histories, and the first analytical catalogue of rubbings of ancient stone and bronze inscriptions. Sima Guang, besides serving as chancellor, wrote a narrative history of China from the Warring States Period (403–221 B.C.E.) to the founding of the Song Dynasty. Su Shi wrote more than twenty-seven hundred poems and eight hundred letters while active in opposition politics. He was also an esteemed painter, calligrapher, and theorist of the arts. Su Song, another high official, constructed an eighty-foot-tall mechanical clock. He adapted the water-powered clock invented in the Tang period by adding a chain-driven mechanism. The clock told not only the time of day but also the day of the month, the phase of the moon, and the position of certain stars and planets in the sky. As in Renaissance Europe a couple of centuries later (discussed in Chapter 15), gifted men made advances in a wide range of fields.

These highly educated men accepted the Confucian responsibility to aid the ruler in the governing of the country. Factional disputes often made government service stressful, especially during the period when the emperor supported the New Policies of the reformer Wang Anshi, which many leading men opposed.

Besides politics, scholars also debated issues in ethics and metaphysics. For several centuries Buddhism had been more vital than Confucianism. Beginning in the late Tang period, Confucian teachers began claiming that the teachings of the Confucian sages contained all the wisdom one needed and that a true Confucian would reject Buddhist teachings. During the eleventh century many Confucian teachers urged students to set their sights not on exam success but on the higher goals of attaining the wisdom of the sages. Metaphysical theories about the workings of the cosmos in terms of *li* (principle) and *qi* (vital energy) were developed in response to the challenge of the sophisticated metaphysics of Buddhism.

**Neo-Confucianism**, as this movement is generally termed, was more fully developed in the twelfth century by the immensely learned Zhu Xi (joo shee) (1130–1200). Besides serving in office, he wrote, compiled, or edited almost a hundred books; corresponded with dozens of other scholars; and still regularly taught groups of disciples, many of whom stayed with him for years at a time. Although he was treated as a political threat during his lifetime, within decades of his death his writings came to be considered orthodox, and in subsequent centuries candidates for the examinations had to be familiar with his commentaries on the classics.

## Women's Lives in Song Times

Thanks to the spread of printing, more books survive from the Song period than from earlier periods, giving us more glimpses of women's lives. Stories, documents, and legal cases show us widows who ran inns, maids who were sent out by their mistresses to do errands, midwives who delivered babies, pious women who spent their days chanting Buddhist sutras, nuns who called on such women to explain Buddhist doctrine, girls who learned to read with their brothers, farmers' daughters who made money by weaving mats, childless widows who accused their nephews of stealing their property, wives who were jealous of the concubines their husbands brought home, and women who used part of their own large dowries to help their husbands' sisters marry well.

Families who could afford it usually tried to keep their wives and daughters within the walls of the house, rather than let them work in the fields or in shops or inns. At home there was plenty for them to do. Not only was there the work of tending children and preparing meals, but spinning, weaving, and sewing were considered women's work as well and took a great deal of time. Families that raised silkworms also needed women to do much of the work of coddling the worms and getting them to spin their cocoons. Within the home women generally had considerable say and took an active interest in issues such as the selection of marriage partners for their children.

Women tended to marry between the ages of sixteen and twenty. Their husbands were, on average, a couple of years older than they were. Marriages were arranged by their parents, who would have either called on a professional matchmaker (most often an older woman) or turned to a friend or relative for suggestions. Before a wedding took place, written agreements were exchanged, listing the prospective bride's and groom's birth dates, parents, and grandparents; the gifts that would be exchanged; and the dowry the bride would bring. The goal was to match families of approximately equal status, but a young man who had just passed the civil service exams would be considered a good prospect even if his family had little wealth.

A few days before the wedding, the bride's family sent her dowry to the groom's family, which at a mini-

---

• **Neo-Confucianism** The revival of Confucian thinking that began in the eleventh century, characterized by the goal of attaining the wisdom of the sages, not exam success.

mum contained boxes full of clothes and bedding. In better-off families, the dowry also included items of substantial value, such as gold jewelry or deeds to land. On the day of the wedding, the groom and some of his friends and relatives went to the bride's home to get her. She would be elaborately dressed and would tearfully bid farewell to everyone in her family. She was carried to her new home in a fancy sedan chair to the sound of music, alerting everyone on the street that a wedding was taking place. Meanwhile, the groom's family's friends and relatives had gathered at his home, ready to greet the bridal party. The bride would kneel and bow to her new parents-in-law and later also to the tablets with the names of her husband's ancestors. A classical ritual still practiced was for the new couple to drink wine from the same cup. A ritual that had become popular in Song times was to attach a string to the bride and groom, literally tying them together. Later they were shown to their new bedroom, where the bride's dowry had already been placed, and people tossed beans or rice on the bed, symbolizing the desired fertility. After teasing them, the guests left them alone and went out to the courtyard for a wedding feast.

The young bride's first priority was to try to win over her mother-in-law, since everyone knew that mothers-in-law were hard to please. One way to do this was to quickly bear a son for the family. Within the patrilineal system, a woman fully secured her position in the family by becoming the mother of one of the men. Every community had older women skilled in midwifery who were called to help when a woman went into labor. If the family was well-to-do, arrangements might be made for a wet nurse to help her take care of the newborn.

Women frequently had four, five, or six children, but likely one or more would die in infancy. If a son reached adulthood and married before the woman herself was widowed, she would be considered fortunate, for she would have always had an adult man who could take care of business for her—first her husband, then her grown son. But in the days when infectious diseases took many people in their twenties and thirties, it was not uncommon for a woman to be widowed while in her twenties, when her children were still very young.

A woman with a healthy and prosperous husband faced another challenge in middle age: her husband could bring home a **concubine** (and more than one if he could afford them). Moralists insisted that it was wrong for a wife to be jealous of her husband's concubines, but contemporary documents suggest that jealousy was very common. Wives outranked concubines and could give them orders in the house, but a concubine had her own ways of getting back through her hold on the husband. The children born to a concubine were considered just as much children of the family as the wife's children, and if the wife had had only daughters and the concubine had a son, the wife would find herself dependent on the concubine's son in her old age.

As a woman's children grew up, she would start thinking of suitable marriage partners. Many women liked the idea of bringing other women from their families of birth—perhaps a brother's daughter—to be their daughters-in-law. No matter who was selected, a woman's life became easier once she had a daughter-in-law to do the cooking and cleaning. Many found more time for religious devotions at this stage of their lives. Their sons, still living with them, could be expected to look after them and do their best to make their late years comfortable.

Neo-Confucianism is sometimes blamed for a decline in the status of women in Song times, largely because one of the best known of the Neo-Confucian teachers, Cheng Yi, once told a follower that it would be better for a widow to die of starvation

**Woman Attendant**

The Song emperors were patrons of a still-extant temple in northern China that enshrined a statue of the "holy mother," the mother of the founder of the ancient Zhou Dynasty. The forty-two maids who attend her, one of whom is shown here, seem to have been modeled on the palace ladies who attended Song emperors. (Taiyuan Jinci/Goddess Hall/Uniphoto Press International Japan/Art and Architecture Collection Ltd.)

• **concubine**  A woman contracted to a man as a secondary spouse; although subordinate to the wife, her sons were considered legitimate heirs.

# Individuals in Society

## Shen Gua

**IN THE ELEVENTH CENTURY IT WAS NOT RARE FOR CHINESE** men of letters to have broad interests, but few could compare to Shen Gua (1031–1095), a man who tried his hand at everything from mathematics, geography, economics, engineering, medicine, divination, and archaeology to military strategy and diplomacy.

Shen Gua's father was an official, and Shen Gua often accompanied him on his assignments, which built up his knowledge of geography. In 1063 he passed the civil service examinations, and in 1066 he received a post in the capital. He eventually held high astronomical, ritual, and financial posts and became involved in waterworks and the construction of defense walls. He was sent as an envoy to the Khitans in 1075 to try to settle a boundary dispute. When a military campaign that he advised failed in 1082, he was demoted and later retired to write.

It is from his book of miscellaneous notes that we know the breadth of his interests. In one note Shen describes how, on assignment to inspect the frontier, he made a relief map of wood and glue-soaked sawdust to show the mountains, roads, rivers, and passes. The emperor was so impressed when he saw it that he ordered all the border prefectures to make relief maps. Elsewhere Shen describes the use of petroleum and explains how to make movable type from clay. Shen Gua often applied a mathematical approach to issues that his contemporaries did not think of in those terms. He once computed the total number of possible situations on a Go board, and another time he calculated the longest possible military campaign given the limits of human carriers, who had to carry their own food as well as food for the soldiers.

Shen Gua is especially known for his scientific explanations. He explained the deflection of the compass from due south. He identified petrified bamboo and from its existence argued that the region where it was found must have been much warmer and more humid in ancient times. He argued against the theory that tides are caused by the rising and setting of the sun, demonstrating that they correlate with the cycles of the moon. He proposed switching from a lunar calendar to a solar one of 365 days, saying that even though his contemporaries would reject his idea, "surely in the future some will adopt my idea." To convince his readers that the sun and the moon were spherical, not flat, he suggested that they cover a ball with fine powder on one side and then look at it obliquely. The powder was the part of the moon illuminated by the sun, and as the viewer looked at it obliquely, the white part would be crescent shaped, like a waxing moon. Shen Gua, however, did not realize that the sun and moon had entirely different orbits, and he explained why they did not collide by positing that both were composed of *qi* (vital energy) and had form but not substance.

Shen Gua also wrote on medicine and criticized his contemporaries for paying more attention to old treatises than to clinical experience. Yet he, too, was sometimes stronger on theory than on observation. In one note he argued that longev-

**Shen Gua played Go with white and black markers on a grid-like board like this one.** (Courtesy of Library of Congress, LC-USZC4-8471/8472)

ity pills could be made from cinnabar. He reasoned that if cinnabar could be transformed in one direction, it ought to be susceptible to transformation in the opposite direction as well. Therefore, since melted cinnabar causes death, solid cinnabar should prevent death.

### QUESTIONS FOR ANALYSIS

1. How did Shen Gua's travels add to his curiosity about the material world?

2. In what ways could Shen Gua have used his scientific interests in his work as a government official?

3. How does Shen Gua's understanding of the natural world compare to that of the early Greeks? (See pages 128–131.)

### LaunchPad
## Online Document Project

**What cultural pursuits interested the scholar-official class?** View images from the Song period, and then complete a quiz and writing assignment based on the evidence and details from this chapter.

*See inside the front cover to learn more.*

# Viewpoints 13.2

## Zhu Xi and Yuan Cai on Family Management

• *The Confucian tradition put considerable emphasis on the ethics and rituals that should govern family life. Filial piety was considered a central virtue in Confucius's* Analects, *and an early Confucian text, the* Greater Learning, *argued that a man who wanted to serve the ruler or bring peace to the realm had to first manage his own family. These Confucian precepts were honored not only in China but also in Korea and Japan.*

*What could one do to bring harmony to his family? Zhu Xi, one of the leading Neo-Confucian philosophers of his day, placed emphasis on ritual. His discussion of the importance of setting up an ancestral shrine is the first item in his influential book* Family Rituals. *Other parts of this book detail the steps to be taken in funerals, weddings, coming-of-age ceremonies, and ancestral rites. His contemporary Yuan Cai (ca. 1140–ca. 1190) was a local government official whose views about how to attain family harmony seem to have come from his personal experience rather than the study of Confucian texts. Yuan Cai's* Precepts for Social Life *also gives advice on arranging marriages, managing servants, and avoiding bankruptcy. These two books, while written in Chinese, circulated in Korea and Japan as well as China, with Zhu Xi's* Family Rituals *becoming especially important in Korea.*

### Zhu Xi on the Offering Hall

" When a man of virtue builds a house his first task is always to set up an offering hall to the east of the main room of his house. For this hall four altars to hold the spirit tablets of the ancestors are made; collateral relatives who died without descendants may have associated offerings made to them there according to their generational seniority. Sacrificial fields should be established and sacrificial utensils prepared. Once the hall is completed, early each morning the master enters the outer gate to pay a visit. All comings and goings are reported there. On New Year's Day, the solstices, and each new and full moon, visits are made. On the customary festivals, seasonal foods are offered, and when an event occurs, reports are made. Should there be flood, fire, robbers, or bandits, the offering hall is the first thing to be saved. The spirit tablets, inherited manuscripts, and then the sacrificial utensils should be moved; only afterward may the family's valuables be taken. As one generation succeeds another, the spirit tablets are reinscribed and moved to their new places. "

### Yuan Cai on Forbearance

" People say that lasting harmony in families begins with the ability to forbear. But knowing how to forbear without knowing how to live with forbearing can lead to a great many errors. Some seem to think that forbearance means to repress anger; that is, when someone offends you, you repress your feelings and do not reveal them. If this happens only once or twice it would be all right. But if it happens repeatedly the anger will come bursting forth like an irrepressible flood.

A better method is to dissipate anger as the occasion arises instead of hiding it in your chest. Do this by saying to yourself, "He wasn't thinking," "He doesn't know any better," "He made a mistake," "He is narrow in his outlook," "How much harm can this really do?" If you keep the anger from entering your heart, then even if someone offends you ten times a day, neither your speech nor your behavior will be affected. You will then see the magnitude of the benefits of forbearance. "

### Yuan Cai on Dislike Among Relatives

" Dislike among blood relatives may start from a very minor incident but end up ingrained. It is just that once two people take a dislike to each other they become irascible, and neither is willing to be the first to cool off. When they are in each other's company day in and day out, they cannot help but irritate each other. If, having reached this state, one of them would be willing to take the initiative in cooling off and would talk to the other, then the other would reciprocate, and the situation would return to normal. This point is worth deep consideration. "

Sources: Patricia Buckley Ebrey, trans., *Chu Hsi's* Family Rituals: *A Twelfth-Century Chinese Manual for the Performance of Cappings, Weddings, Funerals, and Ancestral Rites* (Princeton, N.J.: Princeton University Press, 1991), p. 5. © 1991 Princeton University Press. Reprinted by permission of Princeton University Press; Patricia Buckley Ebrey, trans., *Family and Property in Sung China: Yuan Ts'ai's* Precepts for Social Life (Princeton, N.J.: Princeton University Press, 1984), pp. 186–187. © 1984 Princeton University Press. Reprinted by permission of Princeton University Press.

### QUESTIONS FOR ANALYSIS

1. Would attention to the details of ancestral rites of the sort Zhu Xi outlines help avoid the sorts of problems among relatives that Yuan Cai discusses, or could it make them worse?

2. The ideal Chinese family was one that did not divide during the parents' lifetimes, so that adult brothers and their families all lived together with their elderly parents. What can you infer about problems connected to such large, complex families from these two authors?

than to lose her virtue by remarrying. In later centuries this saying was often quoted to justify pressuring widows, even very young ones, to stay with their husbands' families and not remarry. In Song times, however, widows frequently remarried. (See "Viewpoints 13.2: Zhu Xi and Yuan Cai on Family Management," at left.)

It is true that **foot binding** began during the Song Dynasty, but it was not recommended by Neo-Confucian teachers; rather it was associated with the pleasure quarters and with women's efforts to beautify themselves. Mothers bound the feet of girls aged five to eight with long strips of cloth to keep them from growing and to bend the four smaller toes under to make the foot narrow and arched. The hope was that the girl would be judged more beautiful. Foot binding spread gradually during Song times but was probably still largely an elite practice. In later centuries it became extremely common in north and central China, eventually spreading to all classes. Women with bound feet were less mobile than women with natural feet, but only those who could afford servants bound their feet so tightly that walking was difficult.

## China Under Mongol Rule

As discussed in Chapter 12, the Mongols conquered China in stages, gaining much of north China by 1215 and all of it by 1234, but not taking the south till the 1270s. The north suffered the most devastation. The non-Chinese rulers in the north, the Jin Dynasty of the Jurchen—with 150,000 cavalry, mostly Jurchen, and more than 300,000 Chinese infantrymen—thought they had the strongest army known to history. Yet Mongol tactics frustrated them. The Mongols would take a city, plunder it, and then withdraw, letting the Jin take it back and deal with the resulting food shortages and destruction. Under these circumstances, Jurchen power rapidly collapsed.

Not until Khubilai was Great Khan was the Song Dynasty defeated and south China brought under the control of the Mongols' Yuan Dynasty. Non-Chinese rulers had gained control of north China several times in Chinese history, but none of them had been able to secure control of the region south of the Yangzi River, which required a navy. By the 1260s Khubilai had put Chinese shipbuilders to work building a fleet, crucial to his victory over the Song (see page 339).

Life in China under the Mongols was much like life in China under earlier alien rulers. Once order was restored, people did their best to get on with their lives. Some were deprived of their land, business, or freedom and suffered real hardship. Yet people still spoke Chinese, followed Chinese customary practices in dividing their family property, made offerings at local temples, and celebrated the new year and other customary festi-

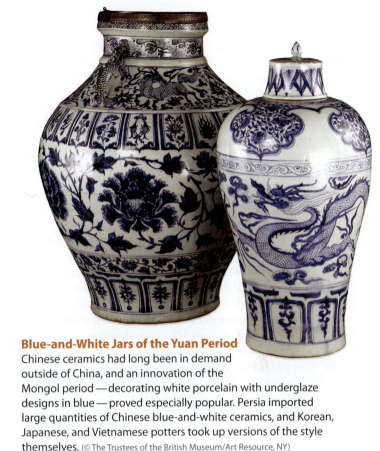

**Blue-and-White Jars of the Yuan Period**
Chinese ceramics had long been in demand outside of China, and an innovation of the Mongol period — decorating white porcelain with underglaze designs in blue — proved especially popular. Persia imported large quantities of Chinese blue-and-white ceramics, and Korean, Japanese, and Vietnamese potters took up versions of the style themselves. (© The Trustees of the British Museum/Art Resource, NY)

vals. Teachers still taught students the classics, scholars continued to write books, and books continued to be printed.

The Mongols, like other foreign rulers before them, did not see anything particularly desirable in the social mobility of Chinese society. Preferring stability, they assigned people hereditary occupations such as farmer, Confucian scholar, physician, astrologer, soldier, artisan, salt producer, miner, and Buddhist monk; the occupations came with obligations to the state. Besides these occupational categories, the Mongols classified the population into four grades, with the Mongols occupying the top grade. Next came various non-Chinese, such as the Uighurs and Persians. Below them were Chinese former subjects of the Jurchen, called the Han. At the bottom were the former subjects of the Song, called southerners.

The reason for codifying ethnic differences this way was to preserve the Mongols' privileges as conquerors. Chinese were not allowed to take Mongol names, and great efforts were made to keep them from passing as

**foot binding** The practice of binding the feet of girls with long strips of cloth to keep them from growing large.

Mongols or marrying Mongols. To keep Chinese from rebelling, they were forbidden to own weapons or congregate in public. Khubilai even prohibited Chinese from dealing in bamboo because it could be used to make bows and arrows.

As the Mongols captured Chinese territory, they recruited Chinese into their armies and government. Although some refused to serve the Mongols, others argued that the Chinese would fare better if Chinese were the administrators and could shield Chinese society from the most brutal effects of Mongol rule. A few Confucian scholars devoted themselves to the task of patiently teaching Mongol rulers the principles of Confucian government.

Nevertheless, government service, which had long been central to the identity and income of the educated elite in China, was not as widely available under the Mongols. The Mongols reinstituted the civil service examinations in 1315, but filled only about 2 percent of the positions in the bureaucracy through them and reserved half of those places for Mongols.

The scholar-official elite without government employment turned to alternative ways to support themselves. Those who did not have land to live off of found work as physicians, fortune-tellers, children's teachers, Daoist priests, publishers, booksellers, or playwrights. Many took leadership roles at the local level, such as founding academies for Confucian learning or promoting local charitable ventures. Through such activities, scholars without government offices could assert the importance of civil over military values and see themselves as trustees of the Confucian tradition.

Since the Mongols wanted to extract wealth from China, they had every incentive to develop the economy. They encouraged trade both within China and beyond its borders and tried to keep paper money in circulation. (See "Viewpoints 12.2: Circulating Paper Money," page 343.) They repaired the Grand Canal, which had been ruined during their initial conquest of north China. Chinese industries with strong foreign markets, such as porcelain, thrived. Nevertheless, the economic expansion of late Tang and Song times did not continue under the alien rule of the Jurchens and Mongols. The economy of north China, with its strong iron industry, contracted under the Jurchens, and the destruction of cities was extensive during the first five decades of Mongol rule of the north.

The Mongols' Yuan Dynasty began a rapid decline in the 1330s as

disease, rebellions, and poor leadership led to disorder throughout the country. When a Chinese strongman succeeded in consolidating the south, the Mongol rulers retreated to Mongolia before he could take Beijing. By 1368 the Yuan Dynasty had given way to a new Chinese-led dynasty: the Ming.

# Korea Under the Koryŏ Dynasty, 935–1392

☐ How did Korean society and culture develop in an age when its northern neighbors were Khitans, Jurchens, and Mongols?

During the Silla period, Korea was strongly tied to Tang China and avidly copied China's model (see page 198). This changed along with much else in North Asia between 800 and 1400. In this period Korea lived more in the shadows of the powerful states of the Khitans, Jurchens, and Mongols than of the Chinese.

The Silla Dynasty began to decline after the king was killed in a revolt in 780. For the next 155 years the kings were selected from several collateral lines, and the majority of them met violent deaths. Rebellions and coups d'état followed one after the other, as different groups of nobles placed their candidates on the throne and killed as many of their opponents as they could. As conditions deteriorated, serfs absconded in large numbers, and independent merchants and seamen of humble origins came to dominate the three-way trade between China, Korea, and Japan.

The dynasty that emerged from this confusion was called Koryŏ (KAW-ree-oh) (935–1392). (The English word *Korea* derives from the name of this dynasty.) During this time Korea developed more independently of the China model than it had in Silla times, just as contemporary Japan was doing (see the next section). This was not because the Chinese model was rejected; the Koryŏ capital was laid out on the Chinese model, and the government was closely patterned on the Tang system. But despite Chinese influence, Korean society remained deeply aristocratic.

The founder of the dynasty, Wang Kon (877–943), was a man of relatively obscure maritime background, and he needed the support of the old aristocracy to maintain control. His successors introduced civil service examinations on the Chinese model, as well as examinations for Buddhist

**The Koryŏ Dynasty, 935–1392**

YUAN DYNASTY

Yalu R.

Kaegyong

1253–1254

1231

1236–1239

KORYŏ KOREA

Sea of Japan

Yellow Sea

Tonggyang

1274–

1281

Korea Strait

JAPAN

→ Mongol invasion
⌐⌐ Wall

clergy, but because the aristocrats were the best educated and the government schools admitted only the sons of aristocrats, this system served primarily to solidify their control. Politics was largely the competition among aristocratic clans for influence at court and marriage of their daughters to the royal princes. Like the Heian aristocrats in Japan (see pages 381–384), the Koryŏ aristocrats wanted to stay in the capital and only reluctantly accepted posts in the provinces.

At the other end of the social scale, the number of people in the serf-slave stratum seems to have increased. This lowborn stratum included not only privately held slaves but also large numbers of government slaves as well as government workers in mines, porcelain factories, and other government industries. Sometimes entire villages or groups of villages were considered lowborn. There were occasional slave revolts, and some freed slaves did rise in status, but prejudice against anyone with slave ancestors was so strong that the law provided that "only if there is no evidence of lowborn status for eight generations in one's official household registration may one receive a position in the government."[3] In China and Japan, by contrast, slavery was a much more minor element in the social landscape.

The commercial economy declined in Korea during this period, showing that it was not closely linked to China's then-booming economy. Except for the capital, there were no cities of commercial importance, and in the countryside the use of money declined. One industry that did flourish was ceramics. Connoisseurs have long appreciated the elegance of the pale green Koryŏ celadon pottery, decorated with designs executed in inlaid white or gray clay.

Buddhism remained strong throughout Korea, and monasteries became major centers of art and learning. As in Song China and Kamakura Japan, Chan (Zen) and Tiantai (Tendai) were the leading Buddhist teachings (see pages 194, 384). The founder of the Koryŏ Dynasty attributed the dynasty's success to the Buddha's protection, and he and his successors were ardent patrons of the church. The entire Buddhist canon was printed in the eleventh century and again in the thirteenth. (The 81,258 individual woodblocks used to print it still survive in a Korean Buddhist monastery.) As in medieval Europe, aristocrats who entered the church occupied the major abbacies. Monasteries played the same roles as they did in China and Japan, such as engaging in money-lending and charitable works. As in Japan (but not China), some monasteries accumulated military power.

Not all cultural advances were connected to monasteries or Buddhism. The most important literary work

**Wooden Blocks for Printing** The Heainsa Buddhist Temple in Korea has preserved the more than eighty thousand woodblocks used to print the huge Buddhist canon in the thirteenth century. The monk shown here is replacing a block. All the blocks are carved on both sides and stabilized by wooden frames that have kept them from warping. (© OUR PLACE THE WORLD HERITAGE COLLECTION, www.ourplaceworldheritage.com)

of the Koryŏ period is *The History of the Three Kingdoms*, compiled in 1145 in Chinese. Modeled on Chinese histories, it is the best source of information on early Korean history.

The Koryŏ Dynasty was preserved in name long after the ruling family had lost most of its power. In 1170 the palace guards massacred the civil officials at court and placed a new king on the throne. The coup leaders scrapped the privileges that had kept the aristocrats in power and appointed themselves to the top posts. After incessant infighting among the generals and a series of coups, in 1196 the general Ch'oe Ch'unghon took control. Ch'oe had a private army of about three thousand warrior-retainers and an even larger number of slaves. The domination of Korea by the Ch'oe family was much like the contemporaneous situation in Japan, where warrior bands were seizing power. Moreover, because the Ch'oes were content to dominate the government while leaving the Koryŏ king on the throne, they had much in common with the Japanese shoguns, who followed a similar strategy.

Although Korea adopted many ideas from China, it could not so easily adopt the Chinese assumption that it was the largest, most powerful, and most advanced society in the world. Korea, from early times, recognized China as being in many ways senior to it, but when strong non-Chinese states emerged to its north in Manchuria, Korea was ready to accommodate them as well. Koryŏ's first neighbor to the north was the Khitan state of Liao, which in 1010 invaded and sacked the capital. To avoid destruction, Koryŏ acceded to vassal status, but Liao invaded again in 1018. This time Koryŏ was able to repel the nomadic Khitans. Afterward a defensive wall was built across the Korean peninsula south of the Yalu River. When the Jurchens and their Jin Dynasty supplanted the Khitans' Liao Dynasty, Koryŏ agreed to send them tribute as well.

As mentioned in Chapter 12, Korea was conquered by the Mongols, and the figurehead Koryŏ kings were moved to Beijing, where they married Mongol princesses, their descendants becoming more Mongol than Korean. This was a time of hardship for the Korean people. In the year 1254 alone, the Mongols enslaved two hundred thousand Koreans and took them away. Ordinary people in Korea suffered grievously when their land was used as a launching pad for the huge Mongol invasions of Japan: nine hundred ships and the provisions for the soldiers on them had to be procured from the Korean countryside. In this period Korea also suffered from frequent attacks by Japanese pirates, somewhat like the depredations of the Vikings in Europe a little earlier (see page 393). The Mongol overlords did little to provide protection, and the harried coastal people had little choice but to retreat inland.

When Mongol rule in China fell apart in the mid-fourteenth century, it declined in Korea as well. Chinese rebels opposing the Mongols entered Korea and even briefly captured the capital in 1361. When the Ming Dynasty was established in China in 1368, the Koryŏ court was unsure how to respond. In 1388 a general, Yi Song-gye, was sent to oppose a Ming army at the northwest frontier. When he saw the strength of the Ming, he concluded that making an alliance was more sensible than fighting, and he led his troops back to the capital, where in 1392 he usurped the throne, founding the Chosŏn Dynasty.

# Japan's Heian Period, 794–1185

☐ How did the Heian form of government contribute to the cultural flowering of Japan in this period?

As described in Chapter 7, during the seventh and eighth centuries the Japanese ruling house pursued a vigorous policy of adopting useful ideas, techniques, and policies from the more advanced civilization of China. The rulers built a splendid capital along Chinese lines in Nara and fostered the growth of Buddhism. Monasteries grew so powerful in Nara, however, that in less than a century the court decided to move away from them and encourage other sects of Buddhism.

The new capital was built about twenty-five miles away at Heian (HAY-ahn; modern Kyoto). Like Nara, Heian was modeled on the Tang capital of Chang'an (although neither of the Japanese capitals had walls, a major feature of Chinese cities). For the first century at Heian the government continued to follow Chinese models, but it turned away from them with the decline of the Tang Dynasty in the late ninth century. The last official embassy to China made the trip in 894. During the Heian period (794–1185), Japan witnessed a literary and cultural flowering under the rule of the Fujiwara family.

## Fujiwara Rule

Only the first two Heian emperors were much involved in governing. By 860 political management had been taken over by a series of regents from the Fujiwara family, who supplied most of the empresses in this period. The emperors continued to be honored, even venerated, because of their presumed divine descent, but the Fujiwaras ruled. Fujiwara dominance represented the privatization of political power and a return to clan politics. Political history thus took a very different course in Japan than in China, where, when a dynasty

**The Tale of Genji** In this scene from a twelfth-century painting illustrating *The Tale of Genji*, Genji has his inkstone and brushes ready to respond to the letter he is reading. (Tokugawa Reimeikai Foundation, Tokyo, Japan/Photo © AISA/The Bridgeman Art Library)

weakened, military strongmen would compete to depose the emperor and found their own dynasties. In Japan for the next thousand years, political contenders sought to manipulate the emperors rather than supplant them.

The Fujiwaras reached the apogee of their glory under Fujiwara Michinaga (r. 995–1027). Like many aristocrats of the period, he was learned in Buddhism, music, poetry, and Chinese literature and history. He dominated the court for more than thirty years as the father of four empresses, the uncle of two emperors, and the grandfather of three emperors. He acquired great landholdings and built fine palaces for himself and his family. After ensuring that his sons could continue to rule, he retired to a Buddhist monastery, all the while continuing to maintain control.

By the end of the eleventh century several emperors who did not have Fujiwara mothers had found a device to counter Fujiwara control: they abdicated but continued to exercise power by controlling their young sons on the throne. This system of rule has been called **cloistered government** because the retired emperors took Buddhist orders, while maintaining control of the government from behind the scenes. Thus for a time the imperial house was a contender for political power along with other aristocratic groups.

## Aristocratic Culture

A brilliant aristocratic culture developed in the Heian period. In the capital at Heian, nobles, palace ladies, and imperial family members lived a highly refined and leisured life. In their society, niceties of birth, rank, and breeding counted for everything. From their diaries we know of the pains aristocratic women took in their dress, selecting the color combinations of the kimonos they wore, layer upon layer. The elegance of one's calligraphy and the allusions in one's poems were matters of intense concern to both men and women at court. Courtiers did not like to leave the capital, and some like the court lady Sei Shonagon shuddered at the sight of ordinary working people. In her *Pillow Book*, she wrote of encountering a group of commoners on a pilgrimage: "They looked like so many basketworms as they crowded together in their hideous clothes, leaving hardly an inch of space between themselves and me. I really felt like pushing them all over sideways."[4] (See "Listening to the Past: *The Pillow Book* of Sei Shonagon," page 382.)

In this period a new script was developed for writing Japanese phonetically. Each symbol was based on a simplified Chinese character and represented one of the syllables used in Japanese (such as *ka, ki, ku, ke, ko*). Although "serious" essays, histories, and government documents continued to be written in Chinese, less formal works such as poetry and memoirs were written in Japanese. Mastering the new writing system took much less time than mastering writing in Chinese

---

• **cloistered government** A system in which an emperor retired to a Buddhist monastery but continued to exercise power by controlling his young son on the throne.

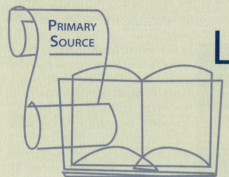

# Listening to the Past

## *The Pillow Book* of Sei Shonagon

*Beginning in the late tenth century Japan produced a series of great women writers. At the time women were much freer than men to write in vernacular Japanese, giving them a large advantage. Lady Murasaki, author of the novel* The Tale of Genji, *is the most famous of the women writers of the period, but her contemporary Sei Shonagon is equally noteworthy. Sei Shonagon served as a lady in waiting to Empress Sadako during the last decade of the tenth century (990–1000). Her only known work is* The Pillow Book, *a collection of notes, character sketches, anecdotes, descriptions of nature, and eccentric lists such as boring things, awkward things, hateful things, and things that have lost their power.*

*The Pillow Book portrays the lovemaking/marriage system among the aristocracy more or less as it is depicted in* The Tale of Genji. *Marriages were arranged for family interests, and a man could have more than one wife. Wives and their children commonly stayed in their own homes, where their husbands and fathers would visit them. But once a man had an heir by his wife, there was nothing to prevent him from establishing relations with other women. Some relationships were long-term, but many were brief, and men often had several lovers at the same time. Some women became known for their amorous conquests, others as abandoned women whose husbands ignored them. The following passage from* The Pillow Book *looks on this lovemaking system with amused detachment.*

❝ It is so stiflingly hot in the Seventh Month that even at night one keeps all the doors and lattices open. At such times it is delightful to wake up when the moon is shining and to look outside. I enjoy it even when there is no moon. But to wake up at dawn and see a pale sliver of a moon in the sky — well, I need hardly say how perfect that is.

I like to see a bright new straw mat that has just been spread out on a well-polished floor. The best place for one's three-foot curtain of state is in the front of the room near the veranda. It is pointless to put it in the rear of the room, as it is most unlikely that anyone will peer in from that direction.

It is dawn and a woman is lying in bed after her lover has taken his leave. She is covered up to her head with a light mauve robe that has a lining of dark violet; the colour of both the outside and the lining is fresh and glossy. The woman, who appears to be asleep, wears an unlined orange robe and a dark crimson skirt of stiff silk whose cords hang loosely by her side, as if they have been left untied. Her thick tresses tumble over each other in cascades, and one can imagine how long her hair must be when it falls freely down her back.

Nearby another woman's lover is making his way home in the misty dawn. He is wearing loose violet trousers, an orange hunting costume, so lightly coloured that one can hardly tell whether it has been dyed or not, a white robe of still silk, and a scarlet robe of glossy, beaten silk. His clothes, which are damp from the mist, hang loosely about him. From the dishevelment of his side locks one can tell how negligently he must have tucked his hair into the black lacquered headdress when he got up. He wants to return and write his next-morning letter before the dew on the morning glories has had time to vanish; but the path seems endless, and to divert himself he hums "the sprouts in the flax fields."

As he walks along, he passes a house with an open lattice. He is on his way to report for official duty, but cannot help stopping to lift up the blind and peep into the room. It amuses him to think that a man has probably been spending the night here and has only recently got up to leave, just as happened to himself. Perhaps that man too had felt the charm of the dew.

Looking around the room, he notices near the woman's pillow an open fan with a magnolia frame and purple paper; and at the foot of her curtain of state he sees some narrow strips of

and aided the spread of literacy, especially among women in court society.

In the Heian period, women played important roles at all levels of society. Women educated in the arts and letters could advance at court as attendants to the ruler's empress and other consorts. Women could inherit property from their parents, and they would compete with their brothers for shares of the family property. In political life, marrying a daughter to an emperor or shogun (see page 384) was one of the best ways to gain power, and women often became major players in power struggles.

The literary masterpiece of this period is **The Tale of Genji**, written in Japanese by Lady Murasaki over several years (ca. 1000–1010). This long narrative depicts a cast of characters enmeshed in court life, with close

• **The Tale of Genji** A Japanese literary masterpiece about court life written by Lady Murasaki.

During the Heian period, noble-women were fashion conscious. Wearing numerous layers of clothing gave women the opportunity to choose different designs and colors for their robes. The layers also kept them warm in drafty homes. (© INTERFOTO/Alamy)

Michinoku paper and also some other paper of a faded colour, either orange-red or maple.

The woman senses that someone is watching her and, looking up from under her bedclothes, sees a gentleman leaning against the wall by the threshold, a smile on his face. She can tell at once that he is the sort of man with whom she need feel no reserve. All the same, she does not want to enter into any familiar relations with him, and she is annoyed that he should have seen her asleep.

"Well, well, Madam," says the man, leaning forward so that the upper part of his body comes behind her curtains, "what a long nap you're having after your morning adieu! You really are a lie-abed!"

"You call me that, Sir," she replied, "only because you're annoyed at having had to get up before the dew had time to settle."

Their conversation may be commonplace, yet I find there is something delightful about the scene.

Now the gentleman leans further forward and, using his own fan, tries to get hold of the fan by the woman's pillow. Fearing his closeness, she moves further back into her curtain enclosure, her heart pounding. The gentleman picks up the magnolia fan and, while examining it, says in a slightly bitter tone, "How standoffish you are!"

But now it is growing light; there is a sound of people's voices, and it looks as if the sun will soon be up. Only a short while ago this same man was hurrying home to write his next-morning letter before the mists had time to clear. Alas, how easily his intentions have been forgotten!

While all this is afoot, the woman's original lover has been busy with his own next-morning letter, and now, quite unexpectedly, the messenger arrives at her house. The letter is attached to a spray of bush-clover, still damp with dew, and the paper gives off a delicious aroma of incense. Because of the new visitor, however, the woman's servants cannot deliver it to her.

Finally it becomes unseemly for the gentleman to stay any longer. As he goes, he is amused to think that a similar scene may be taking place in the house he left earlier that morning. **"**

Source: *The Pillow Book of Sei Shonagon*, edited and translated by Ivan Morris, pp. 60–62. © Ivan Morris 1967. Copyright © 1991 Columbia University Press. Reprinted by permission of Columbia University Press and Oxford University Press.

## QUESTIONS FOR ANALYSIS

1. What sorts of images does Sei Shonagon evoke to convey an impression of a scene?

2. What can you learn from this passage about the material culture of Japan in this period?

3. Why do you think Sei Shonagon was highly esteemed as a writer?

---

attention to dialogue and personality. Murasaki also wrote a diary that is similarly revealing of aristocratic culture. In one passage she tells of an occasion when word got out that she had read the Chinese classics:

Worried what people would think if they heard such rumors, I pretended to be unable to read even the inscriptions on the screens. Then Her Majesty asked me to read to her here and there from the collected works of [the Tang Chinese poet] Bo Juyi, and, because she evinced a desire to know much more about such things, we carefully chose a time when other women would not be present and, amateur that I was, I read with her the two books of Bo Juyi's New Ballads in secret; we started the summer before last.[5]

Despite the reluctance of Murasaki and the lady she served to let others know of their learning, there were, in fact, quite a few women writers in this period. The wife of a high-ranking court official wrote a poetic memoir of her unhappy twenty-year marriage to him and his rare visits. A woman wrote both an autobiography that related her father's efforts to find favor at court and a love story of a hero who travels to China. Another woman even wrote a history that concludes with a triumphal biography of Fujiwara Michinaga.

Buddhism remained very strong throughout the Heian period. A mission sent to China in 804 included two monks in search of new texts. One of the monks, Saichō, spent time at the monasteries on Mount Tiantai and brought back the Buddhist teachings associated with that mountain (called Tendai in Japanese). Tendai's basic message is that all living beings share the Buddha nature and can be brought to salvation. Tendai practices include strict monastic discipline, prayer, textual study, and meditation. Once back in Japan, Saichō established a monastery on Mount Hiei outside Kyoto, which grew to be one of the most important monasteries in Japan. By the twelfth century this monastery and its many branch temples had vast lands and a powerful army of monk-soldiers to protect its interests. Whenever the monastery felt that its interests were at risk, it sent the monk-soldiers into the capital to parade its sacred symbols in an attempt to intimidate the civil authorities.

Kūkai, the other monk on the 804 mission to China, came back with texts from another school of Buddhism—Shingon, "True Word," a form of **Esoteric Buddhism**. Esoteric Buddhism is based on the idea that teachings containing the secrets of enlightenment had been secretly transmitted from the Buddha. People can gain access to these mysteries through initiation into the mandalas (cosmic diagrams), mudras (gestures), and mantras (verbal formulas). On his return to Japan, Kūkai attracted many followers and was allowed to establish a monastery at Mount Kōya, south of Osaka. The popularity of Esoteric Buddhism was a great stimulus to Buddhist art.

# The Samurai and the Kamakura Shogunate, 1185–1333

☐ **What were the causes and consequences of military rule in Japan?**

The gradual rise of a warrior elite over the course of the Heian period finally brought an end to the domination of the Fujiwaras and other Heian aristocratic families. In 1156 civil war broke out between the Taira and Minamoto warrior clans based in western and eastern Japan, respectively. Both clans relied on skilled warriors, later called samurai, who were rapidly becoming a new social class. A samurai and his lord had a double bond: in return for the samurai's loyalty and service, the lord granted him land or income. From 1159 to 1181 a Taira named Kiyomori dominated the court, taking the position of prime minister and marrying his daughter to the emperor. His relatives became governors of more than thirty provinces, managed some five hundred tax-exempt estates, and amassed a fortune in the trade with Song China and Koryŏ Korea. Still, the Minamoto clan managed to defeat the Taira, and the Minamoto leader, Yoritomo, became **shogun**, or general-in-chief. With him began the Kamakura Shogunate (1185–1333). This period is often referred to as Japan's feudal period because it was dominated by a military class whose members were tied to their superiors by bonds of loyalty and supported by landed estates rather than salaries.

## Military Rule

The similarities between military rule in Japan and feudalism in medieval Europe during roughly the same period have fascinated scholars, as have the very significant differences. In Europe feudalism emerged out of the fusion of Germanic and Roman social institutions and flowered under the impact of Muslim and Viking invasions. In Japan military rule evolved from a combination of the native warrior tradition and Confucian ethical principles of duty to superiors.

The emergence of the samurai was made possible by the development of private landholding. The government land allotment system, copied from Tang China, began breaking down in the eighth century (much as it did in China). By the ninth century local lords had begun escaping imperial taxes and control by commending (formally giving) their land to tax-exempt entities such as monasteries, the imperial family, and high-ranking officials. The local lord then received his land back as a tenant and paid his protector a small rent. The monastery or privileged individual received a

- • **Esoteric Buddhism** A sect of Buddhism that maintains that the secrets of enlightenment have been secretly transmitted from the Buddha and can be accessed through initiation into the mandalas, mudras, and mantras.

- • **shogun** The Japanese general-in-chief, whose headquarters was the shogunate.

- • **Bushido** Literally, the "way of the warrior"; the code of conduct by which samurai were expected to live.

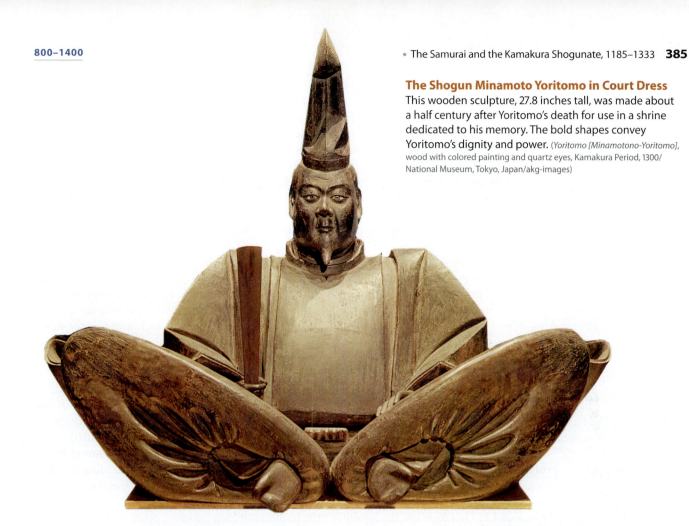

**The Shogun Minamoto Yoritomo in Court Dress**
This wooden sculpture, 27.8 inches tall, was made about a half century after Yoritomo's death for use in a shrine dedicated to his memory. The bold shapes convey Yoritomo's dignity and power. (*Yoritomo [Minamotono-Yoritomo]*, wood with colored painting and quartz eyes, Kamakura Period, 1300/ National Museum, Tokyo, Japan/akg-images)

steady income from the land, and the local lord escaped imperial taxes and control. By the end of the thirteenth century most land seems to have been taken off the tax rolls this way. Each plot of land could thus have several people with rights to shares of its produce, ranging from the cultivator, to a local lord, to an estate manager working for him, to a regional strongman, to a noble or temple in the capital. Unlike peasants in medieval Europe, where similar practices of commendation occurred, those working the land in Japan never became serfs. Moreover, Japanese lords rarely lived on the lands they had rights in, unlike English or French lords who lived on their manors.

Samurai resembled European knights in several ways. Both were armed with expensive weapons, and both fought on horseback. Just as the knight was supposed to live according to the chivalric code, so Japanese samurai were expected to live according to **Bushido** (or "way of the warrior"), a code that stressed military honor, courage, stoic acceptance of hardship, and, above all, loyalty. Physical hardship was accepted as routine, and soft living was despised as weak and unworthy. Disloyalty brought social disgrace, which the samurai could avoid only through *seppuku*, ritual suicide by slashing his belly.

The Kamakura Shogunate derives its name from Kamakura, a city near modern Tokyo that was the seat of the Minamoto clan. The founder, Yoritomo, ruled the country much the way he ran his own estates, appointing his retainers to newly created offices. To cope with the emergence of hard-to-tax estates, he put military land stewards in charge of seeing to the estates' proper operation. To bring order to the lawless countryside, he appointed military governors to oversee the military and enforce the law in the provinces. They supervised the conduct of the land stewards in peacetime and commanded the provincial samurai in war.

Yoritomo's wife, Masako, protected the interests of her own family, the Hōjōs, especially after Yoritomo died. She went so far as to force her first son to abdicate when he showed signs of preferring the family of his wife to the family of his mother. She later helped her brother take power away from her father. Thus the process of reducing power holders to figureheads went one step further in 1219 when the Hōjō family reduced the shogun to a figurehead. The Hōjō

**Kamakura Shogunate, 1185–1333**

family held the reins of power for more than a century until 1333.

The Mongols' two massive seaborne invasions in 1274 and 1281 (see page 339) were a huge shock to the shogunate. The Kamakura government was hard-pressed to gather adequate resources for its defense. Temples were squeezed, farmers were taken away from their fields to build walls, and warriors were promised generous rewards in return for their service. Although the Hōjō regents, with the help of a "divine wind" (kamikaze), repelled the Mongols, they were unable to reward their vassals in the traditional way because little booty was found among the wreckage of the Mongol fleets. Discontent grew among the samurai, and by the fourteenth century the entire political system was breaking down. Both the imperial and the shogunate families were fighting among themselves. As land grants were divided, samurai became impoverished and took to plunder and piracy, or shifted their loyalty to local officials who could offer them a better living.

The factional disputes among Japan's leading families remained explosive until 1331, when the emperor Go-Daigo tried to recapture real power. His attempt sparked an uprising by the great families, local lords, samurai, and even Buddhist monasteries, which had thousands of samurai retainers. Go-Daigo destroyed the Kamakura Shogunate in 1333 but soon lost the loyalty of his followers. By 1338 one of his most important military supporters, Ashikaga Takauji, had turned on him and established the Ashikaga Shogunate, which lasted until 1573. Takauji's victory was also a victory for the samurai, who took over civil authority throughout Japan.

## Cultural Trends

The cultural distance between the elites and the commoners narrowed a little during the Kamakura period. Buddhism was spread to ordinary Japanese by energetic preachers. Honen (1133–1212) propagated the Pure Land teaching, preaching that paradise could be reached through simple faith in the Buddha and repeating the name of the Buddha Amitabha. Neither philosophical understanding of Buddhist scriptures nor devotion to rituals was essential. His follower Shinran (1173–1263) taught that monks should not shut themselves off in monasteries but should marry and have children. A different path was promoted by Nichiren (1222–1282), a fiery and intolerant preacher who proclaimed that to be saved people had only to invoke sincerely the Lotus Sutra, one of the most important of the Buddhist sutras. These lay versions of Buddhism found a receptive audience among ordinary people in the countryside.

It was also during the Kamakura period that **Zen** came to flourish in Japan. Zen teachings originated in Tang China, where they were known as Chan (see page 195). Rejecting the authority of the sutras, Zen teachers claimed the superiority of mind-to-mind transmission of Buddhist truth. When Japanese monks went to China in the twelfth century looking for ways to revitalize Japanese Buddhism, they were impressed by the rigorous monastic life of the Chan/Zen monasteries. One school of Zen held that enlightenment could be achieved suddenly through insight into one's own true nature. This school taught rigorous meditation and the use of kōan riddles to unseat logic and free the mind for enlightenment. This teaching found eager patrons among the samurai, who were attracted to its discipline and strong master-disciple bonds.

Buddhism remained central to the visual arts. Many temples in Japan still house fine sculptures done in this period. In painting, narrative hand scrolls brought to life the miracles that faith could bring and the torments of Hell awaiting unbelievers. All forms of literature were depicted in these scrolls, including *The Tale of Genji*, war stories, and humorous anecdotes.

During the Kamakura period, war tales continued the tradition of long narrative prose works. *The Tale of the Heike* tells the story of the fall of the Taira family and the rise of the Minamoto clan. The tale reached a large and mostly illiterate audience because blind minstrels would chant sections to the accompaniment of a lute. The story is suffused with the Buddhist idea of the transience of life and the illusory nature of glory. Yet it also celebrates strength, courage, loyalty, and pride. The Minamoto warriors from the east are portrayed as the toughest. In one scene one of them dismisses his own prowess with the bow, claiming that other warriors from his region could pierce three sets of armor with their arrows. He then brags about the martial spirit of warriors from the east: "They are bold horsemen who never fall, nor do they let their horses stumble on the roughest road. When they fight they do not care if even their parents or children are killed; they ride over their bodies and continue the battle."[6] In this they stood in contrast to the warriors of the west, who in good Confucian fashion would retire from battle to mourn their parents.

After stagnating in the Heian period, agricultural productivity began to improve in the Kamakura period, and the population grew, reaching perhaps 8.2 million by 1333. Much like farmers in contemporary Song China, Japanese farmers adopted new strains of rice, often double-cropped in warmer regions, made increased use of fertilizers, and improved irrigation for paddy rice. Besides farming, ordinary people made their liv-

---

• **Zen** A school of Buddhism that emphasized meditation and truths that could not be conveyed in words.

ings as artisans, traders, fishermen, and entertainers. Although trade in human beings was banned, those who fell into debt might sell themselves or their children, and professional slave traders kidnapped women and children. A vague category of outcastes occupied the fringes of society, in a manner reminiscent of India. Buddhist strictures against killing and Shinto ideas of pollution probably account for the exclusion of butchers, leatherworkers, morticians, and lepers, but other groups, such as bamboo whisk makers, were also traditionally excluded for no obvious reason.

# Chapter Summary

The countries of East Asia—China, Japan, and Korea—all underwent major changes in the six centuries from 800 to 1400. In China the loosening of the central government's control of the economy stimulated trade and economic growth. Between 800 and 1100 China's population doubled to 100 million, reflecting in part the spread of wet-field rice cultivation, especially in the south. The economic center of China shifted from the north China plain to the south, the milder region drained by the Yangzi River.

In the Song period, the booming economy and the invention of printing allowed for expansion of the scholar-official class, which came to dominate government and society. Men who aspired to this life spent a decade or more studying for the highly competitive civil service examinations. Many educated men pursued interests in literature, antiquities, philosophy, and art. Repeatedly, the Song government chose to pay tribute to its militarily powerful neighbors—first the Khitans, then the Jurchens, then the Mongols—to keep the peace. Eventually, however, Song fell to the Mongols. The Mongols instituted hereditary occupations, ending much of the social mobility that characterized the Song Dynasty.

During the Koryŏ Dynasty, Korea evolved more independently of China than it had previously, in part because it had to placate powerful non-Chinese neighbors. The commercial economy declined, and an increasing portion of the population was unfree, working as slaves for aristocrats or the government. Military strongmen dominated the government, but their armies were no match for the much larger

empires to their north. The period of Mongol domination was particularly difficult.

In Heian Japan, a tiny aristocracy dominated government and society. A series of regents, most of them from the Fujiwara family and fathers-in-law of the emperors, controlled political life. The aristocratic court society put great emphasis on taste and refinement. Women were influential at the court and wrote much of the best literature of the period. The Heian aristocrats had little interest in life in the provinces, which gradually came under the control of military clans.

After a civil war between the two leading military clans, a military government, called the shogunate, was established. The Kamakura Shogunate was dominated by a military class of samurais, who were bound to their lord by loyalty and service in return for land and income. Emperors had little power. Two invasions by the Mongols caused major crises in military control. Although both times the invaders were repelled, defense costs were high. During this period culture was less centered around the capital, and Buddhism spread to ordinary people.

## CHRONOLOGY

| | |
|---|---|
| 794–1185 | Heian period in Japan |
| 804 | Two Japanese Buddhist monks, Saichō and Kūkai, travel to China |
| 935–1392 | Koryŏ Dynasty in Korea |
| 960–1279 | Song Dynasty in China; emergence of scholar-official class; invention of movable type |
| 995–1027 | Fujiwara Michinaga dominant at Heian court |
| ca. 1000–1010 | *The Tale of Genji* |
| 1119 | First reported use of compass |
| 1120s | First government-issued paper money introduced by Song |
| 1126 | Song loss of north China to the Jurchens; Song capital relocated to Hangzhou |
| 1130–1200 | Zhu Xi, Neo-Confucian philosopher |
| 1185–1333 | Kamakura Shogunate in Japan; Zen Buddhism flourishes |
| 1234–1368 | Mongols' Yuan Dynasty in China |
| ca. 1275–1292 | Marco Polo travels in China |

## NOTES

1. *The Travels of Marco Polo, the Venetian*, ed. Manuel Komroff (New York: Boni and Liveright, 1926), p. 227.
2. Ibid., p. 235.
3. Peter H. Lee, ed., *Sourcebook of Korean Civilization* (New York: Columbia University Press, 1993), p. 327.
4. *The Pillow Book of Sei Shonagon*, edited and translated by Ivan Morris, p. 258. © Ivan Morris 1967. Copyright © 1991 Columbia University Press. Reprinted by permission of Columbia University Press and Oxford University Press.
5. Quoted in M. Collcott, M. Jansen, and I. Kumakura, *Cultural Atlas of Japan* (New York: Facts on File, 1988), p. 82, slightly modified.
6. Ibid., p. 101.

## CONNECTIONS

East Asia faced many internal and external challenges between 800 and 1400, and the ways societies responded to them shaped their subsequent histories. In China the first four centuries of this period saw economic growth, urbanization, the spread of printing, and the expansion of the educated class. In Korea and Japan aristocratic dominance and military rule were more typical of the era. All three areas, but especially China and Korea, faced an unprecedented challenge from the Mongols, with Japan less vulnerable because it did not share a land border. The challenges of the period did not hinder creativity in the literary and visual arts; among the greatest achievements of this era are the women's writings of Heian Japan, such as *The Tale of Genji*, and landscape painting of both Song and Yuan China.

Europe during these six centuries, the subject of the next chapter, also faced invasions from outside; in its case, the pagan Vikings were especially dreaded. Europe had a social structure more like that of Korea and Japan than of China, with less centralization and a more dominant place in society for military men. The centralized church in Europe, however, was unlike anything known in East Asian history. These centuries in Europe saw a major expansion of Christendom, especially to Scandinavia and eastern Europe, through both conversion and migration. Although there were scares that the Mongols would penetrate deeper into Europe, the greatest challenge in Europe was the Black Death and the huge loss of life that it caused.

# Review and Explore

## Make It Stick

### LearningCurve
Go online and use LearningCurve to retain what you've read.

## Identify Key Terms

Identify and explain the significance of each item below.

dynastic cycle (p. 365)

compass (p. 367)

scholar-official class (p. 369)

examination system (p. 369)

movable type (p. 370)

Neo-Confucianism (p. 373)

concubine (p. 374)

foot binding (p. 377)

cloistered government (p. 381)

*The Tale of Genji* (p. 382)

Esoteric Buddhism (p. 384)

shogun (p. 384)

Bushido (p. 385)

Zen (p. 386)

## Review the Main Ideas

Answer the focus questions from each section of the chapter.

1.  What made possible the expansion of the Chinese economy, and what were the outcomes of this economic growth? (p. 365)
2.  How did the civil service examinations and the scholar-official class shape Chinese society and culture, and what impact did the Mongol conquest have on them? (p. 369)
3.  How did Korean society and culture develop in an age when its northern neighbors were Khitans, Jurchens, and Mongols? (p. 378)
4.  How did the Heian form of government contribute to the cultural flowering of Japan in this period? (p. 380)
5.  What were the causes and consequences of military rule in Japan? (p. 384)

## Make Connections

Analyze the larger developments and continuities within and across chapters.

1.  What elements in women's lives in Song China were common in other parts of the world as well? What elements were more distinctive?
2.  How did the impact of Mongol rule on China compare to its impact on Muslim lands?
3.  How did being an island country affect Japan's history? What other island countries make good comparisons?
4.  Did the countries of East Asia have more in common at the end of the Mongol period than they did in the seventh or eighth century (discussed in Chapter 7)?

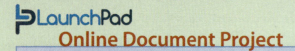
**LaunchPad**
## Online Document Project

### Song Artwork

**What cultural pursuits interested the scholar-official class?**
View images from the Song period, and then complete a quiz and writing assignment based on the evidence and details from this chapter.

*See inside the front cover to learn more.*

## Suggested Reading

Bowring, Richard. *The Religious Traditions of Japan, 500–1600*. 2005. A wide-ranging study that puts Buddhism in the context of local cults.

Chaffee, John W. *The Thorny Gates of Learning in Sung China: A Social History of Examinations*. 1985. Documents the extensive impact of the examination system and the ways men could improve their chances.

Ebrey, Patricia Buckley. *The Inner Quarters: Marriage and the Lives of Chinese Women in the Sung Period*. 1993. Overview of the many facets of women's lives, from engagements to dowries, child rearing, and widowhood.

Ebrey, Patricia Buckley, Anne Walthall, and James B. Palais. *East Asia: A Cultural, Social, and Political History*, 2d ed. 2009. Textbook with strong coverage of this period.

Egan, Ronald. *Word, Image, and Deed in the Life of Su Shi*. 1994. A sympathetic portrait of one of the most talented men of the age.

Farris, Wayne W. *Heavenly Warriors*. 1992. Argues against Western analogies in explaining the dominance of the samurai.

Friday, Karl F. *Hired Swords*. 1992. Treats the evolution of state military development in connection with the emergence of the samurai.

Hansen, Valerie. *Changing the Gods in Medieval China, 1127–1276*. 1990. A portrait of the religious beliefs and practices of ordinary people in Song times.

Ko, Dorothy, JaHyun Kim Haboush, and Joan R. Piggott, eds. *Women and Confucian Cultures in Premodern China, Korea, and Japan*. 2003. Addresses both the elements that the East Asian countries shared and the ways they diverged.

Kuhn, Dieter. *The Age of Confucian Rule: The Song Transformation of China*. 2009. An accessible overview that is especially strong on economic history and material culture.

Lorge, Peter. *War, Politics and Society in Early Modern China, 900–1795*. 2009. Examines dynasties as military powers.

Morris, Ivan. *The World of the Shining Prince: Court Life in Ancient Japan*. 1964. An engaging portrait of Heian culture based on both fiction and nonfiction sources.

Rossabi, Maurice. *China Among Equals*. 1983. Essays on Song, Liao, Jin, and Yuan, as well as Korea.

Seth, Michael J. *A Concise History of Korea*. 2006. Readable and engaging overview of Korean history.

Souyri, Pierre François. *The World Turned Upside Down: Medieval Japanese Society*. 2001. A thought-provoking analysis of both the social system and the mentalities of Japan's Middle Ages.

### Hedwig of Silesia

Noblewomen in medieval Europe played a wide variety of roles. Hedwig of Silesia conducted diplomatic negotiations, ruled her husband's territory when he was away, founded monasteries, and worked to expand Christianity in eastern Europe. (The John Paul Getty Museum, Los Angeles, Ms Ludwig XI 7, fol. 12v [detail], Court Atelier of Duke Ludwig I of Liegnitz and Brieg [illuminator], *Vita beatae Hedwigis*, 1353. Tempera colors, colored washes and ink bound between wood boards covered with red-stained pigskin, 34.1 × 24.8 cm.)

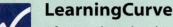

**LearningCurve**

After reading the chapter, go online and use LearningCurve to retain what you've read.

# Chapter Preview

**Political Developments**

**The Christian Church**

**The Crusades**

**The Life of the People**

**Learning and Culture**

**Crises of the Later Middle Ages**

By the fifteenth century scholars in the growing cities of northern Italy had begun to think that they were living in a new era, one in which the glories of ancient Greece and Rome were being reborn. What separated their time from classical antiquity, in their opinion, was a long period of darkness and barbarism, to which a seventeenth-century professor gave the name "Middle Ages." In this conceptualization, the history of Europe was divided into three periods—ancient, medieval, and modern—an organization that is still in use today. Later, the history of other parts of the world was sometimes fit into this three-period schema as well, with discussions of the "classical" period in Maya history, of "medieval" India and China, and of "modern" everywhere.

Today historians often question whether labels of past time periods for one culture work on a global scale, and some scholars are uncertain about whether "Middle Ages" is a just term even for European history. They assert that the Middle Ages was not simply a period of stagnation between two high points but rather a time of enormous intellectual energy and creative vitality. While agrarian life continued to dominate Europe, political structures that would influence later European history began to form, and Christianity continued to spread. People at the time did not know that they were living in an era that would later be labeled "middle" or sometimes even "dark," and we can wonder whether they would have shared this negative view of their own times.

## Political Developments

☐ How did medieval rulers restore order and centralize political power?

Later scholars dated the beginning of the Middle Ages to the fifth century, the time of the fall of the Roman Empire in the West. However, the growth of Germanic kingdoms such as those of the Merovingians and the Carolingians (see Chapter 8) is generally viewed as the beginning of "medieval" politics in Europe, and that is why we begin this chapter with the ninth century. In 800 Charlemagne, the most powerful of the Carolingians, was crowned Holy Roman emperor. After his death his empire was divided among his grandsons, and their kingdoms were weakened by nobles vying for power. In addition, beginning around 800 western Europe was invaded by several different groups. Local nobles were the strongest power, and common people turned to them for protection. By the eleventh century, however, rulers in some parts of Europe had reasserted authority and were slowly building centralized states.

## Invasions and Migrations

From the moors of Scotland to the mountains of Sicily, there arose in the ninth century the prayer "Save us, O God, from the violence of the Northmen." The feared Northmen were pagan Germanic peoples from Norway, Sweden, and Denmark who came to be known as Vikings. They began to make overseas expeditions, which they themselves called *vikings*, and the word came to be used for people who went on such voyages as well.

Viking assaults began around 800, and by the mid-tenth century the Vikings had brought large sections of continental Europe and Britain under their sway. In the east they sailed the rivers of Russia as far as the Black Sea. In the west they established permanent settlements in Iceland and short-lived ones in Greenland and Newfoundland in Canada (Map 14.1).

The Vikings were superb seamen with advanced methods of boatbuilding. Propelled either by oars or by sails, deckless, and about sixty-five feet long, a Viking ship could carry between forty and sixty men — enough to harass an isolated monastery or village. Against these ships navigated by experienced and fearless sailors, the Carolingian Empire, with no navy, was helpless. At first the Vikings attacked and sailed off laden with booty. Later, on returning, they settled down and colonized the areas they had conquered, often marrying local women and adopting the local languages and some of the customs.

Along with the Vikings, groups of central European steppe peoples known as Magyars (MAG-yahrz) also raided villages in the late ninth century, taking plunder and captives and forcing leaders to pay tribute in an effort to prevent further destruction. Moving westward, small bands of Magyars on horseback reached far into Europe. They subdued northern Italy, compelled Bavaria and Saxony to pay tribute, and penetrated into the Rhineland and Burgundy. Western Europeans thought of them as returning Huns, so the Magyars came to be known as Hungarians. They settled in the area that is now Hungary, became Christian, and in the eleventh century allied with the papacy.

From North Africa, the Muslims also began new encroachments in the ninth century. They already ruled most of Spain and now conquered Sicily, driving northward into central Italy and the south coast of France.

From the perspective of those living in what had been Charlemagne's empire, Viking, Magyar, and Muslim attacks contributed to increasing disorder and violence. Italian, French, and English sources often describe this period as one of terror and chaos. People in other parts of Europe might have had a different opinion. In Muslim Spain and Sicily scholars worked in thriving cities, and new crops such as cotton and sugar enhanced ordinary people's lives. In eastern Europe states such as Moravia and Hungary became strong kingdoms. A Viking point of view might be the most positive, for by 1100 descendants of the Vikings not only ruled their homelands in Norway, Sweden, and Denmark but also ruled northern France (a province known as Normandy, or land of the Northmen), England, Sicily, Iceland, and Russia, with an outpost in Greenland and occasional voyages to North America.

## "Feudalism" and Manorialism

The large-scale division of Charlemagne's empire into three parts in the ninth century led to a decentralization of power at the local level. Civil wars weakened the power and prestige of kings, who could do little about regional violence. Likewise, the invasions of the ninth century, especially those of the Vikings, weakened royal authority. The Frankish kings were unable to halt the invaders, and the local aristocracy had to assume responsibility for defense. Thus, in the ninth and tenth centuries, aristocratic families increased their authority in their local territories, and distant and weak kings could not interfere. Common people turned for protection to the strongest power, the local nobles.

The most powerful nobles were those who gained warriors' allegiance, often symbolized in an oath-swearing ceremony of homage and fealty that grew out of earlier Germanic oaths of loyalty. In this ceremony a warrior (knight) swore his loyalty as a **vassal** — from a Celtic term meaning "servant" — to the more powerful individual, who became his lord. In return for the vassal's loyalty, aid, and military assistance, the lord promised him protection and material support. This support might be a place in the lord's household but was more likely land of the vassal's own, called a **fief** (*feudum* in Latin). The fief, which might contain forests, churches, and towns, technically still belonged to the lord, and the vassal had only the use of it. Peasants living on a fief produced the food and other goods necessary to maintain the knight. Most legal scholars and historians have identified these personal ties of loyalty cemented by grants of land rather than allegiance to an abstract state as a political and social system they term **feudalism**. In the last several decades, however, increasing numbers of medieval historians have found the

- **vassal** A knight who has sworn loyalty to a particular lord.
- **fief** A portion of land, the use of which was given by a lord to a vassal in exchange for the latter's oath of loyalty.
- **feudalism** A medieval European political system that defines the military obligations and relations between a lord and his vassals and involves the granting of fiefs.

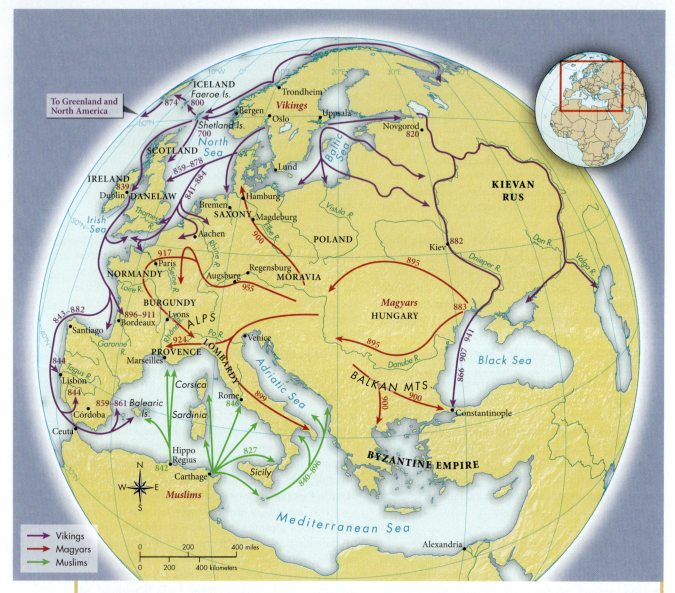

## □ Mapping the Past

**MAP 14.1 Invasions and Migrations of the Ninth and Tenth Centuries** This map shows the Viking, Magyar, and Muslim invasions and migrations in the ninth and tenth centuries. Compare it with Map 8.2 (page 221) on the barbarian migrations of late antiquity to answer the following questions.

**ANALYZING THE MAP** What similarities do you see in the patterns of migration in these two periods? What significant differences?

**CONNECTIONS** How did the Vikings' expertise in shipbuilding and sailing make their migrations different from those of earlier Germanic tribes? How did this set them apart from the Magyar and Muslim invaders of the ninth century?

idea of "feudalism" problematic, because the word was a later invention and the system was so varied and changed over time. They still point to the personal relationship between lords and vassals as the key way political authority was organized and note that the church also received and granted land.

The economic power of the warrior class rested on landed estates, which were worked by peasants under a system of **manorialism**. Free farmers surrendered themselves and their land to the lord's jurisdiction in exchange for protection. The land was given back to them to farm, but they were tied to the land by various payments and services. Most significantly, a peasant lost his or her freedom and became a **serf**, part of the lord's permanent labor force. Unlike slaves, serfs were personally free, but they were bound to the land and unable to leave it without the lord's permission.

By the year 800 perhaps 60 percent of the population of western Europe had been reduced to serfdom. Over the next several centuries unstable conditions and insecurity further increased the need for protection, so that by around 1000 the majority of western Europeans were serfs. While serfs ranged from the highly prosperous to the desperately poor, all had lost their freedom. In eastern Europe the transition was slower but longer lasting. Western European peasants began to escape from serfdom in the later Middle Ages, at the very point that serfs were more firmly tied to the land in eastern Europe, especially in eastern Germany, Poland, and Russia.

## The Restoration of Order

The eleventh century witnessed the beginnings of political stability in western Europe. Foreign invasions gradually declined, and in some parts of Europe lords in control of large territories built up their power even further, becoming kings over growing and slowly centralizing states. In a process similar to that occurring at the same time in the West African kingdom of Ghana (see pages 277–279), rulers expanded their territories and extended their authority by developing larger bureaucracies, armies, judicial systems, and other institutions to maintain control, as well as taxation systems to pay for them. These new institutions and practices laid the foundations for modern national states. Political developments in England, France, and Germany provide good examples of the beginnings of the national state in the central Middle Ages.

Throughout the ninth century the Vikings made a concerted effort to conquer and rule all of Anglo-Saxon England, and in the early eleventh century they succeeded. The Viking Canute (r. 1016–1035) made England the center of his empire, while promoting a policy of assimilation and reconciliation between Anglo-Saxons and Vikings. At the same time, England was divided into local shires, or counties, each under the jurisdiction of a sheriff appointed by the king. When Canute's heir Edward died childless, there were three claimants to the throne. One of these, Duke William of Normandy, crossed the Channel and won the English

**The Norman Conquest, 1066**

throne by defeating and killing his Anglo-Saxon rival, Harold II, at the Battle of Hastings in 1066. Later dubbed "the Conqueror," William (r. 1066–1087) limited the power of the nobles and church officials and built a unified monarchy. He retained the Anglo-Saxon institution of sheriff, but named Normans to the posts.

In 1085 William decided to conduct a systematic survey of the entire country to determine how much wealth there was and who had it. This process was described by a contemporary chronicler:

> He sent his men over all England into every shire and had them find out . . . what or how much everybody had who was occupying land in England, in land or cattle, and how much money it was worth. So very narrowly did he have it investigated, that there was no single . . . yard of land, nor indeed . . . one ox nor one cow nor one pig was there left out, and not put down in his record: and all these records were brought to him afterwards.[1]

The resulting record, called the *Domesday Book* (DOOMZ-day) from the Anglo-Saxon word *doom*, meaning "judgment," provided William and his descendants with vital information for governing the country. Completed in 1086, the book still survives, and it is an invaluable source of social and economic information about medieval England.

In 1128 William's granddaughter Matilda married a powerful French noble, Geoffrey of Anjou. Their son, who became Henry II of England, inherited provinces in northwestern France from his father. When Henry married the great heiress Eleanor of Aquitaine in 1152, he claimed lordship over Aquitaine and other provinces in southwestern France as well. The histories of England and France were thus closely intertwined in the Middle Ages.

In the early twelfth century France consisted of a number of nearly independent provinces, each governed by its local ruler. The work of unifying and enlarging France began under Philip II (r. 1180–1223), also known as Philip Augustus. By the end of his reign Philip was effectively master of northern France, and by 1300

---

- **manorialism** The economic system that governed rural life in medieval Europe, in which the landed estates of a lord were worked by the peasants under the lord's jurisdiction in exchange for his protection.

- **serf** A peasant who lost his or her freedom and became permanently bound to the landed estate of a lord.

most of the provinces of modern France had been added to the royal domain through diplomacy, marriage, war, and inheritance.

In central Europe the German king Otto I (r. 936–973) defeated many other lords to build up his power, based on an alliance with and control of the church. Otto asserted the right to control church appointments, and bishops and abbots had to perform feudal homage for the lands that accompanied their church positions. Under Otto I and his successors, a loose confederation stretching from the North Sea to the Mediterranean developed. In this confederation, later called the Holy Roman Empire, the emperor shared power with princes, dukes, counts, city officials, archbishops, and bishops.

Frederick Barbarossa (r. 1152–1190) of the house of Hohenstaufen tried valiantly to make the Holy Roman Empire a united state. He made alliances with the high nobles and even compelled the great churchmen to become his vassals. When he tried to enforce his authority over the cities of northern Italy, however, they formed a league against him in alliance with the pope, and infantrymen from the cities defeated Frederick's mounted knights. Frederick's absence from the German part of his empire allowed the princes and other rulers of independent provinces to consolidate their power there as well, and Germany did not become a unified state.

## Law and Justice

Throughout Europe in the twelfth and thirteenth centuries, the law was a hodgepodge of customs, feudal rights, and provincial practices. Rulers wanted to blend these elements into a uniform system of rules acceptable and applicable to all their peoples, though their success in doing so varied.

The French king Louis IX (r. 1226–1270) was famous for his concern for justice. Each French province, even after being made part of the kingdom of France, retained its unique laws and procedures. But Louis IX created a royal judicial system, establishing the Parlement of Paris, a kind of supreme court that heard appeals from lower courts.

Under Henry II (r. 1154–1189), England developed and extended a common law—a law common to and accepted by the entire country, unique in medieval Europe. Henry's son John (r. 1199–1216), however, met with serious disappointment after taking the throne. He lost the French province of Normandy to Philip Augustus in 1204 and spent the rest of his reign trying to win it back. Saddled with heavy debt from his father and his brother Richard (r. 1189–1199), John tried to squeeze more money from nobles and town dwellers, creating an atmosphere of resentment. When

John's military campaign failed in 1214, it was clear that the French lands that had once belonged to the English king were lost for good. A rebellion begun by northern barons grew, and in 1215 the barons forced him to attach his seal to the Magna Carta—the "Great Charter," which became the cornerstone of English justice and law.

The Magna Carta was simply meant to assert traditional rights enjoyed by certain groups, but in time it came to signify the broader principle that everyone, including the king and the government, must obey the law. Because later generations referred to the Magna Carta as a written statement of English liberties, it gradually came to have an almost sacred importance.

Statements of legal principles such as the Magna Carta were not how most people experienced the law in medieval Europe. Instead they were involved in actual cases. Judges determined guilt or innocence in a number of ways. In some cases, particularly those in which there was little clear evidence, they ordered a trial by ordeal, in which the accused might be tied hand and foot and dropped in a lake or river. People believed that water was a pure substance and would reject anything foul or unclean, although God could always affect the outcome. Thus a person who sank was considered innocent, while a person who floated was found guilty. Trials by ordeal were relatively rare, and courts increasingly favored more rational procedures, in which judges heard testimony, sought witnesses, and read written evidence if it was available. Violent crimes were often punished by public execution. Hanging was the most common method of execution, although nobles might be beheaded because hanging was seen as demeaning. Executioners were feared figures, but they were also well-paid public officials and were a necessary part of the legal structure.

# The Christian Church

☐ How did the Christian Church enhance its power and create new institutions and religious practices?

Kings and emperors were not the only rulers consolidating their power in the eleventh and twelfth centuries; the papacy did as well, although the popes' efforts were sometimes challenged by medieval kings and emperors. Despite such challenges, monasteries continued to be important places for learning and devotion, and new religious orders were founded. Christianity expanded into Europe's northern and eastern regions, and Christian rulers expanded their holdings in Muslim Spain.

**Córdoba Mosque and Cathedral**  The huge arches of the Great Mosque at Córdoba dwarf the cathedral built in its center after the city was conquered by Christian armies in 1236. During the reconquista (see page 401), Christian kings often transformed mosques into churches, often by simply adding Christian elements such as crosses and altars to existing structures. (© dbimages/Alamy)

## Papal Reforms

During the ninth and tenth centuries the church came under the control of kings and feudal lords, who chose priests, bishops, abbots, and other church officials in their territories, granting them fiefs that provided an income and expecting loyalty and service in return. Church offices were sometimes sold outright—a practice called *simony*. Although the Roman Church encouraged clerical celibacy, many priests were married or living with women. Wealthy Roman families chose popes from among their members; thus popes paid more attention to their families' political fortunes or their own pleasures than to the church's institutional or spiritual health. Not surprisingly, clergy at all levels who had bought their positions or had been granted them for political reasons provided little spiritual guidance and were rarely models of high moral standards.

Serious efforts to reform the church began in the eleventh century. A series of popes believed that secular or lay control over the church was largely responsible for the lack of moral leadership, so they proclaimed the church independent from secular rulers. The Lateran Council of 1059 decreed that the authority and power to elect the pope rested solely in the college of cardinals, a special group of priests from the major churches in and around Rome. The college retains that power today.

Pope Gregory VII (pontificate 1073–1085) vigorously championed reform and the expansion of papal power. He ordered all priests to give up their wives and children or face dismissal, invalidated the ordination of church officials who had purchased their offices, and placed nuns under firmer control of male authorities. He believed that the pope, as the successor of Saint Peter, was the vicar of God on earth and that papal orders were the orders of God. He emphasized the political authority of the papacy, ordering that any church official selected or appointed by a layperson should be deposed, and any layperson, including rulers, who appointed a church official should be excommunicated—cut off from the sacraments and the Christian community.

European rulers immediately protested this restriction of their power, and the strongest reaction came from Henry IV, the ruler of Germany who later became

# Individuals in Society

## Hildegard of Bingen

**THE TENTH CHILD OF A LESSER NOBLE FAMILY, HILDEGARD** (1098–1179) was turned over to the care of an abbey in the Rhineland when she was eight years old. There she learned Latin and received a good education. She spent most of her life in various women's religious communities, two of which she founded herself. When she was a child, she began having mystical visions, often of light in the sky, but told few people about them. In middle age, however, her visions became more dramatic: "And it came to pass . . . when I was 42 years and 7 months old, that the heavens were opened and a blinding light of exceptional brilliance flowed through my entire brain. And so it kindled my whole heart and breast like a flame, not burning but warming . . . and suddenly I understood of the meaning of expositions of the books."* She wanted the church to approve of her visions and wrote first to Saint Bernard of Clairvaux, who answered her briefly and dismissively, and then to Pope Eugenius, who encouraged her to write them down. Her first work was *Scivias* (Know the Ways of the Lord), a record of her mystical visions that incorporates extensive theological learning.

Obviously possessed of leadership and administrative talents, Hildegard left her abbey in 1147 to found the convent of Rupertsberg near Bingen. There she produced *Physica* (On the Physical Elements) and *Causa et Curae* (Causes and Cures), scientific works on the curative properties of natural elements; poems; a religious play; and several more works of mysticism. She carried on a huge correspondence with scholars, prelates, and ordinary people. When she was over fifty, she left her community to preach to audiences of clergy and laity, and she was the only woman of her time whose opinions on religious matters were considered authoritative by the church.

Hildegard's visions have been explored by theologians and also by neurologists, who judge that they may have originated in migraine headaches, as she reports many of the same phenomena that migraine sufferers do: auras of light around objects, areas of blindness, feelings of intense doubt and intense euphoria. The interpretations that she develops come from her theological insight and learning, however, not from her illness. That same insight also emerges in her music, which is what she is best known for today. Eighty of her compositions survive—a huge number for a medieval composer—most of them written to be sung by the nuns in her convent, so they have strong lines for female voices. Many of her songs and chants have been recorded recently by various artists and are available on compact disk, as downloads, and on several Web sites.

Inspired by heavenly fire, Hildegard begins to dictate her visions to her scribe. The original of this elaborately illustrated copy of *Scivias* disappeared from Hildegard's convent during World War II, but fortunately a facsimile had already been made. (Private Collection/The Bridgeman Art Library)

### QUESTIONS FOR ANALYSIS

1. Why do you think Hildegard might have kept her visions secret at first? Why do you think she eventually sought church approval for them?

2. In what ways were Hildegard's accomplishments extraordinary given women's general status in the Middle Ages?

*From *Scivias*, trans. Mother Columba Hart and Jane Bishop, *The Classics of Western Spirituality* (New York/Mahwah: Paulist Press, 1990).

## LaunchPad
### Online Document Project

**Why was Hildegard of Bingen considered a worthy instrument for the transmission of God's word?** Read excerpts from Hildegard's correspondence, and then complete a quiz and writing assignment based on the evidence and details from this chapter.

*See inside the front cover to learn more.*

the Holy Roman emperor. Henry continued to appoint officials, and Gregory responded by excommunicating bishops who supported Henry and threatening to depose him. In January 1077 Henry arrived at the pope's residence in Canossa in northern Italy and, according to a letter later sent by Gregory to his German allies, stood outside in the snow for three days seeking forgiveness. Gregory readmitted the emperor into the Christian community. Although Henry bowed before the pope, he actually won a victory, maintaining authority over his subjects and in 1084 being crowned emperor. This victory was temporary, however, for high nobles within the empire took advantage of further conflicts with the pope to enhance their position, siding with the church to gain power. They subordinated lesser nobles, expanded restrictions on peasants, and prevented later emperors such as Frederick Barbarossa from unifying the empire.

## Monastic Life

Although they were in theory cut off from the world (see page 216), monasteries and convents were deeply affected by issues of money, rank, and power. By the eighth century monasteries and convents dotted the European landscape, and during the ninth and tenth centuries they were often the target of Viking attacks or raids by local looters seeking valuable objects. Some religious communities fled and dispersed, while others fell under the control and domination of local feudal lords. Powerful laymen appointed themselves or their relatives as abbots, took the lands and goods of monasteries, and spent monastic revenues.

Medieval monasteries also provided noble boys with education and opportunities for ecclesiastical careers. Although a few men who rose in the ranks of church officials were of humble origins, most were from high-status families. Social class also defined the kinds of religious life open to women. Kings and nobles usually established convents for their female relatives and other elite women, and the position of abbess, or head of a convent, became the most powerful position a woman could hold in medieval society. (See "Individuals in Society: Hildegard of Bingen," at left.) People of lower social standing did live and work in monasteries, but as lay brothers and sisters who performed manual labor, not religious duties.

Routines within individual monasteries varied widely from house to house and from region to region. In every monastery, however, daily life centered on the liturgy or Divine Office, psalms, and other prayers, which monks and nuns said seven times a day and once during the night. Praying was looked on as a vital service, as crucial as the labor of peasants and the military might of nobles. Prayers were said for peace, rain, good harvests, the civil authorities, the monks' and nuns' families, and their benefactors. Monastic patrons in turn lavished gifts on the monasteries, which often became very wealthy, controlling large tracts of land and the peasants who farmed them.

The combination of lay control and wealth created problems for monasteries as monks and nuns concentrated on worldly issues and spiritual observance and intellectual activity declined. To counteract this problem, new religious orders, such as the Cistercians (sihs-TUHR-shuhnz), founded in 1098, established their houses in isolated areas, rejected the traditional feudal sources of income (such as the possession of mills and serfs), and lived very simply. Their innovative methods of farming, sheep raising, and cloth production brought financial success, however, and by the late twelfth century economic prosperity and political power had begun to compromise the original Cistercian ideals.

In the thirteenth century the growth of cities provided a new challenge for the church. Many urban people thought that the church did not meet their spiritual needs. They turned instead to heresies—that is, to versions of Christianity outside of those approved by the papacy, many of which called on the church to give up its wealth and power. Combating **heresy** became a principal task of new religious orders, most prominently the Dominicans and Franciscans, who preached and ministered to city dwellers; the Dominicans also staffed the papal Inquisition, a special court designed to root out heresy.

## Popular Religion

Apart from the land, the weather, and local legal and social conditions, religion had the greatest impact on the daily lives of ordinary people in medieval Europe. Religious practices varied widely from country to country and even from province to province. But everywhere, religion permeated everyday life.

For Christians, the village church was the center of community life—social, political, and economic as well as religious—with the parish priest in charge of a host of activities. People gathered at the church for services on Sundays and holy days, breaking the painful routine of work. The feasts that accompanied baptisms, weddings, funerals, and other celebrations were commonly held in the churchyard. In everyday life people engaged in rituals and used language heavy with religious symbolism. Before planting began on local lands, the village priest customarily went out and sprinkled the fields with water, symbolizing renewal

---

• **heresy** An opinion, belief, or action counter to doctrines that church leaders defined as correct; heretics could be punished by the church.

and life. Everyone participated in village processions to honor the saints and ask their protection. The entire calendar was designed with reference to Christmas, Easter, and Pentecost, events in the life of Jesus and his disciples.

The Christian calendar was also filled with saints' days. Saints were individuals who had lived particularly holy lives and were honored locally or more widely for their connection with the divine. Veneration of the saints had been an important tool of Christian conversion since late antiquity (see Chapter 8), and the cult of the saints was a central feature of popular culture in the Middle Ages. People believed that the saints possessed supernatural powers that enabled them to perform miracles, and each saint became the special property of the locality in which his or her relics—remains or possessions—rested. In return for the saint's healing powers and support, peasants would offer prayers, loyalty, and gifts. The Virgin Mary, Christ's mother, became the most important saint, with churches built in her honor and special hymns, prayers, and ceremonies created.

Most people in medieval Europe were Christian, but there were small Jewish communities scattered through many parts of Europe, as well as Muslims in the Iberian Peninsula, Sicily, other Mediterranean islands, and southeastern Europe. Increasing suspicion and hostility marked relations among believers in different religions throughout the Middle Ages, but there were also important similarities in the ways that European Christians, Jews, and Muslims understood and experienced their faiths. In all three traditions, every major life transition was marked by a ceremony that involved religious officials or spiritual elements. In all three faiths, death was marked by religious rituals, and the living had obligations to the dead, including prayers and special mourning periods.

## The Expansion of Christianity

The eleventh and twelfth centuries saw not only reforms in monasticism and the papacy but also an expansion of Christianity into Scandinavia, the Baltic lands, eastern Europe, and Spain that had profound cultural consequences. The expansion was accomplished through wars, the establishment of new bishoprics, and the vast migration of Christian colonists into non-Christian territories. As it occurred, more and more Europeans began to think of themselves as belonging to a realm of Christianity that was political as well as religious, a realm they called Christendom.

Christian influences entered Scandinavia and the Baltic lands primarily through the creation of dioceses (church districts headed by bishops). This took place in Denmark and Norway in the tenth and eleventh centuries, and then in Sweden and Finland. In all of these areas, Christian missionaries preached, baptized, and built churches. Royal power advanced institutional Christianity, and traditional Norse religions practiced by the Vikings were outlawed. In eastern Europe the German emperor Otto I (see page 396) planted a string of dioceses along his northern and eastern frontiers, hoping to pacify the newly conquered Slavs in eastern Europe. German nobles built castles and ruthlessly crushed revolts by Slavic peoples.

The church also moved into central Europe, first into Bohemia in the tenth century and from there into Poland and Hungary in the eleventh century. In the twelfth and thirteenth centuries thousands of settlers poured into eastern Europe from the west. These new immigrants, German in descent, name, language, and

**Statue of Saint Anne, the Virgin Mary, and the Christ Child**   Nearly every church had at least one image of the Virgin Mary, the most important figure of Christian devotion in medieval Europe. In this thirteenth-century wooden sculpture, she is shown holding the infant Jesus, and is herself sitting on the lap of her mother, Anne. Statues such as this reinforced people's sense that the heavenly family was much like theirs, with grandparents who sometimes played important roles. (Museo Nazionale del Bargello, Florence, Italy/Scala/Art Resource, NY)

law, settled in Silesia, Mecklenburg, Bohemia, Poland, Hungary, and Transylvania, where they established towns.

The Iberian Peninsula was another area of Christian expansion. In about 950 Caliph Abd al-Rahman III (912–961) of the Umayyad Dynasty of Córdoba ruled most of the peninsula. Christian Spain consisted of the small kingdoms of Castile, León, Catalonia, Aragon, Navarre, and Portugal. In the eleventh century divisions and civil wars in the caliphate of Córdoba allowed Christian armies to conquer an increasingly large part of the Iberian Peninsula. By 1248 Christians held all of the peninsula save for the small state of Granada in the south. As the Christians advanced, they changed the face of Spanish cities, transforming mosques into cathedrals.

Fourteenth-century clerical writers would call the movement to expel the Muslims the **reconquista** (ray-kon-KEES-tah; reconquest)—a sacred and patriotic crusade to wrest the country from "alien" Muslim hands. This religious idea became part of Spanish political culture and of the national psychology. Rulers of the Christian kingdoms of Spain increasingly passed legislation discriminating against Muslims and Jews living under Christian rule, and they attempted to exclude anyone from the nobility who could not prove "purity of blood"—that is, that they had no Muslim or Jewish ancestors. As a consequence of the reconquista, the Spanish and Portuguese also learned how to administer vast tracts of newly acquired territory. In the sixteenth century they used their claims about the rightful dominance of Christianity to justify their colonization of new territories in Mexico, Brazil, Peru, Angola, and the Philippines and relied on their experiences at home to provide models of how to govern.

Spain was not the only place in Europe where "blood" became a way of understanding differences among people and a basis for discriminatory laws. When Germans moved into eastern Europe and English forces took over much of Ireland, they increasingly barred local people from access to legal courts and denied them positions in monasteries or craft guilds. They banned intermarriage between ethnic groups in an attempt to maintain ethnic purity, even though everyone was Christian. As Europeans later came into contact with people from Africa and Asia, and particularly as they developed colonial empires there, these notions of blood also became a way of conceptualizing racial categories.

Date of Christian reconquest

- By 814
- By 910
- By 1037
- By 1097
- By 1150
- By 1190
- By 1275
- By 1492

FRANCE
LEÓN
NAVARRE
ARAGON
CASTILE
PORTUGAL
GRANADA
ATLANTIC OCEAN
Mediterranean Sea
AFRICA

**The Reconquista, ca. 750–1492**

# The Crusades

❑ What were the causes, course, and consequences of the Crusades?

The expansion of Christianity in the Middle Ages was not limited to Europe but extended to the eastern Mediterranean in what were later termed the **Crusades**. Occurring in the late eleventh and early twelfth centuries, the Crusades were wars sponsored by the papacy to recover the holy city of Jerusalem from the Muslims. The word *crusade* was not actually used at the time and did not appear in English until the late sixteenth century. It means literally "taking the cross," a vow to spread Christianity symbolized by the cross that soldiers sewed on their garments. Although people of all ages and classes participated in the Crusades, so many knights did that crusading became a distinctive feature of the upper-class lifestyle. In an aristocratic military society, men coveted reputations as Crusaders; the Christian knight who had been to Jerusalem enjoyed great prestige.

## Background and Motives

In the eleventh century the papacy had strong reasons for wanting to launch an expedition against Muslims in the East. If the pope could muster a large army against the enemies of Christianity, his claim to be the leader of Christian society in the West would be strengthened. Moreover, in 1054 a serious theological disagreement had split the Greek Church of Byzantium and the Roman Church of the West. The pope believed that a crusade would lead to strong Roman influence in Greek territories and eventually the reunion of the two churches.

Popes and other church officials gained support for war in defense of Christianity by promising spiritual benefits to those who joined a campaign or died fighting. Church leaders said that these people would be forgiven for their sins without having to do penance, that is, without having to confess to a priest and carry

- **reconquista** A fourteenth-century term used to describe the long Christian crusade to wrest Spain back from the Muslims; clerics believed it was a sacred and patriotic mission.

- **Crusades** Holy wars sponsored by the papacy for the recovery of the Holy Land from the Muslims.

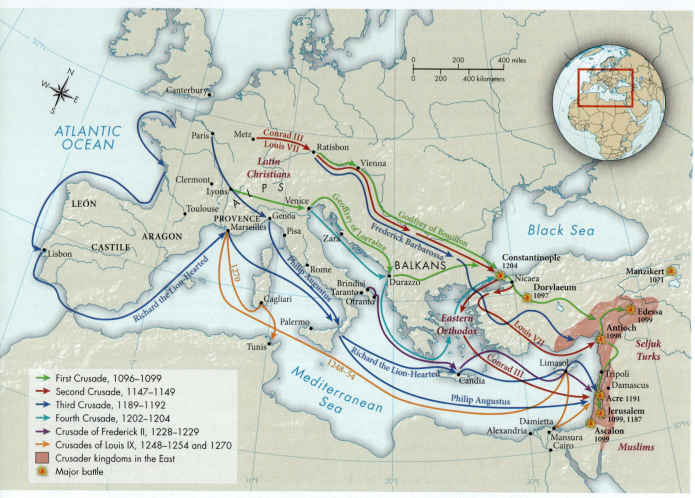

**MAP 14.2 The Crusades, 1096–1270** The Crusaders took many different sea and land routes on their way to Jerusalem, often crossing the lands of the Byzantine Empire, which led to conflict with Eastern Christians. The Crusader kingdoms in the East lasted only briefly.

Legend on map:
- First Crusade, 1096–1099
- Second Crusade, 1147–1149
- Third Crusade, 1189–1192
- Fourth Crusade, 1202–1204
- Crusade of Frederick II, 1228–1229
- Crusades of Louis IX, 1248–1254 and 1270
- Crusader kingdoms in the East
- Major battle

out some action to make up for the sins. Preachers communicated these ideas widely and told stories about warrior-saints who slew hundreds of enemies.

Religious zeal led increasing numbers of people to go on pilgrimages to holy places, including Jerusalem. The Arab Muslims who had ruled Jerusalem and the surrounding territory for centuries allowed Christian pilgrims to travel freely, but in the late eleventh century the Seljuk Turks took over Palestine, defeating both Arab and Byzantine armies, and pilgrimage became more difficult. The Byzantine emperor at Constantinople appealed to western European Christians for support. The emperor's appeal fit well with papal aims, and in 1095 Pope Urban II called for a great Christian holy war against the infidels—a term Christians and Muslims both used to describe the other. Urban urged Christian knights who had been fighting one another to direct their energies against those he claimed were the true enemies of God, the Muslims.

## The Course of the Crusades

Thousands of people of all classes responded to Urban's call, streaming southward and then toward Jerusalem in what became known as the First Crusade. The First Crusade was successful, mostly because of the dynamic enthusiasm of the participants, who had little more than religious zeal. They knew little of the geography or climate of the Middle East, and although there were several counts with military experience, the Crusaders could never agree on a leader. Adding to these disadvantages, supply lines were never set up, starvation and disease wracked the army, and the Turks slaughtered hundreds of noncombatants. Nevertheless, the army pressed on, besieging and taking several cities, including Antioch. (See "Viewpoints 14.1: Christian and Muslim Views of the Fall of Antioch," at right.) After a monthlong siege, the Crusaders took Jerusalem in July 1099 (Map 14.2). Fulcher of Chartres, a chaplain on

# Viewpoints 14.1

## Christian and Muslim Views of the Fall of Antioch

• *Christian and Muslim accounts of the Crusades differ in their basic perspectives—were they a holy war or an invasion?—and sometimes also in their details, which can be revealing. In June 1098 the Crusaders captured the city of Antioch after a siege of more than seven months. They were assisted in this by an Armenian Christian convert to Islam named Firouz, an armor maker and official in the government of Yaghi-Siyan, the Seljuk Turkish ruler of Antioch. The* Gesta Francorum *[The Deeds of the Franks], written by an anonymous Crusader who was an eyewitness, provides a Christian view of this event, and the history of Ibn al-Athir (1160–1223) provides a Muslim view.*

### Gesta Francorum

There was a certain Emir [ruler] of the race of the Turks, whose name was Pirus [i.e., Firouz], who took up the greatest friendship with Bohemund [a Norman leader of the Crusades]. By an interchange of messengers Bohemund often pressed this man to receive him within the city in a most friendly fashion, and, after promising Christianity to him most freely, he sent word that he would make him rich with much honor. Pirus yielded to these words and promises, saying, "I guard three towers, and I freely promise them to him, and at whatever hour he wishes I will receive him within them." . . . All the night they [the Crusaders] rode and marched until dawn, and then began to approach the towers which that person (Pirus) was watchfully guarding. Bohemund straightaway dismounted and gave orders to the rest, saying, "Go with secure mind and happy accord, and climb by ladder into Antioch which, if it please God, we shall have in our power immediately." . . . Now the men began to climb up there in wondrous fashion. Then they reached the top and ran in haste to the other towers. Those whom they found there they straightaway sentenced to death; they even killed a brother of Pirus. . . . [Then] all ran to [a certain gate], and, having broken it open, we entered through it. . . . But Cassianus [Yaghi-Siyan], their lord, fearing the race of the Franks greatly, took flight with the many others who were with him. . . . They killed the Turks and Saracens whom they found there. . . . All the squares of the city were already everywhere full of the corpses of the dead, so that no one could endure it there for the excessive stench. No one could go along a street of the city except over the bodies of the dead.

### Ibn al-Athir

After the siege had been going on for a long time the Franks made a deal with . . . a cuirass [breastplate] maker called Ruzbih [Firouz] whom they bribed with a fortune in money and lands. He worked in the tower that stood over the riverbed, where the river flowed out of the city into the valley. The Franks sealed their pact with the cuirass-maker, God damn him! and made their way to the water-gate. They opened it and entered the city. Another gang of them climbed the tower with ropes. At dawn, when more than 500 of them were in the city and the defenders were worn out after the night watch, they sounded their trumpets. . . . Panic seized Yaghi-Siyan and he opened the city gates and fled in terror, with an escort of thirty pages. His army commander arrived, but when he discovered on enquiry that Yaghi-Siyan had fled, he made his escape by another gate. This was of great help to the Franks, for if he had stood firm for an hour, they would have been wiped out. They entered the city by the gates and sacked it, slaughtering all the Muslims they found there.

Sources: Edward Peters, ed., *The First Crusade: The Chronicle of Fulcher of Chartres and Other Source Materials* (Philadelphia: University of Pennsylvania Press, 1971), pp. 163–166. Copyright © 1971 by the University of Pennsylvania Press. Reprinted by permission of the University of Pennsylvania Press; *Arab Historians of the Crusades*, selected and translated from the Arabic sources by Francesco Gabrieli. Translated from the Italian by E. J. Costello. © 1969 by Routledge & Kegan Paul Ltd. Reproduced by permission of Taylor & Francis Books UK and The University of California Press.

### QUESTIONS FOR ANALYSIS

1. Why did Firouz agree to help the Crusaders, according to the two accounts? Why do you think they differ in this regard?

2. Do either of the two accounts recognize that many people in Antioch, including Firouz and his brother, were Christian? Do you think the Crusaders recognized this?

3. What other similarities and differences do you see in the two accounts?

the First Crusade, described the scene:

> Amid the sound of trumpets and with everything in an uproar they attacked boldly, shouting "God help us!" . . . They ran with the greatest exultation as fast as they could into the city and joined their companions in pursuing and slaying their wicked enemies without cessation. . . . If you had been there your feet would have been stained to the ankles in the blood of the slain. What shall I say? None of them were left alive. Neither women nor children were spared.[2]

With Jerusalem taken, some Crusaders regarded their mission as accomplished and set off for home, but the appearance of more Muslim troops convinced other Crusaders that they needed to stay. Slowly institutions were set up to rule local territories and the Muslim population. Four small "Crusader states"—Jerusalem, Edessa, Tripoli, and Antioch—were established, and castles and fortified towns were built in these states to defend against Muslim reconquest. Reinforcements arrived in the form of pilgrims and fighters from Europe, so that there was constant coming and going by land and more often by sea after the Crusaders conquered port cities. Most Crusaders were men, but some women came along as well, assisting in the besieging of towns and castles by providing water to fighting men or foraging for food, working as washerwomen, and providing sexual services.

Between 1096 and 1270 the crusading ideal was expressed in eight papally approved expeditions, though none after the First Crusade accomplished very much. The Muslim states in the Middle East were politically fragmented when the Crusaders first came, and it took them about a century to reorganize. They did so dramatically under Saladin (Salah al-Din), who unified Egypt and Syria. In 1187 the Muslims retook Jerusalem, but the Christians held onto port towns, and Saladin allowed pilgrims safe passage to Jerusalem. From that point on, the Crusader states were more important economically than politically or religiously, giving Italian and French merchants direct access to Eastern products such as perfumes and silk.

After the Muslims retook Jerusalem, the crusading movement faced other setbacks. During the Fourth Crusade (1202–1204), Crusaders stopped in Constantinople, and when they were not welcomed, they sacked the city and grabbed thousands of relics, which were later sold in Europe. The Byzantine Empire splintered into three parts and soon consisted of little more than the city of Constantinople. Moreover, the assault of one Christian people on another—when one of the goals of the Crusades was reunion of the Greek and Latin Churches—made the split between the churches

permanent and discredited the entire crusading movement in the eyes of many Christians.

In the late thirteenth century Turkish armies, after gradually conquering all other Muslim rulers, turned against the Crusader states. In 1291 the Christians' last stronghold, the port of Acre, fell in a battle that was just as bloody as the first battle for Jerusalem two centuries earlier. Knights then needed a new battlefield for military actions, which some found in Spain, where the rulers of Aragon and Castile continued fighting Muslims until 1492.

## Consequences of the Crusades

The Crusades testified to the religious enthusiasm of the High Middle Ages and the influence of the papacy, gave kings and the pope opportunities to expand their bureaucracies, and provided an outlet for nobles' dreams of glory. The Crusades also introduced some Europeans to Eastern luxury goods, but their immediate cultural impact on the West remains debatable. By the late eleventh century there were already strong economic and intellectual ties with the East; however, the Crusades were a boon to Italian merchants, who profited from outfitting military expeditions as well as from the opening of new trade routes and the establishment of trading communities in the Crusader states.

Despite these advantages, the Crusades had some seriously negative sociopolitical consequences. For one thing, they proved to be a disaster for Jewish-Christian relations. Inspired by the ideology of holy war, Christian armies on their way to Jerusalem on the First Crusade joined with local mobs to attack Jewish families and communities, sometimes burning people alive in the synagogue or Jewish section of town. Later Crusades brought similar violence, enhanced by accusations that Jews engaged in the ritual murder of Christians to use their blood in religious rites.

Legal restrictions on Jews gradually increased throughout Europe. Jews were forbidden to have Christian servants or employees, to hold public office, to appear in public on Christian holy days, or to enter Christian parts of town without a badge marking them as Jews. They were prohibited from engaging in any trade with Christians except money-lending and were banished from England and France.

The Crusades also left an inheritance of deep bitterness in Christian-Muslim relations. Each side dehumanized the other, viewing those who followed the other religion as unbelievers. Whereas Europeans perceived the Crusades as sacred religious movements, Muslims saw them as expansionist and imperialistic. The ideal of a sacred mission to conquer or convert Muslim peoples entered Europeans' consciousness and became a continuing goal. When in 1492 Christopher

Columbus sailed west, he used the language of the Crusades in his diaries, and he hoped to establish a Christian base in India from which a new crusade against Islam could be launched (see page 467).

# The Life of the People

☐ How did the lives of common people, nobles, and townspeople differ, and what new commercial developments increased wealth?

In the late ninth century medieval intellectuals described Christian society as composed of those who pray (the monks), those who fight (the nobles), and those who work (the peasants). This image of society became popular in the Middle Ages, especially among people who were worried about the changes they saw around them. They asserted that the three categories of citizens had been established by God and that every person had been assigned a fixed place in the social order.

This three-category model does not fully describe medieval society—there were degrees of wealth and status within each group. Also, the model does not take townspeople and the emerging commercial classes into consideration, and it completely excludes those who were not Christian, such as Jews, Muslims, and

pagans. Furthermore, those who used the model, generally bishops and other church officials, ignored the fact that each of these groups was made up of both women and men; they spoke only of warriors, monks, and farmers. Despite—or perhaps because of—these limitations, the model of the three categories was a powerful mental construct. Therefore, we can use it to organize our investigation of life in the Middle Ages, broadening it to include groups and issues that medieval authors did not. (See page 399 for a discussion of the life of monks and nuns—"those who pray.")

## The Life and Work of Peasants

The men and women who worked the land in medieval Europe made up probably more than 90 percent of the population, as they did in China, India, and other parts of the world where agriculture predominated. The evolution of localized systems of authority into more centralized states had relatively little impact on the daily lives of these peasants except when it involved warfare. While only nobles fought, their battles often destroyed the houses, barns, and fields of ordinary people, who might also be killed either directly or as a result of the famine and disease that often accompanied war. Villagers might seek protection in the local castle during times of war, but typically they worked and lived without paying much attention to political developments within castle walls.

**Agricultural Work** In this scene from a German manuscript written about 1190, men and women of different ages are sowing seeds and harvesting grain. All residents of a village, including children, engaged in agricultural tasks. (Rheinisches Landesmuseum, Bonn, Germany/Giraudon/The Bridgeman Art Library)

At the same time, since villagers did not perform what were considered "noble" deeds, the aristocratic monks and clerics who wrote the records that serve as historical sources did not spend time or precious writing materials on them. So it is more difficult to find information on the majority of Europeans who were peasants than on the small group at the top of society.

Medieval theologians lumped everyone who worked the land into the category of "those who work," but in fact there were many levels of peasants, ranging from slaves to free and sometimes very rich farmers. Most peasants were serfs, required to stay in the village and perform labor on the lord's land. The number of workdays varied, but serfs usually worked three days a week except in the planting or harvest seasons, when the number of days increased. Serfs were also often obliged to pay fees on common occurrences, such as marriage or inheritance of property. A free person had to do none of these things.

Serfdom was a hereditary condition. A person born a serf was likely to die a serf, though many serfs did secure their freedom, and the economic revival that began in the eleventh century (see pages 407–410) allowed some to buy their freedom. Further opportunities for increased personal freedom came when lords organized groups of villagers to migrate to sparsely settled frontier areas or to cut down forests or fill in swamps so that there was more land available for farming. Those who took on this extra work often gained a reduction in traditional manorial obligations and an improvement of their social and legal conditions.

In the Middle Ages most European peasants, free and unfree, lived in family groups in small villages that were part of a manor, the estate of a lord (see page 393). The manor was the basic unit of medieval rural organization and the center of rural life. Within the manors of western and central Europe, villages were made up of small houses for individual families, a church, and perhaps the large house of the lord. Peasant households consisted of one married couple, their children (including stepchildren), and perhaps one or two other relatives, such as a grandparent or unmarried aunt. In southern and eastern Europe, extended families were more likely to live in the same household or very near

**Baking Bread** In this fourteenth-century French manuscript, women bake bread in a large oven, using a long wooden paddle to insert the loaves, just as modern pizza bakers do. Medieval families cooked in pots and on spits over fires in their own homes, but rarely had ovens because of the danger of fire. Instead they bought their bread, just as they did beer or ale, another staple of the medieval diet. (The Granger Collection, New York — All rights reserved.)

one another. Between one-third and one-half of children died before age five, though many people lived into their sixties.

The arable land of the manor was divided between the lord and the peasantry, with the lord's portion known as the demesne (dih-MAYN) or home farm. A peasant family's land was not usually one particular field but a scattering of strips across many fields, some of which would be planted in grain, some in other crops, and some left unworked to allow the soil to rejuvenate. That way if one field yielded little, strips in a different field might be more bountiful.

The peasants' work was typically divided according to gender. Men and boys were responsible for clearing new land, plowing, and caring for large animals; women and girls were responsible for the care of small animals, spinning, and food preparation. Both sexes harvested and planted, though often there were gender-specific tasks within each of these major undertakings. Women and men worked in the vineyards and in the harvest and preparation of crops needed by the textile industry—flax and plants used for dyeing cloth. Beginning in the eleventh century water mills and windmills aided in some tasks, especially grinding grain, and an increasing use of horses rather than oxen speeded up plowing.

The mainstay of the diet for peasants everywhere—and for all other classes—was bread. Peasants also ate vegetables; animals were too valuable to be used for food on a regular basis, but weaker animals were often slaughtered in the fall so that they did not need to be fed through the winter, and their meat was preserved with salt and eaten on great feast days such as Christmas and Easter. Ale was the universal drink of common people, and it provided needed calories and some relief from the difficult and monotonous labor that filled people's lives.

## The Life and Work of Nobles

The nobility, though a small fraction of the total population, influenced all aspects of medieval culture. Despite political, scientific, and industrial revolutions, nobles continued to hold real political and social power in Europe into the nineteenth century.

In the early Middle Ages noble status was limited to a very few families, but in the eleventh century knights in service to kings began to claim such status because it gave them special legal privileges. Nobles generally paid few taxes, and they had power over the people living on their lands. They maintained order, resolved disputes, and protected their dependents from attacks. They appointed officials who oversaw agricultural production. The liberty and privileges of the noble were inheritable, perpetuated by blood and not by wealth alone.

The nobles' primary obligation was warfare, just as it was for nobles among the Mexica (see pages 315–319) and the samurai in Japan (see page 384). Nobles were also obliged to attend the lord's court on important occasions when the lord wanted to put on great displays, such as on religious holidays or the wedding of a son or daughter.

Originally, most knights focused solely on military skills, but around 1200 a different ideal of knighthood emerged, usually termed **chivalry**. Chivalry was a code of conduct in which fighting to defend the Christian faith and protecting one's countrymen was declared to have a sacred purpose. Other qualities gradually became part of chivalry: bravery, generosity, honor, graciousness, mercy, and eventually gallantry toward women, which came to be called "courtly love." (See "Listening to the Past: Courtly Love Poetry," page 408.) The chivalric ideal—and it was an ideal, not a standard pattern of behavior—created a new standard of masculinity for nobles, in which loyalty and honor remained the most important qualities, but graceful dancing and intelligent conversation were not considered unmanly.

Noblewomen played a large and important role in the functioning of the estate. They were responsible for managing the household's "inner economy"—cooking, brewing, spinning, weaving, and caring for yard animals. When the lord was away for long periods, his wife became the sole manager of the family properties. Often the responsibilities of the estate fell permanently to her if she became a widow.

## Towns, Cities, and the Growth of Commercial Interests

Most people continued to live in villages in the Middle Ages, but the rise of towns and the growth of a new business and commercial class were central to Europe's recovery after the disorders of the tenth century. Several factors contributed to this growth: a rise in population; increased agricultural output, which provided an adequate food supply for new town dwellers; and enough peace and political stability to allow merchants to transport and sell goods.

Towns in Europe were generally enclosed by walls as were towns in China, India, and the Middle East. (The terms *burgher* and *bourgeois* derive from the Old English and Old German words *burg*, *burgh*, *borg*, and *borough* for "a walled or fortified place.") Most towns were first established as trading centers, with a marketplace in the middle, and they were likely to have a mint for coining money and a court for settling disputes. In each town, many people inhabited a small, cramped area. As population increased, towns rebuilt their walls,

• **chivalry** A code of conduct that was supposed to govern the behavior of a knight.

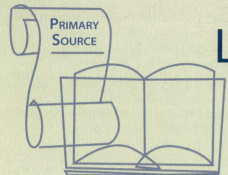

# Listening to the Past

## Courtly Love Poetry

*Whether female or male, troubadour poets celebrated* fin'amor, *a Provençal word for the pure or perfect love a knight was supposed to feel for his lady, which has in English come to be called "courtly love." In courtly love poetry, the writer praises his or her love object, idealizing the beloved and promising loyalty and great deeds. Most of these songs are written by, or from the perspective of, a male lover who is socially beneath his female beloved; her higher status makes her unattainable, so the lover's devotion can remain chaste and pure, rewarded by her handkerchief, or perhaps a kiss, but nothing more.*

*Scholars generally agree that poetry praising pure and perfect love originated in the Muslim culture of the Iberian Peninsula, where heterosexual romantic love had long been the subject of poems and songs. Spanish Muslim poets sang at the courts of Christian nobles, and Provençal poets picked up their romantic themes. Other aspects of courtly love are hotly debated. Was it simply a literary convention, or did it shape actual behavior? Did it celebrate adultery, or was true courtly love pure (and unrequited)? How should we interpret medieval physicians' reports of people (mostly young men) becoming gravely ill from "lovesickness"? Were there actually "courts of love" in which women judged lovers based on a system of rules? Did courtly love lead to greater respect for women or toward greater misogyny, as desire for a beloved so often ended in frustration?*

*It is very difficult to know whether courtly love literature influenced the treatment of real women to any great extent, but it did introduce a new ideal of heterosexual romance into Western literature. Courtly love ideals still shape romantic conventions, and often appear in movies, songs, and novels that explore love between people of different social groups.*

*The following poem was written by Arnaut Daniel, a thirteenth-century troubadour praised by poets from Dante in the thirteenth century to Ezra Pound in the twentieth. Not much is known about him, but his surviving songs capture courtly love conventions perfectly.*

I only know the grief that comes to me,
to my love-ridden heart, out of over-loving,
since my will is so firm and whole
that it never parted or grew distant from her
whom I craved at first sight, and afterwards:
and now, in her absence, I tell her burning words;
then, when I see her, I don't know, so much I have to, what
    to say.

To the sight of other women I am blind, deaf to hearing them
since her only I see, and hear and heed,
and in that I am surely not a false slanderer,
since heart desires her more than mouth may say;
wherever I may roam through fields and valleys, plains and
    mountains
I shan't find in a single person all those qualities
which God wanted to select and place in her.

I have been in many a good court,
but here by her I find much more to praise:
measure and wit and other good virtues,
beauty and youth, worthy deeds and fair disport;
so well kindness taught and instructed her
that it has rooted every ill manner out of her:
I don't think she lacks anything good.

No joy would be brief or short
coming from her whom I endear to guess [my intentions],
otherwise she won't know them from me,
if my heart cannot reveal itself without words,
since even the Rhone [River], when rain swells it,
has no such rush that my heart doesn't stir
a stronger one, weary of love, when I behold her.

Joy and merriment from another woman seems false and ill
    to me,
since no worthy one can compare with her,
and her company is above the others'.
Ah me, if I don't have her, alas, so badly she has taken me!
But this grief is amusement, laughter and joy,
since in thinking of her, of her am I gluttonous and greedy:
ah me, God, could I ever enjoy her otherwise!

And never, I swear, I have liked game or ball so much,
or anything has given my heart so much joy
as did the one thing that no false slanderer
made public, which is a treasure for me only.
Do I tell too much? Not I, unless she is displeased:
beautiful one, by God, speech and voice
I'd lose ere I say something to annoy you.

And I pray my song does not displease you
since, if you like the music and lyrics,
little cares Arnaut whether the unpleasant ones like them
    as well.

Desire for his beloved has so tormented the poet in this thirteenth-century manuscript that his cheeks are flushed and he has become literally bedridden with lovesickness. (Heinrich Von Morungen [ca. 1150–1222], German poet. *Codex Manesse* [ca. 1300]/Photo © Tarker/The Bridgeman Art Library)

*Far fewer poems by female trobairitz have survived than by male troubadours, but those that have survived express strong physical and emotional feelings. The following song was written in the twelfth century by the Countess of Dia. She was purportedly the wife of a Provençal nobleman, though biographies of both troubadours and trobairitz were often made up to fit the conventions of courtly love, so we don't know for sure. The words to at least four of her songs have survived, one of them with the melody, which is very rare.*

I've suffered great distress
From a knight whom I once owned.
Now, for all time, be it known:
I loved him — yes, to excess. His jilting I've
    regretted,
Yet his love I never really returned. Now for my
    sin I can only burn:
Dressed, or in my bed.

O if I had that knight to caress
Naked all night in my arms,
He'd be ravished by the charm
Of using, for cushion, my breast. His love I more
    deeply prize
Than Floris did Blancheor's
Take that love, my core, My sense, my life, my
    eyes!

Lovely lover, gracious, kind,
When will I overcome your fight?
O if I could lie with you one night!
Feel those loving lips on mine! Listen, one thing sets me afire:
Here in my husband's place I want you,
If you'll just keep your promise true: Give me everything I desire.

Sources: First poem used by permission of Leonardo Malcovati, editor and translator of *Prosody in England and Elsewhere: A Comparative Approach* (London: Gival Press, 2006) and online at http://www.trobar.org/troubadours /arnaut_daniel/arnaut_daniel_17.php; three verses from lyrics by the Countess of Dia, often called Beatritz, the Sappho of the Rhone, in *Lyrics of the Middle Ages: An Anthology*, edited and translated by James J. Wilhelm. Reproduced with permission of GARLAND PUBLISHING, INCORPORATED, in the format Republish in a book via Copyright Clearance Center.

## QUESTIONS FOR ANALYSIS

1. Both of these songs focus on a beloved who does not return the lover's affection. What similarities and differences do you see in them?

2. How does courtly love reinforce other aspects of medieval society? What aspects of medieval society does it contradict?

3. Can you find examples from current popular music that parallel the sentiments expressed in these two songs?

expanding the living space to accommodate growing numbers. Residents bargained with lords to make the town politically independent, which gave them the right to hold legal courts, select leaders, and set taxes.

Townspeople also tried to acquire liberties, above all personal freedom, for themselves. It gradually developed that an individual who lived in a town for a year and a day, and was accepted by the townspeople, was free of servile obligations and status. Thus serfs who fled their manors for towns and were able to find work and avoid recapture became free of personal labor obligations. In this way the growth of towns contributed to a slow decline of serfdom in western Europe, although the complete elimination of serfdom took centuries.

Merchants constituted the most powerful group in most towns, and they were often organized into merchant guilds, which prohibited nonmembers from trading, pooled members' risks, monopolized city offices, and controlled the economy of the town. Towns became centers of production as well, and artisans in particular trades formed their own **craft guilds**, including guilds of butchers, weavers, blacksmiths, bakers, silversmiths, and so on. Members of the craft guilds determined the quality, quantity, and price of the goods produced and the number of apprentices and journeymen affiliated with the guild. Formal membership in guilds was generally limited to men, but women often worked in guild shops without official membership.

Artisans generally made and sold products in their own homes, with production taking place on the ground floor. A window or door opened from the main workroom directly onto the street, and passersby could look in and see the goods being produced. The family lived above the business on the second or third floor. As the business and the family expanded, additional stories were added.

Most medieval towns and cities developed with little planning or attention to sanitation. Horses and oxen, the chief means of transportation and power, dropped tons of dung on the streets every year. It was universal practice in the early towns to dump household waste, both animal and human, into the road in front of one's house. The stench must have been abominable, as officials of the king noted in their order to the citizens of one English town in 1298:

The air is so corrupted and infected by the pigsties situated in the king's highways and in the lanes of that town and by the swine feeding and frequently wandering about . . . and by dung and dunghills

and many other foul things placed in the streets and lanes, that great repugnance overtakes the king's ministers staying in that town and . . . the advantage of more wholesome air is impeded. . . . [So] the king, being unwilling longer to tolerate such great and unbearable defects there, orders . . . the pigsties, aforesaid streets and lanes to be cleansed from all dung.[3]

Despite such unpleasant aspects of urban life, people wanted to get into medieval towns because they represented opportunities for economic advancement, social mobility, and improvement in legal status.

## The Expansion of Trade and the Commercial Revolution

The growth of towns went hand in hand with a revival of trade as artisans and craftsmen manufactured goods for local and foreign consumption. As in the city-states of East Africa (see pages 285–291), most trade centered in towns and was controlled by merchants. They began to pool their money to finance trading expeditions, sharing the profits and also sharing the risks. If disaster struck the ship or caravan, an investor's loss was limited to the amount of that individual's investment, a legal concept termed "limited liability" that is essential to the modern capitalist economy.

Italian cities, especially Venice, led the West in trade in general and completely dominated trade with Asia and North Africa. Venetian ships carried salt from the Venetian lagoon; pepper and other spices from North Africa; and slaves, silk, and purple textiles from the East to northern and western Europe. Wealthy European consumers had greater access to foreign luxuries than they had earlier, and their tastes became more sophisticated. Merchants from Florence and Milan were also important traders, and they developed new methods of accounting and record keeping that facilitated the movement of goods and money. The towns of Bruges, Ghent, and Ypres in Flanders were leaders in long-distance trade and built up a vast industry in the manufacture of cloth, aided by ready access to wool from England, just across the Channel. The availability of raw wool also encouraged the development of cloth manufacture within England itself, and commercial families in manufacturing towns grew fabulously rich.

In much of northern Europe, the Hanseatic League (known as the Hansa for short), a mercantile associa-

• Principal Hanseatic town
▲ Hanseatic trading partner

**The Hanseatic League, 1300–1400**

tion of towns formed to achieve mutual security and exclusive trading rights, controlled trade. During the thirteenth century perhaps two hundred cities from Holland to Poland joined the league. The ships of the Hansa cities carried furs, wax, copper, fish, grain, timber, and wine. These goods were exchanged for other products, mainly cloth and salt, from western cities. At cities such as Bruges and London, Hanseatic merchants secured special concessions exempting them from all tolls and allowing them to trade at local fairs. Hanseatic merchants also established foreign trading centers, which they called "factories," because the commercial agents within them were called "factors." (Later the word *factory* would be applied to centers of production as well.)

These developments added up to what historians of Europe have called the **commercial revolution**, a direct parallel to the economic revolution going on in Song Dynasty China at the same time (see pages 369–373). In giving the transformation this name, historians point not only to an increase in the sheer volume of trade and in the complexity and sophistication of business procedures but also to the new attitude toward business and making money. Some even detect a "capitalist spirit" in which making a profit was regarded as a good thing in itself.

The commercial revolution created a great deal of new wealth, which did not escape the attention of kings and other rulers. Wealth could be taxed, and through taxation kings could create strong and centralized states. Through the activities of merchants, Europeans again saw products from Africa and Asia in city marketplaces, as they had in Roman times. The commercial revolution also provided the opportunity for thousands of serfs in western Europe to improve their social position. There were also strong continuities: many people continued to live hand to mouth on low wages; most towns remained small; and the nobility and churchmen continued to determine the preponderant social attitudes, values, and patterns of thought and behavior.

# Learning and Culture

☐ What were the primary educational and cultural developments in medieval Europe?

The towns that became centers of trade and production in the High Middle Ages also developed into cultural and intellectual centers. Trade brought in new ideas as well as merchandise, and in many cities a new type of educational institution—the university—emerged, meeting the needs of the new bureaucratic states and the church for educated administrators. As universities emerged, so did other cultural advancements, such as new forms of architecture and literature.

## Universities and Scholasticism

Since the time of the Carolingian Empire, monasteries and cathedral schools had offered the only formal instruction available. Monasteries, geared to religious concerns, were located in rural environments. In contrast, schools attached to cathedrals and run by the bishop and his clergy were frequently situated in bustling cities, where people of many backgrounds stimulated the growth and exchange of ideas. In the eleventh century in Bologna and other Italian cities, wealthy businessmen established municipal schools; in the twelfth century municipal schools in Italy and cathedral schools in France developed into much larger universities, a transformation parallel to the opening of madrasas in Muslim cities (see page 255).

The growth of the University of Bologna coincided with a revival of interest in Roman law. The study of Roman law as embodied in Justinian's *Code* (see page 210) had never completely died out in the West, but in the eleventh century the discovery of a complete manuscript of the code in a library in northern Italy led scholars to study and teach Roman law intently. They applied it to practical situations, such as cases of inheritance and landownership.

At the Italian city of Salerno, interest in medicine had persisted for centuries. Greek and Muslim physicians there had studied the use of herbs as cures and had experimented with surgery. The twelfth century ushered in a new interest in Greek medical texts and in the work of Arab and Greek doctors. Ideas from this medical literature spread throughout Europe from Salerno and became the basis of training for physicians at other medieval universities. University training gave physicians high social status and allowed them to charge high fees, although their diagnoses and treatments were based on classical theories, not on interactions with patients.

Although medicine and law were important academic disciplines in the Middle Ages, theology was "the queen of sciences," so termed because it involved the study of God, who was said to make all knowledge possible. Paris became the place to study theology, and in the first decades of the twelfth century students from all over Europe crowded into the cathedral school of Notre Dame in that city.

- **craft guilds** Associations of artisans organized to regulate the quality, quantity, and price of the goods produced as well as the number of affiliated apprentices and journeymen.
- **commercial revolution** The transformation of the economic structure of Europe, beginning in the eleventh century, from a rural, manorial society to a more complex mercantile society.

University professors (a term first used in the fourteenth century) were known as "schoolmen" or **Scholastics**. They developed a method of thinking, reasoning, and writing in which questions were raised and authorities cited on both sides of a question. The goal of the Scholastic method was to arrive at definitive answers and to provide a rational explanation for what was believed on faith.

One of the most famous Scholastics was Peter Abelard (1079–1142). Fascinated by logic, which he believed could be used to solve most problems, Abelard used a method of systematic doubting in his writing and teaching. As he put it, "By doubting we come to questioning, and by questioning we perceive the truth." Abelard was censured by a church council, but he was highly popular with students.

Thirteenth-century Scholastics devoted an enormous amount of time to collecting and organizing knowledge on all topics. These collections were published as summae (SOO-may), or reference books. There were summae on law, philosophy, vegetation, animal life, and theology. Thomas Aquinas (1225–1274), a professor at the University of Paris, produced the most famous collection, the *Summa Theologica*, which deals with a vast number of theological questions.

In northern Europe—at Paris and later at Oxford and Cambridge in England—university faculties grouped themselves according to academic disciplines, or schools: law, medicine, arts, and theology. Students lived in privately endowed residential colleges and were considered to be lower-level members of the clergy, so that any student accused of a crime was tried in church, rather than in city, courts. This clerical status, along with widely held ideas about women's lesser intellectual capabilities, meant that university education was restricted to men.

At all universities the standard method of teaching was the lecture—that is, a reading. With this method the professor read a passage from the Bible, Justinian's *Code*, or one of Aristotle's treatises. He then explained and interpreted the passage. Students wrote down everything. Because books had to be copied by hand, they were extremely expensive, and few students could afford them. Examinations were given after three, four, or five years of study, when the student applied for a degree. Examinations were oral and very difficult. If the candidate passed, he was awarded the first, or bachelor's, degree. Further study, about as long, arduous, and expensive as it is today, enabled the graduate to try for the master's and doctor's degrees. Degrees were technically licenses to teach. Most students, however, did not become teachers. They staffed the expanding royal and papal administrations.

## Cathedrals and a New Architectural Style

As we have seen, religious devotion was expressed through daily rituals, holiday ceremonies, and the creation of new institutions such as universities and religious orders. People also wanted permanent visible representations of their piety, and both church and city leaders wanted physical symbols of their wealth and power. These aims found their outlet in the building of tens of thousands of churches, chapels, abbeys, and, most spectacularly, cathedrals. A cathedral is the church of a bishop and the administrative headquarters of a diocese. The word comes from the Greek word *kathedra*, meaning "seat," because the bishop's throne, a symbol of the office, is located in the cathedral.

In the tenth and eleventh centuries cathedrals were built in a style that resembled ancient Roman architecture, with massive walls, rounded stone arches, and small windows—features later labeled Romanesque. In the twelfth century a new style spread out from central France. It was dubbed **Gothic** by later Renaissance architects who thought that only the uncouth Goths could have invented such a disunified style. The basic features of Gothic architecture—pointed arches, high ceilings, and exterior supports called flying buttresses that carried much of the weight of the roof—allowed unprecedented interior light. Stained-glass windows were cut into the stone, so that the interior, one French abbot exclaimed, "would shine with the wonderful and uninterrupted light of most sacred windows, pervading the interior beauty."[4] Between 1180 and 1270 in France alone, eighty cathedrals, about five hundred abbey churches, and tens of thousands of parish churches were constructed in this new style. They are testimony to the deep religious faith and piety of medieval people and also to the civic pride of urban residents, for towns competed with one another to build the largest and most splendid cathedral. In addition to marriages, baptisms, and funerals, there were scores of feast days on which the entire town gathered in the cathedral.

Cathedrals served secular as well as religious purposes. Local guilds met in the cathedrals to arrange business deals, and municipal officials held political meetings there. Pilgrims slept there, lovers courted there, and traveling actors staged plays there. Through its statuary, paintings, and stained-glass windows, the cathedral was designed to teach the people the doc-

- **Scholastics** Medieval professors who developed a method of thinking, reasoning, and writing in which questions were raised and authorities cited on both sides of a question.
- **Gothic** The term for the architectural and artistic style that prevailed in Europe from the mid-twelfth to the sixteenth century.
- **vernacular literature** Literature written in the everyday language of a region rather than Latin; this included French, German, Italian, and English.

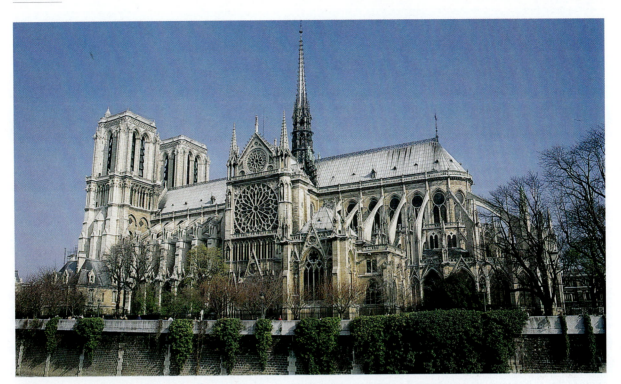

**Notre Dame Cathedral, Paris, begun 1163** This view offers a fine example of the twin towers (left), the spire, the great rose window over the south portal (center), and the flying buttresses that support the walls and the vaults. Like hundreds of other churches in medieval Europe, it was dedicated to the Virgin Mary. With a spire rising more than 300 feet, Notre Dame was the tallest building in Europe at the time of its construction. (David R. Frazier/Photo Researchers, Inc.)

trines of Christian faith through visual images, though these also often showed scenes from the lives of the artisans and merchants who paid for them.

## Vernacular Literature and Drama

Latin was the language used in university education, scholarly writing, and works of literature. By the High Middle Ages, however, no one spoke Latin as his or her first language. The barbarian invasions, the mixture of peoples, and the usual changes in language that occurred over time resulted in a variety of local dialects that blended words and linguistic forms in various ways. As kings increased the size of their holdings, they often ruled people who spoke many different dialects.

In the High Middle Ages, some authors departed from tradition and began to write in their local dialect, that is, in the everyday language of their region, which linguistic historians call the vernacular. This new **vernacular literature** gradually transformed some local dialects into literary languages, such as French, German, Italian, and English, while other local dialects, such as Breton and Bavarian, remained (and remain to this day) means of oral communication.

Stories and songs in the vernacular were composed and performed at the courts of nobles and rulers. In southern Europe, especially in Provence in southern France, poets who called themselves troubadours wrote and sang lyric verses celebrating love, desire, beauty, and gallantry. Troubadours included a few women, with their poetry often chiding knights who did not live up to the ideal. (See "Listening to the Past: Courtly Love Poetry," page 408.) The songs of the troubadours were widely imitated in Italy, England, and Germany, so they spurred the development of vernacular literature there as well. Drama, derived from the church's liturgy, emerged as a distinct art form. Amateurs and later professional actors performed plays based on biblical themes and on the lives of the saints; these dramas were presented in the towns, first in churches and then at the marketplace. By combining comical farce based on ordinary life with serious religious scenes, plays gave ordinary people an opportunity to identify with religious figures and think about their faith.

Beginning in the fourteenth century a variety of evidence attests to the increasing literacy of laypeople. Wills and inventories reveal that many people, not just nobles, possessed books—mainly devotional texts, but also romances, manuals on manners and etiquette, histories, and sometimes legal and philosophical texts. The spread of literacy represents a response to the needs of an increasingly complex society.

# Crises of the Later Middle Ages

☐ Why have the later Middle Ages been seen as a time of calamity and crisis?

During the later Middle Ages, the last book of the New Testament, the book of Revelation, inspired thousands of sermons and hundreds of religious tracts. Revelation deals with visions of the end of the world, with disease, war, famine, and death—often called the "Four Horsemen of the Apocalypse"—triumphing everywhere. It is no wonder that this part of the Bible was so popular. Between 1300 and 1450 Europeans experienced a frightful series of shocks: climate change, economic decline, plague, war, social upheaval, and increased crime and violence. Death and preoccupation with death made the fourteenth century one of the most wrenching periods of history in Europe.

## The Great Famine and the Black Death

In the first half of the fourteenth century Europe experienced a series of climate changes, especially the beginning of a period of colder and wetter weather that historical geographers label the "little ice age." Its effects were dramatic and disastrous. Population had steadily increased in the twelfth and thirteenth centuries, but with colder weather, poor harvests led to scarcity and starvation. The costs of grain, livestock, and dairy products rose sharply. Almost all of northern Europe suffered a terrible famine between 1315 and 1322, with dire social consequences: peasants were forced to sell or mortgage their lands for money to buy food, and the number of vagabonds, or homeless people, greatly increased, as did petty crime. An undernourished population was ripe for the Grim Reaper, who appeared in 1347 in the form of a virulent new disease, later called the **Black Death** (Map 14.3). The symp-

**MAP 14.3 The Course of the Black Death in Fourteenth-Century Europe** The plague followed trade routes as it spread into and across Europe. A few cities that took strict quarantine measures were spared.

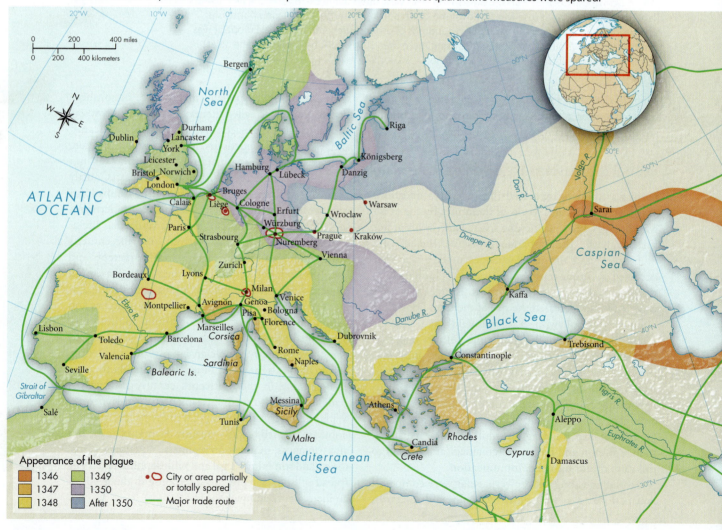

**Procession of Flagellants** In this manuscript illumination from 1349, shirtless flagellants, men and women who whipped and scourged themselves as penance for their and society's sins, walk through the Flemish city of Tournai, which had just been struck by the plague. Many people believed that the Black Death was God's punishment for humanity's wickedness. (The Flagellants at Doornik in 1349, copy of a miniature from the *Chronicle of Aegidius Li Muisis*/Private Collection/The Bridgeman Art Library)

toms of this disease were first described in 1331 in southwestern China, then part of the Mongol Empire (see page 333). From there it spread across Central Asia by way of Mongol armies and merchant caravans, arriving in the ports of the Black Sea by the 1340s. In October 1347 Genoese ships traveling from the Crimea in southern Russia brought the plague to Messina, from which it spread across Sicily and into Italy. From Italy it traveled in all directions.

Most historians and almost all microbiologists identify the disease that spread in the fourteenth century as the bubonic plague, caused by the bacillus *Yersinia pestis*. The disease normally afflicts rats. Fleas living on the infected rats drink their blood and pass the bacteria that cause the plague on to the next rat they bite. Usually the disease is limited to rats and other rodents, but at certain points in history the fleas have jumped from their rodent hosts to humans and other animals. The fourteenth-century disease showed some differences from later outbreaks of bubonic plague; there are no reports of massive rat die-offs, and the disease was often transmitted directly from one person to another through coughing and sneezing. These differences have led a few historians to ask whether the fourteenth-century outbreak was some disease other than the bubonic plague—perhaps something like the Ebola

virus. Debates about the nature of the disease fuel continued study of medical aspects of the plague, with scientists using innovative techniques such as studying the tooth pulp of bodies in medieval cemeteries to see if it contains DNA from plague-causing agents.

Whatever it was, the disease had dreadful effects on the body. The classic symptom was a growth the size of a nut or an apple in the armpit, in the groin, or on the neck. This was the boil, or *bubo*, that gave the disease its name and caused agonizing pain. If the bubo was lanced and the pus thoroughly drained, the victim had a chance of recovery. The secondary stage was the appearance of black spots or blotches caused by bleeding under the skin. Finally, the victim began to cough violently and spit blood. This stage, indicating the presence of millions of bacilli in the bloodstream, signaled the end, and death followed in two or three days. Physicians could sometimes ease the pain but had no cure.

Most people believed that the Black Death was caused by poisons or by "corrupted air" that carried the disease from place to place. They sought to keep poisons from entering the body by smelling or ingesting

● **Black Death** The plague that first struck Europe in 1347, killing perhaps one-third of the population.

strong-smelling herbs, and they tried to remove the poisons through bloodletting. They also prayed and did penance. Anxiety and fears about the plague caused people to look for scapegoats, and they found them in the Jews, who they believed had poisoned the wells of Christian communities and thereby infected the drinking water. This charge led to the murder of thousands of Jews across Europe.

Because population figures for the period before the arrival of the plague do not exist for most countries and cities, only educated guesses can be made about mortality rates. Of a total English population of perhaps 4.2 million, probably 1.4 million died of the Black Death in its several visits. In Italy densely populated cities endured incredible losses. Florence lost between one-half and two-thirds of its population when the plague visited in 1348. The disease recurred intermittently in the 1360s and 1370s and reappeared many times, as late as the early 1700s in Europe. (It still continues to infect rodent and human populations sporadically today.)

In the short term the economic effects of the plague were severe because the death of many peasants disrupted food production. But in the long term the dramatic decline in population eased pressure on the land, and wages and per capita wealth rose for those who survived. The psychological consequences of the plague were profound. (See "Viewpoints 14.2: Italian and English Views of the Plague," at right.) Some people sought release in wild living, while others turned to the severest forms of asceticism and frenzied religious fervor.

## The Hundred Years' War

While the plague ravaged populations in Asia, North Africa, and Europe, a long international war in western Europe added further death and destruction. England and France had engaged in sporadic military hostilities from the time of the Norman Conquest in 1066 (see page 395), and in the middle of the fourteenth century these became more intense. From 1337 to 1453 the two countries intermittently fought one another in what was the longest war in European history, ultimately dubbed the Hundred Years' War, though it actually lasted 116 years.

The Hundred Years' War had a number of causes. Both England and France claimed the duchy of Aquitaine in southwestern France, and the English king Edward III argued that, as the grandson of an earlier French king, he should have rightfully inherited the French throne. Nobles in provinces on the borders of France who were worried about the growing power of the French king supported Edward, as did wealthy wool merchants and clothmakers in Flanders who

depended on English wool. The governments of both England and France promised wealth and glory to those who fought, and each country portrayed the other as evil.

The war, fought almost entirely in France, consisted mainly of a series of random sieges and raids. During the war's early stages, England was successful, primarily through the use of longbows fired by well-trained foot soldiers against mounted knights and, after 1375, by early cannons. By 1419 the English had advanced to the walls of Paris. But the French cause was not lost. Though England scored the initial victories, France won the war.

The ultimate French success rests heavily on the actions of Joan, an obscure French peasant girl whose vision and military leadership revived French fortunes and led to victory. (Over the centuries, she acquired the name "of Arc"—*d'Arc* in French—based on her father's name; she never used this name for herself, but called herself "the maiden"—*la Pucelle* in French.) Born in 1412 to well-to-do peasants, Joan grew up in a pious household. During adolescence she began to hear voices, which she later said belonged to Saint Michael, Saint Catherine, and Saint Margaret. In 1428 these voices told her that the dauphin of France—Charles VII, who was uncrowned as king because of the English occupation—had to be crowned and the English expelled from France. Joan went to the French court disguised as a male for safety and secured the support of the dauphin to travel, dressed as a knight, with the French army to the besieged city of Orléans.

At Orléans, Joan inspired and led French attacks, and the English retreated. As a result of her successes, Charles made Joan co-commander of the entire army, and she led it to a string of military victories in the summer of 1429; many cities surrendered without a fight. Two months after the victory at Orléans, Charles VII was crowned king at Reims.

Joan and the French army continued their fight against the English. In 1430 England's allies, the Burgundians, captured Joan and sold her to the English, and the French did not intervene. The English wanted Joan eliminated for obvious political reasons, but the primary charge against her was heresy, and the trial was conducted by church authorities. She was interrogated about the angelic voices and about why she wore men's clothing. She apparently answered skillfully, but in 1431 the court condemned her as a heretic, and she was burned at the stake in the marketplace at Rouen. (A new trial in 1456 cleared her of all charges, and in 1920 she was canonized as a saint.) Joan continues to be a symbol of deep religious piety to some, of conservative nationalism to others, and of gender-bending cross-dressing to others. Beneath the pious and popu-

# Viewpoints 14.2

## Italian and English Views of the Plague

• *Eyewitness commentators on the plague include the Italian writer Giovanni Boccaccio (1313–1375), who portrayed the course of the disease in Florence in the preface to his book of tales,* The Decameron, *and the English monastic chronicler Henry Knighton (d. 1396), who described the effects of the plague on English towns and villages in his four-volume chronicle of English history.*

### Giovanni Boccaccio

❝ Against this pestilence no human wisdom or foresight was of any avail. . . . Men and women in great numbers abandoned their city, their houses, their farms, their relatives, and their possessions and sought other places, going at least as far away as the Florentine countryside — as if the wrath of God could not pursue them with this pestilence wherever they went but would only strike those it found within the walls of the city! . . . Almost no one cared for his neighbor, and relatives hardly ever visited one another — they stayed far apart. This disaster had struck such fear into the hearts of men and women that brother abandoned brother, uncle abandoned nephew, sister left brother, and very often wife abandoned husband, and — even worse, almost unbelievable — fathers and mothers neglected to tend and care for their children as if they were not their own. . . . So many corpses would arrive in front of a church every day and at every hour that the amount of holy ground for burials was certainly insufficient for the ancient custom of giving each body its individual place; when all the graves were full, huge trenches were dug in all the cemeteries of the churches and into them the new arrivals were dumped by the hundreds; and they were packed in there with dirt, one on top of another, like a ship's cargo, until the trench was filled. . . . Oh how many great palaces, beautiful homes and noble dwellings, once filled with families, gentlemen, and ladies, were now emptied, down to the last servant! ❞

### Henry Knighton

❝ Then that most grievous pestilence penetrated the coastal regions [of England] by way of Southampton, and came to Bristol, and people died as if the whole strength of the city were seized by sudden death. For there were few who lay in their beds more than three days or two and half days; then that savage death snatched them about the second day. In Leicester, in the little parish of St. Leonard, more than three hundred and eighty died; in the parish of Holy Cross, more than four hundred. . . . And so in each parish, they died in great numbers. . . . At the same time, there was so great a lack of priests everywhere that many churches had no divine services. . . . One could hardly hire a chaplain to minister to the church for less than ten marks, whereas before the pestilence, when there were plenty of priests, one could hire a chaplain for five or four marks. . . . Meanwhile, the king ordered that in every county of the kingdom, reapers and other labourers should not receive more than they were accustomed to receive, under the penalty provided in the statute, and he renewed the statute at this time. The labourers, however, were so arrogant and hostile that they did not heed the king's command, but if anyone wished to hire them, he had to pay them what they wanted, and either lose his fruits and crops or satisfy the arrogant and greedy desire of the labourers as they wished. . . . Similarly, those who received day-work from their tenants throughout the year, as is usual from serfs, had to release them and to remit such service. They either had to excuse them entirely or had to fix them in a laxer manner at a small rent, lest very great and irreparable damage be done to the buildings and the land everywhere remain uncultivated. ❞

Sources: Giovanni Boccaccio, *The Decameron*, trans. Mark Musa and Peter Bondanella (New York: W. W. Norton, 1982), pp. 7, 9, 12. Copyright © 1982 by Mark Musa and Peter Bondanella. Used by permission of W. W. Norton & Company, Inc.; Henry Knighton, *Chronicon Henrici Knighton*, in James Bruce Ross and Mary Martin McLaughlin, eds., *The Portable Medieval Reader* (New York: Viking, 1949), pp. 218, 220, 222.

### QUESTIONS FOR ANALYSIS

1. How did the residents of Florence respond to the plague, as described by Boccaccio?

2. What were some of the effects of the plague in England, as described by Knighton?

3. How might the fact that Boccaccio was writing in an urban setting and Knighton was writing from a rural monastery that owned a large amount of land have shaped their perspectives?

## □ Picturing the Past

**Siege of the Castle of Mortagne near Bordeaux**  This miniature of a battle in the Hundred Years' War shows the French besieging an English-held castle. Medieval warfare usually consisted of small skirmishes and attacks on castles. (from *The Coronation of Richard II to 1387* by Jean de Batard Wavrin/© British Library Board. All Rights Reserved./The Bridgeman Art Library)

**ANALYZING THE IMAGE**  What types of weapons are the attackers and defenders using? How have the attackers on the left enhanced their position?

**CONNECTIONS**  This painting shows a battle that occurred in 1377, but it was painted about a hundred years later and shows the military technology available at the time it was painted, not at the time of the actual siege. Which of the weapons represent newer forms of military technology? What impact would you expect them to have on warfare?

lar legends is a teenage girl who saved the French monarchy, which was the embodiment of France. The French army continued its victories without her, and demands for an end to the war increased among the English, who were growing tired of the mounting loss of life and the flow of money into a seemingly bottomless pit. Slowly the French reconquered Normandy and finally ejected the English from Aquitaine. At the war's end in 1453, only the town of Calais remained in English hands.

The long war had a profound impact on the two countries. In England and France the war promoted nationalism—the feeling of unity and identity that binds together a people. It led to technological experimentation, especially with gunpowder weaponry, whose firepower made the protective walls of stone castles obsolete. However, such weaponry also made warfare increasingly expensive. The war also stimulated the development of the English Parliament. Between 1250 and 1450 representative assemblies from several classes of society flourished in many European countries, but only the English Parliament became a powerful national body. Edward III's constant need for money to pay for the war compelled him to summon it many times, and its representatives slowly built up their powers.

## Challenges to the Church

In times of crisis or disaster people of all faiths have sought the consolation of religion, but in the fourteenth century the official Christian Church offered little solace. While local clergy eased the suffering of many, a dispute over who was the legitimate pope weakened the church as an institution. In 1309 pressure by the French monarchy led the pope to move his permanent residence to Avignon in southern France, the location of the papal summer palace. This marked the start of seven successive papacies in Avignon. Not surprising, all these popes were French—a matter of controversy among church followers outside France. Also, the popes largely concentrated on bureaucratic and financial matters to the exclusion of spiritual objectives.

In 1376 one of the French popes returned to Rome, and when he died there several years later Roman citizens demanded an Italian pope who would remain in Rome. The cardinals elected Urban VI, but his tactless, arrogant, and bullheaded manner caused them to regret their decision. The cardinals slipped away from Rome and declared Urban's election invalid because it had come about under threats from the Roman mob. They elected a French cardinal who took the name Clement VII (pontificate 1378–1394) and set himself up at Avignon in opposition to Urban. There were thus two popes, a situation that was later termed the Great Schism.

The powers of Europe aligned themselves with Urban or Clement along strictly political lines. France recognized the Frenchman, Clement; England, France's historic enemy, recognized Urban. The rest of Europe lined up behind one or the other. In all European countries the common people—hard-pressed by inflation, wars, and plague—were thoroughly confused about which pope was legitimate. In the end the schism weakened the religious faith of many Christians and brought church leadership into serious disrepute.

A first attempt to heal the schism led to the installation of a third pope and a threefold split, but finally a church council meeting at Constance (1414–1418)

Allegiance to Rome
Allegiance to Avignon
Official allegiance to Rome but with shifting local allegiances

**The Great Schism, 1378–1417**

successfully deposed the three schismatic popes and elected a new leader, who took the name Martin V (pontificate 1417–1431). The schism was over, but those who had hoped that the council would also reform problems in the church were disappointed. In the later fifteenth century the papacy concentrated on building up its wealth and political power in Italy rather than on the concerns of the whole church. As a result, many people decided that they would need to rely on their own prayers and pious actions rather than on the institutional church for their salvation.

## Peasant and Urban Revolts

The difficult conditions of the fourteenth and fifteenth centuries spurred a wave of peasant and urban revolts across Europe. In 1358, when French taxation for the Hundred Years' War fell heavily on the poor, the frustrations of the French peasantry exploded in a massive uprising called the Jacquerie (zhah-kuh-REE), after a supposedly happy agricultural laborer, Jacques Bonhomme (Good Fellow). Adding to the anger over taxes was the toll taken by the plague and by the famine that had struck some areas. Crowds swept through the countryside, slashing the throats of nobles, burning their castles, raping their wives and daughters, and killing or maiming their horses and cattle. Artisans, small merchants, and parish priests joined the peasants, and residents of both urban and rural areas committed terrible destruction. For several weeks the nobles were on the defensive, until the upper class united to repress the revolt with merciless ferocity. Thousands of the "Jacques," innocent as well as guilty, were cut down.

Taxes and other grievances also led to the 1381 English Peasants' Revolt, involving tens of thousands of people. The Black Death had dramatically reduced the supply of labor, and peasants had demanded higher wages and fewer manorial obligations. Parliament countered with a law freezing wages and binding workers to their manors. Although the law was difficult to enforce, it contributed to an atmosphere of discontent, which was further enhanced by popular preachers who proclaimed that great disparities between rich and poor went against Christ's teachings. Moreover, decades of aristocratic violence, much of it perpetrated against the weak peasantry, had bred hostility and bitterness.

In 1380 Parliament imposed a poll tax on all citizens to fund the Hundred Years' War, requiring rich and poor to pay the same amount and ordering sheriffs to collect it. This tax imposed a greater burden on the poor than on wealthier citizens, and it sparked revolt. Beginning with assaults on the tax collectors, the uprising in England followed much the same course as had the Jacquerie in France. Castles and manors were sacked; manorial records were destroyed; nobles were murdered. Urban discontent merged with rural violence. Apprentices and journeymen, frustrated because the highest positions in the guilds were closed to them, rioted.

The boy-king Richard II (r. 1377–1399) met the leaders of the revolt, agreed to charters ensuring the peasants' freedom, tricked them with false promises, and then proceeded to crush the uprising with terrible ferocity. The nobility tried to use this defeat to restore the labor obligations of serfdom, but they were not successful, and the conversion to money rents continued. In Flanders, France, and England peasant revolts often blended with conflicts involving workers in cities. Unrest also occurred in Italian, Spanish, and German cities. In Florence in 1378 the *ciompi*, or poor propertyless wool workers, revolted and briefly shared government of the city with wealthier artisans and merchants. Rebellions and uprisings everywhere revealed deep peasant and worker frustration with the socioeconomic conditions of the time.

**Suit of Armor**  This fifteenth-century suit of Italian armor protected its wearer, but its weight made movement difficult. Both English and French mounted knights wore full armor at the beginning of the Hundred Years' War, but by the end they wore only breastplates and helmets, which protected their vital organs but allowed greater mobility. This suit has been so well preserved that it was most likely never used in battle; it may have been made for ceremonial purposes. (Armor, Italy, ca. 1400 and later. Steel, brass, textile. Bashford Dean Memorial Collection. Gift of Helen Fahnestock, in memory of her father, Harris C. Fahnestock, 1929 [29.154.3]/The Metropolitan Museum of Art, New York, NY, USA/Image copyright © The Metropolitan Museum of Art/Image source: Art Resource, NY)

# Chapter Summary

Invasions by Vikings, Magyars, and Muslims, along with civil wars, created instability in the ninth and tenth centuries. Local nobles became the strongest powers against external threats, establishing a form of decentralized government later known as feudalism. By the twelfth century rulers in some parts of Europe had reasserted authority and were beginning to develop new institutions of government and legal codes that enabled them to assert power over lesser lords and the general population. The papacy also consolidated its power, though these moves were sometimes challenged by kings and emperors. Monasteries continued to be important places for learning and devotion, and new religious orders were founded. A papal call to retake the holy city of Jerusalem led to the Crusades, nearly two centuries of warfare between Christians and Muslims. Many of the effects of the Crusades were disastrous, including attacks on Jewish communities and more uniformly hostile Christian-Muslim relations.

The vast majority of medieval Europeans were peasants who lived in small villages and worked their own and their lord's land. Most Europeans were Christian, and the village church was generally the center of community life. Nobles were a tiny fraction of the total population, but they exerted great power over all aspects of life. Medieval towns and cities grew initially as trading centers and then became centers of production.

Towns also developed into cultural and intellectual centers, as trade brought in new ideas as well as merchandise. Universities offered courses of study based on classical models, and townspeople built churches and cathedrals as symbols of their Christian faith and their civic pride. New types of vernacular literature arose in which poems, songs, and stories were written down in local dialects.

In the fourteenth century a worsening climate brought poor harvests, which contributed to an international economic depression and fostered disease. The Black Death caused enormous population losses and social, psychological, and economic consequences.

Additional difficulties included the Hundred Years' War, a schism among rival popes that weakened the Western Christian Church, and peasant and worker frustrations that exploded into uprisings.

## CHRONOLOGY

| | |
|---|---|
| 722–1492 | Reconquista, the Christian reconquest of Spain from Muslims |
| ca. 800–950 | Viking, Magyar, and Muslim attacks on Europe |
| 1066–1087 | Reign of William the Conqueror |
| 1086 | *Domesday Book* |
| 1095–1270 | Crusades |
| 1180–1270 | Height of construction of cathedrals in France |
| 1215 | Magna Carta |
| 1225–1274 | Life of Saint Thomas Aquinas, author of *Summa Theologica* |
| 1309–1376 | Papacy in Avignon |
| 1315–1322 | Famine in northern Europe |
| ca. 1337–1453 | Hundred Years' War |
| 1347 | Black Death arrives in Europe |
| 1358 | Jacquerie peasant uprising in France |
| 1378–1417 | Great Schism |
| 1381 | English Peasants' Revolt |
| 1429 | Joan of Arc leads French troops to victory at Orléans |

## NOTES

1. D. C. Douglas and G. E. Greenaway, eds., *English Historical Documents*, vol. 2 (London: Eyre & Spottiswoode, 1961), p. 853.
2. Fulcher of Chartres, *A History of the Expedition to Jerusalem, 1095–1127*, trans. Frances Rita Ryan, ed. Harold S. Fink (Knoxville: University of Tennessee Press, 1969), pp. 121–123.
3. H. Rothwell, ed., *English Historical Documents*, vol. 3 (London: Eyre & Spottiswoode, 1975), p. 854.
4. Erwin Panofsky, trans. and ed., *Abbot Suger on the Abbey Church of St.-Denis and Its Art Treasures* (Princeton, N.J.: Princeton University Press, 1946), p. 101.

## CONNECTIONS

Medieval Europe continues to fascinate us today. We go to medieval banquets, fairs, and even weddings; visit castle-themed hotels and amusement parks; watch movies about knights and their conquests; play video games in which we become warriors, trolls, or sorcerers; and read stories with themes of great quests, some set in the Middle Ages and some set in places that just seem medieval, with humble but brave villagers, beautiful ladies, powerful wizards, and gorgeous warriors on horseback. From all these amusements the Middle Ages emerges as a strange and wonderful time, when people's emotions were more powerful, challenges more dangerous, and friendships more lasting than in the safe, shallow, fast-paced modern world. Characters from other parts of the world often heighten the exoticism: a Muslim soldier joins the fight against a common enemy, a Persian princess rescues the hero and his sidekick, a Buddhist monk teaches martial arts techniques. These characters from outside Europe are fictional, but they also represent aspects of reality, because medieval Europe was not isolated, and political and social structures similar to those in Europe developed elsewhere.

In reality few of us would probably want to live in the real Middle Ages, when most people worked in the fields all day, a banquet meant a piece of tough old rooster instead of the usual meal of pea soup and black bread, and even wealthy lords lived in damp and drafty castles. We do not really want to return to a time when one-third to one-half of all children died before age five and alcohol was the only real pain reliever. But the contemporary appeal of the Middle Ages is an interesting phenomenon, particularly because it stands in such sharp contrast to the attitude of educated Europeans who lived in the centuries immediately afterward. They were the ones who dubbed the period "middle" and viewed the soaring cathedrals as dreadfully "Gothic." They saw their own era as the one to be celebrated, and the Middle Ages as best forgotten.

# Review and Explore

## Make It Stick

 **LearningCurve**
Go online and use LearningCurve to retain what you've read.

## Identify Key Terms

Identify and explain the significance of each item below.

**vassal** (p. 393)          **heresy** (p. 399)          **commercial revolution** (p. 411)

**fief** (p. 393)          **reconquista** (p. 401)          **Scholastics** (p. 412)

**feudalism** (p. 393)          **Crusades** (p. 401)          **Gothic** (p. 412)

**manorialism** (p. 394)          **chivalry** (p. 407)          **vernacular literature** (p. 413)

**serf** (p. 395)          **craft guilds** (p. 410)          **Black Death** (p. 414)

## Review the Main Ideas

Answer the focus questions from each section of the chapter.

1. How did medieval rulers restore order and centralize political power? (p. 392)
2. How did the Christian Church enhance its power and create new institutions and religious practices? (p. 396)
3. What were the causes, course, and consequences of the Crusades? (p. 401)
4. How did the lives of common people, nobles, and townspeople differ, and what new commercial developments increased wealth? (p. 405)
5. What were the primary educational and cultural developments in medieval Europe? (p. 411)
6. Why have the later Middle Ages been seen as a time of calamity and crisis? (p. 414)

## Make Connections

Analyze the larger developments and continuities within and across chapters.

1. What similarities and differences do you see between the institutions and laws established by medieval European rulers and those of the Roman (Chapter 6), Byzantine (Chapter 8), and Chinese (Chapter 13) emperors?
2. What factors over the centuries enabled the Christian Church (Chapters 6, 8) to become the most powerful and wealthy institution in Europe, and what problems did this create?
3. How would you compare the role of trade in economic development in the Islamic world (Chapter 9), Africa (Chapter 10), Southeast Asia (Chapter 12), China (Chapter 13), and Europe in the period from 800 to 1400?

## LaunchPad
### Online Document Project

**Hildegard of Bingen**

**Why was Hildegard of Bingen considered a worthy instrument for the transmission of God's word?**
Read excerpts from Hildegard's correspondence, and then complete a quiz and writing assignment based on the evidence and details from this chapter.

*See inside the front cover to learn more.*

## Suggested Reading

Allmand, Christopher. *The Hundred Years War: England and France at War, ca. 1300–1450*, rev. ed. 2005. Designed for students; examines the war from political, military, social, and economic perspectives and compares the way England and France reacted to the conflict.

Bartlett, Robert. *The Making of Europe: Conquest, Colonization and Cultural Change, 950–1350*. 1993. A broad survey of many of the developments traced in this chapter.

Bennett, Judith M. *A Medieval Life: Cecelia Penifader of Brigstock, c. 1297–1344*. 1998. An excellent brief introduction to all aspects of medieval village life from the perspective of one woman; designed for students.

Brooke, Rosalind, and Christopher Brooke. *Popular Religion in the Middle Ages*. 1984. A readable synthesis of material on the beliefs and practices of ordinary Christians.

Epstein, Steven A. *An Economic and Social History of Later Medieval Europe, 1000–1500*. 2009. Examines the most important themes in European social and economic history, with a wide geographic sweep.

Glick, Leonard B. *Abraham's Heirs: Jews and Christians in Medieval Europe*. 1999. Provides information on many aspects of Jewish life and Jewish-Christian relations.

Herlihy, David. *The Black Death and the Transformation of the West*, 2d ed. 1997. A fine treatment of the causes and cultural consequences of the disease that remains the best starting point for study of the great epidemic.

Janin, Hunt. *The University in Medieval Life, 1179–1499*. 2008. An overview of medieval universities designed for general readers.

Kaeuper, Richard W. *Chivalry and Violence in Medieval Europe*. 2006. Examines the role chivalry played in promoting violent disorder.

Madden, Thomas. *The New Concise History of the Crusades*. 2005. A highly readable brief survey by the pre-eminent American scholar of the Crusades.

Sawyer, Peter, ed. *The Oxford Illustrated History of the Vikings*. 1997. A sound account of the Vikings by an international team of scholars.

Shahar, Shulamit. *The Fourth Estate: A History of Women in the Middle Ages*, 2d ed. 2003. Analyzes attitudes toward women and provides information on the lives of a variety of women, including nuns, peasants, noblewomen, and townswomen.

Shinners, John. *Medieval Popular Religion, 1000–1500*, 2d ed. 2006. An excellent collection of a wide variety of sources that provide evidence about the beliefs and practices of ordinary Christians.

Spufford, Peter. *Power and Profit: The Merchant in Medieval Europe*. 2003. A comprehensive history of medieval commerce, designed for general readers; includes many illustrations.

Tuchman, Barbara. *A Distant Mirror: The Calamitous Fourteenth Century*. 1978. A vivid description of this tumultuous time written for a general audience.

# Europe in the Renaissance and Reformation

## 1350–1600

### Portrait of Baldassare Castiglione

The author and courtier Baldassare Castiglione directs his calm gaze toward the viewer in this portrait by the renowned Italian Renaissance artist Raphael. Individual portraits like this one expressed the ideals of the Renaissance: elegance, balance, proportion, and self-awareness. (© Samuel Courtauld Trust, The Courtauld Gallery, London, UK/The Bridgeman Art Library)

**LearningCurve**
After reading the chapter, go online and use LearningCurve to retain what you've read.

# Chapter Preview

W hile disease, famine, and war marked the fourteenth century in much of Europe, the era also witnessed the beginnings of remarkable changes in many aspects of intellectual and cultural life. First in Italy and then elsewhere, artists and writers thought that they were living in a new golden age, later termed the Renaissance, French for "rebirth." The word *renaissance* was used initially to describe art that seemed to recapture, or perhaps even surpass, the glories of the classical past and then came to be used for many aspects of life of the period. The new attitude diffused slowly out of Italy, with the result that the Renaissance "happened" at different times in different parts of Europe. It shaped the lives of Europe's educated elites, although families, kin networks, religious beliefs, and the rhythms of the agricultural year still remained important.

Religious reformers carried out even more dramatic changes. Calls for reform of the Christian Church began very early in its history and continued throughout the Middle Ages. In the sixteenth century these calls gained wide acceptance, due not only to religious issues and problems within the church but also to political and social factors. In a movement termed the Protestant Reformation, Western Christianity broke into many divisions, a situation that continues today. The Renaissance and the Reformation were very different types of movements, but both looked back to a time they regarded as purer and better than their own, and both offered opportunities for strong individuals to shape their world in unexpected ways. Both have also been seen as key elements in the creation of the "modern" world.

## Renaissance Culture

❑ What were the major cultural developments of the Renaissance?

The **Renaissance** was characterized by self-conscious awareness among fourteenth- and fifteenth-century Italians, particularly scholars and writers known as humanists, that they were living in a new era. Their ideas influenced education and were spread through the new technology of the printing press. Interest in the classical past and in the individual also shaped Renaissance art in terms of style and subject matter. Also important to Renaissance art were the wealthy patrons who helped fund it.

### Wealth and Power in Renaissance Italy

Economic growth laid the material basis for the Italian Renaissance and its cultural achievements. Ambitious merchants gained political power to match their economic power and then used their money to buy luxuries and hire talent in a **patronage** system. Through this system, cities, groups, and individuals commissioned writers and artists to produce specific works. Thus economics, politics, and culture were interconnected.

The Renaissance began in the northern Italian city of Florence, which possessed enormous wealth. From their position as tax collectors for the papacy, Florentine mercantile families began to dominate European banking on both sides of the Alps, setting up offices in major European and North African cities. The profits from loans, investments, and money exchanges allowed banking families to control the city's politics and culture. Although Florence was officially a republic, starting in 1434 the great Medici (MEH-duh-chee) banking family held power almost continually for centuries. They supported an academy for scholars and a host of painters, sculptors, poets, and architects. (See "Individuals in Society: Cosimo and Lorenzo de' Medici," page 428.)

In other Italian cities as well, wealthy merchants and bankers built magnificent palaces and required that all political business be done there. They became patrons of the arts, hiring not only architects to design and build these palaces but also artists to fill them with paintings and sculptures, and musicians and composers to fill them with music. Attractions like these appealed to the rich, social-climbing residents of Venice, Florence, Genoa, and Rome, who came to see life more as an opportunity for enjoyment than as a painful pilgrimage to Heaven.

This cultural flowering took place amid political turmoil. In the fifteenth century five powers dominated the Italian peninsula: Venice, Milan, Florence, the Papal States, and the kingdom of Naples. These powers competed furiously for territory and ruthlessly tried to extend their authority over smaller city-states. While the states of northern Europe were moving toward centralization and consolidation, Italian politics resembled a jungle where the powerful dominated the weak.

In one significant respect, however, the Italian city-states anticipated future relations among competing European states after 1500. Whenever one Italian state appeared to gain a predominant position within the peninsula, other states combined to establish a balance of power against the major threat. In the formation of these alliances, Renaissance Italians invented the machinery of modern diplomacy: permanent embassies with resident ambassadors in capitals where political relations and commercial ties needed continual monitoring.

Although the resident ambassador was one of the great political achievements of the Italian Renaissance, diplomacy did not prevent invasions of Italy. These began in 1494 as Italy became the focus of international ambitions and the battleground of foreign armies, and Italian cities suffered severely from continual warfare for decades. Thus the failure of the city-states to form some type of federal system—or at least to establish a common foreign policy—led to centuries of subjugation by outside invaders. Italy was not to achieve unification until 1870.

## The Rise of Humanism

The Renaissance was a self-conscious intellectual movement. The realization that something new and unique was happening first came to writers in the fourteenth century, especially to the Italian poet and humanist Francesco Petrarch (frahn-CHEH-skoh PEH-trahrk) (1304–1374). For Petrarch, the barbarian migrations (see pages 220–224) had caused a sharp cultural break with the glories of Rome and inaugurated what he called the "dark ages." Along with many of his contemporaries, Petrarch sought to reconnect with the classical past, and he believed that such efforts were bringing on a new golden age of intellectual achievement.

Petrarch and other poets, writers, and artists showed a deep interest both in the physical remains of the Roman Empire and in classical Latin texts. The study of Latin classics became known as the *studia humanitates*, usually translated as "liberal studies" or the "liberal arts." People who advocated it were known as *humanists*, and their program was known as **humanism**. Like all programs of study, humanism contained an implicit philosophy: that human nature and achievements, evident in the classics, were worthy of contemplation. Humanists did not reject religion; instead they sought to synthesize

**Italian States, 1494**

- **Renaissance** A French word meaning "rebirth," used to describe a cultural movement that began in fourteenth-century Italy and looked back to the classical past.

- **patronage** Financial support of writers and artists by cities, groups, and individuals, often to produce specific works or works in specific styles.

- **humanism** A program of study designed by Italians that emphasized the critical study of Latin and Greek literature with the goal of understanding human nature.

# Individuals in Society

## Cosimo and Lorenzo de' Medici

**THE RENAISSANCE IS OFTEN DESCRIBED AS A TIME OF** growing individualism, a development evidenced in the era's many personal portraits and individual biographies. But a person's family also remained important, even for those at the very top of society. The Medici of Florence were one of Europe's wealthiest families and used their money to influence politics and culture. The Medici got their start in banking in the late fourteenth century, with smart bets on what would happen politically in turbulent Italy and the adoption of the best new business practices. By the early fifteenth century the Medici bank had branches in Rome, Pisa, London, and other important European cities, and it served as the pope's primary banker.

Cosimo (1389–1464) and his grandson Lorenzo (1449–1492) were the most influential Medici. Not content with great wealth, Cosimo operated behind the scenes to gain control of the Florentine political system, although he held no office and officially the city remained a republic. Worries about his growing power led the Florentine city council to exile him, but he took his money and his business with him and was soon asked to return.

Cosimo supported artists and thinkers, sponsoring what became known as the Platonic Academy, an informal group of Florence's cultural elite named in honor of Plato's famous academy in ancient Athens. Here Marsilio Ficino and other humanists translated Plato's works into Latin, making Greek learning available to a much wider European audience. Cosimo collected books and manuscripts from all over Europe, assembling an impressive library within the equally impressive Medici palace that he built in the heart of Florence.

Like his grandfather, Lorenzo was the head of the Medici bank and the de facto ruler of Florence. He, too, survived an attempt to oust him, this one led by the rival Pazzi family. The

Pazzi went beyond simply trying to exile the Medici, and instead tried to murder them: Lorenzo was wounded and his brother Giuliano was killed. Medici revenge was swift and many Pazzi were executed, which led the pope—who sided with the Pazzi—to back an invasion of Florence. Lorenzo ended the conflict through personal diplomacy, and the constitution of Florence was modified to favor the Medici.

Lorenzo came to be known during his lifetime—with no irony—as "Lorenzo the Magnificent," primarily for his support for learning and the arts. As they had in Cosimo's day, a group of poets, philosophers, and artists spent much of their time at the Medici palace, where Lorenzo patronized writing in Italian as well as humanist scholarship in Latin and Greek. Lorenzo himself wrote love lyrics, sonnets, pastorals, odes, and carnival songs, many of them meditations on nature or on the fleetingness of human life. The group included the humanists Ficino and Pico della Mirandola and the artists Michelangelo, Leonardo da Vinci, and Botticelli, all of them influenced by Platonic concepts of beauty and love. Botticelli's *Adoration of the Magi*, painted while he was at the Medici court, shows Cosimo (who was dead by the time the picture was painted) kneeling in front of the Virgin Mary as one of the three kings giving gifts to the infant Jesus, while a black-haired Lorenzo stands with other important Florentines on the right.

As Lorenzo reached his forties, many of the Medici bank branches collapsed because of bad loans, and his diplomacy was not successful in maintaining a peaceful balance of power. Like many others in Florence, Lorenzo came under the spell of the charismatic preacher Savonarola, who preached that God would punish Italy for its vice and corruption. Lorenzo died before the prediction appeared to come true when the French invaded Italy in 1494. The Medici were again ousted, but just as before, they returned, and later became the official and hereditary rulers of Florence and its environs as the Grand Dukes of Tuscany.

### QUESTIONS FOR ANALYSIS

1. Renaissance people were fascinated by the quality of virtù, the ability to shape the world around one according to one's will. How did Cosimo and Lorenzo exhibit virtù?

2. The Medici created a model for very wealthy people of how to obtain political and cultural influence. Can you think of more recent examples of those who followed this model?

### LaunchPad
### Online Document Project

**What role did patrons play in shaping Renaissance artistic and intellectual life?** Examine paintings and letters by Renaissance artists, and complete a quiz and writing assignment based on the evidence and details from this chapter.

*See inside the front cover to learn more.*

**Botticelli's *Adoration of the Magi* shows many members of the Medici family and their circle, including the artist himself at the far right.** (De Agostini Picture Library/akg-images)

Christian and classical teachings, pointing out the harmony between them.

Families, religious brotherhoods, workers' organizations, and other groups continued to have meaning in people's lives, but humanists and other Renaissance thinkers increasingly viewed these groups as springboards to far greater individual achievement. They were especially interested in individuals who had risen above their background to become brilliant, powerful, or unique. Such individuals had the admirable quality of *virtù* (vir-TOO), which is not virtue in the sense of moral goodness, but the ability to shape the world around them according to their will. Humanists thought that their recommended course of study in the classics would provide essential skills for future diplomats, lawyers, military leaders, businessmen, and politicians, as well as for writers and artists. Just as Confucian officials did in Song China, they also taught that taking an active role in the world and working for the common good should be the aim of all educated individuals.

Humanists put their educational ideas into practice. They opened schools and academies in Italian cities and courts in which pupils began with Latin grammar and rhetoric, went on to study Roman history and political philosophy, and then learned Greek in order to study Greek literature and philosophy. These classics, humanists taught, would provide models of how to write clearly, argue effectively, and speak persuasively. Gradually humanist education became the basis for intermediate and advanced education for well-to-do urban boys and men.

Humanists disagreed about education for women. Many saw the value of exposing women to classical models of moral behavior and reasoning, but they also wondered whether a program of study that emphasized eloquence and action was proper for women, whose sphere was generally understood to be private and domestic. Humanists never established schools for girls, though through tutors or programs of self-study a few women did become educated in the classics. (See "Viewpoints 15.1: Lauro Quirini and Cassandra Fedele: Women and Humanist Learning," page 430.)

Humanists looked to the classical past for political as well as literary models. The best-known political theorist of this era was Niccolò Machiavelli (1469–1527), who worked as an official for the city of Florence until he was ousted in a power struggle. He spent the rest of his life writing, and his most famous work is the short political treatise *The Prince* (1513). Using the examples of classical and contemporary rulers, *The Prince* argues that the function of a ruler (or a government) is to preserve order and security. The inability to do so would lead to disorder, which might end in civil war or conquest by an outsider, situations clearly not conducive to any people's well-being. To preserve the state, a ruler should use whatever means necessary—brutality, lying,

manipulation—but he should not do anything that would make the populace turn against him. Stealing or cruel actions done for a ruler's own pleasure would lead to resentment and destroy the popular support needed for a strong, stable realm. "It is much safer for the prince to be feared than loved," Machiavelli advised, "but he ought to avoid making himself hated."[1]

*The Prince* is often seen as the first modern guide to politics in the West, though Machiavelli was denounced for writing it, and people later came to use the word *Machiavellian* to mean cunning and ruthless. Machiavelli put a new spin on the Renaissance search for perfection, arguing that ideals needed to be measured in the cold light of the real world.

## Christian Humanism

In the last quarter of the fifteenth century students from the Low Countries, France, Germany, and England flocked to Italy, absorbed the "new learning" of humanism, and carried it back to their own countries. Northern humanists shared the Italians' ideas about the wisdom of ancient texts and felt even more strongly that the best elements of classical and Christian cultures should be combined. These **Christian humanists**, as they were later called, saw humanist learning as a way to bring about reform of the church and to deepen people's spiritual lives.

The Englishman Thomas More (1478–1535) began life as a lawyer, studied the classics, and entered government service. He became best known for his controversial dialogue *Utopia* (1516), a word More invented from the Greek words for "nowhere." *Utopia* describes a community on an island somewhere beyond Europe where all children receive a good humanist education and adults divide their days between manual labor or business pursuits and intellectual activities. The problems that plagued More's fellow citizens, such as poverty and hunger, are solved by a beneficent government. Inequality and greed are prevented because profits from business and property are held in common, not privately. Furthermore, there is religious tolerance, and order and reason prevail. Because Utopian institutions are perfect, however, dissent and disagreement are not acceptable.

More's purposes in writing *Utopia* have been hotly debated. Some view it as a revolutionary critique of More's own hierarchical and violent society, some as a call for an even firmer hierarchy, and others as part of the humanist tradition of satire. It was widely read by learned Europeans in the Latin in which More wrote

---

• **Christian humanists** Humanists from northern Europe who thought that the best elements of classical and Christian cultures should be combined and saw humanist learning as a way to bring about reform of the church and deepen people's spiritual lives.

# Viewpoints 15.1

## Lauro Quirini and Cassandra Fedele: Women and Humanist Learning

• *Italian humanists promoted the value of their new style of education, and several women from the bustling cities of northern Italy obtained humanist education, writing letters, dialogues, and orations. Some male humanists criticized women who publicly shared their ideas, but others celebrated them. The Venetian humanist and nobleman Lauro Quirini (ca. 1420–ca. 1475) wrote to one of these, the learned Isotta Nogarola (1418–1466), praising her accomplishments and advising her on a plan of study. The second document is an excerpt from an oration that the Venetian Cassandra Fedele (1465–1558) gave in Latin at the University of Padua in honor of her (male) cousin's graduation. Fedele applied advice such as Quirini's to her own studies and became the best-known female scholar of her time.*

### Letter from Lauro Quirini to Isotta Nogarola, ca. 1450

❝ This letter asks of you nothing else than that you pursue in the most splendid way, until death, that same course of right living that you have followed since childhood. . . . Rightful therefore, should you also, famous Isotta, receive the highest praises, since you have, if I may so speak, overcome your own nature. For that true virtue that is proper to men you have pursued with remarkable zeal — not the mediocre virtue that many men seek, but that which would befit a man of the most flawless and perfect wisdom. . . . Therefore dissatisfied with the lesser studies, you have applied your noble mind to those highest disciplines, in which there is need for keenness of intelligence and mind. For you are engaged in the art of dialectic, which shows the way to learning the truth. After you have also digested this part of philosophy, which is concerned with human matters, equipped with your nobility of the soul you should also set out for that ample and vast other part [divine matters]. . . . Here you should begin especially with those disciplines that we call by the Greek term mathematics. . . . You should also make use of those studies, moreover, that you have splendidly embraced from your youth, and especially history, for history is as it were the teacher of life. ❞

### Cassandra Fedele, In Praise of Letters, ca. 1485

❝ I shall speak very briefly on the study of the liberal arts, which for humans is useful and honorable, pleasurable and enlightening since everyone, not only philosophers but also the most ignorant man, knows and admits that it is by reason that man is separated from beasts. For what is it that so greatly helps both the learned and the ignorant? What so enlarges and enlightens men's minds the way that an education in and knowledge of literature and the liberal arts do? . . . But erudite men who are filled with the knowledge of divine and human things turn all their thoughts and considerations toward reason as though toward a target, and free their minds from all pain, though plagued by many anxieties. . . .

But enough on the utility of literature since it produces not only an outcome that is rich, precious, and sublime, but also provides one with advantages that are extremely pleasurable, fruitful, and lasting — benefits that I myself have enjoyed. And when I meditate on the idea of marching forth in life with the lowly and execrable weapons of the little woman — the needle and the distaff [the rod onto which yarn is wound after spinning] — even if the study of literature offers women no rewards or honors, I believe women must nonetheless pursue and embrace such studies alone for the pleasure and enjoyment they contain. ❞

Sources: Isotta Nogarola, *Complete Writings, Letterbook, Dialogue on Adam and Eve, Orations*, ed. and trans. Margaret L. King and Diana Robin, pp. 108–113. Reproduced with permission of University of Chicago Press in the format Republish in a book via Copyright Clearance Center; Cassandra Fedele, *Letters and Orations*, ed. and trans. Diana Robin, pp. 159–162. Reproduced with permission of University of Chicago Press in the format Republish in a book via Copyright Clearance Center.

### QUESTIONS FOR ANALYSIS

1. What do Quirini and Fedele view as the best course and purposes of study? How are these different, or similar, for men and women?

2. Quirini is male and Fedele female. Does the gender of the authors shape their ideas about the appropriateness of humanist learning for women? If so, how?

it, and later in vernacular translations, and its title quickly became the standard word for any idealized imaginary society.

Better known by contemporaries than Thomas More was the Dutch humanist Desiderius Erasmus (1466?–1536) of Rotterdam. His fame rested largely on his exceptional knowledge of Greek and the Bible. Erasmus's long list of publications includes *The Education of a Christian Prince* (1504), a book combining idealistic and practical suggestions for the formation of a ruler's character through the careful study of Plutarch, Aristotle, Cicero, and Plato; *The Praise of Folly* (1509), a witty satire poking fun at social, political, and especially religious institutions; and, most important, a critical edition of the Greek New Testament (1516). For Erasmus, education was the key to moral and intellectual improvement, and true Christianity was an inner attitude of the spirit, not a set of outward actions.

## Printing and Its Social Impact

The fourteenth-century humanist Petrarch and the sixteenth-century humanist Erasmus had many similar ideas, but the immediate impact of their ideas was very different because of one thing: the printing press with movable metal type. While Petrarch's works spread slowly from person to person by hand copying, Erasmus's works spread quickly through printing, in which hundreds or thousands of identical copies could be made in a short time.

While printing with movable type was invented in China (see page 370), movable *metal* type was actually developed in the thirteenth century in Korea, though it was tightly controlled by the monarchy and did not have the broad impact there that printing did in Europe. Printing with movable metal type developed in Germany in the middle of the fifteenth century as a combination of existing technologies. Several metalsmiths, most prominently Johann Gutenberg (ca. 1400–1468), transformed the metal stamps used to mark signs on jewelry into type that could be covered with ink and used to mark symbols onto a page. This type could be rearranged for every page and so used over and over. Historians have speculated whether German printers somehow learned of the Korean invention, but there is no evidence that they did. The printing revolution was also enabled by the ready availability of paper, which was made using techniques that had originated in China and spread from Muslim Spain to the rest of Europe.

The effects of the invention of movable-type printing were not felt overnight. Nevertheless, within a half century of the publication of Gutenberg's Bible of 1456, movable type had brought about radical changes. Historians estimate that somewhere between 8 million and 20 million books were printed in Europe between 1456 and 1500, many more than the total number of books that had been produced in the West during the many millennia between the invention of writing and 1456.

Printing transformed both the private and the public lives of Europeans. In the public realm, government and church leaders both used and worried about printing. They printed laws, declarations of war, battle accounts, and propaganda, but they also attempted to censor or ban books and authors whose ideas they thought were wrong. These efforts were rarely effective.

In the private realm, printing enabled people to read identical books so that they could more easily discuss the ideas that the books contained. Although most of the earliest books and pamphlets dealt with religious subjects, printers produced anything that would sell: professional reference sets, historical romances, biographies, poetry, prose fiction, and how-to manuals for the general public. Illustrations increased a book's sales, so printers published both history and pornography full of woodcuts and engravings. Additionally, single-page broadsides and fly sheets allowed public events and "wonders" such as comets and two-headed calves to be experienced vicariously. Since books and other printed materials were read aloud to illiterate listeners, print bridged the gap between the written and oral cultures.

Because many laypeople could not read Latin, printers put out works in vernacular languages, fostering standardization in these languages. Works in these languages were also performed onstage, for plays of all types were popular everywhere. Traveling companies of actors performed before royal courts and in town squares, and in larger cities public theaters offered bawdy comedies and bloody tragedies. In London the works of William Shakespeare (1564–1616) were especially popular. (See "Viewpoints 16.2: Two Views of 'Natural Man,'" page 484.)

## Art and the Artist

No feature of the Renaissance evokes greater admiration than its artistic masterpieces. In Renaissance Italy wealthy merchants, bankers, popes, and princes spent vast sums to commission art as a means of glorifying themselves and their families. Patrons varied in their level of involvement as a work progressed; some simply ordered a specific subject or scene, while others oversaw the work of the artist or architect very closely, suggesting themes and styles and demanding changes while the work was in progress.

As a result of patronage, certain artists gained great public acclaim and adulation, leading many historians to view the Renaissance as the beginning of the concept of the artist as genius. In the Middle Ages, people believed that only God created, albeit through individuals, and artistic originality was not particularly valued. By contrast, Renaissance artists and humanists came to think that a work of art was the deliberate creation of a unique personality, of an individual who transcended traditions, rules, and theories.

In terms of artistic themes, religious topics, such as the Annunciation of the Virgin Mary and the Nativity, remained popular among both patrons and artists, but frequently the patron had himself and his family portrayed in the scene. As the fifteenth century advanced and humanist ideas spread more widely, classical themes and motifs, such as the lives and loves of pagan gods and goddesses, figured increasingly in painting and sculpture, with the facial features of the gods sometimes modeled on those of living people. Classical styles also influenced architecture, as architects designed build-

**Michelangelo's *David* (1501–1504) and the *Last Judgment* (detail, 1537–1541)** Like all Renaissance artists, Michelangelo worked largely on commissions from patrons. Officials of the city of Florence contracted the young sculptor to produce a statue of the Old Testament hero David (left) to be displayed in the city's main square. Michelangelo portrayed David anticipating his fight against the giant Goliath, and the statue came to symbolize the republic of Florence standing up to its larger and more powerful enemies. More than thirty years later, Michelangelo was commissioned by the pope to paint a scene of the Last Judgment on the altar wall of the Sistine Chapel, where he had earlier spent four years covering the ceiling with magnificent frescoes. The massive work shows a powerful Christ standing in judgment, with souls ascending into Heaven while others are dragged by demons into Hell (above). The *David* captures ideals of human perfection and has come to be an iconic symbol of Renaissance artistic brilliance, while the dramatic and violent *Last Judgment* conveys both terror and divine power. (sculpture: Galleria dell'Accademia, Florence, Italy/Ken Welsh/The Bridgeman Art Library; painting: Vatican Museum and Galleries, Vatican City/Alinari/The Bridgeman Art Library)

ings that featured carefully proportioned arches and domes modeled on the structures of ancient Rome.

The individual portrait emerged as a distinct genre in Renaissance art. Rather than reflecting a spiritual ideal, as medieval painting and sculpture tended to do, Renaissance portraits showed human ideals, often portrayed in a more realistic style. The Florentine sculptor Donatello (1386–1466) revived the classical figure, with its balance and self-awareness. Leonardo da Vinci (1452–1519) was particularly adept at portraying female grace and beauty in his paintings of upper-class urban women and biblical figures such as the Virgin Mary. Another Florentine artist, Raphael Sanzio (1483–1520), painted hundreds of portraits and devotional images in his relatively short life, becoming the most sought-after artist in Europe (see page 425).

In the late fifteenth century the center of Renaissance art shifted from Florence to Rome, where wealthy cardinals and popes wanted visual expression of the church's and their own families' power and piety. To meet this demand, Michelangelo Buonarroti (1475–1564) went to Rome from Florence in about 1500 and began the series of statues, paintings, and architectural projects from which he gained an international reputation. For example, he produced sculptures of Moses and of the Virgin Mary holding Jesus after his crucifixion (the Pietà), he redesigned the Capitoline Hill in central Rome, and most famously, between 1508 and 1512, he painted religiously themed frescoes on the ceiling and altar wall of the Sistine Chapel. Pope Julius II, who commissioned Michelangelo for the Sistine Chapel project, demanded that the artist work as fast as he could and frequently visited him to offer suggestions and criticism. Michelangelo complained in person and by letter about the pope's meddling, but his fame did not match the power of the pope, and he kept working.

Though they might show individual genius, Renaissance artists were still expected to be schooled in proper artistic techniques and stylistic conventions, for the notion that artistic genius could show up in the work of the untrained did not emerge until the twentieth century. Therefore, in both Italy and northern Europe most aspiring artists were educated in the workshops of older artists. By the later sixteenth century formal academies were also established to train artists. Like universities, artistic workshops and academies were male-only settings in which students of different ages came together to learn and to create bonds of friendship, influence, patronage, and sometimes intimacy. Several women did become well known as painters during the Renaissance, but they were trained by their artist fathers and often quit painting when they married.

Women were not alone in being excluded from the institutions of Renaissance culture. Though a few

**Donatello, *Gattamelata*, 1450** The Florentine sculptor Donatello's bronze statue of the powerful military captain nicknamed Gattamelata (Honey-Cat) mounted on his horse was erected in the public square of Padua. The first bronze equestrian statue made since Roman times, the larger-than-life-size work seems to capture in metal the shrewd and determined type of ruler Machiavelli described in *The Prince*. (Scala/ Art Resource, NY)

talented artists such as Leonardo and Michelangelo emerged from artisanal backgrounds, most scholars and artists came from families with at least some money. The audience for artists' work was also exclusive, limited mostly to educated and prosperous citizens. Although common people in large cities might have occasionally seen plays such as those of Shakespeare, most people lived in villages with no access to formal schooling or to the work of prominent artists. In general a small, highly educated minority of literary humanists and artists created the culture of and for a social elite. In this way the Renaissance maintained, and even enhanced, a gulf between the learned minority and the uneducated multitude that has survived for many centuries.

***The Chess Game, 1555*** In this oil painting, the Italian artist Sofonisba Anguissola (1532–1625) shows her three younger sisters playing chess, a game that was growing in popularity in the sixteenth century. Each sister looks at the one immediately older than herself, with the girl on the left looking out at her sister, the artist. Anguissola's father, a minor nobleman, recognized his daughter's talent and arranged for her to study with several painters. She became a court painter at the Spanish royal court, where she painted many portraits. Returning to Italy, she continued to be active, painting her last portrait when she was over eighty. (Museum Narodowe, Poznan, Poland/The Bridgeman Art Library)

## Social Hierarchies

☐ What were the key social hierarchies in Renaissance Europe, and how did these hierarchies shape people's lives?

The division between the educated and uneducated was one of many social hierarchies evident in the Renaissance. Other hierarchies were built on those of the Middle Ages, but also developed new features that contributed to modern social hierarchies, such as those of race, class, and gender.

### Race and Slavery

Renaissance people did not use the word *race* the way we do, but often used *race*, *people*, and *nation* interchangeably for ethnic, national, and religious groups — for example, the French race, the Irish people, the Jewish nation. They did make distinctions based on skin color that were in keeping with later conceptualizations of race, but these distinctions were interwoven with other characteristics when people thought about human differences.

Ever since the time of the Roman Republic, a few black Africans had lived in western Europe. They had come, along with white slaves, as the spoils of war.

After the collapse of the Roman Empire and throughout the Middle Ages, Muslim and Christian merchants continued to import black slaves, and long tradition sanctioned the practice of slavery. The black population was especially concentrated in the cities of the Iberian Peninsula, where African slaves sometimes gained their freedom and intermingled with the local population. By the mid-sixteenth century blacks, slave and free, constituted roughly 3 percent of the Portuguese population, and because of intermarriage cities such as Lisbon had significant numbers of people of mixed African and European descent.

In Renaissance Portugal, Spain, and Italy, African slaves supplemented the labor force in virtually all occupations — as servants, agricultural laborers, craftsmen, and seamen on ships. Slaves also formed the primary workforce on the sugar plantations set up by Europeans on the Atlantic islands in the late fifteenth century (see page 477). European aristocrats sometimes had themselves painted with their black servants to indicate their wealth or, in the case of noblewomen, to highlight their fair skin.

Until their voyages down the African coast in the late fifteenth century, Europeans had little concrete knowledge of Africans and their cultures. They perceived Africa as a remote place, the home of strange people isolated by heresy and Islam from superior European civilization. Africans' contact, even as slaves, with Christian Europeans would only "improve" the blacks, they believed. The expanding slave trade reinforced negative preconceptions about the inferiority of black Africans.

• **debate about women** A discussion, which began in the later years of the fourteenth century, that attempted to answer fundamental questions about gender and to define the role of women in society.

## Wealth and the Nobility

The word *class*—as in working class, middle class, upper class—was not used in the Renaissance to describe social division, but by the thirteenth century, and even more so by the fifteenth, the idea of a hierarchy based on wealth was emerging. This was particularly true in cities, where wealthy merchants oversaw vast trading empires, held positions of political power, and lived in splendor rivaling that enjoyed by the richest nobles. (See "Individuals in Society: Cosimo and Lorenzo de' Medici," page 428.)

The development of a hierarchy of wealth did not mean an end to the prominence of nobles, however, and even poorer nobles still had higher status than wealthy commoners. Thus wealthy Italian merchants enthusiastically bought noble titles and country villas in the fifteenth century, and wealthy English and Spanish merchants eagerly married their daughters and sons into often-impoverished noble families. The nobility maintained its status in most parts of Europe not by maintaining rigid boundaries, but by taking in and integrating the new social elite of wealth.

## Gender Roles

Renaissance people would not have understood the word *gender* to refer to categories of people, but they would have easily grasped the concept. Toward the end of the fourteenth century learned men (and a few women) began what was termed the **debate about women** (*querelle des femmes*), an argument about women's character and nature that would last for centuries. Misogynist critiques of women from both clerical and secular authors denounced females as devious, domineering, and demanding. In response, several authors compiled long lists of famous and praiseworthy women exemplary for their loyalty, bravery, and morality. Some writers, including a few women who had gained a humanist education, were interested not only in defending women but also in exploring the reasons behind women's secondary status—that is, why the great philosophers, statesmen, and poets had generally been men. In this they were anticipating more recent discussions about the "social construction of gender" by six hundred years.

## □ Picturing the Past

***Laura de Dianti*, 1523** The Venetian artist Titian portrays a young Italian woman with a gorgeous blue dress and an elaborate pearl and feather headdress accompanied by a young black page with a gold earring. Slaves from Africa and the Ottoman Empire were common in wealthy Venetian households.

(Photographer: Human Bios International AG, CH-8280, Kreuzlingen, www.humanbios.com)

**ANALYZING THE IMAGE** How does the artist convey the message that this woman comes from a wealthy family? How does he use the skin color of the slave to highlight the woman's fair skin, which was one of the Renaissance ideals of female beauty?

**CONNECTIONS** Household slaves worked at various tasks, but they were also symbols of the exotic. What other elements does Titian include in the painting to represent foreign places and the wealth brought to Venice by overseas trade? What does this painting suggest about Venetian attitudes toward slaves, who were part of that trade?

Beginning in the sixteenth century the debate about women also became a debate about female rulers, because in Spain, England, France, and Scotland women served as advisers to child-kings or ruled in their own right. There were no successful rebellions against female rulers simply because they were women, but in part this was because female rulers, especially Queen Elizabeth I of England, emphasized qualities regarded as masculine—physical bravery, stamina, wisdom, duty—whenever they appeared in public.

The dominant notion of the "true" man was that of the married head of household, so men whose class and age would have normally conferred political power but who remained unmarried were sometimes excluded from ruling positions. Actual marriage patterns in Europe left many women unmarried until late in life, but this did not lead to greater equality. Women who worked for wages, as was typical, earned about half to two-thirds of what men did even for the same work. Regulations for German vineyard workers in the early

sixteenth century, for example, specified:

Men who work in the vineyards, doing work that is skilled, are to be paid 16 pence per day; in addition, they are to receive soup and wine in the morning, at midday beer, vegetables and meat, and in the evening soup, vegetables and wine. Young boys are to be paid 10 pence per day. Women who work as haymakers are to be given 6 pence a day. If the employer wants to have them doing other work, he may make an agreement with them to pay them 7 or 8 pence. He may also give them soup and vegetables to eat in the morning—but no wine—milk and bread at midday, but nothing in the evening.[2]

Of all the ways in which Renaissance society was hierarchically arranged—by class, age, level of education, rank, race, occupation—gender was regarded as the most "natural" distinction and therefore the most important one to defend.

**Italian City Scene** In this detail from a fresco, the Italian painter Lorenzo Lotto captures the mixing of social groups in a Renaissance Italian city. The crowd of men in the left foreground includes wealthy merchants in elaborate hats and colorful coats. Two mercenary soldiers (carrying a sword and a pike) wear short doublets and tight hose stylishly slit to reveal colored undergarments, while boys play with toy weapons at their feet. Clothing like that of the soldiers, which emphasized the masculine form, was frequently criticized for its expense and its "indecency." At the right, women sell vegetables and bread, which would have been a common sight at any city marketplace. (Scala/Art Resource, NY)

# Politics and the State in the Renaissance, ca. 1450–1521

☐ How did the nation-states of western Europe evolve in this period?

The High Middle Ages had witnessed the origins of many of the basic institutions of the modern state. Sheriffs, inquests, juries, circuit judges, professional bureaucracies, and representative assemblies all trace their origins to the twelfth and thirteenth centuries. The linchpin for the development of states, however, was strong monarchy. Beginning in the fifteenth century rulers used aggressive methods to build up their governments. They began the work of reducing violence, curbing unruly nobles, and establishing domestic order. As they built and maintained power, they emphasized royal majesty and royal sovereignty and insisted on the respect and loyalty of all subjects.

## France

The Black Death and the Hundred Years' War left France drastically depopulated, commercially ruined, and agriculturally weak (see page 416). Nonetheless, the ruler whom Joan of Arc had seen crowned at Reims, Charles VII (r. 1422–1461), revived the monarchy and France. He reorganized the royal council, giving increased influence to middle-class men, and strengthened royal finances through taxes on certain products and on land. These taxes remained the Crown's chief sources of income until the Revolution of 1789. By establishing regular companies of cavalry and archers — recruited, paid, and inspected by the state — Charles created the first permanent royal army anywhere in Europe.

Two further developments strengthened the French monarchy. The marriage of Louis XII (r. 1498–1515) and Anne of Brittany added the large western duchy of Brittany to the state. Louis XII's successor, Francis I (r. 1515–1547), and Pope Leo X reached a mutually satisfactory agreement about church and state powers in 1516 that gave French kings the power to control the appointment and thus the policies of church officials in the kingdom.

## England

English society suffered severely in the fourteenth and fifteenth centuries. Population, decimated by the Black Death, continued to decline. Between 1455 and 1471 adherents of the ducal houses of York and Lancaster waged civil wars over control of the English throne, commonly called the Wars of the Roses because the symbol of the Yorkists was a white rose and that of the Lancastrians a red one. The chronic disorder hurt trade, agriculture, and domestic industry, and the authority of the monarchy sank lower than it had been in centuries.

The Yorkist Edward IV (r. 1461–1483) succeeded in defeating the Lancastrian forces and after 1471 began to reconstruct the monarchy and consolidate royal power. Henry VII (r. 1485–1509) of the Welsh house of Tudor worked to restore royal prestige, to crush the power of the nobility, and to establish order and law at the local level. Because the government halted the long period of anarchy, it won the key support of the merchant and agricultural upper middle class. Early in his reign Henry VII summoned several meetings of Parliament, primarily to confirm laws, but the center of royal authority was the royal council, which governed at the national level. There Henry VII revealed his distrust of the nobility: very few great lords were among the king's closest advisers, who instead were lesser landowners and lawyers. They were, in a sense, middle class. The royal council handled any business the king put before it — executive, legislative, and judicial.

Secretive, cautious, and thrifty, Henry VII rebuilt the monarchy. He encouraged the cloth industry and built up the English merchant marine. He crushed an invasion from Ireland, secured peace with Scotland through the marriage of his daughter Margaret to the Scottish king, and enhanced English prestige through the marriage of his eldest son, Arthur, to Catherine of Aragon, the daughter of Ferdinand and Isabella of Spain. (Several years after Arthur's death, Catherine would become the wife of his younger brother and the next king of England, Henry VIII; see page 446.) When Henry VII died in 1509, he left a country at peace both domestically and internationally, a substantially augmented treasury, and the dignity and role of the Crown much enhanced.

## Spain

While England and France laid the foundations of unified nation-states during the Renaissance, Spain remained a conglomerate of independent kingdoms. Even the wedding in 1469 of the dynamic and aggressive Isabella of Castile and the crafty and persistent Ferdinand of Aragon did not bring about administrative unity. Isabella and Ferdinand were, however, able to exert their authority in ways similar to the rulers of France and England. They curbed aristocratic power by excluding aristocrats and great territorial magnates from the royal council, and instead appointed only men of middle-class background. The council and various government boards recruited men trained in Roman law, which exalted the power of the Crown. They also secured from the Spanish pope Alexander VI the right to appoint bishops in Spain and in the Hispanic territories in America, enabling them to establish the equivalent of a national church. In 1492 their armies conquered Granada, the last territory held by Arabs in southern Spain.

Ferdinand and Isabella's rule also marked the start of greater persecution of the Jews. In the Middle Ages, the kings of France and England had expelled the Jews from their kingdoms, and many had sought refuge in Spain. During the long centuries of the reconquista (see page 401), Christian kings in Spain had renewed Jewish rights and privileges; in fact, Jewish industry, intelligence, and money had supported royal power. But while Christians of all classes borrowed from Jewish moneylenders and while all who could afford them

sought Jewish physicians, a strong undercurrent of resentment of Jewish influence and wealth festered.

In the fourteenth century anti-Semitism in Spain was aggravated by fiery anti-Jewish preaching, by economic dislocation, and by the search for a scapegoat during the Black Death. Anti-Semitic pogroms, violent massacres and riots directed against Jews, swept the towns of Spain, and perhaps 40 percent of the Jewish population was killed or forced to convert. Those who converted were called *conversos* (kuhn-VEHR-sohz) or New Christians. Conversos were often well educated and held prominent positions in government, the church, medicine, law, and business.

Such successes bred resentment. Aristocrats resented their financial dependence on conversos, the poor hated the converso tax collectors, and churchmen doubted the sincerity of their conversions. Queen Isabella shared

## MAP 15.1  The Global Empire of Charles V, ca. 1556

Charles V exercised theoretical jurisdiction over more European territory than anyone since Charlemagne. He also claimed authority over large parts of North and South America, although actual Spanish control was weak in much of this area.

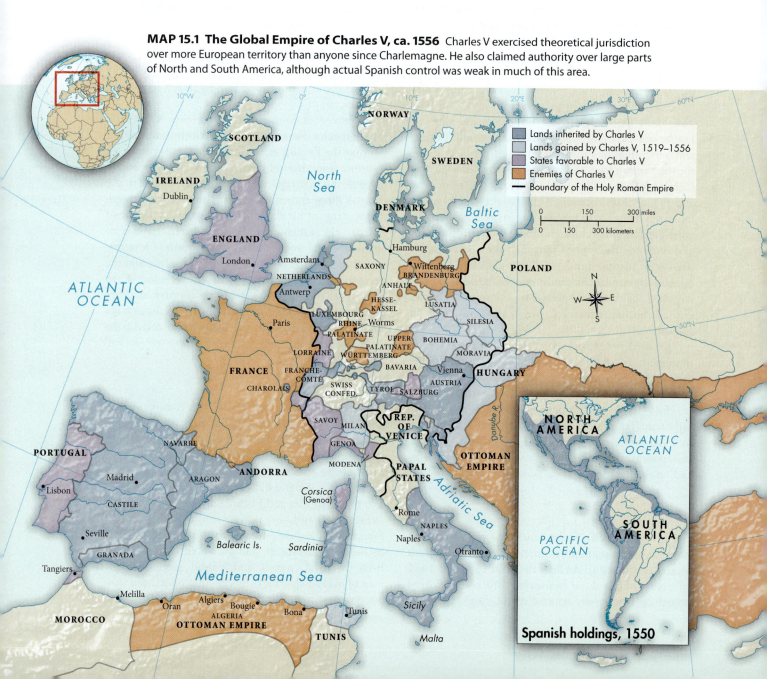

these suspicions, and she and Ferdinand received permission from Pope Sixtus IV to establish an Inquisition to "search out and punish converts from Judaism who had transgressed against Christianity by secretly adhering to Jewish beliefs and performing rites of the Jews."[3] Investigations and trials began immediately, with officials of the Inquisition looking for conversos who showed any sign of incomplete conversion, such as not eating pork.

Recent scholarship has carefully analyzed documents of the Inquisition. Most conversos identified themselves as sincere Christians; many came from families that had received baptism generations before. In response, officials of the Inquisition developed a new type of anti-Semitism. A person's status as a Jew, they argued, could not be changed by religious conversion, but was in the person's blood and was heritable, so Jews could never be true Christians. Under what were known as "purity of blood" laws, having "pure Christian blood" became a requirement for noble status. Ideas about Jews developed in Spain became important components in European concepts of race, and discussions of "Jewish blood" later expanded into discriminatory definitions of the "Jewish race."

In 1492, shortly after the conquest of Granada, Isabella and Ferdinand issued an edict expelling all practicing Jews from Spain. Of the community of perhaps 200,000 Jews, 150,000 fled. Absolute religious orthodoxy and "purity of blood" served as the theoretical foundation of the Spanish national state.

## The Habsburgs

War and diplomacy were important ways that states increased their power in sixteenth-century Europe, but so was marriage. Because almost all of Europe was ruled by hereditary dynasties—the Papal States and a few cities being the exceptions—claiming and holding resources involved shrewd marital strategies, for it was far cheaper to gain land by inheritance than by war.

The benefits of an advantageous marriage stretched across generations, as can be seen most dramatically with the Habsburgs. The Holy Roman emperor Frederick III, a Habsburg who was the ruler of most of Austria, acquired only a small amount of territory—but a great deal of money—with his marriage to Princess Eleanore of Portugal in 1452. He arranged for his son Maximilian to marry Europe's most prominent heiress, Mary of Burgundy, in 1477; she inherited the Netherlands, Luxembourg, and the county of Burgundy in what is now eastern France. Through this union with the rich and powerful duchy of Burgundy, the Austrian house of Habsburg, already the strongest ruling family in the empire, became an international power. The marriage of Maximilian and Mary angered the French, who considered Burgundy French territory, and it inaugu-

rated centuries of conflict between the Habsburgs and the kings of France. Within the empire, German principalities that resented Austria's pre-eminence began to see that they shared interests with France.

Maximilian learned the lesson of marital politics well, marrying his son and daughter to the children of Ferdinand and Isabella, the rulers of Spain, much of southern Italy, and eventually the Spanish New World empire. His grandson Charles V (1500–1558) fell heir to a vast and incredibly diverse collection of states and peoples, each governed in a different manner and held together only by the person of the emperor (Map 15.1). Charles was convinced that it was his duty to maintain the political and religious unity of Western Christendom. This conviction would be challenged far more than Charles ever anticipated.

## The Protestant Reformation

☐ What were the central ideas of Protestant reformers, and why were they appealing to various groups across Europe?

Calls for reform in the church came from many quarters in early-sixteenth-century Europe—from educated laypeople such as Christian humanists and urban residents, from villagers and artisans, and from church officials themselves. This dissatisfaction helps explain why the ideas of Martin Luther, an obscure professor from a new and not very prestigious German university, found a ready audience. Within a decade of his first publishing his ideas (using the new technology of the printing press), much of central Europe and Scandinavia had broken with the Catholic Church in a movement that came to be known as the **Protestant Reformation**. In addition, even more radical concepts of the Christian message were being developed and linked to calls for social change.

## Criticism of the Church

Sixteenth-century Europeans were deeply pious. Despite—or perhaps because of—the depth of their piety, many people were also highly critical of the Roman Catholic Church and its clergy. Papal conflicts with rulers and the Great Schism (see page 419) badly damaged the prestige of church leaders. Papal tax collection methods were also attacked, and some criticized the papacy itself as an institution. Court records, written descriptions of bishops' visitations of parishes,

• **Protestant Reformation** A religious reform movement that began in the early sixteenth century that split the Western Christian Church.

and even popular songs and printed images show widespread anticlericalism, or opposition to the clergy.

In the early sixteenth century, critics of the church concentrated their attacks on clerical immorality, ignorance, and absenteeism. Charges of immorality were aimed at a number of priests who were drunkards, neglected the rule of celibacy, gambled, or indulged in fancy dress. Charges of ignorance applied to barely literate priests who delivered poor-quality sermons and who were obviously ignorant of the Latin words of the Mass.

In regard to absenteeism, many clerics, especially higher ecclesiastics, held several benefices (offices) simultaneously—a practice termed pluralism. However, they seldom visited the communities served by the benefices, let alone performed the spiritual responsibilities those offices entailed. Instead, they collected revenues from all the benefices assigned to them and hired a poor priest to fulfill their spiritual duties, paying him just a fraction of the income.

There was also local resentment of clerical privileges and immunities. Priests, monks, and nuns were exempt from civic responsibilities, such as defending the city and paying taxes. Yet religious orders frequently held large amounts of urban property, in some cities as much as one-third. City governments were increasingly determined to integrate the clergy into civic life. This brought city leaders into opposition with bishops and the papacy, which for centuries had stressed the independence of the church from lay control and the distinction between members of the clergy and laypeople.

## Martin Luther

By itself, widespread criticism of the church did not lead to the dramatic changes of the sixteenth century. Those resulted from the personal religious struggle of a German university professor, Martin Luther (1483–1546). Luther's father wanted him to be a lawyer, but a sense of religious calling led him to join the Augustinian friars, an order whose members often preached to, taught, and assisted the poor. Luther was ordained a priest in 1507 and after additional study earned a doctorate of theology. From 1512 until his death in 1546 he served as professor of the Scriptures at the new University of Wittenberg.

Martin Luther was a very conscientious friar, but his scrupulous observance of the religious routine, frequent confessions, and fasting gave him only temporary relief from anxieties about sin and his ability to meet God's demands. Through his study of Saint Paul's letters in the New Testament, he gradually arrived at a new understanding of Christian doctrine. His understanding is often summarized as "faith alone, grace alone, scripture alone." He believed that salvation and justification (righteousness in God's eyes) come through faith, and that faith is a free gift of God, not the result of human effort. God's word is revealed only in biblical scripture, not in the traditions of the church.

At the same time that Luther was engaged in scholarly reflections and professorial lecturing, Pope Leo X authorized a special Saint Peter's indulgence to finance his building plans in Rome. An **indulgence** was a document, signed by the pope or another church official, that substituted for penance. The archbishop who controlled the area in which Wittenberg was located, Albert of Mainz, also promoted the sale of indulgences, in his case to pay off a debt he had incurred to be named bishop of several additional territories. Albert's sales campaign, run by a Dominican friar who mounted an advertising blitz, promised that the purchase of indulgences would bring full forgiveness for one's own sins or buy release from purgatory for a loved one. One of the slogans—"As soon as coin in coffer rings, the soul from purgatory springs"—brought phenomenal success.

Luther was severely troubled that many people believed that they had no further need for repentance once they had purchased indulgences. He wrote a letter to Archbishop Albert on the subject and enclosed in Latin his "Ninety-five Theses on the Power of Indulgences." His argument was that indulgences undermined the seriousness of the sacrament of penance and competed with the preaching of the Gospel. After Luther's death, biographies reported that the theses were also posted on the door of the church at Wittenberg Castle on October 31, 1517. Such an act would have been very strange—they were in Latin and written for those learned in theology, not for normal churchgoers—but it has become a standard part of Luther lore. In any case, Luther intended the theses for academic debate, but by December 1517 they had been translated into German and were being read throughout central Europe. Luther was ordered to go to Rome, but he was able to avoid this because the ruler of the territory in which he lived protected him. The pope nonetheless ordered him to recant many of his ideas, and Luther publicly burned the letter containing the papal order. In this highly charged atmosphere, the twenty-one-year-old emperor Charles V summoned Luther to appear before the **Diet of Worms**, an assembly of representatives from the territories of

- **indulgence** A papal statement granting remission of a priest-imposed penalty for sin. (No one knew what penalty God would impose after death.)
- **Diet of Worms** An assembly of representatives from the territories of the Holy Roman Empire convened by Charles V in the German city of Worms in 1521. It was here that Martin Luther refused to recant his writings.
- **Protestant** Originally meaning "a follower of Luther," this term came to be generally applied to all non-Catholic western European Christians.

## Selling Indulgences

A German single-page pamphlet shows a monk offering an indulgence, with the official seals of the pope attached, as people run to put their money in the box in exchange for his promise of heavenly bliss, symbolized by the dove above his head. Indulgences were sold widely in Germany, and they were the first Catholic practice that Luther criticized openly. This pamphlet also attacks the sale of indulgences, calling it devilish and deceitful, a point of view expressed in the woodcut by the peddler's riding on a donkey, an animal that had long been used as a symbol of ignorance. Indulgences were often printed as fill-in-the-blank forms. This one, purchased in 1521, has space for the indulgence seller's name at the top, the buyer's name in the middle, and the date at the bottom. (woodcut: akg-images; indulgence: Visual Connection Archive)

the Holy Roman Empire meeting in the city of Worms in 1521. Luther refused to give in to demands that he take back his ideas:

> Unless I am convinced by the evidence of Scripture or by plain reason—for I do not accept the authority of the Pope or the councils alone, since it is established that they have often erred and contradicted themselves—I am bound by the Scriptures I have cited and my conscience is captive to the Word of God. I cannot and will not recant anything, for it is neither safe nor right to go against conscience.[4]

## Protestant Thought and Its Appeal

As he developed his ideas, Luther gathered followers, who came to be called Protestants. The word **Protestant** derives from a "protest" drawn up by a small group of reforming German princes in 1529. At first *Protestant* meant "a follower of Luther," but as many other reformers appeared, it became a general term for all non-Catholic western European Christians.

Catholics and Protestants disagreed on many issues. First, how is a person to be saved? Catholic teaching held that salvation is achieved by both faith and good works. Protestants held that salvation comes by faith alone, irrespective of good works or the sacraments. God, not people, initiates salvation. (See "Listening to the Past: Martin Luther, *On Christian Liberty*," page 442.) Second, where does religious authority reside? Christian doctrine had long maintained that authority rests both in the Bible and in the traditional teaching of the church. For Protestants, however, authority rests in the Bible alone, and for a doctrine or issue to be valid, it has to have a scriptural basis. Third, what is the church? Protestants held that the church is a spiritual priesthood of all believers, an invisible fellowship not fixed in any place or person, which differed markedly from the Roman Catholic practice of looking to a clerical, hierarchical institution headed by the pope in Rome. Fourth, what is the highest form of Christian life? The medieval church had stressed the superiority of the monastic and religious life over the secular. Protestants disagreed and argued that every person should serve God in his or her individual calling.

Pulpits and printing presses spread the Protestant message all over Germany, and by the middle of the sixteenth century people of all social classes had rejected

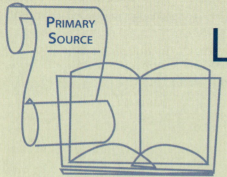

# Listening to the Past

## Martin Luther, *On Christian Liberty*

*The idea of liberty or freedom has played a powerful role in the history of human society and culture, but the meaning and understanding of liberty have undergone continual change and interpretation. In the Roman world, where slavery was a basic institution, liberty meant the condition of being a free man, independent of obligations to a master. In the Middle Ages, possessing liberty meant having special privileges or rights that other persons or institutions did not have. A lord or a monastery, for example, might speak of his or its liberties, and citizens in London were said to possess the "freedom of the city," which allowed them to practice trades and own property without interference.*

*The idea of liberty also has a religious dimension, and the reformer Martin Luther formulated a classic interpretation of liberty in his treatise* On Christian Liberty *(sometimes translated as* On the Freedom of a Christian*), arguably his finest piece. Written in Latin for the pope but translated immediately into German and published widely, it contains the main themes of Luther's theology: the importance of faith, the relationship of Christian faith and good works, the dual nature of human beings, and the fundamental importance of scripture. Luther writes that Christians were freed from sin and death through Christ, not by their own actions.*

❝ A Christian man is the most free lord of all, and subject to none; a Christian man is the most dutiful servant of all, and subject to everyone. Although these statements appear contradictory, yet, when they are found to agree together, they will do excellently for my purpose. They are both the statements of Paul himself, who says, "Though I be free from all men, yet have I made myself a servant unto all" (I Corinthians 9:19), and "Owe no man anything but to love one another" (Romans 13:8). Now love is by its own nature dutiful and obedient to the beloved object. Thus even Christ, though Lord of all things, was yet made of a woman; made under the law; at once free and a servant; at once in the form of God and in the form of a servant.

Let us examine the subject on a deeper and less simple principle. Man is composed of a twofold nature, a spiritual and a bodily. As regards the spiritual nature, which they name the soul, he is called the spiritual, inward, new man; as regards the bodily nature, which they name the flesh, he is called the fleshly, outward, old man. The Apostle speaks of this: "Though our outward man perish, yet the inward man is renewed day by day" (II Corinthians 4:16). The result of this diversity is that in the Scriptures opposing statements are made concerning the same man, the fact being that in the same man these two men are opposed to one another; the flesh lusting against the spirit, and the spirit against the flesh (Galatians 5:17).

We first approach the subject of the inward man, that we may see by what means a man becomes justified, free, and a true Christian; that is, a spiritual, new, and inward man. It is certain that absolutely none among outward things, under whatever name they may be reckoned, has any influence in producing Christian righteousness or liberty, nor, on the other hand, unrighteousness or slavery. This can be shown by an easy argument. What can it profit to the soul that the body should be in good condition, free, and full of life, that it should eat, drink, and act according to its pleasure, when even the most impious slaves of every kind of vice are prosperous in these matters? Again, what harm can ill health, bondage, hunger, thirst, or any other outward evil, do to the soul, when even the most pious of men, and the freest in the purity of their conscience, are harassed by these things? Neither of these states of things has to do with the liberty or the slavery of the soul.

And so it will profit nothing that the body should be adorned with sacred vestment, or dwell in holy places, or be occupied in sacred offices, or pray, fast, and abstain from certain meats, or do whatever works can be done through the body and in the body. Something widely different will be necessary for the justification and liberty of the soul, since the things I have spoken of can be done by an impious person, and only hypocrites are produced by devotion to these things. On the other hand, it will not at all injure the soul that the body should be clothed in profane raiment, should dwell in profane places, should eat and drink in the ordinary fashion, should not pray aloud, and should

Catholic teachings and become Protestant. What was the immense appeal of Luther's religious ideas and those of other Protestants?

Educated people and humanists were attracted by Luther's ideas. He advocated a simpler personal religion based on faith, a return to the spirit of the early church, the centrality of the Scriptures in the liturgy and in Christian life, and the abolition of elaborate ceremonies—precisely the reforms the Christian humanists had been calling for. His insistence that everyone should read and reflect on the Scriptures attracted the literate middle classes, including many priests and monks who became clergy in the new Protestant churches. Luther's ideas also appealed to townspeople who envied the church's wealth and resented paying for it. After cities became Protestant, the city council taxed the clergy and placed them under the jurisdiction of civil courts.

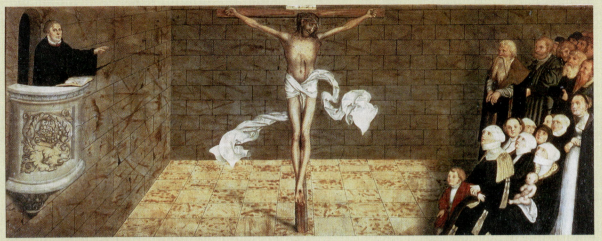

**For effective preaching, especially to the uneducated, Luther urged the minister "to keep it simple for the simple."** (*Martin Luther's Sermon*, detail from a triptych, Lucas Cranach the Elder, 1547 [oil on panel]/ Church of St. Marien, Wittenberg, Germany/Giraudon/The Bridgeman Art Library)

leave undone all the things above mentioned, which may be done by hypocrites. . . .

One thing, and one alone, is necessary for life, justification, and Christian liberty; and that is the most Holy Word of God, the Gospel of Christ, as He says, "I am the resurrection and the life; he that believeth in me shall not die eternally" (John 9:25), and also, "If the Son shall make you free, ye shall be free indeed" (John 8:36), and "Man shall not live by bread alone, but by every word that proceedeth out of the mouth of God" (Matthew 4:4).

Let us therefore hold it for certain and firmly established that the soul can do without everything except the Word of God, without which none at all of its wants is provided for. But, having the Word, it is rich and wants for nothing, since that is the Word of life, of truth, of light, of peace, of justification, of salvation, of joy, of liberty, of wisdom, of virtue, of grace, of glory, and of every good thing. . . .

But you will ask, "What is this Word, and by what means is it to be used, since there are so many words of God?" I answer, "The Apostle Paul (Romans 1) explains what it is, namely the Gospel of God, concerning His Son, incarnate, suffering, risen, and glorified through the Spirit, the Sanctifier." To preach Christ is to feed the soul, to justify it, to set it free, and to save it, if it believes the preaching. For faith alone, and the efficacious use of the Word of God, bring salvation. "If thou shalt confess with thy mouth the Lord Jesus, and shalt believe in thine heart that God hath raised Him from the dead, thou shalt be saved" (Romans 9:9); . . . and "The just shall live by faith" (Romans 1:17). . . .

But this faith cannot consist of all with works; that is, if you imagine that you can be justified by those works, whatever they are, along with it. . . . Therefore, when you begin to believe, you learn at the same time that all that is in you is utterly guilty, sinful, and damnable, according to that saying, "All have sinned, and come short of the glory of God" (Romans 3:23). . . . When you have learned this, you will know that Christ is necessary for you, since He has suffered and risen again for you, that, believing on Him, you might by this faith become another man, all your sins being remitted, and you being justified by the merits of another, namely Christ alone. . . .

And since it [faith] alone justifies, it is evident that by no outward work or labour can the inward man be at all justified, made free, and saved; and that no works whatever have any relation to him. . . . Therefore the first care of every Christian ought to be to lay aside all reliance on works, and strengthen his faith alone more and more, and by it grow in knowledge, not of works, but of Christ Jesus, who has suffered and risen again for him, as Peter teaches (I Peter 5). 🙶

Source: *Luther's Primary Works*, ed. H. Wace and C. A. Buchheim (London: Holder and Stoughton, 1896). Reprinted in *The Portable Renaissance Reader*, ed. James Bruce Ross and Mary Martin McLaughlin (New York: Penguin Books, 1981), pp. 721–726.

**QUESTIONS FOR ANALYSIS**

1. What did Luther mean by liberty?
2. Why, for Luther, was scripture basic to Christian life?

Scholars in many disciplines have attributed Luther's fame and success to the invention of the printing press, which rapidly reproduced and made known his ideas. Many printed works included woodcuts and other illustrations, so that even those who could not read could grasp the main ideas. Hymns were also important means of conveying central points of doctrine, as was Luther's translation of the New Testament into German in 1523.

Luther worked closely with political authorities, viewing them as fully justified in reforming the church in their territories. He instructed all Christians to obey their secular rulers, whom he saw as divinely ordained to maintain order. Individuals may have been convinced of the truth of Protestant teachings by hearing sermons, listening to hymns, or reading pamphlets, but a territory became Protestant when its ruler, whether a noble or a city council, brought in a reformer or two to re-educate the territory's clergy, sponsored public sermons, and confiscated church property. This happened in many of the states of the empire during the 1520s and then moved beyond the empire to Denmark-Norway and Sweden.

## The Radical Reformation and the German Peasants' War

In the sixteenth century the practice of religion remained a public matter. The ruler determined the official form of religious practice in his (or occasionally her) jurisdiction. Almost everyone believed that the presence of a faith different from that of the majority represented a political threat to the security of the state. Few believed in religious liberty; people with different ideas had to convert or leave.

Some individuals and groups rejected the idea that church and state needed to be united, however, and they sought to create a voluntary community of believers as they understood it to have existed in New Testament times. In terms of theology and spiritual practices, these individuals and groups varied widely, though they are generally termed "radicals" for their insistence on a more extensive break with prevailing ideas. Some adopted the custom of baptizing adult believers—for which they were given the title of "Anabaptists" or rebaptizers by their enemies—while others saw all outward sacraments or rituals as misguided. Some groups attempted communal ownership of property, living very simply and rejecting anything they thought unbiblical. Some reacted harshly to members who deviated from the group's accepted practices, but others argued for complete religious tolerance and individualism.

Religious radicals were met with fanatical hatred and bitter persecution, including banishment and execution. Both Protestant and Catholic authorities felt threatened by the social, political, and economic implications of radicals' religious ideas and by their rejection of a state church, which the authorities saw as key to maintaining order. Their community spirit and heroism in the face of martyrdom, however, contributed to the survival of radical ideas. Later, the Quakers, with their pacifism; the Baptists, with their emphasis on inner spiritual light; the Congregationalists, with their democratic church organization; and, in 1787, the authors of the U.S. Constitution, with their opposition to the "establishment of religion" (state churches), would all trace the origins of their beliefs, in part, to the radicals of the sixteenth century.

Another group to challenge state authorities was the peasantry. In the early sixteenth century the economic condition of peasants varied from place to place but was generally worse than it had been in the fifteenth century and was deteriorating. Peasants demanded limitations on the new taxes and labor obligations their noble landlords were imposing. They believed that their demands conformed to the Scriptures and cited Luther as a theologian who could prove that they did.

Wanting to prevent rebellion, Luther initially sided with the peasants, blasting the lords for robbing their subjects. But when rebellion broke out, the peasants who expected Luther's support were soon disillusioned. Freedom for Luther meant independence from the authority of the Roman Church, not opposition to legally established secular powers. Firmly convinced that rebellion would hasten the end of civilized society, he wrote the tract *Against the Murderous, Thieving Hordes of the Peasants*, which said, in part, "Let everyone who can smite, slay, and stab [the peasants], secretly and openly, remembering that nothing can be more poisonous, hurtful or devilish than a rebel."[5] The nobility ferociously crushed the revolt, which became known as the German Peasants' War of 1525. That year, historians estimate, more than seventy-five thousand peasants were killed.

The Peasants' War greatly strengthened the authority of lay rulers. Because Luther turned against the peasants who revolted, the Reformation lost much of its popular appeal after 1525, though peasants and urban rebels sometimes found a place for their social and religious ideas in radical groups. Peasants' economic conditions did moderately improve, however. For example, in many parts of Germany enclosed fields, meadows, and forests were returned to common use instead of being controlled by noble landlords.

## Marriage and Women's Roles

Luther and other Protestants believed that a priest's or nun's vows of celibacy went against human nature and God's commandments. Luther married a former nun, Katharina von Bora (1499–1532), who quickly had several children. Most other Protestant reformers also married, and their wives had to create a new and respectable role for themselves—pastor's wife—to overcome being viewed as simply a new type of priest's concubine. They were living demonstrations of their husband's convictions about the superiority of marriage to celibacy, and they were expected to be models of wifely obedience and Christian charity.

Catholics viewed marriage as a sacramental union that, if validly entered into, could not be dissolved. Protestants saw marriage as a contract in which each partner promised the other support, companionship, and the sharing of mutual goods. They believed that spouses who did not comfort or support one another endangered their own souls and the surrounding community; therefore, most Protestants came to allow divorce. Divorce remained rare, however, because marriage was such an important social and economic institution.

Protestants did not break with medieval scholastic theologians in their view that, within marriage, women were to be subject to men. Women were advised to be cheerful rather than grudging in their obedience, for in doing so they demonstrated their willingness to follow God's plan. Men were urged to treat their wives kindly and considerately, but also to enforce their authority, through physical coercion if necessary. Both continental and English marriage manuals use the metaphor of breaking a horse for teaching a wife obedience, though laws did set limits on the husband's power to control his wife. A few women took the Protestant idea about the priesthood of all believers to heart and wrote religious pamphlets and hymns, but no sixteenth-century Protestants officially allowed women to hold positions of religious authority. Monarchs such as Elizabeth I of England and female territorial rulers of the states of the Holy Roman Empire did determine religious policies, however.

Because the Reformation generally brought the closing of monasteries and convents, marriage became virtually the only occupation for upper-class Protestant women. Recognizing this, women in some convents fought the Reformation or argued that they could still be pious Protestants within convent walls. Most nuns left, however, and we do not know what happened to them. The Protestant emphasis on marriage made unmarried women (and men) suspect, for they did not belong to the type of household regarded as the cornerstone of a proper, godly society.

## The Reformation and German Politics

Criticism of the church was widespread in Europe in the early sixteenth century, and calls for reform came from many areas. Yet such movements could be more easily squelched by the strong central governments of Spain, France, and England. The Holy Roman Empire, in contrast, included hundreds of largely independent states in which the emperor had far less authority than did the monarchs of western Europe. Thus local rulers of the many states in the empire continued to exercise great power.

Luther's ideas appealed to local rulers within the empire for a variety of reasons. Though Germany was not a nation, people did have an understanding of being German because of their language and traditions. Luther frequently used the phrase "we Germans" in his attacks on the papacy, and his appeal to national feeling influenced many rulers. Also, while some German rulers were sincerely attracted to Lutheran ideas, material considerations swayed many others to embrace the new faith. The rejection of Roman Catholicism and the adoption of Protestantism would mean the legal confiscation of lush farmlands, rich monasteries, and wealthy shrines owned by monasteries, bishops, and other officials. Thus many political authorities in the empire used the religious issue to extend their financial and political power and to enhance their independence from the emperor.

The Habsburg Charles V, elected as emperor in 1521, was a vigorous defender of Catholicism, so it is

**Martin Luther and Katharina von Bora** Lucas Cranach the Elder painted this double marriage portrait to celebrate Luther's wedding in 1525 to Katharina von Bora, a former nun. The artist was one of the witnesses at the wedding and, in fact, had presented Luther's marriage proposal to Katharina. The couple quickly became a model of the ideal marriage, and many churches wanted their portraits. More than sixty similar paintings, with slight variations, were produced by Cranach's workshop and hung in churches and wealthy homes. (Painting by Lucas Cranach the Elder [1472–1553], oil on wood/Galleria degli Uffizi, Florence, Italy/akg-images)

not surprising that the Reformation led to religious wars. Protestant territories in the empire formed military alliances, and the emperor could not oppose them effectively given other military engagements. In southeastern Europe Habsburg troops were already fighting the Ottoman Turks, who were expanding their holdings at just the point that the Reformation began. Habsburg soldiers were also engaged in a series of wars with the Valois (VAL-wah) kings of France. The cornerstone of French foreign policy in the sixteenth and seventeenth centuries was the desire to keep the German states divided. Thus Europe witnessed the paradox of the Catholic king of France supporting Lutheran princes in their challenge to his fellow Catholic, Charles V. The Habsburg-Valois wars advanced the cause of Protestantism and promoted the political fragmentation of the German Empire.

Finally, in 1555, Charles agreed to the Peace of Augsburg, which officially recognized Lutheranism and ended religious war in Germany for many decades. Under this treaty, the political authority in each territory of the Holy Roman Empire was permitted to decide whether the territory would be Catholic or Lutheran. Most of northern and central Germany became Lutheran, while southern Germany was divided between Lutheran and Catholic. His hope of uniting his empire under a single church dashed, Charles V abdicated in 1556, transferring power over his Spanish and Netherlandish holdings to his son Philip II and his imperial power to his brother Ferdinand.

## England's Shift Toward Protestantism

States within the Holy Roman Empire and the kingdom of Denmark-Norway were the earliest territories to accept the Protestant Reformation, but by the later 1520s religious change had also come to England, France, and eastern Europe. In all these areas, a second generation of reformers, most prominently John Calvin (see below), built on earlier ideas to develop their own theology and plans for institutional change.

As on the continent, the Reformation in England had economic and political as well as religious causes. The impetus for England's break with Rome was the desire of King Henry VIII (r. 1509–1547) for a new wife. When the personal matter of his need to divorce his first wife became enmeshed with political issues, a complete break with Rome resulted.

In 1527, after eighteen years of marriage, Henry's wife Catherine of Aragon had failed to produce a male child, and Henry had also fallen in love with a court lady in waiting, Anne Boleyn. So Henry petitioned Pope Clement VII for an annulment of his marriage to Catherine. When the pope procrastinated in granting the annulment, Henry decided to remove the English Church from papal authority. In this way, he was able to get the annulment and marry Anne.

Henry used Parliament to legalize the Reformation in England and to make himself the supreme head of the Church of England. Some opposed the king and were beheaded, among them Thomas More, the king's chancellor and author of *Utopia* (see page 429). Anne had a daughter, Elizabeth, but failed to produce a son, so Henry VIII charged her with adulterous incest and in 1536 had her beheaded. His third wife, Jane Seymour, gave Henry the desired son, Edward, but she died a few days after childbirth. Henry went on to three more wives.

Between 1535 and 1539, influenced by his chief minister, Thomas Cromwell, Henry decided to dissolve the English monasteries primarily because he wanted their wealth. Hundreds of former church properties were sold to the middle and upper classes, strengthening the upper classes and tying them to the Tudor dynasty, to which Henry belonged. How did everyday people react to Henry's break from the Catholic Church? Recent scholarship points out that people rarely "converted" from Catholicism to Protestantism overnight. Instead they responded to the local consequences of the shift from Catholicism—for example, the closing of a monastery, the ending of Masses for the dead—with a combination of resistance, acceptance, and collaboration.

Loyalty to the Catholic Church remained particularly strong in Ireland. Ireland had been claimed by English kings since the twelfth century, but in reality the English had firm control of only the area around Dublin known as the Pale. In 1536, on orders from London, the Irish Parliament, which represented only the English landlords and the people of the Pale, approved the English laws severing the church from Rome. The (English) ruling class adopted the new reformed faith, but most of the Irish people remained Roman Catholic. Irish armed opposition to the Reformation led to harsh repression by the English, thus adding religious antagonism to the ethnic hostility that had been a feature of English policy toward Ireland for centuries.

In the short reign of Henry's sickly son Edward VI (r. 1547–1553), strongly Protestant ideas exerted a significant influence on the religious life of the country. The equally brief reign of Mary Tudor (r. 1553–1558), the devoutly Catholic daughter of Catherine of Aragon, witnessed a sharp move back to Catholicism, and many Protestants fled to the continent. Mary's death raised to the throne her half sister Elizabeth (r. 1558–1603) and inaugurated the beginning of religious stability.

Elizabeth had been raised a Protestant, but at the start of her reign sharp differences existed in England. On the one hand, Catholics wanted a Roman Catholic ruler. On the other hand, a vocal number of returning

# Viewpoints 15.2

## Wang Yangming and John Calvin Encourage Proper Behavior

• *Protestant reformers in Europe had clear ideas about virtuous behavior and how to encourage it, and the same was true of Neo-Confucian scholar-officials in China (see page 369). The reformer John Calvin designed ordinances for the city of Geneva that regulated public and family life, while in China the official and military leader Wang Yangming (1472–1529) called for "community compacts," agreements between community members in which all pledged to act in a moral fashion.*

### Wang Yangming, Community Compact for Southern Ganzhou, 1520s

❝ Nothing can be done to change what has already gone by, but something can still be done in the future. Therefore a community compact is now specially prepared to unite and harmonize all of you.

From now on, all of you who enter into this compact should be filial to your parents and respectful to your elders, teach your children, live in harmony with your fellow villagers, help one another when there is death in the family and assist one another in times of difficulty, encourage one another to do good and warn one another not to do evil, stop litigations and rivalry, cultivate faithfulness and promote harmony, and be sure to be good citizens so that together you may establish the custom of humanity and kindness. . . .

Elect from the compact membership an elderly and virtuous person respected by all to be the compact chief and two persons to be assistant chiefs [and other officials]. . . . Have three record books. One of these is to record the names of compact members and their daily movements and activities, and is to be in the charge of the compact executives. Of the remaining record books, one is for the purpose of displaying good deeds and the other for the purpose of reporting evil deeds. . . . To display good deeds, the language used must be clear and decisive, but in reporting mistakes, the language must be indirect and gentle. ❞

### John Calvin, Ecclesiastical Ordinances for the City of Geneva, 1541

❝ [The office of the elders appointed to the Consistory] is to keep watch over the lives of everyone, to admonish in love those whom they see in error and leading disorderly lives. Whenever necessary they shall make a report concerning these to the ministers who will be designated to make brotherly corrections. . . .

If the church deems it wise, it will be well to choose two from the Little Council, four from the Council of Two Hundred, honest men of good demeanor, without reproach and free from all suspicion, above all fearing God and possessed of good and spiritual judgment. It will be well to elect them from every part of the city so as to be able to maintain supervision over all. . . .

If there shall be anyone who lays down opinions contrary to received doctrine, he is to be summoned. If he recants, he is to be dismissed without prejudice. If he is stubborn, he is to be admonished from time to time until it shall be evident that he deserves greater severity. . . .

If anyone is negligent in attending worship so that a noticeable offense is evident for the communion of the faithful, or if anyone shows himself contemptuous of ecclesiastical discipline, he is to be admonished. . . .

For the correction of faults, it is necessary to proceed after the ordinance of our Lord. That is, vices are to be dealt with secretly and no one is to be brought before the church for accusation if the fault is neither public nor scandalous, unless he has been found rebellious in the matter. . . .

Let all these measures be moderate; let there not be such a degree of rigor that anyone should be cast down, for all corrections are but medicinal, to bring back sinners to the Lord. ❞

Sources: *Sources of Chinese Tradition* by William Theodore de Bary and Irene Bloom, eds., pp. 854–855. Reproduced with permission of COLUMBIA UNIVERSITY PRESS in the format Book via Copyright Clearance Center; *The Protestant Reformation*, ed. Hans J. Hillerbrand (New York: Harper Torchbooks, 1968), pp. 174, 177. Material originally appeared (in slightly modified form) in *The Reformation: A Narrative History Related by Contemporary Observers and Participants*, ed. Hans J. Hillerbrand (New York: Harper and Row, 1964), pp. 192–194. Used by permission of the author.

### QUESTIONS FOR ANALYSIS

1. What types of actions do Wang and Calvin encourage and discourage?

2. What similarities and differences do you see in the institutions and procedures Wang and Calvin established to enforce proper conduct?

3. How do these documents reflect Confucian and Protestant Christian values and ideals?

---

exiles wanted all Catholic elements in the Church of England eliminated. Members of the latter group, because they wanted to "purify" the church, were called "Puritans." Shrewdly, Elizabeth chose a middle course between Catholic and Puritan extremes. She referred to herself as the "supreme governor of the Church of England," which allowed Catholics to remain loyal to her without denying the pope. She required her subjects to attend church or risk a fine but did not interfere with their privately held beliefs. The Anglican Church, as the Church of England was called, moved in a moderately Protestant direction.

## Calvinism and Its Moral Standards

In 1509, while Luther was preparing for a doctorate at Wittenberg, John Calvin (1509–1564) was born in Noyon in northwestern France. As a young man he studied law, but in 1533 he experienced a religious crisis, as a result of which he converted from Catholicism to Protestantism. Calvin believed that God had specifically selected him to reform the church. Accordingly, he accepted an invitation to assist in the reformation of the city of Geneva. There, beginning in 1541, Calvin worked assiduously to establish a Christian society ruled by God through civil magistrates and reformed ministers. Geneva thereby became the model of a Christian community for sixteenth-century Protestant reformers.

To understand Calvin's Geneva, it is necessary to understand Calvin's ideas. These he embodied in *The Institutes of the Christian Religion*, first published in 1536 and modified several times afterward. The cornerstone of Calvin's theology was his belief in the absolute sovereignty and omnipotence of God and the total weakness of humanity. Before the infinite power of God, he asserted, men and women are as insignificant as grains of sand.

Calvin did not ascribe free will to human beings, because that would detract from the sovereignty of God. According to his beliefs, men and women could not actively work to achieve salvation; rather, God decided at the beginning of time who would be saved and who damned. This viewpoint constitutes the theological principle called **predestination**. Many people consider the doctrine of predestination, which dates back to Saint Augustine and Saint Paul, to be a pessimistic view of the nature of God. But "this terrible decree," as even Calvin called it, did not lead to pessimism or fatalism. Instead, although Calvinists believed that one's own actions could do nothing to change one's fate, many came to believe that hard work, thrift, and moral conduct could serve as signs that one was among the "elect" chosen for salvation. Any occupation or profession could be a God-given "calling" and should be carried out with diligence and dedication.

Calvin transformed Geneva into a community based on his religious principles. The most powerful organization in the city became the Consistory, a group of laymen and pastors charged with investigating and disciplining deviations from proper doctrine and conduct. (See "Viewpoints 15.2: Wang Yangming and John Calvin Encourage Proper Behavior," page 447.)

Religious refugees from France, England, Spain, Scotland, and Italy visited Calvin's Geneva, which became the model of a Christian community for many. Subsequently, the Reformed Church of Calvin served as the model for the Presbyterian Church in Scotland, the Huguenot (HYOO-guh-naht) Church in France, and the Puritan Churches in England and New England. Calvinism became the compelling force in international Protestantism, first in Europe and then in many Dutch and English colonies around the world.

# The Catholic Reformation

☐ How did the Catholic Church respond to the new religious situation?

Between 1517 and 1547 Protestantism made remarkable advances. Nevertheless, the Roman Catholic Church made a significant comeback. After about 1540 no new large areas of Europe, other than the Netherlands, accepted Protestant beliefs (Map 15.2). Many historians see the developments within the Catholic Church after the Protestant Reformation as two interrelated movements, one a drive for internal reform linked to earlier reform efforts, and the other a Counter-Reformation that opposed Protestants intellectually, politically, militarily, and institutionally. In both movements, papal reforms and new religious orders were important agents.

## Papal Reforms and the Council of Trent

Renaissance popes and advisers were not blind to the need for church reforms, but they resisted calls for a general council representing the entire church, fearing loss of power, revenue, and prestige. This changed beginning with Pope Paul III (pontificate 1534–1549), under whom the papal court became the center of the reform movement rather than its chief opponent.

In 1542 Pope Paul III established the Supreme Sacred Congregation of the Roman and Universal Inquisition, often called the Holy Office, with jurisdiction over the Roman Inquisition, a powerful instrument of the Catholic Reformation. The Inquisition was a committee of six cardinals with judicial authority over all Catholics and the power to arrest, imprison, and execute. Within the Papal States, the Inquisition effectively destroyed heresy (and some heretics).

Pope Paul III also called a general council, which met intermittently from 1545 to 1563 at Trent, an imperial city close to Italy. It was called not only to reform the church but also to secure reconciliation with the Protestants. Lutherans and Calvinists were invited to participate, but their insistence that the Scriptures be the sole basis for discussion made reconciliation impossible.

• **predestination** Calvin's teaching that, by God's decree, some persons are guided to salvation and others to damnation; that God has called people not according to their works but according to his purpose and grace.

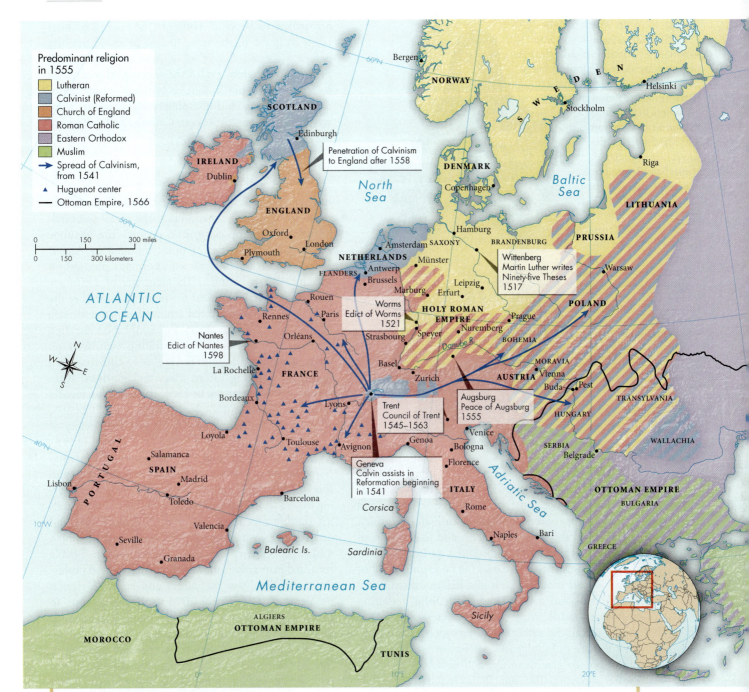

**Predominant religion in 1555**
- Lutheran
- Calvinist (Reformed)
- Church of England
- Roman Catholic
- Eastern Orthodox
- Muslim
- → Spread of Calvinism, from 1541
- ▲ Huguenot center
- ── Ottoman Empire, 1566

0   150   300 miles
0   150   300 kilometers

Penetration of Calvinism to England after 1558

Wittenberg
Martin Luther writes Ninety-five Theses
1517

Worms
Edict of Worms
1521

Nantes
Edict of Nantes
1598

Trent
Council of Trent
1545–1563

Augsburg
Peace of Augsburg
1555

Geneva
Calvin assists in Reformation beginning in 1541

## ☐ Mapping the Past

**MAP 15.2   Religious Divisions in Europe, ca. 1555**   The Reformation shattered the religious unity of Western Christendom. The situation was even more complicated than a map of this scale can show. Many cities within the Holy Roman Empire, for example, accepted a different faith than did the surrounding countryside; Augsburg, Basel, and Strasbourg were all Protestant, though surrounded by territory ruled by Catholic nobles.

**ANALYZING THE MAP**   Which countries in Europe were the most religiously diverse? Which were the least diverse?

**CONNECTIONS**   Where was the first arena of religious conflict in Europe, and why did it develop there and not elsewhere? What nonreligious factors contributed to the religious divisions that developed in sixteenth-century Europe, and to what degree can they explain these divisions?

**Teresa of Ávila** Teresa of Ávila (1515–1582) was a Spanish nun who experienced mystical visions, reformed her religious order, and founded new convents, seeing them as answers to the spread of Protestantism elsewhere in Europe. In this wood carving from 1625, the Spanish artist Gregorio Fernandez shows Saint Teresa book in hand, actively teaching. The influence of her ideas and actions led the pope to give Teresa the title "Doctor of the Church" in 1970, the first woman to be so honored. (Gregorio Fernandez [1576–1636], *Saint Teresa of Ávila*, 1625. Polychromatic Baroque carving on wood, Valladolid, Spain. National Museum of Sculpture/© P. Rotger/Iberfoto/The Image Works)

Nonetheless, the decrees of the Council of Trent laid a solid basis for the spiritual renewal of the Catholic Church. It gave equal validity to the Scriptures and to tradition as sources of religious truth and authority. It reaffirmed the seven sacraments and the traditional Catholic teaching on transubstantiation (the transformation of bread and wine into the body and blood of Christ in the Eucharist). It tackled the disciplinary matters that had disillusioned the faithful, requiring bishops to reside in their own dioceses, suppressing pluralism and the selling of church offices, and forbidding the sale of indulgences. Clerics who kept concubines were to give them up, and bishops were given greater authority. The council also required every diocese to establish a seminary for educating and training clergy. Seminary professors were to determine whether candidates for ordination had vocations, genuine callings to the priesthood. This was a novel idea, since from the time of the early church, parents had determined their sons' (and daughters') religious careers. Finally, great emphasis was placed on preaching to and instructing the laity, especially the uneducated. One decision had especially important social consequences for laypeople. The Council of Trent stipulated that for

a marriage to be valid, consent (the essence of marriage) as given in the vows had to be made publicly before witnesses, one of whom had to be the parish priest. Trent thereby ended the widespread practice of secret marriages in Catholic countries. For four centuries the doctrinal and disciplinary legislation of Trent served as the basis for Roman Catholic faith, organization, and practice.

## New Religious Orders

Just as seminaries provided education, so did new religious orders, which aimed to raise the moral and intellectual level of the clergy and people. The Ursuline (UHR-suh-luhn) order of nuns, founded by Angela Merici (1474–1540), attained enormous prestige for its education of women. The daughter of a country gentleman, Merici worked for many years among the poor, sick, and uneducated around her native Brescia in northern Italy. In 1535 she established the first women's religious order concentrating exclusively on teaching young girls, with the goal of re-Christianizing society by training future wives and mothers. After receiving papal approval in 1565, the Ursulines rapidly spread to France and the New World.

Another important new order was the Society of Jesus, or **Jesuits**. Founded by Ignatius Loyola (1491–1556) in 1540, this order played a powerful international role in strengthening Catholicism in Europe and spreading the faith around the world. While recuperating from a severe battle wound in his legs, Loyola studied the life of Christ and other religious books and decided to give up his military career and become a soldier of Christ. The first Jesuits, whom Loyola recruited primarily from wealthy merchant and professional families, saw the causes and cures of church problems as related not to doctrinal issues but to people's spiritual condition. Reform of the church, as Luther and Calvin understood that term, played no role in the future the Jesuits planned for themselves. Instead their goal was "to help souls." The Society of Jesus developed into a highly centralized, tightly knit organization whose professed members vowed to go anywhere the pope said they were needed. They established schools that adopted the modern humanist curricula and methods and that educated the sons of the nobility as well as the poor. The Jesuits attracted many recruits and achieved phenomenal success for the papacy and the reformed Catholic Church, carrying Christianity to much of South and Central America, India, and Japan before 1550 and to Brazil, North America, and the Congo in the seventeenth century. Within Europe the Jesuits brought almost all of southern Germany and much of eastern Europe back to Catholicism. Also, as confessors and spiritual directors to kings, Jesuits exerted great political influence.

- **Jesuits** Members of the Society of Jesus, founded by Ignatius Loyola and approved by the papacy in 1540, whose goal was the spread of the Roman Catholic faith through humanistic schools and missionary activity.

# Religious Violence

☐ What were the causes and consequences of religious violence, including riots, wars, and witch-hunts?

In 1559 France and Spain signed the Treaty of Cateau-Cambrésis, which ended the long conflict known as the Habsburg-Valois wars. However, over the next century religious differences led to riots, civil wars, and international conflicts. Especially in France and the Netherlands, Protestants and Catholics opposed one another through preaching, teaching, and violence, for each side regarded the other as a poison in the community that would provoke the wrath of God. Catholics and Protestants alike feared people of other faiths, whom they often saw as agents of Satan. Even more, they feared those explicitly identified with Satan: people believed to be witches. This era saw the most virulent witch persecutions in European history, as both Protestants and Catholics tried to make their cities and states more godly.

## French Religious Wars

The costs of the Habsburg-Valois wars, waged intermittently through the first half of the sixteenth century, forced the French to increase taxes and borrow heavily. King Francis I's treaty with the pope (see page 437) gave the French crown a rich supplement of money and offices and also a vested financial interest in Catholicism. Significant numbers of French people, however, were attracted to the "reformed religion," as Calvinism was called. Calvinism drew converts from among reform-minded members of the Catholic clergy, the industrious middle classes, and artisan groups. Additionally, some French nobles became Calvinist, either because of religious conviction or because this allowed them to oppose the monarchy. By the middle of the sixteenth century perhaps one-tenth of the French population had become **Huguenots**, the name given to French Calvinists.

Both Calvinists and Catholics believed that the others' books, services, and ministers polluted the community. Preachers communicated these ideas in sermons, triggering violence at the baptisms, marriages, and funerals of the other faith. Armed clashes between Catholic royalist nobles and Calvinist antimonarchical nobles occurred in many parts of France.

Calvinist teachings called the power of sacred images into question, and mobs in many cities destroyed statues, stained-glass windows, and paintings. Though it was often inspired by fiery Protestant sermons, this iconoclasm is an example of men and women carrying out the Reformation themselves, rethinking the church's system of meaning. Catholic mobs responded by

defending the sacred images, and crowds on both sides killed their opponents, often in gruesome ways.

A savage Catholic attack on Calvinists in Paris on August 24, 1572—Saint Bartholomew's Day—followed the usual pattern. The occasion was the marriage of the king's sister Margaret of Valois to the Protestant Henry of Navarre, which was intended to help reconcile Catholics and Huguenots. Instead Huguenot wedding guests in Paris were massacred, and other Protestants were slaughtered by mobs. Violence spread to the provinces, where thousands were killed. The Saint Bartholomew's Day massacre led to a civil war that dragged on for fifteen years. As a result, agriculture in many areas was destroyed, commercial life declined severely, and starvation and death haunted the land.

What ultimately saved France was a small group of moderates of both faiths called **politiques** (POH-lee-teeks) who believed that only the restoration of a strong monarchy could reverse the trend toward collapse. The politiques also favored officially recognizing the Huguenots. The death of the French queen Catherine de' Medici, followed by the assassination of her son King Henry III, paved the way for the accession of Henry of Navarre (the unfortunate bridegroom of the Saint Bartholomew's Day massacre), a politique who became Henry IV (r. 1589–1610).

Henry's willingness to sacrifice religious principles to political necessity saved France. He converted to Catholicism but also, in 1598, issued the Edict of Nantes (nahnt), which granted liberty of conscience (freedom of thought) and liberty of public worship to Huguenots in 150 fortified towns. By helping restore internal peace in France, the reign of Henry IV and the Edict of Nantes paved the way for French kings to claim absolute power in the seventeenth century.

## Civil Wars in the Netherlands

In the Netherlands a movement for church reform developed into a struggle for Dutch independence. The Catholic emperor Charles V had inherited the seventeen provinces that compose present-day Belgium and the Netherlands (see page 439). In the Netherlands, as elsewhere, corruption in the Roman Catholic Church and the critical spirit of the Renaissance provoked pressure for reform, and Lutheran ideas took root. Charles V had grown up in the Netherlands, however, and he was able to limit the impact of the new ideas. Charles V abdicated in 1556 and transferred power over the Netherlands to his son Philip II, who had grown up in Spain. Although Philip, like his father,

- **Huguenots** French Calvinists.
- **politiques** Catholic and Protestant moderates who sought to end the religious violence in France by restoring a strong monarchy and granting official recognition to the Huguenots.

***Massacre of the Huguenots, 1573*** The Italian artist Giorgio Vasari depicts the Saint Bartholomew's Day massacre in Paris, one of many bloody events in the religious wars that accompanied the Reformation. Here Admiral Coligny, a leader of the French Protestants (called Huguenots), is hurled from a window while his followers are slaughtered. This fresco was commissioned by Pope Gregory XIII to decorate a hall in the Vatican Palace in Rome. Both sides used visual images to win followers and celebrate their victories. (Giorgio Vasari [1511–1574], Sala Regia, Apostolic Palace, Vatican City/De Agostini Picture Library/The Bridgeman Art Library)

In the 1560s Spanish authorities attempted to suppress Calvinist worship and raised taxes, which sparked riots and a wave of iconoclasm. In response, Philip II sent twenty thousand Spanish troops, and from 1568 to 1578 civil war raged in the Netherlands between Catholics and Protestants and between the seventeen provinces and Spain. Eventually the ten southern provinces — the Spanish Netherlands (the future Belgium) — came under the control of the Spanish Habsburg forces. The seven northern provinces, led by Holland, formed the Union of Utrecht (the United Provinces), and in 1581 they declared their independence from Spain. The north was Protestant, and the south remained Catholic. Philip did not accept the independence of the north, and war continued. England was even drawn into the conflict, supplying money and troops to the United Provinces. (Spain launched the Spanish Armada, an unsuccessful invasion of England, in response.) Hostilities ended in 1609 when Spain agreed to a truce that recognized the independence of the United Provinces.

## The Great European Witch-Hunt

Insecurity created by the religious wars contributed to persecution for witchcraft, which actually began before the Reformation in the 1480s but became especially common about 1560. Both Protestants and Catholics tried and executed those accused of being witches, with church officials and secular authorities acting together.

The heightened sense of God's power and divine wrath in the Reformation era was an important factor in the **witch-hunts**, but other factors were also significant. In the later Middle Ages, many educated Christian theologians, canon lawyers, and officials added a demonological component to existing ideas about witches. For them, the essence of witchcraft was making a pact with the Devil that required the witch to do the Devil's bidding. Witches were no longer simply people who used magical power to do harm and get what they wanted, but rather people used by the Devil to do what he wanted. Some demonological theorists also claimed that witches were organized in an international conspiracy to overthrow Christianity.

Trials involving this new notion of witchcraft as diabolical heresy began in Switzerland and southern Germany in the late fifteenth century; became less numerous in the early decades of the Reformation, when

opposed Protestantism, Protestant ideas spread in the Netherlands.

By the 1560s Protestants in the Netherlands were primarily Calvinists. Calvinism's intellectual seriousness, moral gravity, and emphasis on any form of labor well done appealed to middle-class merchants and financiers and to working-class people. Whereas Lutherans taught respect for the powers that be, Calvinism tended to encourage opposition to authorities who were judged to be ungodly.

- **witch-hunts** Campaign against witchcraft in early modern Europe and European colonies in which hundreds of thousands of people, mostly women, were tried, and many of them executed.

Protestants and Catholics were busy fighting each other; and then picked up again about 1560, spreading to much of western Europe and to European colonies in the Americas. Scholars estimate that during the sixteenth and seventeenth centuries somewhere between 100,000 and 200,000 people were officially tried for witchcraft, and between 40,000 and 60,000 were executed. While the trials were secret, executions were not, and the list of charges was read out for all to hear.

Though the gender balance of the accused varied widely in different parts of Europe, between 75 and 85 percent of those tried and executed were women, whom some demonologists viewed as weaker and so more likely to give in to the Devil. Tensions within families, households, and neighborhoods also played a role in witchcraft accusations, as grievances and jealousies led to accusations. Suspects were questioned and tortured by legal authorities, and they often implicated others. The circle of the accused grew, sometimes into a much larger hunt that historians have called a "witch panic." Panics were most common in the part of Europe that saw the most witch accusations in general—the Holy Roman Empire, Switzerland, and parts of France. Most of this area consisted of very small governmental units that were jealous of each other and, after the Reformation, were divided by religion. The rulers of these small territories often felt more threatened than did the monarchs of western Europe, and they saw persecuting witches as a way to demonstrate their piety and concern for order.

Even in the sixteenth century a few individuals questioned whether witches could ever do harm, make a pact with the Devil, or engage in the wild activities attributed to them. Furthermore, doubts about whether secret denunciations were valid or torture would ever yield a truthful confession gradually spread among the same type of religious and legal authorities who had so vigorously persecuted witches. By about 1660 prosecutions for witchcraft had become less common. The last official execution for witchcraft in England was in 1682, though the last one in the Holy Roman Empire was not until 1775.

European ideas about witchcraft traveled across the Atlantic. There were a few trials of European colonists for witchcraft—the most famous of which was at Salem in Massachusetts—but more often indigenous people were accused of being witches. For example, Jean de Léry, a French Protestant explorer in South America, used a description of a witches' ritual from a book of European demonology to describe rituals of the Tupinambá people of Brazil. Another French official speculated in the early seventeenth century that the reason there were so many more witches in Europe than there had been earlier was the coming of European missionaries to the New World. Many of Satan's demons had left Europe centuries earlier when it had become Christian, he commented, but now they had returned. Religious zeal, heightened by the Protestant and Catholic Reformations, had many consequences that were not expected.

## CHRONOLOGY

| | |
|---|---|
| **1434–1737** | Medici family in power in Florence |
| **1450s** | Development of movable metal type in Germany |
| **1469** | Marriage of Isabella of Castile and Ferdinand of Aragon |
| **1492** | Spain conquers Granada; practicing Jews expelled from Spain |
| **1508–1512** | Michelangelo paints ceiling of the Sistine Chapel |
| **1513** | Niccolò Machiavelli writes *The Prince* |
| **1521** | Diet of Worms |
| **1521–1555** | Charles V's wars against Valois kings |
| **1525** | Peasant revolts in Germany |
| **1527** | Henry VIII of England asks Pope Clement VII to annul his marriage to Catherine of Aragon |
| **1536** | John Calvin publishes *The Institutes of the Christian Religion* |
| **1540** | Founding of the Society of Jesus (Jesuits) |
| **1545–1563** | Council of Trent |
| **1555** | Peace of Augsburg |
| **1558–1603** | Reign of Elizabeth I in England |
| **1560–1660** | Height of European witch-hunt |
| **1568–1578** | Civil war in the Netherlands |
| **1572** | Saint Bartholomew's Day massacre |
| **1598** | Edict of Nantes |

# Chapter Summary

The Renaissance was characterized by self-conscious awareness among educated Europeans, particularly scholars and writers known as humanists, that they were living in a new era. Central to humanists were interest in the Latin classics, belief in individual potential, education for a career of public service, and, in northern Europe, the reform of church and society. Their ideas spread as a result of the development of the printing press with movable metal type, which revolutionized communication. Interest in the classical past and in the individual shaped Renaissance art in terms of style and subject matter, and patrons provided the money needed for an outpouring of painting, sculpture, and architecture. Social hierarchies in the Renaissance developed new features that contributed to the modern social hierarchies of race, class, and gender. In politics, feudal monarchies gradually evolved into nation-states, as rulers used war, diplomacy, new forms of taxation, centralized institutions, and strategic marital alliances to build up their power.

Many individuals and groups had long called for reforms in the Catholic Church, providing a ready audience in the early sixteenth century for the ideas of Martin Luther, a German priest and university professor. Luther and other reformers, called Protestants, developed a new understanding of Christian doctrine that emphasized faith and grace; Protestant ideas spread rapidly through preaching, hymns, and the printing press; and soon western Europe was split religiously. Local situations influenced religious patterns. In England the king's need for a church-approved divorce triggered the break with Rome, while in France and eastern Europe the ideas of John Calvin gained wide acceptance, especially among middle-class people and nobles. The Roman Catholic Church responded slowly to the Protestant challenge, but by the middle of the sixteenth century it had begun a process of internal reform along with opposing Protestants intellectually, politically, militarily, and institutionally. This reinvigorated Catholic Church would carry Christian ideas around the world, while in Europe religious differences led to riots, witch persecutions, civil wars, and international conflicts.

## NOTES

1. Niccolò Machiavelli, *The Prince*, trans. Leo Paul S. de Alvarez (Prospect Heights, Ill.: Waveland Press, 1980), p. 101.
2. Stuttgart, Württembergische Hauptstaatsarchiv, General-reskripta, A38, Bü. 2, 1550, trans. Merry Wiesner-Hanks.
3. Quoted in Benzion Netanyahu, *The Origins of the Inquisition in Fifteenth Century Spain* (New York: Random House, 1995), p. 921.
4. Quoted in E. H. Harbison, *The Age of Reformation* (Ithaca, N.Y.: Cornell University Press, 1963), p. 52.
5. Quoted ibid., p. 284.

## CONNECTIONS

The Renaissance and the Reformation are often seen as key to the creation of the modern world. The radical changes of these times contained many elements of continuity, however. Artists, humanists, and religious reformers looked back to the classical era and early Christianity for inspiration, viewing those times as better and purer than their own. Political leaders played important roles in cultural and religious developments, just as they had for centuries in Europe and other parts of the world.

The events of the Renaissance and Reformation were thus linked with earlier developments, and they were also closely connected with another important element in the modern world: European exploration and colonization (discussed in Chapter 16). Renaissance monarchs paid for expeditions' ships, crews, and supplies, expecting a large share of any profits gained and increasingly viewing overseas territory as essential to a strong state. Only a week after Martin Luther stood in front of Charles V at the Diet of Worms declaring his independence in matters of religion, Ferdinand Magellan, a Portuguese sea captain using Spanish ships, was killed by indigenous people in a group of islands off the coast of Southeast Asia. Charles V had provided the backing for Magellan's voyage, the first to circumnavigate the globe. Magellan viewed one of the purposes of his trip as the spread of Christianity, and later in the sixteenth century institutions created as part of the Catholic Reformation, including the Jesuit order and the Inquisition, would operate in European colonies overseas as well as in Europe itself. The islands where Magellan was killed were later named the Philippines, in honor of Charles's son Philip, who sent the ill-fated Spanish Armada against England. The desire for fame, wealth, and power that was central to the Renaissance, and the religious zeal central to the Reformation, were thus key to the European voyages and to colonial ventures as well.

# Review and Explore

## Make It Stick

 **LearningCurve**
Go online and use LearningCurve to retain what you've read.

## Identify Key Terms

Identify and explain the significance of each item below.

Renaissance (p. 426)

patronage (p. 427)

humanism (p. 427)

Christian humanists (p. 429)

debate about women (p. 435)

Protestant Reformation (p. 439)

indulgence (p. 440)

Diet of Worms (p. 440)

Protestant (p. 441)

predestination (p. 448)

Jesuits (p. 450)

Huguenots (p. 451)

politiques (p. 451)

witch-hunts (p. 452)

## Review the Main Ideas

Answer the focus questions from each section of the chapter.

1. What were the major cultural developments of the Renaissance? (p. 426)
2. What were the key social hierarchies in Renaissance Europe, and how did these hierarchies shape people's lives? (p. 434)
3. How did the nation-states of western Europe evolve in this period? (p. 437)
4. What were the central ideas of Protestant reformers, and why were they appealing to various groups across Europe? (p. 439)
5. How did the Catholic Church respond to the new religious situation? (p. 448)
6. What were the causes and consequences of religious violence, including riots, wars, and witch-hunts? (p. 451)

## Make Connections

Analyze the larger developments and continuities within and across chapters.

1. The word *Renaissance*, invented to describe the cultural flowering in Italy that began in the fifteenth century, has often been used for other periods of advance in learning and the arts, such as the "Carolingian Renaissance" that you read about in Chapter 8. Can you think of other, more recent "Renaissances" or ways the term is used today?
2. The "debate about women" was not simply a European phenomenon, as educated men (and occasionally a few educated women) in many cultures discussed women's nature and character. How would you compare ideas about women in classical Islamic society (Chapter 9), Song China (Chapter 13), Heian Japan (Chapter 13), Renaissance Italy, and Protestant Germany? How were these ideas reflected (or not reflected) in women's actual lives?
3. Martin Luther is always on every list of the one hundred most influential people of all time. Should he be? Why or why not? Who else from this chapter should be on such a list, and why?

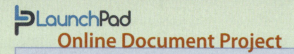
## Online Document Project

### Cosimo and Lorenzo de' Medici

**What role did patrons play in shaping Renaissance artistic and intellectual life?**

Examine paintings and letters by Renaissance artists, and then complete a quiz and writing assignment based on the evidence and details from this chapter.

*See inside the front cover to learn more.*

## Suggested Reading

Bethencourt, Francisco. *The Inquisition: A Global History, 1478–1834*. 2009. A comprehensive study that examines the Inquisition in Spain, Portugal, Italy, and the Iberian empires overseas.

Cameron, Euan. *The European Reformation*, 2d ed. 2012. A thorough analysis of the Protestant and Catholic Reformations throughout Europe.

Earle, T. F., and K. J. P. Lowe, eds. *Black Africans in Renaissance Europe*. 2005. Includes essays discussing many aspects of ideas about race and the experience of Africans in Europe.

Ertman, Thomas. *The Birth of Leviathan: Building States and Regimes in Medieval and Early Modern Europe*. 1997. A good introduction to the creation of nation-states.

Hendrix, Scott. *Luther*. 2009. A brief introduction to his thought; part of the Abingdon Pillars of Theology series.

Hsia, R. Po-Chia. *The World of Catholic Renewal, 1540–1770*, 2d ed. 2005. Situates the Catholic Reformation in a global context and examines colonial Catholicism.

Johnson, Geraldine. *Renaissance Art: A Very Short Introduction*. 2005. Excellent brief survey that includes male and female artists and sets the art in its cultural and historical context.

Levack, Brian. *The Witch-Hunt in Early Modern Europe*, 3d ed. 2007. A good introduction to the vast literature on witchcraft, with helpful bibliographies.

Man, John. *Gutenberg Revolution: The Story of a Genius and an Invention That Changed the World*. 2002. Presents a rather idealized view of Gutenberg but has good discussions of his milieu and excellent illustrations.

Matheson, Peter, ed. *Reformation Christianity*. 2004. This volume in the People's History of Christianity series explores social issues and popular religion.

Nauert, Charles. *Humanism and the Culture of Renaissance Europe*, 2d ed. 2006. A thorough introduction to humanism throughout Europe.

Waley, Daniel, and Trevor Dean. *The Italian City-Republics*, 4th ed. 2010. Analyzes the rise of independent city-states in northern Italy, including discussion of the artistic and social lives of their inhabitants.

Wiesner-Hanks, Merry E. *Women and Gender in Early Modern Europe*, 3d ed. 2008. Discusses all aspects of women's lives as well as ideas about gender.

### Nezahualpilli

At the time of the arrival of Europeans, Nezahualpilli was ruler of the city-state of Texcoco, the second most important city in the Aztec Empire after Tenochtitlan. (Nezahualpilli, portrait from *Codex Ixtlilxochitl*, 1582, pigment on European paper/Bibliothèque Nationale, Paris, France/De Agostini Picture Library/akg-images)

**LearningCurve**
After reading the chapter, go online and use LearningCurve to retain what you've read.

# Chapter Preview

**The Afroeurasian Trade World**

**The European Voyages of Discovery**

**Conquest and Settlement**

**The Era of Global Contact**

**Changing Attitudes and Beliefs**

**B**efore 1500 Europeans were relatively marginal players in a centuries-old trading system that linked Africa, Asia, and Europe. The Indian Ocean was the locus of a vibrant, cosmopolitan Afroeurasian trade world in which Arab, Persian, Turkish, Indian, African, Chinese, and European merchants and adventurers competed for trade in spices, silks, and other goods.

By 1550 the European search for better access to Asian trade goods had led to a new overseas empire in the Indian Ocean and the accidental discovery of the Western Hemisphere. With this discovery South and North America were soon drawn into an international network of trade centers and political empires, which Europeans came to dominate. The era of globalization had begun, creating new political systems and forms of economic exchange as well as cultural assimilation, conversion, and resistance. Europeans sought to impose their values on the peoples they encountered while struggling to comprehend these peoples' societies. The Age of Discovery from 1450 to 1600, as the time of these encounters is known, laid the foundations for the modern world.

## The Afroeurasian Trade World

◻ What was the Afroeurasian trade world like prior to the era of European exploration?

Historians now recognize that a type of world economy, known as the Afroeurasian trade world, linked the products and people of Europe, Asia, and Africa in the fifteenth century. Before Christopher Columbus began his voyages to the New World in 1492, the West was not the dominant player in world trade. Nevertheless, wealthy Europeans were eager consumers of luxury goods from the East, which they received through Venetian and Genoese middlemen.

### The Trade World of the Indian Ocean

The Indian Ocean was the center of the Afroeurasian trade world, serving as a crossroads for commercial and cultural exchanges among China, India, the Middle East, Africa, and Europe (Map 16.1). From the seventh through the fourteenth centuries, the volume of this trade steadily increased, declining only during the years of the Black Death.

Merchants congregated in a series of multicultural, cosmopolitan port cities strung around the Indian Ocean. Most of these cities had some form of autonomous self-government, and mutual self-interest had largely limited violence and attempts to monopolize trade. The most developed area of this commercial web was made up of the ports surrounding the South China Sea. In the fifteenth century the port of Malacca became a great commercial entrepôt (AHN-truh-poh), a trad-

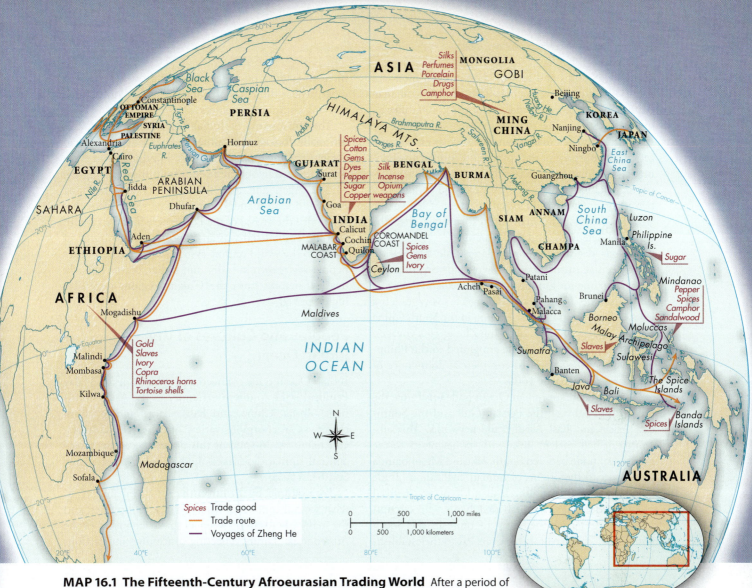

**MAP 16.1 The Fifteenth-Century Afroeurasian Trading World** After a period of decline following the Black Death and the Mongol invasions, trade revived in the fifteenth century. Muslim merchants dominated trade, linking ports in East Africa and the Red Sea with those in India and the Malay Archipelago. The Chinese admiral Zheng He followed the most important Indian Ocean trade routes on his voyages (1405–1433), hoping to impose Ming dominance of trade and tribute.

ing post to which goods were shipped for storage while awaiting redistribution to other places. To Malacca came porcelains, silks, and camphor (used in the manufacture of many medications) from China; pepper, cloves, nutmeg, and raw materials such as sandalwood from the Moluccas; sugar from the Philippines; and textiles, copper weapons, incense, dyes, and opium from India.

The Mongol emperors opened the doors of China to the West, encouraging Europeans like the Venetian trader and explorer Marco Polo to do business there. Marco Polo's tales of his travels from 1271 to 1295 and his encounter with the Great Khan (one of the successors of the famous Mongol ruler Chinggis Khan) fueled Western fantasies about the Orient. Polo vividly recounted the splendors of the Khan's court and the city of Hangzhou, which he described as "the finest and noblest in the world" in which "the number and

wealth of the merchants, and the amount of goods that passed through their hands, was so enormous that no man could form a just estimate thereof."[1]

After the Mongols fell to the Ming Dynasty in 1368, China entered a period of agricultural and commercial expansion, population growth, and urbanization. By the end of the dynasty in 1644, the Chinese population had tripled to between 150 million and 200 million. The city of Nanjing had 1 million inhabitants, making it the largest city in the world, while the new capital, Beijing, had more than 600,000 inhabitants, a population greater than that of any European city (see pages 617–627). Historians agree that China had the most advanced economy in the world until at least the beginning of the eighteenth century.

China also took the lead in exploration, sending Admiral Zheng He's fleet as far west as Egypt. Each of his seven expeditions from 1405 to 1433 involved hundreds of ships and tens of thousands of men (see page 639). In one voyage alone, Zheng sailed more than 12,000 miles, compared to Columbus's 2,400 miles on his first voyage some sixty years later.[2] Although the ships brought back many wonders, such as giraffes and zebras, the purpose of the voyages was primarily diplomatic, to enhance China's prestige and seek tribute-paying alliances. The high expense of the voyages in a period of renewed Mongol encroachment led to the abandonment of the maritime expeditions after the deaths of Zheng He and the emperor.

China's decision to forego large-scale exploration was a decisive turning point in world history, one that left an opening for European states to expand their role in Asian trade. Nonetheless, Zheng He's voyages left a legacy of increased Chinese trading in the South China Sea and Indian Ocean. Following Zheng He's voyages, tens of thousands of Chinese emigrated to the Philippines, where they acquired commercial dominance of the island of Luzon by 1600.

Another center of Indian Ocean trade was India, the crucial link between the Persian Gulf and the Southeast Asian and East Asian trade networks. The subcontinent had ancient links with its neighbors to the northwest: trade between South Asia and Mesopotamia dates back to the origins of human civilization. Trade among ports bordering the Indian Ocean was revived in the Middle Ages by Arab merchants who circumnavigated India on their way to trade in the South China Sea. The need for stopovers led to the establish-

ment of trading posts at Gujarat and on the Malabar coast, where the cities of Calicut and Quilon became thriving commercial centers.

The inhabitants of India's Coromandel coast traditionally looked to Southeast Asia, where they had ancient trading and cultural ties. Hinduism and Buddhism arrived in Southeast Asia from India during the Middle Ages, and a brisk trade between Southeast Asian and Coromandel port cities persisted from that time until the arrival of the Portuguese in the sixteenth century. India itself was an important contributor of goods to the world trading system. Most of the world's pepper was grown in India, and Indian cotton and silk textiles, mainly from the Gujarat region, were also highly prized.

## Peoples and Cultures of the Indian Ocean

Indian Ocean trade connected peoples from the Malay Peninsula (the southern extremity of the Asian continent), India, China, and East Africa, among whom there was an enormous variety of languages, cultures, and religions. In spite of this diversity, certain sociocultural similarities linked these peoples, especially in Southeast Asia.

For example, by the fifteenth century inhabitants of what we call Indonesia, Malaysia, the Philippines, and the many islands in between all spoke languages of the Austronesian family, reflecting continuing interactions

**The Port of Calicut in India**  The port of Calicut, located on the west coast of India, was a center of the Indian Ocean spice trade during the Middle Ages. Vasco da Gama arrived in Calicut in 1498 and obtained permission to trade there, leading to hostilities between the Portuguese and the Arab traders who had previously dominated the port. (Private Collection/The Stapleton Collection/The Bridgeman Art Library)

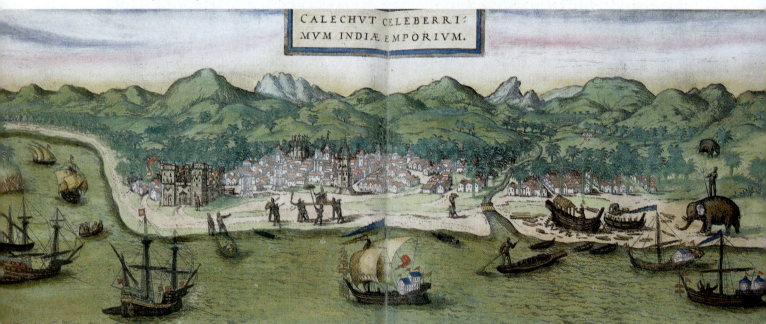

among them. A common environment led to a diet based on rice, fish, palms, and palm wine. Rice, harvested by women, is probably indigenous to the region, and it formed the staple of the diet. The seas provided many varieties of fish, crabs, and shrimp, and fishing served as the chief male occupation, well ahead of agriculture. Also, sugarcane grew in profusion, and it was chewed as a confectionery and used as a sweetener.[3]

In comparison to India, China, or even Europe after the Black Death, Southeast Asia was sparsely populated. People were concentrated in port cities and in areas of intense rice cultivation. Another difference between Southeast Asia and India, China, and Europe was the higher status of women — their primary role in planting and harvesting rice gave them authority and economic power. At marriage, which typically occurred around age twenty, the groom paid the bride (or sometimes her family) a sum of money called **bride wealth**, which remained under her control. This practice was in sharp contrast to the Chinese, Indian, and European dowry, which came under the husband's control. Property was administered jointly, in contrast to the Chinese principle and Indian practice that wives had no say in the disposal of family property. All children, regardless of gender, inherited equally, and when Islam arrived in the region, the rule requiring sons to receive double the inheritance of daughters was never implemented.

Respect for women carried over to the commercial sphere. Women participated in business as partners and independent entrepreneurs, even undertaking long sea voyages to accompany their wares. When Portuguese and Dutch men settled in the region and married local women, their wives continued to play important roles in trade and commerce.

In contrast to most parts of the world other than Africa, Southeast Asian peoples had an accepting attitude toward premarital sexual activity and placed no premium on virginity at marriage. Divorce carried no social stigma and was easily attainable if a pair proved incompatible. Either the woman or the man could initiate a divorce, and common property and children were divided.

## Trade with Africa and the Middle East

On the east coast of Africa, Swahili-speaking city-states engaged in the Indian Ocean trade, exchanging ivory, rhinoceros horn, tortoise shells, copra (dried coconut), and slaves for textiles, spices, cowrie shells, porcelain, and other goods. The most important cities were Mogadishu, Mombasa, and Kilwa, which had converted to Islam by the eleventh century. Peopled by confident and urbane merchants, the cities were known for their prosperity and culture.

**Mansa Musa** This detail from the Catalan Atlas of 1375, a world map created for the Catalan king, depicts a king of Mali, Mansa Musa, who was legendary for his wealth in gold. European desires for direct access to the trade in sub-Saharan gold helped inspire Portuguese exploration of the west coast of Africa in the fifteenth century. (Detail from the *Catalan Atlas*, 1375 [vellum], by Abraham Cresques (1325–1387)/ Bibliothèque Nationale, Paris, France/The Bridgeman Art Library)

West Africa also played an important role in world trade. In the fifteenth century most of the gold that reached Europe came from the Sudan region in West Africa and, in particular, from the kingdom of Mali near present-day Ghana. Transported across the Sahara by Arab and African traders on camels, the gold was sold in the ports of North Africa. Other trading routes led to the Egyptian cities of Alexandria and Cairo, where the Venetians held commercial privileges.

Inland nations that sat astride the north-south caravan routes grew wealthy from this trade. In the mid-thirteenth century the kingdom of Mali emerged as an important player on the overland trade route. In later centuries, however, the diversion of gold away from the trans-Sahara routes would weaken the inland states of Africa politically and economically.

> • **bride wealth** In early modern Southeast Asia, a sum of money the groom paid the bride or her family at the time of marriage. This practice contrasted with the dowry in China, India, and Europe, which the husband controlled.

Gold was one important object of trade; slaves were another. Slavery was practiced in Africa, as it was virtually everywhere else in the world, long before the arrival of Europeans. Arab and African merchants took West African slaves to the Mediterranean to be sold in European, Egyptian, and Middle Eastern markets and also brought eastern Europeans to West Africa as slaves. In addition, Indian and Arab merchants traded slaves in the coastal regions of East Africa.

The Middle East served as an intermediary for trade between Europe, Africa, and Asia and was also an important supplier of goods for foreign exchange, especially silk and cotton. Two great rival empires, the Persian Safavids and the Turkish Ottomans, dominated the region, competing for control over western trade routes to the East. By the mid-sixteenth century the Ottomans had established control over eastern Mediterranean sea routes to trading centers in Syria, Palestine, Egypt, and the rest of North Africa. Their power also extended into Europe as far west as Vienna.

## Genoese and Venetian Middlemen

Compared to the riches and vibrancy of the East, Europe constituted a minor outpost in the world trading system, for European craftsmen produced few products to rival those of Asia. However, Europeans desired luxury goods from the East, and in the late Middle Ages such trade was controlled by the Italian city-states of Venice and Genoa. Venice had opened the gateway to Asian trade in 1304, when it established formal relations with the sultan of Mamluk Egypt and started operations in Cairo. In exchange for European products like Spanish and English wool, German metal goods, and Flemish textiles, the Venetians obtained luxury items like spices, silks, and carpets from middlemen in the eastern Mediterranean and Asia Minor. Because Eastern demand for European goods was low, Venetians funded their purchases through shipping and trade in firearms and slaves.

Venice's ancient trading rival was Genoa. By the time the Crusades ended around 1270, Genoa dominated the northern route to Asia through the Black Sea. From then until the fourteenth century, the Genoese expanded their trade routes as far as Persia and the Far East. In 1291 they sponsored a failed expedition into the Atlantic in search of India. This voyage reveals the early origins of Genoese interest in Atlantic exploration.

In the fifteenth century, with Venice claiming victory in the spice trade, the Genoese shifted focus from trade to finance and from the Black Sea to the western Mediterranean. Located on the northwestern coast of Italy, Genoa had always been active in the western Mediterranean, trading with North African ports, southern France, Spain, and even England and Flan-

ders through the Strait of Gibraltar. When Spanish and Portuguese voyages began to explore the western Atlantic (see page 467), Genoese merchants, navigators, and financiers provided their skills and capital to the Iberian monarchs.

A major element of Italian trade was slavery. Merchants purchased slaves, many of whom were fellow Christians, in the Balkans of southeastern Europe. After the loss of the Black Sea trade routes—and thus the source of slaves—to the Ottomans, the Genoese sought new supplies of slaves in the West, eventually seizing or buying and selling the Guanches (indigenous peoples from the Canary Islands), Muslim prisoners and Jewish refugees from Spain, and, by the early 1500s, both black and Berber Africans. With the growth of Spanish colonies in the New World, Genoese and Venetian merchants became important players in the Atlantic slave trade.

Italian experience in colonial administration, slaving, and international trade served as a model for the Iberian states as they pushed European expansion to new heights. Mariners, merchants, and financiers from Venice and Genoa—most notably Christopher Columbus—played crucial roles in bringing the fruits of this experience to the Iberian Peninsula and to the New World.

## The European Voyages of Discovery

☐ Why and how did Europeans undertake ambitious voyages of expansion?

Europe was by no means isolated before the voyages of exploration and its "discovery" of the New World. But because Europeans did not produce many products desired by Eastern elites, they were modest players in the Indian Ocean trading world. As Europe recovered after the Black Death, new European players entered the scene with novel technology, eager to spread Christianity and to undo Italian and Ottoman domination of trade with the East. A century after the plague, Iberian explorers began the overseas voyages that helped create the modern world, with immense consequences for their own continent and the rest of the planet.

### Causes of European Expansion

European expansion had multiple causes. The first was economic. By the middle of the fifteenth century Europe was experiencing a revival of population and economic activity after the lows of the Black Death. This revival created renewed demand for luxuries, especially spices, from the East. The fall of Constantinople and the subsequent Ottoman control of trade routes created obstacles to fulfilling these demands. European merchants and rulers eager for the profits of trade thus needed to find new sources of precious metal to exchange with the Ottomans or trade routes that bypassed the Ottomans.

Why were spices so desirable? Introduced into western Europe by the Crusaders in the twelfth century, pepper, nutmeg, ginger, mace, cinnamon, and cloves added flavor and variety to the monotonous European diet. Not only did spices serve as flavorings for food, but they were also used in anointing oil and as incense for religious rituals, and as perfumes, medicines, and dyes in daily life. Apart from their utility, the expense and exotic origins of spices meant that they were a high-status good, which European elites could use to demonstrate their social standing.

Religious fervor and the crusading spirit were another important catalyst for expansion. Just seven months separated Isabella and Ferdinand's conquest of the emirate of Granada, the last remaining Muslim state on the Iberian Peninsula, and Columbus's departure across the Atlantic. Overseas exploration thus transferred the militaristic religious fervor of the reconquista (reconquest) to new non-Christian territories. As they conquered indigenous empires, Iberians brought the attitudes and administrative practices developed during the reconquista to the Americas. Conquistadors fully expected to be rewarded with land, titles, and power over conquered peoples, just as the leaders of the reconquista had been.

A third motivation was the dynamic spirit of the Renaissance. Like other men of the Renaissance era, explorers sought to win glory for their amazing exploits and demonstrated a genuine interest in learning more about unknown waters. Scholars have frequently described the European discoveries as an outcome of Renaissance curiosity about the physical universe. The detailed journals kept by European voyagers attest to their fascination with the new peoples and places they visited.

Individual explorers often manifested all of these desires at once. Columbus, a devout Christian, aimed to discover new territories where Christianity could be spread while seeking a direct trade route to Asia. The motives of Portuguese explorer Bartholomew Diaz were, in his own words, "to serve God and His Majesty, to give light to those who were in darkness and to grow rich as all men desire to do." When the Portuguese explorer Vasco da Gama reached the port of Calicut, India, in 1498 and a native asked what he wanted, he replied, "Christians and spices."[4] The bluntest of the Spanish **conquistadors** (kahn-KEES-tuh-dawrz), or conquerors, Hernán Cortés, announced as he prepared to conquer Mexico, "I have come to win gold, not to plow the fields like a peasant."[5]

Ordinary seamen joined these voyages to escape poverty at home, to continue a family trade, or to win a few crumbs of the great riches of empire. Common sailors were ill-paid, and life at sea meant danger, unbearable stench, hunger, and overcrowding. For months at a time, 100 to 120 people lived and worked in a space of 1,600 to 2,000 square feet.

The people who stayed at home had a powerful impact on the voyages of discovery. Merchants provided the capital for many early voyages and had a strong say in their course. To gain authorization and financial support for their expeditions, they sought official sponsorship from the Crown. Competition among European monarchs for the prestige and profit of overseas exploration thus constituted another crucial factor in encouraging the steady stream of expeditions that began in the late fifteenth century.

The small number of Europeans who could read provided a rapt audience for tales of fantastic places and unknown peoples. Cosmography, natural history, and geography aroused enormous interest among educated people in the fifteenth and sixteenth centuries. One of the most popular books of the time was the fourteenth-century text *The Travels of Sir John Mandeville*, which purported to be a firsthand account of the author's travels in the Middle East, India, and China. Although we now know they were fictional, these fantastic tales of cannibals, one-eyed giants, men with the heads of dogs, and other marvels were believed for centuries. Columbus took a copy of Mandeville and the equally popular and more reliable *The Travels of Marco Polo* on his voyage in 1492.

## Technology and the Rise of Exploration

Technological developments in shipbuilding, navigation, and weaponry enabled European expansion. Since ancient times, most seagoing vessels had been narrow, open boats called galleys, propelled by slaves or convicts manning the oars. Though well suited to the placid waters of the Mediterranean, galleys could not withstand the rougher conditions in the Atlantic. The need for sturdier craft, as well as population losses caused by the Black Death, forced the development of a new style of ship that would not require much manpower. Over the course of the fifteenth century the Portuguese developed the **caravel**, a small, light, three-mast sailing ship with triangular lateen sails. The caravel was much

- **conquistador** Spanish for "conqueror"; a Spanish soldier-explorer, such as Hernán Cortés or Francisco Pizarro, who sought to conquer the New World for the Spanish crown.

- **caravel** A small, maneuverable, three-mast sailing ship developed by the Portuguese in the fifteenth century that gave the Portuguese a distinct advantage in exploration and trade.

more maneuverable than the galley. When fitted with cannon, it could dominate larger vessels.

This period also saw great strides in cartography and navigational aids. Around 1410 Arab scholars reintroduced Europeans to **Ptolemy's** *Geography*. Written in the second century, the work synthesized the geographical knowledge of the classical world. It represented a major improvement over medieval cartography, showing the world as round and introducing the idea of latitude and longitude to plot a ship's position accurately. It also contained significant errors. Unaware of the Americas, Ptolemy showed the world as much smaller than it is, so that Asia appeared not very far to the west of Europe. Both the assets and the flaws of Ptolemy's work shaped the geographical knowledge that explorers like Christopher Columbus brought to their voyages.

The magnetic compass made it possible for sailors to determine their direction and position at sea. The astrolabe, an instrument invented by the ancient Greeks and perfected by Muslim navigators, was used to determine the altitude of the sun and other celestial bodies. It permitted mariners to plot their latitude, that is, their precise position north or south of the equator.

Like the astrolabe, much of the new technology that Europeans used on their voyages was borrowed from the East. Gunpowder, the compass, and the sternpost rudder were Chinese inventions. Advances in cartography also drew on the rich tradition of Judeo-Arabic mathematical and astronomical learning in Iberia. In exploring new territories, European sailors thus called on techniques and knowledge developed over centuries in China, the Muslim world, and trading centers along the Indian Ocean.

## The Portuguese in Africa and Asia

For centuries Portugal was a small and poor nation on the margins of European life whose principal activities were fishing and subsistence farming. It would have been hard for a medieval European to predict Portugal's phenomenal success overseas after 1450. Yet Portugal had a long history of seafaring and navigation. Blocked from access to western Europe by Spain, the Portuguese turned to the Atlantic, whose waters they knew better than did other Europeans. Nature favored the Portuguese: winds blowing along their coast offered passage to Africa, its Atlantic islands, and, ultimately, Brazil. Once they had mastered the secret to sailing against the wind to return to Europe (by sailing farther west to catch winds from the southwest), they were ideally poised to lead Atlantic exploration.

**The Portuguese Fleet Embarked for the Indies** This image shows a Portuguese trading fleet in the late fifteenth century bound for the riches of the Indies. Between 1500 and 1635 over nine hundred ships sailed from Portugal to ports on the Indian Ocean in annual fleets composed of five to ten ships. Portuguese sailors used astrolabes, such as the one pictured here, to accurately plot their position. (fleet: British Museum/HarperCollins Publishers/ The Art Archive at Art Resource, NY; astrolabe: © The Trustees of the British Museum/Art Resource, NY)

**Pepper Harvest** To break the monotony of their bland diet, Europeans had a passion for pepper, which — along with cinnamon, cloves, nutmeg, and ginger — was the main object of the Asian trade. We can appreciate the fifteenth-century expression "as dear as pepper": one kilo of pepper cost 2 grams of silver at the place of production in the East Indies and from 1 to 10 grams of silver in Alexandria, Egypt; 14 to 18 grams in Venice; and 20 to 30 grams at the markets of northern Europe. Here natives fill vats, and the dealer tastes a peppercorn for pungency. (Bibliothèque Nationale, Paris, France/Archives Charmet/The Bridgeman Art Library)

In the early phases of Portuguese exploration, Prince Henry (1394–1460), a dynamic younger son of the king, played a leading role. A nineteenth-century scholar dubbed Henry "the Navigator" because of his support for the study of geography and navigation and for the annual expeditions he sponsored down the western coast of Africa. Although he never personally participated in voyages of exploration, Henry's involvement ensured that Portugal did not abandon the effort despite early disappointments.

Portugal's conquest of Ceuta, an Arab city in northern Morocco, in 1415 marked the beginning of European overseas expansion. In the 1420s, under Henry's direction, the Portuguese began to settle the Atlantic islands of Madeira (ca. 1420) and the Azores (1427). In 1443 they founded their first African commercial settlement at Arguin in North Africa. By the time of Henry's death in 1460, his support for exploration was vindicated — in Portuguese eyes — by thriving sugar plantations on the Atlantic islands, the first arrival of enslaved Africans in Portugal (see page 477), and new access to African gold.

The Portuguese next established fortified trading posts, called factories, on the gold-rich Guinea coast and penetrated into the African continent all the way to Timbuktu (Map 16.2). By 1500 Portugal controlled the flow of African gold to Europe. In contrast to the Spanish conquest of the Americas (see page 471), the Portuguese did not establish large settlements in West Africa or seek to control the political or cultural lives of those with whom they traded. Instead they sought easier and faster profits by inserting themselves into pre-existing trading systems. For the first century of their relations, African rulers were equal partners with the Portuguese, protected by their experienced armies and European vulnerability to tropical diseases.

In 1487 Bartholomew Diaz (ca. 1451–1500) rounded the Cape of Good Hope at the southern tip of Africa (Map 16.2), but storms and a threatened mutiny forced him to turn back. A decade later Vasco da Gama (ca. 1469–1524) succeeded in rounding the Cape while commanding a fleet in search of a sea route to India. With the help of an Indian guide, da Gama reached the port of Calicut in India. He returned to Lisbon with spices and samples of Indian cloth, having proved the possibility of lucrative trade with the East via the

**Ptolemy's *Geography*** A second-century-C.E. work that synthesized the classical knowledge of geography and introduced the concepts of longitude and latitude. Reintroduced to Europeans in 1410 by Arab scholars, its ideas allowed cartographers to create more accurate maps.

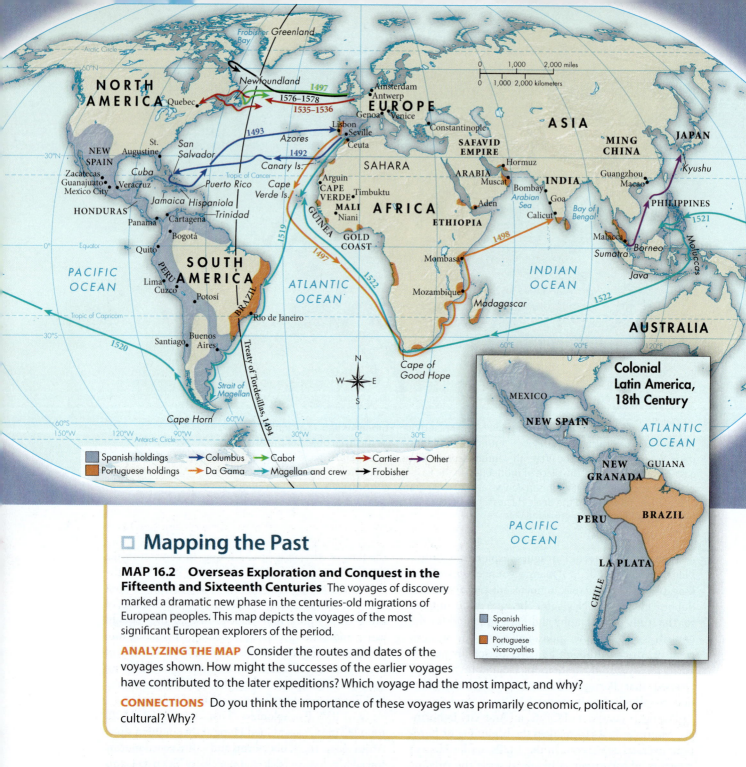

## Mapping the Past

**MAP 16.2 Overseas Exploration and Conquest in the Fifteenth and Sixteenth Centuries** The voyages of discovery marked a dramatic new phase in the centuries-old migrations of European peoples. This map depicts the voyages of the most significant European explorers of the period.

**ANALYZING THE MAP** Consider the routes and dates of the voyages shown. How might the successes of the earlier voyages have contributed to the later expeditions? Which voyage had the most impact, and why?

**CONNECTIONS** Do you think the importance of these voyages was primarily economic, political, or cultural? Why?

Cape route. Thereafter, a Portuguese convoy set out for passage around the Cape every March.

Lisbon became the entrance port for Asian goods into Europe, but this was not accomplished without a fight. Muslim-controlled port city-states had long controlled the rich trade of the Indian Ocean, and they did not surrender it willingly. From 1500 to 1515 the Portuguese used a combination of bombardment and diplomatic treaties to establish trading factories at Goa, Malacca, Calicut, and Hormuz, thereby laying the foundation for a Portuguese trading empire in the

sixteenth and seventeenth centuries. The acquisition of port cities and their trade routes brought riches to Portugal, but, as in Africa, the Portuguese had limited impact on the lives and religious faith of peoples beyond Portuguese coastal holdings. Moreover, Portuguese ability to enforce a monopoly on trading in the Indian Ocean was always limited by the sheer distances involved and the stiff resistance of Indian, Ottoman, and other rivals.

Inspired by the Portuguese, the Spanish had also begun the quest for empire. Theirs was to be a second, entirely different, mode of colonization leading to large-scale settlement and the forced assimilation of huge indigenous populations.

## Spain's Voyages to the Americas

Christopher Columbus was not the first navigator to explore the Atlantic. In the ninth century Vikings established short-lived settlements in Newfoundland, and it is probable that others made the voyage, either on purpose or accidentally, carried by westward currents off the coast of Africa. In Africa, Mansa Musa, emperor of Mali, reportedly came to the throne after the previous king failed to return from a naval expedition he led to explore the Atlantic Ocean. A document by a scholar of the time, al-Umari, quoted Mansa Musa's description of his predecessor as a man who "did not believe that the ocean was impossible to cross. He wished to reach the other side and was passionately interested in doing so."[6] Portugal's achievements in Atlantic navigation made the moment right for Christopher Columbus to attempt to find a westward route across the Atlantic to Asia in the late fifteenth century.

Christopher Columbus, a native of Genoa, was an experienced seaman and navigator. He had worked as a mapmaker in Lisbon and had spent time on Madeira. He was familiar with such fifteenth-century Portuguese navigational aids as *portolans*—written descriptions of the courses along which ships sailed—and the use of the compass as a nautical instrument. Columbus asserted in his journal: "I have spent twenty-three years at sea and have not left it for any length of time worth mentioning, and I have seen every thing from east to west [meaning he had been to England] and I have been to Guinea [North and West Africa]."[7]

Columbus was also a deeply religious man. He had witnessed the Spanish conquest of Granada and shared fully in the religious fervor surrounding that event. Like the Spanish rulers and most Europeans of his age, Columbus understood Christianity as a missionary religion that should be carried to all places of the earth. He thus viewed himself as a divine agent: "God made me the messenger of the new heaven and the new earth of which he spoke in the Apocalypse of St. John . . . and he showed me the post where to find it."[8]

Rejected for funding by the Portuguese in 1483 and by Ferdinand and Isabella in 1486, Columbus finally won the support of the Spanish monarchy in 1492. Buoyed by the success of the reconquista and eager to earn profits from trade, the Spanish crown agreed to make him viceroy over any territory he might discover and to give him one-tenth of the material rewards of the journey.

Columbus and his small fleet left Spain on August 3, 1492. Columbus dreamed of reaching the court of the Mongol emperor, the Great Khan, not realizing that the Ming Dynasty had overthrown the Mongols in 1368. Based on Ptolemy's *Geography* and other texts, he expected to pass the islands of Japan and then land on the east coast of China.

After a brief stop in the Canary Islands, he landed on an island in the Bahamas on October 12, which he christened San Salvador and claimed on behalf of the Spanish crown. In a letter he wrote to Ferdinand and Isabella on his return to Spain, Columbus described the natives as handsome, peaceful, and primitive. Believing he was somewhere off the east coast of Japan, in what he considered the Indies, he called them "Indians," a name that was later applied to all inhabitants of the Americas. Columbus concluded that they would make good slaves and could quickly be converted to Christianity. (See "Listening to the Past: Columbus Describes His First Voyage," page 468.)

**Columbus's First Voyage to the New World, 1492–1493**

First landing on San Salvador Island Oct. 12, 1492

Gulf of Mexico · Cuba · Santiago · Hispaniola · Santo Domingo · Caribbean Sea · ATLANTIC OCEAN

Scholars have identified the inhabitants of the islands as the Taino (TIGH-noh) people, speakers of the Arawak language, who inhabited Hispaniola (modern-day Haiti and the Dominican Republic) and other islands in the Caribbean. From San Salvador, Columbus sailed southwest, landing on Cuba on October 28. Deciding that he must be on the mainland of China near the coastal city of Quinsay (now Hangzhou), he sent a small embassy inland with letters from Ferdinand and Isabella and instructions to locate the grand city. Although they found no large settlement or any evidence of a great kingdom, the sight of Taino people wearing gold ornaments on Hispaniola suggested that gold was available in the region. In January, confident that its source would soon be found, he headed back to Spain to report on his discovery.

On his second voyage, Columbus took control of the island of Hispaniola and enslaved its indigenous peoples. On this and subsequent voyages, he brought with him settlers for the new Spanish territories, along with agricultural seed and livestock. Columbus himself, however, had little interest in or capacity for governing. Arriving in Hispaniola on his third voyage, he found revolt had broken out against his brother, whom Columbus had left behind to govern the colony. An investigatory expedition sent by the Spanish crown arrested Columbus and his brother for failing to maintain order. Columbus returned to Spain in disgrace and a royal governor assumed control of the colony.

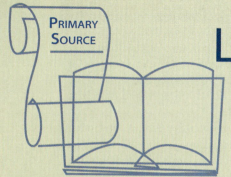
# Listening to the Past

## Columbus Describes His First Voyage

*On his return voyage to Spain in February 1493, Christopher Columbus composed a letter intended for wide circulation and had copies of it sent ahead to Isabella, Ferdinand, and others when his ship docked at Lisbon. Because the letter sums up Columbus's understanding of his achievements, it is considered the most important document of his first voyage.*

❝ Since I know that you will be pleased at the great success with which the Lord has crowned my voyage, I write to inform you how in thirty-three days I crossed from the Canary Islands to the Indies, with the fleet which our most illustrious sovereigns gave me. I found very many islands with large populations and took possession of them all for their Highnesses; this I did by proclamation and unfurled the royal standard. No opposition was offered.

I named the first island that I found "San Salvador," in honour of our Lord and Saviour who has granted me this miracle. . . . When I reached Cuba, I followed its north coast westwards, and found it so extensive that I thought this must be the mainland, the province of Cathay.* . . . From there I saw another island eighteen leagues eastwards which I then named "Hispaniola."† . . .

Hispaniola is a wonder. The mountains and hills, the plains and meadow lands are both fertile and beautiful. They are most suitable for planting crops and for raising cattle of all kinds, and there are good sites for building towns and villages. The harbours are incredibly fine and there are many great rivers with broad channels and the majority contain gold.‡ The trees, fruits and plants are very different from those of Cuba. In Hispaniola there are many spices and large mines of gold and other metals.§ . . .

The inhabitants of this island, and all the rest that I discovered or heard of, go naked, as their mothers bore them, men and women alike. A few of the women, however, cover a single place with a leaf of a plant or piece of cotton which they weave for the purpose. They have no iron or steel or arms and are not capable of using them, not because they are not strong and well built but because they are amazingly timid. All the weapons they have are canes cut at seeding time, at the end of which they fix a sharpened stick, but they have not the courage to make use of these, for very often when I have sent two or three men to a village to have conversation with them a great number of them have come out. But as soon as they saw my men all fled immediately, a father not even waiting for his son. And this is not because we have harmed any of them; on the contrary, wherever I have gone and been able to have conversation with them, I have given them some of the various things I had, a cloth and other articles, and received nothing in exchange. But they have still remained incurably timid. True, when they have been reassured and lost their fear, they are so ingenuous and so liberal with all their possessions that no one who has not seen them would believe it. If one asks for anything they have they never say no. On the contrary, they offer a share to anyone with demonstrations of heartfelt affection, and they are immediately content with any small thing, valuable or valueless, that is given them. I forbade the men to give them bits of broken crockery, fragments of glass or tags of laces, though if they could get them they fancied them the finest jewels in the world.

I hoped to win them to the love and service of their Highnesses and of the whole Spanish nation and to persuade them to collect and give us of the things which they possessed in abundance and which we needed. They have no religion and are not idolaters; but all believe that power and goodness dwell in the sky and they are firmly convinced that I have come from the sky with these ships and people. In this belief they gave me a good reception everywhere, once they had overcome their fear; and this is not because they are stupid — far from it, they are men of great intelligence, for they navigate all those seas, and give a marvellously good account of everything — but because they have never before seen men clothed or ships like these. . . .

Columbus was very much a man of his times. To the end of his life in 1506, he believed that he had found small islands off the coast of Asia. He never realized the scope of his achievement: that he had found a vast continent unknown to Europeans, except for a fleeting Viking presence centuries earlier. He could not know that the lands he discovered would become a crucial new arena for international trade and colonization, with grave consequences for native peoples.

## Spain "Discovers" the Pacific

The Florentine navigator Amerigo Vespucci (veh-SPOO-chee) (1454–1512) realized what Columbus had not. Writing about his discoveries on the coast of modern-day Venezuela, Vespucci stated: "Those new regions which we found and explored with the fleet . . . we may rightly call a New World." This letter, titled *Mundus Novus* (The New World), was the first docu-

In all these islands the men are seemingly content with one woman, but their chief or king is allowed more than twenty. The women appear to work more than the men and I have not been able to find out if they have private property. As far as I could see whatever a man had was shared among all the rest and this particularly applies to food. . . . In another island, which I am told is larger than Hispaniola, the people have no hair. Here there is a vast quantity of gold, and from here and the other islands I bring Indians as evidence.

In conclusion, to speak only of the results of this very hasty voyage, their Highnesses can see that I will give them as much gold as they require, if they will render me some very slight assistance; also I will give them all the spices and cotton they want. . . . I will also bring them as much aloes as they ask and as many slaves, who will be taken from the idolaters. I believe also that I have found rhubarb and cinnamon and there will be countless other things in addition. . . .

So all Christendom will be delighted that our Redeemer has given victory to our most illustrious King and Queen and their renowned kingdoms, in this great matter. They should hold great celebrations and render solemn thanks to the Holy Trinity with many solemn prayers, for the great triumph which they will have, by the conversion of so many peoples to our holy faith and for the temporal benefits which will follow, for not only Spain, but all Christendom will receive encouragement and profit.

This is a brief account of the facts.

Written in the caravel off the Canary Islands.**

15 February 1493

At your orders
THE ADMIRAL 🙶

Source: J. M. Cohen, ed. and trans., *The Four Voyages of Christopher Columbus* (Penguin Classics, 1958), pp. 115–123. Copyright © J. M. Cohen, 1969, London. Reproduced by permission of Penguin Books Ltd.

**Christopher Columbus**, by Ridolfo Ghirlandio. Friend of Raphael and teacher of Michelangelo, Ghirlandio (1483–1561) enjoyed distinction as a portrait painter, and so we can assume that this is a good likeness of the older Columbus.
(Museo Navale di Pegli, Genoa, Italy/Scala/Art Resource, NY)

## QUESTIONS FOR ANALYSIS

1. How did Columbus explain the success of his voyage?

2. What was Columbus's view of the Native Americans he met?

3. Evaluate Columbus's statements that the Caribbean islands possessed gold, cotton, and spices.

4. Why did Columbus cling to the idea that he had reached Asia?

*Cathay is the old name for China. In the logbook and later in this letter Columbus accepts the natives' story that Cuba is an island that they can circumnavigate in something more than twenty-one days, yet he insists here and during the second voyage that it is in fact part of the Asiatic mainland.

†Hispaniola is the second-largest island of the West Indies; Haiti occupies the western third of the island, the Dominican Republic the rest.

‡This did not prove to be true.

§These statements are also inaccurate.

**Actually, Columbus was off Santa Maria in the Azores.

ment to describe America as a continent separate from Asia. In recognition of Amerigo's bold claim, the continent was named for him.

To settle competing claims to the Atlantic discoveries, Spain and Portugal turned to Pope Alexander VI. The resulting **Treaty of Tordesillas** (tawr-duh-SEE-yuhs) in 1494 gave Spain everything to the west of an imaginary line drawn down the Atlantic and Portugal everything to the east. This arbitrary division worked in Portugal's favor when in 1500 an expedition led by Pedro Álvares Cabral landed on the coast of Brazil, which Cabral claimed as Portuguese territory.

The search for profits determined the direction of Spanish exploration and expansion in South America.

- **Treaty of Tordesillas** The 1494 agreement giving Spain everything west of an imaginary line drawn down the Atlantic and giving Portugal everything to the east.

Because its profits from Hispaniola and other Caribbean islands were insignificant compared to Portugal's enormous riches from the Asian spice trade, Spain renewed the search for a western passage to Asia. In 1519 Charles V of Spain commissioned Ferdinand Magellan (1480–1521) to find a direct sea route to the spices of the Moluccas, islands off the southeast coast of Asia. Magellan sailed southwest across the Atlantic to Brazil, and after a long search along the coast he located the treacherous strait off the southern tip of South America that now bears his name (see Map 16.2). After passing through the strait, his fleet sailed north up the west coast of South America and then headed west into the Pacific toward the Malay Archipelago. (Some of these islands were conquered in the 1560s and were named the Philippines for Philip II of Spain.)

Terrible storms, disease, starvation, and violence haunted the expedition. Sailors on two of Magellan's five ships attempted mutiny on the South American coast; one ship was lost, and another ship deserted and returned to Spain before even traversing the strait. Magellan himself was killed in a skirmish in the Malay Archipelago. At this point, the expedition had enough survivors to man only two ships, and one of them was captured by the Portuguese. Finally, in 1522, one ship with only eighteen men returned to Spain, having traveled from the east by way of the Indian Ocean, the Cape of Good Hope, and the Atlantic. The voyage— the first to circumnavigate the globe—had taken close to three years.

Despite the losses, this voyage revolutionized Europeans' understanding of the world by demonstrating the vastness of the Pacific. The earth was clearly much larger than Ptolemy's map had shown. Magellan's expedition also forced Spain's rulers to rethink their plans for overseas commerce and territorial expansion. Although the voyage made a small profit in spices, the westward passage to the Indies was too long and dangerous for commercial purposes. Thus Spain soon abandoned the attempt to oust Portugal from the Eastern spice trade and concentrated on exploiting its New World territories.

## Early Exploration by Northern European Powers

Spain's northern European rivals also set sail across the Atlantic during the early days of exploration, searching for a northwest passage to the Indies. In 1497 John

**Juan Vespucci's World Map, 1526**  As chief pilot to the Spanish crown, Juan Vespucci oversaw constant revisions to royal maps necessitated by ongoing voyages of discovery and exploration. This map shows the progress of Spanish knowledge of the New World some thirty years after Columbus. (The Granger Collection, NYC — All rights reserved.)

Cabot (ca. 1450–1499), a Genoese merchant living in London, landed on Newfoundland. The next year he returned and explored the New England coast. These forays proved futile, and at that time the English established no permanent colonies in the territories they explored.

News of the riches of Mexico and Peru later inspired the English to renew their efforts, this time in the extreme north. Between 1576 and 1578 Martin Frobisher (ca. 1535–1594) made three voyages in and around the Canadian bay that now bears his name. Frobisher brought a quantity of ore back to England with him in hopes that it contained precious metals, but it proved to be worthless.

Early French exploration of the Atlantic was equally frustrating. Between 1534 and 1541 Frenchman Jacques Cartier (1491–1557) made several voyages and explored the St. Lawrence region of Canada, searching for a passage to the wealth of Asia. When this hope proved vain, the French turned to a new source of profit within Canada itself: trade in beavers and other furs. As had the Portuguese in Asia, French traders bartered with local peoples whom they largely treated as autonomous and equal partners. French fishermen also competed with the Spanish and English for the teeming schools of cod they found in the Atlantic waters around Newfoundland.

# Conquest and Settlement

☐ What was the impact of Iberian conquest and settlement on the peoples and ecologies of the Americas?

Before Columbus's arrival, the Americas were inhabited by thousands of groups of indigenous peoples with distinct languages and cultures. These groups ranged from hunter-gatherer tribes organized into tribal confederations to settled agriculturalists to large-scale empires connecting bustling cities and towns. The best estimate is that the peoples of the Americas numbered between 35 and 50 million in 1492. Their lives were radically altered by the arrival of Europeans.

The growing European presence in the New World transformed its land and its peoples forever. Violence, forced labor, and disease wrought devastating losses, while surviving peoples encountered new political, social, and economic organizations imposed by Europeans. Although the exchange of goods and people between Europe and the New World brought diseases to the Americas, it also gave both the New and Old Worlds new crops that eventually altered consumption patterns across the globe.

## Spanish Conquest of the Aztec and Inca Empires

In the first two decades after Columbus's arrival in the New World, the Spanish colonized Hispaniola, Cuba, Puerto Rico, and other Caribbean islands. Based on rumors of a wealthy mainland civilization, the Spanish governor in Cuba sponsored expeditions to the Yucatán coast of the Gulf of Mexico, including one in 1519 under the command of the conquistador Hernán Cortés (1485–1547). Alarmed by Cortés's brash ambition, the governor decided to withdraw his support, but Cortés quickly set sail before being removed from command. Accompanied by eleven ships, 450 men, sixteen horses, and ten cannon, Cortés landed on the Mexican coast on April 21, 1519. His camp soon received visits by delegations of unarmed Aztec leaders bearing gifts and news of their great emperor.

The **Aztec Empire**, also known as the Mexica Empire, comprised the Mexica people and the peoples they had conquered, and it had grown rapidly in size and power in the early fifteenth century. At the time of the Spanish arrival, the empire was ruled by Moctezuma II (r. 1502–1520), from his capital at Tenochtitlan (tay-nawch-teet-LAHN), now Mexico City. The Aztecs were a sophisticated civilization with an advanced understanding of mathematics, astronomy, and engineering and with oral poetry and historical traditions. As in European nations at the time, a hereditary nobility dominated the army, the priesthood, and the state bureaucracy and reaped the gains from the agricultural labor of the common people.

Within weeks of his arrival, Cortés acquired translators who provided vital information on the empire and its weaknesses. (See "Individuals in Society: Doña Marina / Malintzin," page 472.) To legitimize his authority, Cortés founded the settlement of Veracruz and had himself named its military commander. He then burned his ships to prevent any disloyal or frightened followers from returning to Cuba.

Through his interpreters, Cortés learned of strong local resentment against the Aztec Empire. The Aztec state practiced warfare against neighboring peoples to secure captives for religious sacrifices and laborers for agricultural and building projects. Once conquered, subject tribes paid continual tribute to the empire through their local chiefs. Realizing that he could exploit dissensions within the empire to his own advantage, Cortés forged an alliance with Tlaxcala (tlah-SKAH-lah), a subject kingdom of the Aztecs. In October a

● **Aztec Empire** Also known as the Mexica Empire, a large and complex Native American civilization in modern Mexico and Central America that possessed advanced mathematical, astronomical, and engineering technology.

# Individuals in Society

## Doña Marina / Malintzin

**IN APRIL 1519 HERNÁN CORTÉS AND HIS FOLLOWERS** received a number of gifts from the Tabasco people after he defeated them, including a group of twenty female captives. Among them was a young woman the Spanish baptized as Marina, which became Malin in the Nahuatl (NAH-wha-tuhl) language spoken in the Aztec Empire. Her high status and importance were recognized with the honorific title of *doña* in Spanish and the suffix *-tzin* in Nahuatl. Bernal Díaz del Castillo, who accompanied Cortés and wrote the most important contemporary history of the Aztec Empire and its conquest, claimed that Doña Marina (or Malintzin) was the daughter of a leader of a Nahuatl-speaking tribe. According to his account, the family sold Marina to Maya slave traders as a child to protect the inheritance rights of her stepbrother.

Marina possessed unique skills that immediately caught the attention of Cortés. Fluent both in Nahuatl and Yucatec Maya (spoken by a Spanish priest accompanying Cortés), she offered a way for him to communicate with the peoples he encountered. She quickly learned Spanish as well and came to play a vital role as an interpreter and diplomatic guide. Indigenous pictures and writings created after the conquest depict Malintzin as a constant presence beside Cortés as he negotiated with and fought and killed Amerindians. The earliest known images show her interpreting for Cortés as he meets with the Tlaxcalan lord Xicotencatl, forging the alliance that would prove vital to Spanish victory against the Aztecs. Malintzin also appears prominently in the images of the *Florentine Codex*, an illustrated history of the Aztec Empire and its conquest created near the end of the sixteenth century by indigenous artists working under the direction of Friar Bernardino de Sahagún. All the images depict her as a well-dressed woman standing at the center of interactions between the Spanish and Amerindians.

Malintzin bore Cortés a son, Don Martín Cortés, in 1522 and accompanied him on expeditions to Honduras between 1524 and 1526. It is impossible to know the true nature of their personal relationship. Cortés was married to a Spanish woman in Cuba at the time, and Malintzin was a slave, in no position to refuse any demands he made of her. Cortés recognized their child and provided financial support for his upbringing. Malintzin later married one of Cortés's Spanish followers, Juan Jaramillo, with whom she had a daughter. It is unknown when and how she died.

**Doña Marina translating for Hernán Cortés.** (The Granger Collection, NYC — All rights reserved)

Bernal Díaz gave Malintzin high praise. In his history, written decades after the fact, he described her as beautiful and intelligent, revered by native tribesmen, and devotedly loyal to the Spanish. He stated repeatedly that it would have been impossible for them to succeed without her help. Cortés mentioned Malintzin only twice in his letters to Spanish king Charles V. He acknowledged her usefulness as his interpreter but described her only as "an Indian woman of this land," giving no hint of their personal relationship. No writings from Malintzin herself exist.

Malintzin is commonly known in Mexico and Latin America as La Malinche, a Spanish rendering of her Nahuatl name. She remains a compelling and controversial figure. Popular opinion has often condemned La Malinche as a traitor to her people, whose betrayal enabled the Spanish conquest and centuries of subjugation of indigenous peoples. Other voices have defended her as an enslaved woman who had no choice but to serve her masters. As the mother of a *mestizo* (mixed-race) child, she has also been seen as a founder of the mixed-race population that dominates modern Mexico. She will always be a reminder of the complex interactions between indigenous peoples and Spanish conquistadors that led to the conquest and the new culture born from it.

### QUESTIONS FOR ANALYSIS

1. Why was the role of interpreter so important in Cortés's conquest of the Aztec Empire? Why did Malintzin become such a central figure in interactions between Cortés and the Amerindians?

2. What options were open to Malintzin in following her path? If she intentionally chose to aid the Spanish, what motivations might she have had?

### LaunchPad
## Online Document Project

**How did Spanish and Amerindian artists depict Malintzin?**
Examine Spanish and Amerindian representations of Malintzin's role in the conquest, and then complete a quiz and writing assignment based on the evidence and details from this chapter.

*See inside the front cover to learn more.*

combined Spanish-Tlaxcalan force occupied the Aztec city of Cholula, second largest in the empire, and massacred thousands of inhabitants. Strengthened by this display of ruthless power, Cortés formed alliances with other native kingdoms. In November 1519, with a few hundred Spanish men and some six thousand indigenous warriors, he marched on Tenochtitlan.

Historians have long debated Moctezuma's response to the arrival of the Spanish. Unlike other native leaders, he refrained from attacking the Spaniards but instead welcomed Cortés and his men into Tenochtitlan. Moctezuma was apparently deeply impressed by Spanish victories and believed the Spanish were invincible. Sources written after the conquest claimed that the emperor believed Cortés was an embodiment of the god Quetzalcoatl, whose return was promised in Aztec myth.

While it is impossible to verify those claims, it is clear that Moctezuma's weak and hesitant response was disastrous. When Cortés—with incredible boldness—took Moctezuma hostage, the emperor's influence crumbled. During the ensuing attacks and counterattacks, Moctezuma was killed. The Spaniards and their allies escaped from the city suffering heavy losses. Cortés quickly began gathering forces and making new alliances against the Aztecs. In May 1521 he led a second assault on Tenochtitlan, leading an army of approximately one thousand Spanish and seventy-five thousand native warriors.[9]

The Spanish victory in late summer 1521 was hard-won and was greatly aided by the effects of smallpox, which had devastated the besieged population of the city. After establishing a new capital in the ruins of Tenochtitlan, Cortés and other conquistadors began the systematic conquest of Mexico.

More remarkable than the defeat of the Aztec Empire was the fall of the remote **Inca Empire** in Peru. Living in a settlement perched more than 9,800 feet above sea level, the Incas were isolated from the Mesoamerican civilization of the Aztecs. Nonetheless, they too had created a vast empire in the fifteenth century that rivaled those of the Europeans in population and complexity. The Incas' strength lay largely in their bureaucratic efficiency. They divided their empire into four major regions containing eighty provinces and twice as many districts. Officials at each level used the extensive network of roads to transmit information and orders back and forth through the empire. While the Aztecs used a system of glyphs for writing, the Incas had devised a complex system of colored and knotted cords, called khipus, for administrative bookkeeping. The empire

**Inca Women Milking Cows** This illustration of Inca women milking cows is from a collection of illustrations by a Spanish bishop that offers a valuable view of life in Peru in the 1780s. (From *Codex Trujillo*, Bishop Baltasar Jaime Martínez Compañón, Palacio Real, Madrid, Spain/Photo: Albers Foundation/Art Resource, NY)

**Invasion of Tenochtitlan, 1519–1521**

Gulf of Mexico

Texcoco
Otumba
Zautla
Jalapa
Veracruz
Tlaxcala
Cholula
Tenochtitlan

→ Cortés's original route, 1519
→ Cortés's retreat, 1520
→ Cortés's return route, 1520–1521

also benefited from the use of llamas as pack animals (by contrast, no beasts of burden existed in Mesoamerica).

By the time of the Spanish invasion, however, the Inca Empire had been weakened by a civil war over succession and an epidemic of disease, possibly smallpox, spread through trade with groups in contact with Europeans. The Spanish conquistador Francisco Pizarro (ca. 1475–1541) landed on the northern coast of Peru on May 13, 1532, the very day the Inca leader Atahualpa (ah-tuh-WAHL-puh) won control of the empire after five years of fighting his brother for the throne. As Pizarro advanced across the Andes toward Cuzco, the capital of the Inca Empire, Atahualpa was also heading there for his coronation.

Like Moctezuma in Mexico, Atahualpa was aware of the Spaniards' movements. He sent envoys to greet the Spanish and invited them to meet him in the provincial town of Cajamarca. Motivated by curiosity

• **Inca Empire** The vast and sophisticated Peruvian empire centered at the capital city of Cuzco that was at its peak in the fifteenth century.

about the Spanish, he intended to meet with them to learn more about them and their intentions. Instead the Spaniards ambushed and captured him, extorted an enormous ransom in gold, and then executed him on trumped-up charges in 1533. The Spanish then marched on to Cuzco, profiting, as with the Aztecs, from internal conflicts and forming alliances with local peoples. When Cuzco fell in 1533, the Spanish plundered immense riches in gold and silver.

How was it possible for several hundred Spanish conquistadors to defeat powerful empires commanding large armies, vast wealth, and millions of inhabitants? Historians seeking answers to this question have emphasized a combination of factors: the boldness and audacity of conquistadors like Cortés and Pizarro; the military superiority endowed by Spanish firepower and horses; the fervent belief in a righteous Christian God imparted by the reconquista; division within the Aztec and Inca Empires that produced native allies for the Spanish; and, of course, the devastating impact of contagious diseases among the indigenous population. Ironically, the well-organized, urban-based Aztec and Inca Empires were more vulnerable to wholesale takeover than more decentralized and fragmented groups like the Maya, whose independence was not wholly crushed until the end of the seventeenth century.

**The Conquest of Peru, 1532–1533**

### Portuguese Brazil

Unlike Mesoamerica or the Andes, the territory of Brazil contained no urban empires but instead had roughly 2.5 million nomadic and settled people divided into small tribes and many different language groups. In 1500 the Portuguese crown named Pedro Álvares Cabral commander of a fleet headed for the spice trade of the Indies. En route, the fleet sailed far to the west, accidentally landing on the coast of Brazil, which Cabral claimed for Portugal under the terms of the Treaty of Tordesillas. The Portuguese soon undertook a profitable trade with local people in brazilwood, a source of red dye.

In the 1520s Portuguese settlers brought sugarcane production to Brazil. They initially used enslaved indigenous laborers on sugar plantations, but the rapid decline in the indigenous population soon led to the use of forcibly transported Africans. In Brazil the Por-

tuguese thus created a new form of colonization in the Americas: large plantations worked by enslaved people. This model of slave-worked sugar plantations would spread throughout the Caribbean in the seventeenth century.

### Colonial Administration

By the end of the sixteenth century the Spanish and Portuguese had successfully overcome most indigenous groups and expanded their territory throughout modern-day Mexico, the southwestern United States, and Central and South America. In Mesoamerica and the Andes, the Spanish had taken over the cities and tribute systems of the Aztecs and the Incas, basing their control on the prior existence of well-established polities with organized tribute systems.

While early conquest and settlement were conducted largely by private initiatives (authorized and sponsored by the state), the Spanish and Portuguese governments soon assumed more direct control. In 1503 the Spanish granted the port of Seville a monopoly over all traffic to the New World and established the House of Trade, or *Casa de Contratación*, to oversee economic matters. In 1523 Spain created the Royal and Supreme Council of the Indies, with authority over all colonial affairs subject to approval by the king. Spanish territories themselves were divided initially into two **viceroyalties**, or administrative divisions: New Spain, created in 1535, with its capital at Mexico City; and Peru, created in 1542, with its capital at Lima. In the eighteenth century two additional viceroyalties were added: New Granada, with Bogotá as its administrative center; and La Plata, with Buenos Aires as its capital (see Map 16.2).

Within each territory, the viceroy, or imperial governor, exercised broad military and civil authority as the direct representative of Spain. The viceroy presided over the *audiencia* (ow-dee-EHN-see-ah), a board of twelve to fifteen judges that served as his advisory council and the highest judicial body. As in Spain, settlement in the Americas was centered on cities and towns. In each city, the municipal council, or *cabildo*, exercised local authority. Women were denied participation in public life, a familiar pattern from both Spain and pre-colonial indigenous societies.

In Portugal, the India House in Lisbon functioned much like the Spanish House of Trade, and royal representatives oversaw its possessions in West Africa and Asia, as did governors in Spanish America. To secure the vast expanse of Brazil, however, the Portuguese implemented a distinctive system of rule, called **captaincies**, in the 1530s. These were hereditary grants of land given to nobles and loyal officials who bore the costs of settling and administering their territories. Over time, the Crown secured greater power over the captaincies, appointing royal governors to act as administrators. The captaincy of Bahia was the site of the capital, Salvador, home to the governor general and other royal officials.

Throughout the Americas, the Catholic Church played an integral role in Iberian rule. Churches and cathedrals were consecrated, often on precolonial sacred sites, and bishoprics were established. The papacy allowed Portuguese and Spanish officials greater control over the church than was the case at home, allowing them to appoint clerics and collect tithes. This control helped colonial powers use the church as an instrument to indoctrinate indigenous people in European ways of life (see page 479).

## Indigenous Population Loss and Economic Exploitation

From the time of Christopher Columbus in Hispaniola, the conquerors of the New World made use of the **encomienda system** to profit from the peoples and territories they encountered. This system was a legacy of the methods used to reward military leaders in the time of the reconquista, when victorious officers received feudal privileges over conquered areas in return for their service. First in the Caribbean and then on the mainland, conquistadors granted their followers the right to employ groups of Native Americans as laborers and to demand tribute payments from them in exchange for providing food, shelter, and instruction in the Christian faith. Commonly, an individual conquistador was assigned a tribal chieftain along with all the people belonging to his kin group. This system was first used in Hispaniola to work goldfields and then in Mexico for agricultural labor and, when silver was discovered in the 1540s, for silver mining.

A 1512 Spanish law authorizing the use of the encomienda called for indigenous people to be treated fairly, but in practice the system led to terrible abuses, including overwork, beatings, and sexual violence. Spanish missionaries publicized these abuses, leading to debates in Spain about the nature and proper treatment of indigenous people (see page 481). King Charles V responded to such complaints in 1542 with the New Laws, which set limits on the authority of encomienda holders, including their ability to transmit their privileges to heirs.

The New Laws provoked a revolt among elites in Peru and were little enforced throughout Spanish territories. Nonetheless, the Crown gradually gained control over encomiendas in central areas of the empire and required indigenous people to pay tributes in cash, rather than in labor. To respond to a shortage of indigenous workers, royal officials established a new government-run system of forced labor, called *repar-*

*timiento* in New Spain and *mita* in Peru. Administrators assigned a certain percentage of the inhabitants of native communities to labor for a set period each year in public works, mining, agriculture, and other tasks. Laborers received modest wages, which they could use to fulfill tribute obligations. In the seventeenth century, as land became a more important source of wealth than labor, elite settlers purchased *haciendas*, enormous tracts of farmland worked by dependent indigenous laborers and slaves.

Spanish systems for exploiting the labor of indigenous peoples were both a cause of and a response to the disastrous decline in the numbers of such peoples that began soon after the arrival of Europeans. Some indigenous people died as a direct result of the violence of conquest and the disruption of agriculture and trade caused by warfare. The most important cause of death, however, was infectious disease. Having little or no resistance to diseases brought from the Old World, the inhabitants of the New World fell victim to smallpox, typhus, influenza, and other illnesses. Overwork and exhaustion reduced indigenous people's ability to survive infectious disease. Moreover, labor obligations diverted local people from tending to their own crops, leading to malnutrition, starvation, and low fertility rates. Labor obligations also separated nursing mothers from their babies, resulting in high infant mortality rates.

The pattern of devastating disease and population loss established in the Spanish colonies was repeated everywhere Europeans settled. Overall, population declined by as much as 90 percent or more but with important regional variations. In general, densely populated urban centers were worse hit than rural areas, and tropical, low-lying regions suffered more than cooler, higher-altitude ones. Some scholars have claimed that losses may have been overreported, since many indigenous people fled their communities—or listed themselves as mixed race (and thus immune from forced labor)—to escape Spanish exploitation. By the mid-seventeenth century the worst losses had occurred and a slight recovery began.

Colonial administrators responded to native population decline by forcibly combining dwindling indigenous communities into new settlements and imposing the rigors of the encomienda and the repartimiento.

- **viceroyalties** The name for the four administrative units of Spanish possessions in the Americas: New Spain, Peru, New Granada, and La Plata.

- **captaincies** A system established by the Portuguese in Brazil in the 1530s, whereby hereditary grants of land were given to nobles and loyal officials who bore the costs of settling and administering their territories.

- **encomienda system** A system whereby the Spanish crown granted the conquerors the right to forcibly employ groups of Indians; it was a disguised form of slavery.

By the end of the sixteenth century the search for fresh sources of labor had given birth to the new tragedy of the Atlantic slave trade (see page 603).

## Patterns of Settlement

The century after the discovery of silver in 1545 marked the high point of Iberian immigration to the Americas. Although the first migrants were men—conquistadors, priests, and colonial officials—soon whole families began to cross the Atlantic, and the European population began to increase through natural reproduction. By 1600 American-born Europeans, called *Creoles*, outnumbered immigrants. By 1650 European-born and Creole Spaniards numbered approximately 200,000 in Mexico and 350,000 in the remaining colonies. Portuguese immigration to Brazil was relatively slow, and Portuguese-born settlers continued to dominate the colony.

Iberian settlement was predominantly urban in nature. Spaniards settled into the cities and towns of the former Aztec and Inca Empires as the native population dwindled through death and flight. They also established new cities, such as Santo Domingo on Hispaniola and Vera Cruz in Mexico. Settlers were quick to establish urban institutions familiar to them from home: city squares, churches, schools, and universities.

Despite the growing number of Europeans and the rapid decline of the native population, Europeans remained a small minority of the total inhabitants of the Americas. Cortés and his followers had taken native women as concubines and, less frequently, as wives. This pattern was repeated with the arrival of more Iberians, leading to a substantial population of mixed Iberian and Indian descent known as *mestizos* (meh-STEE-zohz). The large-scale arrival of enslaved Africans, starting in Brazil in the mid-sixteenth century, added new ethnic and racial dimensions to the population (see pages 603–611).

## The Era of Global Contact

❑ How was the era of global contact shaped by new commodities, commercial empires, and forced migrations?

The centuries-old Afroeurasian trade world was forever changed by the European voyages of discovery and their aftermath. For the first time, a truly global economy emerged in the sixteenth and seventeenth centuries, and it forged new links among far-flung peoples, cultures, and societies. The ancient civilizations of Europe, Africa, the Americas, and Asia confronted each other in new and rapidly evolving ways. Those confrontations often led to conquest, forced migration, and brutal exploitation, but they also contributed to cultural exchange and renewal.

## The Columbian Exchange

The travel of people and goods between the Old and New Worlds led to an exchange of animals, plants, and diseases, a complex process known as the **Columbian exchange**. As we have seen, the introduction of new diseases to the Americas had devastating consequences. But other results of the exchange brought benefits not only to the Europeans but also to native peoples.

European immigrants wanted to eat foods familiar to them, so they searched the Americas for climatic zones favorable to crops grown in their homelands. Everywhere they settled, the Spanish and Portuguese brought and raised wheat with labor provided by the encomienda system. Grapes and olives brought over from Spain did well in parts of Peru and Chile. Perhaps the most significant introduction to the diet of Native Americans came via the meat and milk of the livestock that the early conquistadors brought with them, including cattle, sheep, and goats. The horse enabled both the Spanish conquerors and native populations to travel faster and farther and to transport heavy loads more easily.

In turn, Europeans returned home with many food crops that became central elements of their diet. Crops originating in the Americas included tomatoes, squash, pumpkins, peppers, and many varieties of beans, as well as tobacco. One of the most important of such crops was maize (corn). Because maize gives a high yield per unit of land, has a short growing season, and thrives in climates too dry for rice and too wet for wheat, it proved an especially important crop for the Old World. By the late seventeenth century, maize had become a staple in Spain, Portugal, southern France, and Italy, and in the eighteenth century it became one of the chief foods of southeastern Europe and southern China.

Even more valuable was the nutritious white potato, which slowly spread from west to east—to Ireland, England, and France in the seventeenth century, and to Germany, Poland, Hungary, and Russia in the eighteenth, contributing everywhere to a rise in population. Ironically, the white potato reached New England from old England in the early eighteenth century. The Portuguese quickly began exporting chili peppers from Brazil to Africa, India, and Southeast Asia along the trade routes they dominated. Chili peppers arrived in continental North America when plantation owners began to plant them as a food source for enslaved Africans, for whom they were a dietary staple.

The initial reaction to these crops was sometimes fear and hostility. Adoption of the tomato and the

**A New World Sugar Refinery in Brazil** Sugar was the most important and most profitable plantation crop in the New World. This image shows the processing and refinement of sugar on a Brazilian plantation. Sugarcane was grown, harvested, and processed by African slaves who labored under brutal and ruthless conditions to generate enormous profits for plantation owners. (Bibliothèque Nationale, Paris, France/Giraudon/The Bridgeman Art Library)

potato, for example, was long hampered by the belief that they were unfit for human consumption and potentially poisonous. Both plants belong to the deadly nightshade family, and both contain poison in their leaves and stems. Consequently, it took time and persuasion for these plants to win over tradition-minded European peasants, who used potatoes mostly as livestock feed. During the eighteenth-century Enlightenment, scientists and doctors played an important role in popularizing the nutritional benefits of the potato.

While the exchange of foods was a great benefit to cultures across the world, the introduction of European pathogens to the New World had a disastrous impact on the native population. The wave of catastrophic epidemic disease that swept the Western Hemisphere after 1492 can be seen as an extension of the swath of devastation wreaked by the Black Death in the 1300s, first on Asia and then on Europe. The world after Columbus was thus unified by disease as well as by trade and colonization.

## Sugar and Early Transatlantic Slavery

Two crucial and interrelated elements of the Columbian exchange were the transatlantic trade in sugar and slaves. Throughout the Middle Ages, slavery was deeply entrenched in the Mediterranean, but it was not based on race; many slaves were European in origin. How, then, did black African slavery enter the European picture and take root in South and then North America? In 1453 the Ottoman capture of Constantinople halted the flow of European slaves from the eastern Mediterranean. Additionally, the successes of the Christian reconquest of the Iberian Peninsula drastically diminished the supply of Muslim captives. Cut off from its traditional sources of slaves, Mediterranean Europe turned to sub-Saharan Africa, which had a long history of slave trading.

As Portuguese explorers began their voyages along the western coast of Africa, one of the first commodities they sought was slaves. In 1444 the first ship returned to Lisbon with a cargo of enslaved Africans. While the first slaves were simply seized by small raiding parties, Portuguese merchants soon found that it was easier and more profitable to trade with African leaders, who were accustomed to dealing in enslaved people captured through warfare with neighboring powers. In 1483 the Portuguese established an alliance with the kingdom of Kongo. The royal family eventually converted to Christianity, and Portuguese merchants intermarried with Kongolese women, creating a permanent Afro-Portuguese community. From 1490 to 1530 Portuguese traders brought between three hundred and two thousand enslaved Africans to Lisbon each year. There they performed most of the manual labor and constituted 10 percent of the city's population.

In this stage of European expansion, the history of slavery became intertwined with the history of sugar. Originally sugar was an expensive luxury, but population increases and greater prosperity in the fifteenth century led to increasing demand. The establishment of sugar plantations on the Canary and Madeira Islands in the fifteenth century testifies to this demand.

● **Columbian exchange** The exchange of animals, plants, and diseases between the Old and the New Worlds.

Sugar was a particularly difficult crop to produce for profit. Seed-stems were planted by hand, thousands to the acre. When mature, the cane had to be harvested and processed rapidly to avoid spoiling. Moreover, sugarcane has a virtually constant growing season, meaning that there was no fallow period when workers could recuperate. The invention of roller mills to crush the cane more efficiently meant that yields could be significantly augmented, but only if a sufficient labor force was found to supply the mills. Europeans solved the labor problem by forcing first native islanders and then transported Africans to perform the backbreaking work.

The transatlantic slave trade that would ultimately result in the forced transport of over 12 million individuals began in 1518, when Spanish king Charles V authorized traders to bring enslaved Africans to New World colonies. The Portuguese brought the first slaves to Brazil around 1550; by 1600 four thousand were being imported annually. After its founding in 1621, the Dutch West India Company transported thousands of Africans to Brazil and the Caribbean, mostly to work on sugar plantations. In the late seventeenth century, with the chartering of the Royal African Company, the English began to bring slaves to Barbados and other English colonies in the Caribbean and mainland North America.

Before 1700, when slavers decided it was better business to improve conditions, some 20 percent of slaves died on the voyage from Africa to the Americas.[10] The most common cause of death was dysentery induced by poor-quality food and water, lack of sanitation, and intense crowding. (To increase profits, slave traders packed several hundred captives on each ship.) Men were often kept in irons during the passage, while women and girls were subject to sexual abuse by sailors. On sugar plantations, death rates among enslaved people from illness and exhaustion were extremely high, leading to a constant stream of new human shipments from Africa. Driven by rising demands for sugar, cotton, tobacco, and other plantation crops, the tragic transatlantic slave trade reached its height in the eighteenth century.

**The Transatlantic Slave Trade**

## The Birth of the Global Economy

With Europeans' discovery of the Americas and their exploration of the Pacific, the entire world was linked for the first time in history by seaborne trade. The opening of that trade brought into being three successive commercial empires: the Portuguese, the Spanish, and the Dutch.

The Portuguese were the first worldwide traders. In the sixteenth century they controlled the sea route to India (Map 16.3). From their fortified bases at Goa on the Arabian Sea and at Malacca on the Malay Peninsula, ships carried goods to the Portuguese settlement at Macao, founded in 1557, in the South China Sea. From Macao Portuguese ships loaded with Chinese silks and porcelains sailed to the Japanese port of Nagasaki and to the Philippine port of Manila, where Chinese goods were exchanged for Spanish silver from New Spain. Throughout Asia the Portuguese traded in slaves. They also exported horses from Mesopotamia and copper from Arabia to India; from India they exported hawks and peacocks for the Chinese and Japanese markets. Back to Portugal they brought Asian spices that had been purchased with textiles produced in India and with gold and ivory from East Africa. They also shipped back sugar from their colony in Brazil, produced by African slaves whom they had transported across the Atlantic.

Becoming an imperial power a few decades later than the Portuguese, the Spanish were determined to claim their place in world trade. This was greatly facilitated by the discovery of immense riches in silver, first at Potosí in modern-day Bolivia and later in Mexico. Silver poured into Europe through the Spanish port of Seville, contributing to steep inflation across Europe. Demand for silver also created a need for slaves to work in the mines. (See "Global Trade: Silver," page 482.)

The Spanish Empire in the New World was basically land based, but across the Pacific the Spaniards built a seaborne empire centered at Manila in the Philippines. The city of Manila served as the transpacific bridge between Spanish America and China. In Manila Spanish traders used silver from American mines to purchase Chinese silk for European markets. The European demand for silk was so huge that in 1597, for example, 12 million pesos of silver, almost the total value of the transatlantic trade, moved from Acapulco in New Spain to Manila (see Map 16.4). After 1640, however, the Spanish silk trade declined in the face of stiff competition from Dutch imports.

In the seventeenth century the Dutch challenged the Spanish and Portuguese Empires. The Dutch East India Company was founded in 1602 with the stated intention of capturing the spice trade from the Portuguese. Drawing on their commercial wealth and long experience in European trade, by the end of the century the Dutch emerged as the most powerful worldwide seaborne trading power (see Chapter 19).

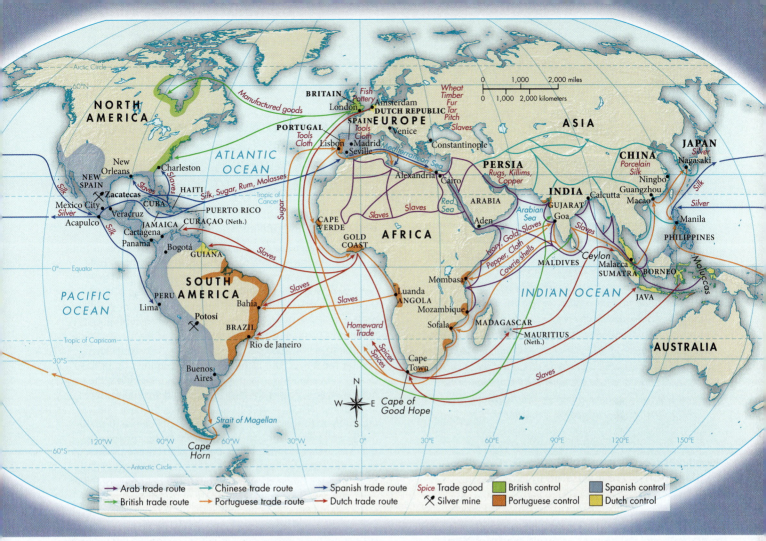

**MAP 16.3  Seaborne Trading Empires in the Sixteenth and Seventeenth Centuries**
By the mid-seventeenth century trade linked all parts of the world except for Australia. Notice that trade in slaves was not confined to the Atlantic but involved almost all parts of the world.

# Changing Attitudes and Beliefs

❑ How did new encounters shape cultural attitudes and beliefs in Europe and the New World?

The age of overseas expansion heightened Europeans' contacts with the rest of the world. These contacts gave birth to new ideas about the inherent superiority or inferiority of different races, in part to justify European participation in the slave trade. Religion became another means of cultural contact, as European missionaries aimed to spread Christianity in both the New World and East Asia, with mixed results. While Christianity was embraced in parts of the New World, it was met largely with suspicion in China and Japan. However, the East-West contacts led to exchanges of influential cultural and scientific ideas.

## Religious Conversion

Converting indigenous people to Christianity was one of the most important justifications for European expansion. Jesuit missionaries were active in Japan and China in the sixteenth and seventeenth centuries, until authorities banned their teachings (see page 644). The first missionaries to the New World accompanied Columbus on his second voyage, and more than 2,500 Franciscans, Dominicans, Jesuits, and other friars crossed the Atlantic in the following century. Later French explorers were also accompanied by missionaries who preached to the Native American tribes who traded with the French.

Catholic friars were among the first Europeans to seek an understanding of native cultures and languages as part of their effort to render Christianity comprehensible to indigenous people. In Mexico they not only learned the Nahuatl language, but also taught it to non-Nahuatl-speaking groups to create a shared language for Christian teaching. They were also the most vociferous opponents of abuses committed by Spanish settlers.

# Viewpoints 16.1

## Christian Conversion in New Spain

● *In justifying their violent conquest of the Aztec and Inca civilizations, Spanish conquistadors emphasized the need to bring Christianity to heathen peoples. For the conquered, the imposition of Christianity and the repression of their pre-existing religions were often experienced as yet another form of loss. The first document describes the response of the recently vanquished Aztec leaders of Tenochtitlan to Franciscan missionaries. Despite resistance, missionaries eventually succeeded in converting much of the indigenous population to Catholicism. In the second document, a firsthand account of the Spanish conquest written a few decades after the fall of Tenochtitlan, Bernal Díaz del Castillo expresses great satisfaction at the Catholic piety of some indigenous communities.*

### Mexica Response to the Franciscans' Explanation of Their Mission in 1524

❝ You have told us that we do not know the One who gives us life and being, who is Lord of the heavens and of the earth. You also say that those we worship are not gods. This way of speaking is entirely new to us, and very scandalous. We are frightened by this way of speaking because our forebears who engendered and governed us never said anything like this. On the contrary, they left us this our custom of worshiping our gods, in which they believed and which they worshiped all the time that they lived here on earth. They taught us how to honor them. And they taught us all the ceremonies and sacrifices that we make. They told us that through them [our gods] we live and are, and that we were beholden to them, to be theirs and to serve countless centuries before the sun began to shine and before there was daytime. They said that these gods that we worship give us everything we need for our physical existence: maize, beans, chia seeds, etc. . . .

All of us together feel that it is enough to have lost, enough that the power and royal jurisdiction have been taken from us. As for our gods, we will die before giving up serving and worshiping them. ❞

### Bernal Díaz del Castillo, from *The True History of the Conquest of New Spain*

❝ It is a thing to be grateful for to God, and for profound consideration, to see how the natives assist in celebrating a holy Mass. . . . There is another good thing they do [namely] that both men, women and children, who are of the age to learn them, know all the holy prayers in their own languages and are obliged to know them. They have other good customs about their holy Christianity, that when they pass near a sacred altar or Cross they bow their heads with humility, bend their knees, and say the prayer "Our Father," which we Conquistadores have taught them, and they place lighted wax candles before the holy altars and crosses, for formerly they did not know how to use wax in making candles. In addition to what I have said, we taught them to show great reverence and obedience to all the monks and priests, and, when these went to their pueblos, to sally forth to receive them with lighted wax candles and to ring the bells, and to feed them very well. . . . Beside the good customs reported by me they have others both holy and good, for when the day of Corpus Christ comes, or that of Our Lady, or other solemn festivals when among us we form processions, most of the pueblos in the neighbourhood of this city of Guatemala come out in procession with their crosses and lighted wax tapers, and carry on their shoulders, on a litter, the image of the saint who is the patron of the pueblo. ❞

Sources: "The Lords and Holy Men of Tenochtitlan Reply to the Franciscans Bernardino de Sahagún, Coloquios y doctrina Cristiana," ed. Miguel León-Portilla, in *Spanish Colonial America: A Documentary History*, ed. Kenneth Mills and William B. Taylor. Reproduced with permission of ROWMAN & LITTLEFIELD PUBLISHERS, INCORPORATED, in the format Book via Copyright Clearance Center; Bernal Díaz, *The True History of the Conquest of New Spain*, in Stuart B. Schwartz, *Victors and Vanquished: Spanish and Nahua Views of the Conquest of Mexico* (Boston: Bedford/St. Martin's, 2000), pp. 218–219.

### QUESTIONS FOR ANALYSIS

1. What reasons do the leaders of Tenochtitlan offer for rejecting the teachings of Franciscan missionaries? What importance do they accord their own religious traditions?

2. What evidence does Díaz provide for the conversion of the indigenous people in the city of Guatemala?

3. How and why do you think the attitudes of indigenous peoples might have evolved from those expressed in the first document to those described in the second? Do you think the second document tells the whole story of religious attitudes under Spanish rule?

Religion had been a central element of pre-Columbian societies, and many, if not all, indigenous people were receptive to the new religion that accompanied the victorious Iberians. (See "Viewpoints 16.1: Christian Conversion in New Spain," at left.) It is estimated that missionaries had baptized between 4 and 9 million indigenous people in New Spain by the mid-1530s.[11] In addition to spreading Christianity, missionaries taught indigenous peoples European methods of agriculture and instilled obedience to colonial masters.

Despite the success of initial conversion efforts, authorities became suspicious about the thoroughness of native peoples' conversion and lingering belief in the old gods. They could not prevent, however, the melding together of Catholic teachings with elements of pagan beliefs and practices. For example, a sixteenth-century apparition of the Virgin Mary in Mexico City, known as the Virgin of Guadalupe, which became a central icon of New World Catholicism, seems to have been associated with the Aztec Mother Earth goddess, Tonantzin.

## European Debates About Indigenous Peoples

Iberian exploitation of the native population of the Americas began from the moment of Columbus's arrival in 1492. Denunciations of this abuse by Catholic missionaries, however, quickly followed, inspiring

Español con India, Mestizo.

Mestizo con Española Castizo.

Mulato con Española, Morisco.

Morisco con Española Chino.

Lobo con China Gibaro.

Gibaro con Mulata Albarazado.

Sanbaigo con Loba Calpamulato.

Calpamulato con Cambuja Tente en el Aire.

## ☐ Picturing the Past

**Mixed Races** The unprecedented mixing of peoples in the Spanish New World colonies inspired great fascination. An elaborate terminology emerged to describe the many possible combinations of indigenous, African, and European blood, which were known collectively as *castas*. This painting belongs to a popular genre of the eighteenth century depicting couples composed of individuals of different ethnic origin and the children produced of their unions. (Schalkwijk/Art Resource, NY)

**ANALYZING THE IMAGE** What do these images suggest about the racial composition of the population of Spanish America and the interaction of people with different racial and ethnic backgrounds? Who do you think the audience might have been, and why would viewers be fascinated by such images?

**CONNECTIONS** What elements of this chapter might suggest that these are romanticized or idealized depictions of relations among different racial and ethnic groups?

# Global Trade

# Silver in vast quantities was discovered in 1545 by the Spanish, at an altitude of fifteen thousand feet, at Potosí in unsettled territory conquered from the Inca Empire. A half century later, 160,000 people lived in Potosí, making its population comparable to that of the city of London. In the second half of the sixteenth century the mine (in present-day Bolivia) yielded perhaps 60 percent of all the silver mined in the world. From Potosí and the mines at Zacatecas and Guanajuato in Mexico, huge quantities of precious metals poured forth.

Mining became the most important industry in the colonies. The Spanish crown claimed the quinto, one-fifth of all precious metals mined in South America, and gold and silver yielded the Spanish monarchy 25 percent of its total income. One scholar has estimated that 260 tons of silver arrived in Europe each year by 1600.* Seville was the official port of entry for all Spanish silver, although a lively smuggling trade existed.

The real mover of world trade was not Europe, however, but China, which in this period had a population approaching 100 million. By 1450 the collapse of its paper currency had led the Ming government to shift to a silver-based currency. Instead of rice, the traditional form of payment, all Chinese now had to pay their taxes in silver. The result was an insatiable demand for the world's production of silver.

Japan was China's original source, and the Japanese continued to ship large quantities of silver ore until the depletion of its mines near the end of the seventeenth century. The discovery of silver in the New World provided a vast and welcome new supply for the Chinese market. In 1571 the Spanish founded a port city at Manila in the Philippines to serve as a bridge point for bringing silver to Asia. Throughout the seventeenth century Spanish galleons annually carried 2 million pesos (or more than fifty tons) of silver from Acapulco to Manila, where Chinese

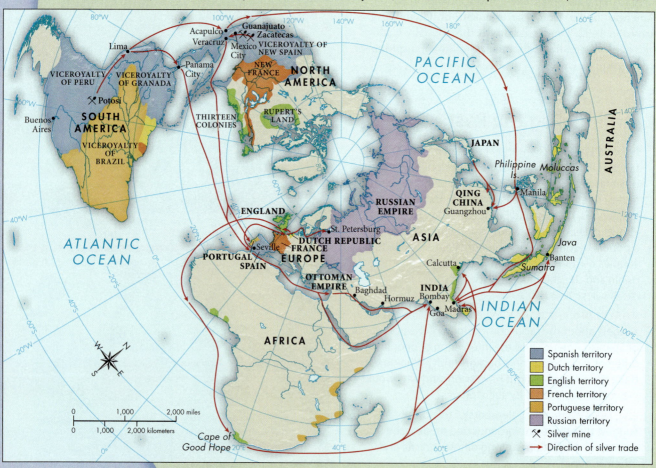

**MAP 16.4** The Global Silver Trade

482 •

merchants carried it on to China. Even more silver reached China through exchange with European merchants who purchased Chinese goods using silver shipped across the Atlantic. European trade routes to China passed through the Baltic, the Mediterranean, and the Ottoman Empire, as well as around the Cape of Good Hope in Africa. Historians estimate that ultimately the majority of the world's silver in this period ended up in China.

In exchange for silver, the Chinese traded high-quality finished goods desired by elites across the world, including fine silks, porcelain, and spices. To ensure continued demand for their products, Chinese merchants adapted them to Western tastes.

Silver had a mixed impact on the regions involved. Spain's immense profits from silver paid for the tremendous expansion of its empire and for the large armies that defended it. However, the easy flow of money also dampened economic innovation. It exacerbated the rising inflation Spain was already experiencing in the mid-sixteenth century. When the profitability of the silver mines diminished in the 1640s, Spain's power was fundamentally undercut.

China experienced similarly mixed effects. On the one hand, the need for finished goods to trade for silver led to the rise of a merchant class and a new specialization of regional production. On the other hand, inflation resulting from the influx of silver weakened the finances of the Ming Dynasty. As the purchasing power of silver declined in China, so did the value of silver taxes. The ensuing fiscal crisis helped bring down the Ming and led to the rise of the Qing in 1644. Ironically, the two states that benefited the most from silver—Ming China and Spain—also experienced political decline as a result of their reliance on it.

The consequences were most tragic elsewhere. In New Spain millions of indigenous laborers suffered brutal conditions and death in the silver mines. Demand for new labor for the mines contributed to the intensification of the African slave trade.

Silver ore mined at Potosí thus built the first global trade system in history. Previously, a long-standing Afroeurasian trading world had involved merchants and consumers from the three Old World continents. Once Spain opened a trade route across the Pacific through Manila, all continents except Australia and Antarctica were linked.

Silver remained a crucial element in world trade through the nineteenth century. When Mexico won independence from Spain in 1821, it began to mint its own silver dollar, which became the most prized coin in trade in East Asia. By the beginning of the twentieth century, when the rest of the world had adopted gold as the standard of currency, only China and Mexico remained on the silver standard, testimony to the central role this metal had played in their histories.

*Artur Attman, *American Bullion in the European World Trade, 1600–1800* (Goteborg, 1986).

vociferous debates in both Europe and the colonies about the nature of indigenous peoples and how they should be treated. Bartolomé de Las Casas (1474–1566), a Dominican friar and former encomienda holder, was one of the earliest and most outspoken critics of the brutal treatment inflicted on indigenous peoples. He wrote:

> To these quiet Lambs . . . came the Spaniards like most c(r)uel Tygres, Wolves and Lions, enrag'd with a sharp and tedious hunger; for these forty years past, minding nothing else but the slaughter of these unfortunate wretches, whom with divers kinds of torments neither seen nor heard of before, they have so cruelly and inhumanely butchered, that of three millions of people which Hispaniola itself did contain, there are left remaining alive scarce three hundred persons.[12]

Mounting criticism in Spain led King Charles V to assemble a group of churchmen and lawyers to debate the issue in 1550 in the city of Valladolid. One side of the **Valladolid debate**, led by Juan Ginés de Sepúlveda, argued that conquest and forcible conversion were both necessary and justified to save indigenous people from the horrors of human sacrifice, cannibalism, and idolatry. He described them as barbarians who belonged to a category of inferior beings identified by the ancient Greek philosopher Aristotle as naturally destined for slavery. To counter these arguments, Las Casas and his supporters depicted indigenous people as rational and innocent children, who deserved protection and tutelage from more advanced civilizations. Both sides claimed victory in the debate, but it had little effect on the situation in the Americas.

Elsewhere in Europe, audiences also debated these questions. (See "Viewpoints 16.2: Two Views of 'Natural Man,'" page 484.) Eagerly reading denunciations of Spanish abuses by critics like Las Casas, they derived the **Black Legend** of Spanish colonialism, the notion that the Spanish were uniquely brutal and cruel in their conquest and settlement of the Americas. This legend helped other European powers overlook their own record of colonial violence and exploitation.

## New Ideas About Race

At the beginning of the transatlantic slave trade, most Europeans would have thought of Africans, if they thought of them at all, as savages in their social customs

---

- **Valladolid debate**  A debate organized by Spanish king Charles V in 1550 in the city of Valladolid that pitted defenders of Spanish conquest and forcible conversion against critics of these practices.

- **Black Legend**  The notion that the Spanish were uniquely brutal and cruel in their conquest and settlement of the Americas, an idea propagated by rival European powers.

# Viewpoints 16.2

## Two Views of "Natural Man"

• *European encounters with the New World produced contentious debates over the nature of native peoples and how to treat them. In contrast to prevailing views of the time, French jurist Michel de Montaigne rejected the notion that there is one universally correct way of life. In his essay "On Cannibals," he argued that indigenous cultures seemed barbaric only because they were unfamiliar and that their natural simplicity was superior to the artifice of European civilization. In his play* The Tempest, *William Shakespeare refuted Montaigne's trust in nature with his harsh portrait of Caliban (a play on the word* cannibal*). Caliban is the primitive and violent inhabitant of a Caribbean island, who has been enslaved by the sorcerer Prospero for the attempted rape of Prospero's daughter Miranda.*

### Montaigne on Natural Virtue

❝I find that there is nothing barbarous and savage in this nation [Brazil], by anything that I can gather, excepting, that everyone gives the title of barbarism to everything that is not in use in his own country: as indeed we have no other level of truth and reason, than the example and idea of the opinions and customs of the place wherein we live; there is always the perfect religion, there the perfect government, and the most exact and accomplished usage of all things. They are savages at the same rate that we say fruits are wild, which nature produces of herself and by her own ordinary progress; whereas in truth, we ought rather to call those wild whose natures we have changed by our artifice and diverted from the common order. In those, the genuine, most useful, and natural virtues and properties are vigorous and sprightly, which we have helped to degenerate in these, by accommodating them to the pleasure of our own corrupted palate. . . .

These nations then seem to me to be . . . not much remote from their original simplicity. The laws of nature . . . govern them still. . . . It is a nation wherein there is no manner of traffic, no knowledge of letters, no science of numbers, no name of magistrate nor political superiority; no use of service, riches or poverty, no contracts, no successions, no dividends, no properties, no employments, but those of leisure, no respect of kindred, but common, no clothing, no agriculture, no metal, no use of corn or wine; and where so much as the very words that signify lying, treachery, dissimulation, avarice, envy, detraction and pardon were never heard of.❞

### William Shakespeare, *The Tempest*

CALIBAN: This island's mine, by Sycorax my mother,
  Which thou takest from me. When thou camest first,
  Thou strokedst me and madest much of me, wouldst give me
  Water with berries in't, and teach me how
  To name the bigger light, and how the less,
  That burn by day and night: and then I loved thee
  And show'd thee all the qualities o' the isle,
  The fresh springs, brine-pits, barren place and fertile:
  Cursed be I that did so! All the charms
  Of Sycorax, toads, beetles, bats, light on you!
  For I am all the subjects that you have,
  Which first was mine own king: and here you sty me
  In this hard rock, whiles you do keep from me
  The rest o' the island.

PROSPERO: Thou most lying slave,
  Whom stripes may move, not kindness! I have used thee,
  Filth as thou art, with human care, and lodged thee
  In mine own cell, till thou didst seek to violate
  The honour of my child.

CALIBAN: O ho, O ho! would't had been done!
  Thou didst prevent me; I had peopled else
  This isle with Calibans.

PROSPERO: Abhorred slave,
  Which any print of goodness wilt not take,
  Being capable of all ill! I pitied thee,
  Took pains to make thee speak, taught thee each hour
  One thing or other: when thou didst not, savage,
  Know thine own meaning, but wouldst gabble like
  A thing most brutish, I endow'd thy purposes
  With words that made them known. But thy vile race,
  Though thou didst learn, had that in't which good natures
  Could not abide to be with; therefore wast thou
  Deservedly confined into this rock,
  Who hadst deserved more than a prison.

CALIBAN: You taught me language; and my profit on't
  Is, I know how to curse. The red plague rid you
  For learning me your language!

Sources: *The Essays of Michel Seigneur de Montaigne*, trans. C. Cotton (London: Alex Murray & Son, 1870), pp. 133–134; William Shakespeare, *The Tempest* (New York: The Macmillan Company, 1915), pp. 25–27.

### QUESTIONS FOR ANALYSIS

1. What evidence does Montaigne provide for his claim that the Brazilians were closer to nature than Europeans? Why does he judge their society to be in some ways superior to that of Europeans?

2. In Shakespeare's play, what advantages does Prospero believe he has given to Caliban, and how does Caliban react to his claims?

3. What contrasting view of "natural man" emerges from these two passages? What evidence do they provide for Europeans' reaction to the peoples encountered in the New World?

and religious practices. They grouped Africans into the despised categories of pagan heathens or Muslim infidels. As Europeans turned to Africa for new sources of slaves, they drew on beliefs about Africans' primitiveness and barbarity to defend slavery and even argue, like Sepúlveda with regard to indigenous Americans, that enslavement benefited Africans by bringing civilization and Christianity to heathen peoples. In 1444 an observer defended the enslavement of the first Africans by Portuguese explorers as necessary "because they lived like beasts, without any of the customs of rational creatures, since they did not even know what were bread and wine, nor garments of cloth, nor life in the shelter of a house; and worse still was their ignorance, which deprived them of knowledge of good, and permitted them only a life of brutish idleness."[13]

Over time, the institution of slavery fostered a new level of racial inequality. Africans gradually became seen as utterly distinct from and wholly inferior to Europeans. In a transition from rather vague assumptions about Africans' non-Christian religious beliefs and general lack of civilization, Europeans developed increasingly rigid ideas of racial superiority and inferiority to safeguard the growing profits gained from plantation slavery. Black skin became equated with slavery itself as Europeans at home and in the colonies convinced themselves that blacks were destined by God to serve them as slaves in perpetuity.

Support for this belief went back to the Greek philosopher Aristotle's argument that some people are naturally destined for slavery and to biblical associations between darkness and sin. A more explicit justification was found in the story of Noah's curse upon the descendants of his disobedient son Ham to be the "servant[s] of servants." Biblical genealogies listing Ham's sons as those who peopled North Africa and Kush (which includes parts of modern Egypt and Sudan) were interpreted to mean that all inhabitants of those regions bore Noah's curse. From the sixteenth century onward, many defenders of slavery cited this story as justification.

After 1700 the emergence of new methods of observing and describing nature led to the use of science to define race. Although previously the term referred to a nation or an ethnic group, henceforth "race" would be used to describe supposedly biologically distinct groups of people whose physical differences produced differences in culture, character, and intelligence. Biblical justifications for inequality thereby gave way to allegedly scientific ones (see page 740).

## CHRONOLOGY

| | |
|---|---|
| 1271–1295 | Marco Polo travels to China |
| 1443 | Portuguese establish first African trading post at Arguin |
| 1492 | Columbus lands on San Salvador |
| 1494 | Treaty of Tordesillas ratified |
| 1518 | Atlantic slave trade begins |
| 1519–1522 | Magellan's expedition circumnavigates the world |
| 1521 | Cortés conquers Aztec Empire |
| 1533 | Pizarro conquers Inca Empire |
| 1571 | Spanish establish port of Manila in the Philippines |
| 1602 | Dutch East India Company founded |

## Chapter Summary

Prior to Columbus's voyages, well-developed trade routes linked the peoples and products of Africa, Asia, and Europe. Overall, Europe played a minor role in the Afroeurasian trade world because it did not produce many products desired by Eastern elites. Nevertheless, Europeans—especially Venetian and Genoese merchants—sought to tap into the goods and wealth of Afroeurasian commerce. As the economy and population recovered from the Black Death, Europeans began to seek more direct and profitable access to the Afroeurasian trade world. Technological developments such as the invention of the caravel and the magnetic compass enabled men like Christopher Columbus and Ferdinand Magellan to undertake ever more ambitious voyages.

In the aftermath of their conquest of the Aztec and Inca Empires, the Spanish established new forms of governance to dominate native peoples and exploit their labor, including the encomienda system. The arrival of Europeans brought enormous population losses to native communities, primarily through the spread of infectious diseases. Disease was one element of the Columbian exchange, a complex transfer of germs, plants, and animals between the Old and New Worlds. Over time, the Columbian exchange brought new crops to both the New and Old Worlds—crops that eventually altered consumption patterns internationally. These exchanges contributed to the creation of the first truly global economy. Tragically, a major component of global trade was the transatlantic slave trade, in which Europeans transported, under horrific conditions, Africans to labor in the sugar plantations and silver mines of the New World. European nations vied for supremacy in global trade, with early Portuguese success in India and Asia being challenged first by the Spanish and then by the Dutch, who took control of trade with the East in the mid-seventeenth century.

Increased contact with the outside world led Europeans to develop new ideas about cultural and racial differences. Debates occurred in Spain and its colonies over the nature of the indigenous peoples of the Americas and how they should be treated. Europeans had long held negative attitudes about Africans; as the slave trade grew, they began to express more rigid notions of racial inequality and to claim that Africans were inherently suited for slavery. Most Europeans, with some important exceptions, shared such views. Religion became another means of cultural contact, as European missionaries aimed to spread Christianity in the New World.

## NOTES

1. Marco Polo, *The Book of Ser Marco Polo, the Venetian: Concerning the Kingdoms and Marvels of the East*, vol. 2, trans. and ed. Colonel Sir Henry Yule (London: John Murray, 1903), pp. 185–186.

2. Thomas Benjamin, *The Atlantic World: Europeans, Africans, Indians and Their Shared History, 1400–1900* (Cambridge: Cambridge University Press, 2009), p. 56.

3. A. Reid, *Southeast Asia in the Age of Commerce, 1450–1680*. Vol. 1: *The Land Under the Winds* (New Haven, Conn.: Yale University Press, 1988), pp. 3–20.

4. Quoted in C. M. Cipolla, *Guns, Sails, and Empires: Technological Innovation and the Early Phases of European Expansion, 1400–1700* (New York: Minerva Press, 1965), p. 132.

5. Quoted in F. H. Littell, *The Macmillan Atlas: History of Christianity* (New York: Macmillan, 1976), p. 75.

6. Quoted in J. Devisse, "Africa in Inter-Continental Relations," in *General History of Africa*. Vol. 4: *Africa from the Twelfth to the Sixteenth Century*, ed. D. T. Niane (Berkeley, Calif.: Heinemann Educational Books, 1984), p. 664.

7. Quoted in F. Maddison, "Tradition and Innovation: Columbus' First Voyage and Portuguese Navigation in the Fifteenth Century," in *Circa 1492: Art in the Age of Exploration*, ed. J. A. Levenson (Washington, D.C.: National Gallery of Art, 1991), p. 69.

8. Quoted in R. L. Kagan, "The Spain of Ferdinand and Isabella," in *Circa 1492: Art in the Age of Exploration*, ed. J. A. Levenson (Washington, D.C.: National Gallery of Art, 1991), p. 60.

9. Benjamin, *The Atlantic World*, p. 141.

10. Herbert S. Klein, "Profits and the Causes of Mortality," in *The Atlantic Slave Trade*, ed. David Northrup (Lexington, Mass.: D. C. Heath, 1994), p. 116.

11. David Carrasco, *The Oxford Encyclopedia of Mesoamerican Cultures* (Oxford: Oxford University Press, 2001), p. 208.

12. Quoted in C. Gibson, ed., *The Black Legend: Anti-Spanish Attitudes in the Old World and the New* (New York: Knopf, 1971), pp. 74–75.

13. Quoted in James H. Sweet, "The Iberian Roots of American Racist Thought," *The William and Mary Quarterly*, Third Series, 54 (January 1997): 155.

## CONNECTIONS

Just three years separated Martin Luther's attack on the Catholic Church in 1517 and Ferdinand Magellan's discovery of the Pacific Ocean in 1520. Within a few short years western Europeans' religious unity and notions of terrestrial geography were shattered. Old medieval certainties about Heaven and earth collapsed. In the ensuing decades Europeans struggled to come to terms with religious differences among Protestants and Catholics at home and with the multitudes of new peoples and places they encountered abroad. While some Europeans were fascinated and inspired by this new diversity, too often the result was suffering and violence. Europeans endured decades of religious civil war, and indigenous peoples overseas underwent massive population losses as a result of European warfare, disease, and exploitation. Tragically, both Catholic and Protestant religious leaders condoned the trade in slaves that ultimately brought suffering and death to millions of Africans.

Even as the voyages of discovery contributed to the fragmentation of European culture, they also played a role in state centralization and consolidation in the longer term. Henceforth, competition to gain overseas colonies became an integral part of European politics. While Spain's enormous profits from conquest ultimately led to a weakening of its power, over time the Netherlands, England, and France used profits from colonial trade to help build modernized, centralized states.

Two crucial consequences emerged from this era of expansion. The first was the creation of enduring contacts among five of the seven continents of the globe—Europe, Asia, Africa, North America, and South America. From the sixteenth century onward, the peoples of the world were increasingly entwined in divergent forms of economic, social, and cultural exchange. The second was the growth of European power. Europeans controlled the Americas and gradually assumed control over existing trade networks in Asia and Africa. Although China remained the world's most powerful economy until at least 1800, the era of European dominance was born.

# Review and Explore

## Make It Stick

 **LearningCurve**
Go online and use LearningCurve to retain what you've read.

## Identify Key Terms

Identify and explain the significance of each item below.

bride wealth (p. 461)

conquistador (p. 463)

caravel (p. 463)

Ptolemy's *Geography* (p. 464)

Treaty of Tordesillas (p. 469)

Aztec Empire (p. 471)

Inca Empire (p. 473)

viceroyalties (p. 474)

captaincies (p. 474)

encomienda system (p. 475)

Columbian exchange (p. 476)

Valladolid debate (p. 483)

Black Legend (p. 483)

## Review the Main Ideas

Answer the focus questions from each section of the chapter.

1. What was the Afroeurasian trade world like prior to the era of European exploration? (p. 458)
2. Why and how did Europeans undertake ambitious voyages of expansion? (p. 462)
3. What was the impact of Iberian conquest and settlement on the peoples and ecologies of the Americas? (p. 471)
4. How was the era of global contact shaped by new commodities, commercial empires, and forced migrations? (p. 476)
5. How did new encounters shape cultural attitudes and beliefs in Europe and the New World? (p. 479)

## Make Connections

Analyze the larger developments and continuities within and across chapters.

1. What range of attitudes toward new and unknown peoples did you encounter in this chapter? How do you explain similarities and differences in attitudes toward such peoples?
2. To what extent did the European voyages of expansion and conquest inaugurate an era of global history? Did this era represent the birth of "globalization"? Why or why not?
3. How did European motivations for expansion compare to those of the Roman Empire, the Arab world under Islam, or the Mongols in Central Asia?

## LaunchPad
### Online Document Project

### Interpreting Conquest

**How did Spanish and Amerindian artists depict Malintzin?**
Examine Spanish and Amerindian representations of Malintzin's role in the conquest, and then complete a quiz and writing assignment based on the evidence and details from this chapter.

*See inside the front cover to learn more.*

## Suggested Reading

Crosby, Alfred W. *The Columbian Exchange: Biological and Cultural Consequences of 1492*, 30th anniversary ed. 2003. An innovative and highly influential account of the environmental impact of Columbus's voyages.

Elliot, J. H. *Empires of the Atlantic World: Britain and Spain in America, 1492–1830*. 2006. A masterful account of the differences and similarities between the British and Spanish Empires in the Americas.

Fernández-Armesto, Felip. *Columbus*. 1992. An excellent biography of Christopher Columbus.

Mann, Charles C. *1491: New Revelations on the Americas Before Columbus*, 2d ed. 2011. A highly readable account of the peoples and societies of the Americas before the arrival of Europeans.

Menard, Russell. *Sweet Negotiations: Sugar, Slavery, and Plantation Agriculture in Early Barbados*. 2006. Explores the intertwined history of sugar plantations and slavery in seventeenth-century Barbados.

Northrup, David, ed. *The Atlantic Slave Trade*. 1994. Collected essays by leading scholars on many different aspects of the slave trade.

Parker, Charles H. *Global Interactions in the Early Modern Age, 1400–1800*. 2010. An examination of the rise of global connections in the early modern period, which situates the European experience in relation to the world's other empires and peoples.

Pérez-Mallaína, Pablo E. *Spain's Men of the Sea: Daily Life on the Indies Fleet in the Sixteenth Century*. 1998. A description of the recruitment, daily life, and career paths of ordinary sailors and officers in the Spanish fleet.

Pomeranz, Kenneth, and Steven Topik. *The World That Trade Created: Society, Culture, and the World Economy, 1400 to the Present*. 1999. Explores the creation of a world market through the rich and vivid stories of merchants, miners, slaves, and farmers.

Restall, Matthew. *Seven Myths of Spanish Conquest*. 2003. A re-examination of common ideas about why and how the Spanish conquered native civilizations in the New World.

Schmidt, Benjamin. *Innocence Abroad: The Dutch Imagination and the New World, 1570–1670*. 2001. Examines changing Dutch attitudes toward the New World, from criticism of the cruelty of the Spanish conquest to eagerness for their own overseas empire.

### Persian Princess

The ruling houses of the Islamic empires were great patrons of art and architecture. This depiction of a princess in a garden is from an early-seventeenth-century palace built by Shah Abbas of the Safavid Dynasty in Persia. (Safavid Dynasty [fresco]. Chehel Sotun, or *The 40 Columns*, Isfahan, Iran/Giraudon/The Bridgeman Art Library)

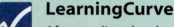

**LearningCurve**

After reading the chapter, go online and use LearningCurve to retain what you've read.

# Chapter Preview

**The Turkish Ruling Houses: The Ottomans, Safavids, and Mughals**

**Cultural Flowering**

**Non-Muslims Under Muslim Rule**

**Shifting Trade Routes and European Penetration**

**Political Decline**

After the decline of the Mongol Empire in the mid-fourteenth century, powerful new Islamic states emerged in south and west Eurasia. By the sixteenth century the Ottoman Empire, centered in Anatolia; the Safavid (sah-FAH-weed) Empire in Persia; and the Mughal (MOO-guhl) Empire in India controlled vast territories from West Africa to Central Asia, from the Balkans to the Bay of Bengal.

Lasting more than six centuries (1299–1922), the Ottoman Empire was one of the largest, best-organized, and most enduring political entities in world history. In Persia (now Iran) the Safavid Dynasty created a Shi'a state and presided over a brilliant culture. In India the Mughal leader Babur and his successors gained control

of much of the Indian subcontinent. Mughal rule inaugurated a period of radical administrative reorganization in India and the flowering of intellectual and architectural creativity. Although these three states were often at war with each other, they shared important characteristics and challenges. For instance, their ruling houses all emerged from Turkish tribal organizations, and they all had to adapt their armies to the introduction of firearms. Over time, they became strongly linked culturally, as merchants, poets, philosophers, artists, and military advisers moved relatively easily across their political boundaries. Before the end of this period, Europeans were also active in trade in these empires, especially in India.

## The Turkish Ruling Houses: The Ottomans, Safavids, and Mughals

☐ How were the three Islamic empires established, and what sorts of governments did they set up?

Before the Mongols arrived in Central Asia and Persia, another nomadic people from the region of modern Mongolia, the Turks, had moved west, gained control over key territories from Anatolia to Delhi in north India, and contributed to the decline of the Abbasid

caliphate in the thirteenth century. The Turks had been quick to join the Mongols and were important participants in the armies and administrations of the Mongol states in Persia and Central Asia. In these regions Turks far outnumbered ethnic Mongols.

As Mongol strength in Persia and Central Asia deteriorated in the late thirteenth to mid-fourteenth centuries, the Turks resumed their expansion. In the late fourteenth century the Turkish leader Timur (1336–1405), also called Tamerlane, built a Central Asian empire from his base in Samarkand that reached into India and through Persia to the Black Sea. Timur campaigned continuously from the 1360s until his death in 1405, aspiring to repeat the achievements of Chinggis

Khan. He did not get involved in administering the new territories but rather appointed lords and let them make use of existing political structures. His conquests were exceptionally destructive and benefited only Samarkand, where craftsmen and other specialists were forced to move to work for the new rulers. After his death, his sons and grandson fought each other for succession. By 1450 his empire was in rapid decline, and power devolved to the local level. Meanwhile, Sufi orders (groups of Islamic mystics) thrived, and Islam became the most important force integrating the region. It was from the many small Turkish chiefs that the founders of the three main empires emerged.

## The Expansion of the Ottoman Empire

The **Ottomans** took their name from Osman (r. 1299–1326), the chief of a band of seminomadic Turks that had migrated into western **Anatolia** while the Mongols still held Persia. The Ottomans gradually expanded at the expense of other small Turkish states and the Byzantine Empire (Map 17.1). The Ottoman ruler called himself "border chief," or leader of the *ghazis* (GAH-zeez), frontier raiders. Although temporarily slowed by defeat at the hands of Timur in 1402, the Ottomans quickly reasserted themselves after Timur's death in 1405.

Osman's campaigns were intended to subdue, not to destroy. The Ottomans built their empire by absorbing the Muslims of Anatolia and by becoming the protector of the Orthodox Church and of the millions of Greek Christians in Anatolia and the Balkans. In 1326 they took Bursa in western Anatolia, and in 1352 they gained a foothold in Europe by seizing Gallipoli. Their victories led more men, including recent converts, to join them as ghazis. In 1389 at Kosovo in the Balkans, the Ottomans defeated a combined force of Serbs and Bosnians. And in 1396 on the Danube River in modern Bulgaria, they crushed King Sigismund of Hungary, who was supported by French, German, and English knights. After the victories in the Balkans, the Ottomans made slaves of many captives and trained them as soldiers. These troops were outfitted with guns and artillery and trained to use them effectively.

In 1453, during the reign of Sultan Mehmet II (r. 1451–1481), the Ottomans conquered Constantinople, capital of the Byzantine Empire, which had lasted a thousand years. The Byzantine emperor, with only about ten thousand men, relied on Constantinople's magnificent system of circular walls and the iron chains that spanned the city's harbor. In response, Mehmet's army carried boats over steep hills to come in behind the chains blocking the harbor and then bombarded the city from the rear. A Transylvanian cannonmaker who had deserted the Greeks for the Turks cast huge bronze cannon on the spot (bringing raw materials to the

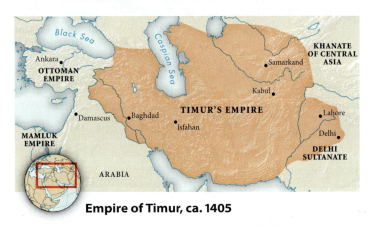

**Empire of Timur, ca. 1405**

scene of military action was easier than moving guns long distances), and these guns were used to weaken the defensive walls.

Once Constantinople was theirs, the Ottoman **sultans** considered themselves successors to both the Byzantine and Seljuk Turk emperors, and they quickly absorbed the rest of the Byzantine Empire. In the sixteenth century they continued to expand through the Middle East and into North Africa.

To begin the transformation of Constantinople (renamed Istanbul) into an imperial Ottoman capital, Mehmet ordered wealthy residents to participate in building mosques, markets, fountains, baths, and other public facilities. To make up for the loss of population through war, Mehmet transplanted inhabitants of other territories to the city, granting them tax remissions and possession of empty houses. He wanted them to start businesses, make Istanbul prosperous, and transform it into a microcosm of the empire.

Gunpowder, which was invented by the Chinese and adapted to artillery use by the Europeans, played an influential role in the expansion of the Ottoman state. In the first half of the sixteenth century, thanks to the use of this technology, the Ottomans gained control of shipping in the eastern Mediterranean, eliminated the Portuguese from the Red Sea and the Persian Gulf, and supported Andalusian and North African Muslims in their fight against the Christian reconquest of Muslim Spain. In 1514, under the superb military leadership of Selim (r. 1512–1520), the Ottomans turned the Safavids back from Anatolia. In addition, the Ottomans added Syria and Palestine (1516) and Egypt (1517). Control of Syria gave them control of the holy cities of Islam. Control of Egypt gave them access to the Indian Ocean, where they competed with the

- **Ottomans** Ruling house of the Turkish empire that lasted from 1299 to 1922.
- **Anatolia** The region of modern Turkey.
- **sultan** An Arabic word originally used by the Seljuk Turks to mean authority or dominion; it was used by the Ottomans to connote political and military supremacy.

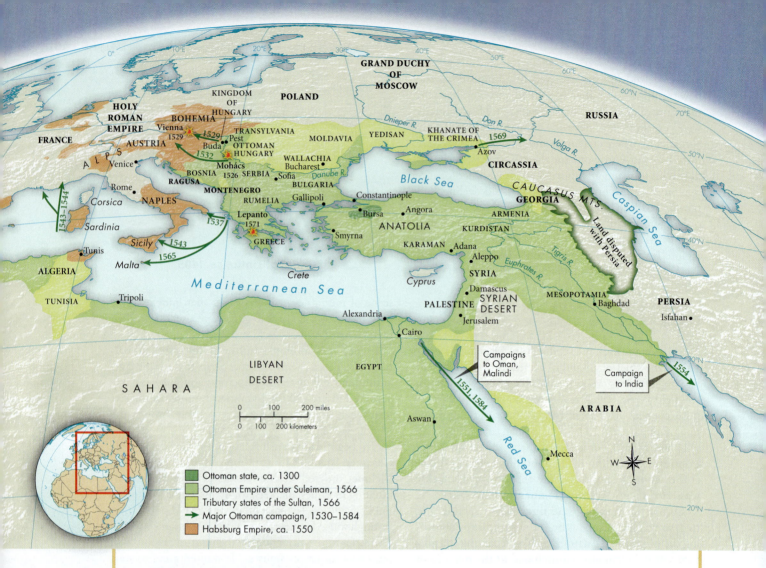

## ☐ Mapping the Past

**MAP 17.1   The Ottoman Empire at Its Height, 1566**   The Ottomans, like their great rivals the Habsburgs, rose to rule a vast dynastic empire encompassing many different peoples and ethnic groups. The army and the bureaucracy served to unite the disparate territories into a single state.

**ANALYZING THE MAP**   Trace the coastlines of the Ottoman Empire. What were the major port cities of the empire? Which regions were encompassed within the empire at its height?

**CONNECTIONS**   If the Ottoman Empire is compared to Europe of the same period (see Map 18.2, page 527), which had more of its territory near the sea? How did proximity to the Mediterranean shape the politics of Ottoman-European relations in this period?

Portuguese for control of shipping. Before long the Ottomans had extended their rule across North Africa to Tunisia and Algeria. For the next four centuries a majority of Arabs lived under Ottoman rule.

Suleiman (r. 1520–1566) extended Ottoman dominion to its widest geographical extent (see Map 17.1). Suleiman's army crushed the Hungarians at Mohács in 1526, killing the king and thousands of his nobles. Three years later the Turks unsuccessfully besieged the Habsburg capital of Vienna. From the late fourteenth

to the early seventeenth centuries, the Ottoman Empire was a key player in European politics. In 1525 Francis I of France and Suleiman struck an alliance; both believed that only their collaboration could prevent Habsburg domination of Europe. The Habsburg emperor Charles V retaliated by seeking an alliance with Safavid Persia. Suleiman renewed the French agreement with Francis's son, Henry II (r. 1547–1559), and this accord became the cornerstone of Ottoman policy in western Europe. Suleiman also allied with the German Protestant princes, forcing the Catholic Habsburgs to grant concessions to the Protestants. Ottoman pressure thus contributed to

● **viziers**   Chief assistants to caliphs.

the official recognition of Lutheran Protestants at the Peace of Augsburg in 1555 and the consolidation of the national monarchy in France.

In eastern Europe to the north of Ottoman lands stood the Grand Duchy of Moscow. In the fifteenth century Ottoman rulers did not regard it as a threat; in 1497 they even gave Russian merchants freedom of trade within the empire. But in 1547 Ivan IV (the Terrible) brought the entire Volga region under Russian control (see Map 17.1). In 1557 Ivan's ally, the Cossack chieftain Dimitrash, tried to take Azov, the northernmost Ottoman fortress. Ottoman plans to recapture the area succeeded in uniting Russia, Persia, and the pope against the Turks.

Though usually victorious on land, the Ottomans did not enjoy complete dominion on the seas. Competition with the Habsburgs and pirates for control of the Mediterranean led the Ottomans to conquer Cyprus in 1570 and settle thousands of Turks from Anatolia there. (Thus began the large Turkish presence on Cyprus that continues to the present day.) In response, Pope Pius V organized a Holy League against the Turks, which won a victory in 1571 at Lepanto off the west coast of Greece with a squadron of more than two hundred Spanish, Venetian, and papal galleys. Still, the Turks remained supreme on land and quickly rebuilt their entire fleet.

To the east, war with Safavid Persia occupied the sultans' attention throughout the sixteenth century. Several issues lay at the root of the long and exhausting conflict: religious antagonism between the Sunni Ottomans and the Shi'a Persians, competition to expand at each other's expense in Mesopotamia, desire to control trade routes, and European alliances. (For more on the Shi'a faith, see page 494.) Finally, in 1638 the Ottomans captured Baghdad, and the treaty of Kasr-I-Shirim established a permanent border between the two powers.

The Ottoman political system reached its classic form under Suleiman I. All authority flowed from the sultan to his public servants: provincial governors, police officers, military generals, heads of treasuries, and **viziers**. In Turkish history Suleiman is known as "the Lawgiver" because of his profound influence on the civil law. He ordered Lütfi Paşa (d. 1562), a poet and juridical scholar of slave origin, to draw up a new general code of laws that prescribed penalties for routine criminal acts such as robbery, adultery, and murder. It also sought to reform bureaucratic and financial corruption, such as foreign merchants' payment of bribes to avoid customs duties, imprisonment without trial, and promotion in the provincial administration because of favoritism rather than ability. The legal code also introduced the idea of balanced government budgets. The head of the religious establishment was given the task of reconciling sultanic law with Islamic law. Suleiman's legal acts influenced many legal codes,

**Sultan Mehmet II** Mehmet was called "the Conqueror" because at age twenty-one he captured Constantinople and ended the Byzantine Empire, but he is also known for his patronage of the arts and appreciation of beauty. (Topkapi Palace Museum, Istanbul, Turkey/Giraudon/The Bridgeman Art Library)

including that of the United States. Today, Suleiman's image appears in the chamber of the U.S. House of Representatives, along with the images of the Athenian lawmaker Solon, Moses, and Thomas Jefferson.

The Ottomans ruled their more distant lands, such as those in North Africa, relatively lightly. Governors of distant provinces collected taxes and maintained trade routes, but their control did not penetrate deeply into the countryside.

## The Ottoman Empire's Use of Slaves

The power of the Ottoman central government was sustained through the training of slaves. Slaves were purchased from Spain, North Africa, and Venice; captured in battle; or drafted through the system known as **devshirme**, by which the sultan's agents compelled Christian families in the Balkans to sell their boys. As the Ottoman frontier advanced in the fifteenth and sixteenth centuries, Albanian, Bosnian, Wallachian, and Hungarian slave boys filled Ottoman imperial needs. The slave boys were converted to Islam and trained for the imperial civil service and the standing army. The brightest 10 percent entered the palace school, where they learned to read and write Arabic, Ottoman Turkish, and Persian in preparation for administrative jobs. Other boys were sent to Turkish farms, where they acquired physical toughness in preparation for military service. Known as **janissaries** (Turkish for "recruits"), they formed the elite army corps. Thoroughly indoctrinated and absolutely loyal to the sultan, the janissary corps threatened the influence of fractious old Turkish families. They played a central role in Ottoman military affairs in the sixteenth century, adapting easily to the use of firearms. The devshirme system enabled the Ottomans to apply merit-based recruitment to military and administrative offices at little cost and provided a means of assimilating Christians living in Ottoman lands. Some Muslims, however, doubted whether janissary converts could be viewed as reliably Muslim.

The Ottoman ruling class consisted partly of descendants of Turkish families that had formerly ruled parts of Anatolia and partly of people of varied ethnic origins who rose through the bureaucratic and military ranks, many beginning as the sultan's slaves. All were committed to the Ottoman way: Islamic in faith, loyal to the sultan, and well versed in the Turkish language and the culture of the imperial court. In return for their services to the sultan, they held landed estates for the duration of their lives. Because all property belonged to the sultan and reverted to him on the holder's death, Turkish nobles, unlike their European counterparts, did not have a local base independent of the ruler. The absence of a hereditary nobility and private ownership of agricultural land differentiates the Ottoman system from European feudalism.

Another distinctive characteristic of the Ottomans was the sultan's failure to marry. From about 1500 on, the sultans did not contract legal marriages but perpetuated the ruling house through concubinage. A slave **concubine** could not expect to exert power the way a local or foreign noblewoman could. (For a notable exception, see "Individuals in Society: Hürrem," at right.) When one of the sultan's concubines became pregnant, her status and her salary increased. If she delivered a boy, she raised him until the age of ten or eleven. Then the child was given a province to govern under his mother's supervision. She accompanied him there, was responsible for his good behavior, and worked through imperial officials and the janissary corps to promote his interests. Because succession to the throne was open to all the sultan's sons, fratricide often resulted upon his death, and the losers were blinded or executed.

Slave concubinage paralleled the Ottoman development of slave soldiers and slave viziers. All held positions entirely at the sultan's pleasure, owed loyalty solely to him, and thus were more reliable than a hereditary nobility. Great social prestige, as well as the opportunity to acquire power and wealth, was attached to being a slave of the imperial household. Suleiman even made it a practice to marry his daughters to top-ranking slave-officials.

## The Safavid Empire in Persia

With the decline of Timur's empire after 1450, Persia was controlled by Turkish lords, with no single one dominant until 1501, when fourteen-year-old Isma'il (1487–1524) led a Turkish army to capture Tabriz and declared himself **shah** (king).

The strength of the early **Safavid** state rested on three crucial features. First, it had the loyalty and military support of nomadic Turkish Sufis known as **Qizilbash** (KIH-zihl-bahsh; a Turkish word meaning "redheads" that was applied to these people because of the red hats they wore). The shah secured the loyalty of the Qizilbash by granting them vast grazing lands, especially on the troublesome Ottoman frontier. In return, the Qizilbash supplied him with troops. Second, the Safavid state utilized the skills of urban bureaucrats and made them an essential part of the civil machinery of government.

The third source of Safavid strength was the Shi'a faith, which became the compulsory religion of the empire. The Shi'a believed that leadership among Muslims rightfully belonged to the Prophet Muhammad's descendants. Because Isma'il claimed descent from a line of twelve infallible imams (leaders) beginning with

---

- **devshirme** A process whereby the sultan's agents swept the provinces for Christian youths to be trained as soldiers or civil servants.

- **janissaries** Turkish for "recruits"; they formed the elite army corps.

- **concubine** A woman who is a recognized spouse but of lower status than a wife.

- **shah** Persian word for "king."

- **Safavid** The dynasty that encompassed all of Persia and other regions; its state religion was Shi'ism.

- **Qizilbash** Nomadic Sufi tribesmen who were loyal to and supportive of the early Safavid state.

- **ulama** Religious scholars whom Sunnis trust to interpret the Qur'an and the Sunna, the deeds and sayings of Muhammad.

- **Mughal** A term meaning "Mongol," used to refer to the Muslim empire of India, although its founders were primarily Turks, Afghans, and Persians.

# Individuals in Society

## Hürrem

**HÜRREM (1505?–1558) WAS BORN** in the western Ukraine (then part of Poland), the daughter of a Ruthenian priest, and was given the Polish name Aleksandra Lisowska. When Tartars raided, they captured and enslaved her. In 1520 she was given as a gift to Suleiman on the occasion of his accession to the throne. The Venetian ambassador (probably relying on sec-ondhand or thirdhand information) described her as "young, graceful, petite, but not beautiful." She was given the Turkish name Hürrem, meaning "joyful."

Hürrem apparently brought joy to Suleiman. Their first child was born in 1521. By 1525 they had four sons and a daughter; sources note that by that year Suleiman visited no other woman. But he waited eight or nine years before breaking Ottoman dynastic tradition by making Hürrem his legal wife, the first slave concu-bine so honored. For the rest of her life, Hürrem played a highly influen-tial role in the political, diplomatic, and philanthropic life of the Ottoman state. First, great power flowed from her position as mother of the prince, the future sultan Selim II (r. 1566–1574). Then, as the intimate and most trusted adviser of the sultan, she was Suleiman's closest confi-dant. During his frequent trips to the far-flung corners of his multiethnic empire, Hürrem wrote him long letters filled with her love and longing for him and her prayers for his safety in battle. She also shared political information about affairs in Istanbul, the activities of the grand vizier, and the attitudes of the janissaries. At a time when some people believed that the sultan's absence from the capital endangered his hold on the throne, Hürrem acted as his eyes and ears for potential threats.

Hürrem was the sultan's contact with her native Poland, which sent more embassies to Istanbul than any other power. Through her correspondence with King Sigismund I, peace between Poland and the Ottomans was maintained. When Sigismund II succeeded his father in 1548, Hürrem sent con-gratulations on his accession, along with two pairs of pajamas (originally a Hindu garment but commonly worn in southwest-ern Asia) and six handkerchiefs. Also, she sent the shah of Persia gold-embroidered sheets and shirts that she had sewn herself, seeking to display the wealth of the sultanate and to keep peace between the Ottomans and the Safavids.

**Hürrem depicted by a contemporary European artist.** (© Mary Evans Picture Library/The Image Works)

The enormous stipend that Sulei-man gave Hürrem permitted her to participate in his vast building pro-gram. In Jerusalem (in the Ottoman province of Palestine) she founded a hospice for fifty-five pilgrims that included a soup kitchen that fed four hundred pilgrims a day. In Istanbul Suleiman built and Hürrem endowed the Haseki (meaning "royal favorite con-cubine") mosque complex and a public bath for women near the Women's Market.

Perhaps Hürrem tried to fulfill two functions hitherto distinct in Ottoman political theory: those of the sultan's favorite and of mother of the prince. She also performed the conflicting roles of slave concubine and imperial wife. Many Turks resented Hürrem's interference at court. They believed she was behind the execution of Suleiman's popular son Mustafa on a charge of treason to make way for her own son to succeed as sultan.

Source: Leslie P. Peirce, *The Imperial Harem: Women and Sovereignty in the Ottoman Empire* (New York: Oxford University Press, 1993).

### QUESTIONS FOR ANALYSIS

1. How does Hürrem compare to powerful women in other places, such as Empress Wu in China, Isabella of Castile, Catherine de' Medici of France, Elizabeth I of England, or any other you know about?
2. What was Hürrem's "nationality"? What role did it play in her life?

### LaunchPad
### Online Document Project

**How did Europeans view the Ottoman Empire?** Examine a Habsburg ambassador's impressions of the Ottoman Empire, and then complete a quiz and writing assignment based on the evidence and details from this chapter.

*See inside the front cover to learn more.*

**Music in a Garden** This illustration of a courtly romance depicts several women in a garden intently listening to a musician, with cups of a beverage in their hands. (The Granger Collection, NYC — All rights reserved.)

Ali (Muhammad's cousin and son-in-law), he was officially regarded as their representative on earth. Isma'il recruited Shi'a scholars outstanding in learning and piety from other lands to instruct and guide his people, and he persecuted and exiled Sunni **ulama**. To this day, Iran remains the only Muslim state in which Shi'ism is the official religion.

Safavid power reached its height under Shah Abbas (r. 1587–1629), who moved the capital from Qazvin to Isfahan. His military achievements, support for trade and commerce, and endowment of the arts earned him the epithet "the Great." In the military realm he adopted the Ottoman practice of building an army of slaves, primarily captives from the Caucasus (especially Armenians and Georgians), who could serve as a counterweight to the Qizilbash, who had come to be considered a threat. He also increased the use of gunpowder weapons and made alliances with European powers against the Ottomans and Portuguese. In his campaigns against the Ottomans, Shah Abbas captured Baghdad, Mosul, and Diarbakr in Mesopotamia (Map 17.2).

Conflict between the Ottomans and the Safavids was not an even match. The Safavids did not have as many people or as much wealth as the Ottomans and continually had to defend against encroachments on their western border. Still, they were able to attract some of the Turks in Ottoman lands who felt that their government had shifted too far from its nomadic roots. After Shah Abbas, Safavid power was sapped by civil war between tribal factions vying for control of the court.

## The Mughal Empire in India

Of the three great Islamic empires of the early modern world, the **Mughal** Empire of India was the largest, wealthiest, and most populous. Extending over 1.2 million square miles at the end of the seventeenth century, with a population between 100 and 150 million, and with fabulous wealth and resources, the Mughal Empire surpassed the other two by a wide margin. In the sixteenth century only the Ming Dynasty in China could compare.

In 1504 Babur (r. 1483–1530), a Turkish ruler forced out of a small territory in Central Asia, captured Kabul and established a kingdom in Afghanistan. An adven-

**MAP 17.2 The Safavid Empire, 1587–1629** In the late sixteenth century the power of the Safavid kingdom of Persia rested on its strong military force, its Shi'a Muslim faith, and its extraordinarily rich trade in rugs and pottery. Many of the cities on the map, such as Tabriz, Qum, and Shiraz, were great rug-weaving centers.

turer who claimed descent from Chinggis Khan and Timur, Babur moved southward in search of resources to restore his fortunes. In 1526, with a force that was small (twelve thousand in number) but was equipped with firearms, Babur defeated the sultan of Delhi at Panipat. Babur's capture of the cities of Agra and Delhi, key fortresses of the north, paved the way for further conquests in northern India. Although many of his soldiers wished to return north with their spoils, Babur decided to stay in India. A gifted writer, Babur wrote an autobiography in Turkish that recounts his military campaigns, describes places and people he encountered, recounts his difficulties giving up wine, and shows his wide-ranging interests in everything from fruit and swimming to a Turkish general who excelled at leapfrog. He was not particularly impressed by India, as can be inferred from this description in his memoirs:

> Hindustan is a country which has few pleasures to recommend it. The people are not handsome. They have no idea of the charms of friendly society, of frankly mixing together, or familiar discourse. They have no genius, no comprehension of mind, no politeness of manner, no kindness or fellow-feeling,

no ingenuity or mechanical invention in planning or executing their handicraft works, no skill or knowledge in design or architecture; they have no horses, no good flesh, no grapes or muskmelons, no good fruits, no ice or cold water, no good food or bread in their bazaars, no baths or colleges, no candles, no torches, not a candlestick.[1]

During the reign of Babur's son Humayun (r. 1530–1540 and 1555–1556), the Mughals lost most of their territories in Afghanistan. Humayun went into temporary exile in Persia, where he developed a deep appreciation for Persian art and literature. The reign of Humayun's son Akbar (r. 1556–1605) may well have been the greatest in the history of India. A boy of thirteen when he succeeded to the throne, Akbar pursued expansionist policies. Under his dynamic leadership, the Mughal state took definitive form and encompassed most of the subcontinent north of the Godavari River. No kingdom or coalition of kingdoms could long resist Akbar's armies. The once-independent states of northern India were forced into a centralized political system under the sole authority of the Mughal emperor.

Akbar replaced Turkish with Persian as the official language of the Mughal Empire, and Persian remained the official language until the British replaced it with English in 1835. To govern this vast region, Akbar developed an administrative bureaucracy centered on four co-equal ministers: finance and revenue; the army and intelligence; the judiciary and religious patronage; and the imperial household, whose jurisdiction included roads, bridges, and infrastructure throughout the empire. Under Akbar's Hindu finance minister, Raja Todar Mal, a uniform system of taxes was put in place. In the provinces imperial governors were appointed by and responsible solely to the emperor. Whereas the Ottoman sultans and Safavid shahs made extensive use of slaves acquired from non-Muslim lands for military and administrative positions, Akbar used the services of royal princes, nobles, and warrior-aristocrats. Initially these men were Muslims from Central Asia, but to reduce their influence, Akbar vigorously recruited Persians and Hindus. No single ethnic or religious faction could challenge the emperor.

Akbar's descendants extended the Mughal Empire further. His son Jahangir (r. 1605–1628) lacked his father's military abilities and administrative genius, but he did succeed in consolidating Mughal rule in Bengal. (See "Viewpoints 17.1: Jahangir and Louis XIV on Priorities for Monarchs," at right.) Jahangir's son Shah Jahan (r. 1628–1658) launched fresh territorial expansion. Faced with dangerous revolts by the Muslims in Ahmadnagar and the resistance of the newly arrived Portuguese in Bengal, Shah Jahan not only crushed this opposition but also strengthened his northwestern frontier. Shah Jahan's son Aurangzeb (r. 1658–1707), unwilling to wait for his father to die, deposed him and confined him for years in a small cell. A puritanically devout and strictly orthodox Muslim, as well as a skillful general and a clever diplomat, Aurangzeb ruled more of India than did any previous Mughal emperor, having extended the realm deeper into south India. His reign, however, also marked the beginning of the empire's decline. His non-Muslim subjects were not pleased with his religious zealotry, and his military campaigns were costly. In the south resistance to Mughal rule led to major uprisings. (For more on Aurangzeb's rule, see page 506.)

**The Mughal Empire, 1526–1857**

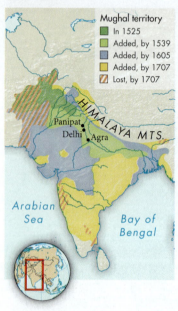

Mughal territory
- In 1525
- Added, by 1539
- Added, by 1605
- Added, by 1707
- Lost, by 1707

HIMALAYA MTS.
Panipat
Delhi · Agra
Arabian Sea
Bay of Bengal

# Cultural Flowering

☐ What cultural advances occurred under the rule of the Ottoman, Safavid, and Mughal Empires?

All three Islamic empires presided over an extraordinary artistic and intellectual flowering in everything from carpetmaking to architecture and gardening, from geography and astronomy to medicine. At the same time, new religious practices (and conflicts) emerged, and new gathering places—coffeehouses—became popular outlets for socializing and exchanging ideas. Artistic and intellectual advances spread from culture to culture, probably because of the common Persian influence on the Turks since the tenth century. This exchange was also aided by common languages. Persian was used as the administrative language by the Mughals in India, and Arabic was a lingua franca of the entire region because of its centrality in Islam. In Ottoman lands both Persian and Arabic were literary languages, but Turkish slowly became the lingua franca of the realm.

## The Arts

One of the arts all three empires shared was carpetmaking. Carpet designs and weaving techniques demonstrate both cultural integration and local distinctiveness. Turkic migrants carried their weaving traditions with them as they moved but also readily adopted new motifs, especially from Persia. In Safavid Persia, Shah Abbas was determined to improve his country's export trade and built the small cottage business of carpet weaving into a national industry. In the capital city of Isfahan alone, factories employed more than twenty-five thousand weavers who produced woolen carpets, brocades, and silks of brilliant color, design, and quality. Women and children were often employed as weavers, especially of the most expensive rugs, because their smaller hands could tie tinier knots.

Another art that spread from Persia to both Ottoman and Mughal lands was miniature painting, especially for book illustration. This tradition had been enriched by the many Chinese artists brought to Persia during the Mongol period. There was also an interplay between carpets and miniature painting. Naturalistic depictions of lotus blossoms, peonies, chrysanthemums, tulips, carnations, birds, and even dragons appear in both book illustrations and carpets.

In Mughal India, as throughout the Muslim world, books were regarded as precious objects. Time, talent, and expensive materials went into their production, and they were highly coveted because they reflected wealth, learning, and power. Akbar reportedly

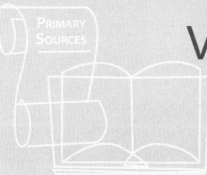
# Viewpoints 17.1

## Jahangir and Louis XIV on Priorities for Monarchs

> • *Jahangir, the fourth Mughal emperor, was as much a patron of the arts as a military commander. Like his great-grandfather, Babur, he wrote a memoir. Jahangir's representation of himself and his actions in the memoir can be compared to that of the French king Louis XIV, less than a century later, whose advice to his heir has been preserved.*

### Jahangir's *Memoirs*

❝ At that period when I took my departure from Lahore for Agra, on the occasion recently described, it happily occurred to me to direct that the different landholders on that route should plant at every town and village, and every stage and halting place, all the way from Lahore to Agra, mulberry and other large and lofty trees affording shade, but particularly those with broad leaves and wide-spreading branches, in order that to all time to come the way-worn and weary traveler might find under their shadow repose and shelter from the scorching rays of the sun during the summer heats. I ordered, moreover, that spacious serrais or places of rest and refreshment, substantially built of brick or stone, so as to be secure against early decay, should be erected at the termination of every eight kosse [twelve miles], for the whole distance, all provided with baths, and to every one a tank or reservoir of fresh water; a certain number of attendants was also allotted to every serrai, for the purpose of sweeping and keeping clean, and in other respects to take care of them. And, lastly, at the passage of every river, whether large or small, convenient bridges were erected, so that the industrious traveler might be able to pursue his objects without obstruction or delay.

In the same manner, all the way from Agra to Bengal, a distance altogether of six months' journey, at similar intervals trees have been planted and rest-houses erected, the former of which have already grown to such a size as to afford abundant shade. And more than this, many benevolent individuals, emulous of evincing their zeal in promoting my views, have at different stages laid out spacious gardens and plantations, containing every description of fruit tree; so that at the period at which I am writing, anyone desirous of traveling to any quarter of my dominions will find at convenient distances spacious buildings for his accommodation, and a refreshing supply of fruit and vegetables for his recreation; in so much, indeed, that he might be led to declare that he is a stranger to the fatigues of travelling. . . .

With regard to the maxims which should govern the policy of sovereign princes, it has been said, that to resolve without the concurrence of men of experience is the most fallacious of proceedings; but I contend, nevertheless, that there is no safety in council, unless founded in rectitude of mind. I maintain, that if we entrust the concerns of the state to the opinions of another, we give to the Almighty an associate in the secrets of the heart. . . . He that conducts the destinies of his country by the judgment of another, must not forget that he will nevertheless be himself responsible, at the awful day of account, for all the exactions, the tyranny, the unjust decisions, violence, and oppression to which the people may have been exposed, through such imprudent delegation. It is from the reigning sovereign that the awful reckoning will be required, not from those who have been his advisers. How much does it then behoove the man who holds the crown and scepter, in every clime, to make himself, by a personal investigation, immediately acquainted with the grievances of his people, so that assured redress may be always attainable, that no one should be within the grasp of oppression in any shape! ❞

### Louis XIV's *Memoirs*

❝ The cleverest private individuals take advice from other clever people about their little concerns. What should be the rule for kings who have in their hands the public weal, and whose resolutions harm or benefit the whole earth? Decisions of such importance should never be formed, if possible, without calling upon all the most enlightened, reasonable and wise among our subjects. . . . Besides, our lofty position in some way separates us from our people to whom our ministers are closer, and are consequently able to see a thousand things of which we know nothing, but on which nevertheless we must make up our minds and take measures. Add to this their age, experience, deliberations, and their greater liberty to obtain information and suggestions from their inferiors, who in their turn gather them from others, step by step down to the lowest.

But when on important occasions they have reported to us all the aspects and all the opposing reasons, all that is done elsewhere in similar cases, all that has been done formerly, and all that might be done today, it is incumbent upon us, my son, to choose what must be actually done. And in regard to that choice I will make bold to tell you that if we do not lack good sense or courage there is no other who can make a better one than us. ❞

Sources: David Price, trans., *Memoirs of the Emperor Jahangueir* (London: The Oriental Translation Committee, 1929), pp. 90–91, slightly modified; Herbert Wilson, trans., *A King's Lessons in Statecraft: Louis XIV: Letters to His Heirs* (New York: Albert and Charles Boni, 1925), pp. 63–64.

### QUESTIONS FOR ANALYSIS

1. Are you more impressed by the similarities between these two monarchs' comments on consultation with advisers or by the differences? What might account for the similarities and the differences?

2. What can you infer about the personalities of these two monarchs from their remarks?

3. Jahangir describes in great detail the improvements to the roads in his empire. Why would a ruler take pride in the improvement of roads?

**Persian "Ardabil" Carpet, ca. 1540**  The Persians were among the first carpet weavers of ancient times and perfected the art over thousands of years. This wool carpet, reputably from the Safavid shrine at Ardabil, is one of only three signed and dated carpets from the Safavid period, when Persian carpetmaking was at its zenith. Hand knotted and hand dyed, it was royally commissioned with a traditional medallion design, consisting of a central sunburst medallion surrounded by radiating pendants. Inscribed on the carpet is an ode by the fourteenth-century poet Hafiz: "I have no refuge in this world other than thy threshold / My head has no resting place other than this doorway." (Victoria & Albert Museum, London, UK/The Bridgeman Art Library)

possessed twenty-four thousand books when he died. The historian Abu'l-Fazl described Akbar's library and love of books:

> His Majesty's library is divided into several parts. . . . Prose works, poetical works, Hindi, Persian, Greek, Kashmirian, Arabic, are all separately placed. In this order they are also inspected. Experienced people bring them daily and read them before His Majesty, who hears every book from beginning to end . . . and rewards the readers with presents of cash either in gold or silver, according to the number of leaves read out by them. . . . There are no historical facts of past ages, or curiosities of science, or interesting points of philosophy, with which His Majesty, a leader of impartial sages, is unacquainted.[2]

## City and Palace Building

In all three empires strong rulers built capital cities and imperial palaces as visible expressions of dynastic majesty. Europeans called Suleiman "the Magnificent" because of the grandeur of his court. With annual state revenues of about $80 million (at a time when Elizabeth I of England could expect $150,000 and Francis I of France perhaps $1 million) and thousands of servants, he had a lifestyle no European monarch could begin to rival. He used his fabulous wealth to adorn Istanbul with palaces, mosques, schools, and libraries, and the city reached about a million in population. The building of hospitals, roads, and bridges and the reconstruction of the water systems of the great pilgrimage sites at Mecca and Jerusalem benefited his subjects. Safavid Persia and Mughal India produced rulers with similar ambitions.

The greatest builder under the Ottomans was Mimar Sinan (1491–1588), a Greek-born devshirme recruit who rose to become imperial architect under Suleiman. A contemporary of Michelangelo, Sinan designed 312 public buildings, including mosques, schools, hospitals, public baths, palaces, and burial chapels. His masterpieces, the Shehzade and Suleimaniye Mosques in Istanbul, which rivaled the Byzantine church of Hagia Sophia, were designed to maximize the space under the dome. His buildings expressed the discipline, power, and devotion to Islam that characterized the Ottoman Empire under Suleiman.

Shah Abbas made his capital, Isfahan, the jewel of the Safavid Empire. He had his architects place a polo ground in the center and surrounded it with palaces, mosques, and bazaars. A seventeenth-century English visitor described one of Isfahan's bazaars as "the surprisingest piece of Greatness in Honour of commerce the world can boast of." In addition to splendid rugs, stalls displayed pottery and fine china, metalwork of exceptionally high quality, and silks and velvets of stunning weave and design. A city of perhaps 750,000 people, Isfahan also contained 162 mosques, 48 schools where future members of the ulama learned the sacred Muslim sciences, 273 public baths, and the vast imperial palace. Mosques were richly decorated with blue tile. Private houses had their own garden courts, and public gardens, pools, and parks adorned the wide streets. Tales of the beauty of Isfahan circulated worldwide, attracting thousands of tourists annually in the seventeenth and eighteenth centuries.

Akbar in India was also a great builder. The birth of a long-awaited son, Jahangir, inspired Akbar to build a new city, Fatehpur Sikri, to symbolize the regime's Islamic foundations. He personally supervised the construction of the city, which combined the Muslim tradition of domes, arches, and spacious courts with the Hindu tradition of flat stone beams, ornate decoration, and solidity. The historian Abu'l-Fazl reported, "His Majesty plans splendid edifices, and dresses the work of his mind and heart in the garment of stone and clay."[3] Completed in 1578, the city included an imperial palace, a mosque, lavish gardens, and a hall of worship, as well as thousands of houses for ordinary people. Unfortunately, because of its bad water supply, the city was soon abandoned.

Of Akbar's successors, Shah Jahan had the most sophisticated interest in architecture. Because his capital at Agra was cramped, in 1639 he decided to found a new capital city at Delhi. In the design and layout of the buildings, Persian ideas predominated, an indication of the number of Persian architects and engineers who had flocked to the subcontinent. The walled palace-fortress alone extended over 125 acres. Built partly of red sandstone, partly of marble, it included private chambers for the emperor; mansions for the wives, widows, and concubines of the imperial household; huge

### Two Masterpieces of Islamic Architecture
Istanbul's Suleimaniye Mosque, designed by Sinan and commissioned by Suleiman I, was finished in 1557. Its interior (right) is especially spacious. The Taj Mahal (above), built about a century later in Agra in northern India, is perhaps the finest example of Mughal architecture. Its white marble exterior is decorated with Arabic inscriptions and floral designs. (mosque: Belinda Images/SuperStock; Taj Mahal: Dinodia/The Bridgeman Art Library)

**Isfahan Tiles** The embellishment of Isfahan under Shah Abbas I created an unprecedented need for tiles, as had the rebuilding of imperial Istanbul after 1453, the vast building program of Suleiman the Magnificent, and a huge European demand. Persian potters learned their skills from the Chinese. By the late sixteenth century Italian and Austrian potters had imitated the Persian and Ottoman tile makers. (Eileen Tweedy/Victoria & Albert Museum, London, UK/The Art Archive at Art Resource, NY)

audience rooms for the conduct of public business (treasury, arsenal, and military); baths; and vast gardens filled with flowers, trees, and thirty silver fountains spraying water. In 1650, with living quarters for guards, military officials, merchants, dancing girls, scholars, and hordes of cooks and servants, the palace-fortress housed fifty-seven thousand people. It also boasted a covered public bazaar. The sight of the magnificent palace left contemporaries speechless. Shah Jahan had a Persian poetic couplet inscribed on the walls:

> If there is a paradise on the face of the earth,
> It is this, it is this.

Beyond the walls, princes and aristocrats built mansions and mosques on a smaller scale. With its fine architecture and its population of between 375,000 and 400,000, Delhi gained the reputation of being one of the great cities of the Muslim world.

For his palace, Shah Jahan ordered the construction of the Peacock Throne. This famous piece, encrusted with emeralds, diamonds, pearls, and rubies, took seven years to fashion and cost the equivalent of $5 million. It served as the imperial throne of India until 1739,

when the Persian warrior Nadir Shah seized it as plunder and carried it to Persia.

Shah Jahan's most enduring monument is the Taj Mahal. Between 1631 and 1648 twenty thousand workers toiled over the construction of this memorial in Agra to Shah Jahan's favorite wife, who died giving birth to their fifteenth child. One of the most beautiful structures in the world, the Taj Mahal is both an expression of love and a superb architectural blending of Islamic and Indian culture.

## Gardens

Many of the architectural masterpieces of this age had splendid gardens attached to them. Gardens represent a distinctive and highly developed feature of Persian culture. They commonly were walled, with a pool in the center and geometrically laid-out flowering plants, especially roses. Identified with paradise in Arab tradition, gardens served not only as centers of prayer and meditation but also as places of leisure and revelry. After the incorporation of Persia into the caliphate in the seventh century, formal gardening spread west and east through the Islamic world, as illustrated by the magnificent gardens of Muslim Spain, southern Italy, and, later, southeastern Europe. The Mongol followers of Timur took landscape architects from Persia back to Samarkand and adapted their designs to nomad encampments. When Babur established the Mughal Dynasty in India, he adapted the Persian garden to the warmer southern climate. Gardens were laid out near palaces, mosques, shrines, and mausoleums, including the Taj Mahal, which had four water channels symbolizing the four rivers of paradise.

Because it evoked paradise, the garden played a large role in Muslim literature. Some scholars hold that to understand Arabic poetry, one must study Arab gardening. The secular literature of Muslim Spain, rife with references such as "a garland of verses," influenced the lyric poetry of southern France, the troubadours, and the courtly love tradition. (See "Listening to the Past: Courtly Love Poetry," page 408.)

Gardens, of course, are seasonal. To remind themselves of paradise during the cold winter months, rulers, city people, and nomads ordered Persian carpets, most of which use floral patterns and have formal garden designs.

## Intellectual Advances and Religious Trends

Between 1400 and 1800 the culture of the Islamic empires developed in many directions. Particularly notable were new movements within Islam as well as advances in mathematics, geography, astronomy, and medicine. Building on the knowledge of earlier Islamic writers and stimulated by Ottoman naval power, the geographer and cartographer Piri Reis produced a map incorporating Islamic and Western knowledge that showed all the known world (1513); another of his maps detailed Columbus's third voyage to the New World. Piri Reis's *Book of the Sea* (1521) contained 129 chapters, each with a map incorporating all Islamic (and Western) knowledge of the seas and navigation and describing harbors, tides, dangerous rocks and shores, and storm areas. In the field of astronomy, Takiyuddin Mehmet (1521–1585), who served as the sultan's chief astronomer, built an observatory at Istanbul. He also produced *Instruments of the Observatory*, which catalogued astronomical instruments and described an astronomical clock that fixed the location of heavenly bodies with greater precision than ever before.

There were also advances in medicine. Under Suleiman the imperial palace itself became a center of medical science, and the large number of hospitals established in Istanbul and throughout the empire testifies to his support for medical research and his concern for the sick. Abi Ahmet Celebi (1436–1523), the chief physician of the empire, produced a study on

**Polo** Two teams of four on horseback ride back and forth on a grass field measuring 200 by 400 yards, trying to hit a 4½-ounce wooden ball with a 4-foot mallet through the opponent's goal. Because a typical match involves many high-speed collisions among the horses, each player has to maintain a string of expensive ponies in order to change mounts several times during the game. Students of the history of sports believe the game originated in Persia, as shown in this eighteenth-century miniature, whence it spread to India, China, and Japan. Brought from India to England, where it became very popular among the aristocracy in the nineteenth century, polo is a fine example of cross-cultural influences. (Private Collection)

kidney and bladder stones. Recurrent outbreaks of the plague posed a challenge for physicians in Muslim lands. Muhammad had once said not to go to a country where an epidemic existed but also not to leave a place because an epidemic broke out. As a consequence, when European cities began enforcing quarantines to control the spread of the plague, early Muslim rulers dismissed such efforts. By the sixteenth century, however, a better understanding of contagion led to a redefinition of the proper response to a plague epidemic and allowed for leaving the city in search of clean air.

In the realm of religion, the rulers of all three empires drew legitimacy from their support for Islam, at least among their Muslim subjects. The Sunni-Shi'a split between the Ottomans and Safavids led to efforts to define and enforce religious orthodoxy on both sides.

For the Safavids this entailed suppressing Sufi movements and Sunnis, even marginalizing—sometimes massacring—the original Qizilbash warriors, who had come to be seen as politically disruptive. Sectarian conflicts within Islam were not as pronounced in Mughal lands, perhaps because even though the Mughals ruled over both Sunni and Shi'a subjects, these subjects were greatly outnumbered by non-Muslims, mostly Hindus.

Sufi fraternities thrived throughout the Muslim world in this era, even when the states tried to limit them. In India Sufi orders also influenced non-Muslims. The mystical Bhakti movement among Hindus involved dances, poems, and songs reminiscent of Sufi practice. The development of the new religion of the Sikhs (seeks) was also influenced by Sufis. The Sikhs traced themselves back to a teacher in the sixteenth century who argued that God did not distinguish between Muslims and Hindus but saw everyone as his children.

Sikhs rejected the caste system (division of society into hereditary groups) and forbade alcohol and tobacco, and men did not cut their hair, covering it instead with a turban. The Sikh movement was most successful in northwest India, where Sikh men armed themselves to defend their communities.

Despite all the signs of cultural vitality in the three Islamic empires, none of them adopted the printing press or went through the sorts of cultural expansion associated with it in China and Europe. Until 1729 the Ottoman authorities prohibited printing books in Turkish or Arabic (Jews, Armenians, and Greeks could establish presses and print in their own languages). Printing was not banned in Mughal India, but neither did the technology spread, even after Jesuit missionaries printed Bibles in Indian languages beginning in the 1550s. The copying of manuscripts was a well-established practice, and those who made their living

## □ Picturing the Past

**Coffee Drinking** This sixteenth-century miniature depicts men drinking coffee at a banquet. (© The Trustees of the Chester Beatty Library, Dublin, Ireland/The Bridgeman Art Library)

**ANALYZING THE IMAGE** What activities are people engaged in? How does the artist convey differences in the ages of those drinking coffee?

**CONNECTIONS** What made coffee a popular drink for people socializing?

this way sometimes organized to keep competition at bay. It also needs to be noted that by the end of this period, scientific knowledge was not keeping up with advances made in Europe (see page 557).

## Coffeehouses and Their Social Impact

In the mid-fifteenth century a new social convention spread throughout the Islamic world—drinking coffee. Arab writers trace the origins of coffee drinking to Yemen Sufis, who sought a trancelike concentration on God to the exclusion of everything else and found that coffee helped them stay awake (similarly, Buddhist monks drank tea to stay awake during long meditation sessions, a practice responsible for the spread of tea in East Asia). Most Sufis were not professional holy men but tradesmen or merchants. Therefore, the use of coffee for pious purposes led to its use as a business lubricant—an extension of hospitality to a potential buyer in a shop. Merchants carried the Yemenite practice to Mecca in about 1490. From Mecca, where pilgrims were introduced to it, coffee drinking spread to Egypt and Syria. In 1555 two Syrians opened a coffeehouse in Istanbul.

Coffeehouses provided a place for conversation and male sociability; there a man could entertain his friends cheaply and more informally than at home. But coffeehouses encountered religious and governmental opposition based on the following arguments: (1) because of its composition, coffee is intoxicating, making it analogous to wine, prohibited to Muslims; (2) coffee drinking was an innovation and therefore a violation of Islamic law; (3) coffeehouses encouraged political discussions, facilitating sedition; (4) coffeehouses attracted unemployed soldiers and other low types, encouraging immoral behavior, such as gambling, using drugs, and soliciting prostitutes; and (5) music at coffeehouses encouraged debauchery. Thus coffeehouses drew the attention of government officials, who considered themselves the guardians of public morality. On the other hand, the coffee trade was a major source of profit that local notables sought to control.

Although debate over the morality of coffeehouses continued through the sixteenth century, their eventual acceptance represented a revolution in Islamic life: socializing was no longer confined to the home. Ultimately, because the medical profession remained divided on coffee's harmful effects and because religious authorities could not prove that coffeehouses violated religious law, coffee drinking could not be forbidden. In the seventeenth century coffee and coffeehouses spread to Europe. (For reaction to another new product that spread quickly despite opposition, see "Listening to the Past: Katib Chelebi on Tobacco," page 506.)

## Non-Muslims Under Muslim Rule

☐ How did Christians, Jews, Hindus, and other non-Muslims fare under these Islamic states?

Drawing on Qur'anic teachings, Muslims had long practiced a religious tolerance unknown in Christian Europe. Muslim rulers for the most part guaranteed the lives and property of Christians and Jews on their promise of obedience and the payment of a poll tax. In the case of the Ottomans, this tolerance was extended not only to the Christians and Jews who had been living under Muslim rule for centuries but also to the Serbs, Bosnians, Croats, and other Orthodox Christians in the newly conquered Balkans. The Ottoman conqueror of Constantinople, Mehmet, nominated the Greek patriarch as official representative of the Greek population. This and other such appointments recognized non-Muslims as functioning parts of the Ottoman society and economy. In 1454 Rabbi Isaac Sarfati sent a letter to the Jews in the Rhineland, Swabia, Moravia, and Hungary, urging them to move to Turkey because of the good conditions for Jews there. A massive migration to Ottoman lands followed. When Ferdinand and Isabella of Spain expelled the Jews in 1492 and later, many immigrated to the Ottoman Empire.

The Safavid authorities made efforts to convert Armenian Christians in the Caucasus, and many seem to have embraced Islam, some more voluntarily than others. Nevertheless, the Armenian Christian Church retained its vitality, and under the Safavids Armenian Christians were prominent merchants in long-distance trade (see page 511).

Babur and his successors acquired even more non-Muslim subjects with their conquests in India, which included not only Hindus but also substantial numbers of Jains, Zoroastrians, Christians, and Sikhs. Over time, the number of Indians who converted to Islam increased, but the Mughal rulers did not force conversion. When the first reliable census was taken in 1901, the Ganges plain, the area of the Indian subcontinent most intensely exposed to Mughal rule and for the longest span of time, had a Muslim population of only 10 to 15 percent. Accordingly, some scholars have argued that in the Indian subcontinent there was an inverse relationship between the degree of Muslim political penetration and conversion to Islam.

Akbar went the furthest in promoting Muslim-Hindu accommodation. He celebrated important Hindu festivals, such as Diwali, the festival of lights, and he wore his uncut hair in a turban as a concession

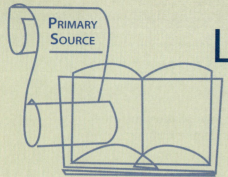

# Listening to the Past

## Katib Chelebi on Tobacco

*Katib Chelebi (1609–1657) was an Ottoman civil servant who spent much of his time as an accountant for the Turkish army, accompanying it on several important campaigns. Over time, he became passionate about learning and pursued not only Islamic law but also ancient Greek philosophy, geography, and modern European sciences. He wrote several important books, including a bibliographical encyclopedia. The book of essays from which the following extract comes also discusses such contemporary issues as coffee, singing, opium, shaking hands, bowing, and bribery.*

### Katib Chelebi, "The Balance of Truth"

❝ When the year 800 after the Hijra approached the year 900 [in the fifteenth century], and when Spanish ships found the New World. The Portuguese and the English were also sailing through the shores in order to pass from the Western seas to the Eastern seas, they arrived at an island,* which is close to the shores noted as Gineya in the *Atlas*. Due to the negative impact of the humidity of the sea air on his nature, a doctor from the crew of the ship suffered from what appeared to be a lymphatic disorder. While he was looking for a cure, employing hot and dry things in accordance with the dictum "Cure is in the opposite," his ship arrived at the aforementioned island, and he saw that some sort of a leaf was burning. Smelling its scent, he understood that it was a hot scent, and he started sucking the smoke through a pipe-like instrument. As he benefited from this, he collected a large quantity of that leaf and used it while he stayed there. The people on the ship, saying "This is a beneficial cure" and following his example, collected a lot of the leaf. They start smoking this way one after another. After the ship arrived in England, smoking spread to France and other places; without knowing about its origin and thinking that it can be used leisurely, people started smoking tobacco. Most of them became addicted and considered it a stimulating drug. As it became a common phenomena in the East and the West, it remained unhindered by prohibition.

It appeared around 1010 A.H. [1601 C.E.]. Since then various preachers mentioned it, and many learned men wrote treatises; some argued that it is religiously prohibited, and others disapproved. Those who were addicted, on the other hand, replied to these with their own treatises. After a while, in the court of the sultan [that is, in Istanbul], Şeyhi Ibrahim Efendi, the surgeon of the Palace, showed extreme care for the topic and talked about it at length and preached in the public seminar of Sultan Mehemmed Mosque and hung on the wall copies of the counsel and religious opinion [*fatwa*] in vain. As he talked about it, people smoked more and became more obstinate. Seeing it doesn't help, he gave in.

Later, towards the end of his reign, Sultan Murad IV [1612–1640] banned coffee houses in order to close down the door of evil acts and tobacco because it caused some fires [in the city]. When people disregarded the prohibition, the power of the Sultan necessitated reprimanding those who by smoking performed the sin of acting against the imperial order. Occasionally, [due to] the sultan's ruthlessness in suppression and in accordance with the dictum "Mankind craves what is forbidden," people's desire and craving to smoke equally increased. Many men were sent to the realm of nothingness due to this crime. At the encampments on the way to the Baghdad campaign, while fifteen to twenty leading soldiers were being executed in the presence of the sultan with extreme torment with the accusation of smoking tobacco, they still carried little pipes, some under their shirts, and some in their pockets and smoked at every opportunity. In Istanbul, there was no end to those who smoked in the barracks and public latrines. Even under such harsh suppression, those who smoked were more than those who didn't. After he [Sultan Murad IV] passed away, at times it was prohibited, and at times it was permitted, and finally, during the time of the late grand mufti Bahai Effendi issued a fatwa ruling that tobacco was permissible; among the people smoking became prevalent and popular once more. Yet, thanks to the fact that the high imperial order chastised the addicts from time to time, some quit. However, in all of the fourth of the world that

to Indian practice. Also, Akbar twice married Hindu princesses, one of whom became the mother of his heir, Jahangir, and he appointed the Spanish Jesuit Antonio Monserrate (1536–1600) as tutor to his second son, Prince Murad. Eventually, Hindus totaled 30 percent of the imperial bureaucracy. In 1579 Akbar abolished the **jizya**, the poll tax on non-Muslims that guaranteed their protection. These actions, especially the abolition of the jizya, infuriated the ulama, and

serious conflict erupted between its members and the emperor. Ultimately, Akbar issued an imperial decree declaring that the Mughal emperor had supreme authority, even above the ulama, in all religious matters, to the dismay of the Muslim religious establishment.

Some of Akbar's successors, above all Aurangzeb, sided more with the ulama. Aurangzeb appointed censors of public morals in important cities to enforce Islamic laws against gambling, prostitution, drinking,

**A man is depicted smoking a long pipe in one of the stalls in a bazaar in this seventeenth-century Turkish painting.** (Miniature from the *Memorie Turchesche* [pen & ink on paper], Venetian School [17th century]/Museo Correr, Venice, Italy/The Bridgeman Art Library)

is inhabited it was being smoked. Such is the story of tobacco. Now, let's consider the contexts for and characteristics of smoking in the form of a few arguments:

The first argument is that people can be prevented through prohibition and can quit tobacco. Since habit is second nature, we need to push aside this possibility. Addicts cannot be made to quit this way. . . .

The second discussion concerns the question of whether tobacco is good or bad with respect to reason. We can neglect the approval of it by addicts, and the intelligent accepted it as bad; either the judgment of good or bad have to be determined by both reason and religious law. . . .

The third argument is about its benefits and harmful effects. There is no doubt that it is financially harmful. However, since it becomes one of the most essential items for the addict, he doesn't mind its financial harm. Its harm on the body is well attested. Since tobacco pollutes the essence of air breathed by people, it is physically harmful.

The fourth argument is whether or not it is an innovation according to religion. It is an innovation according to the religious law, since it appeared in recent times. Moreover, it cannot be argued that it is an acceptable innovation. It is also rationally an innovation, because smoking hasn't been seen or heard of by the intelligent since the time of Adam. . . .

The fifth argument concerns if it is religiously abominable or not. There is no way to deny that it is abominable in reason and in religion; everyone has accepted this argument. Since the scent of tobacco smoke and the scent of its leaves are not abominable in themselves, for it to be accepted as abominable, its excessive use is a condition.† . . .

The sixth argument is about its being unlawful or not. To produce a judgment on a topic through independent reasoning is accepted as a method in books of religious law. There are sufficient conditions collected to proscribe tobacco through an analysis of available proof. Yet it is preferable not to proclaim it forbidden. It is recommended to accept it as religiously permissible in order to protect people from insisting on sin by doing forbidden acts through the application of a legal principle.

The seventh argument is whether or not it is religiously permissible. Since tobacco appeared in recent times, it is not clearly considered and mentioned in books of religious law. Consequently, following the dictum, "In things permissibility is inherent," smoking is considered as permissible and legitimate. **"**

Source: *Mecmu'a-i Ulum* [Journal of Sciences] 1.2 (November 30, 1879): 79–125, trans. Selim S. Kuru.

*Some learned people argue that since the name of the island meant "sheet [*tabaka*]," a sheet of tobacco is named after that. However, this claim couldn't be verified.

†For example, as long as one doesn't drink boza [a slightly intoxicating drink made from millet] to the level that he gets drunk it is not religiously prohibited.

### QUESTIONS FOR ANALYSIS

1. What do you learn about social life in the Ottoman Empire from this essay?

2. What can you infer about the sorts of arguments that were made by Islamic jurists in Katib Chelebi's day?

3. How open-minded was Katib Chelebi? What evidence from the text led you to your conclusion?

and the use of narcotics. He forbade sati—the self-immolation of widows on their husbands' funeral pyres—and the castration of boys to be sold as eunuchs. He also abolished all taxes not authorized by Islamic law. To compensate for the loss of revenue, in 1679 Aurangzeb reimposed the tax on non-Muslims. Aurangzeb's reversal of Akbar's religious tolerance and cultural cosmopolitanism extended further. He ordered the destruction of some Hindu temples and tried to curb Sikhism. He also required Hindus to pay higher customs duties than Muslims. Out of fidelity to Islamic law, he even criticized his mother's tomb, the Taj Mahal: "The lawfulness of a solid construction over a grave is doubtful, and there can be no doubt about the extravagance involved."[4] Aurangzeb's attempts to enforce rigid

• **jizya** A poll tax on non-Muslims.

Islamic norms proved highly unpopular and aroused resistance that weakened Mughal rule. Aurangzeb himself died on an unsuccessful military campaign in 1707 to suppress a rebellion by the Marathas in the southern highlands.

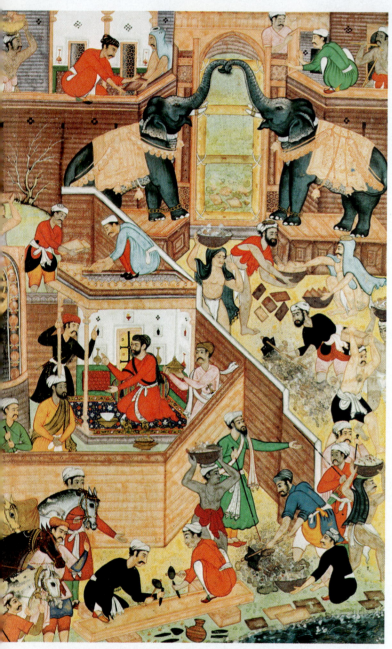

**Emperor Akbar in the City of Fatehpur Sikri** In 1569 Akbar founded the city of Fatehpur Sikri (the City of Victory) to honor the Muslim holy man Sheik Salim Chishti, who had foretold the birth of Akbar's son and heir Jahangir. Akbar is shown here seated on the cushion in the center overseeing the construction of the city. The image is contained in the *Akbarnama*, a book of illustrations Akbar commissioned to officially chronicle his reign. (Victoria & Albert Museum, London, UK/The Bridgeman Art Library)

# Shifting Trade Routes and European Penetration

☐ How were the Islamic empires affected by the gradual shift toward trade routes that bypassed their lands?

It has widely been thought that a decline in the wealth and international importance of the Muslim empires could be directly attributed to the long-term shift in trading patterns that resulted from the discoveries of Columbus, Magellan, and other European explorers. The argument is that new sea routes enabled Europeans to acquire goods from the East without using Muslim intermediaries, so that the creation of European colonial powers beginning in the sixteenth century led directly and indirectly to the eclipse of the Ottomans, Safavids, and Mughals. Recent scholars have challenged these ideas as too simplistic. First, it was not until the eighteenth century that political decline became evident in the three Islamic empires. Second, Turkish, Persian, and Indian merchants remained very active as long-distance traders into the eighteenth century and opened up many new routes themselves. It is true that in the Islamic empires New World crops like potatoes and sweet potatoes fueled population increases less rapidly than in western Europe and East Asia. By 1800 the population of India was about 190 million, that of Safavid lands about 8 million, and that of Ottoman lands about 24 million. (By comparison, China's population stood at about 300 million in 1800 and Russia's about 35 million.) But economic growth does not always correlate with population increases.

Over the centuries covered in this chapter, the Islamic empires became not only more tied to European powers but also more connected to each other. Europeans gained deeper knowledge of Islamic lands, but so did residents of these lands, who more frequently traveled to other Islamic countries and wrote about their travels. (For Ottoman subjects who visited other Islamic countries, see "Viewpoints 17.2: Ottoman Travelers in Muslim Lands," at right.)

## European Rivalry for Trade in the Indian Ocean

Shortly before Babur's invasion of India, the Portuguese had opened the subcontinent to Portuguese trade. In 1510 they established the port of Goa on the west coast of India as their headquarters and through an aggressive policy took control of Muslim shipping in the Indian Ocean and Arabian Sea, charging high fees to let ships through. The Portuguese historian Barrões

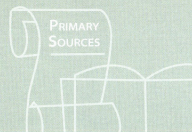

# Viewpoints 17.2

## Ottoman Travelers in Muslim Lands

• *As the Ottoman Empire expanded, soldiers, officers, and administrators were dispatched to distant lands. Just as European travelers wrote of their adventures and the unusual customs they encountered, so too did Ottoman travelers.*

*The first excerpt from such travel writing comes from Sidi Ali Reis (1498–1563), an Ottoman admiral whose ship was blown off course and shipwrecked in northwest India. With the winds against him, he returned overland through India, Afghanistan, and Persia, the journey taking three years (1554–1556). The second excerpt is from Mustafa Ali's "Description of Cairo," written in 1599. Ali was a career official who held a series of posts as a financial administrator and worked on a history of the world. Although he had requested an assignment in Egypt, thinking it would help him with his world history, he found much of which he did not approve there. The final excerpt is from the lengthy travel writings of Evliya Celebi (1611–1682). In this passage he reports on Tabriz, then under Safavid control, which he visited in 1640 in the entourage of an envoy. This region was predominantly Shi'a, which attracted Celebi's attention.*

### Sidi Ali Reis on His Journey Across India, 1554–1556

❝ The Sultan offered to give me an escort by the way of Lahore, warning me to be on my guard against the Djats, a hostile tribe which had its abode there. But whichever route I chose I should have to wait a while yet, and as a matter of fact I waited for a whole month. One night in my dream I saw my mother, who told me that she had seen her highness Fatima in a dream, and had learned from her the glad news that I should soon be coming home, safe and sound.

When next morning I told this dream to my companions they were full of good courage. Sultan Mahmud, when he heard of it, at once consented to my departure. He gave me a beautiful horse, a team of camels, a large and a small tent, and money for the journey. He also provided me with a letter of recommendation to Humayun, and an escort of 250 mounted camel-drivers from Sind. . . . On the second day we came to the spring, but found no water, and many of my companions nearly succumbed to heat and thirst. I gave them some Teriak [opium], of the very best quality, and on the second day they were recovered. After this experience we deemed it advisable to leave the desert and to return to Mav, for the proverb says truly, "A stranger is an ignorant man."

The people of Sind gave us permission to proceed as far as the Machvara, and this river was crossed by boats. On the other side we found 500 Djats awaiting us, but our firearms frightened them and they did not attack. We advanced unmolested, and reached the town of Multan on the fifteenth of Ramazan. ❞

### Mustafa Ali's "Description of Cairo," 1599

❝ Their women, all of them, ride donkeys! Even the spouses of some notables ride on donkeys to the Bulak promenade. Week after week they mount their donkeys and dismount like soldiers. Moreover, when they marry a daughter off they let her ride on a donkey and seventy or eighty women ride [with her], while the only things visible in terms of weapons are their shields. People of intelligence find that this unbecoming behavior constitutes a serious defect for the city of Cairo, because in other lands they put prostitutes on a donkey as a punishment. In Cairo the women mount donkeys by their own free will and expose themselves [to the eyes of the public]; therefore it appears appropriate that for punishment they be put on camels. ❞

### Evliya Celebi on His 1640 Visit to Tabriz

❝ Painters, architects, goldsmiths, and tailors are nowhere to be found so perfect as here. Precious stuffs manufactured here go all over the world; the velvet is much renowned. . . . Among the abundance of delicious fruits are particularly the pears and exquisite apricots; they are not found in such perfection even at Constantinople.

On New Year's day or the beginning of spring, battles are fought in this place by horses trained in the dark during forty or fifty days, by camels, buffaloes, sheep, asses, dogs, and cocks. These fights are peculiar to Persia. Every year on the tenth of the first month, being the feast of A'ashura, all the population of the town assemble under tents. . . . The finest show is in the variegated tent of the Khân, where all the great men of Tabriz are assembled, and where a Hymn on the death of Hussein is recited, in the same manner as the Hymn on the Prophet's birthday is in the Turkish mosques. The hearers listen, sighing and lamenting, but when the reciter arrives at the passage where Hussein is killed by accursed Shabr, a curtain opens behind him, and a severed head and trunk of a body, representing that of the Imam when dead, is thrown on the ground, when there rises such an uproar of cries and lamentations that everybody loses his wits. At this moment some hundred men mingle in the crowd with razors, with which they cut the arms and breasts of all loving believers, who desire to shed their blood on this day in remembrance of the blood shed by the Imam; they make such deep incisions and scars, that the ground appears as if it was blooming with tulips. ❞

Sources: Ármin Vámbéry, trans., *The Travels and Adventures of the Turkish Admiral Sidi Ali Reïs in India, Afghanistan, Central Asia, and Persia, During the Years 1553–1556* (London: Luzac, 1899); Andreas Tietze, trans., *Mustafa Ali's Description of Cairo of 1599* (Vienna: Verlag der Österreichischen Akademie der Wissenschaften, 1975), p. 41; Evliya Effendi, *Narrative of Travels in Europe, Asia, and Africa in the Seventeenth Century*, trans. Joseph von Hammer (London: William H. Allen, 1834), pp. 137–138, slightly modified.

### QUESTIONS FOR ANALYSIS

1. Why do you think these authors wrote about their experiences? Who was their likely audience?

2. Do you see any common themes or issues in these writings?

**MAP 17.3 India, 1707–1805**
In the eighteenth century Mughal power gradually yielded to the Hindu Marathas and to the British East India Company.

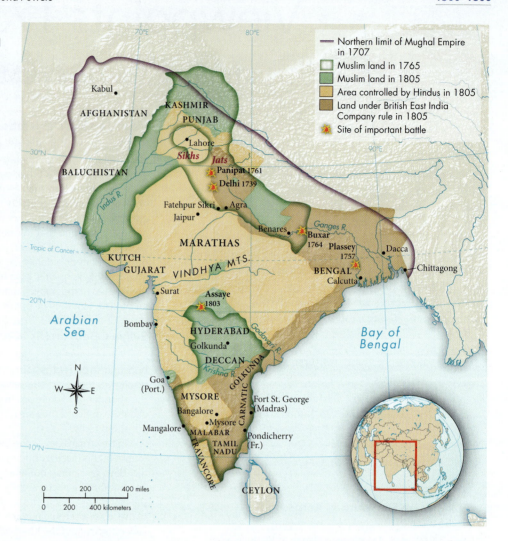

attempted to justify Portugal's seizure of commercial traffic that the Muslims had long dominated:

> It is true that there does exist a common right to all to navigate the seas and in Europe we recognize the rights which others hold against us; but the right does not extend beyond Europe and therefore the Portuguese as Lords of the Sea are justified in confiscating the goods of all those who navigate the seas without their permission.[5]

In short, the Portuguese decided that Western principles of international law should not restrict them in Asia. As a result, they controlled the spice trade over the Indian Ocean for almost a century.

In 1602 the Dutch formed the Dutch East India Company with the stated goal of wresting the enormously lucrative spice trade from the Portuguese. In 1685 they supplanted the Portuguese in Ceylon (Sri Lanka). The scent of fabulous profits also attracted the English. With a charter signed by Queen Elizabeth,

eighty London merchants organized the British East India Company. In 1619 Emperor Jahangir granted a British mission important commercial concessions. Soon, by offering gifts, medical services, and bribes to Indian rulers, the British East India Company was able to set up twenty-eight coastal forts/trading posts. By 1700 the company had founded the cities that became Madras and Calcutta (today called Chennai and Kolkata) and had taken over Bombay (today Mumbai), which had been a Portuguese possession (Map 17.3).

The British called their trading posts **factory-forts**. The term *factory* did not signify manufacturing; it designated the walled compound containing the residences, gardens, and offices of British East India Company officials and the warehouses where goods were stored before being shipped to Europe. The company president exercised political authority over all residents.

Factory-forts existed to make profits from Asian-European trade, which was robust due to the popularity of Indian and Chinese wares in Europe in the late seventeenth and early eighteenth centuries. The European middle classes wanted Indian textiles, which were colorful, durable, cheap, and washable. The upper classes

• **factory-forts** A term first used by the British for their trading post at Surat that was later applied to all European walled settlements in India.

**English Dress Made of Indian Printed Cotton Cloth** Early British traders in India were impressed with the quality of the textiles made there and began ordering designs that would be popular with the English. This dress, created around 1770–1780 in England, is made of printed cotton (chintz) from the southeastern part of India. Chintz became so popular in England that it was eventually banned because it was threatening local textile industries. (Victoria & Albert Museum, London, UK/Art Resource, NY)

desired Chinese wallpaper and porcelains and Indian silks and cottons. Other Indian goods in demand included pepper and other spices, sugar, and opium. To pay for these goods, the British East India Company sold silver, copper, zinc, lead, and fabrics to the Indians. Profits grew even larger after 1700, when the company began to trade with China.

## Merchant Networks in the Islamic Empires

The shifting trade patterns associated with European colonial expansion brought no direct benefit to the Ottomans and the Safavids, whose merchants could now be bypassed by Europeans seeking goods from India, Southeast Asia, or China. Yet merchants from these Islamic empires often proved adaptable, finding ways to benefit from the new trade networks.

In the case of India, the appearance of European traders led to a rapid increase in overall trade, helping Indian merchants and the Indian economy. Some Indian merchants in Calcutta and Bombay, for instance, made gigantic fortunes from trade within Asia carried on European ships. Block-printed cotton cloth, produced by artisans working at home, was India's chief export. Through an Islamic business device involving advancing payment to artisans, banker-brokers supplied the material for production and money for the artisans to live on while they worked; the cloth brokers specified the quality, quantity, and design of the finished products. This procedure resembles the later English "putting-out" or "domestic" system (see page 688), for the very good reason that the English took the idea from the Indians.

Within India the demand for cotton cloth, as well as for food crops, was so great that Akbar had to launch a wide-scale road-building campaign. From the Indian region of Gujarat, Indian merchant bankers shipped their cloth worldwide: across the Indian Ocean to Aden and the Muslim-controlled cities on the east coast of Africa; across the Arabian Sea to Muscat and Hormuz and up the Persian Gulf to the cities of Persia; up the Red Sea to the Mediterranean; by sea also to Malacca, Indonesia, China, and Japan; by land across Africa to Ghana on the west coast; and to Astrakhan, Poland, Moscow, and even the Russian cities on the

distant Volga River. Indian businessmen had branch offices in many of these places, and all this activity produced fabulous wealth for some Indian merchants. Some scholars have compared India's international trade in the sixteenth century with that of Italian firms, such as the Medici. Indian trade actually extended over a far wider area, however. Indian merchants were often devout Hindus, Muslims, Buddhists, or Jains, evidence that undermines the argument of some Western writers, notably Karl Marx (see page 722), that religion retarded Asia's economic development.

Throughout Muslim lands both Jews and Christians were active in commerce. A particularly interesting case involves the Armenian Christians in the Safavid Empire in the sixteenth to eighteenth centuries. Armenian merchants had been trading from their base in Armenia for centuries and were especially known for their trade in Persian silk. When the Portuguese first appeared on the western coast of India in 1498 and began to settle in south India, they found many Armenian merchant communities already there. A few decades later Akbar invited Armenians to settle in his new capital, Agra. In 1603 Shah Abbas captured much of Armenia, taking it from the Ottomans. Because defending this newly acquired border area was difficult, he forced the Armenians to move more deeply into Persia. Among them was the merchant community of Julfa, which was moved to a new suburb of Isfahan that was given the name New Julfa. The old city of Julfa was burned down so that the residents could not return. Shah Abbas made use of the Armenian merchants as royal merchants and financiers, but their economic mainstay continued to be long-distance trade.

Surviving letters and account books have allowed scholars to reconstruct the expanding trading networks of the Armenian merchants—networks that stretched from Venice and Amsterdam in western Europe, Moscow in Russia, and Ottoman-controlled Aleppo and Smyrna to all the major trading cities of India and even regions farther east, including Guangzhou in southern China and Manila in the Philippines. Many Armenian communities in these cities became quite substantial, built churches, and recruited priests. Kinship connections were regularly used to cement commercial relations, and members of the community living in these scattered cities would return to New Julfa to marry, creating new kinship connections. Business, though, was conducted through contracts. The merchant about to take a journey would borrow a sum of money to purchase goods and would contract to pay it back with interest on his return. Using couriers, these Armenian merchants sent long letters describing the trade environment and the prices that could be realized for given goods. These letters were written in a dialect of Armenian known to few outside their community, making it easier to maintain confidentiality in reports on trade conditions.

The Armenian merchants would sail on whatever ships were available, including Dutch and Italian ones. The goods they dealt in included silver, gold, precious stones, indigo and other dyestuffs, silk, cotton cloth, and tea. The merchants could often speak half a dozen languages and were comfortable in both Islamic and Christian lands. In India Armenian merchants reached an agreement with the British East India Company that recognized their rights to live in company cities and observe their own religion. By the 1660s they had settled in Manila, and a few decades later they entered what is now Malaysia and Indonesia. By the end of the seventeenth century a small group of Armenian merchants had crossed the Himalayas from India and established themselves in Lhasa, Tibet. By the mid-eighteenth century they had also settled in the Dutch colony of Batavia (Indonesia). Clearly the Armenian merchants were able to operate profitably in cities European powers dominated.

In the mid-eighteenth century the Armenian community lost its center in New Julfa because of religious persecution by a zealous shah, and the community scattered. Still, Armenian merchants remained prominent in many trading centers, including Russia, the Mediterranean, and especially India, well into the nineteenth century.

## From the British East India Company to the British Empire in India

Britain's presence in India began with the British East India Company and its desire to profit from trade. Managers of the company in London discouraged all unnecessary expenses and financial risks and thus opposed missionary activities or interference in local Indian politics. Nevertheless, the company responded to political instability in India in the early eighteenth century by extending political control. When warlords

**Armenian Brass Bowl** The inscription on this bowl dates it to 1616 and places it in New Julfa, the Armenian quarter of Isfahan. It would have been used by an Armenian Christian priest to wash his hands. (© Ana Melikian 2007)

appeared or an uprising occurred, people from the surrounding countryside flocked into the company's factory-forts, which gradually came to exercise political authority over the territories around them. The company's factories evolved into defensive installations manned by small garrisons of native troops—known as **sepoys**—trained in Western military weapons and tactics.

Britain eventually became the dominant foreign presence in India, despite challenges from the French. From 1740 to 1763 Britain and France were engaged in a tremendous global struggle, and India, like North America in the Seven Years' War, became a battlefield and a prize. The French won land battles, but English sea power proved decisive by preventing the landing of French reinforcements. The Treaty of Paris of 1763 recognized British control of much of India, marking the beginning of the British Empire in India.

How was Britain to govern so large a territory? Eventually, the East India Company was pushed out of its governing role because the English Parliament distrusted the company, believing it was corrupt. The Regulating Act of 1773 created the office of governor general to exercise political authority over the territory controlled by the company. The India Act of 1784 required that the governor general be chosen from outside the company, and it made company directors subject to parliamentary supervision.

Implementation of these reforms fell to three successive governors: Warren Hastings (r. 1774–1785), Lord Charles Cornwallis (r. 1786–1794), and the marquess Richard Wellesley (r. 1797–1805). Hastings sought allies among Indian princes, laid the foundations for the first Indian civil service, abolished tolls to facilitate internal trade, placed the salt and opium trades under government control, and planned a codification of Muslim and Hindu laws. Cornwallis introduced the British style of property relations, in effect converting a motley collection of former Mughal officers, tax collectors, and others into English-style landlords. The result was a new system of landholding in which the rents of tenant farmers supported the landlords. Wellesley was victorious over local rulers who resisted British rule, vastly extending British influence in India. Like most nineteenth-century British governors of India, Wellesley believed that British rule strongly benefited the Indians. With supreme condescension, he wrote that British power should be established over the Indian princes in order "to deprive them of the means of prosecuting any measure or of forming any confederacy hazardous to the security of the British empire, and to enable us to preserve the tranquility of India by exercising a general control over the restless spirit of ambition and violence which is characteristic of every Asiatic government."[6]

# Political Decline

☐ What common factors led to the decline of central power in the Islamic empires in the seventeenth and eighteenth centuries?

By the end of the eighteenth century all three of the major Islamic empires were on the defensive and losing territory (Map 17.4). They faced some common problems—succession difficulties, financial strain, and loss of military superiority—but their circumstances differed in significant ways as well.

The first to fall was the Safavid Empire. Persia did not have the revenue base to maintain the sort of standing armies that the Ottomans and the Mughals had. Decline in the strength of the army encouraged increased foreign aggression. In 1722 the Afghans invaded from the east, seized Isfahan, and were able to repulse an Ottoman invasion from the west. In Isfahan thousands of officials and members of the shah's family were executed. In the following century some potential leaders emerged, but none were able to reunite all of Persia. In this political vacuum, Shi'a religious institutions grew stronger.

The Ottoman Empire also suffered from poor leadership. Early Ottoman practice had guaranteed that the sultans would be forceful men. The sultan's sons gained administrative experience as governors of provinces and military experience on the battlefield as part of their education. After the sultan died, any son who wanted to succeed had to contest his brothers to claim the throne, after which the new sultan would have his defeated brothers executed. Although bloody, this system led to the succession of capable, determined men. After Suleiman's reign, however, the tradition was abandoned. To prevent threats of usurpation, sons of the sultan were brought up in the harem and confined there as adults, denied roles in government. The result was a series of rulers who were minor children or incompetent adults, leaving power in the hands of high officials and the mothers of the heirs. Political factions formed around viziers, military leaders, and palace women. In the contest for political favor, the devshirme was abandoned, and political and military ranks were filled by Muslims.

The Ottoman Empire's military strength also declined. The defeat of the Turkish fleet by the Spanish off the coast of Greece at Lepanto in 1571 marked the loss of Ottoman dominance in the Mediterranean. By the terms of a peace treaty with Austria signed at Karlowitz (1699), the Ottomans lost the major

---

• **sepoys**  The native Indian troops who were trained as infantrymen.

**MAP 17.4 The Muslim World, ca. 1700** The three great Islamic empires were adjacent to each other and of similar physical size. Many of their other neighbors were Muslim as well.

European provinces of Hungary and Transylvania, along with the tax revenues they had provided. Also, the Ottoman armies were depending more on mercenaries, and they did not keep up with the innovations in drill, command, and control that were then transforming European armies. From the late seventeenth century Ottoman armies began losing wars and territory along both northern and eastern borders. In 1774 the empire lost the lands on the northern bank of the Black Sea to Russia. In North Africa the local governors came to act more independently, sometimes starting hereditary dynasties.

In Mughal India the old Turkish practice of letting heirs fight for the throne persisted, leading to frequent struggles over succession, but also to strong rulers. Yet military challenges proved daunting there as well. After defeating his father and brothers, Aurangzeb made it his goal to conquer the south. The stiffest opposition came from the Marathas, a militant Hindu group centered in the western Deccan. From 1681 until his death

in 1707, Aurangzeb led repeated sorties through the Deccan. He took many forts and won several battles, but total destruction of the Maratha guerrilla bands eluded him.

Aurangzeb's death led to thirteen years of succession struggles, shattering the empire. His eighteenth-century successors were less successful than the Ottomans in making the dynasty the focus of loyalty. Mughal provincial governors began to rule independently, giving only minimal allegiance to the throne at Delhi. Meanwhile, the Marathas pressed steadily northward, constituting the gravest threat to Mughal authority. Threats also came from the west. In 1739 the Persian adventurer Nadir Shah invaded India, defeated the Mughal army, looted Delhi, and, after a savage massacre, carried off a huge amount of treasure, including the Peacock Throne. Constant skirmishes between the Afghans and the Marathas for control of the Punjab and northern India ended in 1761 at Panipat, where the Marathas were crushed by the Afghans. At that point, India no longer had a state strong enough to impose order on the subcontinent or check the penetration of the Europeans. Not until 1857, however, did the Mughal Dynasty come to a formal end.

In all three empires fiscal difficulties contributed to strain on the state. A long period of peace in the late sixteenth century and again in the mid-eighteenth century, as well as a decline in the frequency of visits of the plague, led to a doubling of the population. Increased population, coupled with the "little ice age" of the mid-seventeenth century, meant that the land could not sustain so many people, nor could the towns provide jobs for the thousands of agricultural workers who fled to them. The return of demobilized soldiers aggravated the problem. Inflation, famine, and widespread revolts resulted. The economic center of gravity shifted from the capital to the provinces, and politically the empire began to decentralize as well. Power was seized by local notables and military strongmen at the expense of central government officials. There was a positive side to increasing provincial autonomy, however, because it drew more people into political participation, thus laying a foundation for later nationalism. At the time, however, central government officials perceived the growth in provincial power in negative terms.

## CHRONOLOGY

| | |
|---|---|
| 1299–1326 | Reign of Osman, founder of the Ottoman Dynasty |
| 1299–1922 | Ottoman Empire |
| 1336–1405 | Life of Timur |
| ca. mid-1400s | Coffeehouses become center of Islamic male social life |
| 1453 | Ottoman conquest of Constantinople |
| 1501–1524 | Reign of Safavid Shah Isma'il |
| 1501–1722 | Safavid Empire |
| 1520–1558 | Hürrem wields influence in the Ottoman Empire as Suleiman's concubine and then wife |
| 1520–1566 | Reign of Ottoman sultan Suleiman I; period of artistic flowering in Ottoman Empire |
| 1521 | Piri Reis produces *Book of the Sea*, a navigational map book |
| 1526–1857 | Mughal Empire |
| 1556–1605 | Reign of Akbar in Mughal Empire |
| 1570 | Ottomans take control of Cyprus |
| 1571 | First major Ottoman defeat by Christians, at Lepanto |
| 1587–1629 | Reign of Shah Abbas; height of Safavid power; carpet weaving becomes major Persian industry |
| 1631–1648 | Construction of Taj Mahal under Shah Jahan in India |
| 1658–1707 | Reign of Aurangzeb; Mughal power begins to decline |
| 1763 | Treaty of Paris recognizes British control over much of India |

## Chapter Summary

After the decline of the Mongols in Central Asia and Persia, many small Turkic-ruled states emerged in the region from Anatolia through Afghanistan. Three of them went on to establish large empires: the Ottomans in Anatolia, the Safavids in Persia, and the Mughals in India. The Ottoman Empire's political system reached its classic form under Suleiman I. All authority flowed from the sultan to his public servants: provincial governors, police officers, military generals, heads of treasuries, and viziers. In Persia for some time Turkish lords competed for power, with no single one dominant until 1501, when a fourteen-year-old military leader declared himself shah. The strength of this Safavid state rested in part on the skills of urban bureaucrats, who were vital to the civil machinery of government. Babur, from his base in Afghanistan, founded the Mughal Empire in India. His grandson Akbar extended Mughal rule far into India. Whereas the Ottoman sultans and Safavid shahs used slaves acquired from non-Muslim lands for military and administrative positions, Akbar relied on the services of royal princes, nobles, and warrior-aristocrats. All three empires quickly adapted to new gunpowder technologies.

Each of the three Islamic empires presided over an extraordinary artistic and intellectual flowering in everything from carpetmaking and book illustration to architecture and gardening, from geography and astronomy to medicine. Each of these empires drew legitimacy from its support for Islam. There were, however, key differences: the Ottomans and Mughals supported the Sunni tradition, the Safavids the Shi'a tradition.

The three Islamic empires all had a substantial number of non-Muslim subjects. The Ottomans ruled over the Balkans, where most of the people were Christian, and Muslims in India were greatly outnumbered by Hindus.

European exploration opened new trade routes and enabled Europeans to trade directly with India and China, bypassing Muslim intermediaries in the Middle East. Within India British merchants increased their political control in politically unstable areas, leading before the end of the eighteenth century to a vast colonial empire in India.

By the end of the eighteenth century all three of the major Islamic empires were losing territory. The first to fall was the Safavid Empire, which could not maintain the sizable standing armies of the Ottomans and the Mughals. From the late seventeenth century Ottoman armies began losing wars along the northern and eastern borders, resulting in substantial loss of territory. Military challenges proved daunting in Mughal India as well. In all three empires, as central power declined, local notables and military strongmen seized power.

## NOTES

1. *Memoirs of Zehir-Ed-Din Muhammed Baber: Emperor of Hindustan,* trans. John Leyden and William Erskine (London: Longman and Cadell, 1826), p. 333.
2. Quoted in M. C. Beach, *The Imperial Image: Paintings for the Mughal Court* (Washington, D.C.: Freer Gallery of Art, Smithsonian Institution, 1981), pp. 9–10.
3. Quoted in V. A. Smith, *The Oxford History of India* (Oxford: Oxford University Press, 1967), p. 398.
4. Quoted in S. K. Ikram, *Muslim Civilization in India* (New York: Columbia University Press, 1964), p. 202.
5. Quoted in K. M. Panikkar, *Asia and Western Domination* (London: George Allen & Unwin, 1965), p. 35.
6. Quoted in W. Bingham, H. Conroy, and F. W. Iklé, *A History of Asia,* vol. 2 (Boston: Allyn and Bacon, 1967), p. 74.

## CONNECTIONS

From 1300 to 1800 and from North Africa to India, Islamic civilization thrived under three dynastic houses: the Ottomans, the Safavids, and the Mughals. All three empires had a period of expansion when territory was enlarged, followed by a high point politically and culturally, and later a period of contraction, when territories broke away. Two of the empires had large non-Muslim populations. India, even under Mughal rule, remained a predominantly Hindu land, and the Ottomans, in the process of conquering the Balkans, acquired a population that was largely Greek Orthodox Christians. Though all three states supported Islam, the Safavids took Shi'a teachings as orthodox, and the other two favored Sunni teachings. At the cultural level, the borders of these three states were porous, and people, ideas, art motifs, languages, and trade flowed back and forth.

In East Asia the fifteenth through eighteenth century also saw the creation of strong, prosperous, and expanding states, though in the case of China (under the Qing Dynasty) and Japan (under the Tokugawa Shogunate) the eighteenth century was a cultural high point, not a period of decline. The Qing emperors were Manchus, from the region northeast of China proper, reminiscent of the Mughals, who began in Afghanistan. As in the Islamic lands, during these centuries the presence of European powers became an issue in East Asia, though the details were quite different. Although one of the commodities that the British most wanted was the tea produced in China, Britain did not extend political control in China the way it did in India. Japan managed to refuse entry to most European traders after finding their presence and their support for missionary activity disturbing. The next chapter takes up these developments in East Asia.

# Review and Explore

## Make It Stick

 **LearningCurve**
Go online and use LearningCurve to retain what you've read.

## Identify Key Terms

Identify and explain the significance of each item below.

Ottomans (p. 491)          janissaries (p. 494)          ulama (p. 496)

Anatolia (p. 491)          concubine (p. 494)          Mughal (p. 496)

sultan (p. 491)          shah (p. 494)          jizya (p. 506)

viziers (p. 493)          Safavid (p. 494)          factory-forts (p. 510)

devshirme (p. 494)          Qizilbash (p. 494)          sepoys (p. 513)

## Review the Main Ideas

Answer the focus questions from each section of the chapter.

1. How were the three Islamic empires established, and what sorts of governments did they set up? (p. 490)
2. What cultural advances occurred under the rule of the Ottoman, Safavid, and Mughal Empires? (p. 498)
3. How did Christians, Jews, Hindus, and other non-Muslims fare under these Islamic states? (p. 505)
4. How were the Islamic empires affected by the gradual shift toward trade routes that bypassed their lands? (p. 508)
5. What common factors led to the decline of central power in the Islamic empires in the seventeenth and eighteenth centuries? (p. 513)

## Make Connections

Analyze the larger developments and continuities within and across chapters.

1. In what sense were the states of the Ottomans, Safavids, and Mughals empires rather than large states? Do all three equally deserve the term "empire"? Why or why not?
2. How did the expansion of European presence in the Indian Ocean after 1450 impinge on the societies and economies of each of the Islamic empires?
3. What made it possible for Islamic rulers to tolerate more religious difference than European Christian rulers of the same period?

**▷LaunchPad**

**Online Document Project**

> **Impressions of the Ottoman Empire**
>
> **How did Europeans view the Ottoman Empire?**
> Examine a Habsburg ambassador's impressions of the Ottoman Empire, and then complete a quiz and writing assignment based on the evidence and details from this chapter.
>
> *See inside the front cover to learn more.*

## Suggested Reading

Barkey, Karen. *Empire of Difference.* 2008. Places the history of the Ottomans in comparative perspective.

Casale, Giancarlo. *The Ottoman Age of Exploration.* 2011. Lively account of Ottoman rivalry with the Portuguese in the Indian Ocean in the sixteenth century.

Dale, Stephen Frederic. *The Garden of the Eight Paradises: Babur and the Culture of Empire in Central Asia, Afghanistan and India, 1483–1750.* 2004. A scholarly biography that draws on and analyzes Babur's autobiography.

Dale, Stephen Frederic. *The Muslim Empires of the Ottomans, Safavids, and Mughals.* 2010. A comparative study of the three empires, with much on religion and culture.

Findley, Carter Vaughn. *The Turks in World History.* 2005. Takes a macro look at the three Islamic empires as part of the history of the Turks.

Finkel, Caroline. *Osman's Dream: A History of the Ottoman Empire.* 2006. A new interpretation that views the Ottomans from their own perspective.

Inalcik, Halil, and Renda Günsel. *Ottoman Civilization.* 2002. A huge, beautifully illustrated, government-sponsored overview, with an emphasis on the arts and culture.

Jackson, Peter, and Lawrence Lockhart, eds. *The Cambridge History of Iran.* Vol. 6: *The Timurid and Safavid Periods.* 1986. A set of essays by leading scholars on the social and cultural, as well as the political and economic, history of Iran.

Lapidus, Ira M. *A History of Islamic Societies,* 2d ed. 2002. A comprehensive yet lucid survey.

Mukhia, Harbans. *The Mughals of India: A Framework for Understanding.* 2004. A short but thoughtful analysis of the Mughal society and state.

Parker, Charles H. *Global Interactions in the Early Modern Age, 1400–1800.* 2010. Places the Islamic empires in a global context.

Parthasarathi, Prasannan. *Why Europe Grew Rich and Asia Did Not: Global Economic Divergence, 1600–1850.* 2011. Focuses on India and how it compared to Britain in producing cotton and coal and making scientific advances.

Peirce, Leslie P. *The Imperial Harem: Women and Sovereignty in the Ottoman Empire.* 1993. A fresh look at the role of elite women under the Ottomans.

Richards, John F. *The Mughal Empire.* 1993. A coherent narrative history of the period 1526–1720.

Ruthven, Malise, and Azim Nanji. *Historical Atlas of Islam.* 2004. Provides numerous maps illustrating the shifting political history of Islamic states.

**Louis XIV**

In this painting, King Louis XIV receives foreign ambassadors to celebrate a peace treaty. The king grandly occupied the center of his court, which in turn served as the pinnacle for the French people and, at the height of his glory, for all of Europe. (Erich Lessing/Art Resource, NY)

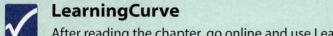

**LearningCurve**

After reading the chapter, go online and use LearningCurve to retain what you've read.

# Chapter Preview

**The Protestant and Catholic Reformations**

**Seventeenth-Century Crisis and Rebuilding**

**Absolutist States in Western and Central Europe**

**Constitutionalism and Empire in England and the Dutch Republic**

**Colonial Expansion and Empire**

**The Russian Empire**

The two centuries that open the period known as the early modern era witnessed crisis and transformation in Europe. What one historian has described as the long European "struggle for stability" originated with conflicts sparked by the Protestant and Catholic Reformations in the early sixteenth century and continued with economic and social breakdown into the late seventeenth century.[1] To consolidate their authority and expand their territories, European rulers increased the size of their armies, imposed higher taxes, and implemented bureaucratic forms of government. Thus, at the same time that powerful empires were emerging and evolving in Asia—the Qing Dynasty in China, the Tokugawa Shogunate in Japan, the Mughal Empire in India, the Ottoman Empire in Turkey, and the Safavid Empire in Iran—European rulers were also building strong imperial states.

Rising state power within Europe raised a series of pressing questions: Who held supreme power? What made it legitimate? Conflicts over these questions led to armed revolt and civil war. Between roughly 1589 and 1715 two basic patterns of government emerged from these conflicts: absolute monarchy and the constitutional state. Almost all subsequent European governments were modeled on one of these patterns, which have also greatly influenced the rest of the world.

Whether a government was constitutional or absolutist, an important foundation of state power was empire and colonialism. Jealous of the riches and prestige the Iberian powers gained from their overseas holdings, England, France, and the Netherlands vied for new acquisitions in Asia and the Americas, while Russia pushed its borders east to the Pacific. This was a distinctive moment in world history when exchange within and among empires produced constant movement of people, goods, and culture, with no one region or empire able to dominate the others entirely.

# The Protestant and Catholic Reformations

☐ How did the Protestant and Catholic Reformations change power structures in Europe and shape European colonial expansion?

In 1500 most of the world's Christians lived in Europe, and those who lived in western Europe belonged to one Christian Church headed by the pope in Rome, now known as the Roman Catholic Church. By 1600, and even more by 1750, Christians could be found throughout the world, but they belonged to many different churches that often competed with one another, sometimes on the battlefield. As a result of a movement of religious reform known as the **Protestant Reformation**, Western Christendom broke into many divisions in the sixteenth century. This splintering happened not only for religious reasons but also because of political and social factors. Religious transformation provided a source of power for many rulers and shaped European colonial expansion.

## The Protestant Reformation

In early-sixteenth-century western Europe, calls for reform in the church came from many quarters, both within and outside the church. Critics of the church concentrated their attacks on clerical immorality, ignorance, and absenteeism. Charges of immorality were aimed at a number of priests who were drunkards, neglected the rule of celibacy, gambled, or indulged in fancy dress. Charges of ignorance applied to barely literate priests who delivered poor-quality sermons and who were obviously ignorant of the Latin words of the Mass.

In regard to absenteeism, many clerics, especially higher ecclesiastics, held several benefices (offices) simultaneously—a practice termed pluralism. However, they seldom visited the communities served by the benefices, let alone performed the spiritual responsibilities those offices entailed. Instead, they collected revenues from all the benefices assigned to them and hired a poor priest to fulfill their spiritual duties, paying him just a fraction of the income.

There was also local resentment of clerical privileges and immunities. Priests, monks, and nuns were exempt from civic responsibilities, such as defending the city and paying taxes. Yet religious orders frequently held large amounts of urban property, in some cities as much as one-third. City governments were increasingly determined to integrate the clergy into civic life. This brought city leaders into opposition with bishops and the papacy, which for centuries had stressed the independence of the church from lay control and the distinction between members of the clergy and laypeople.

**Domestic Scene** The Protestant notion that the best form of Christian life was marriage and a family helps explain its appeal to middle-class urban men and women, such as those shown in this domestic scene. The large covered bed at the back was both a standard piece of furniture in urban homes and a symbol of proper marital sexual relations. (© Mary Evans Picture Library/The Image Works)

This range of complaints helps explain why the ideas of Martin Luther (1483–1546), a priest and professor of theology from the German University of Wittenberg, found a ready audience. Luther and other Protestants—the word comes from a "protest" drawn up by a group of reforming princes in 1529—developed a new understanding of Christian doctrine that emphasized faith, the power of God's grace, and the centrality of the Bible. Protestant ideas were attractive to educated people and urban residents, and they spread rapidly through preaching, hymns, and the printing press.

Luther lived in the Holy Roman Empire, a loose collection of largely independent states in which the emperor had far less authority than did the monarchs of western Europe. The Habsburg emperor, Charles V, may have ruled almost half of Europe along with Spain's overseas colonies, but within the empire local princes, nobles, and cities actually held the most power. Charles V was a staunch supporter of Catholicism, but the ruler of the territory in which Luther lived protected the reformer. Although Luther appeared before

• **Protestant Reformation** A religious reform movement that began in the early sixteenth century and split the Western Christian Church.

**MAP 18.1 Religious Divisions, ca. 1555** In the mid-sixteenth century, much of Europe remained Catholic. The Peace of Augsburg (1555) allowed the ruler of each territory in the Holy Roman Empire to determine the religion of its people. The northern territories of the empire became Lutheran, as did Scandinavia, while much of the southern empire remained Catholic. Sizable Calvinist populations existed in Scotland, the Netherlands, and central Europe. Eastern Europe was dominated by Orthodox Christianity, and the Ottoman Empire to the south and southeast was Muslim.

Charles V when he was summoned, he was not arrested and continued to preach and write.

Luther's ideas appealed to the local rulers of the empire for a variety of reasons. Though Germany was not a nation, people did have an understanding of being German because of their language and traditions. Luther frequently used the phrase "we Germans" in his attacks on the papacy, and his appeal to national feeling influenced many rulers. Also, while some German rulers were sincerely attracted to Lutheran ideas, material considerations swayed many others. The adoption of Protestantism would mean the legal confiscation of lush farmlands, rich monasteries, and wealthy shrines owned by Catholic monasteries and bishops.

Thus many political authorities in the empire used the religious issue to extend their power and to enhance their independence from the emperor. Luther worked closely with political authorities, viewing them as fully justified in reforming the church in their territories. Thus, just as in the Ottoman and Safavid Empires (see Chapter 17), rulers drew their legitimacy in part from their support for religion. By 1530 many parts of the Holy Roman Empire and Scandinavia had broken with the Catholic Church, with independent Protestant Churches set up in each state.

In England the issue of the royal succession triggered that country's break with Rome, and a Protestant church was established during the 1530s under King Henry VIII (r. 1509–1547) and reaffirmed under his daughter Elizabeth I (r. 1558–1603). As in the Holy Roman Empire, Henry dissolved the English monasteries and confiscated church property. Church offi-

**Jesuits** Members of the Society of Jesus, founded by Ignatius Loyola and approved by the papacy in 1540, whose goal was the spread of the Roman Catholic faith through humanistic schools and missionary activity.

cials were required to sign an oath of loyalty to the monarch, and people were required to attend services at the state church, which became known as the Anglican Church.

Protestant ideas also spread into France, the Netherlands, Scotland, and eastern Europe. In all these areas, a second generation of reformers built on earlier ideas to develop their own theology and plans for institutional change. The most important of the second-generation reformers was the Frenchman John Calvin (1509–1564), who reformed the city of Geneva, Switzerland, where a group of laymen and pastors known as the Consistory investigated and disciplined deviations from proper doctrine and conduct. Calvin believed that God was absolutely sovereign and omnipotent and that humans had no free will. Thus men and women could not actively work to achieve salvation, because God had decided at the beginning of time who would be saved and who damned, a theological principle called predestination.

The church in Geneva served as the model for the Presbyterian Church in Scotland, the Huguenot (HYOO-guh-naht) Church in France, and the Puritan Churches in England and New England. Calvinism became the compelling force in international Protestantism, first in Europe and then in many Dutch and English colonies around the world. Calvinism was also the dominant form of Protestantism in France. By the middle of the sixteenth century perhaps one-tenth of the French population was Huguenot (Map 18.1).

## The Catholic Reformation

In response to the Protestant Reformation, by the 1530s the papacy was leading a movement for reform within the Roman Catholic Church. After about 1540 no new large areas of Europe, other than the Netherlands, became Protestant. Many historians see the developments within the Catholic Church after the Protestant Reformation as two interrelated movements, one a drive for internal reform linked to earlier reform efforts and the other a Counter-Reformation that opposed Protestantism spiritually, politically, and militarily.

Under Pope Paul III (pontificate 1534–1549), the papal court became the center of the reform movement. Paul III established the Supreme Sacred Congregation of the Roman and Universal Inquisition, often called the Holy Office, with judicial authority over all Catholics and the power to imprison and execute. He also called a general council of the church, which met intermittently from 1545 to 1563 at the city of Trent. The Council of Trent laid a solid basis for the spiritual renewal of the Catholic Church. It gave equal validity to the Scriptures and to tradition as sources of religious truth and tackled problems that had disillusioned many Christians. Bishops were required to live in their

**Jesuits in China** This European image depicts early Jesuit missionaries baptizing converts in south China. (Archiv Gerstenberg—ullstein bild/The Granger Collection, NYC—All rights reserved.)

dioceses and to establish a seminary for educating and training clergy. Finally, it placed great emphasis on preaching to and instructing the laity. For four centuries the Council of Trent served as the basis for Roman Catholic faith, organization, and practice.

Just as seminaries provided education, so did new religious orders, which aimed to raise the moral and intellectual level of the clergy and people. The Ursuline (UHR-suh-luhn) order of nuns, founded by Angela Merici (1474–1540), attained enormous prestige for its education of women. After receiving papal approval in 1565, the Ursulines rapidly spread to France and the New World.

Another important new order was the Society of Jesus, or **Jesuits**. Founded by Ignatius Loyola (1491–1556) in 1540, this order played a powerful international role in strengthening Catholicism in Europe and spreading the faith around the world. While recuperating from a severe battle wound, Loyola studied religious books and decided to give up his military career and become a soldier of Christ. Recruited primarily from wealthy merchant and professional families, the Society of Jesus developed into a highly centralized organization. They established well-run schools to educate the sons of the nobility as well as the poor. The Jesuits achieved phenomenal success for the papacy and the reformed Catholic Church, carrying Christianity to South and Central America, India, and Japan before 1550 and to Brazil, North America, and the Congo in the seventeenth century. Within Europe the Jesuits brought almost all of southern Germany and much of eastern Europe back to Catholicism. Also, as confessors and spiritual directors to kings, Jesuits exerted great political influence.

## Religious Violence

Religious differences led to riots, civil wars, and international conflicts in Europe during the sixteenth century. The first battleground was Switzerland, where in the 1520s and 1530s Protestants and Catholics fought one another until both sides decided that a treaty was preferable to further fighting. The treaty allowed each part of Switzerland to determine its own religion and ordered each side to give up its foreign alliances, a policy of neutrality that has characterized Switzerland ever since.

In the Holy Roman Empire fighting began in 1546. The empire was a confederation of hundreds of principalities, independent cities, duchies, and other polities loosely united under an elected emperor. The initial success of Emperor Charles V led to French intervention on the side of the Protestants, lest the emperor acquire even more power. In 1555 Charles agreed to the Peace of Augsburg, which officially recognized Lutheranism and ended religious war in Germany for many decades. Under this treaty, the political authority in each territory of the Holy Roman Empire was permitted to decide whether the territory would be Catholic or Lutheran. Most of northern and central Germany became Lutheran, while southern Germany was divided between Lutheran and Catholic. His hope of uniting his empire under a single church dashed, Charles V abdicated in 1556, transferring power over his Spanish and Dutch holdings to his son Philip II and his imperial power to his brother Ferdinand.

In France Calvinists and Catholics each believed that the other's books, services, and ministers polluted the community. Armed clashes between Catholic royalists and Calvinist antiroyalists occurred in many parts of France. A savage Catholic attack on Calvinists in Paris on August 24, 1572 — Saint Bartholomew's Day — occurred at the marriage of the king's sister Margaret of Valois to the Protestant Henry of Navarre, which had been intended to help reconcile Catholics and Huguenots. The Saint Bartholomew's Day massacre initiated a civil war that dragged on for fifteen years, destroying agriculture and commercial life in many areas.

In the Netherlands the movement for church reform developed into a struggle for Dutch independence. In the 1560s Spanish authorities attempted to suppress Calvinist worship and raised taxes. Civil war broke out from 1568 to 1578 between Catholics and Protestants in the Netherlands and between the provinces of the Netherlands and Spain. Eventually the ten southern provinces — the Spanish Netherlands (the future Belgium) — came under the control of the Spanish Habsburg forces. The seven northern provinces, led by Holland, formed the Union of Utrecht (United Provinces of the Netherlands) and in 1581 declared their independence from Spain. The north was Protestant, and the south remained Catholic. Hostilities continued until 1609, when Spain agreed to a truce that recognized the independence of the northern provinces.

The era of religious wars was also the time of the most extensive witch persecutions in European history, as authorities tried to rid their cities and states of people they regarded as linked to the Devil. Both Protestants and Catholics tried and executed those accused of being witches, with church officials and secular authorities acting together. The heightened sense of God's power and divine wrath in the Reformation era was an important factor in the witch-hunts, as were new demonological ideas, legal procedures involving torture, and neighborhood tensions. Between 1450 and 1650 between 100,000 and 200,000 people were officially tried for witchcraft, and between 40,000 and 60,000 were executed. Though the gender balance of the accused varied widely in different parts of Europe, between 75 and 85 percent of those tried and executed were women, whom some demonologists viewed as weaker and so more likely to give in to the Devil.

# Seventeenth-Century Crisis and Rebuilding

☐ How did seventeenth-century European states overcome social and economic crisis to build strong states?

Historians often refer to the seventeenth century as an "age of crisis" because Europe faced population losses, economic decline, and social and political unrest. These difficulties were partially due to climate changes that reduced agricultural productivity. But they also resulted from military competition among European powers, the religious divides of the Reformations, increased taxation, and war. Peasants and the urban poor were especially hard hit by the economic problems, and they frequently rioted against high food prices.

The atmosphere of crisis encouraged governments to take emergency measures to restore order, measures that they successfully turned into long-term reforms that strengthened the power of the state. These included a spectacular growth in army size, as well as increased taxation, the expansion of government bureaucracies, and the acquisition of land or maritime empires. In the long run, European states proved increasingly able to impose their will on the populace.

## The Social Order and Peasant Life

Peasants occupied the lower tiers of a society organized in hierarchical levels. In much of Europe, the monarch occupied the summit, celebrated as a semidivine being chosen by God to embody the state. In Catholic countries, the clergy constituted the first order of society, due to its sacred role interceding with God and the saints on behalf of its flocks. Next came nobles, whose privileged status derived from their ancient bloodlines and centuries of sacrifice on the battlefield. Christian prejudices against commerce and money meant that merchants could never lay claim to the highest honors. However, many prosperous mercantile families had bought their way into the nobility through service to the monarchy in the fifteenth and sixteenth centuries, and they constituted a second tier of nobles. Those lower on the social scale, the peasants and artisans who formed the vast majority of the population, were expected to show humble deference to their betters. This was the "Great Chain of Being" that linked God to his creation in a series of ranked social groups.

In addition to being rigidly hierarchical, European societies were patriarchal, with men assuming authority over women as a God-given prerogative. The family represented a microcosm of the political order. The father ruled his family like a king ruled his domains. Religious and secular law commanded a man's wife, children, servants, and apprentices to respect and obey him. Fathers did not possess the power of life and death, like Roman patriarchs, but they were entitled to use physical violence, imprisonment, and other forceful measures to impose their authority. These powers were balanced by expectations that, like a wise king, a good father would care benevolently for his dependents.

In the seventeenth century the vast majority of Europeans lived in the countryside, as was the case in most parts of the world. The hub of the rural world was the small peasant village centered on a church and a manor. Life was in many ways circumscribed by the village, although one should not underestimate the mobility induced by war, food shortage, and the desire to seek one's fortune or embark on a religious pilgrimage.

In western Europe a small number of peasants owned enough land to feed themselves and possessed the live-

**Estonian Serfs in the 1660s** The Estonians were conquered by German military nobility in the Middle Ages and reduced to serfdom. The German-speaking nobles ruled the Estonian peasants with an iron hand, and Peter the Great reaffirmed their domination when Russia annexed Estonia. (Mansell Collection/Time and Life Pictures/Getty Images)

stock and plows necessary to work their land. Independent farmers were leaders of the peasant village. They employed the landless poor, rented out livestock and tools, and served as agents for the noble lord. Below them were small landowners and tenant farmers who did not have enough land to be self-sufficient. At the bottom were villagers who worked as dependent laborers and servants. Private landowning among peasants was a distinguishing feature of western Europe. In central and eastern Europe the vast majority of peasants toiled as serfs for noble landowners and did not own land in their own right, while in the Ottoman Empire all land belonged to the sultan.

Rich or poor, east or west, bread was the primary element of the European diet. The richest ate a white loaf, leaving brown bread to those who could not afford better. Peasants paid stiff fees to the local miller for grinding grain into flour and sometimes to the lord for the right to bake bread in his oven. Bread was most often accompanied by a soup made of roots, herbs, beans, and perhaps a small piece of salt pork. An important annual festival in many villages was the killing of the family pig. The whole family gathered to help, sharing a rare abundance of meat with neighbors and carefully salting the extra and putting down the lard. In some areas menstruating women were careful to stay away from the kitchen for fear they might cause the lard to spoil.

## Famine and Economic Crisis

Because of crude technology and low crop yield, peasants and urban laborers were constantly threatened by scarcity and famine. In the seventeenth century a period of colder and wetter climate throughout Europe, dubbed the "little ice age" by historians, meant a shorter farming season with lower yields. A bad harvest created food shortages; a series of bad harvests could lead to famine. Recurrent famines significantly reduced the population of early modern Europe through reduced fertility, susceptibility to disease, and outright starvation.

The Estates of Normandy, a provincial assembly, reported on the dire conditions in northern France during an outbreak of plague:

> Of the 450 sick persons whom the inhabitants were unable to relieve, 200 were turned out, and these we saw die one by one as they lay on the roadside. A large number still remain, and to each of them it is only possible to dole out the least scrap of bread. We only give bread to those who would otherwise die. The staple dish here consists of mice, which the inhabitants hunt, so desperate are they from hunger. They devour roots which the animals cannot eat; one can, in fact, not put into words the things one sees. . . .[2]

Industry also suffered. The output of woolen textiles, one of the most important European manufactures, declined sharply in the first half of the seventeenth century. Food prices were high, wages stagnated, and unemployment soared. This economic crisis was not universal: it struck various regions at different times and to different degrees. In the middle decades of the century, for example, Spain, France, Germany, and England all experienced great economic difficul-

ties, but these years were the golden age of the Netherlands (see page 541).

The urban poor and peasants were the hardest hit. When the price of bread rose beyond their capacity to pay, they frequently expressed their anger by rioting. In towns they invaded bakers' shops to seize bread and resell it at a "just price." In rural areas they attacked convoys taking grain to the cities. Women often led these actions, since their role as mothers gave them some impunity in authorities' eyes. Historians have used the term **moral economy** for this vision of a world in which community needs predominate over competition and profit.

## The Thirty Years' War

Harsh economic conditions in the seventeenth century were greatly exacerbated by the decades-long conflict known as the **Thirty Years' War** (1618–1648). Shifts in the balance between the population of Protestants and Catholics in the Holy Roman Empire led to the deterioration of the Peace of Augsburg. Lutheran princes felt compelled to form the Protestant Union (1608), and Catholics retaliated with the Catholic League (1609). Each alliance was determined that the other should make no religious or territorial advance. Dynastic interests were also involved; the Spanish Habsburgs strongly supported the goals of their Austrian relatives, which were the unity of the empire and the preservation of Catholicism within it.

The war began with a conflict in Bohemia (part of the present-day Czech Republic) between the Catholic League and the Protestant Union, but soon spread through the Holy Roman Empire, drawing in combatants from across Europe. After a series of initial Catholic victories, the tide of the conflict turned due to the intervention of Sweden, under its able king Gustavus Adolphus (r. 1594–1632), and then France, whose prime minister, Cardinal Richelieu, intervened on the side of the Protestants to undermine Habsburg power.

The 1648 Peace of Westphalia that ended the Thirty Years' War marked a turning point in European history. The treaties that established the peace not only ended conflicts fought over religious faith but also recognized the independent authority of more than three hundred German princes (Map 18.2), reconfirming the emperor's severely limited authority. The Augsburg agreement of 1555 became permanent, adding Calvinism to Catholicism and Lutheranism as legally permissible creeds. The north German states remained Protestant; the south German states, Catholic. The United Provinces of the Netherlands, known as the Dutch Republic, won official freedom from Spain.

The Thirty Years' War was probably the most destructive event in central Europe prior to the world wars of the twentieth century. Perhaps one-third of urban resi-

---

• **moral economy** The early modern European view that community needs predominated over competition and profit and that necessary goods should thus be sold at a fair price.

• **Thirty Years' War** A large-scale conflict extending from 1618 to 1648 that pitted Protestants against Catholics in central Europe, but also involved dynastic interests, notably of Spain and France.

MAP 18.2 **Europe After the Thirty Years' War** Which country emerged from the Thirty Years' War as the strongest European power? What dynastic house was that country's major rival in the early modern period?

dents and two-fifths of the rural population died, leaving entire areas depopulated. Trade in southern German cities was virtually destroyed. Agricultural areas also suffered catastrophically. Many small farmers lost their land, allowing nobles to enlarge their estates and consolidate their control.[3]

## European Achievements in State-Building

In this context of warfare, economic crisis, and demographic decline, European monarchs took urgent measures to restore order and rebuild their states. Traditionally, historians have distinguished between the absolutist governments of France, Spain, eastern and central Europe, and Russia and the constitutionalist governments of England and the Dutch Republic. Whereas absolutist monarchs gathered all power under their personal control, English and Dutch rulers were obliged to respect laws passed by representative institutions. More recently, historians have emphasized commonalities among these powers. Despite their political differences, all these states sought to protect and expand their frontiers, raise new taxes, consolidate central control, and compete for colonies and trade in the New and Old Worlds. In so doing, they followed a broad pattern of state-building and consolidation of power found across Eurasia in this period.

Rulers who wished to increase their authority encountered formidable obstacles. Without paved roads, telephones, or other modern technology, it took weeks to convey orders from the central government to the provinces and even longer to distant colonies. Rulers also suffered from lack of information about their realms, making it impossible to police and tax the population effectively. Local power structures presented another serious obstacle. Nobles, the church, provincial and national assemblies, town councils, guilds, and other corporate bodies held legal privileges that could not easily be rescinded. Many kingdoms were composed of groups who had different ethnicities or groups who spoke languages different from the Crown's, which further diminished their willingness to obey the monarch's commands.

Nonetheless, over the course of the seventeenth century both absolutist and constitutional governments achieved new levels of power and national unity. They did so by transforming emergency measures of wartime into permanent structures of government and by subduing privileged groups through the combined use of force and economic and social incentives. Increased state authority may be seen in four areas in particular: a tremendous growth in the size and professionalism of armies; much higher taxes; larger and more efficient bureaucracies; and territorial expansion both within Europe and overseas.

Over time, centralized power added up to something close to **sovereignty**. A state may be termed sovereign when it possesses a monopoly over the instruments of justice and the use of force within clearly defined boundaries. In a sovereign state, no nongovernmental system of courts, such as ecclesiastical tribunals, competes with state courts in the dispensation of justice. Also, private armies, such as those of feudal lords, present no threat to central authority. While seventeenth-century states did not acquire full sovereignty, they made important strides toward that goal.

# Absolutist States in Western and Central Europe

☐ How did absolutism evolve in the seventeenth century in Spain, France, and Austria?

Rulers in absolutist states asserted that, because they were chosen by God, they were responsible to God alone. Under the rule of **absolutism**, monarchs claimed exclusive power to make and enforce laws, denying any other institution or group the authority to check their power. Fervent Catholic faith had been a cornerstone of the unification of Spain in the fifteenth century, and it had helped integrate a Habsburg empire encom-

passing much of Europe and Spain's overseas empire. Yet, once the fabulous revenue from American silver declined, Spain's economic stagnation could no longer be disguised, and the country faltered under weak leadership. After the Thirty Years' War, the Austrian Habsburgs gave up on securing real power over the Holy Roman Empire and turned instead to consolidating authority within their own domains.

The decline of Habsburg power opened the door to a French bid for European domination. The Bourbon dynasty steered France's recovery from the religious conflicts of the late sixteenth century. Under Louis XIV, France led Europe in size, population, and military strength. Seen as the epitome of an absolute monarch, in truth Louis's success relied on collaboration with nobles, and thus his example illustrates both the achievements and the compromises of absolutist rule.

## Spain

The discovery of silver at Potosí in 1541 (see page 478) had produced momentous wealth for Spain, allowing it to dominate Europe militarily. Yet Spain had inherent weaknesses that the vast wealth of empire had hidden. It was a combination of different kingdoms with their own traditions and loyalties. Spanish silver had created great wealth but also dependency. While Creoles undertook new industries in the colonies and European nations targeted Spanish colonial trade, industry and finance in Spain itself remained undeveloped.

The impact of these developments became apparent during the first half of the seventeenth century. Between 1610 and 1650 Spanish trade with the colonies in the New World fell 60 percent due to competition from colonial industries and from Dutch and English traders. At the same time, frightful epidemics of disease decimated the enslaved workers who toiled in South American silver mines. Moreover, the mines started to run dry, and the quantity of metal produced steadily declined after 1620.

In Madrid royal expenditures constantly exceeded income. To meet mountainous state debt, the Spanish crown repeatedly devalued the coinage and declared bankruptcy, which resulted in the collapse of national credit. Meanwhile, commerce and manufacturing shrank. In the textile industry, manufacturers were forced out of business by steep inflation that pushed their production costs to the point where they could not compete in colonial and international markets.[4] To make matters worse, in 1609 the Crown expelled some three hundred thousand Moriscos, or former Muslims, significantly reducing the pool of skilled workers and merchants.

Spanish aristocrats, attempting to maintain an extravagant lifestyle they could no longer afford, increased the rents on their estates. High rents and

**Spanish Troops** The long wars that Spain fought over Dutch independence, in support of Habsburg interests in Germany, and against France left the country militarily exhausted and financially drained by the mid-1600s. In this detail from a painting by Peeter Snayers, Spanish troops — thin, emaciated, and probably unpaid — straggle away from battle. (detail, *Troops at the Siege of Aire Sur La Lys*, 1658, by Peeter Snayers [1592–1667]/Prado, Madrid, Spain/Index/The Bridgeman Art Library)

heavy taxes drove the peasants from the land, leading to a decline in agricultural productivity. In cities wages and production stagnated.

Spain's situation worsened with internal conflicts and fresh military defeats during the Thirty Years' War and the remainder of the seventeenth century. In the 1640s Spain faced serious revolts in Catalonia, the economic center of its realm; in Sicily; and in the Spanish Netherlands. In 1643 the French inflicted a crushing defeat on the Spanish army at Rocroi in what is now Belgium. The Treaty of Westphalia, which ended the Thirty Years' War, compelled Spain to recognize the independence of the Dutch Republic, and another treaty in 1659 granted extensive territories to France. Finally, in 1688 the Spanish crown reluctantly recognized the independence of Portugal. With these losses, the era of Spanish dominance in Europe ended.

## The Foundations of French Absolutism

At the beginning of the seventeenth century France's position appeared extremely weak. Struggling to recover from decades of religious civil war, France posed little threat to Spain's predominance in Europe. By the end of the century the countries' positions were reversed.

Henry IV (r. 1589–1610) inaugurated a remarkable recovery by defusing religious tensions and rebuilding France's economy. He issued the Edict of Nantes in 1598, allowing Huguenots (French Protestants) the right to worship in 150 traditionally Protestant towns throughout France. He built new roads and canals to repair the ravages of years of civil war and raised revenue by selling royal offices instead of charging high taxes. Despite his efforts at peace, Henry was murdered in 1610 by a Catholic zealot.

Cardinal Richelieu (1585–1642) became first minister of the French crown on behalf of Henry's young

- **sovereignty** Authority of states that possess a monopoly over the instruments of justice and the use of force within clearly defined boundaries and in which private armies present no threat to central control; seventeenth-century European states made important advances toward sovereignty.

- **absolutism** A political system common to early modern Europe in which monarchs claimed exclusive power to make and enforce laws, without checks by other institutions; this system was limited in practice by the need to maintain legitimacy and compromise with elites.

son Louis XIII (r. 1610–1643). Richelieu designed his domestic policies to strengthen royal control. He extended the use of intendants, commissioners for each of France's thirty-two districts who were appointed by and were responsible to the monarch. They recruited men for the army, supervised tax collection, presided over the administration of local law, checked up on the local nobility, and regulated economic activities in their districts. As the intendants' power increased under Richelieu, so did the power of the centralized French state.

Richelieu's main foreign policy goal was to destroy the Habsburgs' grip on territories that surrounded France. Consequently, Richelieu supported Habsburg enemies, including Protestants during the Thirty Years' War (see page 526). For the French cardinal, interests of state outweighed the traditional Catholic faith of France.

Cardinal Jules Mazarin (1602–1661) succeeded Richelieu as chief minister for the next child-king, the four-year-old Louis XIV, who inherited the throne from his father in 1643. Mazarin's struggle to increase royal revenues to meet the costs of the Thirty Years' War led to the uprisings of 1648–1653 known as the Fronde. In Paris magistrates of the Parlement of Paris, the nation's most important law court, were outraged by the Crown's autocratic measures. These so-called robe nobles (named for the robes they wore in court) encouraged violent protest by the common people. As rebellion spread outside Paris and to the sword nobles (the traditional warrior nobility), civil order broke down completely, and young Louis XIV had to flee Paris.

Much of the rebellion faded, however, when Louis XIV was declared king in his own right in 1651, ending the regency of his mother, Anne of Austria. Because French law prohibited women from inheriting the throne, royal authority was more easily challenged during periods when a queen-regent exercised power through a child-king. The French people were desperate for peace and stability after the disorders of the Fronde and were willing to accept a strong monarch who could restore order. Louis pledged to do just that when he assumed personal rule of his realm at Mazarin's death in 1661.

## Louis XIV and Absolutism

During the long reign of Louis XIV (r. 1643–1715), the French monarchy reached the peak of absolutist development. Louis believed in the **divine right of kings**: God had established kings as his rulers on earth, and they were answerable ultimately to him alone. To sym-

> • **divine right of kings** The belief propagated by absolutist monarchs that they derived their power from God and were only answerable to him.

bolize his central role in the divine order, when he was fifteen years old Louis danced at a court ballet dressed as the sun, thereby acquiring the title "Sun King." However, he also recognized that even though kings were divinely anointed and shared in the sacred nature of divinity, they could not simply do as they pleased. They had to obey God's laws and rule for the good of the people.

Like his counterpart, the Kangxi emperor of China, who inherited his realm only two decades after the Sun King did (see page 628), Louis XIV impressed his subjects with his majestic bearing and his discipline and hard work. (See "Viewpoints 18.1: Descriptions of Louis XIV of France and the Kangxi Emperor of China," at right.) Louis ruled his realm through several councils of state and insisted on taking a personal role in many of the councils' decisions. Despite increasing financial problems, Louis never called a meeting of the Estates General, the traditional French representative assembly composed of the three estates of clergy, nobility, and commoners. The nobility, therefore, had no means of united expression or action. Nor did Louis have a first minister. He alone was in command.

Although personally tolerant, Louis hated division. He insisted that religious unity was essential to his royal dignity and to the security of the state. In 1685 Louis revoked the Edict of Nantes, ordering the Catholic baptism of Huguenots, the destruction of Huguenot churches, the closing of schools, and the exile of Huguenot pastors who refused to renounce their faith. Around two hundred thousand Protestants, including some of the kingdom's most highly skilled artisans, fled France. Louis's insistence on "one king, one law, one religion" contrasts sharply with the religious tolerance exhibited by the Ottoman Empire (see page 505).

Despite his claims to absolute authority, there were multiple constraints on Louis's power. As a representative of divine power, he was obliged to rule in a way that seemed consistent with virtue and benevolent authority. He had to uphold the laws issued by his royal predecessors. Moreover, he also relied on the collaboration of nobles, who maintained authority in their ancestral lands. Without their cooperation, it would have been impossible for Louis to extend his power throughout France or wage his many foreign wars.

## Expansion Within Europe

Louis XIV kept France at war for thirty-three of the fifty-four years of his personal rule. Under the leadership of François le Tellier, marquis de Louvois, Louis's secretary of state for war, France acquired a huge professional army. The French army grew from roughly 125,000 men during the period of France's participation in the Thirty Years' War (1630–1648) to 250,000

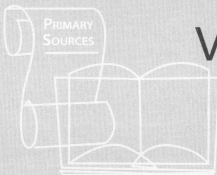

# Viewpoints 18.1

## Descriptions of Louis XIV of France and the Kangxi Emperor of China

• *King Louis XIV of France (1638–1715) and the Kangxi emperor of Ming China (1654–1722) lived remarkably parallel lives. They both inherited their thrones in childhood and learned the art of statecraft from powerful women, in Louis's case his mother, Queen Anne of Austria, and in Kangxi's case his grandmother, Grand Empress Dowager Xiaozhuang. Upon assuming personal control of their realms in adulthood, both men built magnificent palaces and gardens and proved their aptitude for hard work, discipline, and, above all, their thirst for glory and power. Although they never met in person, Louis sent Jesuit fathers to the Chinese court to spread European scientific and mathematical knowledge and the Catholic faith. The Kangxi emperor originally welcomed the Jesuits and was fascinated by the learning and technology they brought, but eventually banned them and Christianity from his realm (see page 644). The following descriptions of Louis XIV and the Kangxi emperor, written by a French courtier and a Jesuit missionary, respectively, underline the similar qualities observers noted in the two rulers.*

### The duc de Saint-Simon, *Memoirs of Louis XIV, His Court, and the Regency*

❝ [He was] the very figure of a hero, so impregnated with a natural but most imposing majesty that it appeared even in his most insignificant gestures and movements, without arrogance but with simple gravity. . . . He was as dignified and majestic in his dressing gown as when dressed in robes of state, or on horseback at the head of his troops.

He excelled in all sorts of exercise and liked to have every facility for it. No fatigue nor stress of weather made any impression on that heroic figure and bearing; drenched with rain or snow, pierced with cold, bathed in sweat or covered with dust, he was always the same. . . .

[He had] the ability to speak well and to listen with quick comprehension; much reserve of manner adjusted with exactness to the quality of different persons; a courtesy always grave, always dignified, always distinguished, and suited to the age, rank, and sex of each individual, and, for the ladies, always an air of natural gallantry. . . .

Nothing could be regulated with greater exactitude than were his days and hours. In spite of all his variety of places, affairs, and amusements, with an almanac and a watch one might tell, three hundred leagues away, exactly what he was doing. . . . If he administered reproof, it was rarely, in few words, and never hastily. He did not lose control of himself ten times in his whole life, and then only with inferior persons, and not more than four or five times seriously. ❞

### Father Joachim Bouvet, *The History of Cang-Hy, the Present Emperour of China*

❝ His whole Deportment is very Majestick, being well proportion'd in his Limbs, and pretty Tall, the Feature of his Face very exact, with a large and brisk Eye, beyond what is observable among others of that Nation; He is a little crooked Nosed, and pitted with the Small-pox, but not so as to be in the least disfigur'd by them.

But the rare Accomplishments of his Mind, surpass infinitely those of his Body. His Natural Genius is such as can be parallel'd but by few, being endow'd with a Quick and piercing Wit, a vast Memory, and Great Understanding; His Constancy is never to be shaken by any sinister Event, which makes him the fittest Person in the World, not only to undertake, but also to accomplish Great Designs.

To be short, his inclinations are so Noble, and in all respects so Answerable to the High Station of so Great a Prince, that his People stand in Admiration of his Person, being equally Charm'd with his Love and Justice, and the Tenderness he shews for his Subjects, and with his virtuous Inclinations; which as they are always guided by the Dictates of Reason, so, they render him an Absolute Master of his Passions. ❞

Sources: J. H. Robinson, ed., *Readings in European History*, vol. 2 (Boston: Ginn, 1906), pp. 285–286; Father Joachim Bouvet, *The History of Cang-Hy, the Present Emperour of China* (London: F. Coggan, 1699), p. 2.

### QUESTIONS FOR ANALYSIS

1. What qualities did the duc de Saint-Simon and Father Bouvet admire in Louis XIV and the Kangxi emperor? What similarities do you find among the qualities they describe?

2. Based on what you have read in this chapter, why was it important for an absolute ruler to possess the qualities they describe? What weaknesses do these excerpts suggest a would-be ruler should avoid, and why?

during the Dutch War (1672–1678) and 340,000 during the War of the League of Augsburg (1688–1697).[5] Uniforms and weapons were standardized, and a system of training and promotion was devised. As in so many other matters, Louis's model was emulated across Europe, amounting to a continent-wide transformation in military capability scholars have referred to as a "military revolution."

During this long period of warfare, Louis's goal was to expand France to what he considered its natural borders. His armies extended French borders to include important commercial centers in the Spanish Netherlands and Flanders as well as the entire province of Franche-Comté between 1667 and 1678. In 1681 Louis seized the city of Strasbourg, and three years later he sent his armies into the province of Lorraine. At that moment the king seemed invincible. In fact, Louis had reached the limit of his expansion. The wars of the 1680s and 1690s brought no additional territories and placed unbearable strains on French resources.

Louis's last war was endured by a French people suffering high taxes, crop failure, and widespread malnutrition and death. This war resulted from a dispute over the rightful successor to the Spanish throne. In 1700 the childless Spanish king Charles II (r. 1665–1700) died. His will bequeathed the Spanish crown and its empire to Philip of Anjou, Louis XIV's grandson (Louis's wife, Maria-Theresa, had been Charles's sister). The will violated a prior treaty by which the European powers had agreed to divide the Spanish possessions between the king of France and the Holy Roman emperor, both brothers-in-law of Charles II. Claiming that he was following both Spanish and French interests, Louis broke with the treaty and accepted the will, thereby triggering the War of the Spanish Succession (1701–1713).

In 1701 the English, Dutch, Austrians, and Prussians formed the Grand Alliance against Louis XIV. War dragged on until 1713, when it was ended by the Peace of Utrecht. This series of treaties allowed Louis's grandson Philip to remain king of Spain on the understanding that the French and Spanish crowns would never be united. France surrendered large territories overseas to England (Map 18.3; see also page 544).

The Peace of Utrecht marked the end of French expansion. Thirty-three years of war had given France the rights to all of Alsace (on France's present-day border with Germany and Switzerland) and some commercial centers in the north. But at what price? In 1714 an exhausted France hovered on the brink of bankruptcy. It is no wonder that when Louis XIV died on

September 1, 1715, many subjects felt as much relief as they did sorrow.

## The Economic Policy of Mercantilism

France's ability to build armies and fight wars depended on a strong economy. Fortunately for Louis, his controller general, Jean-Baptiste Colbert (1619–1683), proved to be a financial genius. Colbert's central principle was that the wealth and the economy of France should serve the state. To this end, from 1665 to his death in 1683, Colbert rigorously applied mercantilist policies to France.

**Mercantilism** is a collection of governmental policies for the regulation of economic activities by and for the state. It derives from the idea that a nation's international power is based on its wealth, specifically its supply of gold and silver. To accumulate wealth, a country always had to sell more goods abroad than it bought. Thus, to reduce imports, Colbert insisted that French industry should produce everything needed by the French people.

To increase exports, Colbert supported old industries and created new ones. He enacted new production regulations, created guilds to boost quality standards, and encouraged foreign craftsmen to immigrate to France. To encourage the purchase of French goods, he abolished many domestic tariffs and raised tariffs on foreign products. In 1664 Colbert founded the Company of the East Indies with hopes of competing with the Dutch for Asian trade. Colbert also sought to increase France's control over and presence in New France (Canada), which was rich in untapped minerals and contained some of the best agricultural land in the world (see page 839).

During Colbert's tenure as controller general, Louis was able to pursue his goals without massive tax increases and without creating a stream of new offices. The constant pressure of warfare after Colbert's death, however, undid many of his economic achievements.

## The Austrian Habsburgs

Absolutism was also the dominant form of monarchical rule among the many states that composed the Holy Roman Empire. Prussia, a minor power with scattered holdings, emerged in the seventeenth and eighteenth centuries under the Hohenzollern dynasty as a major rival to the Austrian Habsburg dynasty (see Chapter 19). Like all of central Europe, the Habsburgs emerged from the Thirty Years' War impoverished and exhausted. Their efforts to destroy Protestantism in the German lands and to turn the weak Holy Roman Empire into a real state had failed. Defeat in central

---

• **mercantilism** A system of economic regulations aimed at increasing the power of the state derived from the belief that a nation's international power was based on its wealth, specifically its supply of gold and silver.

## □ Mapping the Past

**MAP 18.3   Europe After the Peace of Utrecht, 1715**  The series of treaties commonly called the Peace of Utrecht ended the War of the Spanish Succession and redrew the map of Europe. A French Bourbon king succeeded to the Spanish throne. France surrendered the Spanish Netherlands (later Belgium), then in French hands, to Austria and recognized the Hohenzollern rulers of Prussia. Spain ceded Gibraltar to Great Britain, for which it has been a strategic naval station ever since. Spain also granted Britain the *asiento*, the contract for supplying African slaves to America.

**ANALYZING THE MAP**  Identify the areas on the map that changed hands as a result of the Peace of Utrecht. How did these changes affect the balance of power in Europe?

**CONNECTIONS**  How and why did so many European countries possess scattered or discontiguous territories? What does this suggest about European politics in this period? Does this map suggest potential for future conflict?

Europe encouraged the Austrian Habsburgs to turn away from a quest for imperial dominance and to focus inward and eastward in an attempt to unify their diverse holdings.

Habsburg victory over Bohemia during the Thirty Years' War was an important step in this direction. Ferdinand II (r. 1619–1637) drastically reduced the power of the Bohemian Estates, the largely Protestant representative assembly. He also confiscated the land-holdings of Protestant nobles and gave them to loyal Catholic nobles and to the foreign aristocratic merce-naries who led his armies. After 1650 a large portion of the Bohemian nobility was of recent origin and owed its success to the Habsburgs.

With the support of this new nobility, the Habsburgs established direct rule over Bohemia. Under their rule, the condition of the serfs worsened substantially. The Habsburgs also successfully eliminated Protestantism in Bohemia. These changes were important steps in creating absolutist rule.

Ferdinand III (r. 1637–1657) continued to build state power. He centralized the government in the empire's German-speaking provinces, which formed the core Habsburg holdings. For the first time, a permanent standing army was ready to put down any internal opposition. The Habsburg monarchy then turned east toward Hungary, which had been divided between the Ottomans and the Habsburgs in the early sixteenth century. Between 1683 and 1699 the Habsburgs pushed the Ottomans from most of Hungary and Transylvania. The recovery of all the former kingdom of Hungary was completed in 1718.

Despite its reduced strength, the Hungarian nobility effectively thwarted the full development of Habsburg absolutism. Throughout the seventeenth century Hungarian nobles periodically rose in revolt against the Habsburgs. They never triumphed decisively, but neither were they crushed. In 1703, with the Habsburgs bogged down in the War of the Spanish Succession, the Hungarians rose in one last patriotic rebellion under Prince Francis Rákóczy (RAH-coht-see). Rákóczy and his forces were eventually defeated, but the Habsburgs agreed to restore many of the traditional privileges of the Hungarian aristocracy in return for the country's acceptance of Habsburg rule. Thus Hungary was never fully integrated into a centralized, absolute Habsburg state.

Elsewhere, the Habsburgs made significant achievements in state-building by forging consensus with the church and the nobility. A sense of common identity and loyalty to the monarchy grew among elites in Habsburg lands, even to a certain extent in Hungary. German became the language of the state. As in France and Spain, rulers used Catholicism to fuse a collective identity. Vienna became the political and cultural center of the empire. By 1700 it was a thriving city with a population of one hundred thousand and a royal palace to rival that of Louis XIV in France.

## The Absolutist Palace

Through most of the seventeenth century the French court had no fixed home, following the monarch to his numerous residences. In 1682 Louis moved his court and government to the newly renovated palace at Versailles, in the countryside southwest of Paris. The palace quickly became the center of political, social, and cultural life. The king required all great nobles to spend at least part of the year in attendance on him there. Since he controlled the distribution of state power and wealth, nobles had no choice but to obey and compete with each other for his favor at Versailles.

Elaborate formal gardens were a crucial component of the palace. The themes of the sculptures in the Versailles gardens hailed Louis's power, with images of Apollo, the Roman sun god, and Neptune, the sea god, making frequent appearances. The rational orderliness and symmetry of the gardens showed that Louis's force extended even to nature, while its terraces and waterworks served as showcases for the latest techniques in military and civil engineering. Exotic plants and elaborate designs testified to the sovereign's global trading networks and cultivated taste.

Louis further revolutionized court life by establishing an elaborate set of etiquette rituals to mark every moment of his day, from waking up and dressing in the morning to removing his clothing and retiring at night. These rituals may seem absurd, but they were far from meaningless or trivial. The king controlled immense resources and privileges; access to him meant favored treatment for government offices, military and religious posts, state pensions, honorary titles, and a host of other benefits.

Courtiers sought these rewards for themselves and their family members and followers. A system of patronage—in which a higher-ranked individual protected a lower-ranked one in return for loyalty and services—flowed from the court to the provinces. Through this mechanism Louis gained cooperation from powerful nobles. Although they were denied public offices and posts, women played a central role in the patronage system. At court the king's wife, mistresses, and other female relatives recommended individuals for honors, advocated policy decisions, and brokered alliances between noble factions.

With Versailles as the center of European politics, French culture grew in international prestige. French became the language of polite society and international diplomacy, gradually replacing Latin as the language of scholarship and learning. The royal courts of Sweden, Russia, Poland, and Germany all spoke French. France inspired a cosmopolitan European culture in the late seventeenth century that looked to Versailles as its center.

**Austrian Expansion, to 1699**

Austrian Habsburg territory in 1648

Lands taken from Ottomans by Austrian Habsburgs, to 1699

Louis's rival European monarchs soon followed his example, and palace building became a Europe-wide phenomenon. In 1693 Charles XI of Sweden, having reduced the power of the aristocracy, ordered the construction of his Royal Palace, which dominates the center of Stockholm to this day. Another such palace was Schönbrunn, an enormous Viennese Versailles begun in 1695 by Emperor Leopold to celebrate Austrian military victories and Habsburg might. As Frederick the Great of Prussia noted, every descendant of a princely family "imagines himself to be something like Louis XIV. He builds his Versailles, has his mistresses, and maintains his army."[6]

# Constitutionalism and Empire in England and the Dutch Republic

☐ Why and how did the constitutional state triumph in England and the Dutch Republic?

While most European nations developed absolutist states in the seventeenth century, England and the Netherlands evolved toward **constitutionalism**, which is the limitation of government by law. Constitutionalism also implies a balance between the authority and power of the government, on the one hand, and the rights and liberties of the subjects, on the other.

After decades of civil war and an experiment with republicanism, the English opted for a constitutional monarchy in 1688. Under this system of government, England retained a monarch as the titular head of government but vested sovereignty in an elected parliament. For their part, the Dutch rejected monarchical rule in 1648, when their independence from Spain was formally recognized. Instead they adopted a republican form of government in which elected Estates (assemblies) held supreme power.

## Religious Divides and Civil War

In 1603 beloved Queen Elizabeth was succeeded by her Scottish cousin James Stuart, who ruled England as James I (r. 1603–1625). Like Louis XIV, James believed that a monarch had a divine right to his authority and was responsible only to God. James went so far as to lecture the English Parliament's House of Commons: "There are no privileges and immunities which can stand against a divinely appointed King." Such a view ran counter to the long-standing English tradition that a person's property could not be taken away without due process of law. James I and his son Charles I

(r. 1625–1649) considered such constraints a threat to their divine-right prerogative. Consequently, at every meeting of Parliament between 1603 and 1640, bitter squabbles erupted between the Crown and the House of Commons.

Religious issues also embittered relations between the king and the House of Commons. In the early seventeenth century many English people felt dissatisfied with the Church of England established by Henry VIII. Calvinist **Puritans** wanted to take the Reformation further by "purifying" the Anglican Church of Roman Catholic elements—elaborate vestments and ceremonials, bishops, and even the giving and wearing of wedding rings. James I responded to such ideas by declaring, "No bishop, no king." For James, bishops were among the chief supporters of the throne. His son and successor, Charles I, further antagonized subjects by marrying a French Catholic princess and supporting the high-handed policies of archbishop of Canterbury William Laud (1573–1645).

Charles avoided direct confrontation by refusing to call Parliament into session from 1629 to 1640, financing his government through extraordinary stopgap levies considered illegal by most English people. However, when Scottish Calvinists revolted in anger against his religious policies, Charles was forced to summon Parliament to obtain funding for an army to put down the revolt. Angry with the king's behavior and sympathetic with the Scots' religious beliefs, the House of Commons passed the Triennial Act in 1641, which compelled the king to call Parliament every three years. The Commons also impeached Archbishop Laud and then threatened to abolish bishops. King Charles, fearful of a Scottish invasion—the original reason for summoning Parliament—reluctantly accepted these measures. The next act in the conflict was precipitated by the outbreak of rebellion in Ireland, where English governors and landlords had long exploited the people. In 1641 the Catholic gentry of Ireland led an uprising in response to a feared invasion by British anti-Catholic forces.

Without an army, Charles I could neither come to terms with the Scots nor respond to the Irish rebellion. After a failed attempt to arrest parliamentary leaders, Charles left London for the north of England, where he began to raise an army. In response, Parliament

● **constitutionalism** A form of government in which power is limited by law and balanced between the authority and power of the government, on the one hand, and the rights and liberties of the subject or citizen, on the other; it includes constitutional monarchies and republics.

● **Puritans** Members of a sixteenth- and seventeenth-century reform movement within the Church of England that advocated purifying it of Roman Catholic elements, such as bishops, elaborate ceremonials, and wedding rings.

**Puritan Occupations** These twelve engravings depict typical Puritan occupations and show that the Puritans came primarily from the artisan and lower middle classes. The governing classes and peasants made up a much smaller percentage of Puritans, and most generally adhered to the traditions of the Church of England. (Visual Connection Archive)

formed its own army, the New Model Army. During the spring of 1642 both sides prepared for war.

The English Civil War (1642–1649) pitted the power of the king against that of Parliament. After three years of fighting, Parliament's army defeated the king's forces at the Battles of Naseby and Langport in the summer of 1645. Charles refused to concede defeat, and both sides waited for a decisive event. This arrived in the form of the army under the leadership of Oliver Cromwell, a member of the House of Commons and a devout Puritan. In 1647 Cromwell's troops captured the king and dismissed members of the Parliament who opposed Cromwell's actions. In 1649 the remaining representatives, known as the Rump Parliament, put Charles on trial for high treason. Charles was found guilty and beheaded on January 30, 1649, an act that sent shock waves around Europe.

**The English Civil War, 1642–1649**

## The Puritan Protectorate

With the execution of Charles, the monarchy was abolished. The question then became how the country would be governed. One answer was provided by philosopher Thomas Hobbes (1588–1679). Hobbes held a pessimistic view of human nature and believed that, left to themselves, humans would compete violently for power and wealth. The only solution, as he outlined in his 1651 treatise *Leviathan*, was a social contract in which all members of society placed themselves under the absolute rule of a monarch who would maintain peace and order. Hobbes imagined society as a human body in which the monarch served as head and individual subjects together made up the body. Just as the body cannot sever its own head, so Hobbes believed that society could not, having accepted the contract, rise up against its king.

Hobbes's longing for a benevolent absolute monarch was not widely shared in England. Instead a commonwealth, or republican government, was proclaimed. Theoretically, legislative power rested in the surviving members of Parliament, and executive power was lodged in a council of state. In fact, the army that had defeated the king controlled the

**The Massacre at Drogheda**
In September 1649 English forces under Oliver Cromwell laid siege to Drogheda, a town on the east coast of Ireland, and killed approximately three thousand soldiers and civilians when they entered the town. The Drogheda massacre long fostered hatred of Cromwell and English rule in Ireland. (Rue des Archives/The Granger Collection, NYC — All rights reserved.)

government, and Oliver Cromwell controlled the army. Though called the Protectorate, the rule of Cromwell (1653–1658) was a form of military dictatorship. Reflecting Puritan ideas of morality, Cromwell's state forbade sports, kept the theaters closed, and rigorously censored the press.

On the issue of religion, Cromwell favored some degree of tolerance, and the Instrument of Government gave all Christians except Roman Catholics the right to practice their faiths. Cromwell had long associated Catholicism in Ireland with sedition and heresy, and he led an army there to reconquer the country in August 1649. Following Cromwell's reconquest, the English banned Catholicism in Ireland, executed priests, and confiscated land from Catholics for English and Scottish settlers. These brutal acts left a legacy of Irish hatred for England and did little to undermine Catholicism.

The Protectorate collapsed when Cromwell died in 1658 and his ineffectual son succeeded him. Fed up with military rule, the English longed for a return to civilian government and, with it, common law and social stability. By 1660 they were ready to restore the monarchy.

## Constitutional Monarchy

The Restoration of 1660 brought to the throne Charles II (r. 1660–1685), the eldest son of Charles I. Both houses of Parliament were also restored, as was the Anglican Church. However, Charles was succeeded by his Catholic brother James II, arousing fears of a return of Catholicism. A group of eminent persons in Parliament and the Church of England offered the English throne to James's Protestant daughter Mary and her Dutch husband, Prince William of Orange. In December 1688 James II, his queen, and their infant son fled to France. Early in 1689 William and Mary were crowned king and queen of England.

The English called the events of 1688 and 1689 the Glorious Revolution because they believed it replaced one king with another with barely any bloodshed. In truth, William's arrival sparked riots and violence across the British Isles and in North American cities such as Boston and New York. Uprisings by supporters of James, known as Jacobites, occurred in 1689 in Scotland. In Ireland the two sides waged outright war from 1689 to 1691. William's victory at the Battle of the Boyne (1690) and the subsequent Treaty of Limerick (1691) sealed his accession to power.

In England the revolution represented the final destruction of the idea of divine-right monarchy. The men who brought about the revolution framed their intentions in the **Bill of Rights of 1689**, which was formulated in direct response to Stuart absolutism. Law was to be made in Parliament; once made, it could not be suspended by the Crown. Parliament had to be called at least once every three years. The Bill of Rights also established the independence of the judiciary and mandated that there be no standing army in peacetime.

**Bill of Rights of 1689** A bill passed by Parliament and accepted by William and Mary that limited the powers of British monarchs and affirmed those of Parliament.

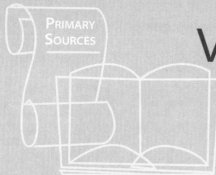
# Viewpoints 18.2

## The Debate over the Extent of Royal Power in England

• *In 1688 King James II of England fled to France, fearing a revolution like the one that led to the trial and execution of his father, Charles I. The crisis was resolved when Parliament invited James's daughter Mary and her husband, William of Orange, to take the throne in James's place. This Glorious Revolution, as it was called, generated furious debate over the extent of royal power in England. Thomas Cartwright, a bishop of the Church of England, spoke out in defense of James and his God-given right to rule. Taking the opposite side, John Locke argued that sovereign power resided in the people, who could reject a monarch if he set himself above the law. In 1689 William and Mary ended the debate by signing the Bill of Rights, which enshrined the rights of Parliament and limited the authority of the monarch.*

### Thomas Cartwright, A Sermon Preached upon the Anniversary Solemnity of the Inauguration of Our Dread Sovereign Lord King James II

❝ Our religion will never suffer us to dispense with our loyalty, to serve any worldly interest or advantage; no, not for its own defense. It sets the crown fast and easy upon the King's head, without catechizing him: for be his heart inclinable to any religion, or none, it leaves him no rival, none to insult or lord it over him. It disclaims all usurpation, popular or papal; neither pope nor presbyter may control him; none but the great God, the only ruler of princes, can over-rule him; to whom 'tis his duty, glory and happiness to be subject. Though the King should not please or humor us; though he should rend off the mantle from our bodies (as Saul did from Samuel), nay though he should sentence us to death (of which, blessed be God and the King, there is no danger), yet if we are living members of the Church of England, we must neither open our mouths, nor lift our hands against him; but honor him before the people and elders of Israel. ❞

### John Locke, *Two Treatises of Government*

❝ But government into whosesoever hands it is put, being as I have before shown, entrusted with this condition, and for this end, that men might have and secure their properties, the prince or senate, however it may have power to make laws for the regulation of property between the subjects one amongst another, yet can never have a power to take to themselves the whole, or any part of the subjects' property without their own consent. For this would be in effect to leave them no property at all.

. . . The constitution of the legislative is the first and fundamental act of society, whereby provision is made for the continuation of their union, under the direction of persons, and bonds of laws, made by persons authorized thereunto, by the consent and appointment of the people, without which no one man, or number of men, amongst them, can have authority of making laws that shall be binding to the rest. When any one, or more, shall take upon them to make laws, whom the people have not appointed so to do, they make laws without authority, which the people are not therefore bound to obey; by which means they come again to be out of subjection, and may constitute to themselves a new legislative, as they think best, being in full liberty to resist the force of those, who, without authority, would impose any thing upon them. ❞

Source: Steven C. A. Pincus, *England's Glorious Revolution, 1688–1689: A Brief History with Documents* (Boston: Bedford/St. Martin's, 2006), pp. 71–72 (Cartwright), 161–164 (Locke).

### QUESTIONS FOR ANALYSIS

1. How does Cartwright justify James's right to rule England? Are there any limitations on royal authority, according to Cartwright?

2. What is the reason for people forming a government, according to Locke? When are they justified in disobeying laws and rejecting the authority of government?

### ◻ Picturing the Past

***The Young Scholar and His Wife*** A new genre of painting emerged in the seventeenth century celebrating the virtues of domestic life and family. It was particularly popular in the wealthy, urban Netherlands, among prosperous families such as the couple depicted here. (*The Young Scholar and His Wife*, 1640, oil on panel by Gonzales Coques [1614–84]/Gemaeldegalerie Alte Meister, Kassel, Germany/© Museumslandschaft Hessen Kassel/The Bridgeman Art Library)

**ANALYZING THE IMAGE** What social and cultural values does this painting seem to celebrate? What insight does the painter offer into masculine and feminine roles in this society? Why do you think the husband and wife are standing separately and not together, as they probably would in a modern family portrait?

**CONNECTIONS** Based on your reading in this chapter, how might the portrait of a more typical European family of 1640 differ from this one? Why would a family in the Netherlands have a different lifestyle from many families in other European countries?

Protestants could possess arms, but the Catholic minority could not. Catholics could not inherit the throne. Additional legislation granted freedom of worship to Protestant dissenters but not to Catholics. William and Mary accepted these principles when they took the throne, and Parliament passed the Bill of Rights in December 1689. The Glorious Revolution and the concept of representative government found its best defense in political philosopher John Locke's *Second Treatise of Civil Government* (1690). Locke (1632–1704) maintained that a government that oversteps its proper function—protecting the natural rights of life, liberty, and property—becomes a tyr-

anny. (See "Viewpoints 18.2: The Debate over the Extent of Royal Power in England," at left.) By "natural rights," Locke meant rights basic to all men because all have the ability to reason. Under a tyrannical government, he argued, the people have the natural right to rebellion.

Although the events of 1688 and 1689 brought England closer to Locke's ideal, they did not constitute a democratic revolution. The Glorious Revolution placed sovereignty in Parliament, and Parliament represented the upper classes. Nondemocratic government lasted in England at least until 1832 and in many ways until 1928, when all women received voting rights.

# Individuals in Society

## Glückel of Hameln

**IN 1690 A JEWISH WIDOW IN THE SMALL GERMAN TOWN** of Hameln in Lower Saxony sat down to write her autobiography. She wanted to distract her mind from the terrible grief she felt over the death of her husband and to provide her twelve children with a record. She told them that she was writing her memoirs "so you will know from what sort of people you have sprung, lest today or tomorrow your beloved children or grandchildren came and know naught of their family." Out of her pain and heightened consciousness, Glückel (1646–1724) produced an invaluable source for scholars.

She was born in Hamburg two years before the end of the Thirty Years' War. In 1649 the merchants of Hamburg expelled the Jews, who moved to nearby Altona, then under Danish rule. When the Swedes overran Altona in 1657–1658, the Jews returned to Hamburg "purely at the mercy of the Town Council." Glückel's narrative unfolds against a background of the constant harassment to which Jews were subjected—special papers, permits, bribes—and in Hameln she wrote, "And so it has been to this day and, I fear, will continue in like fashion."

When Glückel was "barely twelve," her father betrothed her to Chayim Hameln, and they married when she was fourteen. She describes him as "the perfect pattern of the pious Jew," a man who stopped his work every day for study and prayer, fasted, and was scrupulously honest in his business dealings. Only a few years older than Glückel, Chayim earned his living dealing in precious metals and in making small loans on pledges (pawned goods). This work required constant travel to larger cities, markets, and fairs, often in bad weather, always over dangerous roads. Chayim consulted his wife about all his business dealings. As he lay dying, a friend asked if he had any last wishes. "None," he replied. "My wife knows everything. She shall do as she has always done." For thirty years Glückel had been his friend, full business partner, and wife. They had thirteen children, twelve of whom survived their father, eight then unmarried. As Chayim had foretold, Glückel succeeded in launching the boys in careers and in providing dowries for the girls.

Glückel's world was her family, the Jewish community of Hameln, and the Jewish communities into which her children married. Her social and business activities took her across Europe, from Amsterdam to Berlin, from Danzig to Vienna; thus her world was far from narrow or provincial. She took great pride that Prince Frederick of Cleves, later king of Prussia, danced at the wedding of her eldest daughter. The rising prosperity of Chayim's businesses allowed the couple to maintain up to six servants.

Glückel was deeply religious, and her culture was steeped in Jewish literature, legends, and mystical and secular works. Above all, she relied on the Bible. Her language, heavily sprinkled with scriptural references, testifies to a rare familiarity with the Scriptures.

Students who wish to learn about seventeenth-century business practices, the importance of the dowry in marriage, childbirth, Jewish life, birthrates, family celebrations, and even the meaning of life can gain a good deal from the memoirs of this extraordinary woman who was, in the words of one of her descendants, the poet Heinrich Heine, "the gift of a world to me."

Source: *The Memoirs of Glückel of Hameln* (New York: Schocken Books, 1977).

**QUESTIONS FOR ANALYSIS**

1. Consider the ways in which Glückel of Hameln was both an ordinary and an extraordinary woman of her times. Would you call her a marginal or a central person in her society? Why?

2. How might Glückel's successes be attributed to the stabilizing force of absolutism in the seventeenth century?

**LaunchPad**
## Online Document Project

**What factors shaped life for European Jews in the early modern era?** Read excerpts from Glückel of Hameln's memoirs and other accounts of Jewish life, and then complete a quiz and writing assignment based on the evidence and details from this chapter.

*See inside the front cover to learn more.*

**Although no images of Glückel exist, Rembrandt's *The Jewish Bride* suggests the mutual devotion of Glückel and her husband.** (Rijksmuseum, Amsterdam, The Netherlands/The Bridgeman Art Library)

## The Dutch Republic

The independence of the Republic of the United Provinces of the Netherlands was recognized in 1648 in the treaty that ended the Thirty Years' War. Rejecting the rule of a monarch, the Dutch adopted a system of **republicanism**, whereby power rested in the hands of the people and was exercised through elected representatives. Other republics of the time included the Swiss Confederation and several autonomous city-states of Italy and the Holy Roman Empire. Among the Dutch, an oligarchy of wealthy businessmen called regents handled domestic affairs in each province's Estates, or assemblies. The provincial Estates held virtually all the power. A federal assembly, or States General, handled foreign affairs and war, but it did not possess sovereign authority. All issues had to be referred back to the local Estates for approval, and each of the seven provinces could veto any proposed legislation. Holland, the province with the largest navy and the most wealth, usually dominated the republic and the States General.

In each province, the Estates appointed an executive officer, known as the stadholder, who carried out ceremonial functions and was responsible for military defense. Although in theory freely chosen by the Estates, in practice the reigning prince of Orange usually held the office of stadholder in several of the seven provinces of the republic. Tensions persisted between supporters of the House of Orange and those of the staunchly republican Estates, who suspected the princes of harboring monarchical ambitions. When one of them, William III, took the English throne in 1689 with his wife, Mary, the republic simply continued without stadholders for several decades.

Global trade and commerce brought the Dutch the highest standard of living in Europe, perhaps in the world. Salaries were high, and all classes of society ate well. A scholar has described the Netherlands as "an island of plenty in a sea of want." Consequently, the Netherlands experienced very few of the food riots that characterized the rest of Europe.[7]

The moral and ethical bases of their commercial wealth were thrift, frugality, and religious tolerance. Jews enjoyed a level of acceptance and assimilation in Dutch business and general culture unique in early modern Europe. (See "Individuals in Society: Glückel of Hameln," at left.) In the Dutch Republic tolerance not only seemed the right way, but also earned profits by attracting a great deal of foreign capital and investment. After Louis XIV revoked the Edict of Nantes, many Huguenots fled France for the Dutch Republic. They brought with them a high level of artisanal skill and business experience, as well as a loathing for state repression that would help inspire the political views of the Enlightenment (see page 565).

## Colonial Expansion and Empire

□ How did European nations compete for global trade and empire in the Americas and Asia?

For almost a century after the fall of the Aztec capital of Tenochtitlan, the Spanish and Portuguese dominated European overseas trade and colonization (see Chapter 16). In the early seventeenth century, however, England, France, and the Netherlands challenged Spain's monopoly. They eventually succeeded in creating overseas empires, consisting of settler colonies in North America, slave plantations in the Caribbean, and scattered trading posts in West Africa and Asia.

### The Dutch Trading Empire

The so-called golden age of the Dutch Republic in the seventeenth century was built on its commercial prosperity and its highly original republican system of government. The Dutch came to dominate European shipping by putting profits from their original industry (herring fishing) into shipbuilding. They then took aim at Portugal's immensely lucrative Asian trade empire.

In 1599 a Dutch fleet returned to Amsterdam from a voyage to Southeast Asia carrying 600,000 pounds of pepper and 250,000 pounds of cloves and nutmeg. Those who had invested in the expedition received a 100 percent profit. The voyage led to the establishment in 1602 of the Dutch East India Company, founded with the stated intention of capturing the spice trade from the Portuguese.

In return for assisting Indonesian princes in local squabbles and disputes with the Portuguese, the Dutch won broad commercial concessions. Through agreements, seizures, and outright military aggression, they gained control of the western access to the Indonesian archipelago in the first half of the seventeenth century. Gradually, they acquired political domination over the archipelago itself. The Dutch were willing to use force more ruthlessly than the Portuguese and had superior organizational efficiency. These factors allowed them to expel the Portuguese from Ceylon and other East Indian islands in the 1660s and henceforth dominate the production and trade of spices. The company also established the colony of Cape Town on the southern tip of Africa as a provisioning point for its Asian fleets.

Not content with challenging the Portuguese in the Indian Ocean, the Dutch also aspired to a role in the

---

• **republicanism** A form of government in which there is no monarch and power rests in the hands of the people as exercised through elected representatives.

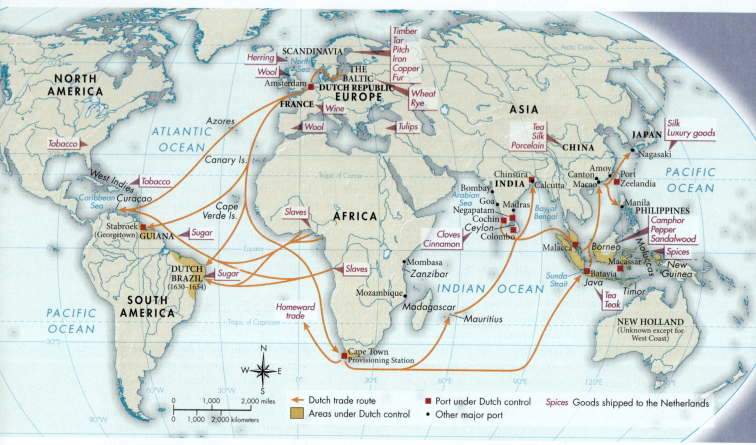

**MAP 18.4 Seventeenth-Century Dutch Commerce** Dutch wealth rested on commerce, and commerce depended on the huge Dutch merchant marine, manned by perhaps forty-eight thousand sailors. The fleet carried goods from all parts of the globe to the port of Amsterdam.

Americas (Map 18.4). Founded in 1621, the Dutch West India Company aggressively sought to open trade with North and South America and capture Spanish territories there. The company captured or destroyed hundreds of Spanish ships, seized the Spanish silver fleet in 1628, and claimed portions of Brazil and the Caribbean. The Dutch also successfully interceded in the transatlantic slave trade, establishing a large number of trading stations on the west coast of Africa. Ironically, the nation that was known throughout Europe as a bastion of tolerance and freedom came to be one of the principal operators of the slave trade starting in the 1640s.

## Colonial Empires of England and France

England and France followed the Dutch in challenging Iberian dominance overseas. Unlike the Iberian powers, whose royal governments financed exploration and directly ruled the colonies, England, France, and the Netherlands conducted the initial phase of colonization through chartered companies with monopolies over settlement and trade in a given area. These corpo-

rate bodies were granted extensive powers over faraway colonies, including the right to monopolize trade, make war, raise taxes, and administer justice.

After an unsuccessful first colony at Roanoke (in what is now North Carolina), the English colony of Virginia, founded at Jamestown in 1607, gained a steady hold by producing tobacco for a growing European market. Indentured servants obtained free passage to the colony in exchange for several years of work and the promise of greater opportunity than in England. In the 1670s English colonists from the Caribbean island of Barbados settled Carolina, where conditions were suitable for large rice plantations. During the late seventeenth century enslaved Africans replaced indentured servants as laborers on tobacco and rice plantations, and a harsh racial divide was imposed.

For the first settlers on the coast of New England, the reasons for seeking a new life in the colonies were more religious than economic. Many of these colonists were radical Protestants escaping Anglican repression. The small and struggling outpost of Plymouth Colony (1620) was followed by Massachusetts Bay Colony (1630), which grew into a prosperous settlement. Religious disputes in Massachusetts led to the dispersion of settlers into the new communities of Providence, Connecticut, Rhode Island, and New Haven. Because New England lacked the conditions for plantation agriculture, slavery was always a minor factor there.

English settlements hugged the Atlantic coastline, but this did not prevent conflicts with the indigenous inhabitants over land and resources. The haphazard nature of English colonization also led to conflicts of authority within the colonies. As the English crown grew more interested in colonial expansion, efforts were made to acquire the territory between New England in the north and Virginia in the south. The goal was to unify English holdings and minimize French and Dutch competition on the Atlantic seaboard. The results of these efforts were the mid-Atlantic colonies: the Catholic settlement of Maryland (1632); New York, captured from the Dutch in 1664; and the Quaker colony of Pennsylvania (1681).

Whereas English settlements were largely agricultural, the French established trading factories in present-day Canada, much like those in Asia and Africa. In 1608 Samuel de Champlain founded the first permanent French settlement at Quebec as a post for trading beaver pelts with local Algonquin and Huron peoples.

The settlement of Ville-Marie, later named Montreal, followed in 1642. Louis XIV's capable controller general, Jean-Baptiste Colbert, established direct royal control over New France (Canada) and tried to enlarge its population by sending colonists.

French immigration to New Canada remained small compared with the stream of settlers who came to British North America; nevertheless, the French were energetic and industrious traders and explorers. Following the waterways of the St. Lawrence River, the Great Lakes, and the Mississippi River, they ventured into much of North America in the 1670s and 1680s. In 1673 the Jesuit Jacques Marquette and the merchant Louis Joliet sailed down the Mississippi and claimed possession of the land on both sides of the river as far south as present-day Arkansas. In 1682 Robert de La Salle traveled the Mississippi to the Gulf of Mexico, opening the way for French occupation of Louisiana.

**European Claims in North America, 1714**

**The Fur Trade** In the early seventeenth century, European fur traders relied on Native Americans' expertise and experience, leading to the equal relations depicted in this scene from the colony of New Sweden (in modern-day Pennsylvania). The action in the background shows violence among indigenous groups, rivalries exacerbated by contact with Europeans and their trade goods. Hudson's Bay Company, the English colonial trading company, issued its own tokens as currency in the fur trade. This token, dating from the mid-nineteenth century, displays the company's crest, which says "a skin for a skin" in Latin. Two stags face each other, with a fox at the top and four beavers on the shield. Traders received tokens for the pelts they sold and could use them to purchase goods from the company's store. European demand for beaver hats, made from the felted pelts of beavers, drove the tremendous expansion of the North American fur trade in the beginning of the seventeenth century. (engraving: From *Geographia Americae with An Account of the Delaware Indians, Based on Surveys and Notes Made 1654–1656*, by Peter Lindestrom, published by The Swedish Colonial Society/Visual Connection Archive; token: © National Maritime Museum, London, UK/The Image Works)

In the first decades of the seventeenth century, English and French captains also challenged Spain's hold over the Caribbean (see Map 19.2, page 579). The English seized control of Bermuda (1612), Barbados (1627), and a succession of other islands. The French took Cayenne (1604), St. Christophe (1625), Martinique and Guadeloupe (1635), and, finally, Saint-Domingue (1697) on the western half of Spanish-occupied Hispaniola. These islands acquired new importance after 1640, when the Portuguese brought sugar plantations to Brazil. Sugar and slaves quickly followed in the West Indies (see pages 477–478), making the Caribbean plantations the most lucrative of all colonial possessions.

The northern European powers also expanded in Africa and Asia. In the 1600s France and England—along with Denmark and other northern European powers—established fortified trading posts, or factories, in West Africa as bases for purchasing slaves and in India and the Indian Ocean for spices and other luxury goods. Thus, by the end of the seventeenth century, a handful of European powers possessed overseas empires that truly spanned the globe.

## Mercantilism and Colonial Wars

Trade to and among European overseas possessions was governed by mercantilist economic policy (see page 532). The acquisition of colonies was intended to favor the wealth and power of the mother country, and to that end, European states—starting with Spain in the sixteenth century—imposed trading monopolies on their overseas colonies and factories. The mercantilist notion of a "zero-sum game," in which any country's gain must come from another country's loss, led to hostile competition and outright warfare among European powers over their colonial possessions.

In England Oliver Cromwell established the first of a series of **Navigation Acts** in 1651, and the restored monarchy of Charles II extended them in 1660 and 1663. The acts required most goods imported into England and Scotland (Great Britain after 1707) to be carried on British-owned ships with British crews or on ships of the country producing the article. Moreover, these laws gave British merchants and shipowners a virtual monopoly on trade with British colonies. The colonists were required to ship their products on British (or American) ships and to buy almost all European goods from Britain. These economic regulations were intended to eliminate foreign competition and to encourage the development of a British shipping

• **Navigation Acts** Mid-seventeenth-century English mercantilist laws that greatly restricted other countries' rights to trade with England and its colonies.

industry whose seamen could serve when necessary in the Royal Navy.

The Navigation Acts were a form of economic warfare against the Dutch, who were far ahead of the English in shipping and foreign trade in the mid-seventeenth century. In conjunction with three Anglo-Dutch wars between 1652 and 1674, the Navigation Acts seriously damaged Dutch shipping and commerce. By the late seventeenth century the Netherlands was falling behind England in shipping, trade, and settlement.

Thereafter France was England's most serious rival in the competition for overseas empire. Rich in natural resources and home to a population three or four times that of England, France was continental Europe's leading military power. It was already building a powerful fleet and a worldwide system of rigidly monopolized colonial trade. But the War of the Spanish Succession, the last of Louis XIV's many wars (see page 532), tilted the balance in favor of England. The 1713 Peace of Utrecht forced France to cede its North American holdings in Newfoundland, Nova Scotia, and the Hudson Bay territory to Britain. Spain was compelled to give Britain control of its West African slave trade—this contract was called the *asiento* (ah-SYEHN-toh)—and to let Britain send one ship of merchandise into the Spanish colonies annually. These acquisitions primed Britain to take a leading role in the growing Atlantic trade of the eighteenth century, including the transatlantic slave trade (discussed in Chapter 19).

## People Beyond Borders

As they seized new territories, European nations produced maps proudly outlining their possessions. The situation on the ground, however, was often much more complicated than the lines on those maps would suggest. Many groups of people lived in the contested frontiers between empires, habitually crisscrossed their borders, or carved out niches within empires where they carried out their own lives in defiance of the official rules.

Restricted from owning land and holding many occupations in Europe, Jews were eager participants in colonial trade and established closely linked mercantile communities scattered across many different empires. Similarly, a community of Christian Armenians in Isfahan in the Safavid Empire formed the center of a trade network extending from London to Manila and Acapulco. Family ties and trust within these minority groups were a tremendous advantage in generating the financial credit and cooperation necessary for international commerce. Yet Jews and Armenians were minorities where they settled and vulnerable to persecution. For example, restrictions existed on the number of slaves Jews could own in Barbados in the early eighteenth century, and the end of Persian tolerance in the same period led to the dispersion of Armenians from Isfahan.

Other groups openly defied the law. The growth in world trade attracted smugglers who routinely violated colonial trade monopolies as well as bandits eager to profit from the vulnerability of fleets laden with precious silver or spices. During the seventeenth century piracy was endemic in the Caribbean islands, as well as in the South China Sea, in the western Indian Ocean, and along the north African coast. States often encouraged predatory attacks by authorizing privateers to raid the ships of countries with which they were at war. A thin line thus separated illegal piracy from legal privateering. Another important group of outlaw communities in the Caribbean islands were Maroons, runaway slaves who took advantage of the mountainous terrain to establish secret settlements where they could live in freedom.

The nomadic Cossacks and Tartars who inhabited the steppes of the Don River basin that bordered the Russian and Ottoman Empires are yet another example of "in-between" peoples. Often depicted as warring pawns of the two great powers whose clients they became, in fact the Cossacks and the Tartars maintained considerable political and cultural autonomy through the seventeenth century and enjoyed a degree of peaceful interaction. By the eighteenth century, however, both Ottoman and Russian rulers had expanded state control in their frontiers and had reined in the raiding and migration of nomadic steppe peoples. As their example suggests, the assertion of state authority in the seventeenth and eighteenth centuries made it progressively harder for all of these groups to retain autonomy from the grip of empire.

## The Russian Empire

☐ How did Russian rulers build a distinctive absolutist monarchy and expand into a vast and powerful empire?

Russia occupied a unique position among Eurasian states. With borders straddling eastern Europe and northwestern Asia, its development into a strong imperial state drew on elements from both continents. Like the Muslim empires in Central and South Asia and the Ming Dynasty in China, the expansion of Russia was a result of the weakening of the great Mongol and Timurid Empires (see Chapters 16 and 17). After declaring independence from the Mongols, the Russian tsars conquered a vast empire, extending through North Asia all the way to the Pacific Ocean. State-building and territorial expansion culminated during the reign of Peter the Great, who turned Russia toward the West by intervening in western European wars and politics and forcing his people to adopt elements of Western culture.

**Russian Peasants** An eighteenth-century French artist visiting Russia recorded his impressions of the daily life of the Russian people in this etching of a fish merchant pulling his wares through a snowy village on a sleigh. Two caviar vendors behind him make a sale to a young mother standing at her doorstep with her baby in her arms. (From Jean-Baptiste Le Prince's second set of Russian etchings, 1765. Private Collection/Gérard PIERSON/www.amis-paris-petersbourg.org)

## Mongol Rule in Russia and the Rise of Moscow

In the thirteenth century the Mongols had conquered Kievan Rus, the medieval Slavic state centered first at Novgorod and then at Kiev, a city on the Dnieper River, which included most of present-day Ukraine, Belarus, and part of northwest Russia. For two hundred years the Mongols forced the Slavic princes to submit to their rule and to render tribute and slaves. The princes of the Grand Duchy of Moscow, also known as Muscovy, a principality within Kievan Rus, became particularly adept at serving the Mongols. They loyally put down uprisings and collected the khan's taxes. Eventually the Muscovite princes were able to destroy the other princes who were their rivals for power. Ivan III (r. 1462–1505), known as Ivan the Great, greatly expanded the principality of Moscow, claiming large territories in the north and east to the Siberian frontier.

By 1480 Ivan III was strong enough to refuse to pay tribute to the Mongols and declare the autonomy of Moscow. To legitimize his new position, Ivan and his successors borrowed elements of Mongol rule. They forced weaker Slavic principalities to render tribute previously paid to Mongols and adopted Mongol institutions such as the tax system, postal routes, and census. Loyalty from the highest-ranking nobles, or boyars, helped the Muscovite princes consolidate their power.

Another source of legitimacy lay in Moscow's claim to the political and religious inheritance of the Byzantine Empire. After the empire's capital, Constantinople, fell to the Ottomans in 1453, the princes of Moscow saw themselves as heirs of the Byzantine caesars (emperors) and guardians of the Orthodox Christian Church. Ivan III's marriage to the daughter of the last Byzantine emperor enhanced Moscow's claim to have inherited imperial authority. The title *tsar*, first taken by Ivan IV in 1547, is a contraction of *caesar*.

## Building the Russian Empire

Developments in Russia took a chaotic turn with the reign of Ivan IV (r. 1533–1584), the famous Ivan the Terrible, who ascended to the throne at age three. His mother died, possibly poisoned, when he was eight, leaving Ivan to suffer insults and neglect from the boyars at court. At age sixteen he suddenly pushed aside his hated advisers and crowned himself tsar.

After the sudden death of his wife, however, Ivan began a campaign of persecution against those he sus-

pected of opposing him. He executed members of leading boyar families, along with their families, friends, servants, and peasants. To replace them, Ivan created a new service nobility, whose loyalty was guaranteed by their dependence on the state for land and titles.

As landlords demanded more from the serfs who survived the persecutions, growing numbers of peasants fled toward recently conquered territories to the east and south. There they joined free groups and warrior bands known as **Cossacks**. Ivan responded by tying serfs ever more firmly to the land and to noble landholders. Simultaneously, he ordered that urban dwellers be bound to their towns and jobs so that he could tax them more heavily. The urban classes had no security in their property, and even the wealthiest merchants were dependent agents of the tsar. These restrictions checked the growth of the Russian middle classes and stood in sharp contrast to economic and social developments in western Europe.

Ivan's reign was successful in defeating the remnants of Mongol power, adding vast new territories to the realm, and laying the foundations for the huge multi-ethnic Russian empire. In the 1550s, strengthened by an alliance with Cossack bands, he conquered the Muslim khanates of Kazan and Astrakhan and brought the fertile steppe region around the Volga River under Russian control. In the 1580s Cossacks fighting for the Russian state crossed the Ural Mountains and began the long conquest of Siberia. Because of the size and distance of the new territories, the Russian state did not initially seek to impose the Orthodox religion and maintained local elites in positions of honor and leadership, buying their loyalty with grants of land. In relying on cooperation from local elites and ruthlessly exploiting the common people, the Russians followed the pattern of the Spanish and other early modern European imperial states.

Following Ivan's death, Russia entered a chaotic period known as the Time of Troubles (1598–1613). While Ivan's relatives struggled for power, the Cossacks and peasants rebelled against nobles and officials. This social explosion from below brought the nobles together. They crushed the Cossack rebellion and elected Ivan's grandnephew, Michael Romanov (r. 1613–1645), the new hereditary tsar. (See "Listening to the Past: A German Account of Russian Life," page 548.) The Romanov dynasty would endure as one of the most successful European absolutist dynasties until the Russian Revolution of 1917.

Despite the turbulence of the period, the Romanov tsars, like their western European counterparts, made further achievements in territorial expansion and state-building. After a long war, Russia gained land to the west in Ukraine in 1667, after allying with Cossacks in rebellion against Poland. By the end of the century it

• **Cossacks** Free groups and outlaw armies living on the borders of Russian territory from the fourteenth century onward. By the end of the sixteenth century they had formed an alliance with the Russian state.

**Peter the Great** This compelling portrait by Grigory Musikiysky captures the strength and determination of the warrior-tsar in 1723, after more than three decades of personal rule. In his hand Peter holds the scepter, symbol of royal sovereignty, and across his breastplate is draped an ermine fur, a mark of honor. In the background are the battleships of Russia's new Baltic fleet and the famous St. Peter and St. Paul Fortress that Peter built in St. Petersburg. Peter the Great commissioned this magnificent new crown (right) for himself for his 1682 joint coronation with his half brother Ivan. (crown: bpk, Berlin/Kremlin Museum, Moscow, Russia/Art Resource, NY; portrait: Hermitage, St. Petersburg, Russia/The Bridgeman Art Library)

had completed the conquest of Siberia to the east. This vast territorial expansion brought Russian power to the Pacific Ocean and was only checked by the powerful Qing Dynasty, which forced Russia to recognize China's northern border. The basis of Russian wealth in Siberia was furs, which the state collected by forced annual tribute payments from local peoples. Profits from furs and other natural resources, especially mining in the eighteenth century, funded expansion of the Russian bureaucracy and the army.

The growth of state power did nothing to improve the lot of the common people. In 1649 a new law code extended serfdom to all peasants in the realm, giving lords unrestricted rights over their serfs and establishing penalties for harboring runaways. The new code also removed the privileges that non-Russian elites had enjoyed within the empire and required conversion to Russian orthodoxy. Henceforth, Moscow maintained strict control of trade and administration throughout the empire.

The peace imposed by harsh Russian rule was disrupted in 1670 by a rebellion led by the Cossack Stenka Razin, who attracted a great army of urban poor and peasants. He and his followers killed landlords and government officials and proclaimed freedom from oppression, but their rebellion was defeated in 1671. The ease with which Moscow crushed the rebellion testifies to the success of the Russian state in unifying and consolidating its empire.

## Peter the Great and Russia's Turn to the West

Heir to his predecessors' efforts at state-building, Peter the Great (r. 1682–1725) embarked on a tremendous campaign to accelerate and complete these processes. Possessing enormous energy and willpower, Peter built on the service obligations of Ivan the Terrible and his successors and continued their tradition of territorial expansion. Peter's ambitions hinged on gaining access to the sea by extending Russia's borders to the Black Sea (controlled by the Ottomans) and to the Baltic Sea (dominated by Sweden).

Peter embarked on his first territorial goal by conquering the Ottoman fort of Azov in 1696 and quickly built Russia's first navy base nearby. In 1697 the tsar

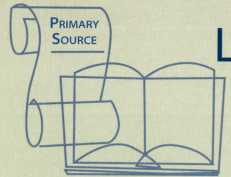
# Listening to the Past

## A German Account of Russian Life

*Seventeenth-century Russia remained a remote and mysterious land for western and even central Europeans, who had few direct contacts with the tsar's dominion. Westerners portrayed eastern Europe as more "barbaric" and less "civilized" than their homelands. Thus they expanded eastern Europe's undeniably harsher social and economic conditions to encompass a very debatable cultural and moral inferiority.*

*Knowledge of Russia came mainly from occasional travelers who had visited Muscovy and sometimes wrote accounts of what they saw. The most famous of these accounts was by the German Adam Olearius (ca. 1599–1671), who was sent to Moscow on three diplomatic missions in the 1630s. These missions ultimately proved unsuccessful, but they provided Olearius with a rich store of information for his* Travels in Muscovy, *from which the following excerpts are taken. Published in German in 1647 and soon translated into several languages (but not Russian), Olearius's unflattering but well-informed study played a major role in shaping European ideas about Russia.*

❝ The government of the Russians is what political theorists call a "dominating and despotic monarchy," where the sovereign, that is, the tsar or the grand prince who has obtained the crown by right of succession, rules the entire land alone, and all the people are his subjects, and where the nobles and princes no less than the common folk — townspeople and peasants — are his serfs and slaves, whom he rules and treats as a master treats his servants. . . .

If the Russians be considered in respect to their character, customs, and way of life, they are justly to be counted among the barbarians. . . . The vice of drunkenness is so common in this nation, among people of every station, clergy and laity, high and low, men and women, old and young, that when they are seen now and then lying about in the streets, wallowing in the mud, no attention is paid to it, as something habitual. If a cart driver comes upon such a drunken pig whom he happens to know, he shoves him onto his cart and drives him home, where he is paid his fare. No one ever refuses an opportunity to drink and to get drunk, at any time and in any place, and usually it is done with vodka. . . .

The Russians being naturally tough and born, as it were, for slavery, they must be kept under a harsh and strict yoke and must be driven to do their work with clubs and whips, which they suffer without impatience, because such is their station, and they are accustomed to it. Young and half-grown fellows sometimes come together on certain days and train themselves in fisticuffs, to accustom themselves to receiving blows, and, since habit is second nature, this makes blows given as punishment easier to bear. Each and all, they are slaves and serfs. . . .

Because of slavery and their rough and hard life, the Russians accept war readily and are well suited to it. On certain occasions, if need be, they reveal themselves as courageous and daring soldiers. . . .

Although the Russians, especially the common populace, living as slaves under a harsh yoke, can bear and endure a great deal out of love for their masters, yet if the pressure is beyond measure, then it can be said of them: "Patience, often wounded, finally turned into fury." A dangerous indignation results, turned not so much against their sovereign as against the lower authorities, especially if the people have been much oppressed by them and by their supporters and have not been protected by the higher authorities. And once they are aroused and enraged, it is not easy to appease them. Then, disregarding all dangers that may ensue, they resort to every kind of violence and behave like madmen. . . . They own little; most of them have no feather beds; they lie on cushions, straw, mats, or their clothes; they sleep on benches and, in winter, like the non-Germans [natives] in Livonia, upon the oven, which serves them for cooking and is flat on the top; here husband, wife, children, servants, and maids huddle together. In some houses in the countryside we saw chickens and pigs under the benches and the ovens. . . . Russians

led a group of 250 Russian officials and young nobles on an eighteen-month tour of western European capitals. Peter was fascinated by foreign technology, and he hoped to forge an anti-Ottoman alliance to strengthen his hold on the Black Sea. Traveling unofficially to avoid lengthy diplomatic ceremonies, Peter met with foreign kings, shipbuilders, and other experts. He failed to secure a military alliance, but he did learn his lessons from the growing power of the Dutch and the English.

To realize his second goal, Peter entered the Great Northern War (1700–1721) against Sweden. After a humiliating defeat at the Battle of Narva in 1700, Peter responded with measures designed to increase state power, strengthen his military, and gain victory. He required all nobles to serve in the army or in the

The brutality of serfdom is shown in this illustration from Olearius's *Travels in Muscovy.* (Courtesy of the Rare Book & Manuscript Library, University of Illinois at Urbana-Champaign)

are not used to delicate food and dainties; their daily food consists of porridge, turnips, cabbage, and cucumbers, fresh and pickled, and in Moscow mostly of big salt fish which stink badly, because of the thrifty use of salt, yet are eaten with relish. . . .

The Russians can endure extreme heat. In the bathhouse they stretch out on benches and let themselves be beaten and rubbed with bunches of birch twigs and wisps of bast (which I could not stand); and when they are hot and red all over and so exhausted that they can bear it no longer in the bathhouse, men and women rush outdoors naked and pour cold water over their bodies; in winter they even wallow in the snow and rub their skin with it as if it were soap; then they go back into the hot bathhouse. And since bathhouses are usually near rivers and brooks, they can throw themselves straight from the hot into the cold bath. . . .

Generally noble families, even the small nobility, rear their daughters in secluded chambers, keeping them hidden from outsiders; and a bridegroom is not allowed to have a look at his bride until he receives her in the bridal chamber. Therefore some happen to be deceived, being given a misshapen and sickly one instead of a fair one, and sometimes a kinswoman or even a maidservant instead of a daughter; of which there have been examples even among the highborn. No wonder therefore that often they live together like cats and dogs and that wife-beating is so common among Russians. . . .

In the Kremlin and in the city there are a great many churches, chapels, and monasteries, both within and without the city walls, over two thousand in all. This is so because every nobleman who has some fortune has a chapel built for himself, and most of them are of stone. The stone churches are round and vaulted inside. . . . They allow neither organs nor any other musical instruments in their churches, saying: Instruments that have neither souls nor life cannot praise God. . . .

In their churches there hang many bells, sometimes five or six, the largest not over two hundredweights. They ring these bells to summon people to church, and also when the priest during mass raises the chalice. In Moscow, because of the multitude of churches and chapels, there are several thousand bells, which during the divine service create such a clang and din that one unaccustomed to it listens in amazement. 99

Source: G. Vernadsky and R. T. Fisher, Jr., eds., *A Source Book for Russian History from Early Times to 1917*, vol. 1 (New Haven: Yale University Press, 1972), pp. 249–251. Reprinted by permission of Yale University Press.

### QUESTIONS FOR ANALYSIS

1. How did Olearius characterize the Russians in general? What evidence did he offer for his judgment?

2. How might Olearius's account help explain Stenka Razin's rebellion (see page 547)?

3. On the basis of these passages, why do you think Olearius's book was so popular and influential in central and western Europe?

civil administration—for life. Peter also created schools and universities to produce skilled technicians and experts. Furthermore, he established an interlocking military-civilian bureaucracy with fourteen ranks, and he decreed that all had to start at the bottom and work toward the top. Drawing on his experience abroad, Peter sought talented foreigners and placed them in his service. These measures gradually combined to make the army and government more powerful and efficient.

Peter also greatly increased the service requirements of commoners. In the wake of the Narva disaster, he established a regular standing army of more than two hundred thousand peasant-soldiers, drafted for life. He added an additional hundred thousand men in special regiments of Cossacks and foreign mercenaries. To

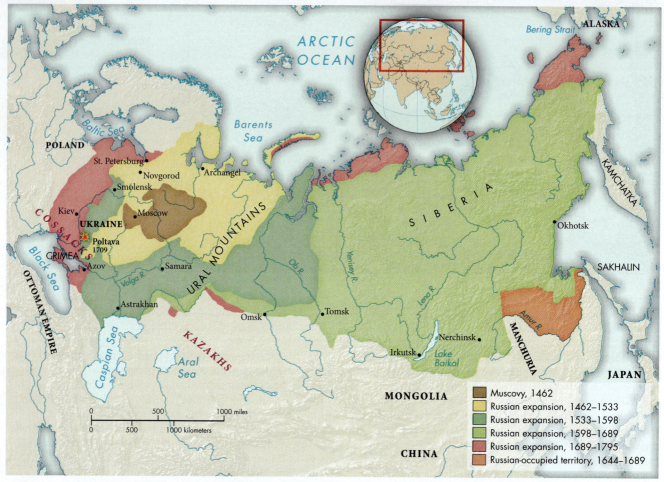

**MAP 18.5  The Expansion of Russia, 1462–1689**  In little more than two centuries, Russia expanded from the small principality of Muscovy to an enormous multiethnic empire, stretching from the borders of western Europe through northern Asia to the Pacific.

fund the army, taxes on peasants increased threefold during Peter's reign. Serfs were also arbitrarily assigned to work in the growing number of factories and mines that supplied the military. Under Peter, Russia's techniques for governing its territories—including the policing of borders and individual identity documents—were far ahead of those of most other imperial powers.

In 1709 Peter's new war machine was able to crush Sweden's army in Ukraine at Poltava in one of the most significant battles in Russian history (Map 18.5). Russia's victory against Sweden was conclusive in 1721, and Estonia and present-day Latvia came under Russian rule for the first time. The cost was high: warfare consumed 80 to 85 percent of all revenues. But Russia became the dominant power in the Baltic and very much a great European power.

After his victory at Poltava, Peter channeled enormous resources into building a new Western-style capital on the Baltic to rival the great cities of Europe.

Originally a desolate and swampy Swedish outpost, the magnificent city of St. Petersburg was designed to reflect modern urban planning with wide, straight avenues; buildings set in a uniform line; and large parks. Each summer, twenty-five thousand to forty thousand peasants were sent to provide construction labor in St. Petersburg without pay.

There were other important consequences of Peter's reign. For Peter, modernization meant westernization, and both Westerners and Western ideas flowed into Russia for the first time. He required nobles to shave their heavy beards and wear Western clothing. He also required them to attend parties where young men and women would mix together and freely choose their own spouses, in defiance of the traditional pattern of strictly controlled marriages. From these efforts a new elite class of Western-oriented Russians began to emerge.

Peter's reforms were unpopular with many Russians. For nobles, one of Peter's most detested reforms was the imposition of unigeniture—inheritance of land by one son alone—cutting off daughters and other sons from family property. For peasants, the reign of the tsar saw a significant increase in the bonds of serfdom, and the gulf between the serfs and the educated nobility increased. Despite the unpopularity of Peter's reforms, his modernizing and westernizing of Russia paved the way for it to move somewhat closer to the European mainstream in its thought and institutions during the Enlightenment, especially under Catherine the Great (see page 576).

## Chapter Summary

Most parts of Europe experienced the first centuries of the early modern era as a time of crisis. Following the religious divides of the sixteenth-century Protestant and Catholic Reformations and the decades of bloodshed they unleashed, Europeans in the seventeenth century suffered from economic stagnation, social upheaval, and renewed military conflict. Despite these obstacles, both absolutist and constitutional European states emerged from the seventeenth century with increased powers and more centralized control. Whether they ruled through monarchical fiat or parliamentary negotiation, European governments increased the size and professionalism of their armies, strengthened their bureaucracies, and raised more taxes. The most successful acquired huge land- or sea-based empires.

Monarchs in Spain, France, and Austria used divine right to claim they possessed absolute power and were not responsible to any representative institutions. As Spain's economic weakness curtailed its role in European politics, Louis XIV's magnificent palace at Versailles became a center of European power and culture. Absolute monarchs overcame the resistance of the nobility both through military force and by affirming existing economic and social privileges. England and the Netherlands defied the general trend toward absolute monarchy, adopting distinctive forms of constitutional rule.

As Spain's power weakened in the early seventeenth century, the Netherlands, England, and France competed for access to overseas trade and territory. Mercantilist competition among these powers led to hostility and war. England emerged in the early eighteenth century with a distinct advantage over its rivals.

In Russia, Mongol conquest and rule set the stage for a harsh tsarist autocracy that was firmly in place by the time of the reign of Ivan the Terrible in the sixteenth century. The reign of Ivan and his successors saw a great expansion of Russian territory, laying the foundations for a huge multiethnic empire. Peter the Great forcibly turned Russia toward the West by adopting Western technology and culture.

## CHRONOLOGY

| | |
|---|---|
| ca. 1500–1650 | Consolidation of serfdom in eastern Europe |
| 1533–1584 | Reign of Ivan the Terrible in Russia |
| 1589–1610 | Reign of Henry IV in France |
| 1598–1613 | Time of Troubles in Russia |
| 1612–1697 | Caribbean islands colonized by France, England, and the Netherlands |
| ca. 1620–1740 | Growth of absolutism in Austria and Prussia |
| 1642–1649 | English Civil War, ending with the execution of Charles I |
| 1643–1715 | Reign of Louis XIV in France |
| 1651 | First of the Navigation Acts |
| 1653–1658 | Oliver Cromwell's military rule in England (the Protectorate) |
| 1660 | Restoration of English monarchy under Charles II |
| 1665–1683 | Jean-Baptiste Colbert applies mercantilism to France |
| 1670–1671 | Cossack revolt led by Stenka Razin |
| 1682 | Louis XIV moves court to Versailles |
| 1682–1725 | Reign of Peter the Great in Russia |
| 1683–1718 | Habsburgs push the Ottoman Turks from Hungary |
| 1685 | Edict of Nantes revoked |
| 1688–1689 | Glorious Revolution in England |
| 1701–1713 | War of the Spanish Succession |

## NOTES

1. Theodore K. Rabb, *The Struggle for Stability in Early Modern Europe* (Oxford: Oxford University Press, 1975), p. 10.
2. Quoted in Cecile Hugon, *Social France in the XVII Century* (London: McMillan, 1911), p. 189.
3. H. Kamen, "The Economic and Social Consequences of the Thirty Years' War," *Past and Present* 39 (April 1968): 44–61.
4. J. H. Elliott, *Imperial Spain, 1469–1716* (New York: Mentor Books, 1963), pp. 306–308.
5. John A. Lynn, "Recalculating French Army Growth," in *The Military Revolution Debate: Readings on the Military Transformation of Early Modern Europe*, ed. Clifford J. Rogers (Boulder, Colo.: Westview Press, 1995), p. 125.
6. Quoted in R. Ergang, *The Potsdam Führer: Frederick William I, Father of Prussian Militarism* (New York: Octagon Books, 1972), p. 13.
7. Simon Schama, *The Embarrassment of Riches: An Interpretation of Dutch Culture in the Golden Age* (New York: Alfred A. Knopf, 1987), pp. 165–170; quotation from p. 167.

## CONNECTIONS

The seventeenth century represented a difficult passage between two centuries of dynamism and growth in Europe. On one side lay the sixteenth century's religious enthusiasm and strife, overseas discoveries, rising populations, and vigorous commerce. On the other side stretched the eighteenth century's renewed population growth, economic development, and cultural flourishing. The first half of the seventeenth century was marked by the spread of religious and dynastic warfare across Europe, resulting in death and widespread suffering. Recurring crop failure, famine, and epidemic disease contributed to a stagnant economy and population loss. In the middle decades of the seventeenth century, the very survival of the European monarchies established in the Renaissance appeared in doubt.

With the re-establishment of order in the second half of the century, maintaining stability was of paramount importance to European rulers. While a few nations placed their trust in constitutionally limited governments, many more were ruled by monarchs proclaiming their absolute and God-given authority. The ability to assume such power depended on cooperation from local elites, who acquiesced to state authority in exchange for privileges and payoffs. In this way, both absolutism and constitutionalism relied on political compromises forged from decades of strife.

As Spain's power weakened, other European nations bordering the Atlantic Ocean sought their own profits and glory from overseas empires. Henceforth, war among European powers would include high-stakes conflicts over territories and trade in the colonies. European rulers' increased control over their own subjects thus went hand in glove with the expansion of European power in the world.

The eighteenth century was to see these power politics thrown into question by new Enlightenment aspirations for human society, which themselves derived from the inquisitive and self-confident spirit of the Scientific Revolution. These movements—both of which would have tremendous worldwide influence—are explored in the next chapter. By the end of the eighteenth century demands for real popular sovereignty, colonial self-rule, and slave emancipation challenged the very bases of order so painfully achieved in the seventeenth century. Chapter 22 recounts the revolutionary movements that swept the late-eighteenth-century Atlantic world, while Chapters 25, 26, and 27 follow the story of European imperialism and the resistance of colonized peoples into the nineteenth century.

# Review and Explore

## Make It Stick

 **LearningCurve**
Go online and use LearningCurve to retain what you've read.

## Identify Key Terms

Identify and explain the significance of each item below.

Protestant Reformation (p. 521)       absolutism (p. 528)             Bill of Rights of 1689 (p. 537)
Jesuits (p. 523)                       divine right of kings (p. 530)  republicanism (p. 541)
moral economy (p. 526)                 mercantilism (p. 532)           Navigation Acts (p. 544)
Thirty Years' War (p. 526)             constitutionalism (p. 535)      Cossacks (p. 546)
sovereignty (p. 528)                   Puritans (p. 535)

## Review the Main Ideas

Answer the focus questions from each section of the chapter.

1. How did the Protestant and Catholic Reformations change power structures in Europe and shape European colonial expansion? (p. 521)
2. How did seventeenth-century European states overcome social and economic crisis to build strong states? (p. 524)
3. How did absolutism evolve in the seventeenth century in Spain, France, and Austria? (p. 528)
4. Why and how did the constitutional state triumph in England and the Dutch Republic? (p. 535)
5. How did European nations compete for global trade and empire in the Americas and Asia? (p. 541)
6. How did Russian rulers build a distinctive absolutist monarchy and expand into a vast and powerful empire? (p. 545)

## Make Connections

Analyze the larger developments and continuities within and across chapters.

1. This chapter has argued that, despite their political differences, rulers in absolutist and constitutionalist nations faced similar obstacles in the mid-seventeenth century and achieved many of the same goals. Based on the evidence presented here, do you agree with this argument? Why or why not?
2. Proponents of absolutism in western Europe believed that their form of monarchical rule was fundamentally different from and superior to what they saw as the "despotism" of Russia and the Ottoman Empire. What was the basis of this belief, and how accurate do you think it was?
3. What common features did the Ming empire in China and the Muslim empires of the Middle East and India share with the Russian and other European empires? How would you characterize interaction among these Eurasian empires?

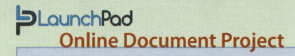

## Online Document Project

### Jewish Life in the Early Modern Era

**What factors shaped life for European Jews in the early modern era?**
Read excerpts from Glückel of Hameln's memoirs and other accounts of Jewish life, and then complete a quiz and writing assignment based on the evidence and details from this chapter.

*See inside the front cover to learn more.*

## Suggested Reading

Benedict, Philip, and Myron P. Gutmann, eds. *Early Modern Europe: From Crisis to Stability.* 2005. A helpful introduction to the many facets of the seventeenth-century crisis.

Burke, Peter. *The Fabrication of Louis XIV.* 1992. Explains the use of architecture, art, medals, and other symbols to promote the king's image.

Elliott, John H. *Imperial Spain, 1469–1716*, 2d ed. 2002. An authoritative account of Spain's rise to imperial greatness and its slow decline.

Gaunt, Peter, ed. *The English Civil War: The Essential Readings.* 2000. A collection showcasing leading historians' interpretations of the Civil War.

Hughes, Lindsey, ed. *Peter the Great and the West: New Perspectives.* 2001. Essays by leading scholars on the reign of Peter the Great and his opening of Russia to the West.

Ingrao, Charles W. *The Habsburg Monarchy, 1618–1815*, 2d ed. 2000. An excellent synthesis of the political and social development of the Habsburg empire in the early modern period.

Mungello, D. E. *The Great Encounter of China and the West, 1500–1800*, 2d ed. 2005. An introduction to China's relations with the West in the early modern period, encompassing politics, religion, science, culture, and the arts.

Parker, Charles. *Global Interactions in the Early Modern Age, 1400–1800.* 2010. A fascinating and accessible account of the global interaction of states, peoples, cultures, and goods in the early modern period.

Romaniello, Matthew. *The Elusive Empire: Kazan and the Creation of Russia, 1552–1671.* 2012. A study of the conquest of Kazan by Ivan the Terrible in 1552 and the Russian empire built in its aftermath.

Schama, Simon. *The Embarrassment of Riches: An Interpretation of Dutch Culture in the Golden Age.* 1987. A lengthy but vivid and highly readable account of Dutch culture in the seventeenth century, including a chapter on the mania for speculation on the tulip market.

Stern, Philip J. *The Company-State: Corporate Sovereignty and the Early Modern Foundations of the British Empire in India.* 2011. A study of the British East India Company and its role in governing India.

### Free People of Color

A sizable mixed-race population emerged in many European colonies in the Americas, including descendants of unions between masters and enslaved African women. The wealthiest of the free people of color, as they were called, were plantation owners with slaves of their own. (Unknown artist, *Portrait of a Young Woman*, pastel on paper, previously attributed to Jean-Etienne Liotard [1702–1789]/Saint Louis Art Museum, Missouri, USA/The Bridgeman Art Library)

**LearningCurve**

After reading the chapter, go online and use LearningCurve to retain what you've read.

# Chapter Preview

**The Scientific Revolution**

**Important Changes in Scientific Thinking and Practice**

**The Enlightenment**

**Economic Change and the Atlantic World**

From the mid-sixteenth century on, age-old patterns of knowledge and daily life were disrupted by a series of transformative developments. The same bold impetus toward exploring and conquering new territories that led Europeans across the Atlantic resulted in momentous new discoveries in astronomy and physics. Just as the authority of ancient models of the globe was overturned, so ancient frameworks for understanding the heavens were challenged and eventually discarded. The resulting conception of the universe and its laws remained in force until Albert Einstein's discoveries in the first half of the twentieth century. Along with new discoveries in botany, zoology, chemistry, and other domains, these developments constituted a fundamental shift in the basic framework for understanding the natural world and the methods for examining it known collectively as the "Scientific Revolution."

In the eighteenth century philosophers extended the use of reason from nature to human society. Self-proclaimed members of an "Enlightenment" movement, they wished to bring the same progress to human affairs that their predecessors brought to the understanding of the natural world. The Enlightenment created concepts of human rights, equality, progress, and tolerance that still guide Western societies. At the same time, some Europeans used their new understanding of reason to explain their own superiority, thus rationalizing attitudes now regarded as racist and sexist.

The expression of new ideas was encouraged by changes in the material world. With the growth of population, the revitalization of industry, and growing world trade, Europeans began to consume at a higher level. Feeding the growth of consumerism was the expansion of transatlantic trade and lower prices for colonial goods, often produced by slaves. During the eighteenth century ships crisscrossing the Atlantic circulated commodities, ideas, and people to all four continents bordering the ocean. As trade became more integrated and communication intensified, an Atlantic world of mixed identities and vivid debates emerged.

# The Scientific Revolution

☐ What revolutionary discoveries were made in the sixteenth and seventeenth centuries, and why did they occur in Europe?

Building on developments in the Middle Ages and the Renaissance, tremendous advances in Europeans' knowledge of the natural world and techniques for establishing such knowledge took place between 1500 and 1700. Collectively known as the "Scientific Revolution," these developments were the result of many more people studying the natural world, who used new methods to answer fundamental questions about the universe and how it operated. The authority of ancient Greek texts was replaced by a conviction that knowledge should be acquired by observation and experimentation and that mathematics could be used to understand and represent the workings of the physical world. By 1700 precise laws governing physics and astronomy were known, and a new emphasis on the practical uses of knowledge had emerged.

For a long time, historians focused on the role of heroic individuals in the development of physics and astronomy. While the work of these scientists constituted highly significant milestones in the creation of modern science, their discoveries must be placed in the broader context of international trade, imperial expansion, and cultural contact. Alongside developments in natural philosophy, historians now emphasize the growth of natural history in this period, spurred by colonial empires and their competition over trade and territory.

## Why Europe?

In 1500 scientific activity flourished in many parts of the world. With the expansion of Islam into the lands of the Byzantine Empire in the seventh and eighth centuries, Muslim scholars inherited ancient Greek learning, which itself was built on centuries of borrowing from older civilizations in Egypt, Babylonia, and India. The interaction of peoples and cultures across the vast Muslim world, facilitated by religious tolerance and the common scholarly language of Arabic, was highly favorable to advances in learning.

In a great period of cultural and intellectual flourishing from 1000 to 1500, Muslim scholars thrived in cultural centers such as Baghdad and Córdoba, the capital of Islamic Spain. They established the world's first universities in Constantinople, Fez (Morocco), and Cairo. In this fertile atmosphere, scholars surpassed the texts they had inherited in areas such as mathematics, physics, astronomy, and medicine. Arab and Persian mathematicians, for example, invented algebra, the concept of the algorithm, and decimal point notation, while Arab astronomers improved on measurements recorded in ancient works.

China was also a vital center of scientific activity, which reached a peak in the mid-fourteenth century. Among its many achievements, papermaking, gunpowder, and the use of the compass in navigation would be the most influential for the West. In Mesoamerica, civilizations such as the Maya and the Aztecs devised complex calendar systems based on astronomical observations and developed mathematics and writing.

Given the multiple world sites of learning and scholarship, it was by no means inevitable that Europe would take the lead in scientific thought or that "modern science" as we know it would emerge. In world history, periods of advancement produced by intense cultural interaction, such as those that occurred after the spread of Islam, are often followed by stagnation and decline during times of conflict and loss of authority. This is what happened in western Europe after the fall of the Western Roman Empire in the fifth century and in the Maya civilization after the collapse of its cultural and political centers around 900. The Muslim world successfully resisted a similar threat after the Mongol invasions.

The re-establishment of stronger monarchies and the growth of trade in the High Middle Ages contributed to a renewal of learning in western Europe. As Europeans began to encroach on Islamic lands in Iberia, Sicily, and the eastern Mediterranean, they became aware of the rich heritage of Greek learning in these regions and the ways scholars had improved upon ancient knowledge. In the twelfth century many ancient Greek texts—including works of Aristotle, Ptolemy, Galen, and Euclid previously unknown in the West—were translated into Latin, along with the commentaries of Arab scholars. A number of European cities created universities in which Aristotle's works dominated the curriculum.

As Europe recovered from the ravages of the Black Death in the late fourteenth and fifteenth centuries, the intellectual and cultural movement known as the Renaissance provided a crucial foundation for the Scientific Revolution. Scholars called humanists, working in the bustling mercantile city-states of Italy, emphasized the value of acquiring knowledge for the practical purposes of life. The quest to restore the glories of the ancient past led to the rediscovery of other classical texts such as Ptolemy's *Geography*, which was translated into Latin around 1410. An encyclopedic treatise on botany by Theophrastus was rediscovered in the 1450s moldering on the shelves of the Vatican library. The fall of Constantinople to the Ottomans in 1453 resulted in a great influx of little-known Greek works, as Christian scholars fled to Italy with their precious texts.

In this period, western European universities established new professorships of mathematics, astronomy, and natural philosophy. The prestige of the new fields was low, especially mathematics, which was reserved for practical problems such as accounting, surveying, and computing planetary tables but not used as a tool to understand the functioning of the physical world itself. Nevertheless, these professorships eventually enabled the union of mathematics with natural philosophy that was to be a hallmark of the Scientific Revolution.

European overseas expansion in the fifteenth and sixteenth centuries provided another catalyst for new thought about the natural world. In particular, the navigational problems of long oceanic voyages in the age of expansion stimulated scientific research and invention. To help solve these problems, inventors developed many new scientific instruments, such as the telescope, barometer, thermometer, pendulum clock, microscope, and air pump. Better instruments, which permitted more accurate observations, often led to important new knowledge. Another crucial technology in this period was printing, which provided a faster and less expensive way to circulate knowledge.

Political and social conflicts were widespread in Eurasia in the sixteenth and early seventeenth centuries, but they had different results. The three large empires of the Muslim world (see Chapter 17) that arose in the wake of the Mongol Empire sought to restore order and assert legitimacy in part by imposing Islamic orthodoxy. Their failure to adopt the printing press (see page 504) can be seen as part of a wider reaction against earlier traditions of innovation. Similarly, in China after the Manchu invasion of 1644, the new Qing Dynasty legitimized its authority through stricter adherence to Confucian tradition. By contrast, western Europe remained politically fragmented into smaller competitive nations, divisions that were augmented by the religious fracturing of the Protestant Reformation. These conditions made it impossible for authorities to impose one orthodox set of ideas and thus allowed individuals to question dominant patterns of thinking.

## Scientific Thought to 1550

For medieval scholars, philosophy was the path to true knowledge about the world, and its proofs consisted of the authority of ancients (as interpreted by Christian theologians) and their techniques of logical argumentation. Questions about the physical nature of the universe and how it functioned belonged to a minor branch of philosophy, called natural philosophy. Natural philosophy was based primarily on the ideas of Aristotle, the great Greek philosopher of the fourth century B.C.E. According to the Christianized version of Aristotle, a motionless earth stood at the center of the universe and was encompassed by ten separate concentric crystal spheres in which were embedded the moon, sun, planets, and stars. Beyond the spheres was Heaven with the throne of God and the souls of the saved. Angels kept the spheres moving in perfect circles.

Aristotle's views also dominated thinking about physics and motion on earth. Aristotle had distinguished between the world of the celestial spheres and that of the earth—the sublunar world. The sublunar realm was made up of four imperfect, changeable elements: air, fire, water, and earth. Aristotle and his followers also believed that a uniform force moved an object at a constant speed and that the object would stop as soon as that force was removed.

Aristotle's cosmology made intellectual sense, but it could not account for the observed motions of the stars and planets and, in particular, provided no explanation

**The Aristotelian Universe as Imagined in the Sixteenth Century** A round earth is at the center, surrounded by spheres of water, air, and fire. Beyond this small nucleus, the moon, the sun, and the five planets were embedded in their own rotating crystal spheres, with the stars sharing the surface of one enormous sphere. Beyond, the heavens were composed of unchanging ether. (Image Select/Art Resource, NY)

for the apparent backward motion of the planets (which we now know occurs as planets closer to the sun periodically overtake the earth on their faster orbits). The ancient Greek scholar Ptolemy offered a theory for this phenomenon. According to Ptolemy, the planets moved in small circles, called epicycles, each of which moved in turn along a larger circle, or deferent. Ptolemaic astronomy was less elegant than Aristotle's neat nested circles and required complex calculations, but it provided a surprisingly accurate model for predicting planetary motion.

The work of Ptolemy also provided the basic foundation of knowledge about the earth. Rediscovered around 1410, his *Geography* presented crucial advances on medieval cartography by representing a round earth divided into 360 degrees with the major latitude marks. Ptolemy's work reintroduced the idea of using coordinates of latitude and longitude to plot points on the earth's surface, a major advantage for long-distance navigation. However, Ptolemy's map reflected the limits of ancient knowledge, showing only the continents of Europe, Africa, and Asia, with land covering three-quarters of the world. Lacking awareness of the Pacific Ocean and the Americas, Ptolemy vastly underestimated the distance west from Europe to Asia.

These two frameworks reveal the strengths and limitations of European knowledge on the eve of the Scientific Revolution. Overcoming the authority of the ancients to develop a new understanding of the natural world, derived from precise techniques of observation and experimentation, was a monumental achievement. Europeans were not the first to use experimental methods—of which there was a long tradition in the Muslim world and elsewhere—but they were the first to separate scientific knowledge decisively from philosophical and religious beliefs and to accord mathematics a fundamental role in understanding the natural world.

## Astronomy and Physics

The first great departure from the medieval understanding of cosmology was the work of the Polish cleric Nicolaus Copernicus (1473–1543). Copernicus studied astronomy, medicine, and church law at the famed universities of Bologna, Padua, and Ferrara before taking up a church position in East Prussia. Copernicus came to believe that Ptolemy's cumbersome rules detracted from the majesty of a perfect creator. He preferred an idea espoused by some ancient Greek and Arab scholars: that the sun, rather than the earth, was at the center of the universe. Without questioning the Aristotelian belief in crystal spheres, Copernicus theorized that the stars and planets, including the earth, revolved around a fixed sun. Fearing the ridicule of other astronomers, Copernicus did not publish his *On the Revolutions of the Heavenly Spheres* until 1543, the year of his death.

One astronomer who agreed with the **Copernican hypothesis** was the Danish astronomer Tycho Brahe (TEE-koh BRAH-hee) (1546–1601). Brahe established himself as Europe's leading astronomer with his detailed observations of a new star that appeared suddenly in 1572 and shone very brightly for almost two years. The new star, which was actually a distant exploding star, challenged the idea that the heavenly spheres were unchanging and therefore perfect. Aided by grants from the king of Denmark, Brahe built the most sophisticated observatory of his day. Upon the king's death, Brahe acquired a new patron in the Holy Roman emperor Rudolph II and built an observatory in Prague. For twenty years Brahe observed the stars and planets with his naked eye in order to create new and improved tables of planetary motions, dubbed the *Rudolphine Tables* in honor of his patron.

Brahe's assistant, Johannes Kepler (1571–1630), carefully re-examined his predecessor's notations and came to believe that they could not be explained by Ptolemy's astronomy. Abandoning the notion of epicycles and deferents, Kepler developed three revolutionary laws of planetary motion. First, he demonstrated that the orbits of the planets around the sun are elliptical rather than circular. Second, he demonstrated that the planets do not move at a uniform speed in their orbits. When a planet is close to the sun it moves more rapidly, and it slows as it moves farther away from the sun. Finally, Kepler's third law stated that the time a planet takes to make its complete orbit is precisely related to its distance from the sun.

Kepler's contribution was monumental. Whereas Copernicus had speculated, Kepler used mathematics to prove the precise relations of a sun-centered (solar) system. His work demolished the old system of Aristotle and Ptolemy, and in his third law he came close to formulating the idea of universal gravitation (see page 560). In 1627 he also completed Brahe's *Rudolphine Tables*, which were used by astronomers for many years.

While Kepler was unraveling planetary motion, a young Florentine named Galileo Galilei (1564–1642) was challenging Aristotelian ideas about motion on earth. Like Kepler and so many early scientists, Galileo was a poor nobleman first marked for a religious career. Instead his fascination with mathematics led to a professorship in which he examined motion and mechanics in a new way. Galileo focused on deficiencies in Aristotle's theories of motion. He measured the movement of a rolling ball across a surface, repeating the action again and again to verify his results. In his famous acceleration experiment, he showed that a uniform

---

• **Copernican hypothesis** The idea that the sun, not the earth, was the center of the universe.

force—in this case, gravity—produced a uniform acceleration. Through another experiment, he formulated the **law of inertia**. He found that rest was not the natural state of objects. Rather, an object continues in motion forever unless stopped by some external force. His discoveries proved Aristotelian physics wrong.

On hearing details about the invention of the telescope in Holland, Galileo made one for himself in 1609. He quickly discovered the first four moons of Jupiter, which clearly demonstrated that Jupiter could not possibly be embedded in an impenetrable crystal sphere as Aristotle and Ptolemy maintained. This discovery provided concrete evidence for the Copernican theory, in which Galileo already believed. Galileo then pointed his telescope at the moon. He wrote in 1610 in *Sidereus Nuncius*:

> By the aid of a telescope anyone may behold [the Milky Way] in a manner which so distinctly appeals to the senses that all the disputes which have tormented philosophers through so many ages are exploded by the irrefutable evidence of our eyes, and we are freed from wordy disputes upon the subject.[1]

Reading these famous lines, one feels a crucial corner in Western civilization being turned. No longer should one rely on established authority. A new method of learning and investigating was being developed, one that proved useful in any field of inquiry.

## Newton's Synthesis

By about 1640 the work of Brahe, Kepler, and Galileo had been largely accepted by the scientific community despite opposition from religious leaders (see page 564). But the new findings failed to explain what forces controlled the movement of the planets and objects on earth. That challenge was taken up by English scientist Isaac Newton (1642–1727).

Born into the lower English gentry, Newton enrolled at Cambridge University in 1661. He arrived at some of his most basic ideas about physics in 1666 at age twenty-four but was unable to prove them mathematically. In 1684, after years of studying optics, Newton returned to physics for eighteen intensive months. The result was his towering accomplishment, a single explanatory system that integrated the astronomy of Copernicus, as corrected by Kepler's laws, with the physics of Galileo and his predecessors. Newton did this through a set of mathematical laws that explain motion and mechanics. These laws were published in 1687 in Newton's *Mathematical Principles of Natural Philosophy* (also known as the *Principia*). Because of their complexity, it took scientists and engineers two hundred years to work out all their implications.

The key feature of the Newtonian synthesis was the **law of universal gravitation**. According to this law, each body in the universe attracts every other body in a precise mathematical relationship, whereby the

**Galileo's Telescopic Observations of the Moon**
Among the many mechanical devices Galileo invented was a telescope that could magnify objects twenty times (other contemporary telescopes could magnify objects only three times). Using this telescope, he obtained the empirical evidence that proved the Copernican system. He sketched many illustrations of his observations, including the six phases of the moon, two of which are shown here. (moon: Biblioteca Nazionale, Florence, Italy/Rabatti-Domingi/akg-images; telescope: Museo delle Scienze, Florence, Italy/akg-images)

**Metamorphoses of the Caterpillar and Moth** Maria Sibylla Merian (1647–1717), the stepdaughter of a Dutch painter, became a celebrated scientific illustrator in her own right. Her finely observed pictures of insects in the South American colony of Suriname introduced many new species. For Merian, science was intimately tied with art: she not only painted but also bred caterpillars and performed experiments on them. Her two-year stay in Suriname, where she was accompanied by a teenage daughter, was a daring feat for a seventeenth-century woman. (bpk, Berlin/Manuscript Division, Staatsbibliothek zu Berlin, Stiftung Preussischer Kulturbesitz/Photo: Ruth Schaut/Art Resource, NY)

force of attraction is proportional to the quantity of matter of the objects and inversely proportional to the square of the distance between them. The whole universe—from Kepler's elliptical orbits to Galileo's rolling balls—was unified in one majestic system. Matter moved on earth and throughout the heavens according to the same laws, which could be understood and expressed in mathematical terms. Newton's synthesis prevailed until the twentieth century.

## Natural History and Empire

At the same time that they made advances in astronomy and physics, Europeans embarked on the pursuit of knowledge about unknown geographical regions and the useful and valuable resources they contained. Because they were the first to acquire a large overseas empire, the Spanish pioneered these efforts. Following the conquest of the Aztec and Inca Empires (see Chapter 16), they sought to learn about and profit from their New World holdings. The Spanish crown sponsored many scientific expeditions to gather information and specimens, out of which emerged new discoveries that reshaped the fields of botany, zoology, cartography, and metallurgy, among others. These accomplishments have attracted less attention from historians in part because of the strict policy of secrecy imposed on scientific discoveries by the Spanish crown.

Plants were a particular source of interest because they offered tremendous profits in the form of spices, medicines, dyes, and cash crops. King Philip II of Spain sent his personal physician, Francisco Hernández, to New Spain for seven years in the 1560s. Hernández filled fifteen volumes with illustrations of three thousand plants previously unknown in Europe. He interviewed local healers about the plants' medicinal properties, thereby benefiting from centuries of Mesoamerican botanical knowledge. In the seventeenth century, for example, the Spanish obtained a monopoly on the world's supply of cinchona bark, which comes from a tree native to the high altitudes of the Andes and is used to treat malaria.

Other countries followed the Spanish example as their global empires expanded, relying both on official expeditions and the private initiative of merchants, missionaries, and settlers. Royal botanical gardens served as living laboratories for cultivating valuable foreign plants. The stream of new information about plant and animal species overwhelmed existing intellectual frameworks. Carl Linnaeus (1707–1778) of Sweden sent his students on exploratory voyages around the world and, based on their observations and the specimens they collected, devised a system of naming and classifying living organisms still used today (with substantial revisions).

New encyclopedias of natural history popularized this knowledge with realistic drawings and descriptions emphasizing the usefulness of animals and plants. Audiences at home eagerly read the accounts of naturalists, who braved the heat, insects, and diseases of tropical jungles to bring home exotic animal, vegetable, and mineral specimens (along with indigenous human subjects). They heard much less about the many local guides, translators, and practitioners of medicine and

- **law of inertia** A law formulated by Galileo stating that motion, not rest, is the natural state of an object and that an object continues in motion forever unless stopped by some external force.

- **law of universal gravitation** Newton's law that all objects are attracted to one another and that the force of attraction is proportional to the object's quantity of matter and inversely proportional to the square of the distance between them.

science who made these expeditions possible and who contributed rich knowledge about the natural world.

## Magic and Alchemy

Recent historical research on the Scientific Revolution has focused on the contribution of ideas and practices that no longer belong to the realm of science, such as astrology and alchemy. For most of human history, interest in astronomy was inspired by the belief that the movement of heavenly bodies influenced events on earth. Many of the most celebrated astronomers were also astrologers. Used as a diagnostic tool in medicine, astrology formed a regular part of the curriculum of medical schools.

Centuries-old practices of magic and alchemy also remained important traditions for natural philosophers. Early modern practitioners of magic strove to understand and control hidden connections they perceived among different elements of the natural world, such as that between a magnet and iron. The idea that objects possessed hidden or "occult" qualities that allowed them to affect other objects was a particularly important legacy of the magical tradition. Belief in occult qualities—or numerology or cosmic harmony—was not antithetical to belief in God. On the contrary, adherents believed that only a divine creator could infuse the universe with such meaningful mystery.

Johannes Kepler exemplifies the interaction among these different strands of interest in the natural world. His duties as court mathematician included casting horoscopes for the royal family, and he based his own life on astrological principles. He also wrote at length on cosmic harmonies and explained elliptical motion through ideas about the beautiful music created by the combined motion of the planets. Kepler's fictional account of travel to the moon, written partly to illustrate the idea of a non-earth-centered universe, caused controversy and may have contributed to the arrest and trial of his mother as a witch in 1620. Kepler also suffered because of his unorthodox brand of Lutheranism, which led to his condemnation by both Lutherans and Catholics.

Another example of the interweaving of ideas and beliefs is Sir Isaac Newton, who was both intensely religious and also fascinated by alchemy, whose practitioners believed (among other things) that base metals could be turned into gold. Critics complained that his idea of universal gravitation was merely a restatement of old magical ideas about the innate sympathies between bodies; Newton himself believed that the attraction of gravity resulted from God's actions in the universe.

## Important Changes in Scientific Thinking and Practice

☐ What intellectual and social changes occurred as a result of the Scientific Revolution?

The Scientific Revolution was not accomplished by a handful of brilliant individuals working alone. Advancements occurred in many fields—medicine, chemistry, and botany, among others—as scholars developed new methods to seek answers to long-standing problems with the collaboration and assistance of skilled craftsmen who invented new instruments and helped conduct experiments. These results circulated in an international intellectual community from which women were usually excluded.

### The Methods of Science

One of the keys to achieving a better understanding of the world was the development of better ways of obtaining knowledge. Two important thinkers, Francis Bacon (1561–1626) and René Descartes (day-KAHRT) (1596–1650), were influential in describing and advocating for improved scientific methods based, respectively, on experimentation and mathematical reasoning.

The English politician and writer Francis Bacon was the greatest early propagandist for the experimental method. Rejecting the Aristotelian and medieval method of using speculative reasoning to build general theories, Bacon argued that new knowledge had to be pursued through empirical research. The researcher who wants to learn more about leaves or rocks, for example, should not speculate about the subject but should rather collect a multitude of specimens and then compare and analyze them to derive general principles. Bacon's contribution was to formalize the empirical method, which had already been used by Brahe and Galileo, into the general theory of inductive reasoning known as **empiricism**.

On the continent more speculative methods retained support. In 1619, as a twenty-three-year-old soldier serving in the Thirty Years' War (1618–1648), the French philosopher René Descartes experienced a life-changing intellectual vision. Descartes saw that there was a perfect correspondence between geometry and algebra and that geometrical spatial figures could be expressed as algebraic equations and vice versa. A major step forward in mathematics, Descartes's discovery of analytic geometry provided scientists with an important new tool.

Descartes used mathematics to elaborate a highly influential vision of the workings of the cosmos. Drawing on ancient Greek atomist philosophies, Descartes

---

● **empiricism** A theory of inductive reasoning that calls for acquiring evidence through observation and experimentation rather than reason and speculation.

developed the idea that matter was made up of identical "corpuscles" (tiny particles) that collided together in an endless series of motions, akin to the working of a machine. All occurrences in nature could be analyzed as matter in motion, and, according to Descartes, the total "quantity of motion" in the universe was constant. Descartes's mechanistic philosophy of the universe depended on the idea that a vacuum was impossible, which meant that every action had an equal reaction, continuing in an eternal chain reaction. Although Descartes's hypothesis about the vacuum proved wrong, his notion of a mechanistic universe intelligible through the physics of motion spread widely.

Descartes's greatest achievement was to develop his initial vision into a whole philosophy of knowledge and science. The Aristotelian cosmos was appealing in part because it corresponded with the evidence of the human senses. When experiments proved that sensory impressions could be wrong, Descartes decided it was necessary to doubt them and everything that could reasonably be doubted, and then, as in geometry, to use deductive reasoning from self-evident truths, which he called "first principles," to ascertain scientific laws. Descartes's reasoning ultimately reduced all substances to "matter" and "mind"—that is, to the physical and the spiritual. The devout Descartes believed that God had endowed man with reason for a purpose and that rational speculation could provide a path to the truths of creation. His view of the world as consisting of two fundamental entities is known as Cartesian dualism. Descartes's thought was particularly influential in France and the Netherlands but less so in England, where experimental philosophy won the day.

Both Bacon's inductive experimentalism and Descartes's deductive mathematical reasoning had flaws. Bacon's inability to appreciate the importance of mathematics and his obsession with practical results illustrated the limitations of antitheoretical empiricism. Likewise, some of Descartes's positions demonstrated the inadequacy of rigid, dogmatic rationalism. He believed, for example, that it was possible to deduce the whole science of medicine from first principles. Although insufficient on their own, Bacon's and Descartes's extreme approaches are combined in the modern scientific method, which began to crystallize in the late seventeenth century.

## Medicine, the Body, and Chemistry

The Scientific Revolution, which began with the study of the cosmos, soon transformed understanding of the microcosm of the human body. For many centuries the ancient Greek physician Galen's explanation of the body carried the same authority as Aristotle's account of the universe. According to Galen, the body contained four humors: blood, phlegm, black bile, and yellow

### MAJOR CONTRIBUTORS TO THE SCIENTIFIC REVOLUTION

| | |
|---|---|
| **Nicolaus Copernicus (1473–1543)** | Published *On the Revolutions of the Heavenly Spheres* (1543); theorized that the stars and planets revolved around a fixed sun |
| **Paracelsus (1493–1541)** | Pioneered the use of chemicals and drugs to address perceived chemical imbalances |
| **Andreas Vesalius (1514–1564)** | Published *On the Structure of the Human Body* (1543) |
| **Tycho Brahe (1546–1601)** | Built observatories and compiled data for the *Rudolphine Tables*, a new table of planetary data |
| **Francis Bacon (1561–1626)** | Advocated experimental method, formalizing theory of inductive reasoning known as empiricism |
| **Galileo Galilei (1564–1642)** | Used telescopic observation to provide evidence for Copernican hypothesis; experimented to formulate laws of physics, such as inertia |
| **Johannes Kepler (1571–1630)** | Used Brahe's data to mathematically prove the Copernican hypothesis; his new laws of planetary motion united for the first time natural philosophy and mathematics; completed the *Rudolphine Tables* in 1627 |
| **William Harvey (1578–1657)** | Discovered blood circulation (1628) |
| **René Descartes (1596–1650)** | Used deductive reasoning to formulate theory of Cartesian dualism |
| **Robert Boyle (1627–1691)** | Founded the modern science of chemistry; created the first vacuum; discovered Boyle's law on the properties of gases |
| **Isaac Newton (1642–1727)** | Introduced the law of universal gravitation, synthesizing the theories of Copernicus and Galileo |

bile. Illness was believed to result from an imbalance of these humors.

Swiss physician and alchemist Paracelsus (1493–1541) was an early proponent of the experimental method in medicine and pioneered the use of chemicals and drugs to address what he saw as chemical, rather than humoral, imbalances. Another experimentalist, Flemish physician Andreas Vesalius (1514–1564), studied anatomy by dissecting human bodies. In 1543, the same year Copernicus published *On the Revolutions of the Heavenly Spheres*, Vesalius issued *On the Structure of the Human Body*. Its two hundred precise drawings revolutionized the understanding of human anatomy, disproving Galen, just as Copernicus and his successors had disproved Aristotle and Ptolemy. The experimental approach also led English royal physician William Harvey (1578–1657)

**Frontispiece to *De Humani Corporis Fabrica* (*On the Structure of the Human Body*)** The frontispiece to Vesalius's pioneering work, published in 1543, shows him dissecting a corpse before a crowd of students. This was a revolutionary new hands-on approach for physicians, who usually worked from a theoretical, rather than a practical, understanding of the body. Based on direct observation, Vesalius replaced ancient ideas drawn from Greek philosophy with a much more accurate account of the structure and function of the body. (© SSPL/Science Museum/The Image Works)

Copernicus and his supporters, including Kepler, on a list of books Catholics were forbidden to read.

Out of caution Galileo Galilei silenced his views on heliocentrism for several years, until 1623 saw the ascension of Pope Urban VIII, a man sympathetic to the new science. However, Galileo's 1632 *Dialogue on the Two Chief Systems of the World* went too far. Published in Italian and widely read, it openly lampooned the Aristotelian view and defended Copernicus. In 1633 Galileo was tried for heresy by the papal Inquisition. Imprisoned and threatened with torture, the aging Galileo recanted, "renouncing and cursing" his Copernican errors.

Thereafter, the Catholic Church became more hostile to science, a change that helped account for the decline of science in Italy (but not in Catholic France) after 1640. At the same time, some Protestant countries, including the Netherlands, Denmark, and England, became quite "pro-science." This was especially true in countries without a strong religious authority capable of imposing religious orthodoxy on scientific questions.

to discover the circulation of blood through the veins and arteries in 1628. Harvey was the first to explain that the heart worked like a pump and to explain the function of its muscles and valves.

Irishman Robert Boyle (1627–1691) was a key figure in the victory of experimental methods in England and helped create the Royal Society in 1660. Boyle's scientific work led to the development of modern chemistry. Following Paracelsus's lead, he undertook experiments to discover the basic elements of nature, which he believed was composed of infinitely small atoms. Boyle was the first to create a vacuum, thus disproving Descartes's belief that a vacuum could not exist in nature, and he discovered Boyle's law (1662), which states that the pressure of a gas varies inversely with volume.

## Science and Religion

It is sometimes assumed that the relationship between science and religion is fundamentally hostile and that the pursuit of knowledge based on reason and proof is incompatible with faith. Yet during the Scientific Revolution most practitioners were devoutly religious and saw their work as contributing to the celebration of God's glory rather than undermining it. However, the concept of heliocentrism, which displaced the earth from the center of the universe, threatened the understanding of the place of mankind in creation as stated in Genesis. All religions derived from the Old Testament—Catholic, Protestant, Jewish, and Muslim—thus faced difficulties accepting the Copernican system. The Catholic Church was initially less hostile than Protestant and Jewish religious leaders, but in the first decades of the sixteenth century its attitude changed. In 1616 the Holy Office placed the works of

## Science and Society

The rise of modern science had many consequences. First, it led to the emergence of a new and expanding social group—the international scientific community. Members of this community were linked together by common interests and values as well as by journals and scientific societies. The personal success of scientists and scholars depended on making new discoveries, and as a result science became competitive. Second, as governments intervened to support and sometimes direct research, the new scientific community became closely tied to the state and its agendas. National academies of science were created under state sponsorship in London in 1662, Paris in 1666, Berlin in 1700, and later across Europe.

It was long believed that the Scientific Revolution was the work of exceptional geniuses and had little relationship to ordinary people and their lives until the late-eighteenth-century Industrial Revolution (see Chapter 23). More recently, historians have emphasized the importance of skilled craftsmen in the rise of science, particularly in the development of the experimental method. Many artisans developed a strong interest in emerging scientific ideas, and, in turn, the practice of

**Popularizing Science** The frontispiece illustration of Fontenelle's *Conversations on the Plurality of Worlds* (1686) invites the reader to share the pleasures of astronomy with an elegant lady and an entertaining teacher. The drawing shows the planets revolving around the sun. (© Roger-Viollet/ The Image Works)

science in the seventeenth century relied heavily on artisans' expertise in making instruments and conducting precise experiments.

Some things did not change in the Scientific Revolution. For example, scholars willing to challenge received ideas about the natural universe did not question traditional inequalities between the sexes. Instead, the emergence of professional science may have worsened the inequality in some ways. When Renaissance courts served as centers of learning, talented noblewomen could find niches in study and research. But the rise of a scientific community raised barriers for women because the universities and academies that furnished professional credentials refused them entry.

There were, however, a number of noteworthy exceptions. In Italy universities and academies did accept women. Across Europe women worked as makers of wax anatomical models and as botanical and zoological illustrators. They were also very much involved in informal scientific communities, attending salons

(see page 580), conducting experiments, and writing learned treatises. Some female intellectuals became full-fledged participants in the philosophical dialogue. In England, Margaret Cavendish, Anne Conway, and Mary Astell all contributed to debates about Descartes's mind-body dualism, among other issues.

# The Enlightenment

☐ What new ideas about society and human relations emerged in the Enlightenment, and what new practices and institutions enabled these ideas to take hold?

The political, intellectual, and religious developments of the early modern period that gave rise to the Scientific Revolution further contributed to a series of debates about key issues in eighteenth-century Europe and the wider world that came to be known as the **Enlightenment**. By shattering the unity of Western Christendom, the conflicts of the Reformation brought old religious certainties into question; the strong states that emerged to quell the disorder soon inspired questions about political sovereignty and its limits. Increased movement of peoples, goods, and ideas within and among the states of Asia, Africa, Europe, and its colonies offered examples of shockingly different ways of life and values. Finally, the tremendous achievements of the Scientific Revolution inspired intellectuals to believe that answers to all the questions being asked could be found through observation and the use of reason. Progress was possible in human society as well as science.

## The Early Enlightenment

Loosely united by certain key questions and ideas, the European Enlightenment (ca. 1690–1789) was a broad intellectual and cultural movement that gained strength gradually and did not reach its maturity until about 1750. Its origins in the late seventeenth century lie in a combination of developments, including political opposition to absolutist rule, religious conflicts between Protestants and Catholics and within Protestantism, and the attempt to apply principles and practices from the Scientific Revolution to human society.

A key crucible for Enlightenment thought was the Dutch Republic, with its proud commitments to religious tolerance and republican rule. When Louis XIV demanded that all Protestants convert to Catholicism,

> • **Enlightenment** An intellectual and cultural movement in late seventeenth- and eighteenth-century Europe and its colonies that used rational and critical thinking to debate issues such as political sovereignty, religious tolerance, gender roles, and racial difference.

around two hundred thousand Huguenots fled the country, many destined for the Dutch Republic. From this haven of tolerance, French Huguenots and their supporters began to publish tracts denouncing religious intolerance and suggesting that only a despotic monarch, not a legitimate ruler, would deny religious freedom. Their challenge to authority thus combined religious and political issues.

These dual concerns drove the career of one important early Enlightenment writer, Pierre Bayle (1647–1706), a Huguenot who took refuge from government persecution in the Dutch Republic. Bayle critically examined the religious beliefs and persecutions of the past in his *Historical and Critical Dictionary* (1697). Demonstrating that human beliefs had been extremely varied and very often mistaken, he concluded that nothing can ever be known beyond all doubt, a view known as skepticism. His influential *Dictionary* was found in more private libraries of eighteenth-century France than any other book.

The Dutch Jewish philosopher Baruch Spinoza (1632–1677) was a key figure in the transition from the Scientific Revolution to the Enlightenment. Deeply inspired by advances in the Scientific Revolution—and in particular by debates about Descartes's thought—Spinoza sought to apply natural philosophy to thinking about human society. He borrowed Descartes's emphasis on rationalism and his methods of deductive reasoning but rejected the French thinker's mind-body dualism. Instead Spinoza came to espouse monism, the idea that mind and body are united in one substance and that God and nature were merely two names for the same thing. He envisioned a deterministic universe in which good and evil were merely relative values, and human actions were shaped by outside circumstances, not free will. Spinoza was excommunicated by the Jewish community of Amsterdam for his controversial religious ideas, but he was heralded by his Enlightenment successors as a model of personal virtue and courageous intellectual autonomy.

German philosopher and mathematician Gottfried Wilhelm von Leibniz (1646–1716), who had developed calculus independently of Isaac Newton, refuted both Cartesian dualism and Spinoza's monism. Instead he adopted the idea of an infinite number of substances, or "monads," from which all matter is composed according to a harmonious divine plan. His *Theodicy* (1710) declared that ours must be "the best of all possible worlds" because it was created by an omnipotent and benevolent God. Leibniz's optimism was later ridiculed by the French philosopher Voltaire in *Candide, or Optimism* (1759).

Out of this period of intellectual turmoil came John Locke's *Essay Concerning Human Understanding* (1690), perhaps the most important text of the early Enlightenment. In this work Locke (1632–1704) set forth a new theory about how human beings learn and form their ideas. Whereas Descartes based his deductive logic on the conviction that certain first principles, or innate ideas, are imbued in humans by God, Locke insisted that all ideas are derived from experience. According to Locke, the human mind at birth is like a blank tablet, or tabula rasa, on which understanding and beliefs are inscribed by experience. Human development is therefore determined by external forces, like education and social institutions, not innate characteristics. Locke's essay contributed to the theory of **sensationalism**, the idea that all human ideas and thoughts are produced as a result of sensory impressions.

Along with Newton's *Principia*, the *Essay Concerning Human Understanding* was one of the dominant intellectual inspirations of the early Enlightenment. Locke's equally important contribution to political theory, *Two Treatises of Civil Government* (1690), argued that real sovereignty rested with an elected Parliament, not in the authority of the Crown.

## The Influence of the Philosophes

Divergences among the early thinkers of the Enlightenment show that, while they shared many of the same premises and questions, the answers they found differed widely. The spread of this spirit of inquiry and debate owed a great deal to the work of the **philosophes**, a group of influential intellectuals in France who proudly proclaimed that they were bringing the light of knowledge to their ignorant fellow creatures.

To appeal to the public and get around the censors, the philosophes wrote novels and plays, histories and philosophies, and dictionaries and encyclopedias, all filled with satire and double meanings to spread their message. One of the greatest philosophes, the baron de Montesquieu (mahn-tuhs-KYOO) (1689–1755) pioneered this approach in *The Persian Letters*, a social satire published in 1721. This work consists of letters supposedly written by two Persian travelers, Usbek and Rica, who as outsiders see European customs in unique ways and thereby allow Montesquieu a vantage point for criticizing existing practices and beliefs.

Disturbed by the growth in royal power under Louis XIV and inspired by the example of the physical sciences, Montesquieu set out to apply the critical method to the problem of government in *The Spirit of Laws* (1748). Arguing that forms of governments were

- **sensationalism** An idea, espoused by John Locke, that all human ideas and thoughts are produced as a result of sensory impressions.

- **philosophes** A group of French intellectuals who proclaimed that they were bringing the light of knowledge to their fellow creatures in the Age of Enlightenment.

- **deism** Belief in a distant, noninterventionist deity, shared by many Enlightenment thinkers.

shaped by history, geography, and customs, Montesquieu identified three main types: monarchies, republics, and despotisms. A great admirer of the English parliamentary system, Montesquieu argued for a separation of powers, with political power divided among different classes and legal estates holding unequal rights and privileges. Montesquieu was no democrat; he was apprehensive about the uneducated poor, and he did not question the sovereignty of the French monarch. But he was concerned that absolutism in France was drifting into tyranny and believed that strengthening the influence of intermediary powers was the best way to prevent it. Decades later, his theory of separation of powers had a great impact on the constitutions of the United States in 1789 and of France in 1791.

The most famous philosophe was François-Marie Arouet, known by the pen name Voltaire (1694–1778). In his long career, Voltaire wrote more than seventy witty volumes, hobnobbed with royalty, and died a millionaire because of shrewd business speculations. His early career, however, was turbulent, and he was twice arrested for insulting noblemen. To avoid a prison term, Voltaire moved to England for three years, and there he came to share Montesquieu's enthusiasm for English liberties and institutions.

Returning to France, Voltaire met Gabrielle-Emilie Le Tonnelier de Breteuil, marquise du Châtelet (1706–1749), a gifted noblewoman. Madame du Châtelet invited Voltaire to live in her country house at Cirey in Lorraine and became his long-time companion (under the eyes of her tolerant husband). Passionate about science, she studied physics and mathematics and published the first French translation of Newton's *Principia*, still in use today. Excluded from the Royal Academy of Sciences because she was a woman, Madame du Châtelet had no doubt that women's limited role in science was due to their unequal education. Discussing what she would do if she were a ruler, she wrote, "I would reform an abuse which cuts off, so to speak, half the human race. I would make women participate in all the rights of humankind, and above all in those of the intellect."[2]

While living at Cirey, Voltaire wrote works praising England and popularizing English scientific progress. Yet, like almost all the philosophes, Voltaire was a reformer, not a revolutionary. He pessimistically concluded that the best form of government was a good monarch, since human beings "are very rarely worthy to govern themselves." Nor did Voltaire believe in social and economic equality. The only realizable equality, Voltaire thought, was that "by which the citizen only depends on the laws which protect the freedom of the feeble against the ambitions of the strong."[3]

Voltaire's philosophical and religious positions were much more radical. Voltaire believed in God, but he rejected Catholicism in favor of **deism**, belief in a dis-

**Voltaire in Conversation** The French philosopher Voltaire is depicted here with his long-time companion, the writer and mathematician Gabrielle-Emilie Le Tonnelier de Breteuil, marquise du Châtelet. (Château de Breteuil/Gianni Dagli Orti/The Art Archive at Art Resource, NY)

tant, noninterventionist deity. Drawing on mechanistic philosophy, he envisioned a universe in which God acted like a great clockmaker who built an orderly system and then stepped aside and let it run. Above all, Voltaire and most of the philosophes hated religious intolerance, which they believed led to fanaticism and cruelty.

The strength of the philosophes lay in their number, dedication, and organization. Their greatest achievement was a group effort — the seventeen-volume *Encyclopedia: The Rational Dictionary of the Sciences, the Arts, and the Crafts*, edited by Denis Diderot (1713–1784) and Jean le Rond d'Alembert (1717–1783). The two men set out in 1751 to find coauthors who would examine the rapidly expanding whole of human knowledge and teach people to think critically about all matters.

Completed in 1765 despite opposition from the French state and the Catholic Church, the *Encyclopedia* contained hundreds of thousands of articles by leading scientists, writers, skilled workers, and progressive priests. Science and the industrial arts were exalted, religion and immortality questioned. Intolerance, legal injustice, and out-of-date social institutions were openly criticized. The *Encyclopedia* also included

## MAJOR FIGURES OF THE ENLIGHTENMENT

| | |
|---|---|
| **Baruch Spinoza** | Early Enlightenment thinker excommunicated from the Jewish community for his concept of a deterministic universe |
| **John Locke** | *Essay Concerning Human Understanding* (1690) |
| **Gottfried Wilhelm von Leibniz** | Early German rational philosopher and scientist |
| **Pierre Bayle** | *Historical and Critical Dictionary* (1697) |
| **Montesquieu** | *The Persian Letters* (1721); *The Spirit of Laws* (1748) |
| **Voltaire** | Renowned French philosophe and author of more than seventy works |
| **Marquise du Châtelet** | French scholar and supporter of equal education for women |
| **David Hume** | Central figure of the Scottish Enlightenment |
| **Jean-Jacques Rousseau** | *The Social Contract* (1762) |
| **Denis Diderot and Jean le Rond d'Alembert** | Editors of *Encyclopedia: The Rational Dictionary of the Sciences, the Arts, and the Crafts* (1765) |
| **Adam Smith** | Author of *An Inquiry into the Nature and Causes of the Wealth of Nations* (1776) |
| **Immanuel Kant** | *What Is Enlightenment?* (1784); *On the Different Races of Man* (1775) |

thousands of articles describing non-European cultures and societies, including acknowledgment of Muslim scholars' contribution to the development of Western science. Summing up the new worldview of the Enlightenment, the *Encyclopedia* was widely read, especially in less expensive reprint editions.

After about 1770 a number of thinkers and writers began to attack the philosophes' faith in reason and progress. The most famous of these was the Swiss intellectual Jean-Jacques Rousseau (1712–1778). Rousseau was both one of the most influential voices of the Enlightenment and, in his rejection of rationalism and social discourse, a harbinger of reaction against Enlightenment ideas. Like other Enlightenment thinkers, Rousseau was passionately committed to individual freedom. Unlike them, however, he attacked rationalism and civilization as destroying, rather than liberating, the individual. Warm, spontaneous feeling, Rousseau believed, had to complement and correct cold intel-

• **general will** A concept associated with Rousseau, referring to the common interests of all the people, who have replaced the power of the monarch.

lect. Moreover, he asserted, the basic goodness of the individual and the unspoiled child had to be protected from the cruel refinements of civilization. Rousseau's ideals greatly influenced the early romantic movement, which rebelled against the culture of the Enlightenment in the late eighteenth century.

Rousseau also called for a rigid division of gender roles, arguing that women and men were radically different beings. According to Rousseau, because women were destined by nature to assume a passive role in sexual relations, they should also be passive in social life and devote themselves to taking care of their husbands and children. (See "Viewpoints 19.1: Jean-Jacques Rousseau and Mary Wollstonecraft on Women's Nature and Education," at right.) Additionally, he believed that women's love for displaying themselves in public, attending salons, and pulling the strings of power was unnatural and had a corrupting effect on both politics and society.

Rousseau's contribution to political theory in *The Social Contract* (1762) was based on two fundamental concepts: the general will and popular sovereignty. According to Rousseau, the **general will** is sacred and absolute, reflecting the common interests of all people, who have displaced the monarch as the holder of sovereign power. The general will is not necessarily the will of the majority, however. At times the general will may be the authentic, long-term needs of the people as correctly interpreted by a farseeing minority. Little noticed before the French Revolution, Rousseau's concept of the general will appealed greatly to democrats and nationalists after 1789.

## Cultural Contacts and Race

The Scientific Revolution and the political and religious conflicts of the late seventeenth century were not the only developments that influenced European thinkers. Europeans' increased interactions with non-European peoples and cultures also helped produce the Enlightenment spirit. In the wake of the great discoveries of the fifteenth and sixteenth centuries, the rapidly growing travel literature taught Europeans that the peoples of China, India, Africa, and the Americas had very different beliefs and customs. Europeans shaved their faces and let their hair grow. Ottomans shaved their heads and let their beards grow. In Europe a man bowed before a woman to show respect. In Siam a man turned his back on a woman when he met her because it was disrespectful to look directly at her. Countless similar examples discussed in travel accounts helped change the perspective of educated Europeans. They began to look at truth and morality in relative, rather than absolute, terms. If anything was possible, who could say what was right or wrong?

The powerful and advanced nations of Asia were obvious sources of comparison with the West. Seventeenth-

# Viewpoints 19.1

## Jean-Jacques Rousseau and Mary Wollstonecraft on Women's Nature and Education

> • *A key eighteenth-century debate centered on the essential characteristics of women and their appropriate education and social roles. Two of the most vociferous participants in this debate were Jean-Jacques Rousseau and Mary Wollstonecraft. Looking to nature as a guiding principle, Rousseau reasoned that women's role in sexual intercourse and conception meant they were intended to be subordinate to men and devote themselves to motherhood and home life. Wollstonecraft responded that human virtue was a universal created by God that could not be differentiated by gender. While acknowledging that women were weaker in some ways than men, she insisted that they should strive to honor their God-given human dignity through education and duty, just like men.*

### Jean-Jacques Rousseau, *Emile, or On Education*

In the union of the sexes each contributes equally to the common aim, but not in the same way. From this diversity arises the first assignable difference in the moral relations of the two sexes. One ought to be active and strong, the other passive and weak. One must necessarily will and be able; it suffices that the other put up little resistance. . . .

Woman and man are made for one another, but their mutual dependence is not equal. Men depend on women because of their desires; women depend on men because of both their desires and their needs. We would survive more easily without them than they would without us. For them to have what is necessary to their station, they depend on us to give it to them, to want to give it to them, to esteem them worthy of it. They depend on our sentiments, on the value we set on their merit, on the importance we attach to their charms and their virtues. By the very law of nature women are at the mercy of men's judgments, as much for their own sake as for that of their children. . . .

To please men, to be useful to them, to make herself loved and honored by them, to raise them when young, to care for them when grown, to counsel them, to console them, to make their lives agreeable and sweet — these are the duties of women at all times, and they ought to be taught from childhood.

### Mary Wollstonecraft, *A Vindication of the Rights of Woman*

Rousseau declares that a woman should never, for a moment, feel herself independent, that she should be governed by fear to exercise her *natural* cunning, and made a coquettish slave in order to render her a more alluring object of desire, a *sweeter* companion to man, whenever he chooses to relax himself. . . .

What nonsense! When will a great man arise with sufficient strength of mind to puff away the fumes which pride and sensuality have thus spread over the subject! If women are by nature inferior to men, their virtues must be the same in quality, if not in degree, or virtue is a relative idea; consequently, their conduct should be founded on the same principles, and have the same aim. . . .

Cultivate their minds, give them the salutary, sublime curb of principle, and let them attain conscious dignity by feeling themselves only dependent on God. Teach them, in common with man, to submit to necessity, instead of giving, to render them more pleasing, a sex to morals.

Further, should experience prove that they cannot attain the same degree of strength of mind, perseverance, and fortitude, let their virtues be the same in kind, though they may vainly struggle for the same degree.

Sources: Jean-Jacques Rousseau, *Emile, or On Education*, trans. Allan Bloom (New York: Basic Books, 1979), pp. 358, 364–365. Reproduced with permission of BASIC BOOKS in the format Republish in a book via Copyright Clearance Center; Mary Wollstonecraft, *A Vindication of the Rights of Woman* (London: Johnson, 1796), pp. 47–48, 71.

### QUESTIONS FOR ANALYSIS

1. How does Rousseau derive his ideas about women's appropriate role in society from his observations about "the union of the sexes," and why does he believe that this is the "law of nature"? What does Wollstonecraft mean when she criticizes writers like Rousseau for giving "a sex to morals"? What arguments does she use to oppose such views?

2. Rousseau and Wollstonecraft differed greatly in their ideas on the essential characteristics of men and women and, as a consequence, on the type of education each sex should receive. For all their differences, are there any issues on which they agree?

---

century Jesuit missionaries served as a conduit for transmission of knowledge to the West about Chinese history and culture. The philosopher and mathematician Leibniz corresponded with Jesuits stationed in China, coming to believe that Chinese ethics and political philosophy were superior but that Europeans had equaled China in science and technology; some schol-

ars believe his concept of monads was influenced by Confucian teaching on the inherent harmony between the cosmic order and human society.[4]

During the eighteenth century Enlightenment opinion on China was divided. Voltaire and some other philosophes revered China—without ever visiting or seriously studying it—as an ancient culture replete with wisdom and learning, ruled by benevolent absolutist monarchs. They enthusiastically embraced Confucianism as a natural religion in which universal moral truths were uncovered by reason. By contrast, Montesquieu and Diderot criticized China as a despotic land ruled by fear.

Attitudes toward Islam and the Muslim world were similarly mixed. As the Ottoman military threat receded at the end of the seventeenth century, some Enlightenment thinkers assessed Islam favorably. Some deists praised Islam as superior to Christianity and Judaism in its rationality, compassion, and tolerance. Others, including Spinoza, saw Islamic culture as superstitious and favorable to despotism. In most cases, writing about Islam and Muslim cultures served primarily as a means to reflect on Western values and practices. Thus Montesquieu's *Persian Letters* used the Persian harem as a symbol of despotic rule that he feared his own country was adopting. Voltaire's play about the life of the Prophet portrayed Muhammad as the epitome of the religious fanaticism the philosophes opposed.

One writer with considerable personal experience in a Muslim country was Lady Mary Wortley Montagu, wife of the English ambassador to the Ottoman Empire. Her letters challenged prevailing ideas by depicting Turkish people as sympathetic and civilized. Montagu also disputed the notion that women were oppressed in Ottoman society.

Apart from debates about Asian and Muslim lands, the "discovery" of the New World and subsequent explorations in the Pacific Ocean also destabilized existing norms and values in Europe. One popular idea, among Rousseau and others, was that indigenous peoples of the Americas were living examples of "natural man," who embodied the essential goodness of humanity uncorrupted by decadent society. Other popular candidates for utopian natural men were the Pacific Island societies explored by Captain James Cook and others from the 1770s on (see page 806).

As scientists developed taxonomies of plant and animal species in response to discoveries in the Americas, they also began to classify humans into hierarchically ordered "races" and to speculate on the origins of such races. The French naturalist Georges-Louis Leclerc, comte de Buffon (1707–1788), argued that humans originated with one species that then developed into distinct races due largely to climatic conditions. Enlightenment thinkers such as David Hume and Immanuel Kant (see page 574) helped popularize these ideas.

Using the word *race* to designate biologically distinct groups of humans was new in European thought. Previously, Europeans had grouped other peoples into "nations" based on their historical, political, and cultural affiliations, rather than on supposedly innate physical differences. Unsurprisingly, when thinkers drew up a hierarchical classification of human species, their own "race" was placed at the top. Europeans had long believed they were culturally superior. The new idea that racial difference was physical and innate rather than cultural taught them they were biologically superior as well. In turn, scientific racism helped legitimate and justify the tremendous growth of slavery that occurred during the eighteenth century by depicting Africans as belonging to a biologically inferior race that was naturally fit for enslavement. (See "Viewpoints 19.2: Malachy Postlethwayt and Olaudah Equiano on the Abolition of Slavery," at right.)

Racist ideas did not go unchallenged. The abbé Raynal's *History of the Two Indies* (1770) fiercely attacked slavery and the abuses of European colonization. *Encyclopedia* editor Denis Diderot adopted Montesquieu's technique of criticizing European attitudes through the voice of outsiders in his dialogue between Tahitian villagers and their European visitors. (See "Listening to the Past: Denis Diderot's 'Supplement to Bougainville's Voyage,'" page 572.) Scottish philosopher James Beattie (1735–1803) responded directly to claims of white superiority by pointing out that Europeans had started out as savage as nonwhites supposedly were and that many non-European peoples in the Americas, Asia, and Africa had achieved high levels of civilization. Former slaves, like Olaudah Equiano (see Chapter 20) and Ottobah Cugoana, published eloquent memoirs testifying to the horrors of slavery and the innate equality of all humans. These challenges to racism, however, were in the minority. More often, Enlightenment thinkers, Thomas Jefferson among them, supported racial inequality.

## The International Enlightenment

The Enlightenment was a movement of international dimensions, with thinkers traversing borders in a constant exchange of visits, letters, and printed materials. Voltaire alone wrote almost eighteen thousand letters to correspondents across Europe. The Republic of Letters, as this international group of scholars and writers was called, was a truly cosmopolitan set of networks stretching from western Europe to its colonies in the Americas, to Russia and eastern Europe, and along the routes of trade and empire to Africa and Asia.

Within this broad international conversation, scholars have identified regional and national particularities. Outside of France, many strains of Enlightenment thought — Protestant, Catholic, and Jewish — sought to reconcile reason with faith, rather than emphasizing the errors of religious fanaticism and intolerance. Some scholars point to a distinctive "Catholic Enlightenment" that aimed to renew and reform the church from within, looking to divine grace rather than human will as the source of social progress.

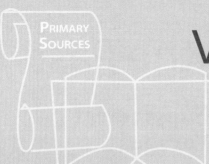

PRIMARY SOURCES

# Viewpoints 19.2

## Malachy Postlethwayt and Olaudah Equiano on the Abolition of Slavery

• As Britain came to dominate transatlantic commerce during the eighteenth century, debate arose over the morality of the slave trade and the country's involvement in it. Malachy Postlethwayt, an economist, rejected criticism of slavery by arguing that African nations treated their subjects much worse than slave traders did and that the benefits of Christianity by far outstripped any disadvantages slaves might endure. In his famous autobiography, former slave Olaudah Equiano (oh-lah-OO-dah ay-kwee-AH-noh) emphasized the cruelties of slavery. He argued, against authors like Postlethwayt, that trade with free peoples in Africa promised much more economic benefit to Britain than did slavery.

### Malachy Postlethwayt, *The National and Private Advantages of the African Trade Considered*

❝ Many are prepossessed against this trade, thinking it a barbarous, inhuman and unlawful traffic for a Christian country to trade in Blacks; to which I would beg leave to observe; that though the odious appellation of slaves is annexed to this trade, it being called by some the slave-trade, yet it does not appear from the best enquiry I have been able to make, that the state of those people is changed for the worse, by being servants to our British planters in America; they are certainly treated with great lenity and humanity: and as the improvement of the planter's estates depends upon due care being taken of their healths and lives, I cannot but think their condition is much bettered to what it was in their own country.

Besides, the negro princes in Africa, 'tis well known, are in perpetual war with each other, and since before they had this method of disposing of their prisoners of war to Christian merchants, they were wont not only to be applied to inhuman sacrifices, but to extreme torture and barbarity, their transportation must certainly be a melioration [improvement] of their condition; provided living in a civilized Christian country, is better than living among savages; Nay, if life be preferable to torment and cruel death, their state cannot, with any color or reason, be presumed to be worsened. ❞

### Olaudah Equiano, Appeal for the Abolition of Slavery

❝ Tortures, murder, and every other imaginable barbarity and iniquity, are practiced upon the poor slaves with impunity. I hope the great slave trade will be abolished. I pray it may be an event at hand. The great body of manufacturers, uniting in the cause, will considerably facilitate and expedite it; and as I have already stated, it is most substantially their interest and advantage, and as such the nation's at large (except those persons concerned in the manufacturing neck yokes, collars, chains, handcuffs, leg bolts, drags, thumb screws, iron muzzles, and coffins; cats, scourges, and other instruments of torture used in the slave trade). In a short time one sentiment will alone prevail, from motives of interest as well as justice and humanity. . . . If the blacks were permitted to remain in their own country, they would double themselves every fifteen years. In proportion to such increase will be the demand for manufactures. Cotton and indigo grow spontaneously in most parts of Africa; a consideration this of no small consequence to the manufacturing towns of Great Britain. It opens a most immense, glorious and happy prospect — the clothing, &c. of a continent ten thousand miles in circumference, and immensely rich in productions of every denomination in return for manufactures. ❞

Sources: Malachy Postlethwayt, *The National and Private Advantages of the African Trade Considered* (London: Jon and Paul Knapton, 1746), pp. 4–5; Olaudah Equiano, *The Interesting Narrative of the Life of Olaudah Equiano*, 2d ed., ed. Robert J. Allison (Boston: Bedford/St. Martin's, 2007), pp. 194–195.

### QUESTIONS FOR ANALYSIS

1. What contrast does Postlethwayt draw between the treatment of African people under slavery and in their home countries? What conclusion does he draw from this contrast?

2. To whom does Equiano address his appeal for abolition of the slave trade? What economic reasons does he provide for trading goods rather than slaves with Africa?

The Scottish Enlightenment, centered in Edinburgh, was marked by an emphasis on common sense and scientific reasoning. After the Act of Union with England in 1707, Scotland was freed from political crisis to experience a vigorous period of intellectual growth. Scottish intellectual revival was also stimulated by the creation of the first public educational system in Europe.

A central figure in Edinburgh was David Hume (1711–1776), whose civic morality and religious skepticism had a powerful impact at home and abroad. Hume strove to apply Newton's experimental methods to what he called the "science of man." Building on Locke's writings on learning, Hume argued that the human mind is really nothing but a bundle of

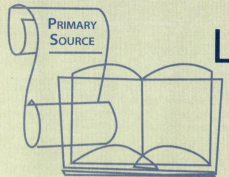
# Listening to the Past

## Denis Diderot's "Supplement to Bougainville's Voyage"

*Denis Diderot was born in a provincial town in eastern France and educated in Paris. Rejecting careers in the church and the law, he devoted himself to literature and philosophy. In 1749, sixty years before Charles Darwin's birth, Diderot was jailed by Parisian authorities for publishing an essay questioning God's role in the creation and suggesting the autonomous evolution of species. Following these difficult beginnings, Diderot's editorial work and writing on the* Encyclopedia *were the crowning intellectual achievements of his life and, according to some, of the Enlightenment itself.*

*Like other philosophes, Diderot disseminated Enlightenment ideas through various types of writing, ranging from scholarly articles in the* Encyclopedia *to philosophical treatises, novels, plays, book reviews, and erotic stories. His "Supplement to Bougainville's Voyage" (1772) was a fictional account of a European voyage to Tahiti inspired by the writings of traveler Louis-Antoine de Bougainville. In this passage, Diderot expresses his own loathing of colonial conquest and exploitation through the voice of an elderly Tahitian man. The character's praise for his own culture allows Diderot to express his Enlightenment idealization of natural man, free from the vices of civilized societies.*

“ He was the father of a large family. When the Europeans arrived he looked upon them with scorn, showing neither astonishment, nor fear, nor curiosity. On their approach he turned his back and retired into his hut. Yet his silence and anxiety revealed his thoughts only too well; he was inwardly lamenting the eclipse of his countrymen's happiness. When Bougainville was leaving the island, as the natives swarmed on the shore, clutching his clothes, clasping his companions in their arms and weeping, the old man made his way forward and proclaimed solemnly, "Weep, wretched natives of Tahiti, weep. But let it be for the coming and not the leaving of these ambitious, wicked men. One day you will know them better. One day they will come back, bearing in one hand the piece of wood you see in that man's belt, and, in the other, the sword hanging by the side of that one, to enslave you, slaughter you, or make you captive to their follies and vices. One day you will be subject to them, as corrupt, vile and miserable as they are. . . ."

Then turning to Bougainville, he continued, "And you, leader of the ruffians who obey you, pull your ship away swiftly from these shores. We are innocent, we are content, and you can only spoil that happiness. We follow the pure instincts of nature, and you have tried to erase its impression from our hearts. Here, everything belongs to everyone, and you have preached I can't

This image depicts the meeting of French explorer Louis-Antoine de Bougainville with Tahitians in April 1768. Of his stay on the island, Bougainville wrote: "I felt as though I had been transported to the Garden of Eden. . . . Everywhere reigned hospitality, peace, joy, and every appearance of happiness." Diderot's philosophical tract was a fictional sequel to Bougainville's account.
(Unknown artist, Tahitians presenting fruit to Bougainville attended by his officers. PIC T2996 NK5066 LOC7321, National Library of Australia)

tell what distinction between 'yours' and 'mine'. . . . If a Tahitian should one day land on your shores and engrave on one of your stones or on the bark of one of your trees, *This land belongs to the people of Tahiti*, what would you think then? You are stronger than we are, and what does that mean? When one of the miserable trinkets with which your ship is filled was taken away, what an uproar you made, what revenge you exacted! At that moment, in the depths of your heart, you were plotting the theft of an entire country! You are not a slave, you would rather die than be one, and yet you wish to make slaves of us. Do you suppose, then, that a Tahitian cannot defend his own liberty and die for it as well? This inhabitant of Tahiti, whom you wish to ensnare like an animal, is your brother. You are both children of Nature. What right do you have over him that he does not have over you? You came; did we attack you? Have we plundered your ship? Did we seize you and expose you to the arrows of our enemies? Did we harness you to work with our animals in the fields? We respected our own image in you.

"Leave us our ways; they are wiser and more decent than yours. We have no wish to exchange what you call our ignorance for your useless knowledge. Everything that we need and is good for us we already possess. Do we merit contempt because we have not learnt how to acquire superfluous needs? When we are hungry, we have enough to eat. When we are cold, we have enough to wear. You have entered our huts; what do you suppose we lack? Pursue as far as you wish what you call the comforts of life, but let sensible beings stop when they have no more to gain from their labours than imaginary benefits. If you persuade us to go beyond the strict bounds of necessity, when will we finish our work? When will we enjoy ourselves? We have kept our annual and daily labours within the smallest possible limits, because in our eyes nothing is better than rest. Go back to your own country to agitate and torment yourselves as much as you like. But leave us in peace. Do not fill our heads with your factitious needs and illusory virtues." 99

Source: Edited excerpts from pages 41–43 in Denis Diderot, *Political Writings*, translated and edited by John Hope Mason and Robert Wokler (Cambridge: Cambridge University Press, 1992). Reprinted by permission of Cambridge University Press.

### QUESTIONS FOR ANALYSIS

1. On what grounds does the speaker argue for the Tahitians' basic equality with the Europeans?

2. What is the good life, according to the speaker, and how does it contrast with the European way of life? Which do you think is the better path, and why?

3. In what ways could Diderot's thoughts here be seen as representative of Enlightenment ideas? Are there ways in which they are not?

4. How realistic do you think this account is? Does it matter? How might defenders of colonial expansion respond to Diderot's criticism?

impressions. These impressions originate only in sensory experiences and our habits of joining these experiences together. Since our ideas ultimately reflect only our sensory experiences, our reason cannot tell us anything about questions that cannot be verified by sensory experience (in the form of controlled experiments or mathematics), such as the origin of the universe or the existence of God. Hume further argued, in opposition to Descartes, that reason alone could not supply moral principles but that they derived instead from emotions and desires, such as feelings of approval or shame. Hume's rationalistic inquiry thus ended up undermining the Enlightenment's faith in the power of reason by emphasizing the superiority of the passions over reason in driving human behavior.

Hume's emphasis on human experience, rather than abstract principle, had a formative influence on another major figure of the Scottish Enlightenment, Adam Smith (1723–1790). In his *Theory of Moral Sentiments* (1759), Smith argued that social interaction produced feelings of mutual sympathy that led people to behave in ethical ways, despite inherent tendencies toward self-interest. By observing others and witnessing their feelings, individuals imaginatively experienced such feelings and learned to act in ways that would elicit positive sentiments and avoid negative ones. Smith believed that the thriving commercial life of the eighteenth century was likely to produce civic virtue through the values of competition, fair play, and individual autonomy. In *An Inquiry into the Nature and Causes of the Wealth of Nations* (1776), Smith attacked the laws and regulations created by mercantilist governments that, he argued, prevented commerce from reaching its full capacity (see Chapter 18). For Smith, ordinary people were capable of forming correct judgments based on their own experience and should therefore not be hampered by government regulations. Smith's **economic liberalism** became the dominant form of economic thought in the early nineteenth century.

Inspired by philosophers of moral sentiments, like Hume and Smith, as well as by physiological studies of the role of the nervous system in human perception, the celebration of sensibility became an important element of eighteenth-century culture. *Sensibility* referred to an acute sensitivity of the nerves and brains to outside stimulus that produced strong emotional and physical reactions. Novels, plays, and other literary genres depicted moral and aesthetic sensibility as a particular characteristic of women and the upper classes. The proper relationship between reason and the emotions (or between *Sense and Sensibility*, as Jane Austen

• **economic liberalism** The theory, associated with Adam Smith, that the pursuit of self-interest in a competitive market suffices to improve living conditions, rendering government intervention unnecessary and undesirable.

## ☐ Picturing the Past

**Enlightenment Culture** An actor performs the first reading of a new play by Voltaire at the salon of Madame Geoffrin in this painting from 1755. Voltaire, then in exile, is represented by a bust statue. (Painting by Gabriel Lemonnier [1743–1824], oil on canvas/De Agostini Picture Library/Gianni Dagli Orti/The Bridgeman Art Library)

**ANALYZING THE IMAGE** Which of these people do you think is the hostess, Madame Geoffrin, and why? Using details from the painting to support your answer, how would you describe the status of the people shown?

**CONNECTIONS** What does this image suggest about the reach of Enlightenment ideas to common people? To women? Does the painting of the bookstore on page 581 suggest a broader reach? Why?

put it in the title of her 1811 novel) became a key question.

After 1760 Enlightenment ideas were hotly debated in the German-speaking states, often in dialogue with Christian theology. Immanuel Kant (1724–1804), a professor in East Prussia, was the greatest German philosopher of his day. Kant posed the question of the age when he published a pamphlet in 1784 titled *What Is Enlightenment?* He answered, "*Sapere Aude* (dare to know)! 'Have the courage to use your own understanding' is therefore the motto of enlightenment." He argued that if intellectuals were granted the freedom to exercise their reason publicly in print, enlightenment would surely follow. Kant was no revolutionary; he also insisted that in their private lives, individuals must obey all laws, no matter how unreasonable, and should be punished for "impertinent" criticism. Like other Enlightenment figures in central and east-central Europe, Kant thus tried to reconcile absolutism and religious faith with a critical public sphere.

Northern Europeans often regarded the Italian states as culturally backward, yet important developments in Enlightenment thought also took place in the

Italian peninsula. After achieving independence from Habsburg rule (1734), the kingdom of Naples entered a period of intellectual flourishing as reformers struggled to lift the heavy weight of church and noble power. In northern Italy a central figure was Cesare Beccaria (1738–1794), a nobleman educated at Jesuit schools and the University of Pavia. His *On Crimes and Punishments* (1764) was a passionate plea for reform of the penal system that decried the use of torture, arbitrary imprisonment, and capital punishment and advocated the prevention of crime over its punishment. The text was quickly translated into French and English and made an impact throughout Europe.

## Enlightened Absolutism and Its Limits

Although Enlightenment thinkers were often critical of untrammeled despotism and eager for reform, their impact on politics was mixed. Outside of England and the Netherlands, especially in central and eastern Europe, most believed that political change could best come from above—from the ruler—rather than from below. Still, government officials' daily involvement in

# Individuals in Society

## Moses Mendelssohn and the Jewish Enlightenment

IN 1743 A SMALL, HUMPBACKED Jewish boy with a stammer left his poor parents in Dessau in central Germany and walked eighty miles to Berlin, the capital of Frederick the Great's Prussia. According to one story, when the boy reached the Rosenthaler Gate, the only one through which Jews could pass, he told the inquiring watchman that his name was Moses and that he had come to Berlin "to learn." The watchman laughed and waved him through. "Go Moses, the sea has opened before you."*

In Berlin the young Mendelssohn studied Jewish law and eked out a living copying Hebrew manuscripts in a beautiful hand. But he was soon fascinated by an intellectual world that had been closed to him in the Dessau ghetto. There, like most Jews throughout central Europe, he had spoken Yiddish — a mixture of German, Polish, and Hebrew. Now, working mainly on his own, he mastered German; learned Latin, Greek, French, and English; and studied mathematics and Enlightenment philosophy. Word of his exceptional abilities spread in Berlin's Jewish community (the dwelling of 1,500 of the city's 100,000 inhabitants). He began tutoring the children of a wealthy Jewish silk merchant, and he soon became the merchant's clerk and later his partner. But his great passion remained the life of the mind and the spirit, which he avidly pursued in his off-hours.

Gentle and unassuming in his personal life, Mendelssohn was a bold thinker. Reading eagerly in works of Western philosophy dating back to antiquity, he was, as a pious Jew, soon convinced that Enlightenment teachings need not be opposed to Jewish thought and religion. He concluded that reason could complement and strengthen religion, although each would retain its integrity as a separate sphere.† Developing this idea in his first great work, "On the Immortality of the Soul" (1767), Mendelssohn used the neutral setting of a philosophical dialogue between Socrates and his followers in ancient Greece to argue that the human soul lived forever. In refusing to bring religion and critical thinking into conflict, he was strongly influenced by contemporary German philosophers who argued similarly on behalf of Christianity. His thoughts reflected the way the German Enlightenment generally supported established religion, in contrast to the French Enlightenment, which attacked it.

Mendelssohn's treatise on the human soul captivated the educated German public, which marveled that a Jew could have written a philosophical masterpiece. In the excitement,

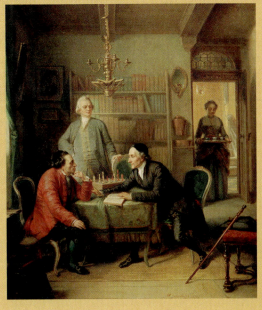

Lavater (right) attempts to convert Mendelssohn, in a painting of an imaginary encounter by Moritz Oppenheim. (Oil on canvas painting by Daniel Moritz Oppenheim [1800–1882]/Judah L. Magnes Memorial Museum/akg-images)

a Christian zealot named Lavater challenged Mendelssohn in a pamphlet to accept Christianity or to demonstrate how the Christian faith was not "reasonable." Replying politely but passionately, the Jewish philosopher affirmed that his studies had only strengthened him in his faith, although he did not seek to convert anyone not born into Judaism. Rather, he urged tolerance in religious matters and spoke up courageously against oppression of Jews.

An Orthodox Jew and a German philosophe, Moses Mendelssohn serenely combined two very different worlds. He built a bridge from the ghetto to the dominant culture over which many Jews would pass, including his novelist daughter Dorothea and his famous grandson, the composer Felix Mendelssohn.

### QUESTIONS FOR ANALYSIS

1. How did Mendelssohn seek to influence Jewish religious thought in his time?

2. How do Mendelssohn's ideas compare with those of the French Enlightenment?

*H. Kupferberg, *The Mendelssohns: Three Generations of Genius* (New York: Charles Scribner's Sons, 1972), p. 3.

†D. Sorkin, *Moses Mendelssohn and the Religious Enlightenment* (Berkeley: University of California Press, 1996), pp. 8ff.

### LaunchPad
## Online Document Project

**How did Moses Mendelssohn fit into the larger Enlightenment debate about religious tolerance?** Examine primary sources written by Mendelssohn and his contemporaries, and then complete a quiz and writing assignment based on the evidence and details from this chapter.

*See inside the front cover to learn more.*

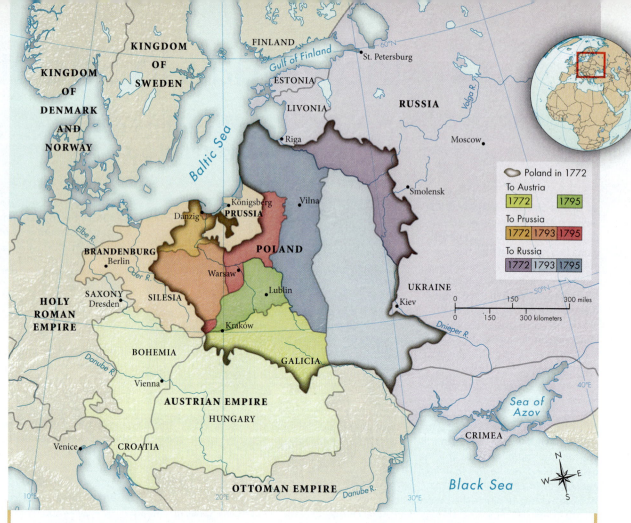

## Mapping the Past

**MAP 19.1    The Partition of Poland, 1772–1795**  In 1772 the threat of war between Russia and Austria arose over Russian gains from the Ottoman Empire. To satisfy desires for expansion without fighting, Prussia's Frederick the Great proposed dividing parts of Poland among Austria, Prussia, and Russia. In 1793 and 1795 the three powers partitioned the remainder, and Poland ceased to exist as an independent nation.

**ANALYZING THE MAP**  Of the three powers that divided the kingdom of Poland, which benefited the most? How did the partition affect the geographical boundaries of each state, and what was the significance? What border with the former Poland remained unchanged? Why do you think this was the case?

**CONNECTIONS**  Why was Poland vulnerable to partition in the later half of the eighteenth century? What does it say about European politics at the time that a country could simply cease to exist on the map? Could that happen today?

complex affairs of state made them naturally attracted to ideas for improving human society. Encouraged and instructed by these officials, some absolutist rulers tried to reform their governments in accordance with Enlightenment ideals. The result was what historians have called the **enlightened absolutism** of the later eighteenth century. (Similar programs of reform in France and Spain will be discussed in Chapter 22.)

Influenced by the philosophes, Frederick II (r. 1740–1786) of Prussia, known as Frederick the Great, and Catherine the Great of Russia (r. 1762–1796) set out to rule in an enlightened manner. Frederick promoted religious tolerance and free speech and improved the educational system. Under his reign, Prussia's laws were

simplified, torture of prisoners was abolished, and judges decided cases quickly and impartially. However, Frederick did not free the serfs of Prussia; instead he extended the privileges of the nobility over them.

Frederick's reputation as an enlightened prince was rivaled by that of Catherine the Great of Russia. When she was fifteen years old, Catherine's family ties to the Romanov dynasty made her a suitable bride for the heir to the Russian throne. Catherine profited from her husband's unpopularity and had him murdered so that she could be declared empress of Russia. Once in power, Catherine pursued three major goals. First, she worked hard to continue Peter the Great's efforts to bring the culture of western Europe to Russia (see page

547). To do so, she patronized Western architects, sculptors, musicians, and Enlightenment philosophes and encouraged Russian nobles to follow her example. Catherine's second goal was domestic reform. Like Frederick, she restricted the practice of torture, allowed limited religious tolerance, and tried to improve education and local government. The philosophes applauded these measures and hoped more would follow.

These hopes were dashed by a massive uprising of serfs in 1733 under the leadership of a Cossack soldier named Emelian Pugachev. Although Pugachev was ultimately captured and executed, his rebellion shocked Russian rulers and ended any reform programs Catherine might have intended to implement. After 1775 Catherine gave nobles absolute control of their serfs and extended serfdom into new areas. In 1785 she formally freed nobles from taxes and state service. Under Catherine the Russian nobility thus attained its most exalted position, and serfdom entered its most oppressive phase.

Catherine's third goal was territorial expansion, and in this respect she was extremely successful. Her armies subjugated the last descendants of the Mongols and the Crimean Tartars and began the conquest of the Caucasus on the border between Europe and Asia. Her greatest coup was the partition of Poland, which took place in stages from 1772 to 1795 (Map 19.1).

Joseph II (r. 1780–1790), the Austrian Habsburg emperor, was perhaps the most sincere proponent of enlightened absolutism. Joseph abolished serfdom in 1781, and in 1789 he decreed that peasants could pay landlords in cash rather than through compulsory labor. This measure was rejected not only by the nobility but also by the peasants it was intended to help, because they lacked the necessary cash. When Joseph died at forty-nine, the Habsburg empire was in turmoil. His brother Leopold II (r. 1790–1792) canceled Joseph's radical edicts in order to re-establish order.

Perhaps the best examples of the limitations of enlightened absolutism are the debates surrounding the possible emancipation of the Jews. For the most part, Jews in Europe were confined to tiny, overcrowded ghettos; were excluded by law from most occupations; and could be ordered out of a kingdom at a moment's notice. Still, a very few did manage to succeed and to obtain the right of permanent settlement, usually by performing some special service for the state, such as banking.

In the eighteenth century an Enlightenment movement known as the **Haskalah** emerged from within

**The Pale of Settlement, 1791**

the European Jewish community, led by the Prussian philosopher Moses Mendelssohn (1729–1786). Christian and Jewish Enlightenment philosophers, including Mendelssohn, began to advocate for freedom and civil rights for European Jews. In an era of growing reason and tolerance, they argued, restrictions on religious grounds could not stand. (See "Individuals in Society: Moses Mendelssohn and the Jewish Enlightenment," page 575.)

Arguments for tolerance won some ground, especially under Joseph II of Austria. Most monarchs, however, refused to entertain the idea of emancipation. In 1791 Catherine the Great established the Pale of Settlement, a territory encompassing modern-day Belarus, Lithuania, Latvia, Moldova, Ukraine, and parts of Poland, in which most Jews were required to live until the Russian Revolution of 1917.

## Economic Change and the Atlantic World

☐ How did economic and social change and the rise of Atlantic trade interact with Enlightenment ideas?

Enlightenment debates took place within a rapidly evolving material world. Agricultural reforms contributed to a rise in population that in turn fueled substantial economic growth in eighteenth-century Europe. A new public sphere emerged in the growing cities in which people exchanged opinions in cafés, bookstores, and other spaces. A consumer revolution brought fashion and imported foods into the reach of common people for the first time.

These economic and social changes were fed by an increasingly integrated Atlantic economy that circulated finished European products, raw materials from the colonies, and enslaved peoples from Africa. Over time, the peoples, goods, and ideas that crisscrossed the ocean created distinctive Atlantic communities and identities.

- **enlightened absolutism** Term coined by historians to describe the rule of eighteenth-century monarchs who, without renouncing their own absolute authority, adopted Enlightenment ideals of rationalism, progress, and tolerance.

- **Haskalah** A Jewish Enlightenment movement led by Prussian philosopher Moses Mendelssohn.

## Economic and Demographic Change

The seventeenth century saw important gains in agricultural productivity in northwestern Europe that slowly spread throughout the continent. Using new scientific techniques of observation and experimentation, a group of scientists, government officials, and a few big landowners devised agricultural practices and tools that raised crop yields dramatically, especially in England and the Netherlands. These included new forms of crop rotation, better equipment, and selective breeding of livestock. The controversial process of **enclosure**, fencing off common land to create privately owned fields, allowed a break with traditional methods but at the cost of reducing poor farmers' access to land.

Colonial plants also provided new sources of calories and nutrition. Introduced into Europe from the Americas—along with corn, squash, tomatoes, and many other useful plants—the humble potato provided an excellent new food source. Containing a good supply of carbohydrates and vitamins A and C, the potato offset the lack of fresh vegetables and fruits in common people's winter diet. The potato had become an important dietary supplement in much of Europe by the end of the eighteenth century.

Increases in agricultural productivity and better nutrition, combined with the disappearance of bubonic plague after 1720 and improvements in sewage and water supply, contributed to the tremendous growth of the European population in the eighteenth century. Growth took place unevenly, with Russia growing very quickly after 1700 and France much more slowly. Nonetheless, the explosion of population was a major phenomenon in all European countries, leading to a doubling of the number of Europeans between 1700 and 1835.

Population growth increased the number of rural workers with little or no land, and this in turn contributed to the development of industry in rural areas. The poor in the countryside increasingly needed to supplement their agricultural earnings with other types of work, and urban capitalists were eager to employ them, at much lower wages than they paid urban workers. **Cottage industry**, which consisted of manufacturing with hand tools in peasant cottages and work sheds, grew markedly in the eighteenth century and became a crucial feature of the European economy.

Rural manufacturing developed most successfully in England, particularly for the spinning and weaving of woolen cloth. By 1500 half of England's textiles were being produced in the countryside. By 1700 English industry was generally more rural than urban and heavily reliant on cottage industry. Most continental countries, with the exception of Flanders and the Dutch Republic, developed rural industry more slowly. The latter part of the eighteenth century witnessed a remarkable expansion of rural industry in certain densely populated regions of continental Europe.

Despite the rise in rural industry, life in the countryside was insufficient to support the rapidly growing population. Many people thus left their small villages to join the tide of migration to the cities, especially after 1750. London and Paris swelled to over five hundred thousand people, while Naples and Amsterdam had populations of more than one hundred thousand. It was in the bustling public life of these cities that the Enlightenment emerged and took root.

## The Atlantic Economy

European economic growth in the eighteenth century was spurred by the expansion of trade across the Atlantic Ocean. Commercial exchange in the Atlantic is often referred to as the triangle trade, designating a three-way transport of goods: European commodities, like guns and textiles, to Africa; enslaved Africans to the colonies; and colonial goods, such as cotton, tobacco, and sugar, back to Europe. This model highlights some of the most important flows of trade but significantly oversimplifies the picture. For example, a brisk intercolonial trade existed, with the Caribbean slave colonies importing food in the form of fish, flour, and livestock from the northern colonies and rice from the south, in exchange for sugar and slaves (Map 19.2).

Moreover, the Atlantic economy was inextricably linked to trade with the Indian and Pacific Oceans. For example, cowries, seashells originating in the Maldives in the Indian Ocean, served as a form of currency in West Africa. European traders obtained them in Asia, packing them alongside porcelains, spices, and silks for the journey home. They then brought the cowries from European ports to the West African coast to be traded for slaves. Indian cotton cloth was also prized in Africa and played a similar role in exchange. The rising economic and political power of Europeans in the eighteenth century thus drew on the connections they established between the long-standing Asian and Atlantic trade worlds.

Over the course of the eighteenth century the economies of European nations bordering the Atlantic Ocean relied more and more on colonial exports. In England sales to the mainland colonies of North America and the West Indian sugar islands—with an important assist from West Africa and Latin America—soared from £500,000 to £4 million (Figure 19.1).

• **enclosure** The controversial process of fencing off common land to create privately owned fields that increased agricultural production at the cost of reducing poor farmers' access to land.

• **cottage industry** Manufacturing with hand tools in peasant cottages and work sheds, a form of economic activity that became important in eighteenth-century Europe.

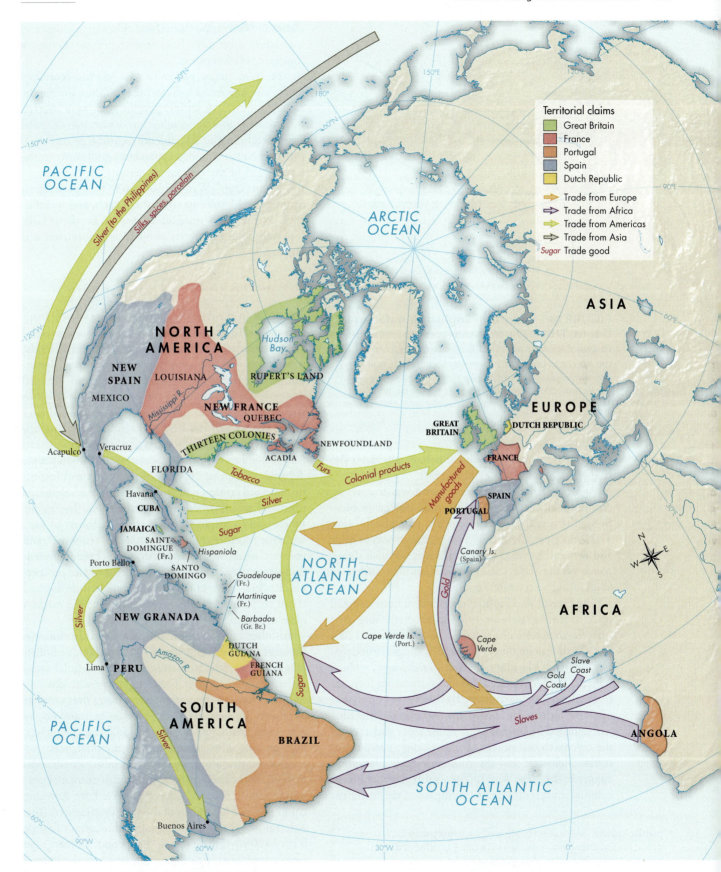

**MAP 19.2 The Atlantic Economy, 1701** The growth of trade encouraged both economic development and military conflict in the Atlantic basin. Four continents were linked together by the exchange of goods and slaves.

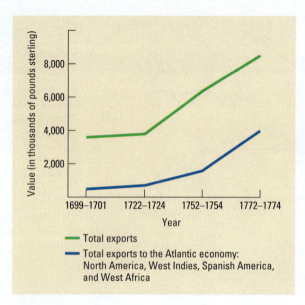

**FIGURE 19.1 Exports of English Manufactured Goods, 1700–1774** While trade between England and Europe stagnated after 1700, English exports to Africa and the Americas boomed and greatly stimulated English economic development. (Source: Data from R. Davis, "English Foreign Trade, 1700–1774," *Economic History Review*, 2nd ser., 15 [1962]: 302–303.)

Exports to England's colonies in Ireland and India also rose substantially from 1700 to 1800.

At the core of this Atlantic world was the misery and profit of the Atlantic slave trade (see pages 603–611). The brutal practice intensified dramatically after 1700 and especially after 1750 with the growth of trade and demand for slave-produced goods. English dominance of the slave trade provided another source of large profits to the home country.

The French also profited enormously from colonial trade in the eighteenth century, even after losing their vast North American territories to England in 1763. The Caribbean colonies of Saint-Domingue (modern-day Haiti), Martinique, and Guadeloupe, which remained in French hands, provided immense fortunes from plantation agriculture. By 1789 the population of Saint-Domingue (sehn daw-MEHNG) included five hundred thousand slaves, whose labor had allowed the colony to become the world's leading producer of coffee and sugar and the most profitable plantation colony in the New World.[5] The wealth generated from colonial trade fostered the confidence of the merchant

classes in Nantes, Bordeaux, and other large cities, and merchants soon joined other elite groups clamoring for more political power.

The third major player in the Atlantic economy, Spain, also saw its colonial fortunes improve during the eighteenth century. Its mercantilist goals were boosted by a recovery in silver production, which had dropped significantly in the seventeenth century. Spanish territory in North America expanded significantly in the second half of the eighteenth century. At the close of the Seven Years' War (1756–1763) (see page 652), Spain gained Louisiana from the French, and its influence extended westward all the way to northern California through the efforts of Spanish missionaries and ranchers.

## Urban Life and the Public Sphere

Urban life in the Atlantic world gave rise to new institutions and practices that encouraged the spread of Enlightenment thought. From about 1700 to 1789 the production and consumption of books grew significantly, and the types of books people read changed dramatically. For example, the proportion of religious and devotional books published in Paris declined after 1750; history and law held constant; the arts and sciences surged. Lending libraries, bookshops, cafés, and Masonic lodges provided spaces in which urban people debated new ideas. Together these spaces and institutions helped create a new **public sphere** that celebrated open debate informed by critical reason. The public sphere was an idealized space where members of society came together to discuss the social, economic, and political issues of the day. Although Enlightenment thinkers addressed their ideas to educated and prosperous readers, even poor and illiterate people learned about such issues as they were debated at the marketplace or tavern.

Another important Enlightenment institution was the salon. In Paris from about 1740 to 1789, a number of talented, wealthy women presided over regular social gatherings named after their elegant private drawing rooms, or **salons**. There they encouraged the exchange of observations on literature, science, and philosophy with great aristocrats, wealthy middle-class financiers, high-ranking officials, and noteworthy foreigners.

Elite women also exercised great influence on artistic taste. Soft pastels, ornate interiors, sentimental portraits, and starry-eyed lovers protected by hovering cupids were all hallmarks of the style they favored. This style, known as rococo, was popular throughout Europe from 1720 to 1780. During this period, women were closely associated with the rise of the novel as a literary genre, as both authors and readers. The novel helped popularize the cult of sensibility, which celebrated strong emotions and intimate family love. Some phi-

- **public sphere** An idealized intellectual space that emerged in Europe during the Enlightenment. Here, the public came together to discuss important social, economic, and political issues.

- **salons** Regular social gatherings held by talented and rich Parisian women in their homes, where philosophes and their followers met to discuss literature, science, and philosophy.

losophes championed greater rights and expanded education for women, claiming that the position and treatment of women were the best indicators of a society's level of civilization and decency.[6]

Economic growth in the second half of the eighteenth century also enabled a significant rise in the consumption of finished goods and new foodstuffs that historians have labeled a "consumer revolution." A boom in textile production and cheap reproductions of luxury items meant that the common people could afford to follow fashion for the first time, if only in a modest manner. Colonial trade made previously expensive and rare foodstuffs, such as sugar, tea, coffee, chocolate, and tobacco, widely available. By the end of the eighteenth century these products, which turned out to be mildly to extremely addictive, had become dietary staples for people of all social classes, especially in Britain.

The consumer revolution was concentrated in large cities in northwestern Europe and North America. This was not yet the society of mass consumption that emerged toward the end of the nineteenth century with the full expansion of the Industrial Revolution. The eighteenth century did, however, lay the foundations for one of the most distinctive features of modern Western life: societies based on the consumption of goods and services obtained through global markets in which many individuals' identities and self-worth are derived from the goods they consume.

## Culture and Community in the Atlantic World

As contacts among the Atlantic coasts of the Americas, Africa, and Europe became more frequent, and as European settlements grew into well-established colonies, new identities and communities emerged. The term *Creole* referred to people of Spanish or other European ancestry born in the Americas. Wealthy Creoles throughout the Atlantic colonies prided themselves on following European ways of life. In addition to their agricultural estates, they maintained townhouses in colonial cities built on the European model, with theaters, plazas, churches, and coffeehouses. They purchased luxury goods made in Europe and sent their children to be educated in the home country.

Over time, however, the colonial elite came to feel that their circumstances gave them different interests and characteristics from people of their home countries. One observer explained that "a turn of mind peculiar to the planter, occasioned by a physical difference of constitution, climate, customs, and education, tends . . . to repress the remains of his former attachment to his native soil."[7] Creoles became "Americanized" by adopting native foods, like chocolate, chili peppers, and squash, and sought relief from tropical disease in native remedies. Also, they began to turn against restrictions from their home countries: Creole traders and planters, along with their counterparts in

**The French Book Trade** Book consumption surged in the eighteenth century and along with it, new bookstores. This appealing bookshop in France with its intriguing ads for the latest works offers to put customers "Under the Protection of Minerva," the Roman goddess of wisdom. Large packets of books sit ready for shipment to foreign countries. (Musée des Beaux-Arts, Dijon, France/Art Resource, NY)

**The Consumer Revolution** From the mid-eighteenth century on, the cities of western Europe witnessed a new proliferation of consumer goods. Items once limited to the wealthy few — such as fans (lower right), watches, snuffboxes, umbrellas, ornamental containers, and teapots — were now reproduced in cheaper versions for middling and ordinary people. The fashion for wide hoopskirts was so popular that the armrests of the chairs of the day, known as Louis XV chairs (left), were specially designed to accommodate them. (fan: Musée Conde, Chantilly, France/Scala/White Images/Art Resource, NY; chair: © RMN–Grand Palais/Art Resource, NY)

English colonies, increasingly resented the regulations and taxes imposed by colonial bureaucrats, and such resentment would eventually lead to revolutions against colonial powers (discussed in Chapter 22).

Not all Europeans in the colonies were wealthy or well educated. Numerous poor and lower-middle-class whites worked as clerks, shopkeepers, craftsmen, and laborers. With the exception of the English colonies of North America, white Europeans made up a minority of the population, outnumbered by indigenous peoples in Spanish America and by the growing numbers of enslaved people of African descent in the Caribbean. Since most European migrants were men, much of the colonial population of the Atlantic world descended from unions—forced or through consent—of European men and indigenous or African women. Colonial attempts to identify and control racial categories greatly influenced developing Enlightenment thought on racial differences.

In the Spanish and French Caribbean, as in Brazil, many slave masters acknowledged and freed their mixed-race children, leading to sizable populations of free people of color. Advantaged by their fathers, some became wealthy landowners and slaveholders in their own right. In the second half of the eighteenth century the prosperity of some free people of color brought a

backlash from the white population of Saint-Domingue in the form of new race laws prohibiting nonwhites from marrying whites and forcing them to adopt distinctive attire. In the British colonies of the Caribbean and the southern mainland, by contrast, masters tended to leave their mixed-race progeny in slavery, maintaining a stark discrepancy between free whites and enslaved people of color.[8] British colonial law forbade marriage between Englishmen and -women and Africans or Native Americans.

Some mixed-race people sought to enter Creole society and obtain its many official and unofficial privileges by passing as white. Where they existed in any number, though, free people of color established their own proud social hierarchies based on wealth, family connections, occupation, and skin color.

Restricted from owning land and holding many occupations in Europe, Jews were eager participants in the new Atlantic economy and established a network of mercantile communities along its trade routes. As in the Old World, Jews in European colonies faced discrimination; for example, restrictions existed on the number of slaves they could own in Barbados in the early eighteenth century.[9] Jews were considered to be white Europeans and thus ineligible to be slaves, but they did not enjoy equal status with Christians. The status of Jews adds one more element to the complexity of Atlantic identities.

## The Atlantic Enlightenment

Enlightenment ideas thrived in the colonies, although with as much diversity and disagreement as in Europe. The colonies of British North America were deeply influenced by the Scottish Enlightenment, with its emphasis on pragmatic approaches to the problems of life. Following the Scottish model, leaders in the colonies adopted a moderate, "common-sense" version of the Enlightenment that emphasized self-improvement and ethical conduct. In most cases, this version of the Enlightenment was perfectly compatible with religion and was chiefly spread through the growing colleges and universities of the colonies, which remained church-based institutions.

Some thinkers went even further in their admiration for Enlightenment ideas. Benjamin Franklin's writings and political career provide an outstanding example of the combination of the pragmatism and economic interests of the Scottish Enlightenment with the constitutional theories of Locke, Montesquieu, and Rousseau. Franklin was privately a deist, but he continued to attend church and respect religious proprieties, a cautious pattern followed by fellow deist Thomas Jefferson and other leading thinkers of the American Enlightenment.

Northern Enlightenment thinkers often depicted Spain and its American colonies as the epitome of the superstition and barbarity they contested. The Catholic Church strictly controlled the publication of books on the Iberian Peninsula and across the Atlantic. Nonetheless, the dynasty that took power in Spain in the early eighteenth century followed its own course of enlightened absolutism, just like its counterparts in the rest of Europe. Under King Carlos III (r. 1759–1788) and his son Carlos IV (r. 1788–1808), Spanish administrators attempted to strengthen colonial rule by posting a standing army in the colonies and increasing royal monopolies and taxes to pay for it. They also ordered officials to gather more accurate information about the colonies as a basis for improving the government. Enlightened administrators debated the status of indigenous peoples and whether it would be better for these peoples (and for the prosperity of Spanish America) if they maintained their distinct legal status or were integrated into Spanish society.

Educated Creoles were well aware of the new currents of thought, and the universities, newspapers, and salons of Spanish America produced their own reform ideas. The establishment of a mining school in Mexico City in 1792, the first in the Spanish colonies, illuminates the practical achievements of reformers. As in other European colonies, Enlightenment thought encouraged Creoles to criticize the policies of the mother country and aspire toward greater autonomy.

## CHRONOLOGY

| | |
|---|---|
| ca. 1500–1700 | Scientific Revolution |
| ca. 1690–1789 | Enlightenment |
| ca. 1700–1789 | Growth of book publishing |
| 1720–1780 | Rococo style in art and decoration |
| 1740–1786 | Reign of Frederick the Great of Prussia |
| ca. 1740–1789 | French salons led by elite women |
| 1762–1796 | Reign of Catherine the Great of Russia |
| 1765 | Philosophes publish *Encyclopedia: The Rational Dictionary of the Sciences, the Arts, and the Crafts* |
| 1780–1790 | Reign of Joseph II of Austria |
| 1791 | Establishment of the Pale of Settlement |
| 1792 | Establishment of mining school in Mexico City as part of reforms |

## Chapter Summary

Decisive breakthroughs in astronomy and physics in the seventeenth century demolished the medieval synthesis of Aristotelian philosophy and Christian theology. Among the most notable discoveries were that the sun, not the earth, was the center of the universe and Newton's universal law of gravitation. Bacon's inductive approach and Descartes's deductive reasoning eventually combined to form the modern scientific method, which relies on both experimentation and reason. The impact of these scientific breakthroughs on intellectual life was enormous, nurturing a new critical attitude in many disciplines. In addition, an international scientific community arose, and state-sponsored academies, which were typically closed to women, advanced scientific research.

Believing that all aspects of life were open to debate and skepticism, Enlightenment thinkers asked challenging questions about religious tolerance, representative government, and racial and sexual difference. Enlightenment thinkers drew inspiration from the new peoples and cultures encountered by Europeans and devised new ideas about race as a scientific and biological category. The ideas of the Enlightenment inspired absolutist rulers in central and eastern Europe, but real reforms were limited. For example, most rulers refused to support emancipation of the Jews.

In the second half of the eighteenth century agricultural reforms helped produce tremendous population growth. Economic growth and urbanization favored the spread of Enlightenment thought by producing a public sphere in which ideas could be debated. The expansion of transatlantic trade made economic growth possible, as did the lowering of prices on colonial goods due to the growth of slave labor. Atlantic trade involved the exchange of commodities among Europe, Africa, and the Americas, but it was also linked with trade in the Indian and Pacific Oceans. The movement of people and ideas across the Atlantic helped shape the identities of colonial inhabitants. At first colonial elites prided themselves on following European ways of life, but over time they developed customs and attitudes apart from those of their homeland.

## NOTES

1. H. Butterfield, *The Origins of Modern Science* (New York: Macmillan, 1951), p. 120.
2. L. Schiebinger, *The Mind Has No Sex? Women in the Origins of Modern Science* (Cambridge, Mass.: Harvard University Press, 1989), p. 64.
3. Quoted in G. L. Mosse et al., eds., *Europe in Review* (Chicago: Rand McNally, 1964), p. 156.
4. D. E. Mungello, *The Great Encounter of China and the West, 1500–1800,* 2d ed. (Lanham, Md.: Rowman & Littlefield, 2005), p. 98.
5. Laurent Dubois and John D. Garrigus, *Slave Revolution in the Caribbean, 1789–1904* (New York: Palgrave, 2006), p. 8.
6. See E. Fox-Genovese, "Women in the Enlightenment," in *Becoming Visible: Women in European History,* 2d ed., ed. R. Bridenthal, C. Koonz, and S. Stuard (Boston: Houghton Mifflin, 1987), esp. pp. 252–259, 263–265.
7. Pierre Marie François Paget, *Travels Round the World in the Years 1767, 1768, 1769, 1770, 1771,* vol. 1 (London, 1793), p. 262.
8. Orlando Patterson, *Slavery and Social Death* (Cambridge, Mass.: Harvard University Press, 1982), p. 255.
9. Erik R. Seeman, "Jews in the Early Modern Atlantic: Crossing Boundaries, Keeping Faith," in *The Atlantic in Global History, 1500–2000,* ed. Jorge Canizares-Esguerra and Erik R. Seeman (Upper Saddle River, N.J.: Pearson Prentice-Hall, 2007), p. 43.

## CONNECTIONS

Hailed as the origin of modern thought, the Scientific Revolution must also be seen as a product of its past. Borrowing from Islamic cultural achievements, medieval universities gave rise to important new scholarship in mathematics and natural philosophy. In turn, the ambition and wealth of Renaissance patrons nurtured intellectual curiosity and encouraged scholarly research and foreign exploration. Natural philosophers starting with Copernicus pioneered new methods of explaining and observing nature while drawing on centuries-old traditions of astrology, alchemy, and magic. A desire to control and profit from empire led the Spanish, followed by their European rivals, to explore and catalogue the flora and fauna of their American colonies. These efforts resulted in new frameworks in natural history and constituted a crucial element of the Scientific Revolution.

Enlightenment ideas of the eighteenth century were a similar blend of past and present, progressive and traditional, homegrown and foreign-inspired. Enlightenment thinkers advocated universal rights and liberties but also preached the biological inferiority of non-Europeans and women. Their principles often served as much to bolster absolutist regimes as to inspire revolutionaries to fight for human rights.

New notions of progress and social improvement would drive Europeans to embark on world-changing revolutions in politics and industry (see Chapters 22 and 23) at the end of the eighteenth century. These revolutions provided the basis for modern democracy and unprecedented scientific advancement. Yet some critics have seen a darker side. For them, the mastery over nature enabled by the Scientific Revolution now threatens to overwhelm the earth's fragile equilibrium, and the Enlightenment belief in the universal application of reason can lead to intolerance of other people's spiritual, cultural, and political values. Ongoing debates about the legacy of these intellectual and scientific developments testify to their continuing importance in today's world.

As the era of European exploration and conquest gave way to empire building, the eighteenth century witnessed increased consolidation of global markets and bitter competition among Europeans. The eighteenth-century Atlantic world thus tied the shores of Europe, the Americas, and Africa in a web of commercial and human exchange, including the tragedy of slavery, discussed in Chapter 20. The Atlantic world maintained strong ties with trade in the Pacific and the Indian Ocean.

# Review and Explore

## Make It Stick

 **LearningCurve**
Go online and use LearningCurve to retain what you've read.

## Identify Key Terms

Identify and explain the significance of each item below.

**Copernican hypothesis** (p. 559)          **philosophes** (p. 566)          **enclosure** (p. 578)

**law of inertia** (p. 560)          **deism** (p. 567)          **cottage industry** (p. 578)

**law of universal gravitation** (p. 560)          **general will** (p. 568)          **public sphere** (p. 580)

**empiricism** (p. 562)          **economic liberalism** (p. 573)          **salons** (p. 580)

**Enlightenment** (p. 565)          **enlightened absolutism** (p. 576)

**sensationalism** (p. 566)          **Haskalah** (p. 577)

## Review the Main Ideas

Answer the focus questions from each section of the chapter.

1. What revolutionary discoveries were made in the sixteenth and seventeenth centuries, and why did they occur in Europe? (p. 557)
2. What intellectual and social changes occurred as a result of the Scientific Revolution? (p. 562)
3. What new ideas about society and human relations emerged in the Enlightenment, and what new practices and institutions enabled these ideas to take hold? (p. 565)
4. How did economic and social change and the rise of Atlantic trade interact with Enlightenment ideas? (p. 577)

## Make Connections

Analyze the larger developments and continuities within and across chapters.

1. How did the era of European exploration and discovery (Chapter 16) affect the ideas of scientists and philosophers discussed in this chapter? In what ways did contact with new peoples and places stimulate new forms of thought among Europeans?
2. What was the relationship between the Scientific Revolution and the Enlightenment? How did new ways of understanding the natural world influence thinking about human society?
3. Compare the policies and actions of seventeenth-century absolutist rulers (Chapter 18) with their "enlightened" descendants described in this chapter. How accurate is the term "enlightened absolutism"?

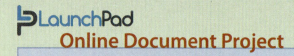

## Online Document Project

### Moses Mendelssohn

**How did Moses Mendelssohn fit into the larger Enlightenment debate about religious tolerance?**
Examine primary sources written by Mendelssohn and his contemporaries, and then complete a quiz and writing assignment based on the evidence and details from this chapter.

*See inside the front cover to learn more.*

## Suggested Reading

Cañizares-Esguerra, Jorge. *Nature, Empire, and Nation: Explorations of the History of Science in the Iberian World.* 2006. Explores the role of Spain and Spanish America in the development of science in the early modern period.

Dear, Peter. *Revolutionizing the Sciences: European Knowledge and Its Ambitions, 1500–1700,* 2d ed. 2009. An accessible and well-illustrated introduction to the Scientific Revolution.

Delborgo, James, and Nicholas Dew, eds. *Science and Empire in the Atlantic World.* 2008. A collection of essays examining the relationship between the Scientific Revolution and the imperial expansion of European powers across the Atlantic.

Ellis, Markman. *The Coffee-House: A Cultural History.* 2004. Recounts the rise of the coffeehouse and its impact on European cultural and social life.

Eze, Emmanuel Chukwudi, ed. *Race and the Enlightenment: A Reader.* 1997. A pioneering source on the origins of modern racial thinking in the Enlightenment.

Liebersohn, Harry. *The Travelers' World: Europe to the Pacific.* 2008. A beautifully written account of Europeans' voyages to the Pacific and the impact of these voyages on Enlightenment ideas.

Mannin, Susan, and Francis D. Cogliano. *The Atlantic Enlightenment.* 2008. A series of essays examining the exchange of Enlightenment ideas, authors, and texts across the Atlantic Ocean.

McMahon, Darrin M. *Happiness: A History.* 2006. Discusses how worldly pleasure became valued as a duty of individuals and societies in the Enlightenment.

Messbarger, Rebecca. *The Lady Anatomist: The Life and Work of Anna Morandi Manzolini.* 2010. The life of an Italian woman artist and scientist, who became a celebrated anatomical sculptor.

Outram, Dorinda. *The Enlightenment,* 2d ed. 2006. An outstanding and accessible introduction to Enlightenment debates that emphasizes the Enlightenment's social context and global reach.

Shapin, Steven. *The Scientific Revolution,* 2d ed. 2008. A concise and well-informed general introduction to the Scientific Revolution.

Sorkin, David. *Moses Mendelssohn and the Religious Enlightenment.* 1996. A brilliant study of the Jewish philosopher and of the role of religion in the Enlightenment.

### Waist Pendant of Benin Worn by Royalty

European intrusion in Africa during the early modern period deeply affected the diverse societies of Africa. The facial features, the beard, and the ruffled collar on this Edo peoples' artifact dating from the sixteenth to the nineteenth centuries are clearly Portuguese, but the braided hair is distinctly African, probably signifying royalty. (Hip Ornament: Portuguese Face, 16th–19th century. Brass, iron. Gift of Mr. and Mrs. Klaus G. Perls, 1991 [1991.162.9]. The Metropolitan Museum of Art, New York, NY, USA/Image copyright © The Metropolitan Museum of Art/Image source: Art Resource, NY)

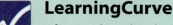

**LearningCurve**

After reading the chapter, go online and use LearningCurve to retain what you've read.

# Chapter Preview

**West Africa in the Fifteenth and Sixteenth Centuries**

**Cross-Cultural Encounters Along the East African Coast**

**The African Slave Trade**

A frican states and societies of the early modern period—from the fifteenth through the eighteenth centuries—included a wide variety of languages, cultures, political systems, and levels of economic development. Kingdoms and stateless societies coexisted throughout Africa, from small Senegambian villages to the Songhai kingdom and its renowned city of Timbuktu in West Africa, and from the Christian state of Ethiopia to the independent Swahili city-states along the East Africa coast. By the fifteenth century Africans had developed a steady rhythm of contact and exchange. Across the vast Sahara, trade goods and knowledge passed back and forth from West Africa to North Africa, and beyond to Europe and the Middle East. The same was true in East Africa, where Indian Ocean traders touched up and down the African coast to deliver goods from Arabia, India, and Asia and to pick up the ivory, gold, spices, and other products

representing Africa's rich natural wealth. In the interior as well, extensive trading networks linked African societies across the vast continent.

Modern European intrusion into Africa beginning in the fifteenth century profoundly affected these diverse societies and ancient trading networks. The intrusion led to the transatlantic slave trade, one of the greatest forced migrations in world history, through which Africa made a substantial, though involuntary, contribution to the building of the West's industrial civilization. In the seventeenth century an increasing desire for sugar in Europe resulted in an increasing demand for slave labor in South America and the West Indies, where sugar was produced. In the eighteenth century Western technological changes created a demand for cotton and other crops that required extensive human labor, thus intensifying the West's "need" for African slaves.

## West Africa in the Fifteenth and Sixteenth Centuries

☐ What types of economic, social, and political structures were found in the kingdoms and states along the west coast and in the Sudan?

In mid-fifteenth-century Africa, Benin and a number of other kingdoms flourished along the two-thousand-mile west coast between Senegambia and the northeastern shore of the Gulf of Guinea. Because much of

that coastal region is covered by tropical rain forest, in contrast to the western Sudan (immediately south of the Sahara), it is called the West African Forest Region (Map 20.1). Further inland, in the region of the Sudan, the kingdoms of Songhai, Kanem-Bornu, and Hausaland benefited from the trans-Saharan caravan trade, which along with goods brought Islamic culture to the region. These West African kingdoms maintained their separate existences for centuries. Stateless societies such as those in the region of Senegambia (modern-day Senegal and the Gambia) existed alongside these more

## ☐ Mapping the Past

**MAP 20.1 West African Societies, ca. 1500–1800** The coastal region of West Africa witnessed the rise of a number of kingdoms in the sixteenth century.

**ANALYZING THE MAP** What geographical features defined each of the kingdoms shown here? Consider rivers, lakes, oceans, deserts, and forests. How might they have affected the size and shape of these kingdoms?

**CONNECTIONS** Compare this map to the spot map of the slave coast of West Africa on page 605. Consider the role that rivers and other geographical factors played in the development of the West African slave trade. Why were Luanda and Benguela the logical Portuguese sources for slaves?

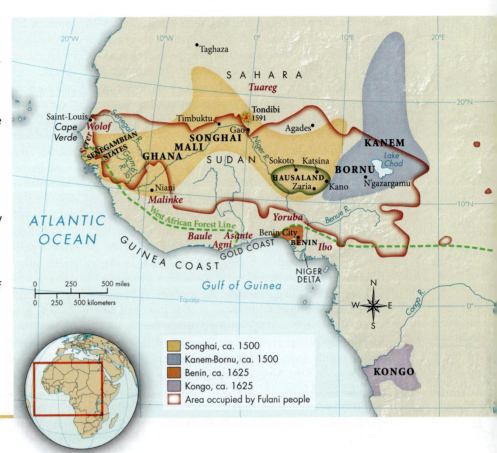

Songhai, ca. 1500
Kanem-Bornu, ca. 1500
Benin, ca. 1625
Kongo, ca. 1625
Area occupied by Fulani people

centralized states. Despite their political differences and whether they were agricultural, pastoral, or a mixture of both, West African cultures all faced the challenges presented by famine, disease, and the slave trade.

## The West Coast: Senegambia and Benin

The Senegambian states possessed a homogeneous culture and a common history. For centuries Senegambia—named for the Senegal and Gambia Rivers—served as an important entrepôt for desert caravan contact with North African and Middle Eastern Islamic civilizations. Through the transatlantic slave trade, Senegambia came into contact with Europe and the Americas. Thus Senegambia felt the impact of Islamic culture to the north and of European influences from the maritime West.

The Senegambian peoples spoke Wolof, Serer, and Pulaar, which all belong to the West African language group. Both the Wolof-speakers and the Serer-speakers had clearly defined social classes: royalty, nobility, warriors, peasants, low-caste artisans such as blacksmiths and leatherworkers, and enslaved persons. The enslaved class consisted of individuals who were pawned for debt, house servants who could not be sold, and people who were acquired through war or purchase. Senegambian slavery varied from society to society but generally

was not a benign institution. In some places slaves were considered chattel property and were treated as harshly as they would be later in the Western Hemisphere.

The word **chattel** originally comes from a Latin word meaning "head," as in "so many head of cattle." It reflects the notion that enslaved people are not human, but subhuman, like beasts of burden or other animals. Thus they can be treated like animals—whipped, beaten, worked to exhaustion, and forced to live in conditions no better than those provided for animals. But in Senegambia and elsewhere in Africa, many enslaved people were not considered chattel property. That is, unlike livestock or other common property, they could not be bought and sold. Some even served as royal advisers and enjoyed great power and prestige.[1] Unlike in the Americas, where slave status passed forever from one generation to the next, in Africa the enslaved person's descendants were sometimes considered free, although the stigma of slavery could attach to the family.

Senegambia was composed of stateless societies, culturally homogeneous ethnic populations where kinship and lineage groups tended to fragment communities. These societies comprised small groups of villages

---

• **chattel** An item of personal property; a term used in reference to enslaved people that conveys the idea that they are subhuman, like animals, and therefore may be treated like animals.

without a central capital. Among these stateless societies, **age-grade systems** evolved. Age-grades were groups of teenage males and females whom the society initiated into adulthood at the same time. Age-grades cut across family ties, created community-wide loyalties, and provided a means of local law enforcement, because each age-grade was responsible for the behavior of all its members.

The typical Senegambian community was a small, self-supporting agricultural village of closely related families. Fields were cut from the surrounding forest, and the average six- to eight-acre farm supported a moderate-size family. Millet and sorghum were the staple grains in northern Senegambia; farther south, forest dwellers cultivated yams as a staple. Senegambians supplemented their diet with plantains, beans, bananas, fish, oysters, and small game such as rabbits and monkeys. Village markets for produce exchange offered opportunities for receiving outside news and for social diversion. Social life centered on the family, and government played a limited role, interceding mostly to resolve family disputes and conflicts between families.

Alongside West African stateless societies like Senegambia were kingdoms and states ruled by kings who governed defined areas through bureaucratic hierarchies. The great forest kingdom of Benin emerged in the fifteenth and sixteenth centuries in what is now

southern Nigeria (see Map 20.1). Over time, the position of its **oba**, or king, was exalted, bringing stability to the state. In the later fifteenth century the oba Ewuare, a great warrior himself, strengthened his army and pushed Benin's borders as far as the Niger River in the east, westward into Yoruba country, and south to the Gulf of Guinea. During the late sixteenth and seventeenth centuries the office of the oba evolved from a warrior-kingship to a position of spiritual leadership.

At its height in the late sixteenth century, Benin controlled a vast territory, and European visitors described a sophisticated society. A Dutch visitor in the early 1600s, possibly Dierick Ruiters, described the capital, Benin City, as possessing a great, wide, and straight main avenue down the middle, with many side streets crisscrossing it. The visitor entered the city through a high, well-guarded gate framed on each side by a very tall earthen bulwark, or wall, with an accompanying moat. There was also an impressive royal palace, with at least four large courtyards surrounded by galleries leading up to it. William Bosman, another Dutch visitor writing a hundred years later, in 1702, described the prodigiously long and broad streets "in which continual Markets are kept, either of Kine [cattle], Cotton, Elephants Teeth, European Wares; or, in short, whatever is to be come at in this Country."[2] Visitors also noted that Benin City was kept scrupulously

clean and had no beggars and that public security was so effective that theft was unknown. The period also witnessed remarkable artistic creativity in ironwork, carved ivory, and especially bronze portrait busts. Over nine hundred brass plaques survive, providing important information about Benin court life, military triumphs, and cosmological ideas.

**The Oba of Benin** The oba's palace walls were decorated with bronze plaques that date from about the sixteenth to eighteenth centuries. This plaque vividly conveys the oba's power, majesty, and authority. The two attendants holding his arms also imply that the oba needs the support of his people. The oba's legs are mudfish, which represent fertility, peace, well-being, and prosperity, but their elongation, suggesting electric eels, relates the oba's terrifying and awesome power to the eel's jolting shock. (National Museum, Lagos, Nigeria/photo: André Held/akg-images)

In 1485 Portuguese and other Europeans began to appear in Benin in pursuit of trade, and over the next couple of centuries Benin grew rich from the profits made through the slave trade and the export of tropical products, particularly pepper and ivory. Its main European trading partners along this stretch of the so-called slave coast were the Dutch and Portuguese. In the early eighteenth century tributary states and stronger neighbors nibbled at Benin's frontiers, challenging its power. Benin, however, survived as an independent entity until the British conquered and burned Benin City in 1898 as part of the European imperialist seizure of Africa (discussed in Chapter 25).

## The Sudan: Songhai, Kanem-Bornu, and Hausaland

The Songhai kingdom, a successor state of the kingdoms of Ghana (ca. 900–1100) and Mali (ca. 1200–1450), dominated the whole Niger region of the western and central Sudan (see Map 20.1). The imperial expansion of Songhai (song-GUY) began during the reign of the Songhai king Sonni Ali (r. ca. 1464–1492) and continued under his eventual successor, Muhammad Toure (r. 1493–1528). From his capital at Gao, Toure extended his rule as far north as the salt-mining center at **Taghaza** in the western Sahara and as far east as Agades and Kano. A convert to Islam, Toure returned from a pilgrimage to Mecca impressed by what he had seen there. He tried to bring about greater centralization in his own territories by building a strong army, improving taxation procedures, and replacing local Songhai officials with more efficient Arabs in an effort to substitute royal institutions for ancient kinship ties.

We know little about daily life in Songhai society because of the paucity of written records and surviving artifacts. Some information is provided by Leo Africanus (ca. 1465–1550), a Moroccan captured by pirates and given as a slave to Pope Leo X. Africanus became a Christian, taught Arabic in Rome, and in 1526 published an account of his many travels, including a stay in the Songhai kingdom.

As a scholar, Africanus was naturally impressed by Timbuktu, the second-largest city of the empire, which he visited in 1513. "Here [is] a great store of doctors, judges, priests, and other learned men, that are bountifully maintained at the King's court," he reported.[3] Many of these Islamic scholars had studied in Cairo and other Muslim learning centers. They gave Timbuktu a reputation for intellectual sophistication, religious piety, and moral justice. (See "Viewpoints 20.1: European Descriptions of Timbuktu and Jenne," page 592.)

Songhai under Muhammad Toure seems to have enjoyed economic prosperity. Leo Africanus noted the abundant food supply, which was produced in the southern savanna and carried to Timbuktu by a large fleet of canoes. The elite had immense wealth, and expensive North African and European luxuries—clothes, copperware, glass and stone beads, perfumes, and horses—were much in demand. The existence of many shops and markets implies the development of an urban culture. In Timbuktu merchants, scholars, judges, and artisans constituted a distinctive bourgeoisie, or middle class. The presence of many foreign merchants, including Jews and Italians, gave the city a cosmopolitan atmosphere. Jews largely controlled the working of gold.

Slavery played an important role in Songhai's economy. On the royal farms scattered throughout the kingdom, enslaved people produced rice—the staple crop—for the royal granaries. Slaves could possess their own slaves, land, and cattle, but they could not bequeath any of this property; the king inherited all of it. Muhammad Toure greatly increased the number of royal slaves. He bestowed slaves on favorite Muslim scholars, who thus gained a steady source of income. Slaves were also sold at the large market at Gao, where traders from North Africa bought them to resell later in Cairo, Constantinople, Lisbon, Naples, Genoa, and Venice.

Despite its considerable economic and cultural strengths, Songhai had serious internal problems. Islam never took root in the countryside, and Muslim officials alienated the king from his people. Muhammad Toure's reforms were a failure. He governed diverse peoples—Tuareg, Mandinka, and Fulani as well as Songhai—who were often hostile to one another, and no cohesive element united them. Finally, the Songhai never developed an effective method of transferring power. Revolts, conspiracies, and palace intrigues followed the death of every king, and only three of the nine rulers in the dynasty begun by Muhammad Toure died natural deaths. Muhammad Toure himself was murdered by one of his sons. His death began a period of political instability that led to the kingdom's slow disintegration.

In 1582 the Moroccan sultanate began to press southward in search of a greater share of the trans-Saharan trade. The Songhai people, lacking effective leadership and believing the desert to be sure protection against invasion, took no defensive precautions. In 1591 a Moroccan army of three thousand soldiers—many of whom were slaves of European origin equipped with European muskets—crossed the Sahara and

- **age-grade systems** Among the societies of Senegambia, groups of men and women whom the society initiated into adulthood at the same time.

- **oba** The title of the king of Benin.

- **Taghaza** A settlement in the western Sahara, the site of the main salt-mining center.

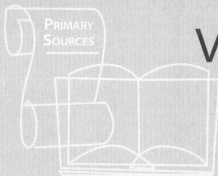

# Viewpoints 20.1

## European Descriptions of Timbuktu and Jenne

> *Timbuktu and Jenne were important cities in the West African empires of Ghana, Mali, and Songhai. The writings of al-Hassan Ibn Muhammad al-Wezaz al-Fasi, also known as Leo Africanus (ca. 1493–ca. 1554?), provide the most authoritative accounts of West Africa between the writings of Ibn Battuta in the fourteenth century and the writings of European travelers in the nineteenth century. The* Tarikh al-Sudan *(History of the Sudan), written by Abd al-Rahman al-Sadi (1594–after 1656), is one of the most important histories of the Mali and Songhai Empires in the fifteenth, sixteenth, and seventeenth centuries.*

### Leo Africanus, On Timbuktu

This name was . . . imposed upon this kingdome from the name of a certain towne so called, which (they say) king *Mense Suleiman* founded in the yeere of the Hegeira 610, and it is situate within twelve miles of a certaine branch of Niger, all the houses whereof are now changed into cottages built of chalke, and covered with thatch. Howbeit there is a most stately temple to be seene, the wals thereof are made of stone and lime; and a princely palace also built by a most excellent workeman of Granada. Here are many shops of artificiers, and merchants, and especially of such as weave linen and cotton cloth. And hither do the Barbarie-merchants bring cloth of Europe. All the women of this region except maid-servants go with their faces covered, and sell all necessarie victuals.

The inhabitants, & especially strangers there residing, are exceeding rich, insomuch, that the king that now is, married both his daughters unto two rich merchants. Here are many wels, containing most sweete water; and so often as the river Niger overfloweth, they conveigh the water thereof by certaine sluces into the towne.

Corne, cattle, milke, and butter this region yeeldeth in great abundance: but salt is verie scarce here; for it is brought hither by land from Tegaza, which is five hundred miles distant. When I myself was here, I saw one camels loade of salt sold for 80 ducates. The rich king of Tombuto hath many plates and scepters of gold, some whereof weigh 1300 pounds: and he keeps a magnificent and well furnished court. . . .

Here are great store of doctors, judges, priests, and other learned men, that are bountifully maintained at the kings cost and charges. And hither are brought divers manuscripts or written books out of Barbarie, which are sold for more money than any other merchandize.

### Al-Sadi, On Jenne

Jenne is a large, well-favoured, and blessed city, characterized by prosperity, good fortune and compassion. God bestowed these things upon that land as innate characteristics. It is the nature of Jenne's inhabitants to be kind and charitable, and solicitous for one another. . . .

Jenne is one of the great markets of the Muslims. Those who deal in salt from the mine of Taghaza meet there with those who deal in gold from the mine of Bitu. These two blessed mines have no equal in the entire world. People discovered their great blessing through going to them for business, amassing such wealth as only God — Sublime is He — could assess. This blessed city of Jenne is the reason why caravans come to Timbuktu from all quarters — north, south, east and west. Jenne is situated to the south and west of Timbuktu beyond the two rivers. . . .

Jenne was founded as a pagan town in the middle of the second century of the *hijira* of the Prophet [150 ANNO HEGIRAE, the Islamic calendar, or 767–768 C.E.]. . . . Its people became Muslims at the end of the sixth century [A.H., or eleventh to twelfth century C.E.]. First, Sultan Kunburu became a Muslim, then people followed his example. When he made up his mind to embrace Islam he ordered that all the Muslim scholars within the city should be assembled. They totaled 4,200, and he made a profession of Islam before them, and told them to call upon God Most High to grant the city three things: firstly, that anyone who fled there from his homeland in poverty and distress should have this translated by God into luxury and ease, so that he may forget his homeland; secondly, that more strangers than local folk should settle there; and thirdly, that those who came to trade there should lose patience and grow weary over selling their goods, and so dispose of them cheaply, allowing the people of Jenne to make a profit.

Sources: Al-Hassan ibn-Mohammad al-Wezaz al-Fasi, *The History and Description of Africa*. Done into English in 1600 by John Pory. Robert Brown, ed. (London: Hakluyt Society, 1896), vol. 3, pp. 824–825; John O. Hunwick, *Timbuktu and the Songhay Empire: Al-Sadi's Tarikh al-Sudan Down to 1613 and Other Contemporary Documents*. Reproduced by permission of BRILL ACADEMIC PUBLISHERS in the format Republish in a book via Copyright Clearance Center.

### QUESTIONS FOR ANALYSIS

1. During the colonial era, and even to the present day, Africa and its inhabitants were described in the most denigrating terms, such as *pagan, savage, illiterate, poor,* and *uncivilized.* How do the descriptions of these two African market and learning centers conform to those characterizations?

2. How important was Islam to the success of these two cities? In what ways?

inflicted a crushing defeat on the Songhai at Tondibi, spelling the empire's end.

East of Songhai lay the kingdoms of Kanem-Bornu and Hausaland (see Map 20.1). Under the dynamic military leader Idris Alooma (r. 1571–1603), Kanem-Bornu subdued weaker peoples and gained jurisdiction over an extensive area. Well drilled and equipped with firearms, his standing army and camel-mounted cavalry decimated warriors fighting with spears and arrows. Idris Alooma perpetuated a form of feudalism by granting land to able fighters in return for loyalty and the promise of future military assistance. Meanwhile, agriculture occupied most people, peasants and slaves alike. Kanem-Bornu shared in the trans-Saharan trade, shipping eunuchs and young girls to North Africa in return for horses and firearms. A devout Muslim, Idris Alooma elicited high praise from ibn-Fartura, who wrote a history of his reign called *The Kanem Wars*:

> So he made the pilgrimage and visited Medina with delight. . . . Among the benefits which God . . . conferred upon the Sultan Idris Alooma was the acquisition of Turkish musketeers and numerous household slaves who became skilled in firing muskets. . . .
>
> Among the most surprising of his acts was the stand he took against obscenity and adultery, so that no such thing took place openly in his time. Formerly the people had been indifferent to such offences. . . . In fact he was a power among his people and from him came their strength.
>
> The Sultan was intent on the clear path laid down by the Qur'an . . . in all his affairs and actions.[4]

Idris Alooma built mosques at his capital city of N'gazargamu and substituted Muslim courts and Islamic law for African tribunals and ancient customary law. His eighteenth-century successors lacked his vitality and military skills, however, and the empire declined.

Between Songhai and Kanem-Bornu were the lands of the Hausa, an agricultural people who lived in small villages. Hausa merchants carried on a sizable trade in slaves and kola nuts with North African communities across the Sahara. Obscure trading posts evolved into important Hausa city-states like Kano and Katsina, through which Islamic influences entered the region. Kano and Katsina became Muslim intellectual centers and in the fifteenth century attracted scholars from Timbuktu. The Muslim chronicler of the reign of King Muhammad Rimfa of Kano (r. 1463–1499) records that the king introduced the Muslim practices of purdah, or seclusion of women; *idal-fitr*, the festival after the fast of Ramadan; and the assignment of eunuchs to high state offices.[5] As in Songhai and Kanem-Bornu, however, Islam made no strong imprint on the Hausa masses until the nineteenth century.

## The Lives of the People of West Africa

Wives and children were highly desired in African societies because they could clear and cultivate the land and because they brought prestige, social support, and security in old age. The results were intense competition for women, inequality of access to them, an emphasis on male virility and female fertility, and serious tension between male generations. Polygyny was almost universal; as recently as the nineteenth century two-thirds of rural wives were in polygynous marriages.

**Queen Mother and Attendants** As in Ottoman, Chinese, and European societies, the mothers of African rulers sometimes exercised considerable political power because of their influence on their sons. African kings granted the title Queen Mother as a badge of honor. In this figure, the long beaded cap, called "chicken's beak," symbolizes the mother's rank, as do her elaborate neck jewelry and attendants. (Culture: Edo peoples. Culture: Court of Benin. Altar Tableau: Queen Mother and Attendants, 18th century. Brass. Front, view #1. Gift of Mr. and Mrs. Klaus G. Perls, 1991 [1991.17.111]. The Metropolitan Museum of Art, New York, NY, USA/Image copyright © The Metropolitan Museum of Art/Image source: Art Resource, NY)

Men acquired wives in two ways. In some cases, couples simply eloped and began their union. More commonly, a man's family gave bride wealth to the bride's family as compensation for losing the fruits of her productive and reproductive abilities. She was expected to produce children, to produce food through her labor, and to pass on the culture in the raising of her children. Because it took time for a young man to acquire the bride wealth, all but the richest men delayed marriage until about age thirty. Women married at about the onset of puberty.

The easy availability of land in Africa reduced the kinds of generational conflict that occurred in western Europe, where land was scarce. Competition for wives between male generations, however, was fierce. On the one hand, myth and folklore stressed respect for the elderly, and the older men in a community imposed their authority over the younger ones through painful initiation rites into adulthood, such as circumcision. On the other hand, in West Africa and elsewhere, societies were not based on rule by elders, as few people lived much beyond forty. Young men possessed the powerful asset of their labor, which could easily be turned into independence where so much land was available.

"Without children you are naked" goes a Yoruba proverb, and children were the primary goal of marriage. Just as a man's virility determined his honor, so barrenness damaged a woman's status. A wife's infidelity was considered a less serious problem than her infertility. A woman might have six widely spaced pregnancies in her fertile years; the universal practice of breast-feeding infants for two, three, or even four years may have inhibited conception. Long intervals between births due to food shortages also may have limited pregnancies and checked population growth. Harsh climate, poor nutrition, and infectious diseases also contributed to a high infant mortality rate.

Both nuclear and extended families were common in West Africa. Nuclear families averaged only five or six members, but the household of a Big Man (a local man of power) included his wives, married and unmarried sons, unmarried daughters, poor relations, dependents, and scores of children. Extended families were common among the Hausa and Mandinka peoples. On the Gold Coast in the seventeenth century, a well-to-do man's household might number 150 people, in the Kongo region in west-central Africa, several hundred. In areas where one family cultivated extensive land, a large household of young adults, children, and slaves probably proved most efficient. Still, although many children might be born, many also died. Families rarely exceeded five or six people; high infant mortality rates and short life spans kept the household numbers low.

In agriculture men did the heavy work of felling trees and clearing the land; women then planted, weeded, and harvested. Between 1000 and 1400, cassava (manioc), bananas, and plantains came to West Africa from Asia. Cassava required little effort to grow and became a staple food, but it had little nutritional value. In the sixteenth century the Portuguese introduced maize (corn), sweet potatoes, and new varieties of yams from the Americas. Fish supplemented the diets of people living near bodies of water. According to former slave Olaudah Equiano, the Ibo people in the mid-eighteenth century ate plantains, yams, beans, and Indian corn, along with stewed poultry, goat, or bullock (castrated steer) seasoned with peppers.[6] However, such a protein-rich diet was probably exceptional.

Disease posed perhaps the biggest obstacle to population growth. Malaria, spread by mosquitoes and rampant in West Africa (except in cool, dry Cameroon), was the greatest killer, especially of infants. West Africans developed a relatively high degree of immunity to malaria and other parasitic diseases, including hookworm (which enters the body through shoeless feet and attaches itself to the intestines), yaws (contracted by nonsexual contact and recognized by ulcerating lesions), sleeping sickness (the parasite enters the blood through the bite of the tsetse [SEHT-see] fly; symptoms are enlarged lymph nodes and, at the end, a comatose state), and a mild nonsexual form of syphilis. Acute strains of smallpox introduced by Europeans certainly did not help population growth, nor did venereal syphilis, which possibly originated in Latin America. As in Chinese and European communities in the early modern period, the sick depended on folk medicine. African medical specialists, such as midwives, bonesetters, exorcists using religious rituals, and herbalists, administered a variety of treatments, including herbal medications like salves, ointments, and purgatives. Still, disease was common where the diet was poor and lacked adequate vitamins.

The devastating effects of famine, often mentioned in West African oral traditions, represented another major check on population growth. Drought, excessive rain, swarms of locusts, and rural wars that prevented land cultivation all meant later food shortages. In the 1680s famine extended from the Senegambian coast to the Upper Nile, and many people sold themselves into slavery for food. In the eighteenth century "slave exports" reached their peak in times of famine, and ships could fill their cargo holds simply by offering food. The worst disaster occurred from 1738 to 1756, when, according to one chronicler, the poor were reduced literally to cannibalism, also considered a metaphor for the complete collapse of civilization.[7]

Because the Americas had been isolated from the Eurasian-African landmass for thousands of years, parasitic diseases common in Europe, Africa, and Asia were unknown in the Americas before the Europeans' arrival. Enslaved Africans taken to the Americas brought with them the diseases common to tropical West Africa, such as yellow fever, dengue fever, malaria, and hookworm. Thus the hot, humid disease environment in the American tropics, where the majority of enslaved Africans lived and worked, became more "African." On the other hand, cold-weather European diseases, such as chicken pox, mumps, measles, and influenza, prevailed in the northern temperate zone in North America and the southern temperate zone in South America. This difference in disease environment partially explains why Africans made up the majority of the unskilled labor force in the tropical areas of the Americas, and Europeans made up the majority of the unskilled labor force in the Western Hemisphere temperate zones, such as the northern United States and Canada.

## Trade and Industry

As in all premodern societies, West African economies rested on agriculture. There was some trade and industry, but population shortages encouraged local self-sufficiency, slowed transportation, and hindered exchange. There were very few large markets, and their relative isolation from the outside world and failure to attract large numbers of foreign merchants limited technological innovation.

For centuries black Africans had exchanged goods with North African merchants in centers such as Gao and Timbuktu. This long-distance trans-Saharan trade was conducted and controlled by Muslim-Berber merchants using camels. The two primary goods exchanged were salt, which came from salt mines in North Africa,

and gold, which came mainly from gold mines in modern-day Mali and, later, modern Ghana.

As elsewhere around the world, water was the cheapest method of transportation, and many small dugout canoes and larger trading canoes plied the Niger and its delta region (see Map 20.1). On land West African peoples used pack animals (camels or donkeys) rather than wheeled vehicles; only a narrow belt of land in the Sudan was suitable for animal-drawn carts. When traders reached an area infested with tsetse flies, they transferred each animal's load to human porters. Such difficulties in transport severely restricted long-distance trade, so most people relied on the regional exchange of local specialties.

West African communities had a well-organized market system. At informal markets on riverbanks, fishermen bartered fish for local specialties. More formal markets existed within towns and villages or on neutral ground between them. Markets also rotated among neighboring villages on certain days. People exchanged cotton cloth, thread, palm oil, millet, vegetables, and small household articles. Local sellers were usually women; traders from afar were men.

**West African Trade Routes**

Taghaza · Timbuktu · S A H A R A · Gao · Benin City · Niger R. · NIGER DELTA

→ Trade route

**Salt Making in the Central Sahara** For centuries camel caravans transported salt south across the Sahara to the great West African kingdoms, where it was exchanged for gold. Here at Tegguida-n-Tessum, Niger, in the central Sahara, salt is still collected by pouring spring water into small pools dug out of the saline soil. The water leaches out the salt before evaporating in the desert sun, leaving deposits of pure salt behind, which are then shaped into blocks for transport. (Afrique Photo, Cliché Naud/Visual Connection Archive)

Salt had long been one of Africa's most critical trade items. Salt is essential to human health; the Hausa language has more than fifty words for it. The salt trade dominated the West African economies in the fifteenth, sixteenth, and seventeenth centuries. The main salt-mining center was at Taghaza (see Map 20.1) in the western Sahara. In the most wretched conditions, slaves dug the salt from desiccated lakes and loaded heavy blocks onto camels' backs. **Tuareg** warriors and later Moors (peoples of Berber and Arab descent) traded their salt south for gold, grain, slaves, and kola nuts, which were used by Muslims as stimulants or aphrodisiacs. **Cowrie shells**, imported from the Maldives in the Indian Ocean by way of Gujarat (see page 511) and North Africa, served as the medium of exchange (and continued to do so long after European intrusion). Gold continued to be mined and shipped from Mali until South American bullion flooded Europe in the sixteenth century. Thereafter, its production in Africa steadily declined. In the late twentieth and early twenty-first centuries gold mining revived in Mali, to the point that gold has been Mali's leading export since 1999. Mali is now Africa's fourth-largest gold producer, after South Africa, Ghana, and Tanzania, and ranked sixteenth in the world in 2011.

West African peoples engaged in many crafts, such as basket weaving and potterymaking. Ironworking, a specialized skill producing articles useful to hunters, farmers, and warriors, became hereditary in individual families; such expertise was regarded as family property. The textile industry had the greatest level of specialization. The earliest fabric in West Africa was made of vegetable fiber. Muslim traders introduced cotton and its weaving in the ninth century, as the fine-quality fabrics found in Mali reveal. By the fifteenth century the Wolof and Mandinka regions had professional weavers producing beautiful cloth, but this cloth was too expensive to compete in the Atlantic and Indian Ocean markets after 1500. Women who spun cotton used only a spindle and not a wheel, which slowed output. Women wove on inefficient broadlooms, men on less clumsy but narrow looms. Although the relatively small quantities of cloth produced on these narrow looms (one to two inches wide) could not compete in a world market, they are the source of the famous multicolored African kente cloth made from threads of cotton, or cotton and silk, by the Akan people of Ghana and the Ivory Coast. The area around Kano, in northern Nigeria, is famous for the deeply dyed blue cloth produced on the narrowest looms in the world and favored by the Tuareg Berber peoples of North Africa.

---

# Cross-Cultural Encounters Along the East African Coast

☐ How did the arrival of Europeans and other foreign cultures affect the East African coast, and how did Ethiopia and the Swahili city-states respond to these incursions?

East Africa in the early modern period faced repeated incursions from foreign powers. At the beginning of the sixteenth century Ethiopia faced challenges from the Muslim state of Adal, and then from Europeans. Jesuit attempts to substitute Roman Catholic liturgical forms for the Coptic Christian liturgies (see below) met with fierce resistance and ushered in a centuries-long period of hostility to foreigners. The wealthy Swahili city-states along the southeastern African coast also resisted European intrusions in the sixteenth century, with even more disastrous results. Cities such as Mogadishu, Kilwa, and Sofala used Arabic as the language of communication, and their commercial economies had long been tied to the trade of the Indian Ocean. The arrival of the Portuguese in 1498 proved catastrophic for those cities, and the Swahili coast suffered economic decline as a result.

## Muslim and European Incursions in Ethiopia, ca. 1500–1630

At the beginning of the sixteenth century the powerful East African kingdom of Ethiopia extended from Massawa in the north to several tributary states in the south (Map 20.2), but the ruling Solomonic dynasty in Ethiopia, in power since the thirteenth century, faced serious external threats. Alone among the states in northeast and eastern Africa, Ethiopia was a Christian kingdom that practiced **Coptic Christianity**, an orthodox form of the Christian faith that originated in Egypt in 451. Christianity had first come to Ethiopia from Egypt when the archbishop in Alexandria appointed Saint Frumentius the first bishop of Ethiopia in 328. By the early 1500s Ethiopia was an island of Christianity surrounded by a sea of Muslim states.

Adal, a Muslim state along the southern base of the Red Sea, began incursions into Ethiopia, and in 1529 the Adal general Ahmad ibn-Ghazi inflicted a disastrous defeat on the Ethiopian emperor Lebna Dengel

---

- **Tuareg** Along with the Moors, warriors who controlled the north-south trans-Saharan trade in salt.

- **cowrie shells** Imported from the Maldives, they served as the medium of exchange in West Africa.

- **Coptic Christianity** Orthodox form of Christianity from Egypt practiced in Ethiopia.

(r. 1508–1540). Ibn-Ghazi followed up his victory with systematic devastation of the land; destruction of many Ethiopian artistic and literary works, churches, and monasteries; and the forced conversion of thousands to Islam. Lebna Dengel fled to the mountains and appealed to Portugal for assistance. A Portuguese force of four hundred men under Cristóvão da Gama came to his aid, but Dengel was killed in battle before the Portuguese arrived. The Muslim occupation of Christian Ethiopia, which began around 1531, ended in 1543, after a joint Ethiopian and Portuguese force defeated a larger Muslim army at the Battle of Wayna Daga, east of Lake Tana, on February 21. During the battle General ibn-Ghazi was killed by a Portuguese musketeer, but not before he had left a horrific legacy of destruction and death that continues to resonate in Ethiopia today.

In the late twelfth century tales of Prester John, rumored to be a powerful Christian monarch ruling a vast and wealthy African empire, reached western Europe. The search for Prester John, as well as for gold and spices, spurred the Portuguese to undertake a series of trans-African expeditions that reached Timbuktu and Mali in the 1480s and the Ethiopian court by 1508. Although Prester John was a mythical figure, Portuguese emissaries triumphantly but mistakenly identified the Ethiopian emperor as Prester John.[8] It was their desire to convert Ethiopians from Coptic Christianity to Roman Catholicism that motivated the Portuguese to aid the Ethiopians in defeating Adal's forces at Wayna Daga in 1543.

No sooner had the Muslim threat ended than Ethiopia encountered three more dangers. The Galla, now known as the Oromo, moved northward in great numbers in the 1530s, occupying portions of Harar, Shoa, and Amhara. The Ethiopians could not defeat them militarily, and the Galla were not interested in assimilation. For the next two centuries the two peoples lived together in an uneasy truce. Simultaneously, the Ottoman Turks seized Massawa and other coastal cities. Then the Jesuits arrived and attempted to force Roman Catholicism on a proud people whose Coptic form of Christianity long antedated the European version. The overzealous Jesuit missionary Alphonse Mendez tried to revamp the Ethiopian liturgy, rebaptize the people, and replace ancient Ethiopian customs and practices with Roman ones. Since Ethiopian national sentiment was closely tied to Coptic Christianity, violent rebellion and anarchy ensued.

In 1633 the Jesuit missionaries were expelled. For the next two centuries hostility to foreigners, weak political leadership, and regionalism characterized Ethiopia. Civil conflicts between Galla and Ethiopians erupted continually. The Coptic Church, though lacking strong authority, survived as the cornerstone of Ethiopian national identity.

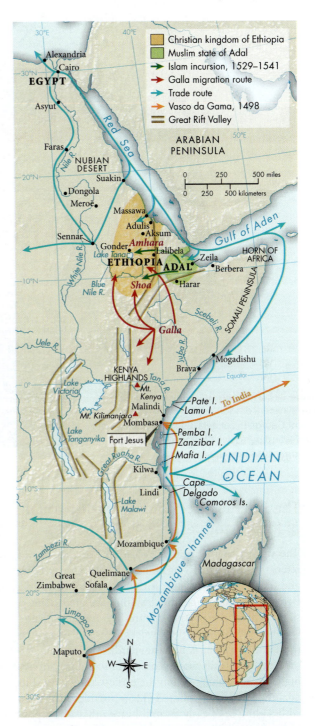

**MAP 20.2 East Africa in the Sixteenth Century**
In early modern times, the Christian kingdom of Ethiopia, first isolated and then subjected to Muslim and European pressures, played an insignificant role in world affairs. But the East African city-states, which stretched from Sofala in the south to Mogadishu in the north, had powerfully important commercial relations with Mughal India, China, the Ottoman world, and southern Europe.

**Saint George in Ethiopian Art** This wall painting of Saint George slaying a dragon resides in the stone-carved Church of Saint George in Lalibela, Ethiopia, and attests to the powerful and pervasive Christian influence on Ethiopian culture. (Galen R. Frysinger)

## The Swahili City-States and the Arrival of the Portuguese, ca. 1500–1600

The word **Swahili** means "People of the Coast" and refers to the people living along the East African coast and on the nearby islands. Although predominantly a Bantu-speaking people, the Swahili have incorporated significant aspects of Arab culture. The Arabic alphabet was used for the first written works in Swahili (although the Latin alphabet is now standard), and roughly 35 percent of Swahili words come from Arabic. Surviving texts in Swahili—from the earliest known Swahili documents dating from 1711—provide historians with a glimpse of early Swahili history that is not possible when studying early nonliterate African societies. By the eleventh century the Swahili had accepted Islam, which provided a common identity and unifying factor for all the peoples along coastal East Africa. Living on the Indian Ocean coast, the Swahili also felt the influences of Indians, Indonesians, Persians, and even the Chinese.

Swahili civilization was overwhelmingly maritime. A fertile, well-watered, and intensely cultivated stretch of land extending down the coast yielded rice, grains, citrus fruit, and cloves. The region's considerable prosperity, however, rested on trade and commerce. The Swahili acted as middlemen in an Indian Ocean–East African economy that might be described as early capitalism. They exchanged ivory, rhinoceros horn, tortoise shells, inlaid ebony chairs, copra (dried coconut meat that yields coconut oil), and inland slaves for Arabian and Persian perfumes, toilet articles, ink, and paper; for Indian textiles, beads, and iron tools; and for Chinese porcelains and silks. In the fifteenth century the cosmopolitan city-states of Mogadishu, Pate, Lamu, Mombasa, and especially Kilwa enjoyed a worldwide reputation for commercial prosperity and high living standards.[9]

The arrival of the Portuguese explorer Vasco da Gama (see Map 16.2, page 466) in 1498 spelled the end of the Swahili cities' independence. Lured by the spice trade, da Gama wanted to build a Portuguese maritime empire in the Indian Ocean. Swahili rulers responded in different ways to Portuguese intrusion. Some, such as the sultan of Malindi, quickly agreed to a trading alliance with the Portuguese. Others, such as the sultan of Mombasa, were tricked into commercial agreements. Swahili rulers who rejected Portuguese overtures saw their cities bombarded and attacked. To

• **Swahili** Meaning "People of the Coast," the term used for the people living along the East African coast and on nearby islands.

secure alliances made between 1502 and 1507, the Portuguese erected forts at the southern port cities of Kilwa, Zanzibar, and Sofala. These fortified markets and trading posts served as the foundation of Portuguese commercial power on the Swahili coast. (See "Listening to the Past: Duarte Barbosa on the Swahili City-States," page 600.) The better-fortified northern cities, such as Mogadishu, survived as important entrepôts for goods to India.

The Portuguese presence in the south did not yield the expected commercial fortunes. Rather than accept Portuguese commercial restrictions, the residents deserted the towns, and the town economies crumbled. Large numbers of Kilwa's people, for example, immigrated to northern cities. The gold flow from inland mines to Sofala slowed to a trickle. Swahili noncooperation successfully prevented the Portuguese from gaining control of the local coastal trade.

In 1589 Portugal finally won an administrative stronghold near Mombasa. Called Fort Jesus, it remained a Portuguese base for over a century. In the late seventeenth century pressures from the northern European maritime powers—the Dutch, French, and English, aided greatly by Omani Arabs—combined with local African rebellions to bring about the collapse of Portuguese influence in Africa. A Portuguese presence remained only at Mozambique in the far south and Angola on the west coast.

The Portuguese had no religious or cultural impact on the Swahili cities. Their sole effect was the cities' economic decline.

## The African Slave Trade

☐ What role did slavery play in African societies before the transatlantic slave trade began, and what was the effect of European involvement?

The exchange of peoples captured in local and ethnic wars within sub-Saharan Africa, the trans-Saharan slave trade with the Mediterranean Islamic world beginning in the seventh century, and the slave traffic across the Indian Ocean all testify to the long tradition and continental dimensions of the African slave trade before European intrusion. The enslavement of human beings was practiced in some form or another all over Africa—indeed, all over the world. Sanctioned by law and custom, enslaved people served critical and well-defined roles in the social, political, and economic organization of many African societies. Domestically these roles ranged from concubines and servants to royal guards and advisers. As was the case later in the Americas, some enslaved people were common laborers. In terms

## ☐ Picturing the Past

### Chinese Porcelain Plates
Embedded in an eighteenth-century Kunduchi pillar tomb, these Chinese plates testify to the enormous Asian-African trade that flourished in the fourteenth to sixteenth centuries. Kunduchi, whose ruins lie north of Dar es Salaam in present-day Tanzania, was one of the Swahili city-states. (Werner Forman Archive/The Bridgeman Art Library)

**ANALYZING THE IMAGE**  How many Chinese plates can you identify? What features identify this as a tomb?

**CONNECTIONS**  Why would a Muslim African want a Chinese plate embedded in his tomb? What does this suggest about his status, occupation, and wealth?

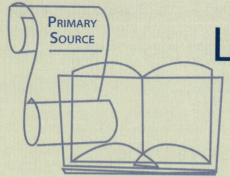

# Listening to the Past

## Duarte Barbosa on the Swahili City-States

*The Portuguese writer, government agent, and traveler Duarte Barbosa made two voyages to India. Arriving first in 1500, he acted for five years as interpreter and translator in Cochin and Cannanore in Kerala (in southwestern India on the Malabar coast), returning to Lisbon in 1506. On his second trip to India in 1511, he served the Portuguese government as chief scribe in the factory of Cannanore (a factory was a warehouse for the storage of goods, not a manufacturing center) and as the liaison with the local Indian rajah (prince). Barbosa returned to Portugal around 1516. In September 1519 he began his greatest adventure, setting off with Ferdinand Magellan to circumnavigate the globe. After Magellan was killed in a battle with native forces in the Philippines, Barbosa took joint command of the expedition, but was himself killed in the Philippines less than a week after Magellan, on May 1, 1521.*

*On the basis of his trips around the Indian Ocean in 1518, Barbosa completed his* Libro de Duarte Barbosa (The Book of Duarte Barbosa), *a geographical and ethnographic survey of peoples, lands, and commerce from the Cape of Good Hope to China. It was based largely on his personal observations. First published in Italian, the book won wide acclaim in Europe, and modern scholars consider its geographical information very accurate. The excerpts below describe some of the city-states along the East African coast of Swahili.*

### Sofala

❝ And the manner of their traffic was this: they came in small vessels named *zambucos* from the kingdoms of Kilwa, Mombasa, and Malindi, bringing many cotton cloths, some spotted and others white and blue, also some of silk, and many small beads, grey, red, and yellow, which things come to the said kingdoms from the great kingdom of Cambaya [in northwest India] in other greater ships. And these wares the said Moors who came from Malindi and Mombasa paid for in gold at such a price that those merchants departed well pleased; which gold they gave by weight.

The Moors of Sofala kept these wares and sold them afterwards to the Heathen of the Kingdom of Benametapa, who came thither laden with gold which they gave in exchange for the said cloths without weighing it. These Moors collect also great store of ivory which they find hard by Sofala, and this also they sell in the Kingdom of Cambaya at five or six cruzados the quintal. They also sell some ambergris, which is brought to them from the Hucicas, and is exceeding good. These Moors are black, and some of them tawny; some of them speak Arabic, but the more part use the language of the country. They clothe themselves from the waist down with cotton and silk cloths, and other cloths they wear over their shoulders like capes, and turbans on their heads. Some of them wear small caps dyed in grain in chequers and other woollen clothes in many tints, also camlets and other silks.

Their food is millet, rice, flesh and fish. In this river as far as the sea are many sea horses, which come out on the land to graze, which horses always move in the sea like fishes; they have tusks like those of small elephants in size, and the ivory is better than that of elephants, being whiter and harder, and it never loses colour. In the country near Sofala are many wild elephants, exceeding great (which the country-folk know not how to tame) ounces, lions, deer and many other wild beasts. It is a land of plains and hills with many streams of sweet water. ❞

### Kilwa

❝ Going along the coast from this town of Mozambique, there is an island hard by the mainland which is called Kilwa, in which is a Moorish town with many fair houses of stone and mortar, with many windows after our fashion, very well arranged in streets, with many flat roofs. The doors are of wood, well carved, with excellent joinery. Around it are streams and orchards and fruit-gardens with many channels of sweet water. It has a Moorish king over it. From this place they trade with Sofala, whence they bring back gold, and from here they spread all over . . . the seacoast [which] is well-peopled with villages and abodes of Moors.

of economics, slaves were commodities for trade, no more or less important than other trade items, such as gold and ivory.

Over time, the trans-Saharan slave trade became less important than the transatlantic trade, which witnessed an explosive growth during the seventeenth and eighteenth centuries. The millions of enslaved Africans forcibly exported to the Americas had a lasting impact on African society and led ultimately to a wider use of slaves within Africa itself.

## The Institution of Slavery in Africa

Islamic practices strongly influenced African slavery. African rulers justified enslavement with the Muslim argument that prisoners of war could be sold and that

Before the King our Lord sent out his expedition to discover India the Moors of Sofala, Cuama, Angoya and Mozambique were all subject to the King of Kilwa, who was the most mighty king among them. And in this town was great plenty of gold, as no ships passed towards Sofala without first coming to this island. . . .

This town was taken by force from its king by the Portuguese, as, moved by arrogance, he refused to obey the King our Lord. There they took many prisoners and the king fled from the island, and His Highness ordered that a fort should be built there, and kept it under his rule and governance. Afterwards he ordered that it should be pulled down, as its maintenance was of no value nor profit to him, and it was destroyed by Antonio de Saldanha. 〞

### Malindi

❝ Journeying along the coast towards India, there is a fair town on the mainland lying along a strand, which is named Malindi. It pertains to the Moors and has a Moorish king over it; the which place has many fair stone and mortar houses of many storeys, with great plenty of windows and flat roofs, after our fashion. The place is well laid out in streets. The folk are both black and white; they go naked, covering only their private parts with cotton and silk cloths. Others of them wear cloths folded like cloaks and waist-bands, and turbans of many rich stuffs on their heads.

They are great barterers, and deal in cloth, gold, ivory, and divers other wares with the Moors and Heathen of the great kingdom of Cambaya; and to their haven come every year many ships with cargoes of merchandize, from which they get great store of gold, ivory and wax. In this traffic the Cambay merchants make great profits, and thus, on one side and the other, they earn much money. There is great plenty of food in this city (rice, millet, and some wheat which they bring from Cambaya), and divers sorts of fruit, inasmuch as there is here abundance of fruit-gardens and orchards. Here too are plenty of round-tailed sheep, cows and other cattle and great store of oranges, also of hens.

The king and people of this place ever were and are friends of the King of Portugal, and the Portuguese always find in them great comfort and friendship and perfect peace, and there the ships, when they chance to pass that way, obtain supplies in plenty. 〞

The walls of the sultan's palace sit silently amid the ruins at Gedi, a historic Swahili site a few miles south of Malindi on the Kenyan coast. Founded in the late thirteenth or early fourteenth century, Gedi survived as a thriving trading community until the early seventeenth century. Although it was not a major Swahili town, excavations have uncovered iron lamps from India, scissors from Spain, a Chinese Ming vase, Persian stoneware, and Venetian beads. Some homes had bathrooms with running water and flush toilets, and the streets had drainage gutters. The dated tomb in the cemetery has "1399" incised in its plaster wall. (© Harry Page/Alamy)

Source: Mansel Longworth Dames, trans., *The Book of Duarte Barbosa,* vol. 1 (London: Bedford Press, 1918).

### QUESTIONS FOR ANALYSIS

1. What seems to have impressed Barbosa? What was his attitude toward the various peoples he saw? What Portuguese or Western prejudices do you discern?

2. What was the Portuguese relationship to the Swahili city-states at the time Barbosa saw them?

3. What was the source of Sofala's gold? Of Sofala's and Malindi's ivory? What did the Indian kingdom of Cambaya use ivory for?

captured people were considered chattel, or personal possessions, to be used any way the owner saw fit. Between 650 and 1600 black as well as white Muslims transported perhaps as many as 4.82 million black slaves across the trans-Saharan trade route.[10] In the 1300s and 1400s the rulers and elites of Mali and Benin imported thousands of white Slavic slave women, symbols of wealth and status, who had been seized in slave raids from the Balkans and Caucasus regions of the eastern Mediterranean by Turks, Mongols, and others.[11] In 1444, when Portuguese caravels landed 235 slaves at Algarve in southern Portugal, a contemporary observed that they seemed "a marvelous (extraordinary) sight, for, amongst them, were some white enough, fair enough, and well-proportioned; others were less white, like mulattoes; others again were black as Ethiops."[12]

**Below Stairs** The prints and cartoons of Thomas Rowlandson (1756–1827) testify to the sizable numbers of blacks in eighteenth-century London, where they worked in naval and military service as well as domestic service. Here the household cook, maid, and footman relax before the kitchen fire. Interracial marriages were not uncommon. (© The Trustees of The British Museum/Art Resource, NY)

Meanwhile, the flow of black people to Europe, begun during the Renaissance, continued. In the seventeenth and eighteenth centuries as many as two hundred thousand Africans entered European societies. Some arrived as slaves, others as servants; the legal distinction was not always clear. Eighteenth-century London, for example, had more than ten thousand blacks, most of whom arrived as sailors on Atlantic crossings or as personal servants brought from the West Indies. In England most were free, not slaves. Initially, a handsome black person was a fashionable accessory, a rare status symbol. Later, English aristocrats considered black servants too ordinary. The duchess of Devonshire offered her mother an eleven-year-old boy, explaining that the duke did not want a Negro servant because "it was more original to have a Chinese page than to have a black one; everybody

had a black one."[13] London's black population constituted a well-organized, self-conscious subculture, with black pubs, black churches, and black social groups assisting the black poor and unemployed. Some black people attained wealth and position, the most famous being Francis Barber, manservant of the sixteenth-century British literary giant Samuel Johnson and heir to Johnson's papers and to most of his sizable fortune. Barber had helped Johnson in revising Johnson's famous *Dictionary of the English Language*, published in 1755, and he is frequently mentioned in the celebrated biography of Johnson by James Boswell. He was a contemporary of another well-known African who lived in London for a while, Olaudah Equiano.

In 1658 the Dutch East India Company (see page 478) began to allow the importation of slaves into the Cape Colony, which the company had founded on the southern tip of Africa in 1652. Over the next century and a half about 75 percent of the slaves brought into the colony came from Dutch East India Company colonies in India and Southeast Asia or from Madagascar; the remaining 25 percent came from Africa. Some of those enslaved at the Cape served as domestic servants or as semiskilled artisans, but most worked long and hard as field hands and at any other menial or manual forms of labor needed by their European masters.

The Dutch East India Company was the single largest slave owner in the Cape Colony, employing its slaves on public works and company farms. Initially, individual company officials collectively owned the most slaves, working them on their wine and grain estates, but by about 1740 urban and rural free burghers (European settlers) owned the majority of the slaves. In 1780 half of all white men at the Cape had at least one slave, as slave ownership fostered a strong sense of racial and economic solidarity in the white master class.

The slave population at the Cape was never large, although from the early 1700s to the 1820s it outnumbered the European free burgher population. When the British ended slavery in the British Empire in 1834, there were around thirty-six thousand slaves in the Cape Colony. In comparison, over three hundred thousand enslaved Africans labored on the Caribbean island of Jamaica, also a British slaveholding colony at the time.

Although in the seventeenth and eighteenth centuries Holland had a Europe-wide reputation for religious tolerance and intellectual freedom (see page 541), in the Cape Colony the Dutch used a strict racial hierarchy and heavy-handed paternalism to maintain control over enslaved

**Cape Colony, ca. 1750**

native and foreign-born peoples. Early accounts of slavery at the Cape often gave the impression that it was a relatively benign institution in comparison with slavery in the Americas. Modern scholars, however, consider slavery in the Cape Colony in many ways as oppressive as slavery in the Americas and the Muslim world. In Muslim society the offspring of a free man and an enslaved woman were free, but in southern Africa such children remained enslaved. Because enslaved males greatly outnumbered enslaved females in the Cape Colony, marriage and family life were almost nonexistent. Because there were few occupations requiring special skills, those enslaved in the colony lacked opportunities to earn manumission, or freedom. And in contrast with North and South America and with Muslim societies, in the Cape Colony only a very small number of those enslaved won manumission; most of them were women, suggesting they gained freedom through sexual or close personal relationships with their owners.[14]

The slave trade expanded greatly in East Africa's savanna and Horn regions in the late eighteenth century and the first half of the nineteenth century. Slave exports from these areas and from Africa's eastern coast amounted to perhaps thirty thousand a year. Why this demand? Merchants and planters wanted slaves to work the sugar plantations on the Mascarene Islands, located east of Madagascar; the clove plantations on Zanzibar and Pemba; and the food plantations along the Kenyan coast. The eastern coast also exported enslaved people to the Americas, particularly to Brazil. In the late eighteenth and early nineteenth centuries, precisely when the slave trade to North America and the Caribbean declined, the Arabian and Asian markets expanded. Only with colonial conquest of Africa by Great Britain, Germany, and Italy after 1870 did suppression of the trade begin. Enslavement, of course, persists even today. (See "Global Trade: Slaves," page 604.)

## The Transatlantic Slave Trade

Although the trade in African people was a worldwide phenomenon, the transatlantic slave trade involved the largest number of enslaved Africans. This forced migration of millions of human beings, extending from the early sixteenth to the late nineteenth centuries, represents one of the most inhumane, unjust, and shameful tragedies in human history. It also immediately provokes a troubling question: why Africa? Why, in the seventeenth and eighteenth centuries, did enslavement in the Americas become exclusively African?

European settlers first enslaved indigenous peoples, the Amerindians, to mine the silver and gold discovered in the New World (see page 478). When they proved ill suited to the harsh rigors of mining, the Spaniards brought in Africans. Although the Dutch had transported Indonesian peoples to work as slaves in the Cape Colony in South Africa, the cost of transporting Chinese or Pacific Island peoples to the Americas was far too great.

One scholar has argued that a pan-European insider-outsider ideology prevailed across Europe. This cultural attitude permitted the enslavement of outsiders but made the enslavement of white Europeans taboo. Europeans could not bear the sight of other Europeans doing plantation slave labor. According to this theory, a similar pan-African ideology did not exist, as Africans had no problem with selling Africans to Europeans.[15] Several facts argue against the validity of this theory. English landlords exploited their Irish peasants with merciless severity, French aristocrats often looked on their peasantry with cold contempt, and Russian boyars treated their serfs with casual indifference and harsh brutality. These and other possible examples contradict the existence of a pan-European ideology or culture that opposed the enslavement of white Europeans. Moreover, the flow of white enslaved Slavic peoples from the Balkans into the eastern Mediterranean continued unabated during the same period.

Another theory holds that in the Muslim and Arab worlds by the tenth century, an association had developed between blackness and menial slavery. The Arab word *abd*, or "black," had become synonymous with *slave*. Although the great majority of enslaved persons in the Islamic world were white, a racial element existed in Muslim perceptions: not all slaves were black, but blacks were identified with slavery. In Europe, after the arrival of tens of thousands of sub-Saharan Africans in the Iberian Peninsula during the fifteenth century, Christian Europeans also began to make a strong association between slavery and black Africans. Therefore, Africans seemed the "logical" solution to the labor shortage in the Americas.[16]

Another important question relating to the African slave trade is this: why were African peoples enslaved in a period when serfdom was declining in western Europe and when land was so widely available and much of the African continent had a labor shortage? The answer seems to lie in a technical problem related to African agriculture. Partly because of the tsetse fly, which causes sleeping sickness and other diseases, and partly because of easily leached lateritic soils (containing high concentrations of oxides), farmers had great difficulty using draft animals. Tropical soils responded poorly to plowing, and most work had to be done with the hoe. Productivity, therefore, was low. Economists maintain that in most societies the value of a worker's productivity determines the value of his or her labor. In precolonial Africa the individual's agricultural productivity was low, so his or her economic value to society was less than the economic value of a European

# Global Trade

## Slaves

**Slaves** are people who are bound to servitude and often traded as property or as a commodity. The traffic in human persons bought and sold for the profits of their labor cannot decently be compared to the buying and selling of other commodities; people are not goods. But most societies, with the remarkable exception of the Aborigines in Australia, have treated people as goods and have engaged in the slave trade. Those who have been enslaved include captives in war, persons convicted of crimes, persons sold for debt, and persons bought and sold for sex. The ancient Greek philosophers, notably Aristotle, justified slavery as "natural." The Middle Eastern monotheistic faiths — Judaism, Christianity, and Islam — while professing the sacred dignity of each individual, and the Asian religious and sociopolitical ideologies of Buddhism and Confucianism, while stressing an ordered and harmonious society, all tolerated slavery and urged slaves' obedience to established authorities. Until the Enlightenment of the eighteenth century, most people everywhere accepted slavery as a "natural phenomenon."

Between 1500 and 1900 the transatlantic African slave trade accounted for the largest number of people bought and sold. As such, and because of ample documentation, it has attracted much attention from scholars, and it also has led many people to identify the institution of slavery with African blacks. From a global perspective, however, the trade was far broader.

Slaves came from all over the world and included people of all races. The steady flow of white women and children from the Crimea, the Caucasus, and the Balkans in the fourteenth to eighteenth centuries for domestic, military, or sexual services in Ottoman lands, Italy, and sub-Saharan Africa; the use of convicts as galley slaves in the Venetian, French, Spanish, and Turkish navies; the enslavement of peoples defeated in war by Aztec, Inca, Sioux, Navajo, and other indigenous peoples of the Americas; the various forms of debt slavery in China and in Russia (where the legal distinction between serf and slave before 1861 was very hazy); the traffic of Indonesian and Pacific Island peoples for slave labor in Dutch South Africa; and the trans-Saharan stream of Africans to Mediterranean

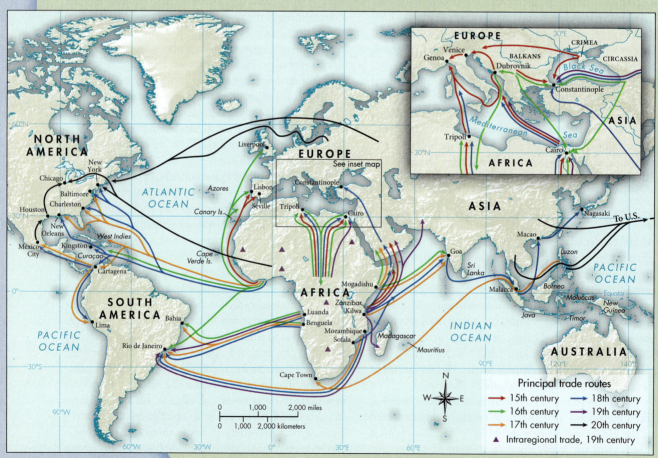

ports that continued at medieval rates into the late nineteenth century—all were different forms of a worldwide practice. Although these forms sometimes had little in common with one another, they all involved the buying and selling of human beings who could not move about freely or enjoy the fruits of their labor.

The price of slaves varied widely over time and from market to market, according to age, sex, physical appearance, buyers' perceptions of the social characteristics of each slave's ethnic background, and changes in supply and demand. The Mediterranean and Indian Ocean markets preferred women for domestic service; the Atlantic markets wanted strong young men for mine and plantation work, for example. We have little solid information on prices for slaves in the Balkans, Caucasus, or Indian Ocean region. Even in the Atlantic trade, it is difficult to determine, over several centuries, the value of currencies, the cost and insurance on transported slaves, and the cost of goods exchanged for slaves. Yet the gold-encrusted cathedrals of Spain and the elegant plantation houses of the southern United States stand as testimony to the vast fortunes made in the slave trade.

How is the human toll of slavery measured? Transformations within societies occurred not only because of local developments but also because of interactions among regions. For example, the virulent racism that in so many ways defines the American experience resulted partly from medieval European habits of dehumanizing the enemy (English versus Irish, German versus Slav, Christian versus Jew and Muslim) and partly from the movement of peoples and ideas all over the globe. American gold prospectors in the 1850s carried the bigotry they had heaped on blacks in the Americas to Australia, where it conditioned attitudes toward Asians and other peoples of color. Racism, like the slave trade, is a global phenomenon.

For all the cries for human rights today, the slave trade continues on a broad scale. The ancient Indian Ocean traffic in Indian girls and boys for "service" in the Persian Gulf oil kingdoms persists, as does the sale of African children for work in Asia. In 2011 an estimated 12 to 27 million people globally are held in one form of slavery or another. The U.S. State Department estimates that 15,000 to 18,000 enslaved foreign nationals are brought to the United States each year and, conservatively, perhaps as many as 50,000 people, mostly women and children, are in slavery in America at any given time. They have been bought, sold, tricked, and held in captivity, and their labor, often as sex slaves, has been exploited for the financial benefit of masters in a global enterprise.

peasant in Europe. Enslaved persons in the Americas were more productive than free producers in Africa. And European slave dealers were very willing to pay a price higher than the value of an African's productivity in Africa.

The incidence of disease in the Americas also helps explain African enslavement. Smallpox took a terrible toll on Native Americans, and between 30 and 50 percent of Europeans exposed to malaria succumbed to that sickness. Africans had developed some immunity to both diseases, and in the Americas they experienced the lowest mortality rate of any people, making them, ironically, the most suitable workers for the environment.

In 1500 a Portuguese fleet en route to India around Africa sailed too far west into the Atlantic and made landfall on the coast of modern Brazil. Although its commander, Pedro Álvares Cabral, did not know where he was, he followed the common practice (see page 469) and immediately claimed the land for King Manuel I, the Portuguese monarch. Colonization began in the early 1530s, and in 1551 the Portuguese founded a sugar colony at Bahia. Between 1551 and 1575, before the North American slave traffic began, the Portuguese delivered more African slaves to Brazil than ever reached British North America (Figure 20.1). Portugal essentially monopolized the slave trade until 1600 and continued to play a significant role in the seventeenth century, though the trade was increasingly taken over by the Dutch, French, and English. From 1690 until the British House of Commons abolished the slave trade in 1807, England was the leading carrier of African slaves.

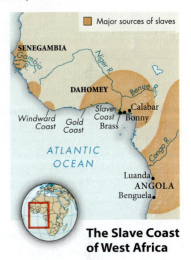

**The Slave Coast of West Africa**

Population density and supply conditions along the West African coast and the sailing time to New World markets determined the sources of slaves. As the demand for slaves rose, slavers moved down the West African coast from Senegambia to the more densely populated hinterlands of the Bight of Benin and the Bight of Biafra (a bight is a bend or curve in the coast). The abundant supply of Africans to enslave in Angola, the region south of the Congo River, and the quick passage from Angola to Brazil and the Caribbean established that region as the major coast for Portuguese slavers.

Transatlantic wind patterns partly determined exchange routes. Shippers naturally preferred the swiftest crossing—that is, from the African port nearest the latitude of the intended American destination. Thus Portuguese shippers carried their cargoes from Angola

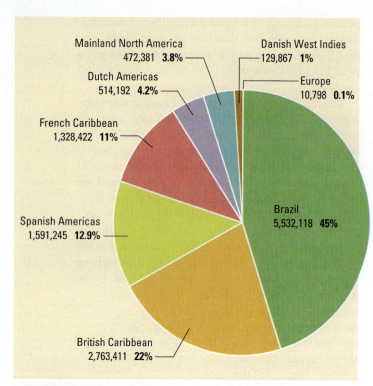

**FIGURE 20.1 Estimated Slave Imports by Destination, 1501–1866** Brazil was the single largest importer of African slaves from 1501 to 1866. But when taken cumulatively, the British, French, Dutch, and Danish colonies of the Caribbean rivaled the much larger colony of Brazil for numbers of slaves imported from Africa. (Source: Data from Emory University. "Assessing the Slave Trade: Estimates," in *Voyages: The Trans-Atlantic Slave Trade Database*. 2009. http://www.slavevoyages.org.)

to Brazil, and British merchants sailed from the Bight of Benin to the Caribbean. The great majority of enslaved Africans were intended for the sugar and coffee plantations extending from the Caribbean islands to Brazil. Angola produced 26 percent of all African slaves and 70 percent of all Portuguese slaves. Trading networks extending deep into the interior culminated at two major ports on the Angolan coast, Luanda and Benguela. The Portuguese acquired a few slaves through warfare but secured the vast majority through trade with African dealers. Whites did not participate in the inland markets, which were run solely by Africans.

Almost all Portuguese shipments went to satisfy the virtually insatiable Brazilian demand for slaves. The so-called **Middle Passage** was the horrific journey experienced by Africans from freedom to enslavement in the Americas. Here is an excerpt from a Portuguese doctor's 1793 report on conditions in Luanda before the voyage across the Atlantic had begun. Be sure to note in this and subsequent quotations how the enslaved peoples are clearly considered, and treated, as chattel:

• **Middle Passage** African slaves' voyage across the Atlantic to the Americas, a long and treacherous journey during which slaves endured appalling and often deadly conditions.

The dwelling place of the slave is simply the dirt floor of the compound, and he remains there exposed to harsh conditions and bad weather, and at night there are only a lean-to and some sheds . . . which they are herded into like cattle.

Their food continues scarce as before . . . limited at times to badly cooked beans, at other times to corn. . . .

And when they reach a port . . . , they are branded on the right breast with the coat of arms of the king and nation, of whom they have become vassals. . . . This mark is made with a hot silver instrument in the act of paying the king's duties, and this brand mark is called a *carimbo*. . . .

In this miserable and deprived condition the terrified slaves remain for weeks and months, and the great number of them who die is unspeakable. With some ten or twelve thousand arriving at Luanda each year, it often happens that only six or seven thousand are finally transported to Brazil.[17]

Conditions during the Middle Passage were even worse. Olaudah Equiano (see "Individuals in Society: Olaudah Equiano," at right) describes the experience of his voyage as a captured slave from Benin to Barbados in the Caribbean:

At last, when the ship we were in had got in all her cargo [of slaves], they made ready with many fearful noises, and we were all put under deck so that we could not see how they managed the vessel. . . . The stench of the hold while we were on the coast was so intolerably loathsome that it was dangerous to remain there for any time, and some of us had been permitted to stay on the deck for the fresh air; but now that the whole ship's cargo were confined together it became absolutely pestilential. The closeness of the place and the heat of the climate, added to the number in the ship, which was so crowded that each had scarcely room to turn himself, almost suffocated us. This produced copious perspirations, so that the air soon became unfit for respiration from a variety of loathsome smells, and brought on a sickness among the slaves, of which many died, thus falling victims to the improvident avarice, as I may call it, of their purchasers. This wretched situation was again aggravated by the galling of the chains, now become insupportable, and the filth of the necessary tubs [of human waste], into which the children often fell and were almost suffocated. The shrieks of the women and the groans of the dying rendered the whole a scene of horror almost inconceivable.[18]

Although the demand was great, Portuguese merchants in Angola and Brazil sought to maintain only a steady trickle of slaves from the African interior to Luanda and across the ocean to Bahia and Rio de

# Individuals in Society

## Olaudah Equiano

**THE TRANSATLANTIC SLAVE TRADE WAS A MASS**
movement involving millions of human beings. It was also the sum of individual lives spent partly or entirely in slavery. Most of those lives remain hidden to us. Olaudah Equiano (1745–1797) represents a rare window into the slaves' obscurity; he is probably the best-known African slave.

In his autobiography, *The Interesting Narrative of the Life of Olaudah Equiano* (1789), Equiano says that he was born in Benin (modern Nigeria) of Ibo ethnicity.* His father, one of the village elders (or chieftains), presided over a large household that included "many slaves," prisoners captured in local wars. All people, slave and free, shared in the cultivation of family lands. One day, when all the adults were in the fields, two strange men and a woman broke into the family compound, kidnapped the eleven-year-old Olaudah and his sister, tied them up, and dragged them into the woods. Brother and sister were separated, and Olaudah was sold several times to various dealers before reaching the coast. As it took six months to walk there, his home must have been far inland. The sea, the slave ship, and the strange appearance of the white crew terrified the boy (see page 606). Equiano's master took him to Jamaica, to Virginia, and then to England, where he placed him in the custody of a kind family. They gave him the rudiments of an education, and he was baptized a Christian.

Equiano soon went to sea as a captain's boy (servant), serving in the Royal Navy during the Seven Years' War (see page 652). On shore at Portsmouth, England, after one battle, Equiano was urged by his master to read, study, and learn basic mathematics. This education served him well, for after a voyage to the West Indies, his master sold him to a Philadelphia Quaker, Robert King, who was a rum and sugar merchant. Equiano worked as a clerk in King's warehouse, as a longshoreman loading and unloading cargo ships, and at sea where he developed good navigational skills; King paid him for his work. Equiano became an entrepreneur himself, buying and selling small goods in the islands and mainland ports. Determined to buy his freedom, Equiano had amassed enough money by 1766, and King signed the deed of manumission. Equiano was twenty-one years old; he had been a slave for ten years.

Equiano returned to London and used his remaining money to hire tutors to teach him hairdressing, mathematics, and how to play the French horn. When money was scarce, he found work as a merchant seaman, traveling to Portugal, Nice, Genoa, Naples, and Turkey. He even participated in an Arctic expedition.

Equiano's *Narrative* reveals a complex and sophisticated man. He had a strong constitution and an equally strong character. His Christian faith undoubtedly sustained him. On the title

**In this 1789 portrait, Olaudah Equiano holds his Bible, open to the book of Acts.** (1789 mezzotint, British Library, London, UK/© British Library Board. All Rights Reserved./The Bridgeman Art Library)

page of his book, he cited a verse from Isaiah (12:2): "The Lord Jehovah is my strength and my song." The very first thought that came to his mind the day he was freed was a passage from Psalm 126: "I glorified God in my heart, in whom I trusted."

Equiano loathed the brutal slavery he saw in the West Indies and the vicious racism he experienced in the North American colonies. He respected the fairness of Robert King, admired British navigational and industrial technologies, and had many close white friends. He once described himself as "almost an Englishman." He was also involved in the black communities in the West Indies and in London. Equiano's *Narrative* is a well-documented argument for the abolition of slavery and a literary classic that went through nine editions before his death.

Olaudah Equiano's *Narrative*, with its horrific descriptions of slavery, proved influential, and after its publication Equiano became active in the abolition movement. He spoke to large crowds in the industrial cities of Manchester and Birmingham in England, arguing that it was in the business interests of manufacturers to support abolition, as Africa was a huge, virtually untapped market for English cloth. Though he died in 1797, ten years before its passage, Equiano significantly advanced the abolitionist cause that led to the Slave Trade Act of 1807.

Source: *Equiano's Travels: The Interesting Narrative of the Life of Olaudah Equiano*, ed. Paul Edwards (Portsmouth, N.H.: Heinemann, 1996).

## QUESTIONS FOR ANALYSIS

1. How typical was Olaudah Equiano's life as a slave? How atypical?
2. Describe Equiano's culture and his sense of himself.

*Recent scholarship has re-examined Equiano's life and raised some questions about his African origins and his experience of the Middle Passage. To explore the debate over Equiano's authorship of the African and Middle Passage portions of his autobiography, see Vincent Carretta, *Equiano, the African: Biography of a Self-Made Man* (New York: Penguin, 2007).

### LaunchPad
### Online Document Project

**What role did slave accounts play in antislavery activism?**
Read several first-person accounts of slavery, and then complete a quiz and writing assignment based on the evidence and details from this chapter.

*See inside the front cover to learn more.*

**Peddlers in Rio de Janeiro** A British army officer sketched this early-nineteenth-century scene of everyday life in Rio de Janeiro, Brazil. The ability to balance large burdens on the head meant that the person's hands were free for other use. Note the player (on the left) of a musical instrument originating in the Congo. On the right a woman gives alms to the man with the holy image in return for being allowed to kiss the image as an act of devotion. We do not know whether the peddlers were free and self-employed or were selling for their owners. (From "Views and Costumes of the City and Neighborhood of Rio de Janeiro, Brazil," in *Drawings Taken by Lieutenant Henry Chamberlain, During the Years 1819 and 1820* [London: Columbian Press, 1822]/Visual Connection Archive)

Janeiro: a flood of slaves would have depressed the American market. Rio, the port capital through which most enslaved Africans passed, commanded the Brazilian trade. Planters and mine operators from the provinces traveled to Rio to buy slaves. Between 1795 and 1808 approximately 10,000 Angolans per year stood in the Rio slave market. In 1810 the figure rose to 18,000; in 1828 it reached 32,000.[19]

The English ports of London, Bristol, and particularly Liverpool dominated the British slave trade. In the eighteenth century Liverpool was the world's greatest slave-trading port. In all three cities, small and cohesive merchant classes exercised great public influence. The cities also had huge stores of industrial products for export, growing shipping industries, and large amounts of ready cash for investment abroad. Merchants generally formed partnerships to raise capital and to share the risks; each voyage was a separate enterprise or venture.

Slaving ships from Bristol plied back and forth along the Gold Coast, the Bight of Benin, Bonny, and Calabar looking for African traders who were willing to supply them with slaves. Liverpool's ships drew enslaved people from Gambia, the Windward Coast, and the Gold Coast. British ships carried textiles, gunpowder and flint, beer and spirits, British and Irish linens, and woolen cloth to Africa. A collection of goods was grouped together into what was called the **sorting**. An English sorting might include bolts of cloth, firearms, alcohol, tobacco, and hardware; this batch of goods was traded for an enslaved individual or a quantity of gold, ivory, or dyewood.[20]

European traders had two systems for exchange. First, especially on the Gold Coast, they established factory-forts. (For more on factory-forts, see page 510 and "Viewpoints 20.2: Perspectives on the Slave Trade," page 609.) These fortified trading posts were expensive to maintain but proved useful for fending off European rivals. Second, they used **shore trading**, in which European ships sent boats ashore or invited African dealers to bring traders and enslaved Africans out to the ships. The English captain John Adams, who made ten voyages to Africa between 1786 and 1800, described the shore method of trading at Bonny:

This place is the wholesale market for slaves, as not fewer than 20,000 are annually sold here; 16,000 of whom are natives of one nation called Ibo. . . . Fairs where the slaves of the Ibo nation are obtained are held every five or six weeks at several villages, which are situated on the banks of the rivers and creeks in the interior, and to which the African traders of Bonny resort to purchase them.

. . . The traders augment the quantity of their merchandise, by obtaining from their friends, the captains of the slave ships, a considerable quantity of goods on credit. . . . Evening is the period chosen for the time of departure, when they proceed in a body, accompanied by the noise of drums, horns, and gongs. At the expiration of the sixth day, they

**sorting** A collection or batch of British goods that would be traded for a slave or for a quantity of gold, ivory, or dyewood.

**shore trading** A process for trading goods in which European ships sent boats ashore or invited African dealers to bring traders and slaves out to the ships.

# Viewpoints 20.2

## Perspectives on the Slave Trade

• *King Nzinga Mbemba (christened Dom Affonso I) (r. 1509–1543) ruled over the Kongo Empire, which included large parts of modern Angola, the Republic of the Congo, the Democratic Republic of the Congo, and Cabinda. Portuguese priests brought Christianity in 1491, and the entire royal family converted to Christianity. Slavery had existed before the Portuguese arrived, and Affonso had profited from it, but by the 1520s the trans-atlantic trade threatened the kingdom's survival. Here Affonso begs the Portuguese king, João VI, to stop the trade.*

*William Bosman, who arrived in West Africa in 1688, was employed by the Dutch East India Company at Elmina Castle (in modern Elmina, Ghana). In letters to his uncle in Holland, Bosman offered a detailed, first-person account of the African slave trade around the port city of Fida (modern Ouidah in Benin).*

### Nzinga Mbemba (Affonso I), Letter to the King of Portugal

❝ July 6, 1526

To Dom João, King our Brother

Sir, Your Highness should know how our Kingdom is being lost . . . caused by the excessive freedom given by your factors and officials to the men and merchants who are allowed to come to this Kingdom to set up shops with goods and many things which have been prohibited by us, and which they spread throughout our Kingdoms and Domains in such an abundance that many of our vassals, whom we had in obedience, do not comply because they have the things in greater abundance than we ourselves; and it was with these things that we had them content and subjected under our vassalage and jurisdiction, so it is doing a great harm not only to the service of God, but the security and peace of our Kingdoms . . . as well.

And we cannot reckon how great the damage is, since the mentioned merchants are taking every day our natives, sons of the land and the sons of our noblemen and vassals and our relatives . . . ; they grab them and get them to be sold; and . . . our country is being completely depopulated. . . . We beg of Your Highness to help and assist us in this matter, commanding your factors that they should not send here either merchants or wares, because it is *our will that in these Kingdoms there should not be any trade of slaves nor outlet for them.* . . . Otherwise we cannot remedy such an obvious damage. Pray Our Lord in His mercy to have Your Highness under His guard. . . . I kiss your hands many times.

At the town of Congo,
The King, Dom Affonso ❞

### William Bosman, *A Description of the Coast of Guinea*

❝ The first business of one of our Factors when he comes to Fida, is to satisfie the Customs of the King . . . , about 100 Pounds in Guinea value. . . . After which we have free License to Trade. . . .

Before we can deal with any Person, we are obliged to buy the King's whole stock of Slaves at a set price; which is commonly one third or one fourth higher than ordinary: After which we [may] deal with all his Subjects. . . . But if there happen to be no stock of Slaves, the Factor must [trust] the Inhabitants with Goods to the value of one or two hundred Slaves; which Commodities they send into the In-land Country, in order to buy with them Slaves at all Markets, and that sometimes two hundred Miles deep in the Country. . . . Most of the Slaves that are offered to us are Prisoners of War, which are sold by the Victors as their Booty.

When these Slaves come to Fida, they are put in Prison . . . ; where, by our Chirurgeons [surgeons], . . . they are thoroughly examined. . . . Those which are approved as good are set on one side; and the lame or faulty are set by as Invalides. . . . These are such as are above five and thirty Years old, or are maimed in the Arms, Legs, Hands or Feet, have lost a Tooth, are grey-haired, or have Films over their Eyes; [or] are affected with any Venereal Distemper, or with several other Diseases.

The Invalides . . . being thrown out, . . . the remainder are numbered, and it is entered who delivered them. In the meanwhile, a burning Iron, with the Arms or Name of the Companies, lies in the Fire; with which ours are marked on the Breast . . . that we may distinguish them from the Slaves of the English, French, or others (which are also marked with their Mark). . . .

We are seldom long detained in the buying . . . , because their price is established, the Women being one fourth or fifth part cheaper than the Men. . . . When we have agreed with the Owners of the Slaves, they are returned to their Prison; where . . . they are kept at our charge. . . . To save Charges, we send them on Board our Ships with the first Opportunity; . . . they come Aboard stark-naked as well Women as Men: In which condition they are obliged to continue, if the Master of the Ship is not so Charitable (which he commonly is) as to bestow something on them to cover their Nakedness. ❞

Sources: Basil Davidson, ed. *The African Past: Chronicles from Antiquity to Modern Times* (Boston: Little, Brown and Company, 1964), pp. 191–192; Copyright © 1964 by Basil Davidson. Reprinted by permission of Curtis Brown, Ltd.; William Bosman, *A New and Accurate Description of the Coast of Guinea, Divided into the Gold, the Slave, and the Ivory Coasts* (London: J. Knapton, 1705), pp. 363–365.

### QUESTIONS FOR ANALYSIS

1. How were Portuguese merchants and foreign goods weakening King Affonso's control over his people and depopulating his country?

2. What steps did a Dutch factor have to take to purchase enslaved Africans at the port of Fida (Ouidah)?

generally return bringing with them 1,500 or 2,000 slaves, who are sold to Europeans the evening after their arrival, and taken on board the ships. . . .

It is expected that every vessel, on her arrival at Bonny, will fire a salute the instant the anchor is let go, as a compliment to the black monarch who soon afterwards makes his appearance in a large canoe, at which time, all those natives who happen to be alongside the vessel are compelled to proceed in their canoes to a respectful distance, and make way for his Majesty's barge. After a few compliments to the captain, he usually enquires after brother George, meaning the King of England, George III, and hopes he and his family are well. He is not pleased unless he is regaled with the best the ship affords. . . . His power is absolute; and the surrounding country, to a considerable distance, is subject to his dominion.[21]

The shore method of buying slaves allowed the ship to move easily from market to market. The final prices of those enslaved depended on their ethnic origin, their availability when the shipper arrived, and their physical health when offered for sale in the West Indies or the North or South American colonies.

The supply of slaves for the foreign market was controlled by a small, wealthy African merchant class or by a state monopoly. By contemporary standards, slave raiding was a costly operation: gathering a band of raiders and the capital for equipment, guides, tolls, and supplies involved considerable expense. Only black African entrepreneurs with sizable capital and labor could afford to finance and direct raiding drives. They exported enslaved men and women because the profits on exports were greater than the profits to be made from using labor in the domestic economy.

The transatlantic slave trade that the British, as well as the Dutch, Portuguese, French, Americans, and others, participated in was part of a much larger trading network that is known as the triangle trade. European merchants sailed to Africa on the first leg of the voyage to trade European manufactured goods for enslaved Africans. When they had filled their ships' holds with enslaved peoples, they headed across the Atlantic on the second leg of the voyage, the Middle Passage. When they reached the Americas, the merchants unloaded and sold their human cargoes and used the profits to purchase raw materials—such as cotton, sugar, and indigo—that they then transported back to Europe, completing the third leg of the commercial triangle.

Enslaved African people had an enormous impact on the economies and cultures of the Portuguese and Spanish colonies of South America and the Dutch, French, and British colonies of the Caribbean and North America. For example, on the sugar plantations of Mexico and the Caribbean; on the North American cotton, rice, and tobacco plantations; and in Peruvian and Mexican silver and gold mines, enslaved Africans not only worked in the mines and fields but also filled skilled, supervisory, and administrative positions and performed domestic service. In the United States enslaved Africans and their descendants influenced many facets of American culture, such as language,

**The African Slave Trade** Enslaved African men, women, and children, captured in the interior, are marched to the coast by their African captors. The guards carry guns obtained from Europeans in the slave trade. The enslaved men are linked together by heavy wooden yokes, making it impossible to escape. (The Granger Collection, NYC — All rights reserved)

music (ragtime and jazz), dance, and diet. Even the U.S. White House and Capitol building, where Congress meets, were built partly by slave labor.[22] But the importance of the slave trade extended beyond the Atlantic world. Both the expansion of capitalism and the industrialization of Western societies, Egypt, and the nations of West, Central, and South Africa were related in one way or another to the traffic in African people.

## Impact on African Societies

What economic impact did European trade have on African societies? Africans possessed technology well suited to their environment. Over the centuries they had cultivated a wide variety of plant foods; developed plant and animal husbandry techniques; and mined, smelted, and otherwise worked a great variety of metals. Apart from firearms, American tobacco and rum, and the cheap brandy brought by the Portuguese, European goods presented no novelty to Africans. They found foreign products desirable because of their low prices. Traders of handwoven Indian cotton textiles, Venetian imitations of African beads, and iron bars from European smelters could undersell African manufacturers. Africans exchanged slaves, ivory, gold, pepper, and animal skins for those goods. African states eager to expand or to control commerce bought European firearms, although the difficulty of maintaining guns often gave gun owners only marginal superiority over skilled bowmen.[23] The kingdom of Dahomey (modern-day Benin in West Africa), however, built its power on the effective use of firearms.

The African merchants who controlled the production of exports gained the most from foreign trade. Dahomey's king, for example, had a gross income in 1750 of £250,000 (almost U.S. $33 million today) from the overseas export of his fellow Africans. A portion of his profit was spent on goods that improved his people's living standard. Slave-trading entrepôts, which provided opportunities for traders and for farmers who supplied foodstuffs to towns, caravans, and slave ships, prospered. But such economic returns did not spread very far.[24] International trade did not lead to Africa's economic development. Africa experienced neither technological growth nor the gradual spread of economic benefits in early modern times.

**Sapi-Portuguese Saltcellar** Contact with the Sapi people of present-day Sierra Leone in West Africa led sixteenth-century Portuguese traders to commission this ivory saltcellar, for which they brought Portuguese designs. But the object's basic features — a spherical container and separate lid on a flat base, with men and/or women supporting, or serving as, beams below — are distinctly African. Here a Portuguese caravel sits on top with a man in the crow's nest. Four men stand below: two finely carved, regally dressed, and fully armed noblemen facing forward and two attendants in profile. (© akg-images/The Image Works)

As in the Islamic world, women in sub-Saharan Africa also engaged in the slave trade. In Guinea these women slave merchants and traders were known as *nhara*, a corruption of the Portuguese term *senhora*, a title used for a married woman. They acquired considerable riches, often by marrying the Portuguese merchants and serving as go-betweens for these outsiders who were not familiar with the customs and languages of the African coast. One of them, Mae Aurélia Correia (1810?–1875?), led a life famous in the upper Guinea coastal region for its wealth and elegance. Between the 1820s and 1840s she operated her own trading vessels and is said to have owned several hundred slaves. Some of them she hired out as skilled artisans and sailors. She and her sister (or aunt) Julia amassed a fortune in gold, silver jewelry, and expensive cloth while living in European-style homes. Julia and her husband, a trader from the Cape Verde Islands, also owned their own slave estates where they produced peanuts.

The intermarriage of French traders and Wolof women in Senegambia created a métis, or mulatto, class. In the emerging urban centers at Saint-Louis, members of this small class adopted the French language, the Roman Catholic faith, and a French manner of life, and they exercised considerable political and economic power. However, European cultural influences did not penetrate West African society beyond the seacoast.

The political consequences of the slave trade varied from place to place. The trade enhanced the power and wealth of some kings and warlords in the short run but promoted conditions of instability and collapse over the long run. In the Kongo kingdom, which was located in parts of modern Angola, the Republic of the

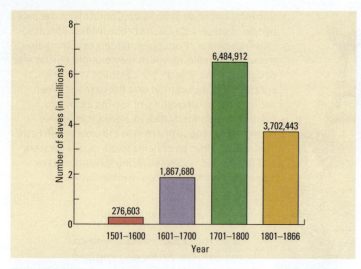

**FIGURE 20.2 The Transatlantic Slave Trade, 1501–1866**
The volume of slaves involved in the transatlantic slave trade peaked during the eighteenth century. These numbers show the slaves who embarked from Africa and do not reflect the 10 to 15 percent of enslaved Africans who died in transit. (Source: Data from Emory University. "Assessing the Slave Trade: Estimates," in *Voyages: The Trans-Atlantic Slave Trade Database.* 2009. http://www.slavevoyages.org.)

Congo, and the Democratic Republic of the Congo, the perpetual Portuguese search for Africans to enslave undermined the monarchy, destroyed political unity, and led to constant disorder and warfare; power passed to the village chiefs. Likewise in Angola, which became a Portuguese proprietary colony (a territory granted to one or more individuals by the Crown for them to govern at their will), the slave trade decimated and scattered the population and destroyed the local economy. By contrast, the military kingdom of Dahomey, which entered into the slave trade in the eighteenth century and made it a royal monopoly, prospered enormously. Dahomey's economic strength rested on the slave trade. The royal army raided deep into the interior, and in the late eighteenth century Dahomey became one of the major West African sources of slaves. When slaving expeditions failed to yield sizable catches and when European demand declined, the resulting depression in the Dahomean economy caused serious political unrest. Iboland, inland from the Niger Delta, from whose great port cities of Bonny and Brass the British drained tens of thousands of enslaved Africans, experienced minimal political effects. A high birthrate kept pace with the incursions of the slave trade, and Ibo societies remained demographically and economically strong.

What demographic impact did the slave trade have on Africa? Between approximately 1501 and 1866 more than 12 million Africans were forcibly exported to the Americas, 6 million were traded to Asia, and 8 million were retained as slaves within Africa. Figure 20.2 shows the estimated number of slaves shipped to the Americas in the transatlantic slave trade. Export figures do not include the approximately 10 to 15 percent who died during procurement or in transit.

The early modern slave trade involved a worldwide network of relationships among markets in the Middle East, Africa, Asia, Europe, and the Americas. But Africa was the crucible of the trade. There is no small irony in the fact that Africa, which of all the continents was most desperately in need of population because of its near total dependence on labor-intensive agriculture and pastoralism, lost so many millions to the trade. Although the British Parliament abolished the slave trade in 1807 and traffic in Africans to Brazil and Cuba gradually declined, within Africa the trade continued at the levels of the peak years of the transatlantic trade, 1780–1820. In the later nineteenth century developing African industries, using slave labor, produced a variety of products for domestic consumption and export. Again, there is irony in the fact that in the eighteenth century European demand for slaves expanded the trade (and wars) within Africa, yet in the nineteenth century European imperialists defended territorial aggrandizement by arguing that they were "civilizing" Africans by abolishing slavery. But after 1880 European businessmen (and African governments) did not push abolition; they wanted cheap labor.

Markets in the Americas generally wanted young male slaves. Consequently, two-thirds of those exported to the Americas were male, one-third female. Asian and African markets preferred young females. Women were sought for their reproductive value, as sex objects, and because their economic productivity was not threatened by the possibility of physical rebellion, as might be the case with young men. As a result, the population on Africa's western coast became predominantly female; the population in the East African savanna and Horn regions was predominantly male. The slave trade therefore had significant consequences for the institutions of marriage, the local trade in enslaved people (as these local populations became skewed with too many males or too many females), and the sexual division of labor. Although Africa's overall population may have shown modest growth from roughly 1650 to 1900, that growth was offset by declines in the Horn and on the eastern and western coasts. While Europe and Asia experienced considerable demographic and economic expansion in the eighteenth century, Africa suffered a decline.[25]

The political and economic consequences of the African slave trade are easier to measure than the human toll taken on individuals and societies. While we have personal accounts from many slaves, ships' captains and crews, slave masters, and others of the horrors of the slave-trading ports along Africa's coasts, the brutality of the Middle Passage, and the inhuman cruelty enslaved Africans endured once they reached the Americas, we know much less about the beginning of the slave's journey in Africa. Africans themselves carried out much of the "man stealing," the term used by Africans to describe capturing enslaved men, women, and children and marching them to the coast, where they were traded to Arabs, Europeans, or others. Therefore, we have few written firsthand accounts of the pain and suffering these violent raids inflicted, either on the person being enslaved or on the families and societies they left behind.

# Chapter Summary

In the early modern world, West African kingdoms and stateless societies existed side by side. Both had predominantly agricultural economies. Stateless societies revolved around a single village or group of villages without a central capital or ruler. Kings ruled over defined areas through bureaucratic hierarchies. The Sudanic empires controlled the north-south trans-Saharan trade in gold, salt, and other items. Led by predominantly Muslim rulers, these kingdoms belonged to a wider Islamic world, allowing them access to vast trade networks and some of the most advanced scholarship in the world. Still, Muslim culture affected primarily the royal and elite classes, seldom reaching the masses.

Europeans believed a wealthy (mythical) Christian monarch named Prester John ruled the Christian kingdom of Ethiopia. This fable attracted Europeans to Ethiopia for centuries, and partly explains why the Portuguese helped the Ethiopians fight off Muslim incursions. Jesuit missionaries tried to convert Ethiopians to Roman Catholicism but were fiercely resisted and expelled in 1633.

Swahili city-states on Africa's southeastern coast possessed a Muslim and mercantile culture. The Swahili acted as middlemen in the East African–Indian Ocean trade network, which, in the late fifteenth and early sixteenth centuries, Portugal sought to conquer and control. Swahili rulers who refused to form trading alliances with the Portuguese were attacked. The Portuguese had little influence on Swahili culture or religion, but their presence caused the economic decline and death of many Swahili cities.

Slavery existed across Africa before Europeans arrived. Enslaved people were treated relatively benignly in some societies but elsewhere as chattel possessions, suffering harsh and brutal treatment. European involvement in the slave trade began around 1550, when the Portuguese purchased Africans to

## CHRONOLOGY

| | |
|---|---|
| **1400–1600s** | Salt trade dominates West African economy |
| **ca. 1464–1591** | Songhai kingdom dominates the western Sudan |
| **1485** | Portuguese and other Europeans first appear in Benin |
| **1493–1528** | Muhammad Toure governs and expands kingdom of Songhai |
| **1498** | Portuguese explorer Vasco da Gama sails around Africa |
| **ca. 1500–1900** | Era of transatlantic slave trade |
| **1502–1507** | Portuguese erect forts at Kilwa, Zanzibar, and Sofala on Swahili coast |
| **1529** | Adal defeats Ethiopian emperor and begins systematic devastation of Ethiopia |
| **1543** | Joint Ethiopian and Portuguese force defeat Muslims in Ethiopia |
| **1571–1603** | Idris Alooma governs kingdom of Kanem-Bornu |
| **1591** | Moroccan army defeats Songhai |
| **1658** | Dutch East India Company allows importation of slaves into Cape Colony |
| **1680s** | Famine from Senegambian coast to Upper Nile |
| **1738–1756** | Major famine in West Africa |
| **1789** | Olaudah Equiano publishes autobiography |

work in Brazil. The Dutch East India Company used enslaved Africans and Southeast Asians in their Cape Colony. African entrepreneurs and merchants partnered in the trade, capturing people in the interior and exchanging them for firearms, liquor, and other goods with European slave ships. Though some kingdoms experienced a temporary rise of wealth and power, over time the slave trade was largely destabilizing. The individual suffering and social disruption in Africa caused by the enslavement of millions of Africans is impossible to estimate.

## NOTES

1. P. D. Curtin, *Economic Change in Precolonial Africa: Senegambia in the Era of the Slave Trade* (Madison: University of Wisconsin Press, 1975), pp. 34–35; J. A. Rawley, *The Transatlantic Slave Trade: A History* (Lincoln: University of Nebraska Press, 2005).
2. Pieter de Marees, *Description of the Gold Kingdom of Guinea*, trans. and ed. Albert van Dantzig and Adam Jones (1602; repr., Oxford: Oxford University Press, 1987), pp. 226–228; William Bosman,

*A New Description of the Coast of Guinea*, ed. John Ralph Willis (London: Frank Cass, 1967), p. 461.

3. Quoted in R. Hallett, *Africa to 1875* (Ann Arbor: University of Michigan Press, 1970), p. 151.

4. A. ibn-Fartura, "The Kanem Wars," in *Nigerian Perspectives*, ed. T. Hodgkin (London: Oxford University Press, 1966), pp. 111–115.

5. "The Kano Chronicle," quoted in *Nigerian Perspectives*, ed. T. Hodgkin (London: Oxford University Press, 1966), pp. 89–90.

6. *Equiano's Travels: The Interesting Narrative of the Life of Olaudah Equiano*, ed. P. Edwards (Portsmouth, N.H.: Heinemann, 1996), p. 4.

7. J. Iliffe, *Africans: The History of a Continent* (Cambridge: Cambridge University Press, 2007), p. 68.

8. See A. J. R. Russell-Wood, *The Portuguese Empire: A World on the Move* (Baltimore: Johns Hopkins University Press, 1998), pp. 11–13.

9. Ibid., pp. 35–38.

10. P. E. Lovejoy, *Transformations in Slavery: A History of Slavery in Africa* (Cambridge: Cambridge University Press, 1992), p. 25, Table 2.1, "Trans-Saharan Slave Trade, 650–1600."

11. Iliffe, *Africans*, p. 77.

12. Quoted in H. Thomas, *The Slave Trade* (New York: Simon and Schuster, 1997), p. 21.

13. G. Gerzina, *Black London: Life Before Emancipation* (New Brunswick, N.J.: Rutgers University Press, 1995), pp. 29–66 passim; quotation from p. 53.

14. R. Shell, *Children of Bondage: A Social History of the Slave Society at the Cape of Good Hope, 1652–1838* (Hanover, N.H.: University Press of New England, 1994), pp. 285–289.

15. See D. Eltis, *The Rise of African Slavery in the Americas* (Cambridge: Cambridge University Press, 2000), chap. 3; and the review/commentary by J. E. Inikori, *American Historical Review* 106.5 (December 2001): 1751–1753.

16. R. Blackburn, *The Making of New World Slavery: From the Baroque to the Modern, 1492–1800* (New York: Verso, 1998), pp. 79–80.

17. R. E. Conrad, *Children of God's Fire: A Documentary History of Black Slavery in Brazil* (Princeton, N.J.: Princeton University Press, 1983), pp. 20–23.

18. *Equiano's Travels*, pp. 23–26.

19. Rawley, *The Transatlantic Slave Trade*, pp. 45–47.

20. Robert W. July, *A History of the African People* (Prospect Heights, Ill.: Waveland Press, 1998), p. 171.

21. J. Adams, "Remarks on the Country Extending from Cape Palmas to the River Congo," in *Nigerian Perspectives*, ed. T. Hodgkin (London: Oxford University Press, 1966), pp. 178–180.

22. J. Thornton, *Africa and Africans in the Making of the Atlantic World* (New York: Cambridge University Press, 1992), pp. 138–142.

23. Robert W. July, *Precolonial Africa: An Economic and Social History* (New York: Scribner's, 1975), pp. 269–270.

24. A. G. Hopkins, *An Economic History of West Africa* (New York: Columbia University Press, 1973), p. 119.

25. P. Manning, *Slavery and African Life: Occidental, Oriental, and African Slave Trades* (New York: Cambridge University Press, 1990), pp. 22–23 and chap. 3, pp. 38–59.

## CONNECTIONS

During the period from 1400 to 1800 many parts of Africa experienced a profound transition with the arrival of Europeans all along Africa's coasts. Ancient trade routes, such as those across the Sahara Desert or up and down the East African coast, were disrupted. In West Africa trade routes that had been purely internal now connected with global trade networks at European coastal trading posts. Along Africa's east coast the Portuguese attacked Swahili city-states in their effort to take control of the Indian Ocean trade nexus.

The most momentous consequence of the European presence along Africa's coast, however, was the introduction of the transatlantic slave trade. For more than three centuries Europeans, with the aid of African slave traders, enslaved millions of Africa's healthiest and strongest men and women. Although many parts of Africa were untouched by the transatlantic slave trade, at least directly, areas where Africans were enslaved experienced serious declines in agricultural production, little progress in technological development, and significant increases in violence.

As we saw in Chapter 17 and will see in Chapter 21, early European commercial contacts with the empires of the Middle East and of South and East Asia were similar in many ways to those with Africa. Initially, the Portuguese, and then the English, Dutch, and French, did little more than establish trading posts at port cities and had to depend on the local people to bring them trade goods from the interior. Tropical diseases, particularly in India and Southeast Asia, took heavy death tolls on the Europeans, as they did in tropical Africa. What is more, while it was possible for the Portuguese to attack and conquer the individual Swahili city-states, Middle Eastern and Asian empires—such as the Ottomans in Turkey, the Safavids in Persia, the Mughals in India, and the Ming and Qing Dynasties in China—were, like the West African kingdoms, economically and militarily powerful enough to dictate terms of trade with the Europeans.

Resistance to enslavement took many forms on both sides of the Atlantic. In Haiti, as discussed in Chapter 22, resistance led to revolution and independence, marking the first successful uprising of non-Europeans against a colonial power. At the end of the nineteenth century, as described in Chapter 25, Europeans used the ongoing Arab-Swahili slave raids from Africa's eastern coast far into the interior as an excuse to invade and eventually colonize much of central and eastern Africa. The racial discrimination that accompanied colonial rule in Africa set the stage for a struggle for equality that led to eventual independence after World War II.

# Review and Explore

## Make It Stick

 **LearningCurve**
Go online and use LearningCurve to retain what you've read.

## Identify Key Terms

Identify and explain the significance of each item below.

**chattel** (p. 589)

**age-grade systems** (p. 590)

**oba** (p. 590)

**Taghaza** (p. 591)

**Tuareg** (p. 596)

**cowrie shells** (p. 596)

**Coptic Christianity** (p. 596)

**Swahili** (p. 598)

**Middle Passage** (p. 606)

**sorting** (p. 608)

**shore trading** (p. 608)

## Review the Main Ideas

Answer the focus questions from each section of the chapter.

1. What types of economic, social, and political structures were found in the kingdoms and states along the west coast and in the Sudan? (p. 588)
2. How did the arrival of Europeans and other foreign cultures affect the East African coast, and how did Ethiopia and the Swahili city-states respond to these incursions? (p. 596)
3. What role did slavery play in African societies before the transatlantic slave trade began, and what was the effect of European involvement? (p. 599)

## Make Connections

Analyze the larger developments and continuities within and across chapters.

1. In what ways did Islam enrich the Sudanic empires of West Africa?
2. Discuss the ways in which Africa came into greater contact with a larger world during the period discussed in this chapter.
3. How did the transatlantic slave trade affect West African society?

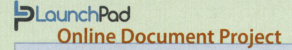

## Online Document Project

### African Voices in the Antislavery Movement

**What role did slave accounts play in antislavery activism?**
Read several first-person accounts of slavery, and then complete a quiz and writing assignment based on the evidence and details from this chapter.

*See inside the front cover to learn more.*

## Suggested Reading

Berger, Iris, E. Frances White, and Cathy Skidmore-Heiss. *Women in Sub-Saharan Africa: Restoring Women to History.* 1999. Necessary reading for a complete understanding of African history.

Cooper, Frederick. *Plantation Slavery on the East Coast of Africa.* 1997. Useful study of slavery as practiced in Africa.

Fredrickson, G. M. *Racism: A Short History.* 2002. Contains probably the best recent study of the connection between African slavery and Western racism.

Klein, Martin, and Claire C. Robertson. *Women and Slavery in Africa.* 1997. Written from the perspective that most slaves in Africa were women.

Law, Robin. *Oyo Empire, c. 1600–c. 1836: A West African Imperialism in the Era of the Atlantic Slave Trade.* 1977. Remains the definitive study of the powerful Oyo Empire in what is today southwestern Nigeria.

Lovejoy, Paul E. *Transformation in Slavery: A History of Slavery in Africa,* 3d ed. 2012. Essential for an understanding of slavery in an African context.

Middleton, J. *The World of the Swahili: An African Mercantile Civilization.* 1992. Introduction to East Africa and the Horn region.

Northrup, D. *Africa's Discovery of Europe, 1450–1850,* 3d ed. 2013. Offers a unique perspective on African-European contact.

Oliver, Roland, and Anthony Atmore. *Medieval Africa, 1250–1800.* 2001. A history of premodern Africa by two renowned historians of the continent.

Pearson, Michael N. *Port Cities and Intruders: The Swahili Coast, India, and Portugal in the Early Modern Era.* 2002. Comprehensive introduction to the Swahili coast and the Indian Ocean trade network.

Powell, Eve Troutt, and John O. Hunwick. *The African Diaspora in the Mediterranean Lands of Islam.* 2002. Important study of Islam and the African slave trade.

Robinson, David. *Muslim Societies in African History.* 2004. Valuable introduction to Islam in Africa by a renowned Africanist.

Shell, R. *Children of Bondage: A Social History of the Slave Society at the Cape of Good Hope, 1652–1938.* 1994. A massive study of Cape slave society filled with much valuable statistical data.

Shillington, K. *History of Africa,* 3d ed. 2012. A soundly researched, highly readable, and well-illustrated survey.

Thorton, J. *Africa and Africans in the Making of the Atlantic World, 1400–1680,* 2d ed. 1998. Places African developments in an Atlantic context.

# Continuity and Change in East Asia

## 1400–1800

### Kabuki Actor
Urban entertainment flourished in Japan under the rule of the Tokugawa shoguns. This late-eighteenth-century woodblock print was made for the many fans of the Kabuki actor Matsumoto Yonesaburo, who specialized in performing female roles. (Private Collection/Photo © Boltin Picture Library/ The Bridgeman Art Library)

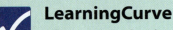

**LearningCurve**

After reading the chapter, go online and use LearningCurve to retain what you've read.

# Chapter Preview

**Ming China, 1368–1644**

**The Manchus and Qing China, to 1800**

**Japan's Middle Ages, ca. 1400–1600**

**The Tokugawa Shogunate, to 1800**

**Maritime Trade, Piracy, and the Entry of Europe into the Asian Maritime Sphere**

The four centuries from 1400 to 1800 were a time of growth and dynamic change throughout East Asia. Although both China and Japan suffered periods of war, each ended up with expanded territories. The age of exploration brought New World crops to the region, leading to increased agricultural output and population growth. It also brought new opportunities for foreign trade and new religions. Another link between these countries was the series of massive Japanese invasions of Korea in the late sixteenth century, which led to war between China and Japan.

In China the native Ming Dynasty (1368–1644) brought an end to Mongol rule. Under the Ming, China saw agricultural reconstruction, commercial expansion, and the rise of a vibrant urban culture. In the early seventeenth century, after the Ming Dynasty fell into disorder, the non-Chinese Manchus founded the Qing Dynasty (1644–1911) and added Taiwan, Mongolia, Tibet, and Xinjiang to their realm. The Qing Empire thus was comparable to the other multiethnic empires of the early modern world, such as the Ottoman, Russian, and Habsburg Empires. In China itself the eighteenth century was a time of peace and prosperity.

In the Japanese islands the fifteenth century saw the start of civil war that lasted a century. At the end of the sixteenth century the world seemed to have turned upside down when a commoner, Hideyoshi (HEE-deh-YOH-shee), became the supreme ruler. He did not succeed in passing on his power to an heir, however. Power was seized by Tokugawa Ieyasu (toh-koo-GAH-wuh ee-eh-YAH-soo). Under the Tokugawa Shogunate (1603–1867), Japan restricted contact with the outside world and social mobility among its own people. Yet Japan thrived, as agricultural productivity increased and a lively urban culture developed.

# Ming China, 1368–1644

☐ What sort of state and society developed in China after the Mongols were ousted?

The story of Ming China begins with a poor boy who rose to become emperor of a new dynasty. This individual, Zhu Yuanzhang (JOO yoowan-JAHNG), proved to be one of the most despotic emperors in Chinese history. Still, peace brought prosperity and a lively urban culture. By the beginning of the seventeenth century, however, the Ming government was beset by fiscal, military, and political problems.

## The Rise of Zhu Yuanzhang and the Founding of the Ming Dynasty

The founder of the **Ming Dynasty**, Zhu Yuanzhang (1328–1398), began life in poverty during the last decades of the Mongol Yuan Dynasty. His home region was hit by drought and then plague in the 1340s, and when he was only sixteen years old, his father, oldest brother, and that brother's wife all died, leaving two penniless boys with three bodies to bury. With no relatives to turn to, Zhu Yuanzhang asked a monastery to accept him as a novice. The monastery itself was short of funds, and the monks soon sent Zhu out to beg for food. For three or four years he wandered through central China. Only after he returned to the monastery did he learn to read.

A few years later, in 1351, members of a religious sect known as the Red Turbans rose in rebellion against the government. Red Turban teachings drew on Manichaean ideas about the incompatibility of the forces of good and evil as well as on the cult of the Maitreya Buddha, who according to believers would in the future bring his paradise to earth to relieve human suffering. The Red Turbans met with considerable success, even defeating Mongol cavalry. When the temple where Zhu Yuanzhang was living was burned down in the fighting, Zhu joined the rebels and rose rapidly.

Zhu and his followers developed into brilliant generals, and gradually they defeated one rival after another. In 1356 Zhu took the city of Nanjing and made it his base. In 1368 his armies took Beijing, which the Mongol emperor and his closest followers had vacated just days before. Then forty years old, Zhu Yuanzhang declared himself emperor of the Ming (Bright) Dynasty. As emperor, he is known as Taizu (TIGH-dzoo) or the Hongwu emperor.

Taizu started his reign wanting to help the poor. To lighten the weight of government taxes and compulsory labor, he ordered a full-scale registration of cultivated land and population so that these burdens could be assessed more fairly. He also tried persuasion. He issued instructions to be read aloud to villagers, telling them to be obedient to their parents, live in harmony with their neighbors, work contentedly at their occupations, and refrain from evil.

Although in many ways anti-Mongol, Taizu retained some Yuan practices. One was setting up provinces as the administrative layer between the central government and the prefectures (local governments a step above counties). Another was the hereditary service obligation for both artisan and military households. Any family classed as a military household had to provide a soldier at all times, replacing those who were injured, who died, or who deserted.

Garrisons were concentrated along the northern border and near the capital at Nanjing. Each garrison was allocated a tract of land that the soldiers took turns cultivating to supply their own food. Although in theory this system should have provided the Ming with a large but inexpensive army, the reality was less satisfactory. Garrisons were rarely self-sufficient. Furthermore, men compelled to become soldiers did not necessarily make good fighting men, and desertion was difficult to prevent. Consequently, like earlier dynasties, the Ming turned to non-Chinese northerners for much of its armed forces. Many of the best soldiers in the Ming army were Mongols in Mongol units. Taizu did not try to conquer the Mongols, and Ming China did not extend into modern Inner Mongolia.

Taizu had deeply ambivalent feelings about men of education and sometimes brutally humiliated them in open court, even having them beaten. His behavior was so erratic that it is most likely that he suffered from some form of mental illness. As Taizu became more literate, he realized that scholars could criticize him in covert ways, using phrases that had double meanings or that sounded like words for "bandit," "monk," or the like. Even poems in private circulation could be used as evidence of subversive thoughts. When literary men began to avoid official life, Taizu made it illegal to turn down appointments or to resign from office. He began falling into rages that only the empress could stop, and

**Ming China, ca. 1600**

---

• **Ming Dynasty** The Chinese dynasty in power from 1368 to 1644; it marked a period of agricultural reconstruction, foreign expeditions, commercial expansion, and vibrant urban culture.

**Forbidden City** The palace complex in Beijing, commonly called the Forbidden City, was built in the early fifteenth century when the capital was moved from Nanjing to Beijing. Audience halls and other important state buildings are arranged on a north-south axis with huge courtyards between them, where officials would stand during ceremonies. (sinopictures/ Wenxiao–ullstein bild/The Granger Collection, NYC — All rights reserved)

after her death in 1382 no one could calm him. In 1376 Taizu had thousands of officials killed because they were found to have taken shortcuts in their handling of paperwork for the grain tax. In 1380 Taizu concluded that his chancellor was plotting to assassinate him, and thousands only remotely connected to the chancellor were executed. From then on, Taizu acted as his own chancellor, dealing directly with the heads of departments and ministries.

The next important emperor, called Chengzu or the Yongle emperor (r. 1403–1425), was also a military man. One of Taizu's younger sons, he took the throne by force from his nephew and often led troops into battle against the Mongols. Like his father, Chengzu was willing to use terror to keep government officials in line.

Early in his reign, Chengzu decided to move the capital from Nanjing to Beijing, which had been his own base as a prince and the capital during Mongol times. Constructed between 1407 and 1420, Beijing was a planned city. Like Chang'an in Sui-Tang times (581–907), it was arranged like a set of boxes within boxes and built on a north-south axis. The main outer walls were forty feet high and nearly fifteen miles around, pierced by nine gates. Inside was the Imperial City, with government offices, and within that the palace itself, called the Forbidden City, with close to ten thousand rooms. Because the Forbidden City survives today, people can still see the series of audience halls with vast courtyards between them where attending officials would stand or kneel.

The areas surrounding Beijing were not nearly as agriculturally productive as those around Nanjing. To supply Beijing with grain, the Yuan Grand Canal connecting the city to the rice basket of the Yangzi River regions was broadened, deepened, and supplied with more locks and dams. The 15,000 boats and the 160,000 soldiers of the transport army who pulled loaded barges from the towpaths along the canal became the lifeline of the capital.

## Problems with the Imperial Institution

Taizu had decreed that succession should go to the eldest son of the empress or to the son's eldest son if the son predeceased his father, the system generally followed by earlier dynasties. In Ming times, the flaws in this system became apparent as one mediocre, obtuse, or erratic emperor followed another. There were emperors who refused to hold audiences, who fell into irrational fits, and who let themselves be manipulated by palace ladies.

Because Taizu had abolished the position of chancellor, emperors turned to secretaries and eunuchs to manage the paperwork. Eunuchs were essentially slaves. Many boys and young men were acquired by dubious means, often from non-Chinese areas in the south, and after they were castrated they had no option but to serve the imperial family. Zheng He, for instance (see page 639), was taken from Yunnan as a boy of ten by a Ming general assigned the task of securing boys to be castrated. Society considered eunuchs the basest of servants, and Confucian scholars heaped scorn on them. Yet Ming emperors, like rulers in earlier dynasties, often preferred the always-compliant eunuchs to high-minded, moralizing civil service officials.

In Ming times, the eunuch establishment became huge. By the late fifteenth century the eunuch bureaucracy had grown as large as the civil service, with each having roughly twelve thousand positions. After 1500 the eunuch bureaucracy grew even more rapidly, and by the mid-sixteenth century seventy thousand eunuchs were in service throughout the country, with ten thousand in the capital. Tension between the two bureaucracies was high. In 1420 Chengzu set up a eunuch-run secret service to investigate cases of suspected corruption and sedition in the regular bureaucracy. Eunuch control over vital government processes, such as appointments, became a severe problem.

In hope of persuading emperors to make reforms, many Ming officials risked their careers and lives by speaking out. In 1376, when Taizu asked for criticism, one official criticized harsh punishment of officials for minor lapses. Incensed, Taizu had him brought to the capital in chains and let him starve to death in prison. In 1519, when an emperor announced plans to make a tour of the southern provinces, over a hundred officials staged a protest by kneeling in front of the palace. The emperor ordered the officials to remain kneeling for three days, then had them flogged; eleven died. The Confucian tradition celebrated these acts of political protest as heroic. Rarely, however, did they succeed in moving an emperor to change his mind.

Although the educated public complained about the performance of emperors, no one proposed or even imagined alternatives to imperial rule. High officials were forced to find ways to work around uncooperative emperors, but they were not able to put in place institutions that would limit the damage an emperor could do. Knowing that strong emperors often acted erratically, many high officials came to prefer weak emperors who let them take care of the government. Emperors, of course, resented the way officials tried to keep them busy doing harmless activities.

## The Mongols and the Great Wall

The early Ming emperors held Mongol fighting men in awe and feared they might form another great military machine of the sort Chinggis Khan (ca. 1162–1227) had put together two centuries earlier. Although in Ming times the Mongols were never united in a pan-Mongol federation, groups of Mongols could and did raid. Twice they threatened the dynasty: in 1449 the khan of the western Mongols captured the Chinese emperor, and in 1550 Beijing was surrounded by the forces of the khan of the Mongols in Inner Mongolia. Fearful of anything that might strengthen the Mongols,

Ming officials were reluctant to grant any privileges to Mongol leaders, such as trading posts along the borders. Instead they wanted the different groups of Mongols to trade only through the formal tribute system. When trade was finally liberalized in 1570, friction was reduced.

Two important developments shaped Ming-Mongol relations: the construction of the Great Wall, and closer relations between Mongolia and Tibet. The Great Wall, much of which survives today, was built as a compromise when Ming officials could agree on no other way to manage the Mongol threat. The wall extends about 1,500 miles from northeast of Beijing into Gansu province. In the eastern 500 miles, the wall averages about 35 feet high and 20 feet across, with lookout towers every half mile. Much of the way, the wall is faced with brick, which gives it an imposing appearance that greatly impressed the first Westerners who saw it.

Whether the wall did much to protect Ming China from the Mongols is still debated. Perhaps of more significance was the spread of Tibetan Buddhism among the Mongols. Tibet in this period was largely ruled by the major Buddhist monasteries. When Tibetan monasteries needed military assistance, they asked competing Mongol leaders for help, and many struggles were decided by Mongol military intervention. The Tibetan Buddhist Tsong-kha-pa (1357–1419) founded the Yellow Hat, or Gelug-pa, sect, whose heads later became known as the Dalai Lamas. In 1577 the third Dalai Lama accepted the invitation of Altan Khan to visit Mongolia, and the khan declared Tibetan Buddhism to be the official religion of all the Mongols. The Dalai Lama gave the khan the title "King of Religion," and the khan swore that the Mongols would renounce blood sacrifice. When the third Dalai Lama's reincarnation was found to be the great-grandson of Altan Khan, the ties between Tibet and Mongolia, not surprisingly, became even stronger. From the perspective of Ming China, the growing influence of Buddhism among the Mongols seemed a positive development, as Buddhist emphasis on nonviolence was expected to counter the Mongols' love of war.

## The Examination Life

In sharp contrast to Europe in this era, Ming China had few social barriers. It had no hereditary aristocracy that could have limited the emperor's absolute power. Although China had no titled aristocracy, it did have an elite whose status was based above all on government office acquired through education. Agricultural land remained the most highly prized form of wealth, but antiques, books, paintings and calligraphies, and urban real estate also brought status. Unlike in many European countries of the era, China's merchants did not become a politically articulate bourgeoisie. Instead

**Portrait of a Scholar-Official** The official Jiang Shunfu arranged to have his portrait painted wearing an official robe and hat and followed by two boy attendants, one holding a lute wrapped in cloth. During Ming and Qing times, the rank of an official was made visible by the badges he wore on his robes. The pair of cranes on Jiang's badge shows he held a first-rank post in the civil service hierarchy. (From *Mingqing renwuxiaoxiang huaxuan* [Nanjing: Nanjing Bowuguan], pl 16/Visual Connection Archive)

the politically active class was that of the scholars who Confucianism taught should aid the ruler in running the state. With the possible exception of the Jewish people, no people have respected learning as much as the Chinese. Merchants tried to marry into the scholar class in order to rise in the world.

Thus, despite the harsh and arbitrary ways in which the Ming emperors treated their civil servants, educated men were eager to enter the government. Reversing the policies of the Mongol Yuan Dynasty, the Ming government recruited almost all its officials through **civil service examinations**. Candidates had to study the Confucian classics and the interpretations of them by the twelfth-century Neo-Confucian scholar Zhu Xi (joo shee) (1130–1200), whose teachings were declared orthodox. To become officials, candidates had to pass examinations at the prefectural, the provincial, and the capital levels. To keep the wealthiest areas from dominating the exams, quotas were established for the number of candidates that each province could send on to the capital.

Of course, boys from well-to-do families had a significant advantage because their families could start their education with tutors at age four or five, though

less costly schools were becoming increasingly available as well. Families that for generations had pursued other careers—for example, as merchants or physicians—had more opportunities than ever for their sons to become officials through the exams. (See "Individuals in Society: Tan Yunxian, Woman Doctor," at right.) Clans sometimes operated schools for their members because the clan as a whole would enjoy the prestige of a successful clansman. Most of those who attended school stayed only a few years, but students who seemed most promising moved on to advanced schools where they practiced essay writing and studied the essays of men who had succeeded in the exams.

The examinations at the prefecture level lasted a day and drew hundreds if not thousands of candidates. The government compound would be taken over to give all candidates places to sit and write. The provincial and capital examinations were given in three sessions spread out over a week. In the first session, candidates wrote essays on passages from the classics. In the second and third sessions, candidates had to write essays on practical policy issues and on a passage from the *Classic of Filial Piety* (a brief text celebrating devotion to parents and other superiors). In addition, they had to show that they could draft state papers such as edicts, decrees, and judicial rulings. Reading the dynastic histories was a good way to prepare for policy questions and state paper exercises.

The provincial examinations were major local events. From five thousand to ten thousand candidates descended on the city and filled up its hostels. Candidates would show up a week in advance to present their credentials and gather the paper, ink, brushes, candles, blankets, and food they needed to survive in their small exam cells. To prevent cheating, no written material could be taken into the cells, and candidates were searched before being admitted. Anyone caught wearing a cheat-sheet (an inner gown covered with the classics in minuscule script) was thrown out of the exam and banned from the next session as well. Clerks used horns and gongs to begin and end each two-day session. During the sessions candidates had time to write rough drafts of their essays, correct them, and then copy neat final versions. Throughout this time,

• **civil service examinations** A highly competitive series of written tests held at the prefecture, province, and capital levels to select men to become officials.

# Individuals in Society

## Tan Yunxian, Woman Doctor

**THE GRANDMOTHER OF TAN YUNXIAN (1461–1554) WAS** the daughter of a physician, and her husband had married into her home to learn medicine himself. At least two of their sons— including Yunxian's father— passed the civil service examination and became officials, raising the social standing of the family considerably. The grandparents wanted to pass their medical knowledge down to someone, and because they found Yunxian very bright, they decided to teach it to her.

Tan Yunxian married and raised four children but also practiced medicine, confining her practice to women. At age fifty she wrote an autobiographical account, *Sayings of a Female Doctor*. In the preface she described how, under her grandmother's tutelage, she had first memorized the *Canon of Problems* and the *Canon of the Pulse*. Then when her grandmother had time, she asked her granddaughter to explain particular passages in these classic medical treatises.

Tan Yunxian began the practice of medicine by treating her own children, asking her grandmother to check her diagnoses. When her grandmother was old and ill, she gave Yunxian her notebook of prescriptions and her equipment for making medicines, telling her to study them carefully. Later, Yunxian herself became seriously ill and dreamed of her grandmother telling her on what page of which book to find the prescription that would cure her. When she recovered, she began her medical career in earnest.

Tan Yunxian's book records the cases of thirty-one patients she treated, most of them women with chronic complaints rather than critical illnesses. Many of the women had what the Chinese classed as women's complaints, such as menstrual irregularities, repeated miscarriages, barrenness, and postpartum fatigue. Some had ailments that men too could suffer, such as coughs, nausea, insomnia, diarrhea, rashes, and swellings. Like other literati physicians, Yunxian regularly prescribed herbal medications. She also practiced moxibustion, the technique of burning moxa (dried artemisia) at specified points on the body with the goal of stimulating the circulation of qi (life energy). Because the physician applying the moxa had to touch the patient, male physicians could not perform moxibustion on women.

Yunxian's patients included working women, and Yunxian seems to have thought that their problems often sprang from overwork. One woman came to her because she had had vaginal bleeding for three years. When questioned, the woman told Yunxian that she worked all day with her husband at their kiln making bricks and tiles. Yunxian's diagnosis was overwork, and she gave the woman pills to replenish her yin energies. A boatman's wife came to her complaining of numbness in her hands. When the woman told Yunxian that she worked in the wind and rain handling the boat, the doctor advised some time off. In another case Yunxian explained to a servant girl that she had gone back to work too soon after suffering a wind damage fever.

Tan Yunxian would have consulted traditional herbals, like this one, with sketches of plants of medicinal value and descriptions of their uses. (Wellcome Trust, London)

By contrast, when patients came from upper-class families, Tan Yunxian believed negative emotions were the source of their problems, particularly if a woman reported that her mother-in-law had scolded her or that her husband had recently brought a concubine home. Yunxian told two upper-class women who had miscarried that they lost their babies because they had hidden their anger, causing fire to turn inward and destabilize the fetus.

Tan Yunxian herself lived a long life, dying at age ninety-three.

Source: Based on Charlotte Furth, *A Flourishing Yin: Gender in China's Medical History, 960–1665* (Berkeley: University of California Press, 1999), pp. 285–295.

### QUESTIONS FOR ANALYSIS

1. Why do you think Tan Yunxian treated only women? Why might she have been more effective with women patients than a male physician would have been?
2. What do you think of Yunxian's diagnoses? Do you think she was able to help many of her patients?

## LaunchPad
### Online Document Project

**What kinds of treatments did Chinese doctors employ?** Examine artwork depicting Chinese medical practices, and then complete a quiz and writing assignment based on the evidence and details from this chapter.

*See inside the front cover to learn more.*

tension was high. Sometimes rumors that the examiners had been bribed to leak the questions led to riots in the exam quarters, and knocked-over candles occasionally caused fires.

After the papers were handed in, clerks recopied them and assigned them numbers to preserve anonymity. Proofreaders checked the copying before handing the papers to the assembled examiners, who divided them up to grade. The grading generally took about twenty days, and most candidates stayed in the vicinity to await the results. Those few who passed (generally from 2 to 10 percent) were invited to the governor's compound for a celebration. By the time they reached home, most of their friends, neighbors, and relatives had already heard their good news. They could not spend long celebrating, however, because they had to begin preparing for the capital exams, less than a year away.

## Everyday Life in Ming China

For civil servants and almost everyone else, everyday life in Ming China followed patterns established in earlier periods. The family remained central to most people's lives, and almost everyone married. Beyond the family, people's lives were shaped by the type of work they did and where they lived.

Large towns and cities proliferated in Ming times and became islands of sophistication in the vast sea of rural villages. In these urban areas small businesses manufactured textiles, paper, and luxury goods such as silks and porcelains. The southeast became a center for the production of cotton and silks; other areas specialized in the grain and salt trades and in silver. Merchants could make fortunes moving these goods across the country.

Printing was invented in Tang times (618–907) and had a great impact on the life of the educated elite in Song times (960–1279), but not until Ming times did it transform the culture of the urban middle classes. By the late Ming period, publishing houses were putting out large numbers of books aimed at general audiences. These included fiction, reference books of all sorts, and popular religious tracts, such as ledgers for calculating the moral value of one's good deeds and subtracting the demerits from bad deeds. To make their books attractive in the marketplace, entrepreneurial book publishers commissioned artists to illustrate them. By the sixteenth century more and more books were being published in the vernacular language (the language people spoke), especially short stories, novels, and plays. Ming vernacular short stories depicted a world much like that of their readers, full of shop clerks and merchants, monks and prostitutes, students and matchmakers. (See "Viewpoints 21.1: Zhang Dai, Engelbert Kaempfer, and Thomas Platter on Urban Amusements," at right.)

The full-length novel made its first appearance during the Ming period. The plots of the early novels were heavily indebted to story cycles developed by oral storytellers over the course of several centuries. *Water Margin* is the episodic tale of a band of bandits, while *The Romance of the Three Kingdoms* is a work of historical fiction based on the exploits of the generals and statesmen contending for power at the end of the Han Dynasty. *The Journey to the West* is a fantastic account of the Tang monk Xuanzang's travels to India; in this book he is accompanied by a pig and a monkey with supernatural powers. *Plum in the Golden Vase* is a novel of manners about a lustful merchant with a wife and five concubines. Competing publishers brought out their own editions of these novels, sometimes adding new illustrations or commentaries.

The Chinese found recreation and relaxation in many ways besides reading. The affluent indulged in an alcoholic drink made from fermented and distilled rice, and once tobacco was introduced from the Americas, both men and women took up pipes. Plays were also very popular. The Jesuit missionary Matteo Ricci, who lived in China from 1583 to 1610, described resident troupes in large cities and traveling troupes that "journey everywhere throughout the length and breadth of the country" putting on plays. The leaders of the troupes would purchase young children and train them to sing and perform. Ricci thought too many people were addicted to these performances:

> These groups of actors are employed at all imposing banquets, and when they are called they come prepared to enact any of the ordinary plays. The host at the banquet is usually presented with a volume of plays and he selects the one or several he may like. The guests, between eating and drinking, follow the plays with so much satisfaction that the banquet at times may last for ten hours.[1]

People not only enjoyed play performances but also avidly read the play scripts. The love stories and social satires of Tang Xianzu, the greatest of the Ming playwrights, were very popular. One of his plays tells the story of a young man who falls asleep while his meal is cooking. In his dream he sees his whole life: he comes in first in the civil service examinations, rises to high office, is unfairly slandered and condemned to death, and then is cleared and promoted. At the point of death, he wakes up, sees that his dinner is nearly ready, and realizes that life passes as quickly as a dream.

More than bread in Europe, rice supplied most of the calories of the population in central and south China. (In north China, wheat, made into steamed or baked bread or into noodles, served as the dietary staple.) In the south, terracing and irrigation of mountain slopes, introduced in the eleventh century, had

# Viewpoints 21.1

## Zhang Dai, Engelbert Kaempfer, and Thomas Platter on Urban Amusements

- *Zhang Dai (1597–1684?) lived the life of a well-to-do urban aesthete in Nanjing in the last decades of the Ming Dynasty, and then saw that life destroyed by the Manchu invasion. In later years, in much reduced circumstances, he wrote with nostalgia about the pleasures of his youth. His account of a popular storyteller can be compared to accounts of two foreign visitors to Japan and England: a German naturalist in Nagasaki, Japan, in 1690–1692, who described the performances put on as entertainment for the gods during a religious festival; and a Swiss visitor to London in 1599, who saw theater troupes.*

### Zhang Dai on a Nanjing Storyteller

❝ Pockmarked Liu of Nanjing . . . is an excellent storyteller. He tells one episode a day, and his fee is one ounce of silver. To engage him you have to make your booking, and forward his retainer, ten days in advance, and even then you may be out of luck. . . . I heard him tell the story of Wu Song killing the tiger on Jingyang Ridge. His version diverged greatly from the original text. He will describe things in the minutest particular, but his choice of what to put in and leave out is nice and neat, and he is never wordy. His bellow is like the boom of a mighty bell, and when he gets to some high point in the action he will let loose such a peal of thunder that the building will shake on its foundations. I remember that when Wu Song goes into the inn to get a drink and finds no one there to serve him, he suddenly gave such a roar as to set all the empty vessels humming and vibrating. To make dull patches come to life like this is typical of his passion for detail.

When he goes to perform in someone's house, he will not loosen his tongue until his hosts sit quietly, hold their breath, and give him their undivided attention. If he spots the servants whispering, or if his listeners yawn or show any signs of fatigue, he will come to an abrupt halt, and be impervious to persuasion to continue. He will often talk till past midnight, still keeping up an unhurried flow, while the servants wipe the tables, trim the lamp, and silently serve tea in cups of tasteful porcelain. His pacing and his inflexions, his articulation and his cadences, are exactly suited to the situation, and lay bare the very body and fibre of the matter. If one plucked all the other storytellers alive by the ear and made them listen to him, I do not doubt but they would be struck dumb with wonder and give up the ghost on the spot. ❞

### Engelbert Kaempfer on Nagasaki Festival Plays

❝ The public spectacles shown upon this occasion are a sort of plays, or rather dramas, acted by eight, twelve, or more persons. The subject is taken out of the history of their gods and heroes. Their remarkable adventures, heroic actions, and sometimes their love intrigues, put in verse, are sung by dancing-actors, whilst others play upon all sorts of musical instruments. If the subject be thought too grave and moving, there is now and then a comical actor jumps out unawares upon the stage, with his gestures and merry discourse in prose, to divert the people. Some of their other plays are composed only of ballets, or dances, like the performances of the Mimic Actors upon the Roman Stage. For the dancers do not speak, but endeavor to express the contents of the story they are about to represent, as naturally as possible, both by their dress, and by their gestures and actions, regulated according to the sound of musical instruments. . . . The Actors are commonly young girls, taken out of the bawdy-houses, as also young boys and children out of those streets, at whose expense the solemnity is performed. They are all magnificently clad, in variously colored silken gowns, suitable to the characters which they are to represent. ❞

### Thomas Platter on London Theater

❝ On September 21st after lunch, about two o'clock, I and my party crossed the water, and there in the house with the thatched roof witnessed an excellent performance of the tragedy of the first Emperor Julius Caesar with a cast of some fifteen people; when the play was over, they danced very marvelously and gracefully together as is their wont, two dressed as men and two as women. . . . Thus daily at two in the afternoon, London has two, sometimes three plays running in different places, competing with each other, and those which play best obtain most spectators. The playhouses are so constructed that they play on a raised platform, so that everyone has a good view. There are different galleries and places, however, where the seating is better and more comfortable and therefore more expensive. For whoever cares to stand below only pays one English penny, but if he wishes to sit he enters by another door and pays another penny, while if he desires to sit in the most comfortable seats, which are cushioned, where he not only sees everything well, but can also be seen, then he pays yet another English penny at another door. And during the performance food and drink are carried round the audience, so that for what one cares to pay one may also have refreshment. ❞

Sources: David Pollard, trans. and ed., *The Chinese Essay* (New York: Columbia University Press, 2000), pp. 89–90. Reproduced with permission of C. HURST & CO. LTD. in the format Book via Copyright Clearance Center; Engelbert Kaempfer, *The History of Japan*, vol. 2:143 (London: J. Mac Lehose and Sons, 1906), pp. 136–137, slightly modified; Clare Williams, trans., *Thomas Platter's Travels in England, 1599* (London: J. Cape, 1937), pp. 166–167.

### QUESTIONS FOR ANALYSIS

1. What similarities do you see in the way the performers in these descriptions entertained their audiences? What differences do you see?

2. What makes foreign visitors' accounts useful? What advantage do local observers have?

**Popular Romance Literature**
Women were among the most avid readers of the scripts for plays, especially romantic ones like *The Western Chamber*, a story of a young scholar who falls in love with a well-educated girl he encounters by chance. In this scene, the young woman looks up at the moon as her maid looks at its reflection in the pond. Meanwhile, her young lover scales the wall. This multicolor woodblock print, made in 1640, was one of twenty-one created to illustrate the play. (RBA 702 405 Min Qiji: *The Romance of the West Chamber*; Museum für Ostasiatische Kunst, Koln, Inv.-No. 62,1 [No. 11]. Photo: © Rheinisches Bildarchiv Köln)

increased rice harvests. Other innovations also brought good results. Farmers began to stock the rice paddies with fish, which continuously fertilized the rice fields, destroyed malaria-bearing mosquitoes, and enriched the diet. Farmers also grew cotton, sugarcane, and indigo as commercial crops. New methods of crop rotation allowed for continuous cultivation and for more than one harvest per year from a single field.

The Ming rulers promoted the repopulation and colonization of war-devastated regions through reclamation of land and massive transfers of people. Immigrants to these areas received large plots and exemption from taxation for many years. Reforestation played a dramatic role in the agricultural revolution. In 1391 the Ming government ordered 50 million trees planted in the Nanjing area to produce lumber for the construction of a maritime fleet. In 1392 each family holding a land grant in Anhui province had to plant two hundred mulberry, jujube, and persimmon trees. In 1396 peasants in the present-day provinces of Hunan and Hubei in central China planted 84 million fruit trees. Historians have estimated that 1 billion trees were planted during Taizu's reign.

Increased food production led to steady population growth and the multiplication of markets, towns, and small cities. Larger towns had permanent shops; smaller towns had periodic markets — some every five days, some every ten days, some only once a month. They sold essential goods — such as pins, matches, oil for lamps, candles, paper, incense, and tobacco — to country people from the surrounding hamlets. Markets usually included moneylenders, pawnbrokers, a tearoom, and sometimes a wine shop where tea and rice wine were sold and entertainers performed.

Tradesmen carrying their wares on their backs and craftsmen — carpenters, barbers, joiners, locksmiths — moved constantly from market to market. Itinerant salesmen depended on the city market for their wares.

## Ming Decline

Beginning in the 1590s the Ming government was beset by fiscal, military, and political problems. The government went nearly bankrupt helping defend Korea against a Japanese invasion (see pages 640–641). Then came a series of natural disasters: floods, droughts, locusts, and epidemics ravaged one region after another. At the same time, a "little ice age" brought a drop in average temperatures that shortened the growing season and reduced harvests. In areas of serious food shortages, gangs of army deserters and laid-off soldiers began scouring the countryside in search of food. Once the gangs had stolen all their grain, hard-pressed farmers joined them just to survive. The Ming government had little choice but to try to increase taxes to deal with these threats, but the last thing people needed was heavier taxes.

Adding to the hardship was a sudden drop in the supply of silver. In place of the paper money that had circulated in Song and Yuan times, silver ingots came into general use as money in Ming times. Even agricultural taxes came to be paid in silver rather than in grain. Much of this silver originated in either Japan or the New World and entered China as payment for the silk and porcelains exported from China. (See "Global Trade: Silver," page 482.) When events in Japan and the Philippines led to disruption of trade, silver imports dropped. This led to deflation in China, which caused real rents to rise. Soon there were riots among urban workers and tenant farmers. In 1642 a group of rebels cut the dikes on the Yellow River, causing massive flooding. A smallpox epidemic soon added to the death toll. In 1644 the last Ming emperor, in despair, took his own life when rebels entered Beijing, opening the way for the start of a new dynasty.

# The Manchus and Qing China, to 1800

☐ Did the return of alien rule with the Manchus have any positive consequences for China?

The next dynasty, the **Qing Dynasty** (1644–1911), was founded by the Manchus, a non-Chinese people who were descended from the Jurchens who had ruled north China during the Jin Dynasty (1127–1234), when south China was controlled by the Song. Manchu men shaved the front of their heads and wore the rest of their hair in a long braid called a queue. In the late sixteenth century the Manchus began expanding their territories, and in 1644 they founded the Qing Dynasty, which brought peace and in time prosperity. Successful Qing military campaigns extended the borders into Mongol, Tibetan, and Uighur regions, creating a multiethnic empire that was larger than any earlier Chinese dynasty.

## The Rise of the Manchus

In the Ming period, the Manchus lived in dispersed communities in what is loosely called Manchuria (the northeast of modern-day China). In the more densely populated southern part of Manchuria, the Manchus lived in close contact with Mongols, Koreans, and Chinese (Map 21.1). They were not nomads but rather hunters, fishers, and farmers. Like the Mongols, they also were excellent horsemen and archers and had a strongly hierarchical social structure, with elites and slaves. Slaves, often Korean or Chinese, were generally acquired through capture. A Korean visitor described many small Manchu settlements, most no larger than twenty households, supported by fishing, hunting for pelts, collecting pine nuts or ginseng, or growing crops such as wheat, millet, and barley. Villages were often at odds with each other over resources, and men did not leave their villages without arming themselves with bows and arrows or swords. Interspersed among these Manchu settlements were groups of nomadic Mongols who lived in tents.

The Manchus credited their own rise to Nurhaci (1559–1626). Over several decades, he united the Manchus and expanded their territories. Like Chinggis Khan, who had reorganized the Mongol armies to reduce the importance of tribal affiliations, Nurhaci created a new social basis for his armies in units called **banners**. Each banner was made up of a set of military companies and included the families and slaves of the soldiers. Each company had a hereditary captain, often from Nurhaci's own lineage. Over time new companies and new banners were formed, and by 1644 there were eight each of Manchu, Mongol, and Chinese banners. When new groups were defeated, their members were distributed among several banners to lessen their potential for subversion.

The Manchus entered China by invitation of the distinguished Ming general Wu Sangui, himself a native of southern Manchuria, who was near the eastern end of the Great Wall when he heard that the rebels had captured Beijing. The Manchus proposed to Wu that they join forces and liberate Beijing. Wu opened the gates of the Great Wall to let the Manchus in, and within a couple of weeks they occupied Beijing. When the Manchus made clear that they intended to conquer the rest of the country and take the throne themselves, Wu and many other Chinese generals joined forces with them. Before long, China was again under alien rule.

In the summer of 1645 the Manchus ordered all Chinese serving in Manchu armies to shave the front of their heads in the Manchu fashion, presumably to make it easier to recognize whose side they were on. Soon this order was extended to all Chinese men. Because so many of those newly conquered by the Qing refused to shave off their hair, Manchu commanders felt justified in ordering the slaughter of defiant cities. After quelling resistance, the Qing put in place policies and institutions that gave China a respite from war and disorder. Most of the political institutions of the Ming Dynasty were taken over relatively unchanged, including the examination system.

After peace was achieved, population growth took off. Between 1700 and 1800 the Chinese population seems to have nearly doubled, from about 150 million to over 300 million. Population growth during the eighteenth century has been attributed to many factors: global warming that extended the growing season, expanded use of New World crops, slowing of the spread of new diseases that had accompanied the sixteenth-century expansion of global traffic, and the efficiency of the Qing government in providing relief in times of famine.

Some scholars have recently argued that China's overall standard of living in the mid-eighteenth century was comparable to Europe's and that the standards

• **Qing Dynasty** The dynasty founded by the Manchus that ruled China from 1644 to 1911.

• **banners** Units of the Qing army, composed of soldiers, their families, and slaves.

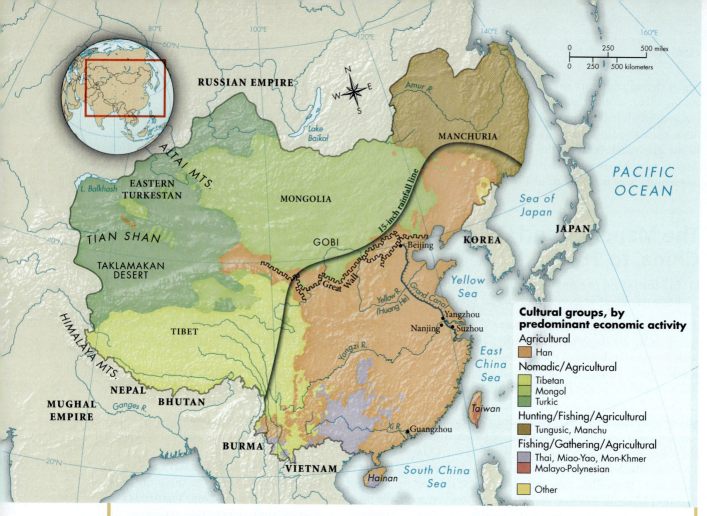

## ☐ Mapping the Past

**MAP 21.1   The Qing Empire, ca. 1800**  The sheer size of the Qing Empire in China almost inevitably led to its profound cultural influence on the rest of Asia.

**ANALYZING THE MAP**  How many different cultural groups are depicted? Which occupied the largest territories? Where was crop agriculture most prevalent?

**CONNECTIONS**  What geographical and political factors limited the expansion of the Qing Empire?

of China's most developed regions, such as the lower Yangzi region, compared favorably to the most developed regions of Europe at the time, such as England and the Netherlands. Life expectancy, food consumption, and even facilities for transportation were at similar levels.

## Competent and Long-Lived Emperors

For more than a century, China was ruled by only three rulers, each of them hard-working, talented, and committed to making the Qing Dynasty a success. Two, the Kangxi and Qianlong emperors, had exceptionally long reigns.

Kangxi (r. 1661–1722) proved adept at meeting the expectations of both the Chinese and the Manchu elites. At age fourteen he announced that he would begin ruling on his own and had his regent imprisoned. Kangxi (KAHNG-shee) could speak, read, and write

Chinese and made efforts to persuade educated Chinese that the Manchus had a legitimate claim to rule, even trying to attract Ming loyalists who had been unwilling to serve the Qing. He undertook a series of tours of the south, where Ming loyalty had been strongest, and he held a special exam to select men to compile the official history of the Ming Dynasty.

Kangxi's son and heir, the Yongzheng emperor (r. 1722–1735), was also a hard-working ruler who took an interest in the efficiency of the government. Because his father had lived so long, he did not come to the throne until his mid-forties and reigned only thirteen years. His successor, however, the Qianlong emperor (r. 1736–1796), like Kangxi had a reign of sixty years, with the result that China had only three rulers in 135 years.

Qianlong (chyan-loong) put much of his energy into impressing his subjects with his magnificence. He understood that the Qing's capacity to hold the multi-

**Presenting a Horse to the Emperor** This detail from a 1757 hand scroll shows the Qianlong emperor, seated, receiving envoys from the Kazakhs. Note how the envoy, presenting a pure white horse, is kneeling to the ground performing the kowtow, which involved lowering his head to the ground as an act of reverence. The artist was Giuseppe Castiglione, an Italian who worked as a painter in Qianlong's court. (by Father Giuseppe Castiglione [1688–1766]; Musée des Arts Asiatiques-Guimet/© RMN–Grand Palais/Art Resource, NY)

ethnic empire together rested on their ability to appeal to all those they ruled. Besides speaking Manchu and Chinese, Qianlong learned to converse in Mongolian, Uighur, Tibetan, and Tangut, and he addressed envoys in their own languages. He became as much a patron of Tibetan Buddhism as of Chinese Confucianism. He initiated a massive project to translate the Tibetan Buddhist canon into Mongolian and Manchu and had huge multilingual dictionaries compiled.

To demonstrate to the Chinese scholar-official elite that he was a sage emperor, Qianlong worked on affairs of state from dawn until early afternoon and then turned to reading, painting, and calligraphy. He was ostentatious in his devotion to his mother, visiting her daily and tending to her comfort with all the devotion of the most filial Chinese son. He took several tours down the Grand Canal to the southeast, in part to emulate his grandfather, in part to entertain his mother, who accompanied him on these tours.

Despite these displays of Chinese virtues, the Qianlong emperor was not fully confident that the Chinese supported his rule, and he was quick to act on any suspicion of anti-Manchu thoughts or actions. During a project to catalogue nearly all the books in China, he began to suspect that some governors were holding back books with seditious content. He ordered full searches for books with disparaging references to the Manchus or to previous alien conquerors like the Jurchens and Mongols. Sometimes passages were deleted or rewritten, but when an entire book was offensive, it was destroyed. So thorough was this book burning that no copies survive of more than two thousand titles.

Through Qianlong's reign, China remained an enormous producer of manufactured goods and led the way in assembly-line production. The government operated huge textile factories, but some private firms were even larger. Hangzhou had a textile firm that gave work to 4,000 weavers, 20,000 spinners, and 10,000 dyers and finishers. The porcelain kilns at Jingdezhen employed the division of labor on a large scale and were able to supply porcelain to much of the world. The growth of the economy benefited the Qing state, and the treasury became so full that the Qianlong emperor was able to cancel taxes on several occasions. When he abdicated in 1796, his treasury had 400 million silver dollars in it.

## Imperial Expansion

The Qing Dynasty put together a multiethnic empire that was larger than any earlier Chinese dynasty. Taiwan was acquired in 1683 after Qing armies pursued a rebel there. Mongolia was acquired next. In 1696 Kangxi led an army of eighty thousand men into Mongolia, and within a few years Manchu supremacy was accepted there. Cannon and muskets gave Qing forces military superiority over the Mongols, who were armed only with bows and arrows. Thus the Qing could dominate the steppe cheaply, effectively ending two thousand years of Inner Asian military advantage.

In the 1720s the Qing established a permanent garrison of banner soldiers in Tibet. By this time, the expanding Qing and Russian Empires were nearing each other. In 1689 the Manchu and the Russian rulers approved a treaty—written in Russian, Manchu,

Chinese, and Latin—defining their borders in Manchuria and regulating trade. Another treaty in 1727 allowed a Russian ecclesiastical mission to reside in Beijing and a trade caravan to make a trip from Russia to Beijing once every three years.

The last region to be annexed was Chinese Turkestan (the modern province of Xinjiang). Both the Han and the Tang Dynasties had stationed troops in the region, exercising loose overlordship, but neither the Song nor the Ming had tried to control the area. The Qing won the region in the 1750s through a series of campaigns against Uighur and Dzungar Mongol forces.

Both Tibet and Turkestan were ruled lightly. The local populations kept their own religious leaders and did not have to wear the queue.

# Japan's Middle Ages, ca. 1400–1600

☐ How did Japan change during this period of political instability?

In the twelfth century Japan entered an age dominated by military men, an age that can be compared to Europe's feudal age. The Kamakura Shogunate (1185–1333) had its capital in the east, at Kamakura. It was succeeded by the Ashikaga Shogunate (1338–1573), which returned the government to Kyoto (KYOH-toh) and helped launch, during the fifteenth century, the great age of Zen-influenced Muromachi culture. The sixteenth century brought civil war over succession to the shogunate, leading to the building of massive castles and the emergence of rulers of obscure origins who eventually unified the realm.

## Muromachi Culture

The headquarters of the Ashikaga shoguns were on Muromachi Street in Kyoto, and the refined and elegant style that they promoted is often called Muromachi culture. The shoguns patronized Zen Buddhism, the school of Buddhism associated with meditation and mind-to-mind transmission of truth. Because Zen monks were able to read and write Chinese, they often assisted the shoguns in handling foreign affairs. Many of the Kyoto Zen temples in this period had rock gardens, seen as aids to Zen meditation.

Zen ideas of simplicity permeated the arts. The Silver Pavilion built by the shogun Yoshimasa (r. 1449–

1473) epitomizes Zen austerity. A white sand cone constructed in the temple garden was designed to reflect moonlight. Yoshimasa was also influential in the development of the tea ceremony, practiced by warriors, aristocrats, and priests, but not by women. Aesthetes celebrated the beauty of imperfect objects, such as plain or misshapen cups or pots. Spare monochrome paintings fit into this aesthetic, as did simple asymmetrical flower arrangements.

The shoguns were also patrons of the **Nō theater**. Nō drama originated in popular forms of entertainment, including comical skits and dances directed to the gods. It was transformed into high art by Zeami (1363–1443), an actor and playwright who also wrote on the aesthetic theory of Nō. Nō was performed on a bare stage with a pine tree painted across the backdrop. One or two actors wearing brilliant brocade robes performed, using stylized gestures and stances. One actor wore a mask indicating whether the character he was portraying was male or female, old or young, a god, a ghost, or a demon. The actors were accompanied by a chorus and a couple of musicians playing drums and flute. Many of the stories concerned ghosts consumed by jealous passions or the desire for revenge. Zeami argued that the most meaningful moments came during silence, when the actor's spiritual presence allowed the audience to catch a glimpse of the mysterious and inexpressible.

## Civil War

Civil war began in Kyoto in 1467 as a struggle over succession to the shogunate. Rival claimants and their followers used arson as their chief weapon and burned down temples and mansions, destroying much of the city and its treasures. In the early phases defeated opponents were exiled or allowed to retire to monasteries. As the conflict continued, violence escalated; hostages and prisoners were slaughtered and corpses mutilated. Once Kyoto was laid waste, war spread to outlying areas. When the shogun could no longer protect cities, merchants banded together to hire mercenaries. In the political vacuum, the Lotus League, a commoner-led religious sect united by faith in the saving power of the Lotus Sutra, set up a commoner-run government that collected taxes and settled disputes. In 1536, during eight days of fighting, the powerful Buddhist monastery Enryakuji attacked the League and its temples, burned much of the city, and killed men, women, and children thought to be believers.

In these confused and violent circumstances, power devolved to the local level, where warlords, called **daimyo** (DIGH-myoh), built their power bases. Unlike earlier power holders, these new lords were not appointed by the court or shogunate and did not send taxes to absentee overlords. Instead they seized what

---

• **Nō theater** A type of Japanese theater in which performers convey emotions and ideas as much through gestures, stances, and dress as through words.

• **daimyo** Regional lords in Japan, many of whom were self-made men.

they needed and used it to build up their territories and recruit more samurai. To raise revenues, they surveyed the land and promoted irrigation and trade. Many of the most successful daimyo were self-made men who rose from obscurity.

The violence of the period encouraged castle building. The castles were built not on mountaintops but on level plains, and they were surrounded by moats and walls made from huge stones. Inside a castle was a many-storied keep, which could be elegantly decorated with painted sliding doors and screens. Though relatively safe from incendiary missiles, the keeps were vulnerable to Western-style cannon, introduced in the 1570s.

## The Victors: Nobunaga and Hideyoshi

The first daimyo to gain a predominance of power was Oda Nobunaga (1534–1582). A samurai of the lesser daimyo class, he recruited followers from masterless samurai who had been living by robbery and extortion. After he won control of his native province in 1559, he immediately set out to extend his power through central Japan. A key step was destroying the military power of the great monasteries. To increase revenues, he minted coins, the first government-issued money in Japan since 958. Also to raise revenues, he promoted trade by eliminating customs barriers and opening the little fishing village of Nagasaki to foreign commerce; it soon became Japan's largest port.

In 1582, in an attempted coup, Nobunaga was forced by one of his vassals to commit suicide. His general and staunchest adherent, Toyotomi Hideyoshi (1537–1598), avenged him and continued the drive toward unification of the daimyo-held lands.

Like the Ming founder, Hideyoshi was a peasant's son who rose to power through military talent. Hideyoshi succeeded in bringing northern and western Japan under his control. In 1582 he attacked the great fortress at Takamatsu. When direct assault failed, his troops flooded the castle to force its surrender. A successful siege of the town of Kagoshima then brought the southern island of Kyushu (KYOO-shoo) under his domination. Hideyoshi soothed the vanquished daimyo as Nobunaga had done—with lands and military positions—but he also required them to swear allegiance and to obey him down to the smallest particular. For the first time in over two centuries, Japan had a single ruler.

Hideyoshi did his best to ensure that future peasants' sons would not be able to rise as he had. His great sword hunt of 1588 collected weapons from farmers, who were no longer allowed to wear swords. Restrictions were also placed on samurai; they were prohibited from leaving their lord's service or switching occupations. To improve tax collection, Hideyoshi ordered a survey of the entire country. His agents collected detailed information about each daimyo's lands and about towns, villages, agricultural produce, and industrial output all over Japan. His surveys not only tightened tax collection, but also registered each peasant household and tied the peasants to the land. With the country pacified, Hideyoshi embarked on an ill-fated attempt to conquer Korea and China that ended only with his death, discussed below (see page 641).

**Hideyoshi's Campaigns in Japan and Korea, 1592–1598**

→ Reunification campaign
→ Campaign against Korea

**Matsumoto Castle** Hideyoshi built Matsumoto Castle between 1594 and 1597. Designed to be impregnable, it was surrounded by a moat and had a base constructed of huge stones. In the sixteenth and early seventeenth centuries Spanish and Portuguese missionaries compared Japanese castles favorably to European castles of the period. (Adina Tovy/Robert Harding World Imagery)

# The Tokugawa Shogunate, to 1800

☐ What was life like in Japan during the Tokugawa peace?

On his deathbed, Hideyoshi set up a council of regents to govern during the minority of his infant son. The strongest regent was Hideyoshi's long-time supporter Tokugawa Ieyasu (1543–1616), who ruled vast territories around Edo (AY-doh; modern-day Tokyo). In 1600 at Sekigahara, Ieyasu smashed a coalition of daimyo defenders of the heir and began building his own government. In 1603 he took the title "shogun." The **Tokugawa Shogunate** that Ieyasu fashioned lasted until 1867. This era is also called the Edo period after the location of the shogunate, starting Tokyo's history as Japan's most important city (Map 21.2). Peace brought many benefits. Towns and cities thrived and became centers for the theater and publishing.

## Tokugawa Government

Over the course of the seventeenth century the Tokugawa shoguns worked to consolidate relations with the daimyo. In a scheme resembling the later residency requirements imposed by Louis XIV in France (see page 534) and Peter the Great in Russia (see page 547), Ieyasu set up the **alternate residence system**, which compelled the lords to live in Edo every other year

and to leave their wives and sons there—essentially as hostages. This arrangement had obvious advantages: the shogun could keep tabs on the daimyo, control them through their wives and children, and weaken them financially with the burden of maintaining two residences.

The peace imposed by the Tokugawa Shogunate brought a steady rise in population to about 30 million people by 1800 (making Tokugawa Japan about one-tenth the size of Qing China). To maintain stability, the early Tokugawa shoguns froze social status. Laws rigidly prescribed what each class could and could not do. Nobles, for example, were strictly forbidden to go sauntering, whether by day or by night, through the streets or lanes in places where they had no business to be. Daimyo were prohibited from moving troops outside their frontiers, making alliances, and coining money. As intended, these rules protected the Tokugawa shoguns from daimyo attack and helped ensure a long era of peace.

The early Tokugawa shoguns also restricted the construction and repair of castles—symbols, in Japan as in medieval Europe, of feudal independence. Continuing Hideyoshi's policy, the Tokugawa regime enforced a policy of complete separation of samurai and peasants. Samurai were defined as those permitted to carry swords. They had to live in castles (which evolved into castle-towns), and they depended on stipends from their lords, the daimyo. Samurai were effectively prevented from establishing ties to the land, so they could not become landholders. Likewise, merchants and arti-

**MAP 21.2 Tokugawa Japan, 1603–1867** The lands that the shogunate directly controlled were concentrated near its capital at Edo. The daimyo of distant places, such as the island of Kyushu, were required to make long journeys to and from Edo every year.

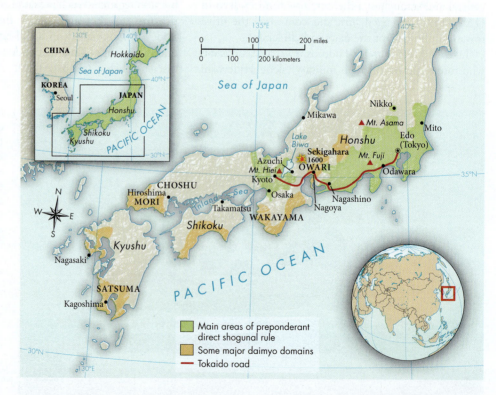

**Daimyo Procession** The system of alternate residence meant that some daimyo were always on the road. The constant travel of daimyo with their attendants between their domains and Edo, the shogun's residence, stimulated construction of roads, inns, and castle-towns. (*Daimyo's Processions Passing Along the Tokaido*, by Utagawa Sadahide [1807–1873]/triptych of polychrome woodblock prints; ink and color on paper, Edo period [1615–1868]. Bequest of William S. Lieberman, 2005, accession 2007.49.290a–c/Metropolitan Museum of Art, New York, NY, USA/Image copyright © The Metropolitan Museum of Art/Image source: Art Resource, NY)

sans had to live in towns and could not own land. Japanese castle-towns evolved into bustling, sophisticated urban centers.

After 1639 Japan limited its contacts with the outside world because of concerns both about the loyalty of subjects converted to Christianity by European missionaries and about the imperialist ambitions of European powers (discussed below). However, China remained an important trading partner and source of ideas. For example, Neo-Confucianism gained a stronger hold among the samurai-turned-bureaucrats, and painting in Chinese styles enjoyed great popularity. The Edo period also saw the development of a school of native learning that rejected Buddhism and Confucianism as alien and tried to identify a distinctly Japanese sensibility.

## Commercialization and the Growth of Towns

During the civil war period, warfare seems to have promoted social and economic change, much as it had in China during the Warring States Period (403–221 B.C.E.). Trade grew, and greater use was made of coins imported from Ming China. Markets began appearing at river crossings, at the entrances to temples and shrines, and at other places where people congregated. Towns and cities sprang up all around the country, some of them around the new castles. Traders and artisans dealing in a specific product—such as comb mak-

ers, sesame oil producers, or metalworkers—began forming guilds. Money-lending was a very profitable business—annual interest rates reached 300 percent. In Kyoto the powerful monastery Enryakuji licensed the moneylenders, in essence running a lucrative protection racket. Foreign trade also flourished, despite chronic problems with pirates who raided the Japanese, Korean, and Chinese coasts (see pages 640–641).

Recent scholarship demonstrates that the Tokugawa era witnessed the foundations of modern Japanese capitalism: the development of a cash economy, the use of money to make more money, the accumulation of large amounts of capital for investment in factory or technological enterprises, the growth of business ventures operating over a national network of roads, and the expansion of wage labor. That these developments occurred simultaneously with, but entirely independent of, similar changes in Europe fascinates and challenges historians.

In most cities, merchant families with special privileges from the government controlled the urban economy. Frequently, a particular family dominated the trade in a particular product and then branched out into other businesses. The family of Kōnoike Shinroku is an example. In 1600 he established a sake (SAH-kay)

- **Tokugawa Shogunate** The Japanese government in Edo founded by Tokugawa Ieyasu. It lasted from 1603 to 1867.

- **alternate residence system** Arrangement in which lords lived in Edo every other year and left their wives and sons there as hostages.

**Interior of Nijo Castle** To assert control over the imperial court and the city of Kyoto, Tokugawa Ieyasu built palace-like Nijo Castle there in 1601–1603. He had the sliding doors painted by leading artists of the period, making the castle as elegant as the imperial palace. (From Fujioka Michio, *Genshoku Nihon no Bijutsu*, Vol. 12: Shiro to Shoin [Tokyo: Shogakkan, 1968]/Visual Connection Archive)

brewery in the village of Kōnoike (sake is an alcoholic beverage made from fermented rice). By 1604 he had opened a branch office in Edo, and in 1615 he opened an office in Osaka and began shipping taxes paid in rice from western Japan to Osaka. In 1656 one of Shinroku's sons founded a banking or money-changing business in Osaka. Forty years later the Kōnoike family was doing business in thirty-two daimyo domains. Eventually, the Kōnoike banking house made loans to and handled the tax-rice for 110 daimyo families. In 1705, with the interest paid from daimyo loans, the Kōnoike bought a tract of ponds and swampland, turned the land into rice paddies, and settled 480 households on the land. (Land reclamation under merchant supervision became a typical feature of Tokugawa business practices.) Involved by this time in five or six business enterprises, the house of Kōnoike had come a long way from brewing sake.

Japanese merchant families also devised distinct patterns and procedures for their business operations. What today is called "family-style management principles" determined the age of apprenticeship (between eleven and thirteen); the employee's detachment from past social relations and adherence to the norms of a particular family business; salaries; seniority as the basis of promotion, although job performance at the middle rungs determined who reached the higher ranks; and the time for retirement. All employees in a family business were expected to practice frugality, resourcefulness, self-denial, and careful accounting. These values formed the basis of what has been called the Japanese "industrious revolution." They help to explain how, after the Meiji (MAY-jee) Restoration of 1867 (see

page 801), Japan was able to industrialize rapidly and compete successfully with the West. (In both Japan and China there was a market for books giving advice on how to get ahead. See "Viewpoints 21.2: Chinese and Japanese Financial Advice," at right.)

In the seventeenth century underemployed farmers and samurai, not to mention the ambitious and adventurous, thronged to the cities. As a result, Japan's cities grew tremendously. Kyoto became the center for the manufacture of luxury goods like lacquer, brocade, and fine porcelain. Osaka was the chief market, especially for rice. Edo was a center of consumption by the daimyo, their vassals, and government bureaucrats. Both Osaka and Edo reached about a million residents.

Two hundred fifty towns came into being in this period. Most ranged in size from 3,000 to 20,000 people, but a few, such as Hiroshima, Kagoshima, and Nagoya, had populations of between 65,000 and 100,000. In addition, perhaps two hundred towns along the main road to Edo emerged to meet the needs of men traveling on the alternate residence system. In the eighteenth century perhaps 4 million people, 15 percent of the Japanese population, resided in cities or towns.

## The Life of the People in the Edo Period

The Tokugawa shoguns brought an end to civil war by controlling the military. Stripped of power and required to spend alternate years at Edo, many of the daimyo and samurai passed their lives in idle pursuit of pleasure. They spent extravagantly on fine silks, paintings, concubines, boys, the theater, and the redecoration of their castles. These temptations, as well as more

# Viewpoints 21.2

## Chinese and Japanese Financial Advice

• *The two passages below offer advice on how to prosper and avoid common mistakes. The first is a short passage from a longer work by a Chinese official, Zhang Ying (1638–1708), addressed to his son. The second, also from a longer work, is by a Japanese contemporary, Ihara Saikaku (1642–1693), and aims as much to entertain as to inform its audience.*

### Zhang Ying, *On Permanent Property*

As regards the things of this world, those that are new invariably become old. Houses after a long time collapse in ruins, clothing eventually wears out. Serfs, cattle and horses after lengthy service grow old and die. Something which in the beginning was bought for a heavy price may not be old after ten years, but after another ten years its value has depreciated to nothing. Only land is a commodity which even after a hundred or a thousand years is always as good as new. Even if agricultural labour is not intensive, if the land is poor and the produce meagre, as soon as it is manured and irrigated it will be renewed. Even if the land is gone to waste and the homestead is covered with weeds, once it is reclaimed it will be renewed. If you construct many ponds, poor land can be enriched, and if you vigorously uproot the weeds then barren soil can be made fertile. From ancient times to the present day there has never been any fear that it will decay or fall into ruin, nor anxiety lest it abscond or suffer attrition. This is really something to be treasured! . . .

In the present age the young men in a family have elegant clothing and spirited horses and are always dancing and carousing. The cost of one fur garment may go up to several tens of taels and that of one feast may be as much as several taels. They do not reflect that in my home area for the past ten years or more, grain has been cheap, and that more than a full ten *shi* are insufficient to provide one feast and a full hundred *shi* or more are not enough to pay for one garment. How can they know the farmers' sufferings? Labouring all year round with soaked bodies and muddy feet, how can it be easy for them to get those hundred *shi*? How much less so when there is unseasonable rain or drought and one year's harvest cannot be made to last until the following year?

### Ihara Saikaku, *This Scheming World*

When a man becomes rich, people always say he's lucky. But this is merely a conventional expression, for in reality he becomes rich and his household thrives solely on account of his own ability and foresight. Even Ebisu, the god of wealth, is unable at will to exercise power over riches.

But be that as it may, our wealthy merchants, for whom the discussion of a pending loan to a feudal lord is a far more engaging pastime than carousing or any other form of merry-making, have recently organized themselves into the Daikoku Club. Shunning a rendezvous in the red-light district, they gather in the guest room of the Buddhist temple in Shimotera, Ikutama. There they meet every month to discuss the financial condition of each individual applicant for a loan. Though they are all well along in years, they take pleasure only in ever-increasing interest and in mounting capital, utterly heedless of the life to come. Although it's quite true that there's nothing more desirable than plenty of money, the proper way for a man to get along in the world should be this: in his youth until the age of twenty-five to be ever alert, in his manly prime up to thirty-five to earn a lot of money, in the prime of discretion in his fifties to pile up his fortune, and at last in his sixties — the year before his sixty-first birthday — to turn over all his business to his eldest son. Thereafter it is proper for him to retire from active affairs and devote the remainder of his days to visiting temples for the sake of his soul.

Sources: Hilary J. Beattie, *Land and Lineage in China* (Cambridge: Cambridge University Press, 1979) pp. 141–143; Ihara Saikaku, *This Scheming World*, trans. Masanori Takatsuka and David C. Stubbs (Rutland, Vt.: Tuttle, 1965), p. 42. Copyright © 1965 by Charles E. Tuttle Publishing Co., Inc. Used by permission of Tuttle Publishing, a member of the Periplus Publishing Group.

### QUESTIONS FOR ANALYSIS

1. How does the advice of these two authors reflect the ways one could get ahead in their respective societies?

2. What common elements do you see in the advice offered in these two passages?

3. How do you think the difference in intended audience explains some of the differences in these two passages?

**Life in the Japanese Entertainment Quarters** This detail from a seventeenth-century six-panel Japanese screen depicts men and women playing instruments and enjoying games. The women are probably professional entertainers (geisha). (detail from screen by Hikone, color on gold paper, Edo Period, early 17th century/De Agostini Picture Library/The Bridgeman Art Library)

sophisticated pleasures and the heavy costs of maintaining alternate residences at Edo, gradually bankrupted the warrior class.

All major cities contained places of amusement for men—teahouses, theaters, restaurants, and houses of prostitution. Desperately poor parents sometimes sold their daughters to entertainment houses (as they did in China and medieval Europe), and the most attractive or talented girls, trained in singing, dancing, and conversational arts, became courtesans, later called geishas (GAY-shahz), "accomplished persons."

Another form of entertainment in the cities was **kabuki theater**, patronized by both merchants and samurai. An art form created by townspeople, kabuki originated in crude, bawdy skits dealing with love and romance. Performances featured elaborate costumes, song, dance, and poetry. Because actresses were thought to corrupt public morals, the Tokugawa government banned them from the stage in 1629. From that time on, men played all the parts. Male actors in female

• **kabuki theater** A popular form of Japanese drama that brings together dialogue, dance, and music to tell stories. The actors wear colorful costumes and dramatic makeup.

dress and makeup performed as seductively as possible to entice the burly samurai who thronged the theaters. Homosexuality, long accepted in Japan, was widely practiced among the samurai, who pursued the actors and spent profligately on them. Some moralists and bureaucrats complained from time to time, but the Tokugawa government decided to accept kabuki and prostitution as necessary evils.

Cities were also the center for commercial publishing. As in contemporary China, the reading public eagerly purchased fiction and the scripts for plays. Ihara Saikaku (1642–1693) wrote stories of the foibles of townspeople in such books as *Five Women Who Loved Love* and *The Life of an Amorous Man*. One of the puppet plays of Chikamatsu Monzaemon (1653–1724) tells the story of the son of a business owner who, caught between duty to his family and love of a prostitute, decides to resolve the situation by double suicide. The art of color woodblock printing also was perfected during this period. Many of the surviving prints, made for a popular audience, depict the theater and women of the entertainment quarters.

Almost as entertaining as attending the theater was watching the long processions of daimyo, their retainers, and their luggage as they passed back and forth to and from Edo twice a year. The shogunate prohibited travel by commoners, but they could get passports to take pilgrimages, visit relatives, or seek the soothing waters of medicinal hot springs. Setting out on foot, groups of villagers would travel to such shrines as Ise, often taking large detours to visit Osaka or Edo to sightsee or attend the theater. Older women with daughters-in-law to run their households were among the most avid pilgrims.

According to Japanese tradition, farmers deserved respect. In practice, however, peasants were often treated callously. In 1649 every village in Japan received these regulations:

Peasants are people without sense or forethought. Therefore they must not give rice to their wives and children at harvest time, but must save food for the future. They should eat millet, vegetables, and other coarse food instead of rice. Even the fallen leaves of plants should be saved as food against famine. . . . During the seasons of planting and harvesting, however, when the labor is arduous, the food taken may be a little better. . . .

They must not buy tea or sake to drink nor must their wives. The husband must work in the fields, the wife must work at the loom. Both must do night work. However good-looking a wife may be, if she neglects her household duties by drinking tea or

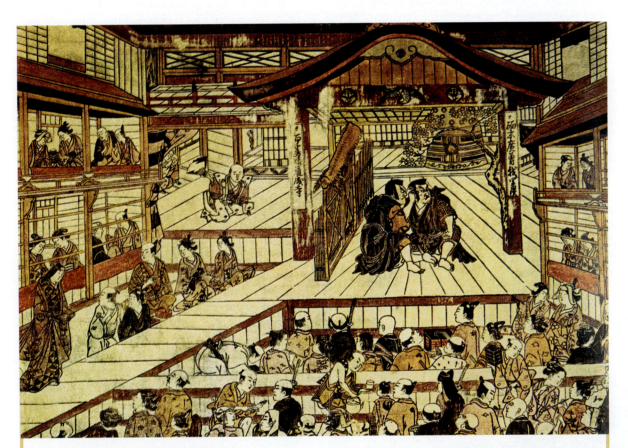

## ☐ Picturing the Past

**Interior View of a Theater** Complex kabuki plays, which dealt with heroes, loyalty, and tragedy and included music and dance, became the most popular form of entertainment in Tokugawa Japan for all classes. Movable scenery and lighting effects made possible the staging of storms, fires, and hurricanes. (woodblock print by Okumura Masanobu, 18th century/Private Collection/J.T. Vintage/The Bridgeman Art Library)

**ANALYZING THE IMAGE** How many people are performing in this scene? Are there more men or women in the audience? How do you distinguish them? Are any of the men samurai?

**CONNECTIONS** What connections do you see between the popularity of kabuki plays and other aspects of Japanese life in this period?

sightseeing or rambling on the hillsides, she must be divorced.

Peasants must wear only cotton or hemp — no silk. They may not smoke tobacco. It is harmful to health, it takes up time, and costs money. It also creates a risk of fire.[2]

During the seventeenth and eighteenth centuries daimyo and upper-level samurai paid for their extravagant lifestyles by raising taxes on their subordinate peasants from 30 or 40 percent of the rice crop to 50 percent. Not surprisingly, this angered peasants, and peasant protests became chronic during the eighteenth century. For example, oppressive taxation provoked eighty-four thousand farmers in the province of Iwaki to revolt in 1739; after widespread burning and destruction, their demands for lower taxes were met. Natural disasters also added to the peasants' misery. In 1783 Mount Asama erupted, spewing volcanic ash that darkened the skies all summer; the resulting crop failures led to famine. When famine recurred again in 1787, commoners rioted for five days in Edo, smashing merchants' stores and pouring sake and rice into the muddy streets. The shogunate responded by trying to control the floating population of day laborers without families in the city. At one point they were rounded up and transported to work the gold mines in an island off

**Edo Craftsman at Work** Less than 3 inches tall, this ivory figure shows a parasol maker seated on the floor (the typical Japanese practice) eating his lunch, his tools by his side. (Photo © Boltin Picture Library/The Bridgeman Art Library)

the north coast, where most of them died within two or three years.

This picture of peasant hardship tells only part of the story. Agricultural productivity increased substantially during the Tokugawa period. Peasants who improved their lands and increased their yields continued to pay the same assessed tax and could pocket the surplus as profit. As those without land drifted to the cities, peasants left in the countryside found ways to improve their livelihoods. At Hirano near Osaka, for example, 61.7 percent of all arable land was sown in cotton. The peasants ginned the cotton locally before transporting it to wholesalers in Osaka. In many rural places, as many peasants worked in the manufacture of silk, cotton, or vegetable oil as in the production of rice.

In comparison to farmers, merchants had a much easier life, even if they had no political power. By contemporary standards anywhere in the world, the Japanese mercantile class lived well. In 1705 the shogunate confiscated the property of a merchant in Osaka "for conduct unbecoming a member of the commercial class." In fact, the confiscation was at the urging of influential daimyo and samurai who owed the merchant gigantic debts. The government seized 50 pairs of gold screens, 360 carpets, several mansions, 48 granaries and warehouses scattered around the country, and hundreds of thousands of gold pieces. Few merchants possessed such fabulous wealth, but many lived very comfortably.

Within a village, some families would be relatively well-off, others barely able to get by. The village headman generally came from the richest family, but he consulted a council of elders on important matters. Women in better-off families were much more likely to learn to read than women in poor families. Daughters of wealthy peasants studied penmanship, the Chinese classics, poetry, and the proper forms of correspondence, and they rounded out their education with travel. By contrast, girls from middle-level peasant families might have had from two to five years of formal schooling, but they were thought incapable of learning the difficult Chinese characters, so their education focused on moral instruction intended to instill virtue.

By the fifteenth and sixteenth centuries Japan's family and marriage systems had evolved in the direction of a patrilocal, patriarchal system more like China's, and Japanese women had lost the prominent role in high society that they had occupied during the Heian period. It became standard for women to move into their husbands' homes, where they occupied positions subordinate to both their husbands and their mothers-in-law. In addition, elite families stopped dividing their property among all their children; instead they retained it for the sons alone or increasingly for a single son who would continue the family line. Marriage, which now had greater consequence, also had a more public character and was marked by greater ceremony. Wedding rituals involved both the exchange of betrothal gifts and the movement of the bride from her parents' home to her husband's home. She brought with her a trousseau that provided her with clothes and other items she would need for daily life, but not with land, which would have given her economic autonomy. On the other hand, her position within her new family was more secure, for it became more difficult for a husband to divorce his wife. She also gained authority within the family. If her husband was away, she managed family affairs. If her husband fathered children with concubines, she was their legal mother.

A peasant wife shared responsibility for the family's economic well-being with her husband. If of poor or middling status, she worked alongside her husband in the fields, doing the routine work while he did the heavy work. If they were farm hands and worked for wages, the wife invariably earned a third or a half less than her husband. Wives of prosperous farmers never worked in the fields, but they reeled silk, wove cloth, helped in any family business, and supervised the maids. When cotton growing spread to Japan in the sixteenth century, women took on the jobs of spinning and weaving it. Whatever their economic status, Japanese women, like women everywhere in the world, tended the children. Families were growing smaller in this period in response to the spread of single-heir inheritance. From studies of household registers, demographic historians have shown that Japanese families restricted the number of children they had by practicing abortion and infanticide, turning to adoption when no heir survived.

How was divorce initiated, and how frequent was it? Among the elite, the husband alone could initiate divorce; all he had to do was order his wife to leave or send her possessions to her parents' home. For the wife, divorce carried a stigma, but she could not prevent it or insist on keeping her children. Widows and divorcées of the samurai elite—where female chastity was the core of fidelity—were not expected to remarry. Among the peasant classes, by contrast, divorce seems to have been fairly common—the divorce rate was at least 15 percent in the villages near Osaka in the eighteenth century. A poor woman wanting a divorce could simply leave her husband's home. It was also possible to secure divorce through a temple. If a married woman entered the temple and performed rites there for three years, her marriage bond was dissolved. Sometimes Buddhist temple priests served as divorce brokers: they went to the village headman and had him force the husband to agree to a divorce. News of the coming of temple officials was usually enough to produce a letter of separation.

# Maritime Trade, Piracy, and the Entry of Europe into the Asian Maritime Sphere

☐ How did the sea link the countries of East Asia, and what happened when Europeans entered this maritime sphere?

In the period 1400–1800 maritime trade and piracy connected China and Japan to each other and also to Korea, Southeast Asia, and Europe. All through the period China and Japan traded extensively with each other as well as with Korea. Both Korea and Japan relied on Chinese coinage, and China relied on silver from Japan. During the fifteenth century China launched overseas expeditions. Japan was a major base for pirates. In the sixteenth century European traders appeared, eager for Chinese porcelains and silks. Christian missionaries followed, but despite initial successes, they were later banned, first by the Japanese government and then by the Chinese government. Political changes in Europe changed the international makeup of the European traders in East Asia, with the dominant groups first the Portuguese, next the Dutch, and then the British.

## Zheng He's Voyages

Early in the Ming period, the Chinese government tried to revive the tribute system of the Han (206–220 C.E.) and Tang (618–907) Dynasties, when China had dominated East Asia and envoys had arrived from dozens of distant lands. To invite more countries to send missions, the third Ming emperor (Chengzu, or Yongle) authorized an extraordinary series of voyages to the Indian Ocean under the command of the Muslim eunuch Zheng He (1371–1433).

Zheng He's father had made the trip to Mecca, and the seven voyages that Zheng led between 1405 and 1433 followed old Arab trade routes. The first of the seven was made by a fleet of 317 ships, of which 62 were huge, 440 feet long. Each expedition involved from twenty thousand to thirty-two thousand men. Their itineraries included stops in Vietnam, Malaysia, Indonesia, Sri Lanka, India, and, in the later voyages, Hormuz (on the coast of Persia) and East Africa (see Map 16.1, page 459). At each stop Zheng He went ashore to visit rulers, transmit messages of China's peaceful intentions, and bestow lavish gifts. Rulers were invited to come to China or send envoys and were offered accommodation on the return voyages. Near the Straits of Malacca, Zheng's fleet battled Chinese

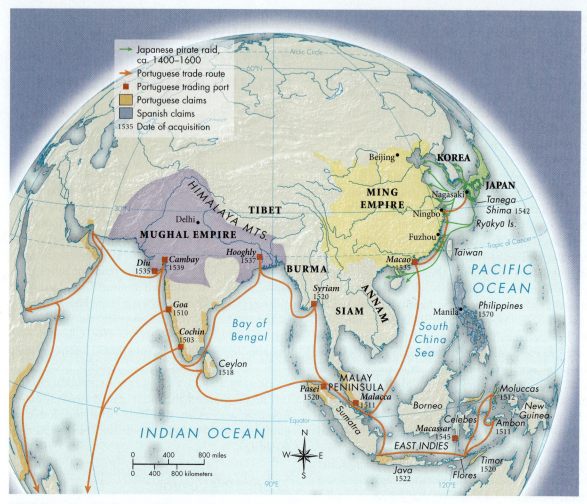

**MAP 21.3 East Asia, ca. 1600** Pirates and traders often plied the same waters as seaborne trade grew in the sixteenth century. The Portuguese were especially active in setting up trading ports.

pirates, bringing them under control. Zheng He made other shows of force as well, deposing rulers deemed unacceptable in Java, Sumatra, and Sri Lanka.

On the return of these expeditions, the Ming emperor was delighted by the exotic things the fleet brought back, such as giraffes and lions from Africa, fine cotton cloth from India, and gems and spices from Southeast Asia. Ma Huan, an interpreter who accompanied Zheng He, collected data on the plants, animals, peoples, and geography that they encountered and wrote a book titled *The Overall Survey of the Ocean's Shores.* Still, these expeditions were not voyages of discovery; they followed established routes and pursued diplomatic rather than commercial goals.

Why were these voyages abandoned? Officials complained about their cost and modest returns. As a consequence, after 1474 all the remaining ships with three or more masts were broken up and used for lumber. Chinese did not pull back from trade in the South China Sea and Indian Ocean, but the government no

longer promoted trade, leaving the initiative to private merchants and migrants.

## Piracy and Japan's Overseas Adventures

One goal of Zheng He's expeditions was to suppress piracy, which had become a problem all along the China coast. Already in the thirteenth century social disorder and banditry in Japan had expanded into seaborne banditry, some of it within the Japanese islands around the Inland Sea (Map 21.3), but also in the straits between Korea and Japan. Japanese "sea bandits" would raid the Korean coast, seizing rice and other goods to take home. In the sixteenth century bands several hundred strong would attack and loot Chinese coastal cities or hold them hostage for ransom. As maritime trade throughout East Asia grew more lively, sea bandits also took to attacking ships to steal their cargo. Although the pirates were called the "Japanese pirates" by both the Koreans and the Chinese, pirate gangs in fact recruited from all countries. The Ryūkyū (ryoo-kyoo) Islands and Taiwan became major bases.

Possibly encouraged by the exploits of these bandits, Hideyoshi, after his victories in unifying Japan, decided to extend his territory across the seas. In 1590, after receiving congratulations from Korea on his victories, Hideyoshi sent a letter asking the Koreans to allow his armies to pass through their country, declaring that his real target was China: "Disregarding the distance of the sea and mountain reaches that lie in between, I shall in one fell swoop invade Great Ming. I have in mind to introduce Japanese customs and values to the four hundred and more provinces of that country and bestow upon it the benefits of imperial rule and culture for the coming hundred million years."[3] He also sent demands for submission to countries of Southeast Asia and to the Spanish governor of the Philippines.

In 1592 Hideyoshi mobilized 158,000 soldiers and 9,200 sailors for his invasion and equipped them with muskets and cannon, which had recently been introduced into Japan. His forces overwhelmed Korean defenders and reached Seoul within three weeks and Pyongyang in two months. A few months later, in the middle of winter, Chinese armies arrived to help defend Korea, and Japanese forces were pushed back from Pyongyang. A stalemate remained in place until 1597, when Hideyoshi sent out new Japanese troops. This time the Ming army and the Korean navy were more successful in resisting the Japanese. In 1598, after Hideyoshi's death, the Japanese army withdrew from Korea, but Korea was left devastated. (See "Listening to the Past: Keinen's Poetic Diary of the Korea Campaign," page 642.)

After recovering from the setbacks of these invasions, Korea began to advance socially and economically. During the Chosŏn Dynasty (1392–1910), the Korean elite (the yangban) turned away from Buddhism and toward strict Neo-Confucian orthodoxy. As agricultural productivity improved, the population grew from about 4.4 million in 1400 to about 8 million in 1600, 10 million in 1700, and 14 million in 1810 (or about half the size of Japan's population and one-twentieth of China's). With economic advances, slavery declined. When slaves ran away, landowners found that it was less expensive to replace them with sharecroppers than to recapture them. Between 1750 and 1790 the slave population dropped from 30 percent to 5 percent of the population. The hold of the yangban elite, however, remained strong. Through the eighteenth century about two dozen yangban families dominated the civil service examinations, leaving relatively few slots for commoners to rise to through study.

## Europeans Enter the Scene

In the sixteenth century Portuguese, Spanish, and Dutch merchants and adventurers began to participate in the East Asian maritime world (see Chapter 16). The trade between Japan, China, and Southeast Asia was very profitable, and the European traders wanted a share of it. They also wanted to develop trade between Asia and Europe.

The Portuguese and Dutch were not reluctant to use force to gain control of trade, and they seized many

**Dutch in Japan** The Japanese were curious about the appearance, dress, and habits of the Dutch who came to the enclave of Deshima to trade. In this detail from a long hand scroll, Dutch traders are shown interacting with a Japanese samurai in a room with Japanese tatami mats on the floor. Note also the Western musical instrument. (Private Collection/The Bridgeman Art Library)

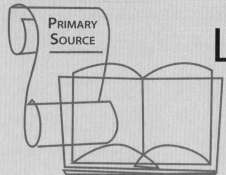
# Listening to the Past

## Keinen's Poetic Diary of the Korea Campaign

*The Buddhist priest Keinen (1534?–1611) was ordered in 1597 to accompany the local daimyo on Hideyoshi's second campaign in Korea and spent seven months there. As a Buddhist, he did not revel in military feats but rather deplored the death and suffering that he observed. Adopting the time-honored form of the poetic diary, Keinen ends each day's entry with a short poem. The excerpt quoted here begins about six weeks after he left home.*

❝ Eighth month, 4th day. Every one is trying to be the first off the ship; no one wants to lag behind. They fall over each other in trying to get at the plunder, to kill people. It is a sight I cannot bear to see.

> A hubbub rises
> as from roiling clouds and mist
> where they swarm about
> in their rage for the plunder
> of innocent people's goods.

VIII.5.

They are burning the houses. As I watched them go up in smoke, I thought that my own existence was like this and was seized by sympathy.

> The "Red Country" is
> what they call it, but black is
> the smoke that rises
> from the burning houses
> where you see flames flying high.

VIII.6.

The very fields and hillsides have been put to the fire, not to speak of the forts. People are put to the sword, or they are shackled with chains and bamboo tubes choking the neck. Parents sobbing for their children, children searching for their parents — never before have I seen such a pitiable sight.

> The hills are ablaze
> with the cries of soldiers
> intoxicated
> with their pyrolatry —
> the battleground of demons.

VIII.7.

Looking at the various kinds of plunder amassed by them all, I formed a desire for such things. Could I really be like this, I thought, and felt ashamed. How can I attain salvation like this, I thought.

> How ashamed I am!
> For everything that I see
> I form desires —
> a creature of delusions,
> my mind full of attachments.

On the same day, as I exerted myself in reflections on my spiritual state, I felt myself more and more ashamed. And yet the Buddha has vowed not to give weight to the weightiest of evil deeds, not to abandon the most abandoned and intemperate!

> Unless it be through
> reliance on the vow of
> Amida Buddha,
> who could obtain salvation
> with such wicked thoughts as mine?

VIII.8.

They are carrying off Korean children and killing their parents. Never shall they see each other again. Their mutual cries — surely this is like the torture meted out by the fiends of hell.

> It is piteous;
> when the four fledglings parted,*
> it must have been thus —
> I see the parents' lament
> over their sobbing children.

VIII.11.

As night fell, I saw people's houses go up in smoke. They have lost everything to the fire, all their grain and all their property.

> How wretched it is!
> Smoke lingers still where the grain
> was burned and wasted;
> so that is where I lay my
> head tonight: on the scorched earth.

VIII.13.

His lordship has set up camp about five leagues this side of Namwon. Unless this fortress is taken, our prospects are dubious; so we are to close in and invest it this evening. The word is that fifty or sixty thousand soldiers from Great Ming are garrisoning the place.

> We'll solve the challenge
> posed even by this fortress
> of the Red Country! —
> The troops rejoice to hear this,
> and they rest their weary feet.

VIII.14.

Rain has been falling steadily since the evening. It comes down in sheets, like a waterfall. We have put up a makeshift tent covered with oil paper only, and it is frightening how the rain pours in. It is impossible to sleep. I had to think of the story "The Devil at One Gulp" in *Tales of Ise.*† The night described in that tale must have been just like this.

> Inexorably,
> fearsome torrents beating down

outposts along the trade routes, including Taiwan. Moreover, they made little distinction between trade, smuggling, and piracy. In 1521 the Ming tried to ban the Portuguese from China. Two years later an expeditionary force commissioned by the Portuguese king to negotiate a friendship treaty defeated its mission by firing on Chinese warships near Guangzhou. In 1557, without informing Beijing, local Chinese officials decided that the way to regulate trade was to allow the Portuguese to build a trading post on uninhabited land near the mouth of the Pearl River. The city they built there—Macao—became the first destination for Euro-

remind me of that
dreadful night when the devil
at one gulp ate his victim.

**VIII.15.**
The fortress is to be stormed before dawn tomorrow. Fascines of bamboo have been distributed to the assault troops. The sun was about to set as they worked their way close in, right up against the edge of the castle's bulwarks, and gunfire opened up from the several siege detachments, accompanied by arrows shot from short-bows. Unthinkable numbers of men were killed. As I saw them dying:

From the fortress, too,
from their short-bows, too.
How many killed? Beyond count
is the number of the dead.

The castle fell to the assault in the course of the night. Lord Hishu's troops were the first inside the walls. Needless to say, he is to get a vermilion-seal letter of commendation.

**VIII.16.**
All in the fortress were slaughtered, to the last man and woman. No prisoners were taken. To be sure, a few were kept alive for exchange purposes.

How cruel! This world
of sorrow and inconstancy
does have one constant—
men and women, young and old
die and vanish; are no more.

**VIII.17.**
Until yesterday they did not know that they would have to die; today, they are transformed into the smoke of impermanence, as is the way of this world of constant change. How can I be unaffected by this!

Look! Everyone, look!
Is this, then, to be called the human
condition?—
a life with a deadline,
a life with a limit: today. **"**

Source: *Sources of Japanese Tradition*, by Wm. Theodore de Bary, Donald Keene, George Tanabe, and Paul Varley. Reproduced with permission of COLUMBIA UNIVERSITY PRESS in the format Book via Copyright Clearance Center.

**Although the Japanese invasion failed, some of the warriors who fought in it were celebrated, such as Kashiwade no Hedeus, shown here fighting a tiger in the hills of Korea.** (Gift of Professor Arthur R. Miller, CBE, on loan from the American Friends of the British Museum/© The Trustees of the British Museum/Art Resource, NY)

**QUESTIONS FOR ANALYSIS**

1. Buddhism teaches the impermanence of phenomena and the need to let go of attachments, and it opposes the taking of life. Which of Keinen's responses can be identified as specifically Buddhist?

2. Does Keinen's use of poetry seem natural, or do you think it seems forced? Explain your response.

3. What would be the purpose of bringing a Buddhist priest opposed to killing on a military campaign?

*An allusion to the proverbial tale of a mother bird's sorrow at her fledglings' departure to the four directions.

†This is a story of an abduction that ends badly. The lady in question, sequestered in a broken-down storehouse to keep her safe from the elements on a dark and stormy night, is devoured "at one gulp" by an ogre who dwells there.

peans going to China until the nineteenth century, and it remained a Portuguese possession until 1999.

European products were not in demand in China, but silver was. Japan had supplied much of China's silver, but with the development of silver mines in the New World, European traders began supplying large quantities of silver to China, allowing the expansion of China's economy.

Chinese were quick to take advantage of the new trading ports set up by European powers. In Batavia harbor (now Jakarta, Indonesia) Chinese ships outnumbered those from any other country by two or three to one. Manila, under Spanish control, and Taiwan and Batavia, both under Dutch control, all attracted thousands of Chinese colonists. Local people felt the intrusion of Chinese more than of Europeans, and riots against Chinese led to massacres on several occasions.

A side benefit of the appearance of European traders was New World crops. Sweet potatoes, maize, peanuts, tomatoes, chili peppers, tobacco, and other crops were quickly adopted in East Asia. Sweet potatoes and maize in particular facilitated population growth because they could be grown on land previously thought too sandy or too steep to cultivate. Sweet potatoes became a common poor people's food.

## Christian Missionaries

The Spanish and Portuguese kings supported missionary activity, and merchant vessels soon brought Catholic missionaries to East Asia. The first to come were Jesuits, from the order founded by Ignatius Loyola in 1540 to promote Catholic scholarship and combat the Protestant Reformation.

The Jesuit priest Francis Xavier had worked in India and the Indies before China and Japan attracted his attention. In 1549, after many misadventures, he landed on Kyushu, Japan's southernmost island (see Map 21.2). After he was expelled by the local lord, he traveled throughout western Japan as far as Kyoto, proselytizing wherever warlords allowed. He soon made many converts among the poor and even some among the daimyo. Xavier then set his sights on China but died on an uninhabited island off the China coast in 1552.

Other missionaries carried on his work, and by 1600 there were three hundred thousand baptized Christians in Japan. Most of them lived on Kyushu,

where the shogun's power was weakest and the loyalty of the daimyo most doubtful. In 1615 bands of Christian samurai supported Tokugawa Ieyasu's enemies at the fierce Battle of Osaka. A couple of decades later, thirty thousand peasants in the heavily Catholic area of northern Kyushu revolted. The Tokugawa shoguns thus came to associate Christianity with domestic disorder and insurrection. Accordingly, what had been mild persecution of Christians became ruthless repression after 1639. Foreign priests were expelled or tortured, and thousands of Japanese Christians suffered crucifixion.

Meanwhile, in China the Jesuits concentrated on gaining the linguistic and scholarly knowledge they would need to convert the educated class. The Jesuit Matteo Ricci studied for years in Macao before setting himself up in Nanjing and trying to win over members of the educated class. In 1601 he was given permission to reside in Beijing, where he made several high-placed conversions. He also interested educated Chinese men in Western geography, astronomy, and Euclidean mathematics.

Ricci and his Jesuit successors believed that Confucianism was compatible with Christianity. The Jesuits thought that both faiths shared similar concerns for morality and virtue, and they viewed the Confucian practice of making food offerings to ancestors as an expression of filial reverence rather than as a form of worship. The Franciscan and Dominican friars, who had taken a vow of poverty, disagreed with the Jesuit position. In 1715 religious and political quarrels in Europe led the pope to decide that the Jesuits' accommodating approach was heretical. Angry at this insult, the Kangxi emperor forbade all Christian missionary work in China.

## Learning from the West

Although both China and Japan ended up prohibiting Christian missionary work, other aspects of Western culture were seen as impressive and worth learning. The closed-country policy that Japan instituted in 1639 restricted Japanese from leaving the country and kept European merchants in small enclaves. Still, Japanese interest in Europe did not disappear. Through the Dutch enclave of Deshima on a tiny island in Nagasaki harbor, a stream of Western ideas and inventions

**Porcelain Vase** Among the objects produced in China that were in high demand in Europe in the seventeenth and eighteenth centuries were colorful porcelains. In this period Chinese potters perfected the use of overglaze enamels, which allowed the application of many colors to a single object. Blue, green, yellow, orange, and red all appear on this 18-inch-tall vase. (Vase, Qing dynasty, Kangxi period [1662–1722], late 17th–early 18th century. Porcelain painted in overglaze famille verte enamels and gold. Bequest of John D. Rockefeller Jr., 1960 [61.200.66], The Metropolitan Museum of Art, New York, NY, USA/Image copyright © The Metropolitan Museum of Art/Image source: Art Resource, NY)

trickled into Japan in the eighteenth century. Western writings, architectural illustrations, calendars, watches, medicine, weapons, and paintings deeply impressed the Japanese. Western portraits and other paintings introduced the Japanese to perspective, shading, and other strategies for bringing more realism to art.

In China, too, both scholars and rulers showed an interest in Western learning. The Kangxi emperor frequently discussed scientific and philosophical questions with the Jesuits at court. When he got malaria, he accepted the Jesuits' offer of the medicine quinine. In addition, he had translations made of a collection of Western works on mathematics and the calendar. The court was impressed with the Jesuits' skill in astronomy and quickly appointed them to the Board of Astronomy. In 1674 the emperor asked them to re-equip the observatory with European instruments. In the visual arts the emperor and his successors employed Italian painters to make imperial portraits. Qianlong also took a fancy to European-style gardens and palaces. Firearms and mechanical clocks were also widely admired. The court established its own clock and watch factory, and in 1673 the emperor insisted that the Jesuits manufacture cannon for him and supervise gunnery practice.

Admiration was not one-sided. In the early eighteenth century China enjoyed a positive reputation in Europe. Voltaire wrote of the rationalism of Confucianism and saw advantages to the Chinese political system because the rulers did not put up with parasitical aristocrats or hypocritical priests. Chinese medical practice also drew European interest. One Chinese practice that Europeans adopted was "variolation," an early form of smallpox inoculation.

## The Shifting International Environment in the Eighteenth Century

The East Asian maritime world underwent many changes from the sixteenth to the eighteenth centuries. As already noted, the Japanese pulled back their own traders and limited opportunities for Europeans to trade in Japan. In China the Qing government limited trading contacts with Europe to Guangzhou in the far south in an attempt to curb piracy. Portugal lost many of its bases to the Dutch, and by the eighteenth century the British had become as active as the Dutch. In the seventeenth century the British and

| CHRONOLOGY | |
|---|---|
| 1368–1644 | Ming Dynasty in China |
| 1405–1433 | Zheng He's naval expeditions |
| 1407–1420 | Construction of Beijing as Chinese capital |
| 1467–1600 | Period of civil war in Japan |
| ca. 1500–1600 | Increased availability of books for general audiences in China |
| 1549 | First Jesuit missionaries land in Japan |
| 1557 | Portuguese set up trading base at Macao |
| 1603–1867 | Tokugawa Shogunate in Japan |
| 1615 | Battle of Osaka leads to persecution of Christians in Japan |
| 1629 | Tokugawa government bans actresses from the stage |
| 1639 | Japan closes its borders |
| 1644–1911 | Qing Dynasty in China |
| 1793 | Lord Macartney's diplomatic visit to China |

Dutch sought primarily porcelains and silk, but in the eighteenth century tea became the commodity in most demand.

By the late eighteenth century Britain had become a great power and did not see why China should be able to dictate the terms of trade. Wanting to renegotiate relations, King George III sent Lord George Macartney to China in 1793 with six hundred cases of British goods, ranging from clocks and telescopes to Wedgwood pottery and landscape paintings. The Qianlong emperor was, however, not impressed. As he pointed out in his formal reply, the Qing Empire "possesses all things in prolific abundance and lacks no product within its own borders"; thus trading with Europe was a kindness, not a necessity.[4] The Qing court was as intent on maintaining the existing system of regulated trade as Britain was intent on doing away with it.

Several members of the Macartney mission wrote books about China on their return, updating European understanding of China. These books, often illustrated, described many elements of Chinese culture and social customs—accounts less rosy than the reports written by the Jesuits a century or two earlier. The British writers, for instance, introduced the idea that Chinese women were oppressed, unable even to sit at the same table with their husbands to eat dinner.

# Chapter Summary

After the fall of the Mongols, China was ruled by the native Ming Dynasty for nearly three centuries. The dynasty's founder ruled for thirty years, becoming more paranoid and despotic over time. Very few of his successors were particularly good rulers, yet China thrived in many ways. Population grew as food production increased. Educational levels were high as more and more men prepared for the civil service examinations. Urban culture was lively, and publishing houses put out novels, short stories, and plays in the vernacular language for large audiences.

In 1644 the Ming Dynasty fell to the non-Chinese Manchus. The Manchu rulers proved more competent than the Ming emperors and were able to both maintain peace and expand the empire to incorporate Mongolia, Tibet, and Central Asia. Population grew steadily under Manchu rule.

During the fifteenth and sixteenth centuries Japan was fragmented by civil war. As daimyo attacked and defeated each other, power was gradually consolidated, until Hideyoshi gained control of most of the country. Japan also saw many cultural developments during this period, including the increasing influence of Zen ideas on the arts and the rise of Nō theater.

After Hideyoshi's death, power was seized by Tokugawa Ieyasu, the founder of the Tokugawa Shogunate. During the seventeenth and eighteenth centuries Japan reaped the rewards of peace. The early rulers tried to create stability by freezing the social structure and limiting foreign contact to the city of Nagasaki. As the wealth of the business classes grew, the samurai, now dependent on fixed stipends, became progressively poorer. Samurai and others in search of work and pleasure streamed into the cities.

Between 1400 and 1800 maritime trade connected the countries of Asia, but piracy was a perpetual problem. Early in this period China sent out naval expeditions looking to promote diplomatic contacts, reaching as far as Africa. In the sixteenth century European traders arrived in China and Japan and soon developed profitable trading relationships. The Chinese economy became so dependent on huge imports of silver acquired through this trade that a cutoff in supplies caused severe hardship. Trade with Europe also brought New World crops and new ideas. The Catholic missionaries who began to arrive in Asia introduced Western science and learning as well as Christianity, until they were banned in both Japan and China. Although the shogunate severely restricted trade, some Western scientific ideas and technology entered Japan through the port of Nagasaki. Chinese, too, took an interest in Western painting, astronomy, and firearms. Because Europeans saw much to admire in East Asia in this period, ideas also flowed from East to West.

## NOTES

1. L. J. Gallagher, trans., *China in the Sixteenth Century: The Journals of Matthew Ricci: 1583–1610* (New York: Random House, 1953), p. 23.
2. Quoted in G. B. Sansom, *A History of Japan, 1615–1867*, vol. 3 (Stanford, Calif.: Stanford University Press, 1978), p. 99.
3. W. T. de Bary et al., eds., *Sources of Japanese Tradition from Earliest Times to 1600* (New York: Columbia University Press, 2001), p. 467. Reproduced with permission of COLUMBIA UNIVERSITY PRESS in the format Book via Copyright Clearance Center.
4. Pei-kai Cheng and M. Lestz, with J. Spence, eds., *The Search for Modern China: A Documentary History* (New York: W. W. Norton, 1999), p. 106.

## CONNECTIONS

During the four centuries from 1400 to 1800, the countries of East Asia became increasingly connected. On the oceans trade and piracy linked them, and for the first time a war involved China and Japan. In both countries, this was a time of economic advance. At the same time, their cultures and social structures were in no sense converging. The elites of the two countries were very different: in Japan elite status was hereditary, while in China the key route to status and power involved doing well on a written examination. In Japan the samurai elite were expected to be skilled warriors, but in China the highest prestige went to men of letters. The Japanese woodblock prints that capture many features of the entertainment quarters in Japanese cities show a world distinct from anything in China.

By the end of this period, East Asian countries found themselves in a rapidly changing international environment, mostly because of revolutions occurring far from their shores. The next two chapters take up the story of these revolutions, first the political ones in America, France, and Haiti, and then the Industrial Revolution that began in Britain. In time, these revolutions would profoundly alter East Asia as well.

# Review and Explore

## Make It Stick

 **LearningCurve**
Go online and use LearningCurve to retain what you've read.

## Identify Key Terms

Identify and explain the significance of each item below.

**Ming Dynasty** (p. 619)

**civil service examinations** (p. 622)

**Qing Dynasty** (p. 627)

**banners** (p. 627)

**Nō theater** (p. 630)

**daimyo** (p. 630)

**Tokugawa Shogunate** (p. 632)

**alternate residence system** (p. 632)

**kabuki theater** (p. 636)

## Review the Main Ideas

Answer the focus questions from each section of the chapter.

1. What sort of state and society developed in China after the Mongols were ousted? (p. 619)
2. Did the return of alien rule with the Manchus have any positive consequences for China? (p. 627)
3. How did Japan change during this period of political instability? (p. 630)
4. What was life like in Japan during the Tokugawa peace? (p. 632)
5. How did the sea link the countries of East Asia, and what happened when Europeans entered this maritime sphere? (p. 639)

## Make Connections

Analyze the larger developments and continuities within and across chapters.

1. How does the Qing Dynasty compare as an empire to other Eurasian empires of its day?
2. How were the attractions of city life in China and Japan of this period similar to those in other parts of Eurasia?
3. Can you think of any other cases in world history in which a farmer's son rose to the top of the power structure the way that Zhu Yuanzhang and Hideyoshi did? Why was this uncommon?

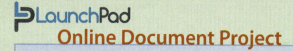

## LaunchPad
## Online Document Project

### Chinese Medicine

**What kinds of treatments did Chinese doctors employ?**
Examine artwork depicting Chinese medical practices, and then complete a quiz and writing assignment based on the evidence and details from this chapter.

*See inside the front cover to learn more.*

## Suggested Reading

Berry, Mary Elizabeth. *The Culture of Civil War in Kyoto*. 1994. Uses diaries and other records to examine how people made sense of violence and social change.

Crossley, Pamela. *The Manchus*. 2002. A lively account that lets one think about Qing history from the rulers' point of view.

Dardess, John W. *Ming China 1368–1644*. 2012. A short but well-informed look at Ming China from its emperors at the top to its outlaws at the bottom.

Elliott, Mark C. *Emperor Qianlong: Son of Heaven, Man of the World*. 2009. Examines the Qing Dynasty at its height from the perspective of a remarkable emperor.

Elvin, Mark. *The Pattern of the Chinese Past*. 1973. Offers an explanation of China's failure to maintain its technological superiority in terms of a "high-level equilibrium trap."

Hanley, Susan B. *Everyday Things in Premodern Japan*. 1999. Shows that the standard of living during the Edo period was comparable to that in the West at the same time.

Hegel, Robert E., trans. *True Crimes in Eighteenth-Century China: Twenty Case Histories*. 2009. Describes various crimes (including neighborhood feuds, murder, and sedition) and how the Chinese government dealt with them at several levels.

Keene, Donald. *Yoshimasa and the Silver Pavilion: The Creation of the Soul of Japan*. 2003. A lively introduction to the aesthetic style associated with Zen and its connection to shogunate patrons.

Mann, Susan. *Precious Records: Women in China's Long Eighteenth Century*. 1997. A well-written analysis of women's lives in the educated class.

McDermott, Joseph. *A Social History of the Chinese Book: Books and Literati Culture in Late Imperial China*. 2006. Places Chinese printing in a comparative perspective.

Mungello, David. *The Great Encounter of China and the West, 1500–1800*. 1999. A short but stimulating examination of the various dimensions of the first phase of Chinese-European relations.

Pomeranz, Kenneth. *The Great Divergence: China, Europe, and the Making of the Modern World Economy*. 2000. Argues that the most advanced areas of China were on a par with the most advanced regions of Europe through the eighteenth century.

Rowe, William T. *China's Last Empire: The Great Qing*. 2009. An up-to-date and thoughtful narrative of the Manchu rulers and the empire over which they presided.

Stanley, Amy. *Selling Women: Prostitution, Markets, and the Household in Early Modern Japan*. 2012. Connects the state, the family, and the market.

Totman, Conrad. *A History of Japan*. 2000. An excellent, well-balanced survey.

Vaporis, Constantine Komitos. *Breaking Barriers: Travel and the State in Early Modern Japan*. 1994. An examination of recreational and religious travel.

Waldron, Arthur. *The Great Wall of China: From History to Myth*. 1990. Places the construction of the current Great Wall in the context of Ming-Mongol relations.

### Jean-Baptiste Belley

Born in Senegal and enslaved in the colony of Saint-Domingue, Jean-Baptiste Belley fought in the American War of Independence and was elected as a deputy to the French National Convention. His career epitomizes the transnational connections of the era of Atlantic revolutions. (*Jean-Baptiste Belley* [1747–1805], Deputy of Santo Domingo at the French Convention, by Anne-Louis Girodet de Roussy-Trioson [1767–1824], 1797, oil on canvas. Inv. MV4616. Photo: Gérard Blot/Châteaux de Versailles et de Trianon, Versailles, France/© RMN–Grand Palais/Art Resource, NY)

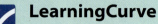

**LearningCurve**

After reading the chapter, go online and use LearningCurve to retain what you've read.

# Chapter Preview

**Background to Revolution**

**The American Revolutionary Era, 1775–1789**

**Revolution in France, 1789–1791**

**Napoleon's Europe, 1799–1815**

**The Haitian Revolution, 1791–1804**

**Revolution in the Spanish Empire**

A great wave of revolution rocked the Atlantic world from 1775 to 1825. As trade goods, individuals, and ideas circulated in ever-greater numbers across the Atlantic Ocean, debates and events in one locale soon influenced those in another. With changing social realities challenging the old order of life and the emergence of Enlightenment ideals of freedom and equality, reformers in many places demanded fundamental changes in politics and government. At the same time, wars fought for dominance of the Atlantic economy burdened European governments with crushing debts, making them vulnerable to calls for reform.

The revolutionary era began in North America in 1775, where the United States of America won freedom from Britain in 1783. Then in 1789 France became the leading revolutionary nation. It established first a constitutional monarchy, then a radical republic, and finally a new empire under Napoleon that would last until 1815. During this period of constant domestic turmoil, French armies brought revolution to much of Europe. Inspired both by the ideals of the revolution on the continent and by internal colonial conditions, the slaves in the French colony of Saint-Domingue rose up in 1791, followed by colonial settlers, indigenous people, and slaves in Spanish America. Their rebellion would eventually lead to the creation of independent nations in the Caribbean, Mexico, and South America. In Europe and its colonies abroad, the world of modern politics was born.

## Background to Revolution

☐ What were the factors behind the age of revolution in the Atlantic world?

The origins of revolutions in the Atlantic world were complex. No one cause lay behind them, nor was revolution inevitable or certain of success. However, a series of shared factors helped set the stage for reform. Among them were fundamental social and economic changes and political crises that eroded state authority.

Another significant cause of revolutionary fervor was the impact of political ideas derived from the Enlightenment. Even though most Enlightenment writers were cautious about political reform, the confidence in reason and progress that they fostered helped inspire a new generation to fight for greater freedom from repressive governments. Perhaps most important, imperial competition and financial crises generated by the expenses of imperial warfare weakened European states and allowed abstract discussions of reform to become pressing realities.

**650** •

## Social Change

Eighteenth-century European society was legally divided into groups with special privileges, such as the nobility and the clergy, and groups with special burdens, such as the peasantry. Nobles were the largest landowners, possessing one-quarter of the agricultural land of France, while constituting less than 2 percent of the population. They enjoyed exemption from many taxes and exclusive rights such as hunting and bearing swords. In most countries, various middle-class groups—professionals, merchants, and guild masters—enjoyed privileges that allowed them to monopolize all sorts of economic activity.

Traditional prerogatives persisted in societies undergoing dramatic change. Due to increased agricultural production, Europe's population rose rapidly after 1750, and its cities and towns swelled in size. Inflation kept pace with demography, making it increasingly difficult for urban people to find affordable food and living space. One way they kept up, and even managed to participate in the new consumer revolution (see pages 580–581), was by working harder and for longer hours. More women and children entered the paid labor force. In another change, men and women in jostling European cities were freer from the constraints of village life, and the rate of illegitimate births soared. More positive developments were increased schooling and a rise in literacy rates, particularly among urban men.

Economic growth created new inequalities between rich and poor. While the poor struggled with rising prices, investors grew rich from the spread of rural manufacture and overseas trade. Old distinctions between landed aristocracy and city merchant began to fade as enterprising nobles put money into trade and rising middle-class bureaucrats and merchants bought landed estates and noble titles. Marriages between proud nobles and wealthy, educated commoners (called the *bourgeoisie* [boor-ZHWAH-ZEE] in France) served both groups' interests, and a mixed-caste elite began to take shape.

Another social change involved the racial regimes established in European colonies. By the late eighteenth century European law accepted that only Africans and people of African descent were subject to slavery. Even free people of color—a term for nonslaves of African or mixed African-European descent—were subject to special laws restricting their property, occupations, marriage, and even clothing. In Spanish America they had to pay a special tax to the Crown. Racial privilege conferred a new dimension of entitlement on European settlers in the colonies, and they used extremely brutal methods to enforce it. The contradiction between slavery and the Enlightenment ideals of liberty and equality was all too evident to educated people of color.

In Spanish America and Brazil, people of European and African descent intermingled with the very large

**The Three Estates** French inhabitants were legally divided into three orders, or estates: the clergy, the nobility, and everyone else. In this political cartoon from 1789 a peasant of the third estate struggles under the weight of a happy clergyman and a plumed nobleman. The caption—"Let's hope this game ends soon"—sets forth a program of reform that any peasant could understand. (Musée de la Ville de Paris, Musée Carnavalet, Paris, France/ The Bridgeman Art Library)

indigenous population. Demographers estimate that indigenous people still accounted for 60 to 75 percent of the population of Latin America at the end of the colonial period, in spite of the tremendous population losses of the sixteenth and seventeenth centuries. The colonies that became Peru and Bolivia had indigenous majorities; the regions that became Argentina and Chile had European majorities. Until the reforms of Charles III, indigenous people and Spaniards were required by law to live in separate communities, although many of the former secretly fled to Spanish cities and haciendas to escape forced labor obligations. Mestizos (meh-STEE-zohz), people of mixed European and indigenous descent, held a higher social status than other nonwhites, but a lower status than Europeans who could prove the "purity" of their blood.

## Demands for Liberty and Equality

In addition to destabilizing social changes, the ideals of liberty and equality helped fuel revolutions in the Atlantic world. The call for liberty was first of all a call for individual human rights. Supporters of the cause of individual liberty (who became known as "liberals" in the early nineteenth century) demanded freedom to worship according to the dictates of their consciences, an end to censorship, and freedom from arbitrary laws and from judges who simply obeyed orders from the government. The Declaration of the Rights of Man and of the Citizen, issued at the beginning of the French Revolution, proclaimed, "Liberty consists in being able to do anything that does not harm another person." In the context of the monarchical and absolutist forms of government then dominating Europe, this was a truly radical idea.

The call for liberty was also a call for a new kind of government. Reformers believed that the people had sovereignty—that is, that the people alone had the authority to make laws limiting an individual's freedom of action. In practice, this system of government meant choosing legislators who represented the people and were accountable to them. Monarchs might retain their thrones, but their rule should be constrained by the will of the people.

Equality was a more ambiguous idea. Eighteenth-century liberals argued that, in theory, all citizens should have identical rights and liberties and that the nobility had no right to special privileges based on birth. However, they accepted a number of distinctions. First, most eighteenth-century liberals were men of their times, and they generally believed that equality between men and women was neither practical nor desirable. Women played an important informal role in the Atlantic revolutions, but in each case male legislators limited formal political rights—the right to vote, to run for office, to participate in government—to men. Second, few questioned the superiority of people of European descent over those of indigenous or African origin. Even those who believed that the slave trade was unjust and should be abolished, such as Thomas Jefferson, usually felt that emancipation was so socially and economically dangerous that it needed to be indefinitely postponed.

Finally, liberals never believed that everyone should be equal economically. Great differences in wealth and income between rich and poor were perfectly acceptable, so long as every free white male had a legally equal chance at economic gain. However limited they appear to modern eyes, these demands for liberty and equality were revolutionary, given that a privileged elite had long existed with little opposition.

The two most important Enlightenment references for late-eighteenth-century liberals were John Locke and the baron de Montesquieu. Locke maintained that England's long political tradition rested on "the rights of Englishmen" and on representative government through Parliament. He argued that if a government oversteps its proper function of protecting the natural rights of life, liberty, and private property, it becomes a tyranny. Montesquieu was also inspired by English constitutional history and the Glorious Revolution of 1688–1689, which placed sovereignty in Parliament (see pages 537–539). He, too, believed that powerful "intermediary groups"—such as the judicial nobility of which he was a proud member—offered the best defense of liberty against despotism.

The belief that representative institutions could defend their liberty and interests appealed powerfully to the educated middle classes. Yet liberal ideas about individual rights and political freedom also appealed to some progressive members of the hereditary nobility. Representative government did not mean democracy, which liberal thinkers tended to equate with mob rule. Rather, they envisioned voting for representatives as being restricted to men who owned property—those with "a stake in society." The blurring of practical distinctions between landed aristocrats and wealthy commoners meant that there was no clear-cut opposition between nobles and non-nobles on political issues.

The Atlantic revolutions began with aspirations for equality and liberty among the social elite. Soon, however, dissenting voices emerged as some revolutionaries became frustrated with the limitations of liberal notions of equality and liberty and clamored for a fuller realization of these concepts. Depending on location, their demands included political rights for women and free people of color, the emancipation of slaves, better treatment of indigenous people, and government regulations to reduce economic inequality. The age of revolution was thus characterized by bitter conflicts over how far reform should go and to whom it should apply.

## The Seven Years' War

The roots of revolutionary ideology could be found in Enlightenment texts, but it was by no means inevitable that such ideas would result in revolution. Many members of the educated elite were satisfied with the status quo or too intimidated to challenge it. Instead events—political, economic, and military—created crises that opened the door for radical action. One of the most important was the global conflict known as the Seven Years' War (1756–1763).

The war's battlefields stretched from central Europe to India to North America (where the conflict was known as the French and Indian War), pitting a new alliance of England and Prussia against the French, Austrians, and, later, Spanish. Its origins were in conflicts left unresolved at the end of the War of the Austrian Succession in 1748, during which Prussia had seized

• **Treaty of Paris**   The 1763 peace treaty that ended the Seven Years' War, according vast French territories in North America and India to Britain and Louisiana to Spain.

the Austrian territory of Silesia. In central Europe, Austria's monarch Maria Theresa vowed to win back Silesia and to crush Prussia, thereby re-establishing the Habsburgs' traditional leadership in German affairs. By the end of the Seven Years' War, Maria Theresa had almost succeeded, but Prussia survived with its boundaries intact.

Unresolved tensions also lingered in North America, particularly regarding the border between the French and British colonies. The encroachment of English settlers into territory claimed by the French in the Ohio Valley resulted in skirmishes that soon became war. Although the inhabitants of New France were greatly outnumbered — Canada counted 55,000 inhabitants, compared to 1.2 million in the thirteen English colonies — French forces achieved major victories until 1758. Both sides relied on the participation of Native American tribes with whom they had long-standing trade contacts and actively sought new indigenous allies during the conflict. The tide of the conflict turned when the British diverted resources from the war in Europe, using superior sea power to destroy the French fleet and choke French commerce around the world. In 1759 the British laid siege to Quebec for four long months, finally defeating the French in a battle that sealed the fate of France in North America.

British victory on all colonial fronts was ratified in the 1763 **Treaty of Paris**. Canada and all French territory east of the Mississippi River passed to Britain, and France ceded Louisiana to Spain as compensation for Spain's loss of Florida to Britain. France also gave up most of its holdings in India, opening the way to British dominance on the subcontinent (Map 22.1).

By 1763 Britain had realized its goal of monopolizing a vast trading and colonial empire, but at a tremendous cost in war debt. France emerged from the conflict humiliated and broke, but with its profitable Caribbean colonies intact. In the aftermath of

**MAP 22.1 European Claims in North America and India Before and After the Seven Years' War, 1755–1763**  As a result of the war, France lost its vast territories in North America and India. In an effort to avoid costly conflicts with Native Americans living in the newly conquered territory, the British government in 1763 prohibited colonists from settling west of the Appalachian Mountains. One of the few remaining French colonies in the Americas, Saint-Domingue (on the island of Hispaniola) was the most profitable plantation in the New World.

war, British, French, and Spanish governments had to increase taxes to repay loans, raising a storm of protest and demands for political reform. Since the Caribbean colony of Saint-Domingue remained French, revolutionary turmoil in the mother country would directly affect its population. The seeds of revolutionary conflict in the Atlantic world were thus sown.

# The American Revolutionary Era, 1775–1789

☐ Why and how did American colonists forge a new, independent nation?

Increased taxes and government control sparked colonial protests in the New World, where the era of liberal political revolution began. After revolting against their home country, the thirteen mainland colonies of British North America succeeded in establishing a new unified government. Participants in the revolution believed they were demanding only the traditional rights of English men and women. But those traditional rights were liberal rights, and in the American context they had strong democratic and popular overtones. In founding a government firmly based on liberal principles, the Americans set an example that would have a forceful impact on France and its colonies. Yet the revolution was a grievous disappointment to the one-fifth of the American population living in slavery who were denied freedom under the new government despite its liberal principles.

## The Origins of the Revolution

The high cost of the Seven Years' War doubled the British national debt. Anticipating further expenses to defend newly conquered territories, the British government broke with tradition and announced that it would maintain a large army in North America and tax the colonies directly. In 1765 Parliament passed the Stamp Act, which levied taxes on a long list of commercial and legal documents, diplomas, newspapers, almanacs, and playing cards. These measures seemed perfectly reasonable to the British, for a much heavier stamp tax already existed in Britain, and proceeds from the tax were to fund the defense of the colonies. Nonetheless, the colonists vigorously protested the Stamp Act by rioting and by boycotting British goods. Thus Parliament reluctantly repealed it.

This dispute raised important political questions. To what extent could the British government reassert its power while limiting the authority of elected colonial bodies? Who had the right to make laws for Americans? The British government replied that Americans were represented in Parliament, albeit indirectly (like most British people), and that Parliament ruled throughout the empire. Many Americans felt otherwise. In the words of John Adams, a major proponent of colonial independence, "A Parliament of Great Britain can have no more rights to tax the colonies than a Parliament of Paris." Thus British colonial administration and parliamentary supremacy came to appear as grave threats to existing American liberties.

Americans' resistance to these threats was fed by the great degree of independence they had long enjoyed. In British North America, unlike in England and Europe, no powerful established church existed, and religious freedom was taken for granted. Colonial assemblies made the important laws, which were seldom overturned by the British government. Also, the right to vote was much more widespread than in England. In many parts of colonial Massachusetts, for example, as many as 95 percent of adult males could vote.

Moreover, greater political equality was matched by greater social and economic equality, at least for the free population. No hereditary nobility exercised privileges over peasants and other social groups. Instead independent farmers dominated colonial society. This was particularly true in the northern colonies, where the revolution originated.

In 1773 disputes over taxes and representation flared up again. Under the Tea Act of that year, the British government permitted the financially hard-pressed East India Company to ship tea from China directly to its agents in the colonies rather than through London middlemen, who sold to independent merchants in the colonies. Thus the company secured a profitable monopoly on the tea trade, and colonial merchants were excluded. The price on tea was actually lowered for colonists, but the act generated a great deal of opposition because of its impact on local merchants.

In protest, Boston men disguised as Native Americans held a rowdy Tea Party in which they boarded East India Company ships and threw tea from them into the harbor. In response, the so-called Coercive Acts of 1774 instated a series of harsh measures. The acts closed the port of Boston, curtailed local elections, and expanded the royal governor's power. County conventions in Massachusetts urged that the acts be "rejected as the attempts of a wicked administration to enslave America." Other colonial assemblies joined in the denunciations. In September 1774 the First Continental Congress—consisting of colonial delegates who sought at first to peacefully resolve conflicts with Britain—met in Philadelphia. The more radical members

● **Declaration of Independence** The 1776 document in which the American colonies declared independence from Great Britain and recast traditional English rights as universal human rights.

**The Signing of the Declaration of Independence, July 4, 1776** John Trumbull's famous painting shows the dignity and determination of America's revolutionary leaders. An extraordinarily talented group, they succeeded in rallying popular support without losing power to more radical forces in the process. (Photo © Boltin Picture Library/The Bridgeman Art Library)

of this assembly argued successfully against concessions to the English crown. The British Parliament also rejected compromise, and in April 1775 fighting between colonial and British troops began at Lexington and Concord.

## Independence from Britain

As fighting spread, the colonists moved slowly toward open calls for independence. The uncompromising attitude of the British government and its use of German mercenaries did much to dissolve loyalties to the home country and to unite the separate colonies. *Common Sense* (1775), a brilliant attack by the recently arrived English radical Thomas Paine (1737–1809), also mobilized public opinion in favor of independence. A runaway bestseller with sales of 120,000 copies in a few months, Paine's tract ridiculed the idea of a small island ruling a great continent. In his call for freedom and republican government, Paine expressed Americans' growing sense of separateness and moral superiority.

On July 4, 1776, the Second Continental Congress adopted the **Declaration of Independence**. Written by Thomas Jefferson and others, this document boldly listed the tyrannical acts committed by George III

(r. 1760–1820) and confidently proclaimed the natural rights of mankind and the sovereignty of the American states. The Declaration of Independence in effect universalized the traditional rights of English people and made them the rights of all mankind. (See "Viewpoints 22.2: Declarations of Independence," page 679.)

After the Declaration of Independence, the conflict often took the form of a civil war pitting patriots against Loyalists, those who maintained an allegiance to the Crown. The Loyalists, who numbered up to 20 percent of the total white population,

**Loyalist Strength in the Colonies, ca. 1774–1776**

tended to be wealthy and politically moderate. They were few in number in New England and Virginia, but more common in the Deep South and on the western frontier. British commanders also recruited Loyalists

## KEY EVENTS OF THE AMERICAN REVOLUTION

| | |
|---|---|
| **1765** | Britain passes the Stamp Act |
| **1773** | Britain passes the Tea Act |
| **1774** | Britain passes the Coercive Acts in response to the Tea Party in the colonies; the First Continental Congress refuses concessions to the English crown |
| **April 1775** | Fighting begins between colonial and British troops |
| **July 4, 1776** | The Second Continental Congress adopts the Declaration of Independence |
| **1777–1780** | The French, Spanish, and Dutch side with the colonists against Britain |
| **1783** | The Treaty of Paris recognizes the independence of the American colonies |
| **1787** | The U.S. Constitution is signed |
| **1791** | The first ten amendments to the Constitution are ratified (the Bill of Rights) |

ity to protect neutral shipping rights and succeeded in hampering Britain's naval power.

Thus by 1780 Britain was engaged in an imperial war against most of Europe as well as the thirteen colonies. In these circumstances, and in the face of severe reverses in India, in the West Indies, and at Yorktown in Virginia, a new British government decided to cut its losses and end the war. American officials in Paris were receptive to negotiating a deal with England alone, for they feared that France wanted a treaty that would bottle up the new United States east of the Allegheny Mountains and give British holdings west of the Alleghenies to France's ally, Spain. Thus the American negotiators deserted their French allies and accepted the extraordinarily favorable terms Britain offered.

Under the Treaty of Paris of 1783, Britain recognized the independence of the thirteen colonies and ceded all its territory between the Allegheny Mountains and the Mississippi River to the Americans. Out of the bitter rivalries of the Old World, the Americans snatched dominion over a vast territory.

## Framing the Constitution

The liberal program of the American Revolution was consolidated by the federal Constitution, the Bill of Rights, and the creation of a national republic. Assembling in Philadelphia in the summer of 1787, the delegates to the Constitutional Convention were determined to end the period of economic depression, social uncertainty, and leadership under a weak central government that had followed independence. The delegates thus decided to grant the federal, or central, government important powers: regulation of domestic and foreign trade, the right to tax, and the means to enforce its laws.

Strong rule would be placed squarely in the context of representative self-government. Senators and congressmen would be the lawmaking delegates of the voters, and the president of the republic would be an elected official. The central government would operate in Montesquieu's framework of checks and balances, under which authority was distributed across three different branches—the executive, legislative, and judicial branches—which would prevent one interest from gaining too much power. The power of the federal government would in turn be checked by that of the individual states.

When the results of the Constitutional Convention were presented to the states for ratification, a great public debate began. The opponents of the proposed Constitution—the **Antifederalists**—charged that the framers of the new document had taken too much power from the individual states and made the federal government too strong. Moreover, many Anti-

from enslaved people by promising freedom to any slave who left his master to fight for the mother country.

Many wealthy patriots—such as John Hancock and George Washington—willingly allied themselves with farmers and artisans in a broad coalition. This coalition harassed the Loyalists and confiscated their property to help pay for the war, causing sixty thousand to eighty thousand of them to flee, mostly to Canada. State governments extended the right to vote to many more men, including free African American men in some cases, but not to women.

On the international scene, the French wanted revenge against the British for the humiliating defeats of the Seven Years' War. Thus they sympathized with the rebels and supplied guns and gunpowder from the beginning of the conflict. By 1777 French volunteers were arriving in Virginia, and a dashing young nobleman, the marquis de Lafayette (1757–1834), quickly became one of the most trusted generals of George Washington, who was commanding American troops. In 1778 the French government offered a formal alliance to the American ambassador in Paris, Benjamin Franklin, and in 1779 and 1780 the Spanish and Dutch declared war on Britain. Catherine the Great of Russia helped organize the League of Armed Neutral-

• **Antifederalists** Opponents of the American Constitution who felt it diminished individual rights and accorded too much power to the federal government at the expense of the states.

federalists feared for the individual freedoms for which they had fought. To overcome these objections, the Federalists promised to spell out these basic freedoms as soon as the new Constitution was adopted. The result was the first ten amendments to the Constitution, which the first Congress passed shortly after it met in New York in March 1789. These amendments, ratified in 1791, formed an effective Bill of Rights to safeguard the individual. Most of them — trial by jury, due process of law, the right to assemble, freedom from unreasonable search — had their origins in English law and the English Bill of Rights of 1689. Other rights — the freedoms of speech, the press, and religion — reflected natural-law theory and the strong value colonists had placed on independence from the start.

## Limitations of Liberty and Equality

The American Constitution and the Bill of Rights exemplified the strengths and the limits of what came to be called classical liberalism. Liberty meant individual freedoms and political safeguards. Liberty also meant representative government, but it did not mean democracy, with its principle of one person, one vote. Equality meant equality before the law, not equality of political participation or wealth. It did not mean equal rights for slaves, Native Americans, or women.

A vigorous abolitionist movement during the 1780s led to the passage of emancipation laws in all northern states, but slavery remained prevalent in the South, and discord between pro- and antislavery delegates roiled the Constitutional Convention of 1787. The result was a compromise stipulating that an enslaved person would count as three-fifths of a person in tallying population numbers for taxation and proportional representation in the House of Representatives. This solution levied higher taxes on the South, but also guaranteed slaveholding states greater representation in Congress, which they used to oppose emancipation. Congress did ban participation in the international slave trade from 1808, but did not prohibit the sale of enslaved people between states.

The new republic also failed to protect the Native American tribes whose lands fell within or alongside the territory ceded by Britain at the Treaty of Paris. The 1787 Constitution promised protection to Native Americans and guaranteed that their land would not be taken without consent. Nonetheless, the federal government forced tribes to concede their land for meager returns; state governments and the rapidly expanding population paid even less heed to the Constitution and often simply seized Native American land for new settlements.

Although lacking the voting rights enjoyed by so many of their husbands and fathers in the relatively democratic colonial assemblies, women played a vital role in the American Revolution. As household provisioners, women were essential participants in boycotts of British goods, like tea, which squeezed profits from British merchants and fostered the revolutionary spirit. After the outbreak of war, women raised funds for the Continental Army and took care of homesteads, workshops, and other businesses when their men went off to fight. Yet despite Abigail Adams's plea to her husband, John Adams, that the framers of the Declaration of Independence should "remember the ladies," women did not receive the right to vote in the new Constitution, an omission confirmed by a clause added in 1844.

# Revolution in France, 1789–1791

☐ How did the events of 1789 result in a constitutional monarchy in France, and what were the consequences?

No country felt the consequences of the American Revolution more deeply than France. Hundreds of French officers served in America and were inspired by the experience. French intellectuals and publicists engaged in passionate analysis of the federal Constitution as well as the constitutions of the various states of the new United States. Yet the French Revolution did not mirror the American example. It was more radical and more complex, more influential and more controversial, more loved and more hated. For Europeans and most of the rest of the world, it was the great revolution of the eighteenth century, the revolution that opened the modern era in politics.

## Breakdown of the Old Order

As did the American Revolution, the French Revolution had its immediate origins in the financial difficulties of the government. The efforts of the ministers of King Louis XV (r. 1715–1774) to raise taxes to meet the expenses of the War of the Austrian Succession and the Seven Years' War were thwarted by the high courts, known as the parlements. The noble judges of the parlements resented this threat to their exemption from taxation and decried the government's actions as a form of royal despotism.

When renewed efforts to reform the tax system similarly failed in 1776, the government was forced to finance its enormous expenditures during the American war with borrowed money. As a result, the national debt soared. In 1786 the finance minister informed King

Louis XVI (r. 1774–1792) that the nation was on the verge of bankruptcy. Fully 50 percent of France's annual budget went to interest payments on the ever-increasing debt. Another 25 percent went to maintain the military, while 6 percent was absorbed by the royal family and the court. Less than 20 percent of the national budget served the productive functions of the state, such as transportation and general administration.

Spurred by a depressed economy and falling tax receipts, Louis XVI's minister of finance revived old proposals to impose a general tax on all landed property as well as to form provincial assemblies to help administer the tax. He convinced the king to call an assembly of notables in 1787 to gain support for the idea. The assembled notables, mainly important noblemen and high-ranking clergy, declared that such sweeping tax changes required the approval of the **Estates General**, the representative body of all three estates, which had not met since 1614. Louis XVI's efforts to reject their demands failed, and in July 1788 he reluctantly called the Estates General into session.

## The National Assembly

As its name indicates, the Estates General was a legislative body with representatives from the three orders of society: the clergy, nobility, and commoners. On May 5, 1789, the twelve hundred newly elected delegates of the three estates gathered in Versailles for the opening session of the Estates General. They met in an atmosphere of deepening crisis. A poor grain harvest in 1788 caused sharp increases in the price of bread, and inflation spread quickly through the economy. As a result, demand for manufactured goods collapsed, and thousands of artisans and small traders lost work.

The Estates General was almost immediately deadlocked by arguments about voting procedures. Controversy had begun during the electoral process itself when the government confirmed that, following precedent, each estate should meet and vote separately. Critics had demanded instead a single assembly dominated by the third estate. In his famous pamphlet "What Is the Third Estate?" the abbé Emmanuel Joseph Sieyès argued that the nobility was a tiny, overprivileged minority and that commoners constituted the true strength of the French nation. (See "Listening to the Past: Abbé Sieyès, 'What Is the Third Estate?'" page 660.) The government granted the third estate as many delegates as the clergy and the nobility combined,

but then nullified the reform by granting one vote per estate, meaning that the two privileged estates could always outvote the third. The issue came to a crisis in June 1789 when delegates of the third estate refused to meet until the king ordered the clergy and nobility to sit with them in a single body. On June 20 the delegates of the third estate, excluded from their hall because of "repairs," moved to a large indoor tennis court where they swore the famous Oath of the Tennis Court, pledging not to disband until they had been recognized as a **National Assembly** and had written a new constitution.

The king's response was disastrously ambivalent. Although he made a conciliatory speech accepting the deputies' demands, he called a large army toward the capital to bring the Assembly under control, and on July 11 he dismissed his finance minister and other liberal ministers. On July 14, 1789, several hundred common people, angered by the king's actions and fearing he would use violence to disband the National Assembly, stormed the Bastille (ba-STEEL), a royal prison, to obtain weapons for the city's defense. Ill-judged severity on the part of the Crown thus led to the first episodes of popular violence, just as the Coercive Acts of 1774 had pushed British colonists toward the fight for independence.

Uprisings also rocked the countryside. In the summer of 1789 throughout France peasants began to rise in insurrection against their lords, ransacking manor houses and burning feudal documents that recorded their obligations. In some areas peasants reoccupied common lands enclosed by landowners and seized forests. Fear of marauders and vagabonds hired by vengeful landlords—called the Great Fear by contemporaries—seized the rural poor and fanned the flames of rebellion.

The National Assembly responded to the swell of popular anger with a surprise maneuver on the night of August 4, 1789. By a decree of the Assembly, all the old noble privileges—peasant serfdom where it still existed, exclusive hunting rights, fees for having legal cases judged in the lord's court, the right to make peasants work on the roads, and a host of other dues—were abolished along with tithes paid to the church. From this point on, French peasants would seek mainly to protect and consolidate this victory. On August 27, 1789, the Assembly further issued the Declaration of the Rights of Man and of the Citizen. This clarion call of the liberal revolutionary ideal guaranteed equality before the law, representative government for a sovereign people, and individual freedom. It was quickly disseminated throughout France, the rest of Europe, and around the world.

The National Assembly's declaration had little practical effect for the poor and hungry people of Paris. The

---

• **Estates General** Traditional representative body of the three estates of France that met in 1789 in response to imminent state bankruptcy.

• **National Assembly** French representative assembly formed in 1789 by the delegates of the third estate and some members of the clergy, the first estate.

**The Tennis Court Oath, June 20, 1789** Painted two years after the event shown, this dramatic painting by Jacques-Louis David depicts a crucial turning point in the early days of the Revolution. On June 20 delegates of the third estate arrived at their meeting hall in the Versailles palace to find the doors closed and guarded. Fearing the king was about to dissolve their meeting by force, the deputies reassembled at a nearby indoor tennis court and swore a solemn oath not to disperse until they had been recognized as the National Assembly. (Musée de la Ville de Paris, Musée Carnavalet, Paris, France/Giraudon/The Bridgeman Art Library)

economic crisis worsened after the fall of the Bastille, as aristocrats fled the country and the luxury market collapsed. Foreign markets also shrank, and unemployment among the urban working class grew. In addition, women—the traditional managers of food and resources in poor homes—could no longer look to the church, which had been stripped of its tithes, for aid.

## Constitutional Monarchy

The next two years, until September 1791, saw the consolidation of the liberal revolution. In June 1790 the National Assembly abolished the nobility, and in July the king swore to uphold the as-yet-unwritten constitution, effectively enshrining a constitutional monarchy. The king remained the head of state, but all lawmaking power now resided in the National Assembly, elected by the wealthiest half of French males. The constitution finally passed in September 1791 was the first in French history. It legalized divorce and broadened women's rights to inherit property and to obtain financial support for illegitimate children from fathers, but excluded women from political office and voting.

This decision was attacked by a small number of men and women who believed that the rights of man should be extended to all French citizens. Olympe de Gouges (1748–1793), a self-taught writer and woman of the people, protested the evils of slavery as well as the injustices done to women. In September 1791 she published her "Declaration of the Rights of Woman." This pamphlet echoed its famous predecessor, the Declaration of the Rights of Man and of the Citizen, proclaiming, "Woman is born free and remains equal to man in rights." De Gouges's position found little sympathy among leaders of the Revolution, however.

In addition to ruling on women's rights, the National Assembly replaced the complicated patchwork of historic provinces with eighty-three departments of approximately equal size, a move toward more rational and systematic methods of administration. The deputies prohibited monopolies, guilds, and workers' associations and abolished barriers to trade within France

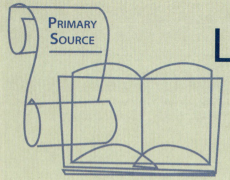

# Listening to the Past

## Abbé Sieyès, "What Is the Third Estate?"

*In the flood of pamphlets that appeared after Louis XVI's call for a meeting of the Estates General, the most influential was written in 1789 by a Catholic priest named Emmanuel Joseph Sieyès. In "What Is the Third Estate?" the abbé Sieyès vigorously condemned the system of privilege that lay at the heart of French society. The term* privilege *combined the Latin words for "private" and "law." In Old Regime France, no one set of laws applied to all; over time, the monarchy had issued a series of particular laws, or privileges, that enshrined special rights and entitlements for select individuals and groups. Noble privileges were among the weightiest.*

*Sieyès rejected this entire system of legal and social inequality. Deriding the nobility as a foreign parasite, he argued that the common people of the third estate, who did most of the work and paid most of the taxes, constituted the true nation. His pamphlet galvanized public opinion and played an important role in convincing representatives of the third estate to proclaim themselves a National Assembly in June 1789. Sieyès later helped bring Napoleon Bonaparte to power, abandoning the radicalism of 1789 for an authoritarian regime.*

" 1. What is the Third Estate? Everything.
   2. What has it been until now in the political order? Nothing.
   3. What does it want? To become something.

. . . What is a Nation? A body of associates living under a *common* law and represented by the same *legislature*.

Is it not more than certain that the noble order has privileges, exemptions, and even rights that are distinct from the rights of the great body of citizens? Because of this, it [the noble order] does not belong to the common order, it is not covered by the law common to the rest. Thus its civil rights already make it a people apart inside the great Nation. It is truly *imperium in imperio* [a law unto itself].

As for its *political* rights, the nobility also exercises them separately. It has its own representatives who have no mandate from the people. Its deputies sit separately, and even when they assemble in the same room with the deputies of the ordinary citizens, the nobility's representation still remains essentially distinct and separate: it is foreign to the Nation by its very principle, for its mission does not emanate from the people, and by its purpose, since it consists in defending, not the general interest, but the private interests of the nobility.

The Third Estate therefore contains everything that pertains to the Nation and nobody outside of the Third Estate can claim to be part of the Nation. What is the Third Estate? EVERYTHING. . . .

By Third Estate is meant the collectivity of citizens who belong to the common order. Anybody who holds a legal privilege of any kind leaves that common order, stands as an exception to the common law, and in consequence does not belong to the Third Estate. . . . It is certain that the moment a citizen acquires privileges contrary to common law, he no longer belongs to the common order. His new interest is opposed to the general interest; he has no right to vote in the name of the people. . . .

In vain can anyone's eyes be closed to the revolution that time and the force of things have brought to pass; it is none the less real. Once upon a time the Third Estate was in bondage and the noble order was everything that mattered. Today the Third is everything and nobility but a word. Yet under the cover of this word a new and intolerable aristocracy has slipped in, and the people has every reason to no longer want aristocrats. . . .

What is the will of a Nation? It is the result of individual wills, just as the Nation is the aggregate of the individuals who com-

in the name of economic liberty. Thus the National Assembly applied the spirit of the Enlightenment in a thorough reform of France's laws and institutions.

The National Assembly also imposed a radical reorganization on religious life. It granted religious freedom to the small minority of French Jews and Protestants. (See "Viewpoints 22.1: The Question of Jewish Citizenship in France," page 662.) Furthermore, in November 1789 it nationalized the property of the Catholic Church and abolished monasteries. The government used all former church property as collateral to guarantee a new paper currency, the assignats (A-sihg-nat), and then sold the property in an attempt to put the state's finances on a solid footing.

Imbued with the rationalism and skepticism of the eighteenth-century Enlightenment philosophes, many delegates distrusted popular piety and "superstitious religion." Thus, in July 1790, with the Civil Constitution of the Clergy, they established a national church with priests chosen by voters. The National Assem-

pose it. It is impossible to conceive of a legitimate association that does not have for its goal the common security, the common liberty, in short, the public good. No doubt each individual also has his own personal aims. He says to himself, "protected by the common security, I will be able to peacefully pursue my own personal projects, I will seek my happiness where I will, assured of encountering only those legal obstacles that society will prescribe for the common interest, in which I have a part, and with which my own personal interest is so usefully allied." . . .

Advantages which differentiate citizens from one another lie outside the purview of citizenship. Inequalities of wealth or ability are like the inequalities of age, sex, size, etc. In no way do they detract from the *equality* of citizenship. These individual advantages no doubt benefit from the protection of the law; but it is not the legislator's task to create them, to give privileges to some and refuse them to others. The law grants nothing; it protects what already exists until such time that what exists begins to harm the common interest. These are the only limits on individual freedom. I imagine the law as being at the center of a large globe; we the citizens without exception, stand equidistant from it on the surface and occupy equal places; all are equally dependent on the law, all present it with their liberty and their property to be protected; and this is what I call the *common rights* of citizens, by which they are all alike. All these individuals communicate with each other, enter into contracts, negotiate, always under the common guarantee of the law. If in this general activity somebody wishes to get control over the person of his neighbor or usurp his property, the common law goes into action to repress this criminal attempt and puts everyone back in their place at the same distance from the law. . . .

It is impossible to say what place the two privileged orders [the clergy and the nobility] ought to occupy in the social order: this is the equivalent of asking what place one wishes to assign to a malignant tumor that torments and undermines the strength of the body of a sick person. It must be *neutralized*. We must re-establish the health and working of all organs so thoroughly that they are no longer susceptible to these fatal schemes that are capable of sapping the most essential principles of vitality. **"**

Source: *The French Revolution and Human Rights: A Brief Documentary History*, pp. 65, 67, 68–70. Edited, translated, and with an introduction by Lynn Hunt. © 1996 by Bedford/St. Martin's. Reprinted by permission of the publisher.

This bust, by the sculptor Pierre Jean David d'Angers, shows an aged and contemplative Sieyès reflecting, perhaps, on his key role in the outbreak and unfolding of the French Revolution. (Galerie David d'Angers, Angers, France/Erich Lessing/Art Resource, NY)

## QUESTIONS FOR ANALYSIS

1. What criticism of noble privileges does Sieyès offer? Why does he believe nobles are "foreign" to the nation?

2. How does Sieyès define the nation, and why does he believe that the third estate constitutes the nation?

3. What relationship between citizens and the law does Sieyès envision? What limitations on the law does he propose?

bly then forced the Catholic clergy to take an oath of loyalty to the new government. The pope formally condemned this measure, and only half the priests of France swore the oath. Many sincere Christians, especially those in the countryside, were also upset by these changes in the religious order. The attempt to remake the Catholic Church, like the abolition of guilds and workers' associations, sharpened the conflict between the educated classes and the common people that had been emerging in the eighteenth century.

## The National Convention

The outbreak and progress of revolution in France produced great excitement and a sharp division of opinion in Europe and the United States. Liberals and radicals saw a triumph of liberty over despotism, while conservative leaders were deeply troubled by the aroused spirit of reform. In 1790 Edmund Burke published *Reflections on the Revolution in France*, one of the great expressions of European conservatism. He derided abstract

# Viewpoints 22.1

## The Question of Jewish Citizenship in France

*• In August 1789 the legislators of the French Revolution adopted the Declaration of the Rights of Man and of the Citizen, enshrining full legal equality under the law for French citizens. Who exactly could become a citizen and what rights they might enjoy quickly became contentious issues. After granting civil rights to Protestants in December 1789, the National Assembly began to consider the smaller but more controversial population of French Jews. Eager to become citizens, the Jews of Paris, Alsace, and Lorraine presented a joint petition to the National Assembly in January 1790. Their appeal was met with negative reactions in some quarters, including from the bishop of Nancy in Lorraine, a province on France's eastern border with a relatively large Jewish population.*

### Jewish Petition to the National Assembly, January 28, 1790

A great question is pending before the supreme tribunal of France. *Will the Jews be citizens or not?* . . .

In general, civil rights are entirely independent from religious principles. And all men of whatever religion, whatever sect they belong to, whatever creed they practice, provided that their creed, their sect, their religion does not offend the principles of a pure and severe morality, all these men, we say, equally able to serve the fatherland, defend its interests, contribute to its splendor, should all equally have the title and the rights of citizen.

. . . Reflect, then, on the condition of the Jews. Excluded from all the professions, ineligible for all the positions, deprived even of the capacity to acquire property, not daring and not being able to sell openly the merchandise of their commerce, to what extremity are you reducing them? You do not want them to die, and yet you refuse them the means to live; you refuse them the means, and you crush them with taxes. . . .

Everything is changing; the lot of the Jews must change at the same time; and the people will not be more surprised by this particular change than by all those which they see around them everyday. This is therefore the moment, the true moment to make justice triumph: attach the improvement of the lot of the Jews to the revolution.

### La Fare, Bishop of Nancy, On the Admissibility of Jews to Full Civil and Political Rights, Spring 1790

Thus, Sirs, assure each Jewish individual his liberty, security, and the enjoyment of his property. You owe it to this individual who has strayed into our midst; you owe him nothing more. He is a foreigner to whom, during the time of this passage and his stay, France owes hospitality, protection and security. But it cannot and should not admit to public posts, to the administration, to the prerogatives of the family a tribe that, regarding itself everywhere as foreign, never exclusively embraces any region; a tribe whose religion, customs, and physical and moral regime essentially differ from that of all other people; a tribe whose eyes turn constantly toward the common fatherland that should one day reunite its dispersed members. . . .

There are also moral and local considerations that should, if not guide, then at least enlighten the legislation regarding the Jewish nation. . . .

The prejudices of the people against the Jews are only too well-known. From time to time, they explode into violence: recently in Alsace, some people committed the most criminal excesses against the Jews. A few months ago, similar misfortunes menaced them in Nancy. . . .

From this account it is easy to understand the habitual disposition of the people; it is a fire always ready to be lit. Any extension that a decree of the National Assembly would hasten to give to the civil existence of the Jews, before opinion has been prepared in advance and led by degrees to this change, could occasion great disaster.

Source: *The French Revolution and Human Rights: A Brief Documentary History*, pp. 93–96 (Jewish petition) and pp. 97–98 (La Fare). Edited, translated, and with an introduction by Lynn Hunt. © 1996 by Bedford/St. Martin's. Reprinted by permission of the publisher.

### QUESTIONS FOR ANALYSIS

1. On what basis do the Jews of Paris, Alsace, and Lorraine argue for their inclusion in citizenship rights? How do they describe the constraints of the Jewish population prior to the Revolution?

2. How does the Bishop of Nancy characterize the Jews' relationship to the French nation, and why does he believe it disqualifies them for citizenship? What dangers does he see in granting citizenship to French Jews?

principles of "liberty" and "rights" and insisted on the importance of inherited traditions and privileges as a bastion of social stability. He predicted that reform like that occurring in France would lead only to chaos and tyranny. Burke's work intensified the international debate over the French Revolution.

The kings and nobles of continental Europe, who had at first welcomed the revolution in France as weakening a competing power, now feared its impact. In June 1791 the royal family was arrested and returned to Paris after a failed attempt to escape France. To the monarchs of Austria and Prussia, the arrest of a crowned monarch was unacceptable. Two months later they issued the Declaration of Pillnitz, proclaiming their willingness to intervene in France to restore Louis XVI's rule, if necessary.

The new French representative body, called the Legislative Assembly, was dominated by members of the **Jacobin Club**. Political clubs had proliferated in Parisian neighborhoods since the beginning of the Revolution, drawing men and women to debate the issues of the day. The Jacobins and other deputies reacted with patriotic fury to the Declaration of Pillnitz. They said that if the kings of Europe were attempting to incite war against France, then "we will incite a war of people against kings."[1] In April 1792 France declared war on Francis II of Austria, the Habsburg monarch.

France's crusade against tyranny went poorly at first. Prussian forces joined Austria against the French, who broke and fled at their first military encounter with this First Coalition of antirevolutionary foreign powers. The Legislative Assembly declared the country in danger, and volunteers rallied to the capital. In August the Assembly suspended the king from all his functions, imprisoned him, and called for a legislative and constitutional assembly to be elected by universal male suffrage.

The fall of the monarchy marked a rapid radicalization of the Revolution. In late September 1792 a new assembly, called the National Convention, was elected by universal manhood suffrage. The Convention proclaimed France a republic, a nation in which the people, instead of a monarch, held sovereign power. Under the leadership of the **Mountain**, the radical faction of the Jacobin Club led by Maximilien Robespierre and Georges Jacques Danton, the Convention tried the king for treason. By a narrow majority, it found him guilty, and on January 21, 1793, Louis was executed by the guillotine, a recent invention intended to provide quick, humane executions. His wife, Marie Antoinette, suffered the same fate later that year.

In February 1793 the National Convention declared war on Britain, the Dutch Republic, and Spain. Republican France was now at war with almost all of Europe, and it faced mounting internal opposition. Peasants in western France revolted against being drafted into the army, with the Vendée region of Brittany emerging as the epicenter of revolt. Devout Catholics, royalists, and foreign agents encouraged their rebellion, and the counter-revolutionaries were able to recruit veritable armies to fight for their cause.

By March 1793 the National Convention was locked in a political life-and-death struggle between two factions of the Jacobin Club, the radical Mountain and the more moderate **Girondists**. With the middle-class delegates so bitterly divided, the laboring poor of Paris once again emerged as the decisive political factor. The laboring poor and the petty traders were often known as the **sans-culottes** (san-koo-LAHT; "without breeches") because their men wore trousers instead of the knee breeches of the aristocracy and the bourgeoisie. They demanded radical political action to guarantee them their daily bread. The Mountain, sensing an opportunity to outmaneuver the Girondists, joined with sans-culotte activists to engineer a popular uprising. On June 2, 1793, armed sans-culottes invaded the Convention and forced its deputies to arrest twenty-nine Girondist deputies for treason. All power passed to the Mountain.

This military and political crisis led to the most radical period of the Revolution, which lasted from spring 1793 until summer 1794. To deal with threats from within and outside France, the Convention formed the Committee of Public Safety in April 1793. Led by Robespierre, the Committee held dictatorial power to deal with the national emergency, allowing it to use whatever force necessary to defend the Revolution. Robespierre and the Committee of Public Safety advanced on several fronts in 1793 and 1794. First, they collaborated with the sans-culottes, who continued pressing the common people's case for fair prices

**Areas of French Insurrection, 1793**

- **Jacobin Club** A political club during the French Revolution to which many of the deputies of the Legislative Assembly belonged.
- **Mountain** Led by Robespierre, the Jacobin Club's radical faction, which led the French National Convention in 1793.
- **Girondists** A moderate group in the Jacobin Club that fought for control of the French National Convention in 1793.
- **sans-culottes** The laboring poor of Paris, so called because the men wore trousers instead of the knee breeches of the aristocracy and middle class; the term came to refer to the militant radicals of the city.

## □ Picturing the Past

**Contrasting Visions of the Sans-Culottes** These two images offer profoundly different representations of a sans-culotte woman. The image on the left was created by a French artist, while the image on the right is English. The French words above the image on the right read in part, "Heads! Blood! Death! . . . I am the Goddess of Liberty! . . . Long Live the Guillotine!" (left: Musée de la Ville de Paris, Musée Carnavalet, Paris, France/Archives Charmet/The Bridgeman Art Library; right: by James Gillray [1757–1815]. © Courtesy of the Warden and Scholars of New College, Oxford, UK/The Bridgeman Art Library)

**ANALYZING THE IMAGE** How would you describe the woman on the left? What qualities does the artist seem to ascribe to her, and how do you think these qualities relate to the sans-culottes and the French Revolution? How would you characterize the facial expression and attire of the woman on the right? How does the inclusion of the text contribute to your impressions of her?

**CONNECTIONS** What does the contrast between these two images suggest about differences between French and English perceptions of the sans-culottes and of the French Revolution? Why do you think the artists have chosen to depict women?

and a moral economic order. In September 1793 Robespierre and his coworkers established a planned economy with egalitarian social overtones. Rather than let supply and demand determine prices, the government set maximum allowable prices for key products. Though the state was too weak to enforce all its price regulations, it did fix the price of bread in Paris at levels the poor could afford.

The government also put the people to work producing arms, munitions, and uniforms for the war effort. The government told craftsmen what to produce, nationalized many small workshops, and requisitioned raw materials and grain. These economic reforms amounted to an emergency form of socialism, which thoroughly frightened Europe's propertied classes and greatly influenced the subsequent development of socialist ideology.

Second, while radical economic measures supplied the poor with bread and the armies with weapons, the **Reign of Terror** (1793–1794) enforced compliance with republican beliefs and practices. Special revolu-

• **Reign of Terror** The period from 1793 to 1794, during which Robespierre's Committee of Public Safety tried and executed thousands suspected of treason and a new revolutionary culture was imposed.

tionary courts tried "enemies of the nation" for political crimes. As a result, some forty thousand French men and women were executed or died in prison. Presented as a necessary measure to save the republic, the Terror was a weapon directed against all suspected of opposing the revolutionary government. As Robespierre himself put it, "Terror is nothing more than prompt, severe inflexible justice."[2] For many Europeans of the time, however, the Reign of Terror represented a frightening perversion of the ideals of 1789.

In their efforts to impose unity, the Jacobins also took actions to suppress women's participation in political debate, which they perceived as disorderly and a distraction from women's proper place in the home. On October 30, 1793, the National Convention declared, "The clubs and popular societies of women, under whatever denomination are prohibited." Among those convicted of sedition was writer Olympe de Gouges, who was sent to the guillotine in November 1793.

The third element of the Committee's program was to bring about a cultural revolution that would transform former royal subjects into republican citizens. The government sponsored revolutionary art and songs as well as secular holidays and open-air festivals to celebrate republican virtues. It also attempted to rationalize daily life by adopting the decimal system for weights and measures and a new calendar based on ten-day weeks. A campaign of de-Christianization aimed to eliminate Catholic symbols and beliefs. Fearful of the hostility aroused in rural France, however, Robespierre called for a halt to de-Christianization measures in mid-1794.

The final element in the program of the Committee of Public Safety was its appeal to a new sense of national identity and patriotism. With a common language and a common tradition reinforced by the revolutionary ideals of popular sovereignty and democracy, many French people developed an intense emotional attachment to the nation, and they saw the war against foreign opponents as a life-and-death struggle between good and evil. This was the birth of modern nationalism, the strong identification with one's nation, which would have a profound effect on subsequent European history.

To defend the nation, a decree of August 1793 imposed a draft on all unmarried young men. By January 1794 French armed forces outnumbered those of their enemies almost four to one.[3] Well trained, well equipped, and constantly indoctrinated, the enormous armies of the republic were led by young, impetuous generals. These generals often had risen from the ranks, and they personified the opportunities the Revolution offered gifted sons of the people. By spring 1794 French armies were victorious on all fronts and domestic revolt was largely suppressed. The republic was saved.

## KEY EVENTS OF THE FRENCH REVOLUTION

| | |
|---|---|
| **May 5, 1789** | Estates General meets at Versailles |
| **June 20, 1789** | Oath of the Tennis Court |
| **July 14, 1789** | Storming of the Bastille |
| **July–August 1789** | Great Fear |
| **August 4, 1789** | National Assembly abolishes feudal privileges |
| **August 27, 1789** | National Assembly issues Declaration of the Rights of Man and of the Citizen |
| **July 1790** | Civil Constitution of the Clergy establishes a national church; Louis XVI agrees to a constitutional monarchy |
| **June 1791** | Royal family is arrested while attempting to flee France |
| **August 1791** | Austria and Prussia issue the Declaration of Pillnitz |
| **April 1792** | France declares war on Austria |
| **August 1792** | Legislative Assembly takes Louis XVI prisoner and suspends him from functions |
| **September 1792** | National Convention declares France a republic and abolishes monarchy |
| **January 21, 1793** | Louis XVI is executed |
| **February 1793** | France declares war on Britain, the Dutch Republic, and Spain; revolts take place in some provinces |
| **March 1793** | Struggle between Girondists and the Mountain |
| **June 1793** | Sans-culottes invade the National Convention; Girondist leaders are arrested |
| **September 1793** | Price controls are instituted to aid the poor |
| **1793–1794** | Reign of Terror |
| **Spring 1794** | French armies are victorious on all fronts |
| **July 1794** | Robespierre is executed; Thermidorian reaction begins |
| **1795** | Economic controls are abolished, and suppression of the sans-culottes begins |
| **1795–1799** | Directory rules |
| **1798–1799** | Austria, Britain, and Russia form the Second Coalition against France |
| **1799** | Napoleon Bonaparte overthrows the Directory and seizes power |

## The Directory

The success of French armies led the Committee of Public Safety to relax emergency economic controls, but they extended the political Reign of Terror. The revolutionary tribunals sent many critics to the guillotine, including long-standing collaborators who Robespierre believed had turned against him. A group of radicals and moderates in the Convention, knowing that they might be next, organized a conspiracy. They howled down Robespierre when he tried to speak to the National Convention on July 27, 1794—a date known as 9 Thermidor according to France's newly adopted republican calendar. The next day it was Robespierre's turn to be guillotined.

The respectable middle-class lawyers and professionals who had led the liberal Revolution of 1789 then reasserted their authority. This period of **Thermidorian reaction**, as it was called, harkened back to the beginnings of the Revolution, rejecting the radicalism of the sans-culottes in favor of moderate policies that favored property owners. In 1795 the National Convention abolished many economic controls, let prices rise sharply, and severely restricted local political organizations through which the sans-culottes exerted their strength. In addition, the middle-class members of the National Convention wrote a new constitution restricting eligibility to serve as a deputy to men of substantial means. Real power lay with a new five-man executive body, called the Directory. France's new rulers continued to support military expansion abroad, but war was no longer so much a crusade as a response to economic problems. Large, victorious armies reduced unemployment at home. However, the French people quickly grew weary of the corruption and ineffectiveness that characterized the Directory. This general dissatisfaction revealed itself clearly in the national elections of 1797, which returned a large number of conservative and even monarchist deputies. Fearing for their survival, the Directory used the army to nullify the elections and began to govern dictatorially. Two years later Napoleon Bonaparte ended the Directory in a coup d'état (koo day-TAH) and substituted a strong dictatorship for a weak one. While claiming to uphold revolutionary values, Napoleon would install authoritarian rule.

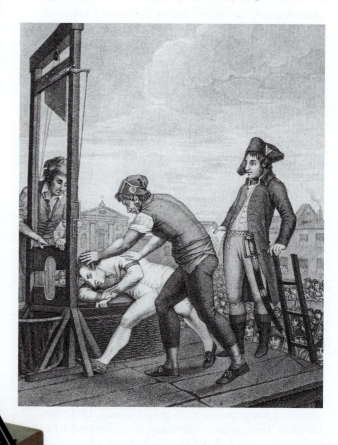

**The Execution of Robespierre**
Completely wooden except for the heavy iron blade, the guillotine was devised by a French revolutionary doctor named Guillotin as a humane method of execution. The guillotine was painted red for Robespierre's execution, a detail not captured in this black-and-white engraving of the 1794 event. Large crowds witnessed the execution in a majestic public square in central Paris, then known as the Place de la Revolution and now called the Place de la Concorde (Harmony Square). (Robespierre: Photo © Tarker/The Bridgeman Art Library; model of guillotine: Musée de la Ville de Paris, Musée Carnavalet, Paris, France/Giraudon/The Bridgeman Art Library)

# Napoleon's Europe, 1799–1815

☐ How did Napoleon Bonaparte assume control of France and much of Europe, and what factors led to his downfall?

For almost fifteen years, from 1799 to 1814, France was in the hands of a keen-minded military dictator of exceptional ability. Napoleon Bonaparte (1769–1821) realized the need to put an end to civil strife in France in order to create unity and consolidate his rule. And he did. But Napoleon saw himself as a man of destiny, and the glory of war and the dream of universal empire proved irresistible.

## Napoleon's Rule of France

Born on the Mediterranean island of Corsica into an impoverished noble family, Napoleon left home and became a lieutenant in the French artillery in 1785. Rising rapidly in the new army, Napoleon was placed in command of French forces in Italy and won brilliant victories there in 1796 and 1797. His next campaign, in Egypt, was a failure, but Napoleon returned to France before the fiasco was generally known, and his reputation remained intact. French aggression in Egypt and elsewhere provoked the British to organize a new alliance in 1798, the Second Coalition, which included Austria and Russia.

Napoleon soon learned that some prominent members of the legislature were plotting against the Directory. The dissatisfaction of these plotters stemmed not so much from the fact that the Directory was a dictatorship as from the fact that it was a weak dictatorship. To these disillusioned revolutionaries, ten years of upheaval and uncertainty had made firm rule much more appealing than liberty and popular politics.

The young Napoleon, nationally revered for his heroism, was an ideal figure of authority. On November 9, 1799, Napoleon and his conspirators ousted the Directors, and the following day soldiers disbanded the legislature. Napoleon was named first consul of the republic, and a new constitution consolidating his position was overwhelmingly approved in a plebiscite in December 1799. Republican appearances were maintained, but Napoleon became the real ruler of France.

Napoleon's domestic policy centered on using his popularity and charisma to maintain order and end civil strife. He did so by appeasing powerful groups in France, offering them favors in return for loyal service. Napoleon's bargain with the middle class was codified in the famous Civil Code of March 1804, also known as the **Napoleonic Code**, which reasserted two of the fundamental principles of the Revolution of 1789:

equality of all male citizens before the law and absolute security of wealth and private property. Napoleon and the leading bankers of Paris established the privately owned Bank of France in 1800, which served the interests of both the state and the financial oligarchy. Napoleon won over peasants by defending the gains in land and status they had won during the Revolution.

At the same time, Napoleon consolidated his rule by recruiting disillusioned revolutionaries for the network of government officials; they depended on him and came to serve him well. Nor were members of the old nobility slighted. In 1800 and again in 1802 Napoleon granted amnesty to one hundred thousand noble émigrés on the condition that they return to France and take a loyalty oath. Members of this returning elite soon occupied high posts in the expanding centralized state. Napoleon also created a new imperial nobility to reward his most talented generals and officials.

Furthermore, Napoleon sought to restore the Catholic Church in France so that it could serve as a bulwark of social stability. Napoleon and Pope Pius VII (pontificate 1800–1823) signed the Concordat of 1801. Under this agreement the pope gained the right for French Catholics to practice their religion freely, but Napoleon gained political power: his government now nominated bishops, paid the clergy, and exerted great influence over the church in France.

The domestic reforms of Napoleon's early years were his greatest achievement. Much of his legal and administrative reorganization has survived in France to this day, but order and unity had a price: authoritarian rule. Women lost many of the gains they had made in the 1790s. Under the Napoleonic Code, women were dependents of either their fathers or their husbands, and they could not make contracts or have bank accounts in their own names. Napoleon aimed at re-establishing a family monarchy, where the power of the husband and father was as absolute over the wife and the children as that of Napoleon over his subjects. He also curtailed free speech and freedom of the press and manipulated voting in the occasional elections. After 1810 political suspects were held in state prisons, as they had been during the Terror.

## Napoleon's Expansion in Europe

Napoleon was above all a great military man. After coming to power in 1799, he sent peace feelers to

- **Thermidorian reaction** A reaction in 1794 to the violence of the Reign of Terror, resulting in the execution of Robespierre and the loosening of economic controls.

- **Napoleonic Code** French civil code promulgated in 1804 that reasserted the 1789 principles of the equality of all male citizens before the law and the absolute security of wealth and private property.

**The Coronation of Napoleon, 1804** In this detail from a grandiose painting by Jacques-Louis David, Napoleon, instead of the pope, prepares to crown his wife, Josephine, in an elaborate ceremony in Notre Dame Cathedral. Napoleon, the ultimate upstart, also crowned himself. Pope Pius VII, seated glumly behind the emperor, is reduced to being a spectator. (Jacques-Louis David [1748–1825]/Louvre, Paris, France/The Bridgeman Art Library)

Austria and Britain, the dominant powers of the Second Coalition. When these overtures were rejected, French armies led by Napoleon decisively defeated the Austrians. Subsequent treaties with Austria in 1801 and Britain in 1802 consolidated France's hold on the territories its armies had won up to that point.

In 1802 Napoleon was secure but still driven to expand his power. Aggressively redrawing the map of German-speaking lands so as to weaken Austria and encourage the secondary states of southwestern Germany to side with France, Napoleon tried to restrict British trade with all of Europe. He then plotted to attack Britain, but his Mediterranean fleet was destroyed by Lord Nelson at the Battle of Trafalgar on October 21, 1805. Renewed fighting had its advantages, however, for the first consul used his high status as a military leader to have himself proclaimed emperor in late 1804.

Austria, Russia, and Sweden joined with Britain to form the Third Coalition against France shortly before the Battle of Trafalgar. Yet the Austrians and the Russians were no match for Napoleon, who scored a brilliant victory over them at the Battle of Austerlitz in December 1805. Russia decided to pull back, and Austria accepted large territorial losses in return for peace as the Third Coalition collapsed.

Napoleon then reorganized the German states to his liking. In 1806 he abolished many tiny German states as well as the Holy Roman Empire and established by decree the German Confederation of the Rhine, a union of fifteen German states minus Austria, Prussia, and Saxony. Naming himself "protector" of the confederation, Napoleon firmly controlled western Germany.

Napoleon's intervention in German affairs alarmed the Prussians, who mobilized their armies. In October 1806 Napoleon attacked them and won two more brilliant victories at Jena and Auerstädt, where the Prussians were outnumbered two to one. The war with Prussia, now joined by Russia, continued into the following spring. After Napoleon's larger armies won another victory, Alexander I of Russia was ready to

**German Confederation of the Rhine, 1806**

**Francisco Goya, *The Third of May 1808*** Spanish master Francisco Goya created a passionate and moving indictment of the brutality of war in this painting from 1814, which depicts the close-range execution of Spanish rebels by Napoleon's forces in May 1808. Goya's painting evoked the bitterness and despair of many Europeans who suffered through Napoleon's invasions. (Museo del Prado, Madrid, Spain/The Bridgeman Art Library)

negotiate for peace. In the treaties of Tilsit in 1807, Prussia lost half its population through land concessions, while Russia accepted Napoleon's reorganization of western and central Europe and promised to enforce Napoleon's economic blockade against British goods.

## The Grand Empire and Its End

Increasingly, Napoleon saw himself as the emperor of Europe, not just of France. The so-called **Grand Empire** he built had three parts. The core, or first part, was an ever-expanding France, which by 1810 included Belgium, Holland, parts of northern Italy, and much German territory on the east bank of the Rhine (Map 22.2). The second part consisted of a number of dependent satellite kingdoms. The third part comprised the independent but allied states of Austria, Prussia, and Russia. After 1806 both satellites and allies were expected to support Napoleon's **Continental System**, a blockade in which no ship coming from Britain or its colonies was permitted to dock at any port that was controlled by the French. The blockade was intended to halt all trade between Britain and continental Europe,

thereby destroying the British economy and its military force.

The impact of the Grand Empire on the peoples of Europe was considerable. In the areas incorporated into France and in the satellites, Napoleon abolished feudal dues and serfdom. Yet he had to put the prosperity and special interests of France first in order to safeguard his power base. Levying heavy taxes in money and men for his armies, Napoleon came to be regarded more as a conquering tyrant than as an enlightened liberator. Thus French rule sparked patriotic upheavals and encouraged the growth of reactive nationalism.

The first great revolt occurred in Spain. In 1808 Napoleon deposed Spanish king Ferdinand VII and placed his own brother Joseph on the throne. A coalition of Catholics, monarchists, and patriots rebelled against this attempt to turn Spain into a satellite of

- **Grand Empire** The empire over which Napoleon and his allies ruled, encompassing virtually all of Europe except Great Britain.

- **Continental System** A blockade imposed by Napoleon to halt all trade between continental Europe and Britain, thereby weakening the British economy and military.

Map legend:
- French empire
- Dependent states
- Allied with Napoleon
- ✹ French victory
- ✹ French defeat

## ☐ Mapping the Past

**MAP 22.2   Napoleonic Europe in 1812**   At the height of the Grand Empire in 1810, Napoleon had conquered or allied with every major European power except Britain. But in 1812, angered by Russian repudiation of his ban on trade with Britain, Napoleon invaded Russia with disastrous results. Compare this map with Map 18.3 (page 533), which shows the division of Europe in 1715.

**ANALYZING THE MAP**   How had the balance of power shifted in Europe from 1715 to 1812? What changed, and what remained the same? What was the impact of Napoleon's wars on Germany, the Italian peninsula, and Russia?

**CONNECTIONS**   Why did Napoleon achieve vast territorial gains where Louis XIV did not?

France. French armies occupied Madrid, but the foes of Napoleon fled to the hills and waged uncompromising guerrilla warfare. Events in Spain sent a clear warning: resistance to French imperialism was growing.

Yet Napoleon pushed on. In 1810, when the Grand Empire was at its height, Britain still remained at war with France, helping the guerrillas in Spain and Portugal. The Continental System was a failure. Instead

of harming Britain, the system provoked the British to set up a counter-blockade, which created hard times for French consumers. Perhaps looking for a scapegoat, Napoleon turned on Alexander I of Russia, who in 1811 openly repudiated Napoleon's prohibitions against British goods.

Napoleon's invasion of Russia began in June 1812 with a force that eventually numbered 600,000, probably the largest force yet assembled in a single army. Only one-third of this army was French, however; nationals of all the satellites and allies were drafted into the operation. Originally planning to winter in the Russian city of Smolensk, Napoleon recklessly pressed on toward Moscow (see Map 22.2). The Battle of Borodino that followed was a draw. Alexander ordered the evacuation of Moscow, which the Russians then burned in part, and he refused to negotiate. Finally, after five weeks in the scorched city, Napoleon ordered a disastrous retreat. The Russian army, the Russian winter, and starvation cut Napoleon's army to pieces. When the frozen remnants staggered into Poland and Prussia in December, 370,000 men had died and another 200,000 had been taken prisoner.[4]

Leaving his troops to their fate, Napoleon raced to Paris to raise another army. Meanwhile, Austria and Prussia deserted Napoleon and joined Russia and Britain in the Treaty of Chaumont in March 1814, by which the four powers formed the Quadruple Alliance to defeat the French emperor. Less than a month later, on April 4, 1814, a defeated Napoleon abdicated his throne. After this unconditional abdication, the victorious allies exiled Napoleon to the island of Elba off the coast of Italy.

In February 1815 Napoleon staged a daring escape from Elba. Landing in France, he issued appeals for support and marched on Paris. French officers and soldiers who had fought so long for their emperor responded to the call. But Napoleon's gamble was a desperate long shot, for the allies were united against him. At the end of a frantic period known as the Hundred Days, they crushed his forces at Waterloo on June 18, 1815, and imprisoned him on the island of St. Helena, off the western coast of Africa. The restored Bourbon dynasty took power under Louis XVIII, a younger brother of Louis XVI.

# The Haitian Revolution, 1791–1804

☐ How did slave revolt on colonial Saint-Domingue lead to the creation of the independent nation of Haiti in 1804?

The events that led to the creation of the independent nation of Haiti constitute the third, and perhaps most extraordinary, chapter of the revolutionary era in the Atlantic world. Prior to 1789 Saint-Domingue, the French colony that was to become Haiti, reaped huge profits through a ruthless system of slave-based plantation agriculture. News of revolution in France lit a powder keg of contradictory aspirations among white planters, free people of color, and slaves. While revo-

lutionary authorities debated how far to extend the rights of man on Saint-Domingue, free people of color and, later, the enslaved took matters into their own hands, rising up to claim their freedom. They succeeded, despite invasion by the British and Spanish and Napoleon Bonaparte's bid to reimpose French control. In 1804 Haiti became the only nation in history to claim its freedom through slave revolt.

## Revolutionary Aspirations in Saint-Domingue

On the eve of the French Revolution, Saint-Domingue—the most profitable of all Caribbean colonies—was even more rife with social tensions than France itself. The colony, which occupied the western third of the island of Hispaniola, was inhabited by a variety of social groups who resented and mistrusted one another. The European population included French colonial officials, wealthy plantation owners and merchants, and poor artisans and clerks. Vastly outnumbering the white population were the colony's five hundred thousand enslaved people, along with a sizable population of some forty thousand free people of African and mixed African and European descent. Members of this last group referred to themselves as "free people of color."

Legal and economic conditions on Saint-Domingue vastly favored the white population. Most of the island's enslaved population performed grueling toil in the island's sugar plantations. The highly outnumbered planters used extremely harsh methods, such as beating, maiming, and executing slaves, to maintain their control. The 1685 Code Noir (Black Code) that legally regulated slavery was intended to provide minimal standards of humane treatment, but its tenets were rarely enforced. Masters calculated that they could earn more by working slaves ruthlessly and purchasing new ones when they died than by providing the food, rest, and medical care needed to allow the enslaved population to reproduce naturally. This meant that a constant inflow of newly enslaved people from Africa was necessary to work the plantations.

Despite their brutality, slaveholders on Saint-Domingue freed a certain number of their slaves, mostly their own mixed-race children, thereby producing one of the largest populations of free people of color in any slaveholding colony. The Code Noir had originally granted free people of color the same legal status as whites: they could own property, live where they wished, and pursue any education or career they desired. From the 1760s on, however, colonial administrators began rescinding these rights, and by the time of the French Revolution many aspects of the lives of free people of color were ruled by discriminatory laws.

The political and intellectual turmoil of the 1780s, with its growing rhetoric of liberty, equality, and fraternity, raised new challenges and possibilities for each of Saint-Domingue's social groups. For enslaved people, who constituted approximately 90 percent of the population, news of abolitionist movements in France led to hopes that the mother country might grant them freedom. Free people of color looked to reforms in Paris as a means of gaining political enfranchisement and reasserting equal status with whites. The white elite, however, was determined to protect its way of life, including slaveholding. They looked to revolutionary ideals of representative government for the chance to gain control of their own affairs, as had the American colonists before them.

The National Assembly frustrated the hopes of all these groups. Cowed by colonial representatives who claimed that support for free people of color would result in slave insurrection, the Assembly refused to extend French constitutional safeguards to the colonies. After dealing this blow to the aspirations of nonwhites, the Assembly also reaffirmed French monopolies over colonial trade, thereby angering planters as well. Like the American settlers did earlier, the colonists chafed under the rule of the mother country.

In July 1790 Vincent Ogé (aw-ZHAY) (ca. 1750–1791), a free man of color, returned to Saint-Domingue from Paris determined to win rights for his people. He raised an army of several hundred and sent letters to the new Provincial Assembly of Saint-Domingue demanding political rights for all free citizens. When Ogé's demands were flatly refused, he and his followers turned to armed insurrection. After initial victories,

his army was defeated, and Ogé was tortured and executed by colonial officials. Revolutionary leaders in Paris were more sympathetic to Ogé's cause. In May 1791, responding to what it perceived as partly justified grievances, the National Assembly granted political rights to free people of color born to two free parents who possessed sufficient property. When news of this legislation arrived in Saint-Domingue, the white elite was furious, and the colonial governor refused to enact it. Violence then erupted between groups of whites and free people of color in parts of the colony.

## The Outbreak of Revolt

Just as the sans-culottes helped push forward more radical reforms in France, the second stage of revolution in Saint-Domingue also resulted from decisive action from below. In August 1791 slaves, who had witnessed the confrontation between whites and free people of color for over a year, took events into their own hands. Groups of slaves held a series of nighttime meetings to plan a mass insurrection. In doing so, they drew on their own considerable military experience; the majority of slaves had been born in Africa, and many had served in the civil wars of the kingdom of Kongo and other conflicts before being taken into slavery.[5] They also drew on a long tradition of slave resistance prior to 1791, which had ranged from work slowdowns, to running away, to taking part in African-derived religious rituals and dances known as *vodou* (or voodoo). According to some sources, the August 1791 pact to take up arms was sealed by such a voodoo ritual.

**Saint-Domingue Slave Life**
Although the brutal conditions of plantation slavery left little time or energy for leisure, slaves on Saint-Domingue took advantage of their day of rest on Sunday to engage in social and religious activities. The law officially prohibited slaves of different masters from mingling together, but such gatherings were often tolerated if they remained peaceful. This image depicts a fight between two slaves, precisely the type of unrest and violence feared by authorities. (Musée du Nouveau Monde, La Rochelle, France/Scala/White Images/Art Resource, NY)

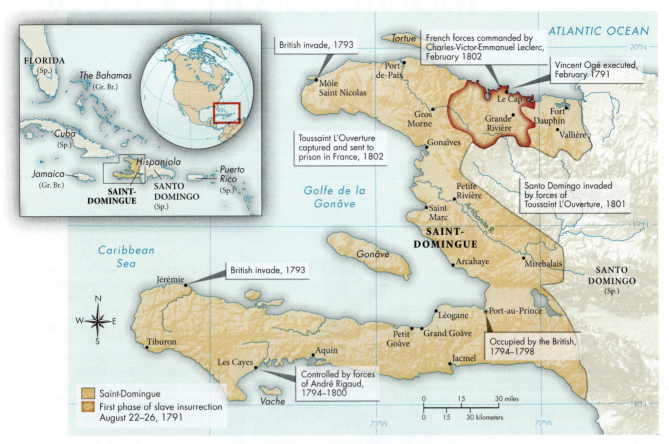

**MAP 22.3 The War of Haitian Independence, 1791–1804** Neighbored by the Spanish colony of Santo Domingo, Saint-Domingue was the most profitable European colony in the Caribbean. In 1791 slave revolts erupted in the north near Le Cap, which had once been the capital. In 1770 the French had transferred the capital to Port-au-Prince, which in 1804 became capital of the newly independent Haiti.

Revolts began on a few plantations on the night of August 22. Within a few days the uprising had swept much of the northern plain, creating a slave army estimated at around 2,000 individuals. By August 27 it was described by one observer as "10,000 strong, divided into 3 armies, of whom 700 or 800 are on horseback, and tolerably well-armed."[6] During the next month enslaved combatants attacked and destroyed hundreds of sugar and coffee plantations.

On April 4, 1792, as war loomed with the European states, the National Assembly issued a decree extending full citizenship rights, including the right to vote, to free people of color. As in France, voting rights and the ability to hold public office applied to men only. The Assembly hoped this measure would win the loyalty of free men of color and their aid in defeating the slave rebellion.

Warfare in Europe soon spread to Saint-Domingue (Map 22.3). Since the beginning of the slave insurrection, the Spanish colony of Santo Domingo, on the eastern side of the island of Hispaniola, had supported rebel slaves. In early 1793 the Spanish began to bring

slave leaders and their soldiers into the Spanish army. Toussaint L'Ouverture (TOO-sahn LOO-vair-toor) (1743–1803), a freed slave who had joined the revolt, was named a Spanish officer. In September the British navy blockaded the colony, and invading British troops captured French territory on the island. For the Spanish and British, revolutionary chaos provided a tempting opportunity to capture a profitable colony.

Desperate for forces to oppose France's enemies, commissioners sent by the newly elected National Convention promised freedom to slaves who fought for France. By October 1793 the commissioners had abolished slavery throughout the colony. On February 4, 1794, the Convention ratified the abolition of slavery and extended it to all French territories, including the Caribbean colonies of Martinique and Guadeloupe.

The tide of battle began to turn when Toussaint L'Ouverture switched sides, bringing his military and political skills, along with four thousand well-trained soldiers, to support the French war effort. By 1796 the French had regained control of the colony, and L'Ouverture had emerged as a key military leader. (See

# Individuals in Society

## Toussaint L'Ouverture

**LITTLE IS KNOWN OF THE EARLY LIFE OF SAINT-DOMINGUE'S** brilliant military and political leader Toussaint L'Ouverture. He was born in 1743 on a plantation outside Le Cap owned by the Count de Bréda. According to tradition, L'Ouverture was the eldest son of a captured African prince from modern-day Benin. Toussaint Bréda, as he was then called, occupied a privileged position among slaves. Instead of performing backbreaking labor in the fields, he served his master as a coachman and livestock keeper. He also learned to read and write French and some Latin, but he was always more comfortable with the Creole dialect.

During the 1770s the plantation manager emancipated L'Ouverture, who subsequently leased his own small coffee plantation, worked by slaves. He married Suzanne Simone, who already had one son, and the couple had another son during their marriage. In 1791 he joined the slave uprisings that swept Saint-Domingue, and he took on the *nom de guerre* (war name) L'Ouverture, meaning "the opening." L'Ouverture rose to prominence among rebel slaves allied with Spain and by early 1794 controlled his own army. A devout Catholic who led a frugal and ascetic life, L'Ouverture impressed others with his enormous physical energy, intellectual acumen, and air of mystery. In 1794 he defected to the French side and led his troops to a series of victories against the Spanish. In 1795 the National Convention promoted L'Ouverture to brigadier general.

Over the next three years L'Ouverture successively eliminated rivals for authority on the island. First he freed himself of the French commissioners sent to govern the colony. With a firm grip on power in the northern province, L'Ouverture defeated General André Rigaud in 1800 to gain control in the south. His army then marched on the capital of Spanish Santo Domingo on the eastern half of the island, meeting little resistance. The entire island of Hispaniola was now under his command.

With control in his hands, L'Ouverture was confronted with the challenge of building a post-emancipation society, the first of its kind. The task was made even more difficult by the chaos wreaked by war, the destruction of plantations, and bitter social and racial tensions. For L'Ouverture the most pressing concern was to re-establish the plantation economy. Without revenue to pay his army, the gains of the rebellion could be lost. He therefore encouraged white planters to return and reclaim their property. He also adopted harsh policies toward former slaves, forcing them back to their plantations and restricting their ability to acquire land. When they resisted, he sent troops across the island to enforce submission. L'Ouverture's 1801 constitution reaffirmed his draconian labor policies and named L'Ouverture governor for life, leaving Saint-Domingue as a colony in name alone. In June 1802 French forces arrested L'Ouverture and jailed him at Fort de Joux in France's Jura Mountains near the Swiss border. He died of pneumonia on April 7, 1803, leaving his lieutenant, Jean Jacques Dessalines, to win independence for the new Haitian nation.

**Equestrian portrait of Toussaint L'Ouverture.** (Bibliothèque Nationale, Paris, France/Archives Charmet/The Bridgeman Art Library)

### QUESTIONS FOR ANALYSIS

1. Toussaint L'Ouverture was both slave and slave owner. How did each experience shape his life and actions?
2. What did L'Ouverture and Napoleon Bonaparte have in common? How did they differ?

## LaunchPad
### Online Document Project

**How did the French Revolution affect France's Caribbean colonies?** Examine reactions of slaves and free men of color to the French Revolution, and then complete a quiz and writing assignment based on the evidence and details from this chapter.

*See inside the front cover to learn more.*

"Individuals in Society: Toussaint L'Ouverture," at left.) In May 1796 he was named commander of the western province of Saint-Domingue (see Map 22.3). The increasingly conservative nature of the French government during the Thermidorian reaction, however, threatened to undo the gains made by former slaves and free people of color.

## The War of Haitian Independence

With Toussaint L'Ouverture acting increasingly as an independent ruler of the western province of Saint-Domingue, another general, André Rigaud (1761–1811), set up his own government in the southern peninsula. Tensions mounted between L'Ouverture and Rigaud. While L'Ouverture was a freed slave of African descent, Rigaud belonged to an elite group of free people of color. This elite resented the growing power of former slaves like L'Ouverture, who in turn accused the elite of adopting the prejudices of white settlers. Civil war broke out between the two sides in 1799, when L'Ouverture's forces, led by his lieutenant, Jean Jacques Dessalines (1758–1806), invaded the south. Victory over Rigaud in 1800 gave L'Ouverture control of the entire colony.

This victory was soon challenged by Napoleon, who had his own plans for using the profits from a re-established system of plantation slavery as a basis for expanding the French empire. Napoleon ordered his brother-in-law, General Charles-Victor-Emmanuel Leclerc (1772–1802), to lead an expedition to the island to crush the new regime. In 1802 Leclerc landed in Saint-Domingue and ordered the arrest of Toussaint L'Ouverture. The rebel leader was deported to France, along with his family, where he died in 1803.

It was left to L'Ouverture's lieutenant, Jean Jacques Dessalines, to unite the resistance, and he led it to a crushing victory over French forces. On January 1, 1804, Dessalines formally declared the independence of Saint-Domingue and the creation of the new sovereign nation of Haiti, the name used by the pre-Columbian inhabitants of the island.

Haiti, the second independent state in the Americas and the first in Latin America, was born from the only successful large-scale slave revolt in history. This event spread shock and fear through slaveholding societies in the Caribbean and the United States, bringing to life their worst nightmares of the utter reversal of power and privilege. Fearing the spread of slave rebellion to the United States, President Thomas Jefferson refused to recognize Haiti. The liberal proponents of the American Revolution thus chose to protect slavery at the expense of revolutionary ideals of universal human rights. Yet Haitian independence had fundamental repercussions for world history, helping spread the idea

that liberty, equality, and fraternity must apply to all people. The next phase of Atlantic revolution soon opened in the Spanish-American colonies.

## KEY EVENTS OF THE HAITIAN REVOLUTION

| | |
|---|---|
| **1760s** | Colonial administrators begin rescinding the rights of free people of color |
| **July 1790** | Vincent Ogé leads a failed rebellion to gain rights for free people of color |
| **August 1791** | Slave revolts begin |
| **April 4, 1792** | National Assembly enfranchises all free blacks and free people of color |
| **September 1793** | British troops invade Saint-Domingue |
| **February 4, 1794** | National Convention ratifies the abolition of slavery and extends it to all French territories |
| **May 1796** | Toussaint L'Ouverture is named commander of Saint-Domingue |
| **1800** | After invading the south of Saint-Domingue, L'Ouverture gains control of the entire colony |
| **1802** | French general Charles-Victor-Emmanuel Leclerc arrests L'Ouverture and deports him to France |
| **1803** | L'Ouverture dies |
| **1804** | After defeating French forces, Jean Jacques Dessalines declares the independence of Saint-Domingue and the creation of the sovereign nation of Haiti |

# Revolution in the Spanish Empire

☐ Why and how did the Spanish and Portuguese colonies of North and South America shake off European domination and develop into national states?

In 1800 the Spanish Empire in the Americas stretched from the headwaters of the Mississippi River in present-day Minnesota to the tip of Cape Horn in the Antarctic (Map 22.4). Spain believed that the great wealth of the Americas existed for its benefit, a stance that fostered bitterness and the desire for independence in the colonies. Between 1806 and 1825 the Spanish colonies in Latin America were convulsed by upheavals that ultimately resulted in their separation from Spain. Until 1898 Spain did, however, retain its Caribbean colonies of Cuba and Puerto Rico.

## The Origins of the Revolutions Against Colonial Powers

The Latin American movements for independence drew strength from unfair taxation and trade policies, Spain's declining control over its Latin American colonies, racial and class discrimination, and the spread of revolutionary ideas. By the eighteenth century the Spanish colonies had become self-sufficient producers of foodstuffs, wine, textiles, and consumer goods, though Spain maintained monopolies on alcohol and tobacco and the colonies traded with each other. In Peru, for example, domestic agriculture supported the large mining settlements, and the colony did not have to import food. Craft workshops owned by the state or by private individuals produced consumer goods for the working class; what was not manufactured locally was bought from Mexico and transported by the Peruvian merchant marine.

Spain's humiliating defeat in the War of the Spanish Succession (1701–1713; see page 544) prompted demands for sweeping reform of all of Spain's institutions, including its colonial policies and practices. The new Bourbon dynasty, descended from the ruling house of France, initiated a decades-long effort known as the Bourbon reforms, which aimed to improve administrative efficiency and increase central control. Reform took on new urgency after Spain's expensive and lackluster participation in the Seven Years' War. Under Charles III (r. 1759–1788), Spanish administrators drew on Enlightenment ideals of rationalism and progress to strengthen colonial rule and thereby increase the fortunes and power of the Spanish state. They created a permanent standing army and enlarged colonial militias. To bring the church under tighter control, they expelled the powerful and wealthy Jesuit order (which had already been exiled from Portugal, Brazil, and France). They also ceased the appointment of Creoles to state posts and followed the Bourbon tradition of dispatching intendants (government commissioners) from the mother country with extensive new powers over justice, administration, tax collection, and military affairs.

Additionally, Spain ended its centuries-old policy of insisting on monopoly over trade with its colonies. Instead it adopted a policy of free trade in order to compete with Great Britain and Holland in the struggle for empire. In Latin America these actions stimulated the production of agricultural commodities that were in demand in Europe, such as coffee, sugar, leather, and salted beef. Between 1778 and 1788 the volume of Spain's trade with the colonies soared, possibly by as much as 700 percent.[7] Colonial manufacturing, however, which had been growing steadily, suffered a heavy blow under free trade. Colonial textiles and china, for example, could not compete with cheap Spanish products.

Madrid's tax reforms also aggravated discontent. Like Great Britain, Spain believed its colonies should bear some of the costs of their own defense. Accordingly, Madrid raised the prices of its monopoly products—tobacco and liquor—and increased sales taxes on many items. War with revolutionary France in the 1790s led to additional taxes and forced loans. As a result, protest movements in Latin America, like those in British North America in the 1770s, claimed that the colonies were being unfairly taxed. Moreover, new taxes took a heavy toll on indigenous communities, which bore the brunt of all forms of taxation and suffered from the corruption and brutality of tax collectors. Riots and protest movements met with harsh repression.

Political conflicts beyond the colonies also helped drive aspirations for independence. The French Revolution and the Napoleonic Wars, which involved France's occupation of Spain and Britain's domination of the seas, isolated Spain from Latin America. As Spain's control over its Latin American colonies diminished, foreign traders, especially from the United States, swarmed into Spanish-American ports. In 1796 the Madrid government made exceptions to its trade restrictions for countries not engaged in the Napoleonic Wars, such as the United States, thus acknowledging Spain's inability to supply the colonies with needed goods and markets.

Racial, ethnic, and class privileges also fueled discontent. The **Creoles**—people of Spanish or other European descent born in the Americas (see page 581)—resented the economic and political dominance of the **peninsulares** (puh-nihn-suh-LUHR-ayz), as the colonial officials and other natives of Spain or Portugal were called. In 1800 there were about thirty thousand peninsulares and 3.5 million Creoles. Peninsulares controlled the rich export-import trade, intercolonial trade, and mining industries and increasingly replaced Creoles in administrative positions. The Creoles wanted to free themselves from Spain and Portugal and to rule the colonies themselves. They had little interest in improving the lot of the Indians, the mestizos of mixed Spanish and Indian background, or the mulattos of mixed Spanish and African heritage.

As in Saint-Domingue, a racial backlash against the growing numbers and social prominence of people of mixed racial origin occurred in the last quarter of the eighteenth century. In 1776 King Charles III outlawed marriages between whites and any person with Indian or African blood. The cabildos (municipal councils) of

• **Creoles** People of Spanish or other European descent born in the Americas.

• **peninsulares** A term for natives of Spain and Portugal.

**MAP 22.4 Latin America in ca. 1780 and 1830** By 1830 almost all of Central America, South America, and the Caribbean islands had won independence. Note that the many nations that now make up Central America were unified when they first won independence from Mexico. Similarly, modern Venezuela, Colombia, and Ecuador were still joined in Gran Colombia.

cities like Lima, Caracas, and Buenos Aires issued ordinances prohibiting nonwhites from joining guilds, serving in the militia, and mixing with whites in public.

A final factor contributing to rebellion was cultural and intellectual ideas. One set of such ideas was the Enlightenment thought of Montesquieu, Voltaire, and Rousseau, which had been trickling into Latin America for decades (see Chapter 19). North American ships calling at South American ports introduced the subversive writings of Thomas Paine and Thomas Jefferson. In 1794 the Colombian Antonio Nariño translated and published the French Declaration of the Rights of Man and of the Citizen. (Spanish authorities sentenced him to ten years in an African prison, but he lived to become the father of Colombian independence.) By 1800 the Creole elite throughout Latin America was familiar with liberal Enlightenment political thought and its role in inspiring colonial revolt.

Another important set of ideas consisted of indigenous traditions of justice and political rule, which often looked back to an idealized precolonial past. During the eighteenth century these ideas served as a rallying point for Indians and non-Indians alike, roused by anger against the Spanish. As Spain was increasingly reviled as cruel and despotic, indigenous culture and history were celebrated. Creoles took advantage of indigenous symbols, but this did not mean they were prepared to view Indians and mestizos as equals.

## Resistance, Rebellion, and Independence

The mid-eighteenth century witnessed frequent Andean Indian rebellions against increased taxation and other impositions of the Bourbon crown. In 1780, under the leadership of a descendant of the Inca rulers who took the name Tupac Amaru II, a massive insurrection exploded. Indian chieftains from the Cuzco region (see Map 22.4) gathered a powerful force of Indians and people of mixed race. Rebellion swept across highland Peru, where many Spanish officials were executed. Creoles joined forces with Spaniards and Indian nobles to crush the rebellion, shocked by the radical social and economic reforms promised by its leaders. A hundred thousand Indians were killed and vast amounts of property destroyed. The government was obliged to concede to some of the rebels' demands by abolishing the repartimiento system, which required Indians to buy goods solely from tax collectors, and establishing assemblies of local representatives in Cuzco.

As news of the rebellion of Tupac Amaru II trickled northward, it helped stimulate the 1781 Comuneros Revolt in the New Granada viceroyalty (see Map 22.4). In this uprising, an Indian and mestizo peasant army commanded by Creole captains marched on Bogotá to protest high taxation and state monopolies on liquor and tobacco. Dispersed by the ruling Spanish, who made promises they did not intend to keep, the revolt in the end did little to improve the Indians' lives.

These two revolts (and the many smaller riots and uprisings that broke out through the eighteenth century) shook authorities, but their ties to the independence movements that followed are indirect. Led from below, these uprisings did not question monarchical rule or the colonial relationship between Spain and Spanish America. Instead two events outside of Spanish America did more to shape the ensuing struggle for independence. First, the revolution on Saint-Domingue and the subsequent independence of the nation of Haiti in 1804 convinced Creole elites, many of whom were slaveholders, of the dangers of slave revolt and racial warfare (see Map 22.3). Their plans and strategies would henceforth be shaped by their determination to avoid a similar outcome in Spanish America.

Second, in 1808 Napoleon Bonaparte deposed Spanish king Ferdinand VII and placed his own brother on the Spanish throne (see page 669). The Creoles in Latin America claimed that the removal of the legitimate king shifted sovereignty to the people—that is, to themselves. Like the patriots in British North America, the Creoles who led the various movements for independence had no desire for a radical redistribution of property or a new social order. They merely rejected the authority of the Spanish crown. Cabildos in cities like Buenos Aires and Caracas took power into their own hands, ostensibly on behalf of Ferdinand, the deposed king.

The great hero of the movement for independence was Simón Bolívar (1783–1830), who was born into a wealthy land- and slave-owning family and went on to become a very able general. Under his leadership, a regional congress in Caracas declared the independence of the United States of Venezuela in July 1811 and quickly drafted a constitution guaranteeing freedom of the press and racial equality. (See "Viewpoints 22.2: Declarations of Independence," at right.) The republic failed after only one year, but Bolívar continued to fight royalist forces for the next eight years, with assistance from the newly formed Haitian republic. His victories over Spanish armies won him the presidency of the new republic of Gran Colombia (formerly the New Granada viceroyalty) in 1819.

Bolívar dreamed of a continental union and in 1826 summoned a conference in Panama City of the American republics he had liberated, which included the future nations of Venezuela, Colombia, Ecuador, Peru, and Bolivia. The meeting achieved little, however. The territories of Gran Colombia soon splintered (see Map 22.4), and a sadly disillusioned Bolívar went into exile, saying, "America is ungovernable."

Under Spain, Mexico had been united with Central America as the Viceroyalty of New Spain. In 1808, after

# Viewpoints 22.2

## Declarations of Independence

- *Within fifty years of the drafting of the Declaration of Independence by Thomas Jefferson and others in 1776, some twenty other independence movements in Europe and the Americas had issued similar proclamations. The rapid spread of this new type of political declaration testifies to the close connections among revolutionary movements in this period. Many of the later declarations of independence modeled themselves self-consciously on the language and arguments of the 1776 text, excerpted below, but they also reflected the unique circumstances in which they were created, as demonstrated by the Venezuelan declaration, also excerpted below.*

### A Declaration by the Representatives of the United States of America, July 4, 1776

We hold these Truths to be self-evident, that all Men are created equal, that they are endowed by their Creator with certain unalienable Rights, that among these are Life, Liberty, and the Pursuit of Happiness — That to secure these Rights, Governments are instituted among Men, deriving their just Powers from the Consent of the Governed, that whenever any Form of Government becomes destructive of these Ends, it is the Right of the People to alter or to abolish it, and to institute new Government, laying its Foundation on such Principles, and organizing its Powers in such Form, as to them shall seem most likely to effect their Safety and Happiness. Prudence, indeed, will dictate that Governments long established should not be changed for light and transient Causes; and accordingly all Experience hath shewn, that Mankind are more disposed to suffer, while Evils are sufferable, than to right themselves by abolishing the Forms to which they are accustomed. But when a long Train of Abuses and Usurpations, pursuing invariably the same Object, evinces a Design to reduce them under absolute Despotism, it is their Right, it is their Duty, to throw off such Government, and to provide new Guards for their future Security. . . . The History of the present King of Great-Britain is a History of repeated Injuries and Usurpations, all having in direct Object the Establishment of an Absolute Tyranny over these States.

### Venezuelan Declaration of Independence, July 5, 1811

In the Name of the All-powerful God, We, the Representatives of the united Provinces . . . , forming the American Confederation of Venezuela, in the South Continent, in Congress assembled, considering the full and absolute possession of our Rights, which we recovered justly and legally from the 19th of April, 1810, in consequence of the occurrences in Bayona,* and the occupation of the Spanish Throne by conquest, and the succession of a new Dynasty, constituted without our consent, . . . calling on the SUPREME BEING to witness the justice of our proceedings and the rectitude of our intentions, do implore his divine and celestial help; and ratifying, at the moment in which we are born to the dignity which his Providence restores to us, the desire we have of living and dying free, and of believing and defending the holy Catholic and Apostolic Religion of Jesus Christ. We, therefore, in the name and by the will and authority which we hold from the virtuous People of Venezuela, DO declare solemnly to the world, that its united Provinces are, and ought to be, from this day, by act and right, Free, Sovereign, and Independent States; and that they are absolved from every submission and dependence on the Throne of Spain . . . and that a free and independent State, thus constituted, has full power to take that form of Government which may be conformable to the general will of the People, to declare war, make peace, form alliances, regulate treaties of commerce, limits, and navigation; and to do and transact every act, in like manner as other free and independent States.

Sources: The Declaration of Independence (1776); *Interesting Official Documents Relating to the United Provinces of Venezuela* (London: Longman and Co., 1812), pp. 3, 18–19.

### QUESTIONS FOR ANALYSIS

1. What justification does the first declaration offer for the independence of the United States of America from Great Britain? What influences from Enlightenment thought are evident in this text?

2. What similarities and differences do you find between the declaration of the United States of America and that of Venezuela?

*The forced abdication of Spanish king Ferdinand VII in favor of Joseph Bonaparte.

## KEY EVENTS IN EARLY LATIN AMERICAN REVOLUTIONS

| | |
|---|---|
| **1759–1788** | Reign of Charles III, who instituted administrative and economic reforms |
| **1794** | Colombian Antonio Nariño publishes the French Declaration of the Rights of Man and of the Citizen |
| **July 1811** | Regional congress in Caracas declares independence of the United States of Venezuela |
| **1822** | Proclamation of Brazil's independence from Portugal |
| **1826** | Call by Simón Bolívar for Panama conference on Latin American union |
| **1830s** | New Spain breaks up into five separate countries |
| **1888** | Emancipation of slaves in Brazil |

Napoleon's coup, the Spanish viceroy assumed control of the government of New Spain from its capital in Mexico City. Meanwhile, groups of rebels plotted to overthrow royalist power. Under the leadership of two charismatic priests, poor Creoles and indigenous peasants rose up against the Spanish. This movement from below fell to royalist forces, but in 1821 a new movement commanded by Creole elites succeeded in winning independence from Spain.

**Triumph of Bolívar** Bolívar was treated as a hero everywhere he went in South America. (akg-images)

Although Creole officers dominated rebel armies, their success depended on a rank and file largely composed of nonwhites. These included many blacks and free people of color, who had come to dominate the colonial militias. In Mexico many indigenous people also fought for the patriots, but elsewhere Indians were often indifferent to independence or felt their status was more secure with the royal government than with the Creoles.

In the 1830s regional separatism resulted in New Spain's breakup into five separate countries. The failure of political union in New Spain and Gran Colombia isolated individual countries, prevented collective action, and later paved the way for the political and economic intrusion of the United States and other powers. Spain's Caribbean colonies of Puerto Rico and Cuba remained loyal, in large part due to fears that slave revolt would spread from neighboring Haiti.

Brazil followed a different path to independence. When Napoleon's troops entered Portugal, the royal family fled to Brazil and made Rio de Janeiro the capital of the Portuguese Empire. The new government immediately lifted the old mercantilist restrictions and opened Brazilian ports to the ships of all friendly nations. The king returned to Portugal in 1821, leaving his son Pedro in Brazil as regent. Under popular pressure, Pedro proclaimed Brazil's independence in 1822, issued a constitution, and even led resistance against Portuguese troops. He accepted the title Emperor Pedro I (r. 1822–1831). Even though Brazil was a monarchy, Creole elites dominated society as they did elsewhere in Latin America. The reign of Pedro I's successor, Pedro II (r. 1831–1889), witnessed the expansion of the coffee industry, the beginnings of the rubber industry, and massive immigration.

## The Aftermath of Revolution in the Atlantic World

The Atlantic revolutions shared many common traits. They had common origins in imperial competition, war debt, social conflict, and Enlightenment ideals. Over the course of revolution, armed struggle often took on the form of civil war, in which the participation of ordinary people—sans-culottes, slaves, free people of color, mestizos, and Indians—played a decisive role. Perhaps their most important similarity was in the democratic limitations of the regimes these revolutions created and the frustrated aspirations they bequeathed to subsequent generations.

For the most part, the elite liberals who led the revolutions were not democrats and had no intention of creating regimes of economic or social equality. The constitutions they wrote generally restricted voting rights and the capacity to be elected to government to landowners and middle-class men. Indigenous people may have gained formal equality as citizens, yet they found that the actual result was the removal of the privileged status they had negotiated with their original conquerors. Thus they suffered the loss of rights over their land and other resources. Moreover, none of the postrevolutionary constitutions gave women a role in political life.

The issue of slavery, by contrast, divided the revolutions. The American Revolution was led in part by slaveholding landowners, who were determined to retain slavery in its aftermath, while the more radical French republic abolished it throughout the French empire (a measure soon reversed by Napoleon). The independent nation of Haiti was built on the only successful slave revolt in history, but the need for revenue from plantation agriculture soon led to the return of coercive labor requirements, if not outright slavery. In Latin America, independence speeded the abolition of slavery, bringing an immediate ban on the slave trade and gradual emancipation from the 1820s to the 1850s. Still, Cuba and Brazil, which had enormous slave populations, did not end slavery until 1886 and 1888, respectively.

The aftermaths of the Atlantic revolutions brought extremely different fortunes to the new nations that emerged from them. France returned to royal rule with the restoration of the Bourbon monarchy in 1815. A series of revolutionary crises ensued in the nineteenth century as succeeding generations struggled over the legacies of monarchicalism, republicanism, and Bonapartism. It was not until 1871 that republicanism finally prevailed (see Chapter 24). The transition to an independent republic was permanent and relatively smooth in the United States, where war was brief and limited, colonial assemblies had long practiced self-governance, and manufacturing and trade recovered quickly with renewed ties with Britain. Nevertheless, the unresolved conflict over slavery would lead to catastrophic civil war in 1860.

The newly independent nations of Latin America had difficulty achieving political stability when the wars of independence ended. The economic lives of most Latin American countries were disrupted during the years of war. Mexico and Venezuela in particular suffered great destruction of farmland and animals. Between 1836 and 1848 Mexico lost half its territory to the United States, and other countries, too, had difficulty defending themselves from their neighbors. (See "Viewpoints 27.1: Mexican and American Perspectives on the U.S.-Mexican War," page 822.) The Creole leaders of the revolutions had little experience in government, and the wars left a legacy of military, not civilian, leadership.

## CHRONOLOGY

| | |
|---|---|
| 1715–1774 | Reign of Louis XV in France |
| 1743–1803 | Life of Toussaint L'Ouverture |
| 1756–1763 | Seven Years' War |
| 1763 | Treaty of Paris |
| 1774–1792 | Reign of Louis XVI in France |
| 1775 | Thomas Paine publishes *Common Sense* |
| 1775–1783 | American Revolution |
| 1789–1799 | French Revolution |
| 1790 | Edmund Burke publishes *Reflections on the Revolution in France* |
| 1791–1804 | Haitian Revolution |
| 1799–1814 | Reign of Napoleon Bonaparte in France |

## Chapter Summary

From 1775 to 1825 a wave of revolution swept through the Atlantic world. Its origins included long-term social and economic changes, Enlightenment ideals of liberty and equality, and the costs of colonial warfare. British efforts to raise taxes after the Seven Years' War aroused violent protest in the American colonies. In 1776 the Second Continental Congress issued the Declaration of Independence, and by 1783 Britain had recognized the independence of the thirteen colonies. Following ratification of a new constitution, Congress passed ten amendments to safeguard individual liberties but denied equal rights to women and nonwhites.

In 1789 delegates to the Estates General defied royal authority to declare themselves a National Assembly, which promulgated France's first constitution in 1791. Led by the Jacobin Club, the Assembly waged war on Austria and Prussia and proclaimed France a republic. From the end of 1793, under the Reign of Terror, the Revolution pursued internal and external enemies ruthlessly and instituted economic controls to aid the poor. The weakness of the Directory government after the fall of Robespierre enabled charismatic general Napoleon Bonaparte to claim control of France. Napoleon's relentless military ambitions allowed him to spread French power through much of Europe but ultimately led to his downfall.

After a failed uprising by free men of color, slaves rose in revolt in the French colony of Saint-Domingue in August 1791. Their revolt, combined with the outbreak of war and the radicalization of the French Revolution, led to the enfranchisement of free men of color, the emancipation of slaves who fought for France, and ultimately the abolition of slavery throughout the colony in late 1793. Like Napoleon Bonaparte, Toussaint L'Ouverture was an unknown soldier who claimed glory and power, only to endure exile and defeat. After his exile, his forces won independence for the new Haitian nation in 1804.

Latin American independence movements drew strength from Spain's unpopular policies. External events—the outbreak of the Haitian Revolution and Napoleon's seizure of the Spanish throne—accelerated the path toward revolt. Under the leadership of Simón Bolívar, the United States of Venezuela claimed independence in 1811. Led by Creole officers but reliant on nonwhite soldiers, rebel armies successfully fought Spanish forces over the next decade. Despite Bolívar's efforts to build a unified state, in the 1830s New Spain split into five separate countries. In Brazil the royal regent proclaimed independence in 1822 and reigned as emperor of the new state.

## NOTES

1. Quoted in L. Gershoy, *The Era of the French Revolution, 1789–1799* (New York: Van Nostrand, 1957), p. 150.
2. Cited in Wim Klooster, *Revolutions in the Atlantic World: A Comprehensive History* (New York: New York University Press, 2009), p. 74.
3. T. Blanning, *The French Revolutionary Wars, 1787–1802* (London: Arnold, 1996), pp. 116–128.
4. Donald Sutherland, *France, 1789–1815: Revolution and Counterrevolution* (New York: Oxford University Press, 1986), p. 420.
5. John K. Thornton, "'I Am the Subject of the King of Congo': African Political Ideology and the Haitian Revolution," *Journal of World History* 4.2 (Fall 1993): 181–214.
6. Quoted in Laurent Dubois, *Avengers of the New World: The Story of the Haitian Revolution* (Cambridge, Mass.: Harvard University Press, 2004), p. 97.
7. See B. Keen and M. Wasserman, *A Short History of Latin America* (Boston: Houghton Mifflin, 1980), pp. 109–115.

## CONNECTIONS

The Atlantic world formed an essential context for a great revolutionary wave in the late eighteenth and early nineteenth centuries. The movement of peoples, commodities, and ideas across the Atlantic Ocean in the eighteenth century created a world of common debates, conflicts, and aspirations. Moreover, the high stakes of colonial empire heightened competition among European states, leading to a series of wars that generated crushing costs for overburdened treasuries. For both the British in their North American colonies and the French at home, the desperate need for new taxes weakened government authority and opened the door to revolution. In turn, the ideals of the French Revolution inspired slaves and free people of color in Saint-Domingue to rise up and claim the promise of liberty, equality, and fraternity for people of all races.

The chain reaction did not end with the liberation movements in Spanish America that followed the Haitian Revolution. Throughout the nineteenth and early twentieth centuries periodic convulsions occurred in Europe, the Americas, and elsewhere as successive generations struggled over political rights first proclaimed by late-eighteenth-century revolutionaries. Meanwhile, as dramatic political events unfolded, a parallel economic revolution was gathering steam. This was the Industrial Revolution, originating around 1780 and accelerating through the end of the eighteenth century (see Chapter 23). After 1815 the twin forces of industrialization and democratization would combine to transform Europe and the world.

# Review and Explore

## Make It Stick

### LearningCurve
Go online and use LearningCurve to retain what you've read.

## Identify Key Terms

Identify and explain the significance of each item below.

Treaty of Paris (p. 653)

Declaration of Independence (p. 655)

Antifederalists (p. 656)

Estates General (p. 658)

National Assembly (p. 658)

Jacobin Club (p. 663)

Mountain (p. 663)

Girondists (p. 663)

sans-culottes (p. 663)

Reign of Terror (p. 664)

Thermidorian reaction (p. 666)

Napoleonic Code (p. 667)

Grand Empire (p. 669)

Continental System (p. 669)

Creoles (p. 676)

peninsulares (p. 676)

## Review the Main Ideas

Answer the focus questions from each section of the chapter.

1. What were the factors behind the age of revolution in the Atlantic world? (p. 650)
2. Why and how did American colonists forge a new, independent nation? (p. 654)
3. How did the events of 1789 result in a constitutional monarchy in France, and what were the consequences? (p. 657)
4. How did Napoleon Bonaparte assume control of France and much of Europe, and what factors led to his downfall? (p. 667)
5. How did slave revolt on colonial Saint-Domingue lead to the creation of the independent nation of Haiti in 1804? (p. 671)
6. Why and how did the Spanish and Portuguese colonies of North and South America shake off European domination and develop into national states? (p. 675)

## Make Connections

Analyze the larger developments and continuities within and across chapters.

1. What were major differences and similarities among the British North American, French, Haitian, and Spanish American Revolutions?
2. How did the growth of empire and transatlantic trade contribute to the outbreak of revolution on both sides of the ocean?
3. To what extent would you characterize the revolutions discussed in this chapter as Enlightenment movements (Chapter 19)?

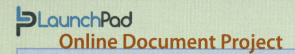

## Online Document Project

### The Rights of Which Men?

**How did the French Revolution affect France's Caribbean colonies?**
Examine reactions of slaves and free men of color to the French Revolution, and then complete a quiz and writing assignment based on the evidence and details from this chapter.

*See inside the front cover to learn more.*

## Suggested Reading

Adelman, Jeremy. *Sovereignty and Revolution in the Iberian Atlantic.* 2006. An examination of independence movements in both Spanish and Portuguese America.

Armitage, David, and Sanjay Subrahmanyam, eds. *The Age of Revolutions in Global Context, c. 1760–1840.* 2009. Presents the age of revolution as a global phenomenon encompassing Europe, the Americas, and Asia.

Auslander, Leora. *Cultural Revolutions: Everyday Life and Politics in Britain, North America, and France.* 2009. An innovative interpretation of the revolutions in England, America, and France as cultural revolutions that politicized daily life.

Bell, David A. *The Cult of the Nation in France: Inventing Nationalism, 1680–1800.* 2001. Traces early French nationalism through its revolutionary culmination.

Broers, Michael. *Europe Under Napoleon.* 2002. Probes Napoleon's impact on the territories he conquered.

Calloway, Colin G. *The Scratch of a Pen: 1763 and the Transformation of North America.* 2006. A study of the dramatic impact of the Seven Years' War on the British and French colonies of North America.

Desan, Suzanne. *The Family on Trial in Revolutionary France.* 2004. Studies the effects of revolutionary law on the family, including the legalization of divorce.

Dubois, Laurent. *Avengers of the New World: The Story of the Haitian Revolution.* 2004. An excellent and highly readable account of the revolution that transformed the French colony of Saint-Domingue into the independent state of Haiti.

Englund, Steven. *Napoleon: A Political Life.* 2004. A good biography of the French emperor.

Goulda, Eliga H., and Peter Onuf, eds. *Empire and Nation: The American Revolution in the Atlantic World.* 2005. A collection of essays placing the American Revolution in its wider Atlantic context, including studies of its impact on daily life in the new republic and the remaining British Empire.

Hunt, Lynn. *Politics, Culture, and Class in the French Revolution,* 2d ed. 2004. A pioneering examination of the French Revolution as a cultural phenomenon that generated new festivals, clothing, and songs, and even a new calendar.

Klooster, Wim. *Revolutions in the Atlantic World: A Comparative History.* 2009. An accessible and engaging comparison of the revolutions in North America, France, Haiti, and Spanish America.

Sepinwall, Alyssa, ed. *Haitian History: New Perspectives.* 2013. A collection of essays showcasing the most important new scholarship on the Haitian Revolution.

Sutherland, Donald. *France, 1789–1815: Revolution and Counterrevolution.* 1986. An overview of the French Revolution that emphasizes its many opponents as well as its supporters.

Wood, Gordon S. *The American Revolution: A History.* 2003. A concise introduction to the American Revolution by a Pulitzer Prize–winning historian.

Tanzania
  gold in, 596
  Kunduchi in, 599(i)
Tariff(s), in France, 532
Tartars, 336, 545, 577. See also Mongols
Tawantinsuyu, Inca Empire as, 305, 306
Taxation
  of British North American colonies, 654
  in China, 365
  of clergy, 442
  colonial protests against, 654, 676
  English Peasants' Revolt and, 419–420
  in France, 437, 657–658
  in India, 498
  in Japan, 631, 634, 638
  medieval, 411
  Mongol, 341
  by Napoleon, 669
  nobility exempted from, 651
  of non-Muslims in Mughal Empire, 506,
    507
  in Russia, 550
  in Spanish America, 676
Tax-farming, 341
Tea
  Britain and, 516
  trade in, 366–367(b), 366(m), 654
Tea Act (U.S., 1773), 654
Tea ceremony, in Japan, 367(b)
Teaching, in universities, 412
Technology. See also Industrialization;
    Science(s)
  in Americas, 299
  in Central Asia, 345
  Chavín, 305
  exploration and, 367, 463–464
  military, 339
  sciences and, 558
Tecuhtli (Aztec lords), 319
Tegguida-n-Tessum, Niger, 595(i)
Telescope, 558, 560, 560(i)
Tempest, The (Shakespeare), 484(b)
Temples
  at Borobudur, 357
  of Huitzilopochtli, 318
  Inca, 307
  in India, 348(i)
  in Japan, 386, 630
  Olmec, 302–303
Temujin. See Chinggis Khan (Mongols)
Tenant farmers
  in Europe, 525
  in India, 513
Tendai (Tiantai) Buddhism, 379, 384
Tennis Court Oath (France), 659(i)
Tenochtitlan (Mexico City), 315, 316, 318,
    471
  Cortés in, 323, 473
  pyramid in, 318(b), 320(i)
Teosinte, 301
Teotihuacan, 310, 311, 313–314
Tepanec Alliance, 315, 316
Teresa of Ávila, 450(i)
Terror, the. See Reign of Terror
Texcoco
  Lake, 315
  ruler of, 457(i)

Textiles and textile industry. See also Cloth
    and clothing
  in China, 629
  in England, 578
  in India, 351, 510, 511–512, 511(i)
  in West Africa, 596
Thai people, 356
Theater
  in China, 624
  in Japan, 630, 636, 637(i)
  vernacular, 413, 431
Theodicy (Leibniz), 566
Theology. See also Religion
  Protestant, 442–443(b), 445
  study of, 411
Theophrastus, botany treatise by, 557
Theory of Moral Sentiments (Smith), 573
Thermidorian reaction, 666
Thermometer, 558
Third Coalition, against France, 668
Third estate (France), 658, 660–661(b). See
    also Estates (French orders)
Third of May 1808 (Goya), 669(i)
Thirty Years' War, 526–527, 529, 530
  Europe after, 527(m), 532, 533
This Scheming World (Ihara Saikaku), 635(b)
Thomas Aquinas (Saint), 412
Tiantai (Tendai) Buddhism, 379
Tibet
  Armenian merchants in, 512
  China and, 365, 621, 627
  Mongols and, 341
Tikal, 310, 311
Tile makers, 502(i)
Tilsit, treaties of, 669
Timbuktu, 591, 592(b)
  Portugal and, 465, 597
  trade in, 595
Time. See Clocks
Time of Troubles, in Russia, 546
Timur (Tamerlane, Turks), 342, 349–351,
    490–491, 491(m), 494
  landscape architects of, 503
Timurid Empire. See Timur
Tithes
  in colonies, 475
  to French church, 658
Titian, 435(i)
Titicaca, Lake, 300, 301, 305
Tiwanaku (Andean city-state), 305
Tizoc (Aztec Empire), 320
Tlacaelel (Aztec adviser), 317, 318(b), 318(i)
Tlaloc (Chac, god), 314
Tlatelolco, Mexico, 315
Tlatoani (Aztec ruler), 316, 317, 320, 321
Tlaxcala people, 323, 324, 471
Tobacco, 644
  in American colonies, 542
  Chelebi on, 506–507(b)
  smoking and, 507(i)
Todar Mal, Raja, 498
Tokharians, 332
Tokugawa Ieyasu (Japan), 632, 634(i), 644
Tokugawa Shogunate (Japan), 632–639,
    632(m)
  Christianity and, 644
  lifestyle under, 637(i)

Tokyo (Edo), Japan, 632, 632(m), 634
Tolerance. See Religious toleration
Toltecs, 314–315, 315(m)
Tomato, 476–477, 644
Tondibi, battle at, 593
Tools
  in Americas, 299
  on Easter Island, 358
Topiltzin-Quetzalcoatl (god), 315
Tordesillas, Treaty of, 469, 474
Tortillas, 301, 301(i)
Toure, Muhammad (Songhai), 591
Toussaint L'Ouverture. See L'Ouverture,
    Toussaint
Towns. See Cities and towns; Villages
Trade. See also Commerce; Cross-cultural
    connections; Global trade; Maritime
    trade; Mercantilism; Silk Road; Sil-
    ver; Slave trade; Spice trade;
    Trans-Saharan trade
  African, 461–462, 588, 595–596
  in Afroeurasia, 458–462, 459(m)
  in Americas, 299, 304, 458
  Armenian, 511–512
  Atlantic economy and, 578–580, 579(m)
  in Benin, 591
  in Brazil, 680
  British factory-forts and, 510–511
  in Canada, 543
  Chinese, 366–367(b), 366(m), 367, 369,
    378, 621, 639–640, 645
  Chinese silver imports and, 626–627
  colonial, 580
  Crusades and, 404
  Dutch, 541–542
  in Enlightenment, 577
  in France, 659–660
  fur, 471, 543, 543(i)
  by Genoa, 462
  Hanseatic League and, 410–411
  in Hausaland, 593
  India and, 346, 347, 352(b), 352(m), 357,
    460, 460(i), 511–512
  in Indian Ocean region, 458–460,
    508–511
  in Japan, 633
  in Korea, 378
  Maya, 310–311, 311(m)
  medieval, 407, 410–411
  Mesoamerican, 303
  in Middle East, 462
  Mongol, 339
  nomadic, 331
  Olmec, 302
  opium, 367(b)
  Portugal and, 465–466, 478
  sorting and, 608
  in Southeast Asia, 355–356
  Spain and, 478
  in Spanish America, 528, 676
  Swahili, 598–599
  in tea, 366–367(b), 366(m)
  in Teotihuacan, 310, 313–314
  Thirty Years' War and, 527
  by Venice, 462
Trade routes. See also Silk Road
  in Africa, 461

| | Africa | The Americas |
|---|---|---|
| **10,000 B.C.E.** | *Homo sapiens* evolve, ca. 250,000 years ago<br>Farming begins in Nile River Valley, ca. 9000<br>Domestication of cattle; plow agriculture, ca. 7000<br>Unification of Egypt, 3100–2660 | Possible migration into Americas begins, ca. 20,000–30,000<br>Farming begins, ca. 8000<br>Maize domesticated in Mexico, ca. 3000 |
| **2500 B.C.E.** | Egypt's Old Kingdom, 2660–2180<br>Egypt's Middle Kingdom, 2080–1640<br>Hyksos migrate into Egypt, 1640–1570 | First cities in Peru; earliest mound building in North America, ca. 2500<br>Textiles become important part of Peruvian culture, ca. 2500<br>Farmers in southwestern North America grow maize, ca. 2000 |
| **1500 B.C.E.** | Egypt's New Kingdom, ca. 1550–1070<br>Ironworking spreads throughout Africa, ca. 1500 B.C.E.–300 C.E.<br>Akhenaten institutes monotheistic worship of Aton, ca. 1360 | Olmec civilization in Mexico, ca. 1500–300<br>Earliest cities in the Andes built by Chavin people, ca. 1200 |
| **1000 B.C.E.** | Political fragmentation of Egypt; rise of small kingdoms, ca. 1100–653<br>Bantu migrations across central and southern Africa, ca. 1000 B.C.E.–1500 C.E.<br>Persians conquer Egypt, 525 | Olmec center at San Lorenzo destroyed; power passes to La Venta, ca. 900 |
| **500 B.C.E.** | Ptolemy conquers Egypt, 323 | |
| **250 B.C.E.** | Scipio Africanus defeats Hannibal at Zama, 202<br>Meroë becomes iron-smelting center, ca. 100 | Hopewell culture flourishes in North America, ca. 200 B.C.E.–600 C.E. |

| Asia and Oceania | Europe | Middle East |
| --- | --- | --- |
| Farming begins in Yellow River Valley, ca. 9000<br><br>Domestication of cattle; plow agriculture begins, ca. 7000 | Farming spreads to Greece, ca. 6500<br>Smelting of copper in Balkans, ca. 5500<br>Farming spreads to Britain, ca. 4000 | Farming begins; domestication of goats and sheep in the Fertile Crescent, ca. 9000<br><br>Invention of pottery wheel in Mesopotamia, ca. 5000<br><br>First writing in Sumeria; city-states emerge, ca. 3500 |
| Harappan civilization, ca. 2800–1800 | Minoan culture emerges, ca. 2000<br><br>Arrival of Greeks in peninsular Greece; founding of Mycenaean kingdom, ca. 1650 | Smelting of iron begins in Mesopotamia, ca. 2500<br><br>Akkadian empire, ca. 2331–2200<br><br>Hammurabi's law code, ca. 1790 |
| Shang Dynasty; first writing in China, ca. 1500–1050<br><br>Vedic Age: Aryans dominate in North India; caste system develops; the *Rigveda*, ca. 1500–500 | Mycenaeans conquer Minoan Crete, ca. 1450<br><br>Greek Dark Age; evolution of the polis, ca. 1100–800 | Hittites expand empire in Mesopotamia, ca. 1600<br><br>Moses leads Hebrews out of Egypt, ca. 1300–1200<br><br>United Hebrew kingdom, ca. 1020–930 |
| Early Zhou Dynasty, ca. 1050–400<br>*Upanishads*, foundation of Hinduism, 750–500<br>Life of Confucius, 551–479<br>Persians conquer parts of India, 513<br>Founding of Buddhism and Jainism, ca. 500 | Fall of Minoan and Mycenaean cultures, ca. 1000<br><br>Rise of Sparta and Athens, 800–500<br>Roman Republic founded, 509 | Assyrian Empire, ca. 800–612<br>Spread of Zoroastrianism, ca. 600–500<br>Babylonian captivity of Hebrews, 587–538<br>Cyrus the Great founds Persian Empire, 550 |
| Warring States period; golden age of Chinese philosophy, 403–221<br>Brahmanic religion develops into Hinduism, ca. 400 B.C.E.–200 C.E.<br>Zhuangzi and development of Daoism, 369–268<br>Alexander the Great invades India, 326<br>Seleucus establishes Seleucid Empire, 323<br>Mauryan Empire, ca. 322–185<br>Reign of Ashoka; Buddhism spreads in central Asia, 269–232 | Flowering of Greek art and philosophy, 500–400<br>Persian wars, 499–479<br>Peloponnesian War, 431–404<br>Roman expansion, 390–146<br>Conquests of Alexander the Great, 336–323<br>Punic Wars; destruction of Carthage, 264–146 | Persian Empire falls to Alexander the Great, 330<br><br>Alexander the Great dies in Babylon, 323 |
| Qin Dynasty unifies China; construction of Great Wall, 221–206<br>Han Dynasty, 206 B.C.E.–220 C.E.<br>Han government controls Silk Road across central Asia, 114<br>Chinese armies conquer Nam Viet, 111<br>*Bhagavad Gita*, ca. 100 B.C.E.–100 C.E. | Late Roman republic, 133–27<br>Julius Caesar killed, 44<br>Octavian seizes power, rules imperial Rome as Augustus, 27 B.C.E.–14 C.E. | |

| | Africa | The Americas |
|---|---|---|
| **1 C.E.** | Expansion of Bantu-speaking peoples into eastern and southern Africa, ca. 100 | Moche civilization flourishes in Peru, ca. 100–800 |
| **200 C.E.** | Aksum (Ethiopia) controls Red Sea trade, ca. 250 | |
| **300** | Christianity comes to Ethiopia from Egypt, 328<br>Aksum accepts Christianity, ca. 350 | Hohokam use irrigation to enhance farming in southwestern North America, ca. 300<br>Classical era in Mesoamerican and North America; Maya and other groups develop large advanced states, 300–900<br>Peak of Teotihuacan civilization in Mexico, ca. 450 |
| **500** | Political and commercial ascendancy of Aksum, ca. 500–700<br>Christian missionaries convert Nubian rulers, ca. 600<br>Muslim conquest of Egypt; Islam introduced to Africa, 642<br>Height of African Mediterranean slave trade, ca. 650–1500 | Peak of Maya civilization, ca. 600–900 |
| **700** | Expansion of Islam into Ethiopia weakens state, 700–800<br>Berbers control trans-Saharan trade, ca. 700–900<br>Islam spreads across Sahara, 800–900<br>Kingdom of Ghana, ca. 900–1300 | Teotihuacan destroyed, 750<br>Period of crop failure, disease, and war in Mesoamerica; collapse of Maya civilization, 800–1000<br>Toltec hegemony, ca. 980–1000 |
| **1000** | Islam penetrates sub-Saharan Africa, ca. 1000–1100<br>Great Zimbabwe built, flourishes, ca. 1100–1400 | Inca civilization in South America, ca. 1000–1500<br>Peak of Cahokia culture in North America, ca. 1150<br>Toltec state collapses, 1174 |
| **1200** | Kingdom of Mali, ca. 1200–1450<br>Mongols conquer Baghdad; fall of Abbasid Dynasty, 1258 | Cahokia's decline begins after earthquake, ca. 1200 |

| Asia and Oceania | Europe | Middle East |
|---|---|---|
| Shakas and Kushans invade eastern Parthia and India, ca. 1–100<br>Maritime trade between Chinese and Roman ports begins, ca. 100<br>Roman attacks on Parthian empire, ca. 100–200<br>Chinese invent paper, 105 | Roman Empire at greatest extent, 117 | Life of Jesus, ca. 3 B.C.E.–29 C.E. |
| Buddhism gains popularity in China, Japan, and Korea, ca. 200–600<br>Age of Division in China, 220–589<br>Fall of the Parthian empire; rise of the Sassanid, ca. 226 | Life of Diocletian: reforms Roman Empire; divides into western and eastern halves, 284–305 | Sassanid dynasty in Persia, 226–651 |
| Three Kingdoms Period in Korea, 313–668<br>China divides into northern and southern regimes, 316<br>Gupta Empire unites northern India, ca. 320–480<br>Huns invade India, ca. 450 | Life of Constantine: legalizes Christianity; founds Constantinople, 306–337<br>Christianity official state religion of Roman Empire, 380<br>Germanic raids on western Europe, 400s<br>Clovis rules Gauls, ca. 481–511 | |
| Sui Dynasty restores order in China, 581–618<br>Prince Shōtoku introduces Chinese-style government in Japan, 604<br>Tang Dynasty in China; cultural flowering, 618–907<br>Korea unified, 668 | Reign of Justinian; *Code* and *Digest*, 527–565<br>*Rule* of Saint Benedict, 529 | Life of Muhammad, 570–632<br>Publication of the Qur'an, 651<br>Umayyad Dynasty; expansion of Islam, 661–750 |
| Creation of Japan's first capital at Nara, 710<br>Islam reaches India, 713<br>Heian era in Japan, 794–1185<br>Khmer Empire of Cambodia founded, 802<br>Koryŏ Dynasty in Korea, 935–1392<br>North Vietnam gains independence from China, 939<br>Song Dynasty in China; invention of movable type, 960–1279 | Muslims defeat Visigothic kingdom in Spain, 711<br>Christian reconquest of Spain from Muslims, 722–1492<br>Carolingians defeat Muslims at Poitiers, 732<br>Viking, Magyar invasions, ca. 800–950<br>Treaty of Verdun divides Carolingian Empire, 843 | Abbasid caliphate; Islamic capital moved to Baghdad, 750–1258<br>Height of Muslim learning and creativity, ca. 800–1300 |
| Construction of Angkor Wat, ca. 1100–1150<br>Muslim conquests lead to decline of Buddhism in India, ca. 1100–1200<br>China divided into Song and Jin empires, 1127<br>Kamakura Shogunate in Japan, 1185–1333 | Latin, Greek churches split, 1054<br>Norman Conquest of England, 1066<br>Crusades, 1095–1270<br>Growth of trade and towns, ca. 1100–1400 | Seljuk Turks take Baghdad, 1055 |
| Easter Island's most prosperous period, ca. 1200–1300<br>Turkish sultanate at Dehli, 1206–1526<br>Peak of Khmer Empire, 1219<br>Mongol's Yuan Dynasty in China, 1234–1368<br>Mongols invade Japan, 1274, 1281<br>Marco Polo travels in China, ca. 1275–1292<br>Mongol conquest of Song China, 1276 | Magna Carta, 1215<br>Life of Thomas Aquinas; *Summa Theologica*, 1225–1274<br>Mongol raids into eastern Europe; Mongols gain control of Kieven Russia, 1237–1241 | Mongols conquer Baghdad, 1238<br>Ottoman Empire, 1299–1922 |

| | Africa | The Americas |
|---|---|---|
| **1300** | Height of Swahili city-states in East Africa, ca. 1300–1500<br>Mansa Musa rules Mali, ca. 1312–1337<br>Ibn Battuta's travels, 1325–1354 | Construction of Aztec city Tenochtitlan begins, ca. 1325 |
| **1400** | Songhai Empire, ca. 1464–1591<br>Arrival of Portuguese in Benin, 1485<br>Da Gama reaches East Africa; Swahili coast enters period of economic decline, 1498 | Height of Inca Empire, 1438–1532<br>Reign of Montezuma I; height of Aztec culture, 1440–1467<br>Inca city of Machu Picchu built, 1450<br>Columbus reaches Americas, 1492 |
| **1500** | Portugal dominates East Africa, ca. 1500–1600<br>Era of transatlantic slave trade, ca. 1500–1900<br>Muslim occupation of Christian Ethiopia, 1531–1543<br>Height of Kanem-Bornu, 1571–1603 | Portuguese reach Brazil, 1500<br>Atlantic slave trade begins, 1518<br>Cortés arrives in Mexico, 1519<br>Aztec Empire falls, 1521<br>Pizarro conquers Inca Empire, 1533<br>First English colony in North America founded at Roanoke, 1585 |
| **1600** | Dutch West India Company founded; starts to bring slave coast of West Africa under its control, 1621<br>Jesuit missionaries expelled from Ethiopia, 1633<br>Dutch East India Company settles Cape Town, 1652<br>Importation of slaves into Cape Colony begins, 1658 | British settle Jamestown, 1607<br>Champlain founds first permanent French settlement at Quebec, 1608<br>Caribbean islands colonized by French, English, Dutch, 1612–1697<br>English seize New Amsterdam from Dutch, 1664 |
| **1700** | Major famine in West Africa, 1738–1756 | Silver production quadruples in Mexico and Peru, ca. 1700–1800<br>Colonial dependence on Spanish goods, ca. 1700–1800 |
| **1750** | Peak of transatlantic slave trade, 1780–1820<br>Olaudah Equiano publishes autobiography, 1789<br>British seize Cape Town, 1795<br>Napoleon's army invades Egypt, 1798 | Seven Years' War, 1756–1763<br>Quebec Act, 1774<br>American Revolution, 1775–1783<br>Comunero revolution in New Granada, 1781<br>Haitian Revolution, 1791–1804 |

| Asia and Oceania | Europe | Middle East |
|---|---|---|
| Ashikaga Shogunate, 1336–1573<br>Mongols defeated in China, 1368<br>Ming Dynasty in China, 1368–1644<br>Timur conquers the Delhi sultanate, 1398 | Hundred Years' War, ca. 1337–1453<br>Black Death arrives in Europe, 1347<br>Great Schism, 1378–1417 | |
| Maritime trade and piracy connects East Asia and Southeast Asia with Europe, ca. 1400–1800<br>Zheng He's maritime expeditions to India, Middle East, Africa, 1405–1433<br>Reign of Sultan Mehmed II, 1451–1481 | Development of movable type in Germany, ca. 1450<br>Italian Renaissance, ca. 1450–1521<br>Age of Discovery, ca. 1450–1650<br>Ottomans capture Constantinople; end of Byzantine Empire, 1453<br>Unification of Spain; Jews expelled, 1492 | Ottoman Empire conquers Byzantine Empire under rule of Sultan Mehmet II, 1451–1481 |
| Increased availability of books in China, 1500–1600<br>Barbur defeats Delhi sultanate; founds Mughal Empire, 1526<br>Japan unified under Toyotomi Hideyoshi, 1537–1598<br>First Christian missionaries land in Japan, 1549<br>Akbar expands Mughal Empire, 1556–1605<br>Spain founds port city of Manila in the Philippines, 1571 | Michelangelo paints Sistine Chapel, 1508–1512<br>Luther's Ninety-five Theses, 1517<br>English Reformation begins, 1527<br>Scientific revolution, ca. 1540–1690<br>Council of Trent, 1545–1563<br>Peace of Augsburg ends religious wars in Germany, 1555<br>Netherlands declares independence from Spain, 1581 | Safavid Empire in Persia, 1501–1722<br>Peak of Ottoman power; cultural flowering under Suleiman, 1520–1566<br>Battle of Lepanto, 1571<br>Height of Safavid Empire under Shah Abbas, 1587–1629 |
| Tokogawa Shogunate in Japan, 1603–1867<br>Japan closes its borders, 1639<br>Manchus establish Qing Dynasty in China, 1644–1911<br>Dutch expel Portuguese in East Indies; gain control of spice trade, ca. 1660<br>French arrive in India, ca. 1670 | Thirty Years' War, 1619–1648<br>Growth of absolutism in Austria and Prussia, 1620–1740<br>English civil war, 1642–1649<br>Habsburgs expel Ottomans from Hungary, 1683–1718<br>Revocation of Edict of Nantes, 1685<br>Glorious Revolution in England, 1688–1689<br>The Enlightenment, ca. 1690–1789 | Shah Abbas captures much of Armenia from the Ottomans, 1603 |
| Height of Edo urban culture in Japan, ca. 1700<br>Christian missionary work forbidden in China, 1715<br>Persian invaders loot Delhi, 1739<br>French and British fight for control of India, 1740–1763 | Growth of book publishing, ca. 1700–1789<br>War of the Spanish Succession, 1701–1713<br>Peace of Utrecht, 1713 | Afghans seize Isfahan from Persians, 1722 |
| Treaty of Paris gives French colonies in India to Britain, 1763<br>Cook claims land in Australia for Britain, 1770<br>East India Act, 1784<br>First British convict-settlers arrive in Australia, 1788 | Watt produces first steam engine, 1769<br>Industrial Revolution in Great Britain, ca. 1780–1850<br>French Revolution, 1789–1799<br>Romantic movement in literature and the arts, ca. 1790s–1890s<br>National Convention declares France a republic, 1792 | Ottoman ruler Selim III introduces reforms, 1761–1808 |

| | Africa | The Americas |
|---|---|---|
| **1800** | Muhammad Ali modernizes Egypt, 1805–1848<br>Slavery abolished in British Empire, 1807 | Latin American wars of independence, 1806–1825<br>Brazil wins independence, 1822<br>Political instability in most Latin American countries, 1825–1870<br>U.S.-Mexican War, 1846–1848 |
| **1850** | Suez Canal opens, 1869<br>Western and central Sudan unite under Islam, 1880<br>European "scramble for Africa"; decline of slave trade, 1880–1900<br>Battle of Omdurman, 1898<br>South African War, 1899–1902 | U.S. Civil War, 1861–1865<br>Dominion of Canada formed, 1867<br>Latin American neocolonialism, ca. 1870–1929<br>Diaz controls Mexico, 1876–1911<br>Immigration from Europe and Asia to the Americas, 1880–1914<br>Spanish-American War, 1898 |
| **1900** | Union of South Africa formed, 1910<br>Native Land Act in South Africa, 1913<br>Du Bois organizes first Pan-African congress, 1919 | Mexican Revolution, 1910<br>Panama Canal opens, 1914<br>Mexico adopts constitution, 1917 |
| **1920** | Cultural nationalism in Africa, 1920s<br>Gold Coast farmers organize cocoa holdups, 1930–1931 | U.S. consumer revolution, 1920s<br>Stock market crash in U.S.; Great Depression begins, 1929<br>Revolutions in six South American countries, 1930<br>Flowering of Mexican culture, 1930s<br>New Deal begins in United States, 1933 |
| **1940** | Decolonization in Africa, 1946–1964<br>Apartheid system in South Africa, 1948–1991 | "Mexican miracle," 1940s–1970s<br>Surprise attack by Japan on Pearl Harbor, 1941<br>United Nations established, 1945 |
| **1950** | Egypt declared a republic; Nasser named premier, 1954<br>French-British Suez invasion, 1956<br>Morocco, Tunisia, Sudan, and Ghana gain independence, 1956–1957<br>France offers commonwealth status to its territories; only Guinea chooses independence, 1958<br>Belgian Congo gains independence; violence follows, 1959 | Cuban revolution, 1953–1959<br>Military rule ends in Venezuela, 1958<br>Castro takes power in Cuba, 1959 |

| Asia and Oceania | Europe | Middle East |
|---|---|---|
| British found Singapore, 1819<br>Java War, 1825–1830<br>Opium War, 1839–1842<br>Treaty of Nanjing; Manchus surrender Hong Kong to British, 1842 | Napoleonic Europe, 1804–1814<br>Congress of Vienna, 1814–1815<br>European economic penetration of non-Western countries, ca. 1816–1880<br>Greece wins independence, 1830<br>Revolutions in France, Austria, and Prussia, 1848 | Ottoman Empire launches Tanzimat reforms, 1839 |
| Taiping Rebellion, 1851–1864<br>Perry opens Japan to trade; Japan begins to industrialize, 1853<br>Great Mutiny/Revolt in India, 1857<br>Meiji Restoration in Japan, 1867<br>Indian National Congress, 1885<br>French acquire Indochina, 1893<br>Sino-Japanese War, 1894–1895<br>U.S. gains Philippines, 1898 | Unification of Italy, 1859–1870<br>Freeing of Russian serfs, 1861<br>Unification of Germany, 1866–1871<br>Massive industrialization surge in Russia, 1890–1900 | Crimean War, 1853–1856<br>Ottoman state declares partial bankruptcy; European creditors take over, 1875 |
| Boxer Rebellion in China, 1900<br>Commonwealth of Australia, 1901<br>Russo-Japanese War, 1904–1905<br>Muslim League formed, 1906<br>Korea becomes province of Japan, 1910<br>Chinese revolution; fall of Qing Dynasty, 1911<br>Chinese republic, 1912–1949<br>Amritsar Massacre in India, 1919 | Revolution in Russia, 1905<br>World War I, 1914–1918<br>Bolshevik Revolution and civil war in Russia, 1917–1922<br>Treaty of Versailles, 1919 | Young Turks seize power in Ottoman Empire, 1908<br>Turkish massacre of Armenians, 1915–1917<br>Sykes-Picot Agreement divides Ottoman Empire, 1916<br>Balfour Declaration establishes Jewish homeland in Palestine, 1917 |
| Gandhi launches nonviolent campaign against British rule in India, 1920<br>Jiang Jieshi unites China, 1928<br>Japan invades China, 1931<br>Mao Zedong's Long March, 1934<br>Sino-Japanese War, 1937–1945<br>Japan conquers Southeast Asia, 1939–1942 | Mussolini seizes power in Italy, 1922<br>Stalin takes power in U.S.S.R., 1927<br>Great Depression, 1929–1933<br>Hitler gains power in Germany, 1933<br>Civil war in Spain, 1936–1939<br>World War II, 1939–1945 | Large numbers of European Jews immigrate to Palestine, 1920s–1930s<br>Turkish republic recognized; Kemal begins to modernize and secularize, 1923<br>Reza Shah leads Iran, 1925–1941<br>Iraq gains independence, 1932 |
| Japan announces "Asia for Asians"; signs alliance with Germany and Italy, 1940<br>United States drops atomic bombs on Hiroshima and Nagasaki, 1945<br>Chinese civil war; Communists win, 1945–1949<br>Philippines gain independence, 1946<br>Independence and separation of India and Pakistan, 1947 | Marshall Plan, 1947<br>NATO formed, 1949<br>Soviet Union and Communist China sign 30-year alliance, 1949 | Arabs and Jews at war in Palestine; Israel created, 1948 |
| Japan begins long period of rapid economic growth, 1950<br>Korean War, 1950–1953<br>Vietnamese nationalists defeat French; Vietnam divided, 1954<br>Mao announces Great Leap Forward in China, 1958 | Death of Stalin, 1953<br>Warsaw Pact, 1955<br>Revolution in Hungary, 1956<br>Common Market formed, 1957 | Turkey joins NATO, 1953<br>Suez crisis, 1956 |

| | Africa | The Americas |
|---|---|---|
| **1960** | Mali and Nigeria gain independence, 1960 <br> Biafra declares independence from Nigeria, 1967 | U.S. Alliance for Progress promotes development and reform in Latin America, 1961 <br> Cuban missile crisis, 1962 <br> U.S. Civil Rights Act; United States starts Vietnam War, 1964 <br> Military dictatorship in Brazil, 1964–1985 <br> Military takeovers lead to brutal dictatorships in Argentina, 1966, 1976 |
| **1970** | Growth of Islamic fundamentalism, 1970s to present | U.S. Watergate scandal, 1972 <br> Nixon visits China; reconciliation between U.S. and China, 1972 <br> Military coup in Chile, 1973 <br> Revolution in Nicaragua, 1979 |
| **1980** | Blacks win long civil war with white settlers in Zimbabwe, 1980 <br> AIDS epidemic, 1980s to present <br> South African government opens talks with African National Congress, 1989 | Democratic wave gains momentum throughout Latin America, 1980s <br> Nationalization of Mexico's banking system, 1982 <br> Argentina restores civilian rule, 1983 <br> Brazilians elect first civilian government in twenty years, 1985 |
| **1990** | Nelson Mandela freed in South Africa, 1990 <br> Rwandan genocide, 1994 <br> Second Congo War, 1998 to present | Canada, Mexico, and United States form free-trade area (NAFTA), 1994 <br> Haiti establishes democratic government, 1994 <br> Socialist "Bolivarian revolution" in Venezuela, 1999 |
| **2000** | Civil war and genocide in Darfur, 2003 to present <br> Mugabe increases violence against opponents after losing Zimbabwean election, 2008 | Terrorist attack on United States, 2001 <br> Economic, social, and political crisis in Argentina, 2002 <br> Formation of the Union of South American Nations, 2008 <br> Raúl Castro succeeds his ailing brother Fidel as president of Cuba, 2008 |
| **2010** | Populist uprisings and protests break out in Tunisia, Egypt, and elsewhere in North Africa, 2010–2011 <br> South Sudan becomes an independent nation, 2011 <br> Nelson Mandela dies, 2013 | Catastrophic earthquake in Haiti, 2010 <br> U.S. withdraws combat troops from Iraq, 2010 <br> U.S. begins troop drawdown in Afghanistan, 2011 <br> Jorge Mario Bergoglio from Argentina elected as Pope Francis, 2013 |

| Asia and Oceania | Europe | Middle East |
| --- | --- | --- |
| Sino-Soviet split becomes apparent, 1960<br>Vietnam War, 1964–1975<br>Great Proletarian Cultural Revolution launched in China, 1965 | Building of Berlin Wall, 1961<br>Student revolution in France, 1968<br>Soviet invasion of Czechoslovakia, 1968 | OPEC founded, 1960<br>Arab-Israeli Six-Day War, 1967 |
| Bangladesh breaks away from Pakistan, 1971<br>Communist victory in Vietnam War, 1975<br>China pursues modernization, 1976 to present | Helsinki Accord on human rights, 1975<br>Soviet invasion of Afghanistan, 1979 | Revival of Islamic fundamentalism, 1970s to present<br>Arab-Israeli Yom Kippur War, 1973<br>OPEC oil embargo, 1973<br>Civil war in Lebanon, 1975–1990<br>Islamic revolution in Iran, 1979<br>Camp David Accords, 1979 |
| Japanese foreign investment surge, 1980–1992<br>Sikh nationalism in India, 1984 to present<br>China crushes democracy movement, 1989 | Soviet reform under Gorbachev, 1985–1991<br>Communism falls in eastern Europe, 1989–1990 | Iran-Iraq War, 1980–1988<br>Palestinians start the intifada, 1987 |
| Collapse of Japanese stock market, 1990–1992<br>Economic growth and political repression in China, 1990 to present<br>Congress Party in India embraces Western capitalist reforms, 1991<br>Kyoto Protocol on global warming, 1997<br>Hong Kong returns to Chinese rule, 1997 | Conservative economic policies, 1990s<br>End of Soviet Union, 1991<br>Civil war in Yugoslavia, 1991–2001<br>Maastricht Treaty creates single currency, 1992<br>Creation of European Union, 1993 | Persian Gulf War, 1990–1991<br>Israel and Palestinians sign peace agreement, 1993<br>Assassination of Israeli prime minster Yitzak Rabin, 1995 |
| China joins World Trade Organization, 2001<br>India and Pakistan come close to all-out war, 2001<br>North Korea withdraws from 1970 Nuclear Non-Proliferation Treaty, 2003<br>Tsunami in Southeast Asia, 2004<br>Terrorist attack in Mumbai, India, 2008 | Resurgence of Russian economy under Putin, 2000–2008<br>Euro note enters circulation, 2002<br>Madrid train bombing, 2004<br>London subway and bus bombing, 2005 | Israel begins construction of West Bank barrier, 2003<br>Wars in Iraq and Afghanistan, 2003 to present<br>Hamas establishes Palestinian Authority government, 2007 |
| Massive earthquake in Japan, 2011<br>Al-Qaeda leader Osama bin Laden killed in Pakistan, 2011<br>Typhoon Haiyan kills thousands in the Philippines, 2013 | European financial crisis intensifies, 2010<br>France legalizes same-sex marriage, 2013<br>Russia annexes Crimea region in Ukraine, 2014 | Populist uprisings and protests across the Middle East, 2010–2011<br>Civil war in Syria begins; refugee crisis intensifies, 2011<br>Egyptian President Mohamed Morsi ousted following protests, 2013 |

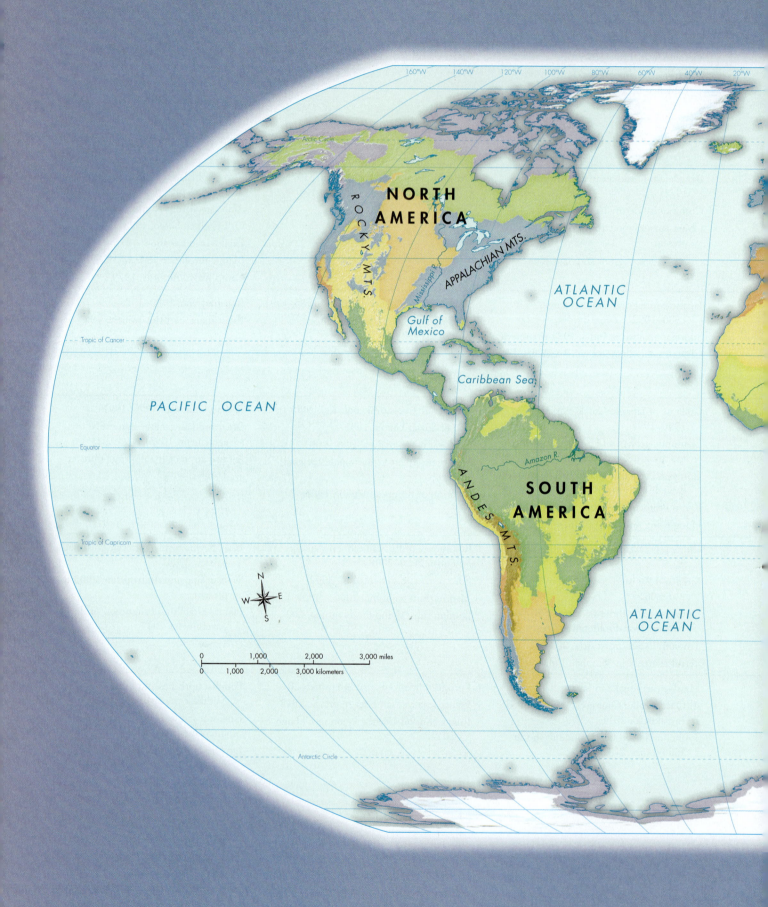

160°W  140°W  120°W  100°W  80°W  60°W  40°W  20°W

Arctic Circle

**NORTH
AMERICA**

R O C K Y   M T S.

Mississippi R.

APPALACHIAN MTS.

Gulf of
Mexico

Tropic of Cancer

Caribbean Sea

ATLANTIC
OCEAN

PACIFIC  OCEAN

Equator

A N D E S   M T S.

Amazon R.

**SOUTH
AMERICA**

Tropic of Capricorn

ATLANTIC
OCEAN

N
W   E
S

0           1,000        2,000        3,000 miles
0    1,000   2,000    3,000 kilometers

Antarctic Circle

EUROPE

ALPS

Mediterranean Sea

SAHARA

AFRICA

Nile R.

Congo R.

Zambezi R.

KALAHARI
DESERT

URAL MTS.

Volga R.

Ob R.

ASIA

GOBI

HIMALAYA MTS.

Ganges R.

Yellow R. (Huang He)

Yangzi R.

ARABIAN
DESERT

Arabian
Sea

Bay of
Bengal

South
China
Sea

PACIFIC OCEAN

INDIAN OCEAN

AUSTRALIA

Arctic Circle

Tropic of Cancer

Equator

Tropic of Capricorn

Antarctic Circle

80°N

60°N

40°N

20°N

0°

20°S

40°S

60°S

80°S

20°E  40°E  60°E  80°E  100°E  120°E  140°E  160°E

**Vegetation zones**

- Tundra
- Northern forest
- Temperate forest
- Temperate grassland
- Desert and dry shrub
- Mediterranean shrub
- Mountain grassland
- Tropical grassland and savanna
- Tropical forest
- Permanent ice cover

# About the Authors

**John P. McKay** (Ph.D., University of California, Berkeley) is professor emeritus at the University of Illinois. He has written or edited numerous works, including the Herbert Baxter Adams Prize–winning book *Pioneers for Profit: Foreign Entrepreneurship and Russian Industrialization, 1885–1913*.

**Patricia Buckley Ebrey** (Ph.D., Columbia University), professor of history at the University of Washington in Seattle, specializes in China. She has published numerous journal articles and *The Cambridge Illustrated History of China*, as well as several monographs. In 2010 she won the Shimada Prize for outstanding work of East Asian Art History for *Accumulating Culture: The Collections of Emperor Huizong*.

**Roger B. Beck** (Ph.D., Indiana University) is Distinguished Professor of African and twentieth-century world history at Eastern Illinois University. His publications include *The History of South Africa*, a translation of P. J. van der Merwe's *The Migrant Farmer in the History of the Cape Colony, 1657–1842*, and more than a hundred articles, book chapters, and reviews. He is a former treasurer and Executive Council member of the World History Association.

**Clare Haru Crowston** (Ph.D., Cornell University) teaches at the University of Illinois, where she is currently associate professor of history. She is the author of *Fabricating Women: The Seamstresses of Old Regime France, 1675–1791*, which won the Berkshire and Hagley Prizes. She edited two special issues of the *Journal of Women's History*, has published numerous journal articles and reviews, and is a past president of the Society for French Historical Studies.

**Merry E. Wiesner-Hanks** (Ph.D., University of Wisconsin–Madison) taught first at Augustana College in Illinois, and since 1985 at the University of Wisconsin–Milwaukee, where she is currently UWM Distinguished Professor in the department of history. She is the coeditor of the *Sixteenth Century Journal* and the author or editor of more than twenty books, most recently *The Marvelous Hairy Girls: The Gonzales Sisters and Their Worlds* and *Gender in History*. She is the former Chief Reader for Advanced Placement World History.

**Jerry Dávila** (Ph.D., Brown University) is Jorge Paulo Lemann Professor of Brazilian History at the University of Illinois. He is the author of *Dictatorship in South America*; *Hotel Trópico: Brazil and the Challenge of African Decolonization*, winner of the Latin Studies Association Brazil Section Book Prize; and *Diploma of Whiteness: Race and Social Policy in Brazil, 1917–1945*. He has served as president of the Conference on Latin American History.